Mating

Intelligence

Sex, Relationships,
and the Mind's
Reproductive System

Mating

Intelligence

Sex, Relationships, and the Mind's Reproductive System

Edited by
Glenn Geher • Geoffrey Miller

LEA Lawrence Erlbaum Associates
Taylor & Francis Group

New York   London

Cover design by Tomai Maridou.

Lawrence Erlbaum Associates
Taylor & Francis Group
270 Madison Avenue
New York, NY 10016

Lawrence Erlbaum Associates
Taylor & Francis Group
2 Park Square
Milton Park, Abingdon
Oxon OX14 4RN

Printed in the United States of America on acid-free paper
10 9 8 7 6 5 4 3 2 1

International Standard Book Number-13: 978-0-8058-5749-8 (Softcover) 978-0-8058-5748-1 (Hardcover)

Visit the Taylor & Francis Web site at
http://www.taylorandfrancis.com

and the LEA Web site at
http://www.erlbaum.com

Contents

Foreword: The Future of Mating Intelligence

David M. Buss

Within the field of psychology, research and theory on human mating has gone from being a fringe area studied by a few "soft" psychologists to one of the most theoretically and empirically commanding domains in the entire discipline. Indeed, the area of mating shows all the hallmarks of a rapidly maturing science—cogent theories that have stood the test of time and a rapidly cumulating body of empirical findings. At the same time, new theoretical and empirical breakthroughs continue at an exciting pace, and many key areas still await intrepid researchers. This book on mating intelligence highlights some of the cutting-edge work and points the way to important domains for new discoveries.

HISTORICAL CONTEXT OF MATING INTELLIGENCE

It is worthwhile placing the current volume in historical context. The evolutionary psychology of human mating can be traced back to Charles Darwin, who developed the most important theoretical foundation for the study of mating today—the theory of sexual selection (Darwin, 1859, 1871). After his original formulation of natural selection (sometimes called "survival selection"), Darwin remained deeply troubled by phenomena that his theory could not explain. Examples included sex differences (e.g., why are male elephant seals four times the size of female elephant seals, given that both have faced the same problems of survival?) and the elaborate ornamentation of some species that seemed detrimental to survival (e.g., enormous antlers, brilliant plumage). Darwin even noted that "The sight of a feather in a peacock's tail, whenever I gaze at it, makes me sick!" (Darwin in a letter to Asa Gray, Apr. 3, 1860).

Darwin's troubles ceased, at least in part, when he formulated the theory of sexual selection—the evolution of characteristics due to *mating advantage* rather than *survival advantage*. Darwin identified two causal processes by which sexual selection could occur. The first is *intrasexual selection* or same-sex competition. If members of one sex compete with one another, and the victors gain preferential mating access to members of the opposite sex, then sexual selection favors an increase in the frequency of qualities linked with success in the contests (assuming the qualities had some heritable basis). The qualities favored by intrasexual selection need not be physical. They could, for example, involve "scramble competition" for reproductively relevant resources or the ability to ascend status hierarchies, if elevation in status hierarchies gave individuals preferential access to mates. Conversely, heritable qualities linked with losing intrasexual competitions would decrease in frequency over time.

The second causal process of sexual selection is *intersexual selection*, which Darwin sometimes called "female choice." If members of one sex display some consensus about the qualities they desired in the opposite sex, then those possessing the desired qualities have a mating advantage. If the desired qualities have some degree of heritability, they will increase in frequency over time. For example, if females prefer males with brilliant plumage or better territories or superior resource-acquisition skills, then sexual selection would favor the evolution of these qualities in males in succeeding generations.

Sexual selection theory, although initially discounted by many biologists of Darwin's day, has emerged as one of the most important theories in evolutionary biology (e.g., Fisher, 1930/1958; Trivers, 1972; Andersson, 1994; Kokko et al., 2003). It has also provided an overarching theoretical framework for research on human mating strategies (Buss, 1989, 1994/2003; Buss & Schmitt, 1993; Gangestad & Simpson, 2000; Kenrick & Keefe, 1992; Miller, 2000; Townsend, 1998). Many conceptual and empirical advances have been made in sexual selection theory, and these have been reflected in a profusion of research on human mating strategies. I'll mention a few.

First, although Darwin initially conceptualized intersexual selection as mainly "female choice" and intrasexual competition as mainly male-against-male competition, work on humans has documented that *both processes apply to both sexes.* Thus, both sexes have elaborate and well-honed mate preferences (Buss, 1989; Buss & Schmitt, 1993; Kenrick & Keefe, 1992; Li et al., 2002), and both sexes compete vigorously for access to desirable mates (Buss, 1988a; Schmitt & Buss, 1996; Tooke & Camire, 1991). Many aspects of mate competition have been empirically documented in both men and women, including *tactics of mate attraction* (Buss, 1988a), *derogation of competitors* (Buss & Dedden, 1990), *tactics of mate retention* (Buss, 1988b; Buss & Shackelford, 1997), and *tactics of mate poaching* (Schmitt & Buss, 2001; Schmitt, 2004).

Second, the importance of "good genes" in both mate preferences and mate competition has been increasingly recognized (Buss & Schmitt, 1993; Gangestad & Thornhill, 1997; Gangestad & Simpson, 2000; Greiling & Buss, 2000; Miller, 2000). Hypotheses about the importance of good genes in mating go back to Fisher (1915) and they come in several varieties (Greiling & Buss, 2000). One version focuses on qualities such as symmetry and masculinity as markers of good health, low mutation load, or ability to withstand environmental insult—qualities that can be passed on to children (e.g., Gangestad & Thornhill, 1997; Gangestad et al., 2005). Another version focuses on "sexy son genes" (Fisher, 1915, 1930/1958). Women might prefer to mate with males who are especially attractive or desirable to females, not because they will bear more offspring, but because they will bear "sexy sons" who will give them more grandchildren (obviously, no conscious intent is implied by this class of hypotheses). Yet another version of good-genes theory focuses on qualities such as ability to produce humor, music, and art—courtship displays that have no direct pragmatic utility for the mate selector, but are preferred because they signal heritable fitness to the mate selector (Miller, 2000). Of course, all these hypotheses about "good genes" are likely to involve fitness signals of one sort or another. Even qualities that serve utilitarian functions for the mate selector—such as preferring mates who have the physical formidability to offer protection, or the qualities that lead to good parenting skills—are likely to be partly heritable, and thus are also markers of "good genes." In short, good-genes sexual selection has become increasingly recognized as an important and complex process in human mating.

A third development has been the increasing recognition that *the two components of sexual selection can be causally related to each other* (Buss, 1988a). The mate preferences of one sex can determine the domains in which members of the opposite sex compete. If women prefer men who can provide resources or offer protection, for example, then, over evolutionary time, men will compete with each other to display resource-providing and athleticism and other protection-indicating abilities. Conversely, the domains in which males compete (e.g., physical contests, hierarchy negotiation skills) can, in turn, influence the evolution of female mate preferences.

A fourth development has been the increasing recognition of *the importance of sexual conflict* and its relationships to sexual selection (Arnqvist & Rowe, 2005). Theoretical developments in sexual-conflict theory have increasingly led to research on human mating, including the domains of sexual aggression and coercion (Buss, 1989b; Malamuth, 2005; Thornhill & Palmer, 2000), sexual harassment (Browne, 2006), and sexual deception (Haselton, Buss, Angleitner, & Oubaid, 2005).

All of these developments in sexual selection theory, and others, have proved to be exceptionally fruitful for evolutionary biologists and evolutionary psychologists in theory and research on mating strategies. Sexual selection theory, in its modern manifestations, remains the most powerful overarching theoretical framework, guiding most research on human sexual strategies since the seminal article by Trivers (1972) on parental investment and sexual selection. It has also guided, explicitly or implicitly, most of the chapters in this volume on mating intelligence.

THE VALUE OF THE CONSTRUCT OF
MATING INTELLIGENCE

This volume brings together a wonderful collection of chapters on many facets of the new construct of mating intelligence. These include how mating intelligence is related to how individuals search for mates (Penke and colleagues; De Backer, Braeckman, & Farinpour); the critically important, but often neglected, role of personality in mating strategies (Nettle & Clegg); deception in mating strategies (O'Sullivan); how the existence of children changes the adaptive problems an individual faces, and hence alters mating strategies (Weekes-Shackelford, Easton, & Stone); how different "mating budgets" influence mate preferences (Li); the role of mutation load in mating (Keller); how mental disorders undermine the successful deployment of mating strategies (Shaner, Miller, & Mintz); the role of creativity and humor in mate selection (Kaufman, Kozbelt, Bromley, & Miller); the relationship between emotional intelligence and mating intelligence in partner selection and relationship quality (Casey, Garrett, Brackett, & Rivers); the possible conceptual independence of mating intelligence and general intelligence (Kanazawa); and the role of ecological factors such as climatic variation on mating intelligence (Ash & Gallup; Figueredo and colleagues). The volume concludes with excellent chapters on frequently asked questions about mating intelligence (Miller), and an integrative model of mating intelligence (Geher, Camargo, & O'Rourke) that provides a foundation for future research in this field.

One of the truly important features of *Mating Intelligence* is that it focuses both on species-typical mating mechanisms as well as individual differences. The field of evolutionary psychology, with some important exceptions, has focused—theoretically and empirically—primarily on universal psychological mechanisms. The incorporation of individual differences into theories and research has been much slower. This book highlights the importance and necessity of understanding both classes of mechanisms within a unified theoretical framework, and thus heralds a more comprehensive understanding of the psychology of human mating.

Since mating intelligence is a new construct, it is worthwhile to scrutinize it, evaluate its worth, note its limitations, and offer suggestions for future work in this domain. I see the primary benefit of the construct of mating intelligence as a *heuristic one*—it guides researchers to new domains of inquiry that may have been neglected, and points to phenomena that may have been overlooked. I would single out the heuristic value that mating intelligence focuses on relative success or failure in the deployment of various mating strategies. This focus has some historical precedent, albeit without the phrase "mating intelligence." For example, there has been empirical research on which tactics are more and less effective at mate attraction (Buss, 1988a; Schmitt & Buss, 1996), which tactics are more and less effective at mate retention (Buss, 1988b), and which tactics are more and less effective at promoting successful sexual encounters (Greer & Buss, 1994). Nonetheless, an explicit focus on the effectiveness of varied mating tactics, as how they are deployed with differential effectiveness by different by individuals in different circumstances, will guide future mating researchers to important discoveries.

This focus will also guide researchers to a fuller exploration of the cognitive abilities underlying mating tactics, such as the psychological mechanisms that lead to successful mate poaching, sexual deception, or successful mate retention. An abilities focus has proven effective in many domains, including the constructs of general intelligence, social intelligence, and emotional intelligence. An abilities focus, as conceptualized by the notion of mating intelligence, should prove fruitful in research on human mating.

SEXUAL SELECTION THEORY PROVIDES A FRAMEWORK FOR CONCEPTUALIZING MATING INTELLIGENCE

One way to organize the emerging study of mating intelligence is to specify the major adaptive problems that need to be solved in order to successfully mate and reproduce. Darwin's initial theory of sexual selection, with important modern modifications, provides such a provisional framework. Identifying the major adaptive problems of mating is the key to assessing how intelligently they are solved.

Table 1 presents a sampling of some of the key mating adaptations that can be deployed more or less successfully, and hence more or less intelligently, for solving problems of mating. The adaptive problems are large in number and require formidable abilities to solve successfully. Those involved in *mate selection,* for example, include calibrating or adjusting one's mate preferences based on: one's current mate value; anticipated future mate value trajectory; whether one is seeking a short-term mate, long-term mate, or extra-pair-copulation partner; operational sex ratio; parasite prevalence in the local ecology; one's history of successes and failures of courtship efforts; and many others. Adaptations involved in *intrasexual competition* include: initial mate attraction adaptations (e.g., flirtation, displays of fitness indicators) to evaluate interest and evoke interest from potential mates; subsequent mate attraction tactics to escalate commitment; sexual persistence adaptations and possibly sexual coercion adaptations; mate deception adaptations; adaptations to monitor, intimidate, and derogate intrasexual rivals; mate poaching adaptations; mate retention adaptations; and many others.

Success at solving many of these adaptive problems requires formidable cognitive skills. These include *mind-reading skills* to gauge and evoke

TABLE 1
Mating Intelligence Adaptations: A Selected Sample Framed by Sexual Selection Theory

Mate Preference Adaptations

1. Calibrate mate preferences to one's current mate value
2. Calibrate mate preferences to anticipated future mate value trajectory
3. Calibrate mate preferences to gains or losses of mate value
4. Adjust mate preferences based on whether one is seeking short-term or long-term mate
5. Calibrate mate preferences to operational sex ratio
6. Calibrate mate preferences to parasite prevalence in local ecology
7. Calibrate mate preferences to number and quality of available potential mates
8. Adjust mate preferences based on phase of ovulation cycle
9. Adjust mate preferences based on the local intensity of intrasexual competition
10. Adjust mate preferences based on successes and failures in mating attempts
11. Adjust mate preferences based on current adaptive needs (e.g., whether one has dependent children)
12. Adjust mate preferences after a breakup, based in part on assessment of causes of relationship failure (e.g., mate value discrepancy)

Intrasexual Competition Adaptations

1. Deploy initial round of mate-attraction tactics (flirtation, courtship displays) in order to:
    a. evaluate interest from target (mind reading)
    b. evoke interest from target (mind reading)
    c. allow closer and fuller assessment of mate quality
2. Deploy subsequent mate-attraction tactics (courtship displays) designed to:
    a. fulfill the desires of potential mate (e.g., displays of mate quality; commitability)
    b. escalate comment
    c. allow more thorough evaluation of mate quality, compatibility, exploitability, etc.
3. Sexual persistence adaptations
4. Sexual coercion adaptations
5. Mate-deception adaptations (e.g., mislead targeted mate about one's mate value or future intentions)(mind reading)
6. Assess and monitor mate value of key intrasexual rivals
7. Deter intrasexual rivals through intimidation
8. Derogate intrasexual rivals to targeted mate
9. Interfere with intrasexual rival's courtship tactics
10. Damage social reputations of intrasexual rivals

TABLE 1 (continued)

11. Mate poaching adaptations, such as . . .
    a. drive wedge in existing relationship
    b. deploy attraction tactics that better fulfill targeted mate's desires
    c. derogate partner of targeted mate
12. Mate retention adaptations, such as . . .
    a. monitor intrasexual rival's interest in one's mate
    b. drive off intrasexual rivals
    c. cloister mate to remove from proximity to intrasexual rivals

mating interest, to monitor a mate's commitment, to anticipate a mate's infidelity or defection, and to carry out successful deception. They include *self-assessment abilities* to evaluate one's mate value, one's future mate value trajectory, and shifts in mate value as a consequence of key life events (e.g., rise or loss of status; gain or loss of a key social ally). They include the *other-assessment abilities,* such the capability as to monitor the mate value and mate-value trajectories of mates and intrasexual rivals. And they include *the ability to anticipate satellite adaptive problems* that follow from deploying particular adaptive solutions. Successful mate guarding, for example, may activate counter-mate guarding adaptations in the mate or in the mate's kin, which create problems that must be solved.

The degree to which success at solving each mating problem is correlated with success at solving other mating problems is an intriguing issue that remains to be determined empirically. Possible outcomes include (1) a "g" in the mating intelligence realm, indicating a positive manifold in the mating intelligence matrix analogous to the "g" in the domain of cognitive abilities; (2) some level of specificity to mating intelligence— those successful at long-term mating may not necessarily be successful at short-term mating, and vice-versa (this outcome would be expected if their exist heritable individual differences in sexual strategies, or if some individuals, through effort and practice, "specialize" in one sexual strategy and hence improve their performance on that strategy to the detriment of performance on other strategies). Only extensive empirical work will reveal the structure of mating intelligence, but the findings will surely be fascinating and provide key insights into human mating.

Future work on mating intelligence will also have to deal with some uncomfortable issues, including important adaptive problems not covered by this volume, but that might be included in future work. I'll mention one—*sexual coercion.* Although there is debate about whether males have evolved adaptations to rape (Thornhill & Palmer, 2000), there is tremendous consensus on the point that *male sexual coercion has been a recurrent adaptive problem for women over human evolutionary history* (Buss, 2003). Thus, an important domain of mating intelligence would involve the tactics that women bring to bear on solving this adaptive problem— perhaps selecting mates who can function as "body guards," avoiding circumstances in which there is an elevated risk of rape, deflecting unwanted sexual attention, avoiding men who display cues correlated with sexual aggression, and even successfully solving the "satellite" adaptive problems caused by being raped, such as avoiding damage to reputation or mate value (Buss, 2003). Women, their mates, their friends, and their kin are likely to differ in their mating intelligence in this realm. The key point is that work on mating intelligence will benefit from a comprehensive treatment of the adaptive problems of mating, including sensitive and controversial ones such as sexual coercion.

Another key issue centers on providing *criteria for gauging and measuring mating intelligence.* A sensible criterion is given by the existing framework of evolutionary psychology—success at solving the adaptive problems of mating, such as successful mate attraction, mate retention, mate poaching, mate switching, and so on. Thus, research on mating intelligence could fruitfully move toward an explicit focus on which tactics are successful at solving mating problems, individual differences in the successful deployment of these tactics, and delineation of the contexts in which certain individual's deployment of specific tactics are effective. This will prove to be much more complicated that it might appear at first blush. One reason is that the success of a tactic typically depends critically on context. Consider the tactic a woman might use to attract a mate— wearing skimpy clothing, showing cleavage, and sucking seductively on a straw. This tactic proves highly effective at attracting short-term mates, but actually backfires in attracting long-term mates (Buss & Schmitt, 1993; Greer & Buss, 1994). Tactic effectiveness is highly context-dependent.

Another complexity is that solutions to one mating problem can produce a cascade of consequences for other adaptive problems. To take one simple example, successful mate poaching (luring a desirable individual away from an existing relationship for a sexual encounter or long-term mateship) may create satellite adaptive problems such as retribution from the poachee's previous mate, or damage to one's social reputation. In the extreme, successful mate poaching (surely an indicator of mating intelligence) may lead to getting ostracized, injured, or even killed (perhaps not so intelligent after all). In short, success at solving the adaptive problems of mating is highly dependent on circumstances and must be examined within the broader context of the cascade of satellite adaptive problems for which the solution has relevance.

Temporal context, the dimension anchored by short-term and long-term mating, will be critical for evaluating all forms of mating intelligence

(Buss & Schmitt, 1993). Mate preferences of both sexes shift as a function of temporal context. Women, for example, place a greater premium on physical attractiveness and immediate resource display in short-term than long-term mating contexts. Sexual fidelity is extremely important for men in long-term mating, but is largely irrelevant in short-term mating. Consequently, success at short-term mating will require the deployment of different tactics than success at long-term mating.

SUMMARY

Mating intelligence offers a fresh framework that is likely to have heuristic value in guiding researchers to new domains of mating and discovering new mating phenomena. Given the early stage of theorizing, much work remains to be done. This work includes a comprehensive identification of the adaptive problems of mating (e.g., sexual coercion); developing measures to assess individual differences in the formidable skills and abilities required for solving each of these adaptive problems; exploring the cascading consequences of each solution for other adaptive problems; and empirically examining the relations among these abilities and determining their statistical structure. Readers of this volume undoubtedly will offer additional suggestions for advancing and clarifying the framework of mating intelligence. Regardless, all readers will enjoy the many mating insights offered by this volume.

REFERENCES

Andersson, M. (1994). Sexual selection. Princeton, NJ: Princeton University Press.

Arnqvist, G., & Rowe, L. (2005). *Sexual conflict.* Princeton, NJ: Princeton University Press.

Browne, K. R. (2006). Sex, power, and dominance: The evolutionary psychology of sexual harassment. *Managerial and Decision Economics, 27,* 145–158.

Buss, D. M. (1988a). The evolution of human intrasexual competition: Tactics of mate attraction. *Journal of Personality and Social Psychology, 54,* 616–628.

Buss, D. M. (1988b). From vigilance to violence: Tactics of mate retention. *Ethology and Sociobiology, 9,* 291–317.

Buss, D. M. (1989). Sex differences in human mate preferences: Evolutionary hypotheses testing in 37 cultures. *Behavioral and Brain Sciences, 12,* 1–49.

Buss, D. M. (1994/2003). *The Evolution of Desire: Strategies of Human Mating.* New York: Basic Books.

Buss, D. M., & Barnes, M. F. (1986). Preferences in human mate selection. *Journal of Personality and Social Psychology, 50,* 559–570.

Buss, D. M., & Dedden, L. A. (1990). Derogation of competitors. *Journal of Social and Personal Relationships, 7,* 395–422.

Buss, D. M., & Schmitt, D. P. (1993). Sexual strategies theory: An evolutionary perspective on human mating. *Psychological Review, 100,* 204–232.

Buss, D. M., & Shackelford, T. K. (1997). From vigilance to violence: Mate retention tactics in married couples. *Journal of Personality and Social Psychology, 72,*
346-361.

Darwin, C. (1859). *The origin of species.* London: Murray.

Darwin, C. (1871). *The descent of man and selection in relation to sex.* London:
Murray.

Fisher, R. A. (1915). The evolution of sexual preference. *Eugenics Review, 7,*
184–192.

Fisher, R. A. (1930/1958). *The genetical theory of natural selection.* New York: Dover

Gangestad, S. W., & Buss, D. M. (1993). Pathogen prevalence and human mate
preferences. *Ethology and Sociobiology, 14,* 89–96.

Gangestad, R. W., Thornhill, R., & Garver-Apgar, C. E. (2005). Adaptations to
ovulation. In D. M. Buss (Ed), *The handbook of evolutionary psychology* (pp.
344–371). New York: Wiley.

Gangestad, S. W., & Simpson, J.A. (2000). The evolution of human mating: The
role of trade-offs and strategic pluralism. *Behavioral and Brain Sciences, 23,*
675–687.

Gangestad, S. W., & Thornhill, R. (1997). Human sexual selection and developmental stability. In J. A. Simpson & D.T. Kenrick (Eds.), *Evolutionary social
psychology* (pp. 169–195). Mahwah, NJ: Lawrence Erlbaum Associates.

Garver-Apgar, C., Gangestad, S. W., Thornhill, R., Miller, R. D., & Olp, J. J. (2006).
Major histocompatibility complex alleles, sexual responsivity, and unfaithful-
ness in romantic couples. *Psychological Science, 17,* 830–835.

Greer, A., & Buss, D. M. (1994). Tactics for promoting sexual encounters. *The Journal of Sex Research, 5,* 185–201.

Greiling, H., & Buss, D. M. (2000). Women's sexual strategies: The hidden dimension of extra-pair mating. *Personality and Individual Differences, 28,* 929–963.

Haselton, M., Buss, D. M., Oubaid, V., & Angleitner, A. (2005). Sex, lies, and strategic interference: The psychology of deception between the sexes. *Personality
and Social Psychology Bulletin, 31,* 3–23.

Kenrick, D.T., & Keefe, R.C. (1992). Age preferences in mates reflect sex differences in reproductive strategies. *Behavioral and Brain Sciences, 15,* 75–133.

Kokko, H., Brooks, R., Jennisons, M. D., & Morley, J. (2003). The evolution of mate
choice and mating biases. *Proceedings of the Royal Society of London Series B—
Biological Sciences, 270,* 653–664.

Li, N. P., Bailey, J. M., Kenrick, D. T., & Linsemeier, J. A. W. (2002). The necessities
and luxuries of mate preferences: Testing the tradeoffs. *Journal of Personality
and Social Psychology, 82,* 947–955.

Malamuth, N. M., Huppin, M., & Paul, B. (2005). Sexual coercion. In D. M. Buss
(Ed.), *The handbook of evolutionary psychology* (pp. 394–418). New York: Wiley.

Miller, G. F. (1998). How mate choice shaped human nature: A review of sexual
selection and human evolution. In C. Crawford & D. Krebs (Eds.), *Handbook
of evolutionary psychology* (pp. 87–129). Mahwah, NJ: Lawrence Erlbaum
Associates.

Miller, G. F. (2000). *The mating mind: How sexual choice shaped the evolution of human
nature.* New York: Doubleday.

Schmitt, D. P. and 121 members of the International Sexuality Description Project
(2004). Patterns and universals of mate poaching across 53 nations: The

effects of sex, culture, and personality on romantically attracting another person's partner. *Journal of Personality and Social Psychology, 86,* 560–584.

Schmitt, D. P., & Buss, D. M. (1996). Strategic self-promotion and competitor derogation: Sex and context effects on perceived effectiveness of mate attraction tactics. *Journal of Personality and Social Psychology, 70,* 1185–1204.

Schmitt, D. P., & Buss, D. M. (2001). Human mate poaching: Tactics and temptations for infiltrating existing relationships. *Journal of Personality and Social Psychology, 80,* 894–917.

Thornhill, R., & Palmer, C. (2000). *A natural history of rape: Biological bases of sexual coercion.* Cambridge, MA: MIT Press.

Tooke, W., & Camire, L. (1991). Patterns of deception in intersexual and intrasexual mating strategies. *Ethology and Sociobiology, 12,* 345–364.

Townsend, J. (1998). *What women want, what men want.* New York: Oxford University Press.

Trivers, R. (1972). Parental investment and sexual selection. In B. Campbell (Ed.), *Sexual Selection and the Descent of Man.* Chicago: Aldine-Atherton.

Preface

Glenn Geher and Geoffrey Miller

This book presents *mating intelligence*—a new construct designed to build bridges between two major areas of psychological research: human mating and intelligence. As evolutionary psychologists with keen interests in understanding human mating, we are convinced that the evolution of psychological processes tied to mating was integral to the evolution of human intelligence. From the perspective we present, it is a mistake to consider mating psychology and intelligence as unrelated aspects of the human mind. We see mating intelligence as comprising two major aspects of human psychology: (a) psychological mechanisms designed specifically for mating purposes—such as the ability to feel attraction to appropriate mates, and to assess one's own attractiveness in a local mating market—and (b) mental fitness indicators—aspects of human intelligence such as creativity, humor, and music that may have evolved specifically for courtship-display purposes.

In addition to presenting a framework for understanding the interface between mating and intelligence, we hope that this book helps expand the horizons of evolutionary psychology in general, to address some of the more intimate and enjoyable aspects of human nature that have been neglected so far. In our minds, evolutionary psychology represents the single most coherent, interesting, important, and reasonable approach to understanding human behavior. One of the goals of this book is to help evolutionary psychology realize its untapped potential to guide research across new areas of psychology. When one looks carefully for the *Darwinized* areas of psychology, obvious gaps emerge. Evolutionary psychology has strongly influenced research on the more superficial and negative aspects of human mating, such as physical attractiveness, sexual jealousy, and short-term lust, but it has not much addressed some deeper, more positive aspects of mating, such as mental and moral attractiveness, sexual intimacy, and long-term love.

Evolutionary psychology needs a rejuvenating tonic. It needs to crossbreed with new fields before it suffers from inbreeding depression and intellectual stagnation. Granted, it has succeeded brilliantly in developing research programs on sexual strategies, reciprocity, kinship, and other core aspects of human nature that were too long neglected in mainstream psychology. These research programs have become Kuhnian normal science—not exactly treading water, but no longer surfing the big waves of a radical paradigm shift. A sense of premature complacency can sometimes be discerned in the leading evolutionary psychology conference (the annual Human Behavior and Evolution Society meeting) and journals *(Evolution and Human Behavior, Human Nature, Evolutionary Psychology).*

One area for improvement in evolutionary psychology pertains to the study of individual differences, including personality, intelligence, and mental illness. In fact, while many evolutionarily informed researchers have documented important human universals in the domain of mating, the entire notion of individual differences, going back to Darwin's long-estranged cousin, Francis Galton, generally falls by the wayside. The mating intelligence construct is an attempt to reconcile the Darwinian tradition of adaptationist research on human universals with the Galtonian tradition of behavior-genetic and psychometric research on individual differences—with the hope of introducing ways of evolutionizing the study of personality, intelligence, and mental illness.

We are both evolutionary psychologists fascinated by human mating, but we had slightly different viewpoints and backgrounds in editing this book, and we think all the chapters have benefited from this creative tension. Glenn's background in emotional intelligence research and social psychology led him to focus a bit more on Theory of Mind in mating—how we understand the specific, moment-by-moment beliefs, desires, and preferences of potential or established sexual partners. Geoffrey's interest in psychometrics and behavior genetics led him to focus a bit more on trait assessment in mating—how we rate the general, stable, heritable personality and cognitive traits of sexual partners. These perspectives are fully complementary: They concern different person-perception and social-attribution tasks, at different levels of description, over different timeframes. Some chapters in this book address one; others address the other; some address both.

We hope that this book shows active young researchers how enthralling and rewarding it is to do research on the more psychologically profound aspects of human mating. There are already vast storehouses of knowledge on human intelligence, personality, psychopathology, Theory of Mind, social attribution, person perception, intimate relationships, and sexuality. These are all directly relevant to understanding mating intelligence. They are the fertile fields waiting for us to cross-breed with them—to our mutual benefit and delight.

The content of this book is organized into several sections. The primary content-based sections address (a) mechanisms for mate search, (b) flexible mating strategies as an element of mating intelligence, (c) mental fitness indicators, (d) mating intelligence and individual-difference factors, and (e) the ecological context of mating intelligence. In our two concluding chapters, we reconsider the nature of the mating intelligence construct to help guide future research on the interface between mating psychology and intelligence.

The intended audience for this book includes students and researchers across the behavioral sciences who are interested in human sexuality, mating, social interaction, personality, intelligence, behavior genetics, and evolutionary psychology. We genuinely hope that this book provides some new ideas and methods for building bridges between these areas. This book is especially targeted to advanced undergraduates and graduate students interested in human behavior. The book may be useful in courses concerning evolutionary psychology, intimate relationships, human sexuality, personality psychology, intelligence, and social psychology.

While many people helped with this project, we are particularly thankful to our outstanding contributors for their tireless and thought-provoking work and, in particular, to David Buss, the author of our foreword, whose support, guidance, and effort on behalf of this book have been enormous. Further, we owe special thanks to Debra Riegert, Rebecca Larsen, and all the folks at Erlbaum who have been competent, professional, and helpful across the duration of this project. We also thank the reviewers of the book proposal, David Barash, Dennis Krebs, and Timothy Ketelaar.

Much of the work here was assisted by undergraduate and graduate students at SUNY New Paltz who helped with this book and with the SUNY New Paltz Mating Intelligence Research Project, including Mike Camargo, Elisabeth DeWispelaere, Jason Diffenderfer, Krystle Hearns, John Johnson, Jill Lavallee, Justin Lee, Heather Mangione, Nilerisha Mollette, Jeremy Murphy, Regina Musicaro, Erin Stenglein, and Erica White.

Additionally, our formulation of mating intelligence has benefited a great deal from many discussions, seminars, and collaborations with individuals from the Human Evolutionary Behavioral Sciences program at the University of New Mexico, especially: Paul Andrews, Christine Apgar-Garver, Jim Boone, Dinah Caruthers, Laura Dane, Rachael Falcon, Steve Gangestad, Gil Greengross, Richard Harper, Paul Hooper, Chris Jenkins, Brent Jordan, Rex Jung, Hilly Kaplan, Yann Klimentidis, Jane Lancaster, Mark Prokosch, Glenn Scheyd, Jon Sefcek, Paul Swegel, Ilanit Tal, Randy Thornhill, Josh Tybur, Paul Watson, Ethan White, and Ron Yeo. For helpful discussions and correspondence about behavior genetics, intelligence, personality, creativity, and/or sexual selection, thanks to: Tim Bates, Ian Deary, A. J. Figueredo, Linda Gottfredson, Matt Keller, Arthur Jensen, Mike Neale, Dan Nettle, Robert Plomin, and Matt Ridley.

Finally, we thank Kathleen Geher and Rosalind Arden, our wives, for their support during the duration of this project and for many provocative discussions about everything related to mating and intelligence.

Mating Intelligence

Sex, Relationships, and the Mind's Reproductive System

I

Introduction

Chapter 1

Mating Intelligence: Toward an Evolutionarily Informed Construct

Glenn Geher
State University of New York at New Paltz

Geoffrey Miller
University of New Mexico

Jeremy Murphy
State University of New York at New Paltz

This book introduces a new construct called 'Mating Intelligence' (MI) which concerns cognitive processes that uniquely apply to the domain of human mating, sexuality, and intimate relationships. This MI construct encompasses both species-typical psychological adaptations (such as the perceptual, cognitive, and decision-making processes for evaluating an individual's potential as a long-term mate), and a set of individual differences in the efficiencies, parameters, and design details of those traits. Although we all have some ability to assess who is attractive (a species-typical adaptation), some of us are better at this than are others (i.e., we show individual differences in adaptive functioning).

We propose the construct with some trepidation, because most new constructs in psychology are a waste of time. They may succeed in getting a new technical term associated with the name of a tenure-seeking researcher, but rarely lead to cumulative, consilient scientific progress (McGrath, 2005). Technically, new constructs rarely show good discriminant validity (predicting behavior differently from existing constructs) or

good incremental validity (predicting behavior better than existing constructs) (see, e.g., Gottfredson, 2003; Judge, Erez, Bono & Thoresen, 2002).
The burden of proof should rightly be against researchers trying to intro-
duce a new way of parsing human nature or a new individual-differences
variable.

This is especially true in intelligence and personality research, where
most new constructs turn out to be little more than the good old-fashioned
g factor (general intelligence, IQ), and/or one or more of the 'Big Five' personality traits (openness, conscientiousness, extroversion, agreeableness,
emotional stability). For example, some evidence suggests that 'political
authoritarianism' corresponds empirically to low intelligence plus low
openness (i.e., conservatism), high conscientiousness (i.e., sense of duty),
and low agreeableness (i.e., aggressiveness) (Heaven & Bucci, 2001; Jost,
Glaser, Kruglanski, & Sulloway, 2003; Schultz & Searleman, 2002). Many
other newly introduced constructs turn out to be little more than statistical
sub-factors of general intelligence. For example, Howard Gardner's 'multiple intelligences' (Gardner, 1983) all correlate positively with general
intelligence, but often can't be measured with as much reliability and
validity, so they look more attractively elusive and mystical (see Gordon,
1997; Hunt, 2001; Klein, 2003; Pyryt, 2000). Similar problems afflict Robert
Sternberg's construct of 'practical intelligence' (Gottfredson, 2003).

On the other hand, there are a few constructs—notably 'social intelligence' (Cantor & Kihlstrom, 1987) and 'emotional intelligence' (Salovey
& Mayer, 1990)—that have provoked progressive research traditions in
the last several decades. Research on social intelligence (including Theory of Mind, Machiavellian intelligence, autism, and face perception) has
arguably been the most important innovation in developmental psychology and comparative psychology in the last 30 years (e.g., Reader &
Laland, 2002). It has yielded thousands of papers on the 'mind-reading'
skills of apes, children, and adults. Research on emotional intelligence
has had a similar impact in business management, organizational behavior, clinical psychology, and relationship research (e.g., George, 2000).
Both constructs are also informing the emerging fields of social neuroscience and affective neuroscience (e.g., Bar-On, Tranel, Denburg, &
Bechara, 2003).

For both social and emotional intelligence, though, the development
of reliable, valid individual-differences measures of the constructs has
proven somewhat frustrating and elusive (e.g., Davies, Stankov, &
Roberts, 1998; Geher, 2004; cf. Mayer, Caruso, & Salovey, 1999)—especially
in finding measures that show good discriminant validity beyond well-
established measures of general intelligence and personality (De Raad,
2005). Some evidence for discriminant validity has been published for
some emotional intelligence scales (e.g., Livingstone & Day, 2005; Petrides
& Furnham, 2001, 2003; Tett, Fox, & Wang, 2005). However, skeptics

suggest that social intelligence is just general intelligence plus extroversion, or that emotional intelligence is just general intelligence plus agreeableness and emotional stability (see, e.g., De Raad, 2005; Matthews, Zeidner, & Roberts, 2004; Schulte, Ree, & Carretta, 2004).

Although such criticisms are important, they often miss the crucial tension that makes these constructs scientifically productive—these constructs bridge the gap between research on human universals and research on individual differences. They unify the experimental psychology tradition of Wilhelm Wundt and the correlational psychology tradition of Francis Galton. They identify not just a distinctive part of human nature, but a cluster of human differences that are socially salient and important. The human-universal aspect of these constructs helps researchers identify key adaptive problems, social functions, and cognitive mechanisms. The individual-differences aspect helps researchers develop valid ability tests that can drive comparative research across species, sexes, ages, populations, families, individuals, and psychopathologies.

For instance, emotional intelligence is a set of mental abilities (to read facial expressions, identify emotions in self and other, and control one's own emotions under trying situations), but it is also a partly-heritable, partly-trainable dimension of variation that is helpful to appreciate in school, work, and family life (Ciarrochi, Forgas, & Mayer, 2006). We all have emotional intelligence in some form, to a far higher degree than most other species. But we differ in how well it works, and even small individual differences in emotional intelligence can yield huge differences in life-outcomes—getting promoted versus fired, driving to a second honeymoon versus a divorce hearing. We suspect that Mating Intelligence will also turn out to have two faces—a set of universal mechanisms, and a dimension of individual differences—as a psychological construct.

A HISTORY OF MUTUAL NEGLECT BETWEEN MATING RESEARCH AND INTELLIGENCE RESEARCH

We aim for 'mating intelligence' to serve a research-motivating function like the 'social intelligence' and 'emotional intelligence' constructs did. Specifically, we hope it will build bridges between mating research (including evolutionary psychology, human sexuality, and relationship research) and intelligence research (including psychometrics and behavior genetics). These two fields have neglected each other for over a century.

Human intelligence research has neglected the central adaptive challenge in the life of any sexually reproducing species—finding mates and having offspring. To quantify this neglect, we examined all volumes of the premier international journal *Intelligence* since its inception in 1977. We searched in SciSearch for *Intelligence* articles that included all keywords we could list related to mating (e.g., *mating, mate, marriage, sex*) in the title or abstract. We then read the abstracts to see if they genuinely concerned mating issues. As of November 2005, only 3 of 811 articles (0.8 percent) in *Intelligence* have dealt directly with human mating (Benbow, Zonderman, & Stanley, 1983; Kanazawa & Kovar, 2004; Rushton, 2004). Another 43 articles concern sex differences unrelated to the context of mating behavior (e.g., Deary, Thorpe, Wilson, Starr, & Whalley, 2003).

Equally, mating research has neglected intelligence—the most reliably measurable, predictive, heritable construct in the history of psychology (Jensen, 1998). Evolutionary psychology has been at the forefront of human mating research since about 1990, and its premier journal is *Evolution and Human Behavior*. Since changing its name from *Ethology and Sociobiology* in 1997, only 1 of its 311 research articles (Flinn, Geary, & Ward, 2005), as of November 2005, has dealt directly with intelligence (according to a similar keyword search in SciSearch). Another 6 concern sex differences in specific cognitive abilities (e.g., Silverman, Choi, Mackewn, Fisher, Moro & Olshansky, 2000), but do not directly relate intelligence to mating behavior. Similarly, the premier journal in relationship research, the *Journal of Social and Personal Relationships*, contains only 2 of 939 articles directly concerning intelligence since its inception in 1985 (Rowatt, Cunningham, & Druen, 1999; Sprecher & Regan, 2002).

More generally, although SciSearch returns 44,111 results for 'mating' and 27,974 results for 'intelligence' in all journals since 1950 (out of 51,477,995 total records), the combination of 'mating' and 'intelligence' appear in only 40 relevant articles. (In descending order of citation impact, the top 10 were: Crow, 1993, 1995; Feingold, 1992; Lykken & Tellegen, 1993; Miller & Todd, 1998; Furlow, Gangestad, & Armijo-Prewitt, 1998; Eaves, 1973; Hatfield & Sprecher, 1995; Li, Bailey, Kenrick, & Linsenmeier, 2002; Rushton & Nicholson, 1988). Most of these concerned assortative mating for intelligence. (Another 60-odd articles concerned different 'mating' strategies in genetic algorithms, an artificial 'intelligence' optimization method, based on early work by Todd & Miller, 1991). Those 40 relevant mating/intelligence articles are only twice as many as would be expected by chance (24), given the base-rate frequency of 'mating' (.000857) and 'intelligence' (.000543) in the whole scientific literature of 51 million papers since 1950. In fact, 'mating' is less likely to be associated with 'intelligence' (121 total papers) than with 'cockroach' (168 papers), 'Norway' (178), or 'steel' (182). Thus, 'mating' and 'intelligence' do not seem very closely connected in the minds of scientists.

Indeed, we could find only three areas of overlap between mating research and intelligence research.

First, as mentioned above, there is the literature of assortative mating for intelligence, which is important to ascertain mostly for technical reasons in behavior genetics (overlooked assortative mating can bias estimates of heritability from twin and adoption studies).

Second, there are sporadic references to mate preferences for intelligence, creativity, adaptability, and other aspects of general intelligence in the evolutionary psychology literature on human mate choice—including research on cross-cultural preferences, personal ads, and sperm-donor preferences (e.g., Buss, 1989; Dunbar, Marriott, & Duncan, 1997; Haselton & Miller, 2006; Kenrick et al., 1990; Li et al., 2002; Scheib, 1994).

Third, there is the clinical psychology literature on mental illnesses that undermine mating intelligence in particular ways that are not entirely explained by reduced general intelligence. These mating-intelligence disorders include the following: Borderline personality disorder includes highly unstable evaluations of the commitment level and mate value of a potential mate, and of one's own mate value (Skodol, Gunderson, Pfohl, Widiger, Livesley, & Siever, 2002). Anorexia—severe, sometimes fatal under-eating—often includes misconceptions that the other sex is attracted to a much thinner body form than they actually prefer, and such misconceptions are often driven by media stereotypes and adolescent peer-group gossip (Groesz, Levine, & Murnen, 2002; Paxton, Schutz, Wertheim, & Muir, 1999). Asperger's syndrome and autism are characterized by deficits in social understanding and communication abilities that result in pervasive, consistent problems in attracting, retaining, and understanding sexual partners (Ashton, 2002; Baron-Cohen, Wheelwright, Skinner, Martin, & Cubley, 2001; Baron-Cohen, Richler, Bisarya, Gurunathan, & Wheelwright, 2003). Narcissistic personality disorder—extreme arrogance, grandiosity, self-involvement, and showing off—can be construed as obsessive over-investing in conspicuous, public fitness-displays to attract multiple short-term mates (Buss & Shackelford, 1997; Gabriel, Critelli, & Ee, 1994; Robins & Beer, 2001). Antisocial personality disorder (psychopathy)—a pervasive pattern of callous, exploitative, impulsive, violent, and promiscuous behavior—can be construed as over-reliance on deceptive, coercive, and short-term mating tactics (see Dunsieth, Nelson, Bursman-Lovins, Holcomb, Bechman, Welge, Roby, Taylor, Soutullo, & McElroy, 2004; Krueger, Hicks, Patrick, Carlson, Iacono, & McGue, 2002). All these personality disorders seriously reduce long-term mating success, relationship satisfaction, and marital stability (Grant, Hasin, Stinson, Dawson, Chou, Ruan, & Pickering, 2004; Skodol, Gunderson, McGlashan, Dyck, Stout, Bender, Grilo, Shea, Zanatini, Morey, Sanislow, & Oldham, 2002), so can be viewed partly as disorders of Mating Intelligence. However, antisocial personality disorder in males often increases short-term reproductive success (Moffitt, Caspi, Harrington, & Milne, 2002)—insofar as this represents a successful 'alternative strategy' in male mating behavior, this emphasizes the point that Mating Intelligence can have a very dark side indeed.

Clearly, none of these research areas has developed an integrated view of Mating Intelligence as a major adaptive domain of human cognitive functioning. We think this century of mutual neglect between mating research and intelligence research has been harmful in many ways. It led mating researchers to neglect the romantic attractiveness of intelligence in its diverse manifestations. It led relationship researchers to neglect intelligence as an explanatory variable in predicting relationship formation, satisfaction, conflict, and dissolution. It led intelligence researchers to focus on the predictive validity of general intelligence in the public domains of education and employment rather than the private domains of relationships and family life, making it easier for critics to portray the 'general intelligence' construct as exclusively concerned with modern book-learning. It led sex-differences researchers to spend decades on sterile debates about cognitive differences between men and women, without any sexual-selection theory from mating research to drive sex-differences predictions, or sophisticated psychometrics from intelligence research to clarify the nature of the cognitive differences.

Each of these scientific problems led to lost opportunities in applied psychology—decades of delay in understanding the real-world effects of intelligence differences in the domains of human mating, relationships, sexuality, marriage, and family life—and in understanding all their associated 'social' (i.e., sexual) problems, such as teen pregnancy, sexually transmitted diseases, abortion, single motherhood, spousal abuse, depression, suicide, divorce, rape, sexual discrimination, and so forth. Research on happiness ('subjective well-being') consistently shows that the quality of intimate relationships (especially sexual relationships) is a major predictor of overall life-satisfaction—often more important than education, income, or occupational status (DePaulo & Morris, 2005; Diener, Oishi, & Lucas, 2005; Lucas, 2005; Mroczek & Spiro, 2005). By neglecting to study the links between mating, intelligence, and human happiness, psychologists have done a great disservice to humanity. Our proximal goal with this book is to spark more interdisciplinary research on mating intelligence, but our ultimate goal is to promote the happiness of human individuals and the sustainability of human societies by shedding more light on the most intimate and important sources of satisfaction in life.

AN EVOLUTIONARY PSYCHOLOGY CONTEXT FOR MATING INTELLIGENCE

If the 1960s is often characterized as the era of the *cognitive revolution* (Martel Johnson & Erneling, 1997), then the 1990s and the current decade must surely qualify as the period of the *evolution revolution* in psychology. A recent content analysis of articles featured in *Behavioral and Brain Sciences*, an elite interdisciplinary journal, revealed that more than 30 percent of articles published in the last decade include *evolution* in the title or as a keyword (Wilson, Garruto, McLeod, Regan, Tan-Wilson, unpublished manuscript). Evolution has come of age in psychology, not just in the new field of evolutionary psychology proper, but in the prominence of adaptationist analysis across many areas of traditional psychology—perceptual, cognitive, social, developmental, and abnormal.

However, many areas of psychology have been slow to incorporate evolutionary principles. Intelligence research is a case in point. To be sure, much work has addressed the heritability of intelligence (e.g., Plomin & Spinath, 2004), and the evolutionary origins of 'human intelligence' (e.g., Sternberg & Kaufman, 2002). Yet the behavior genetics work on intelligence has rarely connected to the evolutionary stories to yield an integrated evolutionary genetic theory of the selection pressures that shaped human intelligence to have the structure, dimensions of variance, and types of heritability that it does. In particular, competing theories of intelligence (e.g., Jensen vs. Sternberg vs. Gardner) have never been resolved by appeal to evolutionary principles. Also, the unitary nature of the g factor (general intelligence) has not been reconciled with evolutionary psychology's 'massive modularity' claim that the human cognitive architecture is composed of hundreds of distinct psychological adaptations. Further, although some new constructs, such as emotional intelligence (Salovey & Mayer, 1990), seem more closely related to core adaptive challenges of humans as social primates, work on such constructs has generally progressed separately from evolutionary psychology (Geher & Renstrom, 2004).

In the past several years, evolutionary psychologists have provided insights into many aspects of human behavior that would not have been possible without the broad and powerful explanatory nature of evolutionary theory. Many such findings deal with issues of human mating (e.g., Buss, 2003), including diverse topics such as sexual jealousy (Buss, Larsen, Westen, & Semmelroth, 1992), the effects of body symmetry on attractiveness ratings (Gangestad & Thornhill, 1997), and the phenomenology of short and long-term mating strategies across the sexes (Schmitt, Shackelford, & Buss, 2002).

This focus on human mating taken by evolutionary psychology is not capricious. In general, evolutionary psychology underscores reproductive success as the ultimate arbiter of whether some trait is likely to replicate across generations and thereby become species-typical. Mating processes influence reproductive success more directly than any other class of human behaviors. As such, the mating domain deserves a special status in evolutionary psychology. In the words of David Buss:

> Because differential reproduction is the engine that drives the evolution-
> ary process, the psychological mechanisms surrounding reproduction
> should be especially strong targets of selection. (Buss, 2004, p. 103)

Yet, in spite of all the evolutionary psychology work on human mating, evolutionary theorizing about the origins of human intelligence has
neglected the mating domain as a possible source of selection pressures, or
an adaptive arena in which intelligence matters.

The book is a first step in trying to synthesize insights concerning
human mating and human intelligence within an evolutionary framework. With few exceptions, existing conceptions of intelligence are devoid
of mating-related content. Similarly, mating research in evolutionary psychology generally ignores intelligence, except as a vaguely defined trait
that seems sexually attractive for obscure reasons (see Miller, 2000, for an
exception). Likewise, human sexuality research and intimate relationships
research neglects intelligence differences between people. These facts are
troubling given the centrality of both mating and intelligence in human
psychology. So we have a situation in which two important areas of psychology, intelligence and mating psychology, need to be synthesized.
Given the utility of short, memorable phrases as labels for emerging
research areas, we think it is useful to label this synthesized construct *mating intelligence* (MI).

MATING INTELLIGENCE (MI) DEFINED

Roughly, we think of mating intelligence (MI) as the mind's reproductive
system: the total set of psychological capacities for sexual courtship, competition, and rivalry; for relationship-formation, commitment, coordination, and termination; for flirtation, foreplay, and copulation; for mate-
search, mate-choice, mate-guarding, and mate-switching; and for many
other behavioral capacities that bring mainly reproductive (rather than
survival) payoffs. MI is not a single capacity, a single adaptation, a single
brain region, or a single 'group factor' under the g factor (general intelligence). Rather, it is a collective noun that covers dozens or hundreds of
distinct adaptations, exaptations, learned skills, and *ad hoc* tactics for mating. MI forms a coherent category only at the functional level (capacities
evolved, learned, or invented *for* mating). As is addressed in Miller's 'Frequently Asked Questions' chapter in this volume, MI is probably not best
conceived as a coherent category at the level of genetics (we don't expect
distinct MI genes), neuroscience (we don't expect distinct MI cortical
areas), or cognitive processes (we don't expect distinct MI modes of
Bayesian inference).

Some of the many MI capacities may be human universals that show
very high efficiency and adaptiveness across all neurologically normal,
sexually mature adults; thus, they might show little variation between
individuals and low correlations with general intelligence. In later chapters, we often refer to these as 'mating mechanisms,' to emphasize their
efficient, reliable functioning. Other MI capacities might show high variance and heritability, and might have high g-loadings (high correlations
with general intelligence or IQ). In later chapters, we often refer to these as
'mental fitness indicators,' to emphasize their conspicuous variation across
individuals. Thus, the relationships between MI, general intelligence,
social intelligence, and emotional intelligence will vary from capacity to
capacity—sometimes closely connected, sometimes not.

Even within mating mechanisms that operate efficiently within all
normal humans, we might still expect substantial adaptive differences in
their design details, including perceptual inputs, decision parameters, and
behavioral outputs, across sexes, ages, levels of mental and physical attractiveness, and many other cross-individual and cross-situational variables.

DIFFERENT VIEWS OF MI

As will become clear from the diversity of ideas included in this volume,
different researchers have different views of MI. This theoretical diversity
is not unusual in intelligence research (see Geher, 2004). One of this book's
goals is to provide a forum for these different voices, in hopes of moving
toward a consensual MI framework that can fruitfully guide future
research, and that is well-rooted in the current theories and findings of
evolutionary psychology, human sexuality research, intimate relationship
research, and intelligence research.

As a starting point, we sketch four distinct views of MI as they have
been articulated by or as they have influenced various contributors to this
volume (see Table 1.1.):

A. *The SUNY New Paltz Mating Intelligence Project.* The authors from the
    State University of New York (SUNY) at New Paltz (Glenn Geher,
    Jeremy Murphy) do empirical research on MI construed as *a set of
    inter-related cognitive abilities that bear directly on mating-relevant issues
    and that show variability across individual adults.* We think of MI as par-
    tially independent of general intelligence, and as distinct from other
    domains of (e.g., social intelligence, emotional intelligence). From
    this perspective, MI must include all mating-relevant domains that
    have proven important in the extant literature on evolutionary psy-
    chology and human sexuality (e.g., factors that predict success in
    attracting and retaining short- and long-term mates, reactions to dif-

TABLE 1.1.
Four Conceptions of Mating Intelligence

	SUNY New Paltz Mating Intelligence Project	Cosmides and Tooby (2002)	Kanazawa (2004)	Miller (2000)
Conception of Mating Intelligence	Set of task-specific cognitive abilities to handle ancestral mating problems	Set of task-specific cognitive abilities to handle ancestral mating problems	Set of task-specific cognitive abilities to handle ancestral mating problems	Focused on sexually selected creative courtship abilities that show high variability, heritability, and difficulty
Relation to General Intelligence (g)	Modest positive correlations with g (as with social & emotional intelligence)	Slight positive correlations with g, which is a 'bundling together' of domain-specific abilities	No correlation with g, except when mating involves evolutionarily novel problems	High positive correlations with general intelligence; Reliable, valid g-indicators
Understanding Lewinskygate	Clinton's sometimes ill-judged mating decisions are largely unrelated to his high general intelligence	Clinton's affair-seeking reflects ancestral mating adaptations for extra-pair copulation by high-status males	Clinton's affair-seeking reflects ancestral mating adaptations for extra-pair copulation by high-status males	Clinton's ability to attract young females reveals his general genetic and phenotypic quality, including general intelligence

ferent kinds of infidelity, etc.; see Buss, 2003). Also, this perspective emphasizes 'cross-sex mind-reading'—our social-cognitive abilities to understand the beliefs and desires of the opposite sex, and to make accurate mating-relevant judgments of their psychological traits. For example, we are interested in whether males can accurately judge which personal advertisement (among three describing potential male marriage partners) will prove most attractive to female raters. We are provisionally defining high MI as the ability to make accurate judgments of this sort across several different mating-related tasks. Other key MI-demanding tasks include detecting sexual interest from a potential mate, detecting sexual infidelity by a partner, and detecting sexual envy from a rival. Readers who are familiar with ability-based methods of measuring emotional intelligence (e.g., Brackett & Salovey, 2004; Mayer et al., 2000) will recognize this framework as similar. This MI-as-ability view has influenced mainly the chapters in this volume first-authored by Glenn Geher, James Casey, and Scott Kaufman.

B. *Cosmides and Tooby's Conception of Domain-Specific Psychological Adaptations.* In their foundational papers in evolutionary psychology, Cosmides and Tooby emphasize massive modularity as a hallmark of adaptations that comprise the human mind. Their view of 'intelligences' is no exception. Cosmides and Tooby (2002) divide intelligences into two distinct categories: *dedicated intelligences* and *improvisational intelligence*. A dedicated intelligence is a reliably developing, universal human ability to solve a set of adaptively important, ancestrally recurring problems. For instance, in their work on the cheater-detection module (Cosmides & Tooby, 1992), they argue that selection favored specialized cognitive modules that allowed us to detect individuals who cheat on implicit social contracts (who take without giving in return). Improvisational intelligence, on the other hand, concerns abilities to solve evolutionarily novel problems such as driving cars, learning calculus, or investing in pensions. They conceive of this more domain-general kind of intelligence as being comprised of a 'bundling together' of several dedicated intelligences. From this perspective, 'Mating Intelligence' is *a class of domain-specific dedicated intelligences attuned to ancestral mating challenges, plus whatever forms of improvisational intelligence deal with evolutionarily novel mating challenges* (e.g., single's ads, contraception, divorce courts). This MI-as-domain-specific-adaptations view has influenced virtually all the chapters in this book, especially those first-authored by Lars Penke, Charlotte de Backer, Norm Li, Maureen O'Sullivan, Viviana Weekes-Shackelford, Jessica Ash, and Aurelio José Figueredo.

C. *Kanazawa's Separation of Mating Domains from General Intelligence.* In a recent set of papers on the evolution of intelligence (Kanazawa & Kovar, 2004; Kanazawa, 2004, Kanazawa, this volume; cf. Borsboom & Dolan, 2006), Satoshi Kanazawa agrees with Cosmides and Tooby that massively modular, domain-specific adaptations (including MI capacities) sufficed for most problem solving in our evolutionary past. However, he argues that humans also evolved a new, domain-specific adaptation, 'general intelligence,' for solving evolutionarily novel problems (e.g., new ways of hunting, socializing, making tools). From this perspective, mating (as an evolutionarily ancient domain) should have little connection to general intelligence (as an adaptation for evolutionary novelty), so MI abilities should be uncorrelated with measures of general intelligence, and mating research and intelligence research should proceed without much cross-talk.

D. *Miller's Focus on MI as Mental Fitness Indicators.* In previous work, one of us (Geoffrey Miller) has extended the Cosmides/Tooby framework in a different direction, arguing that many human domain-specific mental traits evolved through sexual selection as 'mental fitness indicators' (Miller, 2000a, b). In this view, many unique human capacities for language, art, music, humor, and creativity evolved to attract sexual partners, and they did so because they were reliable signals of general intelligence (a brain with high 'neurodevelopmental stability') and good genes (a genotype with relatively few harmful mutations). This view predicts substantial correlations between general intelligence and many sexually attractive mental fitness indicators, but does not predict such correlations between general intelligence and most other components of MI. This fitness indicator framework has influenced the chapters first-authored by Lars Penke, Daniel Nettle, Matthew Keller, Andrew Shaner, Scott Kaufman, and Geoffrey Miller.

MATING INTELLIGENCE VERSUS TRADITIONAL NORMS OF RATIONALITY

These four views differ in their emphasis on MI as a way of understanding others versus a way of impressing them, in their predictions about MI's relationship with general intelligence, and in their views about mismatches between ancestral and modern mating conditions. What they have in common is a biologically grounded view of 'intelligence' as adaptive behavior rather than rational choice. In traditional social stereotypes, 'intelligence' implies cold, rational, analytical calculation. In traditional economics and other social sciences that use Rational Choice Theory, 'intelligence' implies the maximization of expected subjective utilities given consistent, transitive preferences. In research on judgment and decision-making, 'intelligence' implies adherence to rather narrow procedural norms of logical reasoning and statistical inference. None of these meanings fit very well with this book's emphasis on the hottest domain of human cognition—mating—which seems both too carnal and too transcendental to fit into such narrow, workaday meanings of 'intelligence.'

As with social and emotional intelligence, mating intelligence can embody hidden forms of adaptive logic that violate traditional norms of rationality, including traditional criteria of 'intelligence,' narrowly construed. For example, mating intelligence is what makes high-school kids distracted when they're taking the SAT test—they might pay so much attention to the socio-sexual cues of interest from their peer group that they miss some analytical reasoning questions. Their parents and their college admission boards might despair over this, but the kids are tuned into the evolutionarily salient forms of intelligence that really count.

Mating Intelligence is not just distracting from academic tasks; it has been under different kinds of selection pressures that favor different performance criteria. For example, many analytical reasoning tasks assume that the reasoner's goal should be to maximize accuracy—the probability of a 'correct' response. By contrast, most evolutionary psychologists now understand that animals and humans are under selection not to maximize raw accuracy in decision-making, but to maximize expected benefits and to minimize expected costs (Haselton & Buss, 2000; Haselton & Nettle, 2005). When fitness costs and benefits of different errors are very different (e.g., failing to notice a saber-toothed cat vs. false-alarming to a rock as if it were a saber-toothed cat), then selection can favor extremely biased responses (e.g., a very low threshold for detecting predators) rather than raw accuracy. Selection favors tendencies to commit errors that are less harmful.

For example, accuracy-maximization might favor young men who go around assuming that most young women are not interested in having a short-term sexual affair with them. However, benefit-maximization might favor young men evolving the opposite assumption (that all women secretly desire them), because, if they are motivated to court many women (as a result of such biased assumptions), the reproductive benefits of finding the very women who say 'yes' may vastly outweigh the reproductive costs (e.g., slightly lower social status due to the embarrassment of being rejection) of the many women who say 'no' (Haselton & Buss, 2000). From a narrow rationality perspective, the young men who assume that all women want them are showing severe social-cognitive inaccuracies, judgment biases, and probably narcissistic personality disorder. However, from an evolutionary perspective, those young men may be showing an adaptive bias that has consistently maximized the reproductive success of their male ancestors—however annoying it was to their female non-ancestors. In this case, male Mating Intelligence would look very low on first inspection (very inaccurate), but rather high on closer examination.

Another recently documented case of adaptive bias is that women tend to perceive men as less committed in relationships than they really are (Haselton & Buss, 2001). Here again the reasons concern an asymmetry in the costs of under-perceiving a male's commitment (which may annoy him, but motivate more conspicuous commitment-displays and attentiveness), versus over-perceiving commitment (which could lead to impulsive sex, pregnancy, abandonment by the male, and subsequent death of the child through lack of paternal investment). It is much worse to be impregnated by a commitment-pretending psychopath than to doubt a truly committed partner's intentions. Thus, women doubt male commitment, and men feign more commitment than they feel—a never-ending arms race of romantic skepticism and excess that has shaped both female and male Mating Intelligence.

A third example of adaptive biases in MI comes from the Ideal Standards Model of Fletcher and Simpson (2000), which explicitly considers which mating contexts should favor raw judgment accuracy versus adaptively biased judgment. According to this perspective, there are times during the mating process when raw accuracy is most adaptive (and should be typical), while there are other times when specific biases are most adaptive (and should prevail). Consider, for instance, the mate-selection phase of the game. When initially assessing the value of a potential mate as a long-term partner, accuracy is crucial. Assessments of kindness, fertility, strength, and social status are key to acquiring a mate who would be good for the long haul. However, when you find yourself in the throes of a long-term relationship with several shared children who need much parental support, focusing on your partner's many annoying habits that have unfolded across the relationship may not be best for everyone involved. Rather, holding an idealized, biased, overly rosy picture of one's partner at this stage may be best for both proximal relationship satisfaction and ultimate survival of offspring (see Murray, Holmes, & Griffin, 1996, for evidence suggesting that such biased perceptions of partners do, in fact, emerge in healthy long-term relationships).

Thus, high MI may not correspond in any simple way to traditional narrow norms of procedural rationality, such as logical deduction or statistical induction. MI researchers may often benefit from viewing human mating tasks from a formal decision-making perspective, as long as they remember that evolution maximizes reproductive success—not personal happiness, relationship stability, parental love, or accuracy in understanding the other sex. To test a formal decision-making model of some mating task—one that includes explicit performance criteria—a good first step might be to see whether people who score higher on general intelligence (e.g., traditional IQ tests) also tend to score higher on the mating task performance criteria. If they do not, there is probably something wrong with the formal model and its performance criteria (see Stanovich & West, 2000).

Another major misconception about Mating Intelligence derives from stereotypes about nerds, geeks, and highly intelligent but socially awkward engineers. Some of the most conspicuously 'intelligent' individuals in modern society are physicists, software engineers, and members of other highly technical professions that require years of obsessive dedication to achieving academic credentials at the cost of one's social and sexual maturation. The result is that the most successful members of these professions are often males with some degree of Asperger syndrome—a keen interest in abstract systems of thought rather than human relationships

(Baron-Cohen et al., 2001; 2003). Such nerds would tend to score very highly on traditional tests of General Intelligence, but very poorly on tests of Mating Intelligence. This is likely a source of continuing frustration to their girl-friends, spouses, and co-workers (see Aston, 2002). The nerd-prevalence rate—especially in academic settings—can thereby give the false impression that General Intelligence must be uncorrelated—or even negatively correlated—with Mating Intelligence in the general population.

MATING INTELLIGENCE IN RELATION TO SOCIAL INTELLIGENCE

Social Intelligence (a.k.a. Machiavellian Intelligence, Theory of Mind, mind-reading) concerns our abilities to understand the beliefs and desires of others (Cantor & Kihlstrom, 1987). As such, it clearly overlaps with any reasonable notion of Mating Intelligence, because human heterosexual relationships depend upon understanding the beliefs and desires of oppo-site-sex partners and same-sex rivals. For example, successful mating depend on assessing each potential mate's beliefs, desires, and preferences through their verbal and non-verbal signals; remembering a vast array of social information about each potential mate's relatives, friends, offspring, previous lovers, and would-be lovers; sorting through conflicting social information (gossip) about each potential mate that is generated or repeated by other individuals with their own socio-sexual agendas; and assessing each potential mate's relative social status in the local dominance hierarchy and mating market. In a highly social primate species such as ours, the sexually successful must be socially competent.

Social intelligence becomes even more important in longer-term rela-tionships, as partners must coordinate their foraging, parenting, and social efforts given somewhat conflicting interests, agendas, personalities, and preferences. Indeed, for people who have been successfully married a long time, one's mental model of one's spouse is probably the most accurate and detailed understanding of another human that one ever develops in his or her lifetime. This is one reason why the death of a spouse is so traumatic.

From this point of view, MI is a sub-set of Social Intelligence, but Social Intelligence also concerns Theory of Mind applied to non-sexual relation-ships with parents, offspring, siblings, kin, friends, allies, trading partners, enemies, dominants, subordinates, peers, mentors, pupils, and other groups. MI might thereby be classed alongside research on Parenting Intel-ligence, Trading Intelligence, Status Intelligence, and Group-Competition Intelligence.

However, MI is not entirely subsumed by Social Intelligence, because it also includes some psychological adaptations that do not concern under-standing the beliefs and desires of others. For example, male adaptations for being attracted to facial beauty and for having stronger orgasms given sperm competition are clear components of MI, but do not obviously depend on Theory of Mind. So, Mating Intelligence and Social Intelligence are partially overlapping, but partially distinct constructs.

What can MI research learn from Social Intelligence research? Kihlstrom and Cantor (2000) argue that social intelligence is an important psychological construct in principle, but that it has shown a limited capacity in practice to guide progressive empirical research. Ever since Thorndike (1920, as cited in Kihlstrom & Cantor, 2000) defined social intelligence as the ability to understand and interact with others, there have been countless attempts to develop reliable, valid measures of social intelligence. However, many early measures of social intelligence (e.g., the George Washington Social Intelligence Test) correlated so heavily with measurements of general intelligence that the social intelligence construct seemed to have little discriminative validity (Kihlstrom & Cantor, 2000). Perhaps social intelligence was just general intelligence applied to social problems, rather than a distinctive set of psychological processes.

In fact, social intelligence research seemed to flourish only after it gave up any connection to psychometric research on individual differences, and turned into the study of adaptive species-typical capacities for certain kinds of social inference (e.g., Theory of Mind research in primates, children, and autistics—see Whiten & Byrne, 1997). For example, Gardner (1983) posited distinctions between general intelligence, 'intrapersonal intelligence' (ability to understand one's own thoughts and feelings), and 'interpersonal intelligence' (ability to understanding the thoughts and feelings of others), but he never demonstrated that the latter can be operationalized into reliable, valid individual-differences measures that are distinct from the g factor. Instead, his arguments for the adaptive importance of these 'intelligences' inspired work in comparative, evolutionary, developmental, and clinical psychology on domain-specific, species-typical capacities for social cognition. In the last 25 years, there has been an explosion of research on 'social intelligence,' but it has almost nothing to do with mainstream intelligence research.

MATING INTELLIGENCE IN RELATION TO EMOTIONAL INTELLIGENCE

MI also overlaps partially with Emotional Intelligence, such that neither is a clear super-set of the other. Emotional Intelligence concerns abilities to understand and influence the emotions of others and of oneself (Salovey & Mayer, 1990). It has been better operationalized than Social Intelligence as an individual-differences construct. For example, the four-part model of emotional intelligence developed by Mayer, Salovey, and colleagues (e.g.,

Mayer, Salovey, & Caruso, 2000) has proven valid and useful in several ways (Matthews et al., 2004). This currently dominant model views emotional intelligence as comprised of four somewhat distinct capacities (to identify, understand, and manage emotions, and to modulate emotions adaptively to promote effective cognition) that vary between individuals, but that tend to positively inter-correlate with each other and with general intelligence. Emotional Intelligence researchers still disagree about the best ways to define and operationalize the construct (see Geher, 2004), but agree that Emotional Intelligence is important across many domains of human social life.

Such emotional-comprehension and emotional-influence capacities are certainly a crucial part of human mating, which activates virtually the whole range of human emotions (e.g., interest, lust, love, surprise, disgust, happiness, sadness, jealousy, envy, hate, rage, fear, anxiety, anticipation, orgasm). Successful courtship demands exemplary abilities to influence a potential mate's emotional state—to maximize interest, lust, and love; to minimize disgust and hate; to optimize levels of jealousy and anxiety; and to create romantic contexts conducive to orgasm. It also requires very high levels of emotional self-control, which are often (unconsciously) tested to the breaking point by potential mates. But there is much more to MI than just Emotional Intelligence, because MI includes many other mating-related adaptations for perception, cognition, memory, learning, planning, decision-making, and motor control. Most mating is very emotionally charged, because the fitness stakes are so high, but human sexuality is not driven exclusively by 'basic emotions' (such as 'lust' or 'jealousy') as normally construed.

MATING INTELLIGENCE: IS BILL CLINTON AN EXEMPLAR?

Bill Gates exemplifies general intelligence; Oprah Winfrey exemplifies Emotional Intelligence. Who exemplifies Mating Intelligence? Several conceptual issues about MI can be clarified by asking whether former U.S. President Bill Clinton captures this construct.

By nearly all accounts, Clinton is extremely intelligent: despite a humble background in a small Arkansas town, he graduated from Georgetown University, visited Oxford as a Rhodes scholar, and got a law degree from Yale University (see Clinton, 2004). As an orator and writer, he has proven articulate, insightful, and highly persuasive to many voters and political peers. The media have consistently portrayed him as one of America's most intelligence presidents. For example, LaRouche (2002) wrote "Clinton was, personally, perhaps the most intelligent President of the Twentieth Century . . ."

Clinton embodies both the light and dark side of mating intelligence: he shows high general intelligence, but is especially strong on mating-relevant abilities: verbal fluency, moral vision, humor, charisma, mind-reading. He's also renowned for showing 'bad sexual judgment' that actually would have had high reproductive payoffs in prehistory—not just with White House intern Monica Lewinsky, but in allegedly dozens of extramarital affairs with many women throughout his adult life, some of whom would have become pregnant if contraception did not exist. So, he would have had a lot of kids—and that's evolutionary success, not political scandal.

Different reactions to 'Lewinskygate' (the 1998 political scandal following the Lewinsky affair) highlight the vastly different implicit views of Mating Intelligence held by media pundits and most psychologists (including intimate relationship researchers, sexuality researchers, and marriage counselors) versus views held by normal voters and evolutionary psychologists. To the former groups, Clinton's affairs revealed reckless impulsiveness, poor judgment, and the pursuit of short-term lust over long-term political respectability and marital stability. Why seek a few minutes of pleasant fellatio when the potential costs were so high—months of embarrassing impeachment hearings and divorce court? The apparent 'poor judgment' shown by Clinton warranted a chapter (written by Diane Halpern) in Robert Sternberg's (2002) book *Why Smart People Can Be So Stupid*. Halpern's cognitive analysis of Clinton's decision-making focused on his individual learning history regarding infidelity (e.g., his father's behavior), and his social learning processes (e.g., the example of other presidents who were highly promiscuous without impeachment). While these learning processes might have influenced Clinton to some extent, they amount to little more than post hoc explanations of apparent psychopathology.

By contrast, to the normal voters and evolutionary psychologists, sexual promiscuity by high-status male social primates comes as no surprise. Indeed, it is both the statistical norm across species, cultures, and history, and the whole adaptive point of status-striving by males (Betzig, 1986; Buss, 2003). As all animal behavior researchers know, males generally compete for resources and status in order to maximize their reproductive success, typically by attracting many females. This may explain Clinton's 'surprisingly' resilient public opinion ratings throughout the Lewinsky-gate scandal—almost 70 percent of American voters approved of his presidency even as the House of Representatives was voting on impeachment (Lawrence & Bennett, 2001; Sonner & Wilcox, 1999; Shah, Watts, Domke, & Fan, 2002).

Consider intelligence as "purposive adaptation to, and selection and shaping of, real-world environments relevant to one's life" (Sternberg, 1985, p. 45). If we interpret this adaptive notion of intelligence in clear evolutionary terms (where 'adaptive' means promoting reproductive success) rather than vague socio-economic terms (where 'adaptive' might mean promoting personal wealth, happiness, political respectability, or marital stability), then we can understand why Mating Intelligence for high-status leaders in complex hierarchical societies typically leads to the organization of formal harem systems that produce hundreds of offspring (Betzig, 1986). From that perspective, the Moroccan despot Moulay Ismail the Bloodthirsty (1672–1727), who sired over 600 sons and killed thousands of male sexual rivals with his own sword (Betzig, 1986), could be viewed as embodying a very high level of adaptive Mating Intelligence. True, he was also a sexist, oppressive, patriarchal psychopath, but evolutionary adaptiveness rarely equals moral virtue (ask any predator or parasite). In this perspective, Clinton was showing impaired Mating Intelligence only to the extent that he used contraception, chose some indiscreet female partners, and provoked sexual envy by lower-status male rivals.

In thinking about Mating Intelligence, we must realize that there is often a mismatch between what is currently adaptive versus what would have been adaptive under ancestral, prehistoric conditions (Tooby & DeVore, 1987). Psychological adaptations in general, and mechanisms of Mating Intelligence in general, have been shaped by prehistoric selection pressures to take advantage of typical fitness opportunities and to avoid typical fitness costs as they would have confronted our ancestors. Evolution cannot anticipate the future. It cannot have shaped human Mating Intelligence to perform optimally given evolutionary novelties such as contraception, religiously imposed monogamy, the American Constitution's impeachment process, or right-wing sexual hypocrisy.

Thus, in judging Clinton's Mating Intelligence, it is only marginally relevant to ask whether Clinton's liaison with Lewinsky resulted in a Clinton-Lewinsky baby (an actual reproductive benefit) or an impeachment (an actual status cost). However, it may be worthwhile to review some of the mating cues that may have influenced Clinton's behavior. At the time of the affair in 1995, Monica Lewinsky (b. 1973) was 22 (near peak fertility), and Clinton's wife Hilary (b. 1947) was 48 (with negligible fertility, approaching menopause). From a strictly reproductive viewpoint, Hilary had an expected future reproductive value of zero, and Monica had the potential for several offspring. Although Hilary (a graduate of Yale Law School) doubtless had higher intelligence and leadership potential than Monica, those heritable qualities could no longer be passed on to offspring. Thus, from a strict evolutionist perspective, Clinton's behavior looks adaptive—a hallmark of mating intelligence.

Clinton's liaisons with Lewinsky provide insights directly into how to best understand the construct at hand: MI. To provide applications of the different conceptions of MI presented in this chapter, we may consider how each conception differentially pertains to the scandal. The provisional

SUNY New Paltz conception of MI takes the tack that MI is comprised of mating-relevant cognitive abilities which should be generally unrelated to g. From this perspective, we may conceptualize Clinton's mating-relevant decision-making as reflecting short-term mating tactics that are not rooted in Clinton's relatively high level of intelligence. More simply, from this perspective, he is a smart man who may not tend to make particularly smart decisions when it comes to relationships.

Cosmides and Tooby's (2002) modularistic perspective on intelligence provides a similar account of Lewinskygate. They see (and provide good evidence for; see Cosmides & Tooby, 2005) the human mind as comprised of multiple, discrete modules designed to address specific adaptive hurdles presented to our ancestors across evolutionary time. From this perspective, mating-relevant decision-making may be broken into multiple discrete, (and largely independent) psychological components. This framework would potentially conceive of Lewinskygate as representative of Clinton's cheating-in-monogamous-relationships module, shaped not primarily by his own experiences (as suggested by Halpern, 2002), but, rather, by selection pressures that favored sexual infidelity in males given certain conditions in our ancestral past. From this perspective, g barely enters the picture; domain-general intelligence is largely irrelevant to such domain-specific behavioral patterns.

Kanazawa's (2004) framework for understanding the relationship between intelligence and mating would conceive of Lewinskygate in a relatively straightforward manner. From this vantage point, general intelligence evolved primarily to deal with evolutionarily novel situations. Whether (and under what conditions) one should cheat in a monogamous relationship characterizes ancestral psychology. Given the evolutionarily familiar nature of infidelity, psychological mechanisms tied to infidelity should be altogether independent of general intelligence. This analysis is consistent with the SUNY New Paltz MI analysis stated prior; Clinton is a smart man—and his high level of general intelligence buys him no benefits when it comes to most mating-relevant decision-making.

Miller's (2000) account of general intelligence as rooted in mating-relevant pressures across evolutionary history potentially provides a very different view of Lewinskygate. From this perspective, g and MI are largely one-and-the-same. As such, the fact that Clinton is high in g corresponds to an increased likelihood of his ability to acquire mates and of engaging in behaviors that should positively correlate with outcomes associated with reproductive success. His ability to effectively utilize his power, charm, and physical features in a coordinated effort to attract reproductively viable and attractive young women speaks to relatively high fitness levels and his ability to advertise such fitness well. From this perspective, Lewinskygate does not necessarily reflect unintelligent behavior. As a testament to this perspective, note that Clinton's marriage, presidency, and place in history may largely have been unaffected by the scandal.

A further point regarding MI that is addressed by the current case study corresponds to whether MI is best conceptualized in terms of *accurate* versus *biased* decision-making. One may envision Clinton having thought something like, "The odds of getting caught are pretty much zero, and the costs associated with getting caught are not likely to be great . . ." Such thoughts did not necessarily capture the reality of the contingencies of the situation accurately. As such, from an accuracy-corresponds-to-intelligence perspective, such thinking would seem unintelligent.

However, modern-day evolutionary social psychologists (and other social psychologists in general [see Taylor & Brown, 1988]) have made the case that erroneous judgments which are biased in ways that are likely to increase genetic fitness are essentially more adaptive (in the evolutionary sense) than relatively accurate judgments across many kinds of situations (e.g., Krebs & Denton, 1997). From this perspective, we can think of the aforementioned hypothetical presidential thoughts as biased in exactly that kind of fitness-enhancing manner. In effect, such judgments are somewhat similar to judgments by males of females' sexual interest which tend to overestimate such interest (as found in Haselton and Buss' [2000] work on error management theory). Given that such judgments represent *overestimates*, they are inaccurate by definition. However, from an evolutionary perspective, it is easy to see how such biased judgments may impel behavior that is more likely to lead to reproductive success compared with alternative behaviors, thus being *adaptive* in the relatively ultimate sense of the word.

This analysis of Clinton's scandalous behavior was designed to provide a context that allows for a discussion of issues that underlie disparate conceptualizations of MI. Are there dedicated intelligences pertaining to domains underlying human mating that are distinct from *g*? Are cognitive factors associated with mating conceptually and empirically conflated with *g*? Is MI best conceptualized as a set of accurate decision-making skills? Is MI, rather, better conceptualized as the tendency to make judgments in mating-relevant contexts that are biased in such a way so as to likely increase an individual's overall likelihood of successful reproduction?

MATING DOMAINS RELEVANT TO MATING INTELLIGENCE

In our attempt to delineate the areas of psychology that need to be considered in the development of MI as a construct, we have, heretofore considered sexual selection and the shaping of human intelligence, whether intelligent mating decisions are relatively accurate versus erroneous, how MI relates to general intelligence, and how MI relates to extant constructs related to social intelligence. We also believe that it is crucial to address the multiple behavioral domains that underlie human mating. In the development of such an organization of these domains, we start with the theory of sexual selection. Sexual selection is divisible into (a) selection occurring due to the preferences of an individual for certain characteristics in a mate, and, separately, (b) selection occurring as a result of several individuals of the same sex competing for a mate (Buss, 2003). More simply, we are speaking formerly of inter-sexual choice, and secondly of intra-sexual competition. Seeing as these terms relate to the process of sexual selection, it follows that the interplay of both choice and rivalry in mating would lead to specific adaptations. These mating-relevant adaptations, to some extent, must themselves represent a part of what we are labeling MI.

Adaptations arising from mate-choice have obvious corollaries in the animal kingdom, such as the example of the peacock's plumage. In the domain of human mating, desires of one sex (e.g., females' desire for a wealthy mate) may select qualities of the other sex (e.g., males' tendencies to seek and display wealth). Thus, qualities desired in potential mates and qualities advertised to potential mates, by both sexes, likely comprise important domains of MI. An important implication of this point regarding MI is that it may well be structured differently across the sexes so as to take into account specific selective pressures that have differentially acted across the sexes over evolutionary history. For instance, an important component of MI in males may be to effectively advertise wealth (regardless of actual levels of wealth); an important component of MI in females may be to effectively advertise youth (regardless of actual age). The integrative model of MI presented in the final chapter of this book (Geher, Camargo, & O'Rourke) addresses this notion of MI as sex-differentiated.

Alternately, the latter half of our division of sexual selection—intra-sexual rivalry, may have played a similarly large role in the shaping of MI. The common example used within this sub-category is the size of the stag's horns. Presumably, such large horns evolved through a form of ritualized inter-locking of horns, in which winners (often the males with the biggest horns) gained access to females. Similarly, in male humans, much of the sexual dimorphism, characterized by larger and stronger males, developed through competition between males for the same mate. Again, given variability in intra-sexual tactics designed to obtain mates across the sexes, it is likely that MI regarding male intra-sexual rivalry differs from MI regarding female intra-sexual rivalry in some important ways. Males who are high in intra-sexual MI may be effective at dominating mixed-sex social situations, for instance. Females who are high in intra-sexual

MI may be effective at framing rivals as overly promiscuous without coming across as overly catty.

Adaptations in both males and females could presumably have arisen in the form of cognitive skills devoted to the judgment and assessment of potential rivals. These assessment skills would reduce the cost of competing with a rival who is clearly more adept or more fit than oneself. Also, adaptations for impressing or deterring rivals could arise in the form of a kind of socially intelligent adeptness at boasting, deceiving, or all around showing-off.

In this manner, it is apparent how cognitive abilities in the domain of mating could arise variably in the human species as a result of sexual selection at the level of inter-sexual choice or, alternatively, at the level of intra-sexual competition. A host of abilities might be identified as sexually selected adaptations. We suggest that MI can be conceptualized as addressing the different mating domains derived from sexual-selection theory.

THIS BOOK

This introductory section 1 contains the foreword by David Buss, the preface, and this introductory Chapter 1. The book is organized into six further sections.

Section 2 addresses mate search—the process of searching through potential sexual partners to find the most attractive ones who will reciprocate one's interest. In Chapter 2, Penke, Todd, Lenton, and Fasolo, consider the complexities that arise from mutual mate choice in humans—the fact that both men and women tend to be choosy about their long-term partners. They examine simple mate-search heuristics that learn to take into account one's own attractiveness, to avoid wasting time on the unattainable (whose mate value is much higher than one's own) or the undeserving (whose mate value is much lower than one's own.) In Chapter 3, De Backer, Braeckman, and Farinpour examine mate search in the context of newspaper personal ads, to assess one important component of MI: how accurate each sex is at understanding the distinctive traits sought by the other sex.

Section 3 concerns strategic flexibility in mating intelligence: How we adapt our mating preferences, goals, strategies, and tactics to local environmental circumstances and to our own strengths and weaknesses as potential mates. In Chapter 4, Li analyzes adaptive shifts in mate preferences in an economic 'mating market' framework, considering how individuals shift from favoring 'necessities' (e.g., female fertility, male resources) to favoring 'luxuries' (e.g., intelligence, creativity, sense of humor) in mates as their own mate value increases. In Chapter 5, Nettle and Clegg

analyze major human personality traits as distinct mating strategies that
may flourish under different social, sexual, and environmental conditions.
In Chapter 6, O'Sullivan analyzes the darker side of mating intelligence by
considering several domains of human mating where deception and self-
deception can have adaptive benefits. In Chapter 7, Weekes-Shackelford,
Easton, and Stone consider how women's mate preferences shift adaptively depending on whether the women already have children from previous relationships—mating intelligence should work differently for vir-
gins versus matriarchs, and in choosing a first boy-friend versus a
potential stepfather to one's teenagers.

Section 4 concerns aspects of MI that we call 'mental fitness indicators'—traits that display intelligence, personality, mental health, or other
qualities of brain function, that vary conspicuously across individuals, and
that are romantically attractive. In Chapter 8, Keller analyzes the role of
genetic mutations in maintaining heritable variation in the quality of mental fitness indicators, and how such indicators can work as reliable cues
of 'good genes' in mate choice. In Chapter 9, Shaner, Miller, and Mintz consider the 'mental disorders' such as schizophrenia and depression, that can
result when these mental fitness indicators develop poorly, and explain
why such disorders are so often associated with poor MI and so harmful to
mating success and intimate relationships.

Section 5 considers MI in relation to other well-studied individual
differences, such as general intelligence, social intelligence, emotional
intelligence, creativity, and sense of humor. In Chapter 10, Kaufman,
Kozbelt, Bromley and Miller review the theoretical and empirical relationships between MI, creativity, sense of humor, general intelligence, and
certain personality traits. In Chapter 11, Casey, Garrett, Brackett, and
Rivers review emotional intelligence in relation to intimate relationships
and MI. In Chapter 12, Kanazawa argues that MI and general intelligence
are independent constructs, because they evolved to guide adaptive
behavior in different domains (mating in the case of MI; mastery of
evolutionarily novel econiches and technologies in the case of general
intelligence).

Section 6 puts MI in its ecological context, since human adaptations for
mating must have always been shaped in various ways by the surrounding social, cultural, ecological, and climatic environments. In Chapter 13,
Ash and Gallup consider the possible role of prehistoric climate variability
in favoring the emergence of larger human brains and human intelligence—factors which may have set the paleoclimatic stage for the evolution of mating intelligence. In Chapter 14, Figueredo, Brumbach, Jones,
Sefcek, Vásquez, and Jacobs develop an integrative framework for considering the evolution of life-history strategies, including mating strategies, in relation to local socio-ecological variables.

Section 7 includes two concluding chapters. In Chapter 15, Miller tries to answer some 'frequently asked questions' about MI, summarizing several themes throughout the book and briefly touching on some topics not covered elsewhere (such as MI in homosexual relationships, and the genetic and neural bases of MI). In Chapter 16, Geher, Camargo, and O'Rourke provide a unifying framework for understanding MI by drawing a major distinction between mating mechanisms (i.e., universal mating-relevant adaptations) and mental fitness indicators (i.e., courtship-display abilities) of MI. That chapter also sketches out some possible directions for future theoretical and empirical research on MI.

WHAT THE MATING INTELLIGENCE CONSTRUCT CAN OFFER TO SCIENCE

The MI construct, at best, offers different benefits to different areas of basic and applied research. Here we sketch out a few that seem most salient to us at the moment:

- intelligence research: MI offers an additional, evolutionarily central, emotionally important domain of challenging psychological problems in which to investigate the role of the g factor and specific intelligences; one in which there might even be specific learning disabilities and cognitive deficits that have gone undiagnosed by professionals (though often noted by spouses!)
- evolutionary psychology: MI offers a way to integrate psychometrics and behavior genetics into the study of human universals, in a domain where individual differences are highly salient
- clinical psychology: MI offers a new perspective on certain psychological dysfunctions, psychopathologies, and anxieties that make people unhappy, especially because they interfere with mate acquisition, mate choice, and general relationship functioning
- psychiatry: MI offers a new perspective on issues in 'cosmetic psychopharmacology'—if MI is a legitimate domain of psychological functioning, then drugs that 'merely' make people more psychologically attractive (e.g., more confident, happy, empathic, creative) are more than superficial band-aids on 'real, underlying problems'; they're absolutely central to human well-being
- educational psych: MI highlights a whole domain of learnable skills and cognitive-developmental challenges that are virtually ignored in public schooling and higher education—we train people for decades to be productive workers, but devote hardly any time to being happy, loving, empathic sexual partners.

CONCLUSION

In sum, this book is necessarily challenging in many ways. It is ambitious in both its breadth and its goals. It was designed to bridge an important and conspicuous gap in the psychological literature; the gap between scholarship on human mating and scholarship on intelligence. As implied by Miller's (2000) work on human mating, intelligence and mating are, given our evolutionary heritage, intimately related. This book represents our match-making effort to induce these major areas of psychology to cross-fertilize each other.

The integration of these heretofore disparate ideas into one coherent construct should lead to useful and productive scholarship in psychology. With that said, there are clear challenges in the development of this construct. First, extant theories that *do* address the interplay between mating and intelligence have a somewhat heterogeneous quality; they tend to disagree on important points (e.g., Kanazawa's [2004] ideas on the relationship between general intelligence and mating success versus Miller's [2000] ideas on this same topic). Further, little empirical work has been conducted dealing with (a) ways to operationally define MI, (b) the factorial structure of MI, and (c) the correlates of MI. To develop a coherent model of MI, ideas pertaining to the evolution of intelligence, species-typical aspects of human mating, social intelligences, general intelligence, and the idea of mental-fitness indicators need to be integrated. While this integration is challenging, the high quality of the contributors to this volume coupled with the inclusion of an organizing model presented in the final chapter should serve to help work toward a coherent and useful framework for understanding MI.

ACKNOWLEDGMENTS

Kathleen Bauman Geher, Alice Andrews, and David Buss provided helpful feedback for which we are grateful. Further, we thank Elisabeth DeWispelaere and Jill Lavallee for their work on some of the content analyses summarized in this chapter. Additionally, Michelle Coombs was extremely helpful in assisting with the citations.

REFERENCES

Aston, M. C. (2002). *The other half of Asperger syndrome: A guide to an intimate relationship with a partner who has Asperger Syndrome.* Shawnee Mission, KN: Autism Asperger Publishing.
Bar-On, R., Tranel, D., Denburg, N. L., & Bechara, A. (2003). Exploring the neurological substrate of emotional and social intelligence. *Brain, 126,* 1790–1800.

Baron-Cohen, S., Richler, J., Bisarya, D., Gurunathan, N., & Wheelwright, S. (2003). The systemizing quotient: an investigation of adults with Asperger syndrome or high-functioning autism, and normal sex differences. *Philosophical Transactions of the Royal Society of London B, 358*(1430), 361–374.

Baron-Cohen, S., Wheelwright, S., Skinner, R., Martin, J., & Clubley, E. (2001). The Autism-Spectrum Quotient (AQ): Evidence from Asperger syndrome/high-functioning autism, males and females, scientists and mathematicians. *Journal of Autism and Developmental Disorders, 31*, 5–17.

Benbow, C. P., Zonderman, A. B., & Stanley, J. C. (1983). Assortative marriage and the familiality of cognitive abilities in families of extremely gifted students. *Intelligence, 7*, 153–161.

Borsboom, D., & Dolan, C. V. (2006). Why g is not an adaptation: A comment on Kanazawa (2004). *Psychological Review, 113*, 433–437.

Brackett, M. A., & Salovey, P. (2004). Measuring emotional intelligence with the Mayer-Salovey-Caruso Emotional Intelligence Test (MSCEIT). In G. Geher (Ed.), *Measuring emotional intelligence: Common ground and controversy.* New York: Nova Science Publishers.

Buss, D. M. (1989). Sex differences in human mate selection: Evolutionary hypotheses tested in 37 cultures. *Behavioral and Brain Sciences, 12*, 1–49.

Buss, D. M. (2003). *The evolution of desire: Strategies of human mating.* New York: Basic Books.

Buss, D. M., Larsen, R. J., Westen, D., & Semmelroth, J. (1992). Sex differences in jealousy: Evolution, physiology, and psychology. *Psychological Science, 3*, 251–255.

Buss, D. M., & Shackelford, T. K. (1997). Susceptibility to infidelity in the first year of marriage. *Journal of Research in Personality, 31*, 193–221.

Cantor, N., & Kihlstrom, J. F. (1987). *Personality and social intelligence.* Englewood Cliffs, NJ: Prentice Hall.

Clinton, B. (2004). *My life.* New York: Knopf.

Cosmides, L., & Tooby, J. (2002). Unraveling the enigma of human intelligence: Evolutionary psychology and the multimodular mind. In R. J. Sternberg & J. C. Kaufman (Eds.), *The evolution of intelligence.* Mahwah, NJ: Lawrence Erlbaum Associates.

Crow, T. J. (1993). Sexual selection, Machiavellian intelligence, and the origins of psychosis. *Lancet, 342*, 594–598.

Crow, T. J. (1995). A Darwinian approach to the origins of psychosis. *British Journal of Psychiatry, 167*, 12–25.

Davies, M., Stankov, L., & Roberts, R. D. (1998). Emotional intelligence: In search of an elusive construct. *Journal of Personality and Social Psychology, 75*, 989–1015.

De Raad, B. (2005). The trait-coverage of emotional intelligence. *Personality and Individual Differences, 38*, 673–687.

Deary, I. J., Thorpe, G., Wilson, V., Starr, J. M., & Whalley, L. J. (2003). Population sex differences in IQ at age 11: The Scottish mental survey 1932. *Intelligence, 31*, 533–542.

DePaulo, B. M., & Morris, W. L. (2005). Singles in society and in science. *Psychological Inquiry, 16*, 57–83.

Diener, E., Oishi, S., & Lucas, R. E. (2003). Personality, culture, and subjective well-being: Emotional and cognitive evaluations of life. *Annual Review of Psychology, 54*, 403–425.

Dunbar, R. I. M., Marriott, A., & Duncan, N. D. C. (1997). Human conversational behavior. *Human Nature, 8,* 231–246.

Dunsieth, N. W., Nelson, E. B., Bursman-Lovins, L. A., Holcomb, J. L., Beckman, D., Welge, J. A., Roby, D., Taylor, P., Soutullo, C. A., & McElroy, S. L. (2004). Psychiatric and legal features of 113 men convicted of sexual offenses. *Journal of Clinical Psychiatry, 65,* 293–300.

Eaves, L. J. (1973). Assortative mating and intelligence: Analysis of pedigree data. *Heredity, 30,* 199–210.

Feingold, A. (1992). Gender differences in mate selection preferences: A test of the parental investment model. *Psychological Bulletin, 112,* 125–139.

Fletcher, G. J. O., & Simpson, J. A. (2000). Ideal standards in close relationships: Their structure and functions. *Current Directions in Psychological Science, 9,* 102–105.

Flinn, M. V., Geary, D. C., & Ward, C. V. (2005). Ecological dominance, social competition, and coalitionary arms races: Why humans evolved extraordinary intelligence. *Evolution* and *Human Behavior, 26,* 10–46.

Furlow, B., Gangestad, S. W., & Armijo-Prewitt, T. (1998). Developmental stability and human violence. *Proceedings of the Royal Society of London B, 265,* 1–6.

Gabriel, M. T., Critelli, J. W., & Ee, J. S. (1994). Narcissistic illusions in self-evaluations of intelligence and attractiveness. *Journal of Personality, 62,* 143–155.

Gardner, H. (1983). *Frames of mind: The theory of multiple intelligences.* New York: Basic Books.

Geher, G. (Ed.). (2004). *Measuring emotional intelligence: Common ground and controversy.* New York: Nova Science Publishers.

Geher, G., & Renstrom, K. L. (2004). Measuring the emotion-perception component of emotional intelligence. In S. P. Shohov (Ed.), *Advances in psychology research.* New York: Nova Science.

George, J. M. (2000). Emotions and leadership: The role of emotional intelligence. *Human Relations, 53,* 1027–1055.

Gordon, R. A. (1997). Everyday life as an intelligence test: Effects of intelligence and intelligence context. *Intelligence, 24,* 203–320.

Gottfredson, L. S. (2003). Dissecting practical intelligence theory: Its claims and evidence. *Intelligence, 31,* 343–397.

Grant, B. F., Hasin, D. S., Stinson, F. S., Dawson, D. A., Chou, S. P., Ruan, W. J., & Pickering, R. P. (2004). Prevalence, correlates, and disability of personality disorders in the United States: Results from the National Epidemiologic Survey on Alcohol and Related Conditions. *Journal of Clinical Psychiatry, 65,* 948–958.

Groesz, L. M., Levine, M. P., & Murnen, S. K. (2002). The effect of experimental presentation of thin media images on body satisfaction: A meta-analytic review. *International Journal of Eating Disorders, 31,* 1–16.

Halpern, D. F. (2002). Sex, lies, and audiotapes. In R. Sternberg (Ed.), *Why smart people can be so stupid.* New Haven, CT: Yale University Press.

Haselton, M., & Miller, G. F. (2006). Women's fertility across the cycle increases the short-term attractiveness of creative intelligence compared to wealth. *Human Nature, 17,* 50–73.

Hatfield, E., & Sprecher, S. (1995). Men's and women's preferences in marital partners in the United States, Russia, and Japan. *Journal of Cross-Cultural Psychology, 26,* 728–750.

Heaven, P. C. L., & Bucci, S. (2001). Right-wing authoritarianism, social dominance orientation and personality: An analysis using the IPIP measure. *European Journal of Personality, 15*, 49–56.

Hunt, E. (2001). Multiple views on multiple intelligences. *Contemporary Psychology, 46*, 5–7.

Jensen, A. (1998). *The g factor: The science of mental ability*. London: Praeger.

Jost, J. T., Glaser, J., Kruglanski, A. W., & Sulloway, F. J. (2003). Political conservatism as motivated social cognition. *Psychological Bulletin, 129*, 339–375.

Judge, T. A., Erez, A., Bono, J. E., & Thoresen, C. J. (2002). Are measures of self-esteem, neuroticism, locus of control, and generalized self-efficacy indicators of a common core construct? *Journal of Personality and Social Psychology, 83*, 693–710.

Kanazawa, S. (this volume). The independence of mating intelligence and general intelligence. In G. Geher & G. F. Miller, (Eds.), *Mating intelligence: Sex, relationships, and the mind's reproductive system*. Mahwah, NJ: Lawrence Erlbaum Associates.

Kanazawa, S. (2004). General intelligence as a domain-specific adaptation. *Psychological Review, 111*, 512–523.

Kanazawa, S., & Kovar, J. L. (2004). Why beautiful people are more intelligent. *Intelligence, 32*, 227–243.

Kenrick, D. T., Sadalla, E. K., Groth, G., & Trost, M. R. (1990). Evolution, traits, and the stages of human courtship: Qualifying the parental investment model. *Journal of Personality, 58*, 97–116.

Kihlstrom, J. F., & Cantor, N. (2000). Social intelligence. In R. J. Sternberg (Ed.), *Handbook of intelligence*. Cambridge University Press.

Klein, P. D. (2003). Rethinking the multiplicity of cognitive resources and curricular representations: alternatives to 'learning styles' and 'multiple intelligences'. *Journal of Curriculum Studies, 35*, 45–81.

Krueger, R. F., Hicks, B. M., Patrick, C. J., Carlson, S. R., Iacono, W. G., & McGue, M. (2002). Etiologic connections among substance dependence, antisocial behavior, and personality: Modeling the externalizing spectrum. *Journal of Abnormal Psychology, 111*, 411–424.

LaRouche, L. H. (2002). Peace between two presidents. In Executive Intelligence Review. Retrieved August 10, 2005, from http://www.larouchepub.com/pr_lar/2002/020302ari_flei_ltr.html

Lawrence, R. G., & Bennett, W. L. (2001). Rethinking media politics and public opinion: Reactions to the Clinton-Lewinsky scandal. *Political Science Quarterly, 116*, 425–446.

Li, N. P., Bailey, J. M., Kenrick, D. T., & Linsenmeier, J. A. W. (2002). The necessities and luxuries of mate preferences: Testing the tradeoffs. *Journal of Personality and Social Psychology, 82*, 947–955.

Livingstone, H. A., & Day, A. L. (2005). Comparing the construct and criterion-related validity of ability-based and mixed-model measures of emotional intelligence. *Educational and Psychological Measurement, 65*, 851–873.

Lucas, R. E. (2005). Time does not heal all wounds—A longitudinal study of reaction and adaptation to divorce. *Psychological Science, 16*, 945–950.

Lykken, D. T., & Tellegen, A. (1993). Is human mating adventitious or the result of lawful choice: A twin study of mate selection. *Journal of Personality and Social Psychology, 65,* 56–68.

Martel Johnson, D., & Erneling, C.E. (Eds.) (1997). *The future of the cognitive revolution.* New York: Oxford University Press.

Mayer, J. D., Caruso, D. R., & Salovey, P. (1999). Emotional intelligence meets traditional standards for an intelligence. *Intelligence, 27,* 267–298.

McGrath, R. E. (2005). Conceptual complexity and construct validity. *Journal of Personality Assessment, 85,* 112–124.

Miller, G. F. (1997). Protean primates: The evolution of adaptive unpredictability in competition and courtship. In A. Whiten & R. W. Byrne (Eds.), *Machiavellian Intelligence II: Extensions and evaluations* (pp. 312–340). Cambridge University Press.

Miller, G. F. (2000a). *The mating mind: How sexual choice shaped the evolution of human nature.* New York: Doubleday.

Miller, G. F. (2000b). Sexual selection for indicators of intelligence. In G. Bock, J. Goode, & K. Webb (Eds.), *The nature of intelligence* (pp. 260–275). Novartis Foundation Symposium 233. New York: John Wiley.

Miller, G. F., & Todd, P. M. (1998). Mate choice turns cognitive. *Trends in Cognitive Sciences, 2,* 190–198.

Miller, G. F. (this volume). Mating intelligence: Frequently asked questions. In G. Geher & G. F. Miller, (Eds.), *Mating Intelligence: Sex, Relationships, and The Mind's Reproductive System.* Mahwah, NJ: Lawrence Erlbaum Associates.

Moffitt, T. E., Caspi, A., Harrington, H., & Milne, B. J. (2002). Males on the life-course-persistent and adolescence-limited antisocial pathways: Follow-up at age 26 years. *Development and Psychopathology, 14,* 179–207.

Mroczek, D. K., & Spiro, A. (2005). Change in life satisfaction during adulthood: Findings from the veterans affairs normative aging study. *Journal of Personality and Social Psychology, 88,* 189–202.

Paxton, S. J., Schutz, H. K., Wertheim, E. H., & Muir, S. L. (1999). Friendship clique and peer influences on body image concerns, dietary restraint, extreme weight-loss behaviors, and binge eating in adolescent girls. *Journal of Abnormal Psychology, 108,* 255–266.

Petrides, K. V., & Furnham, A. (2001). Trait emotional intelligence: Psychometric investigation with reference to established trait taxonomies. *European Journal of Personality, 15,* 425–448.

Petrides, K. V., & Furnham, A. (2003). Trait emotional intelligence: Behavioural validation in two studies of emotion recognition and reactivity to mood induction. *European Journal of Personality, 17,* 39–57.

Plomin, R., & Spinath, F. M. (2004). Intelligence: Genetics, genes, and genomic. *Journal of Personality and Social Psychology, 86,* 112–129.

Pyryt, M. C. (2000). Finding "g": Easy viewing through higher order factor analysis. *Gifted Child Quarterly, 44,* 190–192.

Reader, S. M., & Laland, K. N. (2002). Social intelligence, innovation, and enhanced brain size in primates. *Proceedings of the National Academy of Sciences USA, 99,* 4436–4441.

Robins, R. W., & Beer, J. S. (2001). Positive illusions about the self: Short-term benefits and long-term costs. *Journal of Personality and Social Psychology, 80*, 340–352.

Rowatt, W. C., Cunningham, M. R., & Druen, P. B. (1999). Lying to get a date: The effect of facial physical attractiveness on the willingness to deceive prospective dating partners. *Journal of Social and Personal Relationships, 16*, 209–223.

Rushton, J. P. (2004). Placing intelligence into an evolutionary framework, or how g fits into the r-K matrix of life history traits including longevity. *Intelligence, 32*, 321–328.

Rushton, J. P., & Nicholson, I. R. (1988). Genetic similarity theory, intelligence, and human mate choice. *Ethology and Sociobiology, 9*, 45–57.

Salovey, P., & Mayer, J. D. (1990). Emotional intelligence. *Imagination, Cognition, and Personality, 9*, 185–211.

Scheib, J. E. (1994). Sperm donor selection and the psychology of female mate choice. *Ethology and Sociobiology, 15*, 113–129.

Schmitt, D. P., Shackelford, T. K., & Buss, D. M. (2001). Are men really more 'oriented' toward short-term mating than women? A critical review of theory and research. *Psychology, Evolution, and Gender, 3*, 211–239.

Schulte, M. J., Ree, M. J., & Carretta, T. R. (2004). Emotional intelligence: Not much more than g and personality. *Personality and Individual Differences, 37*, 1059–1068.

Schultz, P. W., & Searleman, A. (2002). Rigidity of thought and behavior: 100 years of research. *Genetic, Social, and General Psychology Monographs, 128*, 165–207.

Shah, D. V., Watts, M. D., Domke, D., & Fan, D. P. (2002). News framing and cueing of issue regimes—Explaining Clinton's public approval in spite of scandal. *Public Opinion Quarterly, 66*, 339–370.

Silverman, I., Choi, J., Mackewn, A., Fisher, M., Moro, J., Olshansky, E. (2000). Evolved mechanisms underlying wayfinding: Further studies on the hunter-gatherer theory of spatial sex differences. *Evolution and Human Behavior, 21*, 201–213.

Skodol, A. E., Gunderson, J. G., Pfohl, B., Widiger, T. A., Livesley, W. J., & Siever, L. J. (2002). The borderline diagnosis I: Psychopathology comorbidity, and personality structure. *Biological Psychiatry, 51*, 936–950.

Skodol, A. E., Gunderson, J. G., McGlashan, T. H., Dyck, I. R., Stout, R. L., Bender, D. S., Grilo, C. M., Shea, M. T., Zanatini, M. C., Morey, L. C., Sanislow, C. A., & Oldham, J. M. (2002). Functional impairment in patients with schizotypal, borderline, avoidant, or obsessive-compulsive personality disorder. *American Journal of Psychiatry, 159*, 276–283.

Sonner, M. W., & Wilcox, C. (1999). Forgiving and forgetting: Public support for Bill Clinton during the Lewinsky scandal. *PS: Political Science and Politics, 32*, 554–557.

Sprecher, S., & Regan, P. C. (2002). Liking some things (in some people) more than others: Partner preferences in romantic relationships and friendships. *Journal of Social and Personal Relationships, 19*, 463–481.

Stanovich, K. E., & West, R. F. (2000). Individual differences in reasoning: Implications for the rationality debate? *Behavioral and Brain Sciences, 23*, 645–726.

Sternberg, R. J. (1985). *Beyond IQ.* New York: Cambridge University Press.

Sternberg, R. J., & Kaufman, J. C. (Eds.) (2002). *Evolution of intelligence.* Mahwah, NJ: Lawrence Erlbaum Associates.

Taylor, S. E., & Brown, J. D. (1988). Illusion and well-being: A social psychological perspective on mental health. *Psychological Bulletin, 103,* 193–210.

Tett, R. P., Fox, K. E., & Wang, A. (2005). Development and validation of a self-report measure of emotional intelligence as a multidimensional trait domain. *Personality and Social Psychology Bulletin, 31,* 859–888.

Todd, P. M., & Miller, G. F. (1991). On the sympatric origin of species: Mercurial mating in the Quicksilver Model. In R. K. Belew & L. B. Booker (Eds.), *Proceedings of the Fourth Conference on Genetic Algorithms* (pp. 547–554). San Mateo, CA: Morgan Kaufmann.

Tooby, J., & DeVore, I. (1987). The reconstruction of hominid behavioral evolution through strategic modeling. In W. G. Kinzey (Ed.), The evolution of human behavior. New York: State University of New York Press.

Whiten, A., & Byrne, R. W. (Eds.) (1997). *Machiavellian intelligence II: Extensions and evaluations.* New York: Cambridge University Press.

Wilson, D. S., Garruto, R., McLeod, K. J., Regan, P. M., Tan-Wilson, A. *Grant proposal for NSF IGERT grant.* Unpublished Manuscript.

II

Mate Search and Mating Intelligence

Chapter 2

How Self-Assessments Can Guide Human Mating Decisions

Lars Penke
*Humboldt University, Berlin and International
Max Planck Research School LIFE, Berlin*

Peter M. Todd
*Indiana University and Max Plank Institute for
Human Development, Berlin*

Alison P. Lenton
University of Edinburgh

Barbara Fasolo
London School of Economics

From puberty onward, mating becomes a major focus of thought: Whom shall I date? Shall I stay with my current partner, or look for someone else? Can I find someone better? Will she like me? Will he leave me for someone else? How popular with the opposite sex am I, compared to my peers? These types of questions, which sometimes persist throughout adulthood, point to the complexity of mating decisions.

These decisions roughly fall into two categories: Mate-choice decisions and mating-tactic decisions. *Mate choice* concerns the target of one's mating effort: which available members of the opposite sex should an individual pursue for a mating relationship (Darwin, 1871; Jennions & Petrie, 1997; Miller & Todd, 1998; Miller, 2000a; Kokko, Brooks, Jennions, & Morley, 2003; Geary, Vigil, & Byrd-Craven, 2004). Should I go with the most popular guy, or with the one who tries hardest to win my heart? Should I court highly attractive girls, or would I be better off with the girl-next-door? *Mating tactic* decisions, on the other hand, concern how an individual should allocate his or her overall efforts (i.e., time, money, energy, and other resources) in the mating area: Should I invest my resources in finding, choosing, and courting new potential mates, or in stabilizing and protecting a committed relationship (and potentially investing in the resulting offspring)? Within a mixed mating strategy (Gangestad & Simpson, 2000; Gross, 1996), more investment in the former translates into the decision to adopt a *short-term* mating tactic, while more investment in the latter implies the decision to adopt a *long-term* mating tactic. (Note that we use the term "tactic" here to broadly describe the poles of a dimension of effort allocation in the mating domain. Other authors apply the term in a more narrow sense to specific behaviors that promote long-term or short-term mating, e.g., Buss & Shackelford, 1997; Greer & Buss, 1994.) Throughout this chapter, we will use the term "*mating decisions*" to refer to both *mate choice* decisions and *mating tactic* decisions.

It is important to note that, while cogitation about the opposite sex is often a reflective, deliberate process, not all mating decisions are consciously made. Indeed, the biological literature often defines the preferences that guide mating decisions as any traits that bias the mating success of opposite-sex individuals, be they cognitive, behavioral, physiological, or morphological (Halliday, 1983; Maynard Smith, 1987; Pomiankowski, 1988; Arnquist & Rowe, 2005). This definition carefully circumvents not only the involvement of consciousness, but the necessity of cognition in general. For example, females may implement mate choice by evolving more acidic reproductive tracts, which make it harder for sperm to reach their eggs—they are thereby selecting for more robust sperm, but are not using cognition to do so. Mate choice mechanisms like these appear to be quite widespread in nature (Jennions & Petrie, 2000). We will concentrate on cases where cognition does play a role in human mating decisions, and argue that these decisions are informed by affective experiences that result from self-assessments (i.e., cognitive processes based on internal representations of the self, see Baumeister, 1997), no matter if they are consciously reflected or not.

From an evolutionary perspective, mating decisions are extremely important for any sexually reproducing species: The opposite sex is the only means by which one can transmit one's own genes to the next generation, and therefore successful mating is a prime determinant of an individual's fitness (Darwin, 1871). We could thus expect that the proximate mechanisms that guide mating decisions were under especially strong selective pressures over evolutionary time, resulting in specially designed psychological adaptations as parts of our Mating Intelligence (Buss, 1995). However, clear descriptions of such mechanisms are generally absent from the literature (Miller, 1997; Miller & Todd, 1998; Mata, Wilke, & Todd, 2005; Penke & Denissen, 2006).

We will argue that, despite the seeming complexity of mating decisions, simple heuristics can enable individuals to make adaptive choices in this domain (Gigerenzer, Todd, & the ABC group, 1999). These heuristics exemplify the principles of bounded rationality because they selectively exploit the natural structure of the social environment, steered by specific evolved capacities (e.g., sexual lust, Diamond, 2004; Fisher, Aron, Mashek, Li, & Brown, 2002; aesthetic preferences for mate qualities, Grammer, Fink, Møller, & Thornhill, 2003; Miller, 2000a; the desire for sexual variety, Buss & Schmitt, 1993; Schmitt et al., 2003; and the adult attachment system, Hazen & Diamond, 2000; Fraley & Shaver, 2000). For example, an aesthetic preference that values symmetry in a potential mate's face as attractive would lead to adaptive mate choice decisions, because facial symmetry is an honest indicator of genetic qualities that buffer against environmental disturbances (pathogens, toxins, etc.) during development (Thornhill & Gangestad, 1999a) and will be passed to offspring if present in a chosen mate. However, if the social environment deviates from those natural conditions under which this mating competence evolved (e.g., because environmental disturbances became uncommon or are efficiently counteracted by cultural innovations, as in Western cultures today), the validity of symmetry as a cue for genetic quality might be compromised, and consequently the adaptive value of the heuristic is attenuated. The greater male desire for sexual variety, on the other hand, is an evolved capacity that apparently endows men with the mating heuristic "Consider having a short-term sexual affair whenever given the opportunity" (see Clark & Hatfield, 1989). Since the adaptive value of this heuristic mechanism depends on the lesser minimal parental investment of men compared to women (Trivers, 1972), it will remain adaptive as long as the social environment consists of women who get pregnant and men who do not (Hagen, 2005). In interaction with certain general self-related motives (i.e., self-esteem maintenance, Baumeister, 1997; social comparison, Gilbert, Price, & Allan, 1995; Festinger, 1954), heuristics like these are able to produce adaptive mating decisions under realistic assumptions of information availability. As we will see, the inclusion of self-related motives can also help us to explain how individual differences in mating decisions can result from a universal component of Mating Intelligence—mate preference adaptations (see also Keller, this volume).

To support our contentions, we first provide a short, selective review on what is known about the nature of human mating decisions. Next, we explain the advantages that decisions based on simple heuristics have when compared to more complex mechanisms that try to optimize decisions. In the focal part of this chapter, we discuss the nature of some of these heuristics, including those based on self-assessments, which we suggest can guide mate choice decisions for long-term committed relationship partners (a task quite similar for both sexes). *Self-assessments* are cognitive representations of one's identity and abilities. They include an important affective-evaluative component (self-esteem), and appear to exist for various hierarchically integrated life domains (Baumeister, 1997). Mating is one of these domains (Kirkpatrick & Ellis, 2001). Mating-related self-assessments include self-perceptions of attractiveness, popularity, and ability to draw the attention and manipulate the behavior of potential or actual mates. We also address how sex differences complicate mating dynamics in a manner that is predictable from evolutionary theorizing, and show that, despite these complications, simple heuristics informed by self-assessments remain capable of solving mate choice problems. Finally, we consider self-related decision mechanisms relevant to mating tactic choices. Throughout this chapter, we will focus on mating decisions in heterosexual individuals. However, most aspects should generalize to homosexuals, who tend to have mate choice preferences like heterosexuals of the opposite sex (Bailey, Kim, Hills, & Linsenmeier, 1997) and desires for sexual variety and romantic attachment like heterosexuals of their own sex (Schmitt et al., 2003; Diamond, 2003).

THE NATURE OF HUMAN MATING DECISIONS

As one would expect from the important role that mating decisions have in the evolutionary process, there is ample evidence that the targets of sexual interest are not random in humans: People mate assortatively with regard to many characteristics, including physical attractiveness, intelligence, education, socioeconomic status, height, age, values, and attitudes (Buss, 1984; Lykken & Tellegen, 1993; Kenrick & Keefe, 1992; Mascie-Taylor & Vandenberg, 1988; Mascie-Taylor, 1989; Nagoshi, Johnson, & Honbo, 1992; Philips et al., 1988; Plomin, DeFries, & Roberts, 1977; Reynolds, Baker, & Pedersen, 2000; Tambs, Sundet, & Berg, 1993; Vandenberg, 1972; Watkins & Meredith 1981; Watson et al., 2004). This evidence for assortative mating in humans is primarily based on the resemblance among mating partners, a finding that could, theoretically, stem from passive processes such as random mating in environments that are stratified for these characteristics (i.e., social homogamy, Kalmijn, 1998; Lykken & Tellegen, 1993). An example of this would be that brighter people end up going to universities instead of joining the work force early in life. Since mere opportunity might lead students to marry people they meet at the university while workers marry people they met at work, assortative mating could in principle be a by-product of cognitive stratification by university entrance requirements. However, in more sophisticated studies that are able to separate active and passive sources of mate assortment, there is good evidence that active mate choice plays a sizeable role, meaning that people selectively decide whom to mate with and whom not (Mascie-Taylor & Vandenberg, 1988; Nagoshi et al., 1992; Reynolds, Baker, & Pedersen, 2000; Watson et al., 2004).

The preferences, desires, and ideals on which people report basing their mating decisions have been studied extensively. The overall pattern of results can be summarized as follows:

1. Both men and women prefer mates who are in good overall condition, as revealed by cues of physical attractiveness (Langlois et al., 2000; Rhodes, 2006; Thornhill & Grammer, 1999; but see also Weeden & Sabini, 2005, vs. Grammer, Fink, Møller, & Manning, 2005), healthy appearance (Jones et al., 2001; 2004; Roberts et al., 2005), good cognitive functioning (i.e., general intelligence, Miller, 2000a, b, and absence of mental disorders, Keller & Miller, 2006; Shaner, Miller, & Mintz, 2004), pleasant scent (Gangestad & Thornhill, 1998; Rikowski & Grammer, 1999; Thornhill & Gangestad, 1999b; Thornhill et al., 2003), behavioral displays (Gangestad et al., 2004; Miller, 2000a, b), sexually dimorphic hormonal markers in the face (reviewed in Rhodes, 2006), body build (Kasperk et al., 1997; Singh, 1993; Swami & Tovée, 2005), and voice (Dabbs & Mallinger, 1999; Feinberg et al., 2005; Puts, 2006). While some authors assume that these traits signal different kinds of mate qualities (Cunningham et al., 1995), many of them have been linked to the direct mating benefits of fecundity (Buss, 1989; Jasienska, Ziomkiewicz, Ellison, Lipson, & Thune, 2004; Manning, Scutt, & Lewisjones, 1998; Singh, 1993), as well as to the indirect benefits of low genetic mutation load and other heritable qualities ("good genes," Gangestad & Simpson, 2000; Gangestad & Thornhill, 2003; Grammer et al., 2003; Hunt, Bussière, Jennions, & Brooks, 2004; Miller, 2000b, this volume; Keller, this volume), suggesting that they indeed represent cues which signal a single underlying quality (Grammer et al., 2002). Brunswik (1956) introduced the concept of "vicarious functioning" in the context of his famous lens model of perception to describe such a constellation where different cues are independently perceived as indicators of the same latent trait (see Miller & Todd, 1998). Further, the preference for good overall condition may reflect more an avoidance of bad condition in a mate than a direct attraction to good condition per se (Arnquist & Rowe, 2005; Grammer et al., 2002; Zebrowitz & Rhodes, 2004). Indifferent to the question of whether this part of our person perception system is more closely linked with an approach or avoidance motivation, we will refer to the preference for good overall condition as *condition preference*.

2. For long-term committed relationships, both men and women want a dependable, kind, and trustworthy mate to whom they can securely attach (Buss, 1989; Kenrick, Sadalla, Groth, & Trost, 1990; Li, Bailey, Kenrick, & Linsenmeier, 2002; Fletcher, Tither, O'Loughlin, Friesen, & Overall, 2004). That is, both sexes possess an attachment system that motivates stable, monogamous pair-bonding with an appropriate partner (Fraley & Shaver, 2000; Hazan & Diamond, 2000). There are general reasons (e.g., risk of desertion, loss of support and investments, and opportunity costs), as well as sex-specific reasons (e.g., risk of cuckoldry for men, risk of losing paternal investment for women) (Buss & Schmitt, 1993) for the human desire for attachment. The attachment system likely evolved to facilitate biparental care for offspring (Miller & Fishkin, 1997; Fraley, Brumbaugh, & Marks, 2005). We will refer to the preference for a dependable, kind, and trustworthy mate as *attachment preference*.

3. Additionally, women have a stronger preference than men for mates who can provide resources (e.g., hunted meat in prehistoric times, earned income today) or at least have a high resource-acquisition and maintenance potential, which facilitates successful child rearing (Buss, 1989; Li et al., 2002). We will refer to this rather female-specific preference as *resource preference*. Men, on the other hand, have on average a much greater desire for sexual variety than women, and therefore tend to be strongly attracted to women who are easily sexually accessible and to refrain from committed relationships. This preference would allow for a great number of sexual partners with relatively low costs, an aim that is generally much more attractive to men than women (Buss & Schmitt, 1993; Schmitt et al., 2003). We will refer to this rather male-specific preference as *variety preference*. Both of these sex-specific preferences can ultimately be explained by sex differences in the minimal investment in the reproductive process, which is higher for women than for men on the level of gametes (i.e., anisogamy: female egg cells are bigger than male sperm), physiology (i.e., gestation, placentation, child birth, lactation), and postnatal childcare (Trivers, 1972).

This core structure of mate preferences has been found to be cross-culturally universal (Buss, 1989; Buss et al., 1990; Marlowe, 2004; Schmitt et al., 2003; Schmitt 2005a, b). However, following the Brunswikian ecological psychology approach, there can be cultural variation in the actual cues that serve as indicators of the underlying qualities preferred in mate choice (Hamon & Ingoldsby, 2003; Marlowe, Apicella, & Reed, 2005; Miller & Todd, 1998). This is completely in line with the modern evolutionary psychological approach, which assumes that mate preferences develop ontogenetically from evolved innate capacities (aesthetic valuations, learning preparedness) in interaction with a given sociocultural and environmental context (cp. Barrett, 2006; Cummins & Cummins, 1999; Tooby, Cosmides, & Barrett, 2005).

The relative importance a population puts on these qualities also varies across cultures (Eagly & Wood, 2000; Hamon & Ingoldsby, 2003), but partly in a predictable functional relationship to environmental factors such as pathogen prevalence and harshness of the environment (Gangestad & Buss, 1993; Gangestad, Haselton, & Buss, 2006; Nelson & Morrison, 2005; Penton-Voak, Jacobson, & Trivers, 2004; Swami & Tovée, 2005). Environmentally contingent shifts of preferences, in turn, are intertwined with shifts in the average mating tactic of populations (Gangestad & Simpson, 2000; Low, 1990; Schmitt, 2005b), which in turn relate to the social evolution of cultural differences in the degree of individual freedom of mate choice (Hamon & Ingoldsby, 2003). However, individuals in every culture still have to face similar trade-offs in their mate choices between these qualities, as revealed by the culturally universal structure of self-reported preferences (Shackelford, Schmitt, & Buss, 2005; see also Fletcher et al., 2004; Gangestad & Simpson, 2000).

To summarize, both data and theory suggest that humans are endowed with four broad classes of preferences that guide their mating decisions. Two of them, the condition and the attachment preferences, play important roles in both male and female mating behavior, while the other two, the resource and the variety preferences, are rather sex-specific, the former being much more important for women and the latter for men. The aesthetic and affective valuations of the four associated kinds of mate qualities, which lead to their perceptual and motivational effects in the mating process, can be regarded as evolved and innate capacities present in every human being. Making these quality evaluations is necessary for adaptive mating decisions based on simple heuristics. The directly observable cues to these mate qualities might vary between human populations and most of them are likely learned over ontogenetic development, a process that is also steered by the evolved innate capacities. Beyond that, two other things have to be learned in order to make a successful mating decision: (1) The range of qualities in the present population of potential mates, which is necessary to evaluate whether a mate with a certain quality is actually high or low on that dimension, and (2) how an individual should solve the conflicts between the four preference classes that are likely to occur "in the wild". The next section will be on the range problem, while the rest of the chapter will address the trade-offs between conflicting preferences in men and women, and the role that self-assessments play in this process.

SIMPLE HEURISTICS AS MATING
DECISION MECHANISMS

To decide whether a potential mate is worth pursuing, we need to compare him or her to the other possibilities we might be able to pursue
instead. One way is to compare him or her to the other potential mates
we have previously encountered and rejected; the problem is that if we
decide that one of those previous mates was actually more attractive overall, we often have little chance of being able to return to that person and try
again, because he or she is likely to have found someone else. Instead, we
can look to the future—but how can we tell who else might await us in
the months ahead, and how attractive that person might be? This is the
twin challenge of sequential mate search: Not being able to go back in
time, nor look ahead to the future, and so struggling to make a good *yes*
or *no* choice concerning the person before us right here and now.

In a situation like this, where the distribution of available alternatives
is unknown, there is no way to return to previous options, and it is hard
to switch to another option once a committed choice has been made, a
good approach is to search with an 'aspiration level': a minimum threshold of apparent mate value for saying 'yes' to the current potential mate.
Aspiration-level search is a simple heuristic method that Herbert Simon
(1990) called *satisficing*. (This situation has been studied mathematically
in probability theory as the 'Dowry Problem' or 'Secretary Problem'—see
Ferguson, 1989.) In particular, satisficing search can be divided into two
phases: In the first phase, potential mates are just looked at without a selection being made, so that the searcher can gather information about the
available range of mate values. For example, this would include young
adolescents being keenly interested in observing and evaluating individuals of the opposite sex, but being 'too shy' to actually court them—because
they're still learning who's worth courting. This information is used to
set an aspiration level—the minimum mate value that the searcher will try
to get in further search. The second phase then consists of looking at additional potential mates, until one is found who exceeds the aspiration level
set in phase 1. Search is stopped at that point and that individual is pursued: one gets a 'crush' on him or her and invests substantial mating effort
in attracting his or her romantic attention. Once the aspiration level is set,
the length of the second search phase is out of the searcher's control—it
depends on the more or less random sequence of mates encountered from
the mating market. But how long the *first* phase should be for setting
the aspiration, and how the aspiration level is set, depends on the goals
of the searcher.

If the searcher is trying to maximize the chance of picking the single
highest-value mate, the *optimal* way to set the aspiration level is to search

long enough in phase 1 that enough information is obtained about the available mate qualities to make a good decision, but not *so* long that the searcher passes by the best alternative in phase 1 without selecting him or her. The aspiration level is then set to the highest mate value seen so far. Mathematically, the length of phase 1 that optimizes this balance is to look at N/e of the available alternatives, where N is the 'search horizon length' or expected number of potential mates whom one will meet in a lifetime, and $e \approx 2.718$ is the base of the natural logarithm system (see Ferguson, 1989, for an explanation of why this exact formula works best). This optimal phase 1 length is 37 percent of N, so the optimal approach in this case is to follow the "37 percent rule": In phase 1, look at 37 percent of the potential mates; then set the aspiration level to equal the *highest overall mate value* seen among all those individuals; and then continue search in phase 2 until someone is found whose mate value exceeds the aspiration level. (For example, if a woman expects to meet a constant number of new potential mates each year from puberty [around age 13] until fertility declines [around age 40], then the woman should take about 10 years [37 percent of 27 years reproductive life-span] to form her aspiration level during phase 1, and start 'searching in earnest' [phase 2] around age 23 for the first male ['Mr. Right'] who exceeds that aspiration level.)

This method gives a better than 1 in 3 chance of picking the *highest mate value* out of N individuals, but it requires searching through 74 percent of those individuals on average before it says to stop. (In the example above, the woman would not find 'Mr. Right' until she was 33 years old on average—having wasted 20 years of potential fertility.) In contrast, if a searcher has the more reasonable and modest goal of selecting a mate in the top 10 percent of the quality distribution, he or she would do best by setting an aspiration level after only seeing about 14 percent of the potential mates to be encountered (Todd & Miller, 1999), which would lead to a choice being made after seeing 40 percent of the potential mates on average. (In the example above, this aspiration level could be set by age 17 and a mate would be chosen by age 24 on average.) Other goals also require relatively little amounts of search to set an aspiration level that reflects the range of mate values likely to be encountered. Thus, successful mate search in this kind of situation can rely on a simple satisficing mechanism that constantly adjusts a searcher's condition preferences (in terms of their aspiration level) upwards with each successively better potential mate that is encountered.

There is ample evidence that both men and women set their aspiration levels as assumed in the simulations: People reduce their evaluations of potential mates (i.e., behave as if their aspiration level is higher) after exposure to highly attractive members of the opposite sex (Kenrick & Gutierres, 1980; Kenrick, Gutierres, & Goldberg, 1989; Melamed & Moss,

1975). Further, even the attraction to current romantic partners can be affected by changes in the comparison group (Kenrick et al., 1989; Kenrick, Neuberg, Zierk, & Krones, 1994; Weaver, Masland, & Zillman, 1984). These are social equivalents of the 'contrast effects' known from psychophysics (Helson, 1964).

The literature on development during adolescence provides support that a learning period (phase 1 in the simulations) indeed precedes serious mate choice attempts during adulthood. Adolescent romantic relationships tend to be very experimental and appear to be aimed at developing one's Mating Intelligence instead of finding a lifetime mate (Furman, 2002). In this vein, Locke and Bogin (2006) argued that the evolution of the human-specific adolescence period was driven by the increasingly complex nature of culturally transmitted human mating cues and rituals (cf. Miller, 2000a). There is mounting evidence that this learning period now extends well beyond biological adolescence and into early adulthood, at least in Western societies (Arnett, 2000). One reason might be that the much greater mobility nowadays leads to an evolutionarily novel degree of instability in peer groups, including the group of available mates. These changes might impose a recurring need to update one's aspiration level. For example, if someone moves from his or her small hometown to a big city, most of his or her peer group likely changes, including the group of potential mates. The exposure there to more potential mates will also on average mean exposure to more *attractive* potential mates, which would raise this person's aspiration level and make him or her pickier than he or she tended to be in the smaller social environment of the hometown.

SIMPLE HEURISTICS FOR LONG-TERM PARTNER CHOICE

While such satisficing heuristics based on aspiration levels are quite plausible models for mate choice in an uncertain social environment, they still contain an unrealistic oversimplification: The assumption that mate choice is one-sided. Such heuristics resemble more the sequential-choice processes of consumers shopping for wares on an economic market than those of singles making *mutual* choices on a mating market. If someone samples cars and makes a choice, the car won't reject this person as its new owner; but if the same person samples potential mates and decides on Brad Pitt or Angelina Jolie, his or her chosen mate is quite likely to say *no* in return. In humans, long-term mate choice must be mutual—except in rare cases of abduction, coercion, or slavery. An individual's failure to understand this mutuality constraint in human mating represents a major failure of Mating Intelligence, and typically leads to unrequited love, sexual stalking, or "erotomania" (De Clerembault's syndrome).

In general, conceptualizing the social dynamics of mating decisions in a market framework is highly promising, since it allows for unifying scientific progress from the fields of psychology (social exchange theory, Baumeister & Vohs, 2004; Kelley & Thibaut, 1978; Thibaut & Kelley, 1959), economics (e.g. modeling of marriage decisions, Choo, & Siow, 2006; Wong, 2003) and biology (biological market theory, Hammerstein & Hagen, 2005; Noë & Hammerstein, 1995).

"Shopping" for mates on a mating market with mutual choice is a highly competitive endeavor. If individuals base their mate choices on aspiration levels learned solely by observing the conditions of available mates, they might be able to find someone who closely matches their condition preference in a fast and frugal manner, but they would also risk wasting their courting efforts if their proposals are declined by the ones chosen, who have *their own* aspiration levels for *their* mate choice decisions. Further risks of making mate choices without reference to one's own condition include opportunity costs (i.e., lost chances to find other mates), and being abandoned for someone better later on in a relationship (Kenrick, Groth, Trost, & Sadalla, 1993). This last risk, which is basically relevant only in committed, long-term romantic relationships, puts individuals' condition preference in conflict with their attachment preference: The better a mate's condition, the more attractive he or she is to any of his or her alternative mates, and the greater the probability that he or she will attract and consider better alternatives. Needless to say, if one is completely deserted by a mate (i.e., all contact is broken off), this person is no longer available to satisfy the attachment preference. But even if both "stay friends" or switch over to a polygamous relationship (which are alternatives that could still stimulate the condition preference in some way), the attachment preference will not be as satisfied anymore. The reason for this is that meeting a preference for good condition is fundamentally different from meeting a preference for secure attachment. Attachment relationships develop in a process of mutual responsiveness and trust, requiring spending plenty of time with each other and paying careful attention to the other's needs (Fraley & Shaver, 2000; Hazan & Diamond, 2000). Exactly these "spendings" and "payments" make being a secure attachment figure literally costly: Since time and attention are always limited resources, no one can be a "safe haven" for a large number of people simultaneously. In contrast, if someone is in good overall condition, it is rather easy to be attractive for many potential mates. To put it another way, while good condition is a characteristic of a mate (i.e., an individual trait), secure attachment is a characteristic of a relationship with a mate (i.e., a dyadic trait).

In a similar vein, seeking attachment is fundamentally different from seeking a mate in good overall condition. For all individuals except those in the best condition, almost all potential mates who match their condition preference will contradict their attachment preference, as these individuals will seek mates with high levels of condition themselves. For example, a woman may feel awe and lust at the sight of Brad Pitt's condition as he is acting in a movie, but may not feel the warm glow of secure attachment she gets from sitting next to her boyfriend during the movie, even though he may be in comparatively less good condition. This is because her boyfriend is responsive to her needs, while Brad Pitt never pays attention to her. Because she knows from her experiences that men like Brad Pitt are out there on the mating market, her aspiration level for condition might tell her to go for someone better. But her need for a secure attachment figure might never be satisfied by any of those "Brad Pitts," simply because none of them will care for her long enough in the presence of alternative women in better condition. Due to the forces of the mating market, only men with a similar (or lower) rank on condition will consider her such a good choice that they bother giving her enough time and attention to make the development of a secure attachment relationship possible. Of course, the reverse is also true for the men she chooses. Taken together, this leads to (monogamous) assortative mating for condition at the population level in spite of absolute condition ideals at the individual level, caused by a trade-off between the preferences for condition and attachment.

A direct implication of these mating market dynamics is that the preferences of one sex become social constraints on the choices of the other sex: We can strive for mates in top condition, but as long as we fail to take into account how well we are able to fit to the condition preference of potential mates, we may get rejected most of the time, and we are especially unlikely to end up in a long-term attachment relationship. Instead of running into these kinds of emotional disasters over and over again, it would be adaptive for individuals to track their own value on the mating market, that is, their ability to live up to the condition preferences of the opposite sex, and to adjust their own condition preference accordingly (Dawkins, 1982; Kenrick et al., 1993; Trivers, 1972; Todd & Miller, 1999).

In this way, self-assessment processes (as defined above) become relevant for mate choice decisions. Tracking one's own mate value can be regarded as a special, domain-specific function of self-esteem, for which Kirkpatrick and Ellis (2001, 2006) coined the term *mate value sociometer*. Note that this framework accords an interpersonal function to self-esteem (see already Cooley, 1902; Mead, 1934). As such, it is an instance of 'sociometer theory' (Leary et al., 1995; Leary & Baumeister, 2000), which proposes that general self-esteem is an evolved mechanism which monitors one's overall risk of social exclusion. Penke and Denissen (2006) argue that being rejected by a courted mate for not reaching his or her condition preferences can be regarded as a form of social exclusion, namely

2. SELF-ASSESSMENTS AND MATING DECISIONS

exclusion from mating. Repeated experiences of this kind imply a severe threat to an individual's reproductive fitness, since they might portend a lifelong exclusion from mating in general. It would therefore be highly adaptive if the general human motive of self-esteem maintenance (Baumeister, 1997) used domain-specific cues of reductions in one's own value on the mating market to motivate either striving for the improvement of mate value (e.g., through getting in better physical shape, learning courtship skills, or seeking higher status, though improvement of condition itself might be difficult, since cues to condition follow the biological principle of honest signaling—Kokko et al., 2003; Miller, 2000a; Zahavi, 1975; Zahavi & Zahavi, 1997), the downward adjustment of the condition preference, or the reallocation of one's general life-effort from short-term to long-term mating (or from mating in general to investment in kin).

But before a mate value sociometer can serve a regulatory function in mating decisions, it has to be properly calibrated; a mate-value sociometer must acquire some validity to be of any use. People have to learn their own mate value relative to other members of their sex. Todd and Miller (1999) argued that this happens by experiences of acceptance and rejection in flirtatious interactions with the opposite sex, especially during the adolescent years (see also Penke & Denissen, 2006). Complementary to that, another general self-related cognitive process can help to accomplish mate value sociometer calibration in a more indirect manner: the motive for social comparison (Festinger, 1954; Gilbert, Price, & Allan, 1995; Mussweiler, 2003). Studies have shown that people are especially likely to compare themselves with same-sex peers on traits that are preferred in mate choice decisions of the opposite sex, and to adjust their self-appraisals accordingly (Gutierres, Kenrick, & Partch, 1999; Brown, Novick, Lord, & Richards, 1992), especially when the competitors appear real and are not professional models (Cash, Cash, & Butters, 1983). This finding is similar to the contrast effects people show in adjusting their aspiration level for mate choices based on condition preferences, as discussed above. Since direct rejection by a potential mate can be a very painful experience, especially for those singles who lack prior experiences of mating success (Penke & Denissen, 2006), social comparisons with one's own sex might add helpful information at low embarrassment cost.

We argued earlier that when it comes to choosing a mate for a long-term, committed relationship, most people face a trade-off between their preferences for condition and attachment. This trade-off might be handled by the mate value sociometer. There is empirical evidence suggesting that people indeed use their mate value sociometer to adjust their condition preference until it roughly matches their own condition (Buston & Emlen, 2003; Kenrick et al., 1993; Little, Jones, Penton-Voak, Burt, & Perrett, 2002; Pawlowski & Dunbar, 1999; Regan, 1998a, b). Srivastava and Beer (2005) showed that an insufficiently satisfied attachment preference (as indicated by an insecure attachment style) increases the sensitivity of the sociometer mechanism to signs of social exclusion. This implies that larger adjustments of the condition preference can be expected when people are in need of attachment, after even minimal experiences of rejection by mates. For example, someone who lacks secure social support from good friends or family members might be much more willing to accept a mate lacking in physical attractiveness or other desirable features, if that mate could instead become a "safe haven" soon. Someone who is better integrated in his or her social environment might also desire a long-term relationship, but because getting a new attachment figure is a less urgent goal for such a person, there is no need to compromise the condition preference as much in this case. It might also be that there are stable interindividual differences in the sensitivity of people's sociometers that are more due to genetic differences than due to differential social integration. Indeed, it might well be that personality differences in neuroticism (i.e., emotional stability), which are highly related to sociometer sensitivity, only exist because the optimal level of sociometer sensitivity differs between environments, so that the genetic variation underlying this personality dimension could not be eroded by natural selection (Denissen & Penke, 2006).

Todd and colleagues (Todd & Billari, 2003; Todd, Billari, & Simão, 2005; Todd & Miller, 1999) developed agent-based computer simulations of the mutual mate choice process outlined so far. These models typically simulate a mating market composed of 100 males and 100 females, each with a condition value drawn from a uniform distribution from 0 (minimum) to 100 (maximum). As in real life, individuals do not innately know their own condition value, but they can accurately assess the values of all potential mates they encounter. Individuals meet in male-female pairs, assess each other, and decide whether to make a romantic proposal to each other. This meeting and assessing process happens in two phases, as in the one-sided (non-mutual) satisficing mate search mechanisms discussed earlier. In the first "adolescent" phase, proposals and rejections do not result in actual pairing, but they can be used to set or adjust an aspiration level that will determine to whom future proposal offers are made. In the following "adult" phase, the aspiration level set during the adolescent phase is fixed and used to make decisions in the rest of the search. These proposal and rejection decisions are now "real," in that mutual proposals result in a long-term pair being made and the couple leaving the mating market simulation. The necessity for mutual agreement is what makes this scenario different from the one-sided case described above—from one searcher's perspective, the decisions of potential mates as to whether they judge the searcher as a suitable mate as well are critical to that searcher's mating success, so the searcher's own decision mechanism, based on his or her mate value sociometer, should take these others' perspectives into account.

Search strategies can be sensitive to the decisions of potential mates in different ways. The information available to these strategies at each time-step is the mate value of the current potential mate being encountered, and whether that individual makes an offer or a rejection to the searcher. A reasonable approach is to use the assessments that others make about oneself as a cue about one's own mate value, which only the others can see clearly. So one could raise one's self-appraisal, and hence one's aspiration level, every time an attractive offer is received and, similarly, one could lower it after every unattractive rejection. This also fits with our intuitions about how romantic successes and failures can induce the mate value sociometer to go up and down, which in turn can affect how high or low people aim in their next romantic endeavors. For example, we feel great after an attractive person reciprocates a kiss passionately, or terrible after a less attractive person shows disinterest. To specify a decision mechanism in more detail, all individuals start with an initial aspiration level of 50 (the middle of the 0–100 mate value range), which corresponds to assuming oneself to be just average. Then, during the adolescent learning period, for every proposal from someone more attractive than one's current aspiration level, raise one's aspiration level to be partway to the other's attractiveness value. Any proposals from someone less attractive than one's aspiration level are to be expected, and so do not have any effect. Just the reverse happens for rejections: for every rejection from someone below one's current aspiration level, lower the aspiration level toward the other's attractiveness. As each individual's aspiration level changes over the course of the adolescence period, he or she influences the learning of everyone else's aspiration levels via the combined effect of the proposals and rejections made.

Simulations of populations using such a simple rule produce results similar to patterns of human mate choice, with most individuals finding marriage partners of similar overall mate value in a relatively short period of time (Todd & Miller, 1999). In addition, the behavior of these proposed search mechanisms can be assessed against population-level outcome measures. For instance, demographers have long puzzled over a frequently observed skewed-bell shape distribution of ages at which people first get married (Coale, 1971). When Todd and colleagues created an agent-based demographic model of a population of males and females looking for marriage partners with the mutual sequential search heuristic just described, they found that the "ages" at which the individuals got married fit the observed demographic data (Todd & Billari, 2003; Todd, Billari, & Simão, 2005).

To recap, mating markets are characterized by mutual choices, with both sexes showing a preference for a partner in good condition as well as a secure attachment relationship. When it comes to long-term relationships like marriage, the attachment preference becomes paramount for either sex. Since market dynamics frequently result in conflicts between both preferences, people need to adjust their condition ideal in these cases.

It is assumed that this is accomplished by an aspiration level for condition that reflects one's self-perceived mate value, as learned from past and present interactions with the opposite sex and from social comparison processes. This special instance of self-esteem has been called the mate-value sociometer. We therefore propose that mate-choice decisions are guided by simple heuristics based on satisficing aspiration levels not only when it comes to evaluating a potential mate of high condition in a sequential search process, but also when it comes to acquiring the best mate for a secure attachment relationship. Thus, the accurate calibration and use of one's mate-value sociometer during adolescence and beyond is an important aspect of human Mating Intelligence.

THE COMPLICATION OF MATING DECISIONS BY SEX DIFFERENCES

So far, our discussion of mating decisions and their underlying mechanisms has ignored sex differences. This is somewhat defensible as long as we concentrate on long-term mate choice, where male and female mate preferences converge (Kenrick et al., 1993; Li & Kenrick, 2006), and men and women face similar trade-offs between condition and attachment preferences (cf. Miller & Fishkin, 1997). However, as Trivers' (1972) seminal parental investment theory implies, a discussion of mating decisions that neglects sex differences completely would surely miss a basic point.

One sex difference that follows from parental investment theory is the greater female preference for resources (Buss, 1989; Feingold, 1992; Li et al., 2002). Bearing a child is a very costly endeavor for the female body, just as successfully raising a child is costly in terms of time, money, energy, and other efforts. Although the child-bearing costs are inevitably a female burden (though it can be eased by male support), the child-rearing ones can easily be shared between both parents. In humans, the quality of parental investment a male can provide depends heavily on the quantity of resources he can provide. The implied prediction is that women, but not men, have evolved a resource preference (i.e., preferring males who are reliable providers) in addition to their condition and attachment preferences, which has to be taken into account when they make mate choices. This extension is hardly necessary for biologists studying mating in non-human animals, since physical condition is so closely intertwined with resource acquisition and resource-holding ability in most species that they are often equated (Hunt et al., 2004; Rowe & Houle, 1996). To some degree, both are overlapping in humans, too. Intelligence, for example, predicts both genetic quality (Miller, 2000b, this volume) and occupational success (Schmidt & Hunter, 2004). But specifically human phenomena such as wealth inheritance, extensive political alliances, and complex financial markets lead to many cases where condition and wealth diverge: Some men happen to possess a significant amount of money, even though they would have lacked the condition to earn it on their own. The consequence is that women sometimes face an additional trade-off between their condition preference and their resource preference, due to an imperfect correlation between these variables. (In fact, a study by Waynforth, 2001, suggests that this trade-off is the only reason for the well-known finding that men have a stronger preference for physical attractiveness in mates than women do; see also Li et al., 2002).

A straightforward solution to this difficult trade-off is for the female (but not the male) ideal of overall mate value to be based on both the overall physical condition *and* the overall resource provision of a mate. Taking this into account, it is logical to then assume that women looking for a long-term mate use a combination of both their condition preference *and* their resource preference as a starting point for setting their aspiration level in the simple mate choice heuristics outlined above. Accordingly, the mate value sociometer of men should track their individual combination of condition and resources, and not just condition alone. An alternative solution arises if women are not able to find one man who fulfills the three-way trade-off between the condition, resource, and attachment preference. Gangestad and Simpson (2000; Thornhill & Gangestad, 2003) propose that women switch to a pluralistic conditional mating strategy in this situation: Securing resources and attachment in a committed relationship with a long-term mate that might not satisfy their condition preference, and acquiring good genes from extra-pair matings with men of good condition when conception is likely, during peak fertility in the ovulatory cycle (Thornhill & Gangestad, 2003; Gangestad, Thornhill, & Garver-Apgar, 2005a, b, but see also Pawlowski, 1999; Roney, 2005).

Another important sex difference is the greater male desire for sexual variety. In all cultures studied so far, men report a much higher number of desired sexual partners over any period of time, a greater willingness to have sex with someone after a short period of time, a greater active search for short-term mating partners, more positive attitudes towards sexual promiscuity than women (Buss & Schmitt, 1993; Schmitt et al., 2003; Schmitt, 2005a, b), and fewer feelings of regret after having short-term sexual affairs than women report (Townsend, 1995; Townsend, Kline, & Wasserman, 1995). These are the largest psychological sex differences found so far (Hyde, 2005; Schmitt et al., 2003).

In the terminology of mating decisions, these sex differences translate into a greater male variety preference (i.e., a preference for easily sexually accessible mates), and a strategic male tendency to allocate more effort to courting new mates than to investing in an established relationship and resulting offspring (i.e., to invest more in short-term mating tactic). This is, again, related to the fact that minimal parental investment is smaller in males than in females from the level of gametes onward, allowing males a higher reproductive potential than females (Trivers, 1972). Physiologically, any fertile man would be able to produce a seemingly endless number of offspring in his lifetime, which is not true for women due to pregnancy and lactation. But since every child has to have a father and a mother, and the number of reproductive-aged men and women is roughly the same in most human populations most of the time, the actual offspring numbers has to be equal for men and women on average. Thus fertile women become the limited resource for male reproductive success. Even though this has the implication that hardly any man will ever actually receive his full potential reproductive success (Kokko & Jennions, 2003), it still implies that a greater variety preference and a short-term mating orientation is the optimal default value with the highest potential payoff for men (Buss & Schmitt, 1993; Schmitt, Shackelford, & Buss, 2001), and that men should not be very discriminating when it comes to short-term, purely sexual affairs (Kenrick et al., 1990, 1993), at least above a certain minimal threshold of female condition that makes fecundity likely. However, how successful a man will be in pursuing a short-term tactic is heavily dependent on his condition, because women, who need not care about trading off their attachment preference in the short-term context anymore, show a much greater condition preference when seeking short-term mates (Kenrick et al., 1990; Li et al., 2002; Regan 1998a, b). Under these circumstances, the only way for men to compensate for a lack of condition might be immediate resource provision (Buss & Schmitt, 1993). That is, men can "pay" to have short-term sex with choosy women through being extremely attractive (offering good condition) or extremely generous (offering good resources). The former is called *romance*, the latter is called *prostitution*. Overall, this analysis reflects Darwin's (1871) prediction of competitive males and choosy females (see also Trivers, 1972).

Hill and Reeve (2004) modeled aspects of these dynamical trade-offs of preferences in a game theory framework and took sex differences into account. They assumed that both men and women choose their mates in a competitive mating market, where all individuals have a certain condition (dependent on genetic quality and a sex- and age-dependent decline function) and resource value. When two (or more) men courted one woman, they offered their condition and attempted to overbid their competitor by providing enough resources to yield a higher overall mate value (condition plus resources—which is an oversimplification in these models since, as we argued above, condition and resources are likely related in men; however, we do not expect that any of the conclusions Hill and Reeve drew from their model would be substantively altered by a more realistic assumption of correlated mate value components). In this model, resource-generosity could influence male mating success over and above condition. The condition and provided resources of the "winning" man were then combined with the condition and resources of the woman to influence their joint reproductive fitness (number of offspring) as a couple. For women, the relative preference for male resources versus male condition was partly dependent on her own resources and partly a preset constant. This constant was meant to reflect relative environmental demands for paternal investment vs. good genes, as discussed by Gangestad and Simpson (2000), but was not dynamically modeled. However, when more than one woman was interested in the same man, he could lower his resource offerings until all but one women refused to accept it anymore. He was therefore left with resources to invest in additional female reproductive partners (satisfying his variety preference). These models predicted not only assortative mating for overall mate value, but, more importantly, that both the competition between potential mates and same-sex competitors on the mating market would influence the overall value of the mate (or mates) an individual will end up with. Interestingly, Hill and Reeve emphasized that competitors on either side do not necessarily need to be immediately present. This maps nicely onto the sequential nature of mate choice in uncertain social environments, as outlined above. Hill and Reeve further support a sociometer-type mutual search mechanism by suggesting that, to make adaptive mating decisions, men and women should monitor their own relative mate value and the distribution of mate values in the population of potential mates, in order to avoid unnecessary mating costs. Their models can thus be taken as further formal evidence for the plausibility of the simple mate choice heuristics we propose.

PARADIGMS FOR STUDYING MATE CHOICE: BOUNDARIES AND LIMITATIONS

To recap, decades of research in various disciplines provide us with useful conceptualizations and elaborated theories about mate choice decision mechanisms. The current knowledge on relevant aspects of human nature and the structure of our social environment can be integrated in precisely specified decision models, which in turn can be evaluated using computer simulations and game theory. However, the most important test is still provided by reality: Are these models valid descriptions of how people make their mate choices?

Unfortunately, we encounter a methodological problem at this point: real mating decisions are intimate processes for which a detailed assessment "in the wild" is not easily done. As a consequence, informative field experiments are difficult to design (for a notable exception, see Clark & Hatfield, 1989), and many factors have to remain uncontrolled. Instead, most empirical research on mate choice decision making seeks refuge in more convenient approaches, typically relying on self-reports (Cooper & Sheldon, 2002), either of recalled past choices, present preferences and desires, or hypothetical decisions based on vignettes. All these approaches are compromised in their validity by the fact that subjects have insufficient conscious insight into the relevant processes that lead to their decisions (Wilson, 2002). Another widespread approach is to let participants report their attraction to isolated aspects of potential mates that were artificially generated or extracted from real individuals. Example include line drawings differing in body built (Singh, 1993) or foot size (Fessler et al., 2005), computer morphs of still faces with neutral expression (Rhodes, 2006), vocal recordings altered for voice pitch (Puts, 2006), videotapes of men flirting with video screens (Gangestad et al., 2004), and jars with sweaty t-shirts (Thornhill & Gangestad, 1999b). These studies are experimentally more controlled, but might artificially alter the natural occurrence and interrelations of the cues utilized in mate choice. How relevant each of these cues becomes once it is embedded in its natural environment cannot be predicted with any certainty from these studies.

But most importantly, almost all paradigms used to study mate choice so far have failed to take its mutual nature into account: Usually, participants in mate-choice studies do not experience the reactions of potential mates, and trade-offs between preferences, if considered at all, are either enforced by the researchers (e.g., Buss, 1989; Fletcher et al., 2004; Li & Kenrick, 2006; Li et al., 2002) or indirectly inferred from self-ratings (e.g., Buston & Emlen, 2003; Kenrick et al., 1993; Regan, 1998a, b) instead of being a natural consequence of the dyadic interaction. In some ways, this is also true for retrospective reports from existing couples, even though their relationship was once formed in a process of mutual choice: because it is difficult to disentangle initial choices from retrospective memory-shifts (e.g., due to reduction of cognitive dissonance, Festinger, 1957), it is difficult to tell which preferences affected the couple formation in hindsight. Finally, studies of romantic relationship development offer some hope, but due to their mostly unpredictable onset, even these studies (e.g., Fletcher, Simpson, & Thomas, 2000) are normally done with already-existing couples, providing little knowledge about the initial mating decisions that led to them.

Therefore, mate-choice research is faced with a solid body of theoretical models and many supportive empirical hints from a variety of methodologically limited paradigms on the one hand, but a dearth of sufficiently ecologically valid studies to evaluate their predictions on the other hand. But an interesting solution to this predicament has recently appeared with the emergence of "speed-dating."

THE SPEED-DATING PARADIGM FOR STUDYING INITIAL MATE-CHOICE DECISIONS

Speed-dating is essentially a faster, more formalized type of sequential mate choice than what usually occurs "in the wild." Speed-dating events are held by commercial firms in many Western countries. The design of these events is largely similar: Single people interested in finding a partner sign up and are assigned to events, usually according to age (and sometimes other demographic variables). The event itself involves seven to thirty men meeting a similar number of women during a single evening. Usually the women stay seated at assigned tables, while the men take turns talking to each woman for a prescribed time interval of three to ten minutes (depending on the company organizing the event). After each of these accelerated "dates," each participant marks a card indicating how interested he or she is in meeting that person again, usually via a categorical decision ("I would like to meet again" vs. "I would not like to meet again"; in some cases, a third category is offered in which participants can indicate that they would consider this person for "friendship,"—i.e., resource investment without immediate sexual access—if not for a romantic/sexual partner). Only those pairs of participants who expressed mutual consensus regarding the desire to meet again are provided with each other's contact information (e.g., phone numbers or e-mail addresses) after the event. Speed-dating thus provides a microcosm for studying Mating Intelligence with a combination of laboratory-like control and ecological realism, since real mate-choice decisions of real singles can be observed systematically. A unique advantage of the speed-dating paradigm is that it allows for a separate assessment of male and female choices in the couple-formation process (based on each individual's marked cards indicating interest or disinterest in each prospect), which is, as we argued above, virtually impossible after relationships have been formed.

Although speed-dating events may be somewhat different from the process of normal dating, they are not as problematic as they might appear at first glance. For example, the artificially set length of the dating interactions might look too short for serious mate choices, but research on person perception in the minimal information paradigm has repeatedly shown that people are surprisingly accurate in judging others after very brief periods of time. This is not only the case for superficial traits like physical attractiveness, but also for less directly observable personality characteristics, such as broad personality traits and general intelligence

(Ambady, Bernieri, & Richeson, 2000; Borkenau, Mauer, Riemann, Spinath, & Angleitner, 2004). Furthermore, studies of speed-dating events can of course only capture the initial "screening" stage of the mate-choice process—not every speed-dating match will result in a marriage. However, the initial stage is crucial, since it determines which pairings have any chance at all to result in committed romantic relationships, for if the initial decision is a negative one, the potential partner will be dropped from further consideration.

A more severe limitation of the speed-dating paradigm might be hidden in a less obvious design feature: Participants at speed-dating events know in advance that they will not experience direct face-to-face rejections of their choices, and this knowledge might influence their choice behavior. Embarrassment is minimized, so individuals may set higher aspirations in their choices. However, it is not clear at the moment what kind of effect, if any, this lack of direct rejection has. We do not know, for example, if people can tell (or, maybe more importantly from a sociometer perspective, feel) if their choices were reciprocated. Neither do we know if prior knowledge about the setting (like how many potential partners they will meet or the indirect format of acceptance and rejection) really alters people's behavior during dating interactions or the choice process. These aspects clearly await further research.

Kurzban and Weeden (2005) were among the first to examine mate-choice decisions and mating success in the context of speed-dating events. In particular, they examined more than 10,000 speed-dating participants, scattered over many events in the United States, to explore the role of mate value (assessed by self-report questionnaires in advance) in initial mating decisions. Just as Darwin (1871) and Trivers (1972) predicted, Kurzban and Weeden found that women were much more selective than men: While men chose, on average, every second woman, women only wanted to meet every third man again. Both mean male and female success at the events (i.e., the number of times they were chosen, regardless of whether they themselves reciprocated the choice) was mainly predicted by visible indicators of good condition (like lower-than-average body mass index given a generally overweight population), suggesting that condition preferences influenced the choices of both sexes. Resource indicators (like income and education) had surprisingly little impact on male success (in terms of number of offers they received). However, having more resources made men more selective (in terms of number of choices made), and having indicators of good condition increased selectivity in both sexes. Greater selectivity, in turn, was related to higher condition preferences in both sexes. This pattern is consistent with our hypothesized trade-off between the attachment preference and the condition preference across both sexes, regulated by the mate value sociometer (though the evidence is indirect here).

In an intensive study of a single speed-dating event in Germany, Todd, Penke, Fasolo, and Lenton (2006; Todd, Fasolo, & Lenton, 2004) were able to examine the mating-decision processes in far greater detail. Before the event run by the German FastDating company, 20 of the women and 26 of the men reported via an online survey their demographic information, their mate choice preferences for condition (physical appearance), resources (wealth and status), and attachment (family values), and their self-evaluations regarding these same three dimensions. Additionally, all participants were rated for physical attractiveness by two raters during the event. As in the study by Kurzban and Weeden (2005), women were, on average, more selective than the men, though both sexes were much more selective in the German sample than in the U.S. sample. Also in concordance with Kurzban and Weeden, indicators of good condition best predicted success at the event, especially observer-rated attractiveness. Indeed, self-reported age and observer-rated attractiveness together explained 83 percent of the variance in female speed-dating success (i.e., younger, more beautiful women received more offers of interest from men). However, male success was significantly less well predicted by condition indicators, which explained only about a quarter of the variance in their success (though this was statistically significant). Just as in the American sample, resource indicators failed to improve this prediction.

Novel results appeared, however, when self-reported preferences and self-perceptions were added to the picture: First of all, across the sexes, self-reported condition, resource, and attachment preferences showed no statistically significant link to actual choices, as assessed by the mean self-perceptions in these domains of all chosen dating partners. This could either mean that the participants in the sample were generally unable to indicate their preferences accurately, that the cues for the preferred qualities could not be assessed within the context of these short meetings, or that the general trade-offs between conflicting preferences that occur in real choices altered the preferred ideals they reported in the questionnaires in a manner that blurred the linear relationships.

The last interpretation appears more likely if the generally low male selectivity is taken as the behavioral expression of a high variety preference: Although men might have high condition and attachment preferences for a long-term relationship with a single woman, their variety preference might lead them to accept a wider array of female characteristics. Especially in the speed-dating context, where courting approaches are facilitated and rejections are covert by design, many men might take the opportunity to maximize their chances for mating success, be it long-term quality or short-term quantity. This would explain the lack of a relationship between male self-perceptions and choices at speed-dating events.

However, the strong relation between condition and speed-dating success in women suggests that men are still not totally indiscriminating with respect to condition, though any condition level above a certain minimal threshold might do (in line with the "avoid-the-worst" heuristic of attractiveness judgments proposed by Grammer et al., 2002; see also Arnquist & Rowe, 2005; Zebrowitz & Rhodes, 2004). Indeed, the two women who were not chosen by any man during the German speed-dating event had an observer-rated attractiveness which was more than one standard deviation below the mean of those women who were chosen at least once. Thus, replacing condition preference (beyond some minimal threshold) and attachment preference with a high-variety preference might be the best description of typical male mate-choice decisions in the speed-dating context.

If an indifference towards the outcome (long-term vs. short-term relationship) is a viable interpretation of the typical male mating tactic in the speed-dating context, we further should expect no downward adjustments of preferences due to mate value self-perceptions. This was indeed the case: Men's self-perceptions in the condition, resource, and attachment domains, as well as an overall aggregate of these self-perceptions that reflected the mate value sociometer (cf. Penke & Denissen, 2006), were generally unrelated to the mean self-perceptions of each man's chosen partners in each individual domain and overall. Similar results emerged when the men's choices were evaluated by observer-rated attractiveness.

Female results were notably different: Besides being choosier overall and showing at least a slight correspondence between reported preferences and actual choices, women showed some tendency to adjust their choice behavior to their self-perceptions. This effect was especially true for self-perceived physical attractiveness, which was positively related to the average self-reported condition, resources, attachment, and overall mate value of their choices. Given that physical attractiveness, literally the most visible aspect of condition, almost perfectly predicted female speed-dating success, it was highly adaptive for women to adjust their choice thresholds upwards according to their own attractiveness.

The overall pattern of results thus suggests that low mate-choice costs lead men to satisfy their variety preference by indifferently choosing any woman who falls above a minimal condition threshold, while women stayed choosy and appeared to fine-tune social-comparison processes to the situation (meaning, in this context, that their mate-value sociometer mainly reflected their physical attractiveness), adjusting their mate choices accordingly. An interesting implication is that, at least as long as choices are not very costly for men, direct mate assortment (i.e., assortative mating that is not an indirect result of social homogamy) is primarily a result of female, not male, choices. However, since the main results stem from a fairly small sample, this interpretation awaits replication. The bottom line is that mate-choice behavior in the speed-dating paradigm appears consistent with the interactive operation of mate preferences as proposed in this chapter. The outlined simple heuristic for mate choice decisions based on learned aspiration levels was especially well supported in women, but seemed to be overridden by the variety preference in men, at the cost of their preferences for condition and attachment.

MATING TACTIC DECISIONS

The evidence from the speed-dating paradigm also reveals how interrelated our mate-choice and mating-tactic decisions are (see also Simpson & Oriña, 2003). For men, choosing a short-term mating tactic means giving strong priority to their variety preference, which imposes severe trade-offs against their condition and attachment preferences. While female condition indicates fecundity and is therefore necessarily preferred to some minimal degree (Grammer et al., 2002; Todd et al., 2006; Zebrowitz & Rhodes, 2004), the preference for a secure attachment partner can be abandoned when all effort is allocated towards short-term mating. For women, a short-term tactic means a similar drastic reduction in their attachment preference, which ultimately would have more severe consequences for them than for men (Trivers, 1972). Their much lower variety preference (Schmitt et al., 2001, 2003) would not provide much motivational compensation to make this trade-off. Instead, only an increase in their aspiration level for condition (or possibly the resources if they are provided immediately, see Buss & Schmitt, 1993) might motivate women to trade off their attachment preference and choose a short-term tactic. As a consequence, only men with high mate value will be able to successfully pursue a short-term tactic, while a similar relationship between mate value and proclivity toward promiscuity does not exist for women (Gangestad & Simpson, 2000). Since an allocation of effort to short-term tactics implies both direct and opportunity costs when such attempts remain unsuccessful (except in rare cases that mirror the low-cost speed-dating context in this regard), men, but not women, should adjust their mating tactic decisions to the level of their mate value sociometer. Exactly this relationship was found by Landolt, Lalumiere, and Quinsey (1995) for hypothetical mating decisions in college students.

Penke and Denissen (2006) took a closer look at how the mate value sociometer might guide male mating tactic decisions. They integrated the domain-specific interpretation of sociometer theory (Kirkpatrick & Ellis, 2001) with the social risk hypothesis by Allen and Badcock (2003), who regard general self-esteem as the phenomenological output of a psychological mechanism that weighs an individual's overall social value against his or her overall social burden (i.e., the overall costs someone induces to his or her social environment). This mechanism produces a depressed mood if the social value/social burden ratio drops too low, thereby motivating the individual to shun socially risky behaviors (i.e. social behaviors with high outcome variance, such as sexual courtship) that might provoke social exclusion. Since short-term mating tactics are proximately more rewarding and ultimately more adaptive for men than for women, and since, as a consequence, women become especially selective when choosing a short-term mate, only a small fraction of men with extraordinarily high mate value will be able to successfully pursue a short term tactic. Put differently, even though most men would prefer a variety of short-term mates, the high standards that women have for short-term mates would lead to their rejection of most of these men. Female mate preferences thus create a potential threat of social exclusion for short-term oriented men, namely an exclusion from mating. (Needless to say, this would severely endanger reproductive fitness.) Therefore, allocating effort to short-term tactics is a risky social behavior with both high potential costs and benefits for men, which, according to the motivational mechanism proposed by Allen and Badcock (2003), should be avoided as a consequence of depressive affect when general self-esteem is low. To be adaptive, the social cues that should trigger the avoidance response of this mechanism are signs of rejection by potential mates, as tracked by the mate value sociometer. This interpretation is consistent with the literature on depression, which is often triggered by failure in courtship, relationships, or status-striving, and which often results in a dramatic reduction in short-term mating effort.

But while the evocation of depressive mood by a low mate-value sociometer would have highly adaptive de-motivational effects on men who might otherwise unsuccessfully try to allocate their efforts in short-term tactics, it would be rather maladaptive for men who are successful in pursuing short-term tactics (because their potential benefit of fathering many offspring is so high), as well as for men who already chose to reallocate their efforts to a long-term relationship with a single mate and to providing paternal investment to their children (who would also shun any social risk in non-mating domains only because of their low mate value sociometer). Therefore, Penke and Denissen (2006) proposed, and subsequently found, that the influence of general self-esteem on the mate value sociometer shifts adaptively in men, but not in women, with lifestyle aspects that indicate short-term mating success (such as lifetime number of one-night stands) and mating tactic choice (such as involvement in a committed long-term relationship or having children): The self-esteem of men with a history of low short-term mating success was especially sensitive to a low mate-value sociometer, while the influence was much smaller for those with high short-term mating success, but also for those in stable romantic relationships and especially fathers. The effects were much weaker and seldom significant in women, but replicated for different operationalizations of the mate value sociometer in men (i.e., both the Mate Value Scale by Landolt et al., 1995, and an aggregate of diverse self-perceptions of traits preferred in mate choice).

These adaptive sociometer contingencies allow men of very high mate value to stay motivated to seek multiple mating partners even when sometimes unsuccessful in this endeavor, while simultaneously motivating the avoidance of such tactics in men with suboptimal mate values, for whom gaining independence from their mate-value sociometers by choosing a long-term mating tactic becomes an attractive alternative. Consequently, they are a plausible mechanism for male mating tactic decisions based on self-assessments.

Interestingly, these cognitive-level results parallel effects that were recently found on the endocrinological level: Free testosterone, which is a major determinant of sexual motivation (Regan, 1999) and which influences sexual-variety fantasies (Leitenberg & Henning, 1995), is also lower in men committed to a romantic relationship compared to singles (Burnham et al., 2003; Gray et al., 2004a, b), in fathers compared to non-fathers (Gray, Kahlenberg, Barrett, Lipson, & Ellison, 2002), and in men who invest more in their romantic relationships compared to those who invest less (Gray et al., 2002). Therefore, testosterone has been called a *hormonal index of effort allocation* in the reproductive domain (i.e., the current mating-tactic decision) (Ellison, 2001; Gray et al., 2004a, b). It is thus plausible that testosterone relates to adaptive shifts in the contingency of self-esteem on the mate value sociometer, constituting its physiological basis. In other words, free testosterone might be the endocrinological mediator of male mating-tactic decisions.

Overall, there is no evidence for a similar guidance of female mating-tactic decisions by self-assessments (Landolt et al., 1995; Penke & Denissen, 2006). This is hardly surprising, given that there is less need for women to base these decisions on their own mate value. Indeed, female mating tactic decisions appear to be much more dependent on ecological factors than are male decisions (Baumeister, 2000), especially those environmental cues that indicate the current relative importance of biparental care compared to good genes for reproductive success (Gangestad & Simpson, 2000; Schmitt, 2005b). How women use and process such environmental cues in order to reach adaptive mating tactic decisions is largely unknown (but see Swami & Tovée, 2005) and, as such, remains an interesting area for future research on Mating Intelligence.

CONCLUSION

Human mating decisions take place in a dynamic mating market characterized by mutual mate choice, high interindividual variability in preferred characteristics (condition and resources) in both sexes, and conflicting optimal allocations of reproductive effort between the sexes. Even though these dynamics can get rather complex and each individual enters the market naïve with regard to its local structure, simple mating heuristics can nonetheless guide adaptive mating decisions by taking advantage of environmental regularities.

In line with the principle of bounded rationality, these mating heuristics develop from evolved and innate capacities in interaction with the local environment's ecological and social structure. The capacities include broad motives, such as sexual lust, the adult attachment system, the desire for sexual variety, the needs for social comparison and self-esteem maintenance, and the avoidance of social risks (which is triggered by the sociometer mechanism). They also include highly specific cognitive biases, such as the learning preparednesses for and aesthetic valuations of cues to condition and resources in mates. In line with the sex-specific optimal reproductive strategies of both sexes, some of these capacities show large sex differences, leading to a "default" orientation of men towards short-term and of women towards long-term tactics. The environment not only provides the cultural context in which the concrete cues for condition and resources are learned, but also information about the distribution of these mate qualities in both potential mates and competitors on the mating market, and on their relative importance for indicating successful reproduction. All this information is initially learned during adolescence, but is constantly updated throughout the reproductive lifespan. The proposed influences of preferences, self-assessments, and sex on mate choice and mating tactic decisions are summarized in Table 21.1.

A direct implication of the heuristics approach is that a high degree of Mating Intelligence can be achieved by fairly simple cognitive operations. The necessary competences are basically present in everyone, since they are part of our universal human nature. However, what can seriously distort the adaptiveness of mating heuristics is invalid environmental input. When high social requirements for spatial mobility lead to instable peer groups and thereby hinder social comparison processes, when adolescents develop their attractiveness standards via exposure to artificial hyperstimuli in the media, when American school programs bias sociometers by trying to maximize the self-esteem of every student, or when unrealistic models of the competitive mating market are internalized as a result of hyper-egalitarian ideologies of human uniformity, we can expect systematic failures of Mating Intelligence.

Although the role of self-assessments for human mating decisions has been proposed repeatedly by various authors and supportive correlations have sometimes been demonstrated, detailed descriptions of *how* such cognitive representations might come about and influence mating decisions are almost absent from the literature. The simple heuristics we outlined in this chapter fill much of this gap. Although they can be further improved in some details and require rigorous empirical testing in the future, they are concrete and realistic specifications of the psychological adaptations that guide human mating and thus constitute important components of Mating Intelligence.

TABLE 2.1.

Summary of Mating Decisions and the Role Played by Preferences and Self-Assessments Therein

Mating tactic decision

Sex	
♂	Preferably short-term; mainly based on the adaptive contingency of general self-esteem on the mate value sociometer
♀	Preferably long-term; mainly based on ecological cues (pathogen prevalence, environmental harshness); strategic pluralism possible

Mate choice decision

Mating tactic	Sex	Condition preference	Resource preference	Attachment preference	Variety preference	Role of self-assessments in decision making
Long-term	♂	+	–	+	–	Adjust condition preference according to mate value sociometer (which tracks a combination of own condition and resources relative to male competitors)
	♀	+	+	++	$(+)^1$	Adjust combination of condition preference and resource preference according to mate value sociometer (which tracks condition relative to female competitors)
Short-term	♂	$(+)^2$	–	–	++	None known
	♀	++	$(++)^3$	–	–	None known

Notes: ++: very important, +: important, –: unimportant, [1]: strategic pluralism possible to satisfy both the condition and the resource preference, [2]: only minimal threshold necessary, [3]: possibly a substitute for the condition preference when resources can be received immediately

ACKNOWLEDGMENTS

We would like to thank the editors Glenn Geher and Geoffrey Miller for helpful comments on an earlier draft.

REFERENCES

Ambady, N., Bernieri, F. J., & Richeson, J. A. (2000). Toward a histology of social behavior: Judgmental accuracy from thin slices of the behavioral stream. In M. P. Zanna (Ed.), *Advances in Experimental Social Psychology* (Vol. 32, pp. 201–271). San Diego: Academic Press.

Arnett, J. J. (2000). Emerging adulthood: A theory of development from the late teens through the twenties. *American Psychologist, 55,* 469–480.

Arnquist, G., & Rowe, L. (2005). Sexual conflict. Princeton, NJ: University Press.

Bailey, J. M., Kim, P. Y., Hills, A., & Linsenmeier, J. A. W. (1997). Butch, femme, or straight acting? Partner preferences of gay men and lesbians. *Journal of Personality and Social Psychology, 73,* 960–973.

Barrett, H. C. (in press). Modularity and design reincarnation. In P. Carruthers, S. Laurence, & S. Stich (Eds.), *The innate mind: Culture and cognition* (pp. 119–117). Oxford: Oxford University Press.

Baumeister, R. F. (1997). Identity, self-concept, and self-esteem: The self lost and found. In R. Hogan & J. Johnson (Eds.), *Handbook of personality psychology* (pp. 681–710). San Diego, CA: Academic Press.

Baumeister, R. F. (2000). Gender differences in erotic plasticity: The female sex drive as socially flexible and responsive. *Psychological Bulletin, 126,* 347–374.

Baumeister, R. F., & Vohs, K. D. (2004). Sexual economics: Sex as female resource for social exchange in heterosexual interactions. *Personality and Social Psychology Review, 8,* 339–363.

Borkenau, P., Mauer, N., Riemann, R., Spinath, F. M., & Angleitner, A. (2004). Thin slices of behavior as cues of personality and intelligence. *Journal of Personality and Social Psychology, 86,* 599–614.

Brown, J. D., Novick, N. J., Lord, K. A., & Richards, J. M. (1992). When Gulliver travels: Social context, psychological closeness, and self-appraisals. *Journal of Personality and Social Psychology, 62,* 717–727.

Brunswik, E. (1956). Perception and the representative design of experiments. Berkeley: University of California Press.

Burnham, T. C., Chapman, J. F., Gray, P. B., McIntyre, M. H., Lipson, S. F., & Ellison, P. T. (2003). Men in committed, romantic relationships have lower testosterone. *Hormones and Behavior, 44,* 119–122.

Buss, D. M. (1984). Marital assortment for personality dimensions: Assessment with three different data sources. *Behavior Genetics, 14,* 111–123.

Buss, D. M. (1989). Sex differences in human mate preferences: Evolutionary hypotheses tested in 37 cultures. *Behavioral and Brain Sciences, 12,* 1–49.

Buss, D. M. (1995). Evolutionary psychology: A new paradigm for psychological science. *Psychological Inquiry, 6,* 1–30.

Buss, D. M., Abbott, M., Angleitner, A., Asherian, A., Biaggio, A., Blanco-Villasensor, A., et al. (1990). International preferences in selecting mates: A study of 37 cultures. *Journal of Cross-Cultural Psychology, 21,* 5–47.

Buss, D. M., & Schmitt, D. P. (1993). Sexual Strategies Theory: An evolutionary perspective on human mating. *Psychological Review, 100,* 204–232.

Buss, D. M., & Shackelford, T. K. (1997). From vigilance to violence: Mate retention tactics in married couples. *Journal of Personality and Social Psychology, 72,* 346–361.

Buston, P. M., & Emlen, S. T. (2003). Cognitive processes underlying human mate choice: The relationship between self-perception and mate preference in Western society. *Proceedings of the National Academy of Science USA, 10,* 8805–8810.

Cash, T. F., Cash, D. W., & Butters, J. W. (1983). "Mirror, mirror, on the wall . . . ?": Contrast effects and self-evaluations of physical attractiveness. *Personality and Social Psychology Bulletin, 9,* 351–358.

Choo, E., & Siow, A. (2006). Who marries whom and why? *Journal of Political Economy, 114,* 175–201.

Clark, R. D., & Hatfield, E. (1989). Gender differences in receptivity to sexual offers. *Journal of Psychology and Human Sexuality, 2,* 39–55.

Coale, A. J. (1971). Age Patterns of Marriage. *Population Studies, 25,* 193–214.

Cooley, C. H. (1902). *Human nature and the social order.* New York: Scribner.

Cooper, M. L., & Sheldon, M. S. (2002). Seventy years of research on personality and close relationships: Substantive and methodological trends over time. *Journal of Personality, 70,* 783–812.

Cummins, D. D., & Cummins, R. (1999). Biological preparedness and evolutionary explanation. *Cognition, 73,* B37–B53.

Cunningham, M. R., Roberts, A. R., Wu, C.-H., Barbee, A. P., & Druen, P. B. (1995). Their ideas of beauty are, on the whole, the same as ours: Consistency and variability in the cross-cultural perception of female attractiveness. *Journal of Personality and Social Psychology, 68,* 261–279.

Dabbs, J. M., Jr., & Mallinger, A. (1999). High testosterone levels predict low voice pitch among men. *Personality and Individual Differences, 27,* 801–804.

Darwin, C. (1871). *The descent of man and selection in relation to sex.* London: Murray.

Dawkins, R. (1982). *The extended phenotype.* San Francisco: W. H. Freeman.

Denissen, J. J. A., & Penke, L. (2006). *Sociometer sensitivity: Reactions to cues of social exclusion as the fundamental feature of neuroticism.* Manuscript under review.

Diamond, L. M. (2003). What does sexual orientation orient? A biobehavioral model distinguishing romantic love and sexual desire. *Psychological Review, 110,* 173–192.

Diamond, L. M. (2004). Emerging perspectives on distinctions between romantic love and sexual desire. *Current Directions in Psychological Science, 13,* 116–119.

Eagly, A. H., & Wood, W. (1999). The origins of sex differences in human behavior: Evolved dispositions versus social roles. *American Psychologist, 54,* 408–423.

Ellison, P. T. (2001). *On fertile ground: A natural history of human reproduction.* Cambridge: Harvard University Press.

Feinberg, D. R., Jones, B. C., DeBruine, L. M., Moore, F. R., Smith, M. J., Cornwell, R., et al. (2005). The voice and face of woman: One ornament that signals quality? *Evolution and Human Behavior, 26,* 398–408.

Feingold, A. (1992). Gender differences in mate selection preferences: A test of the parental investment model. *Psychological Bulletin, 112,* 125–139.

Ferguson, T. S. (1989). Who solved the secretary problem? *Statistical Science, 4*, 282–296.

Fessler, D. M. T., Nettle, D., Afshar, Y., de Andrade Pinheiro, I., Bolyanatz, A., Borgerhoff Mulder, M., Cravalho, M., Delgado, T., Gruzd, B., Oliveira Correia, M., Khaltourina, D., Korotayev, A., Marrow, J., Santiago de Souza, L., & Zbarauskaite, A. (2005). A cross-cultural investigation of the role of foot size in physical attractiveness. *Archives of Sexual Behavior, 34*, 267–276.

Festinger, L. (1954). A theory of social comparison processes. *Human Relations, 7*, 117–140.

Festinger, L. (1957). *A theory of cognitive dissonance.* Stanford, CA: University Press.

Fisher, H. E., Aron, A., Mashek, D., Li, H., & Brown, L. L. (2002). Defining the brain systems of lust, romantic attraction, and attachment. *Archives of Sexual Behavior, 31*, 413–419.

Fletcher, G. J. O., Simpson, J. A., & Thomas, G. (2000). Ideals, perceptions, and evaluations in early relationship development. *Journal of Personality and Social Psychology, 79*, 933–940.

Fletcher, G. J. O., Tither, J. M., O'Loughlin, C., Friesen, M., & Overall, N. (2004). Warm and homely or cold and beautiful? Sex differences in trading off traits in mate selection. *Personality and Social Psychology Bulletin, 30*, 659–672.

Fraley, R., Brumbaugh, C. C., & Marks, M. J. (2005). The evolution and function of adult attachment: A comparative and phylogenetic analysis. *Journal of Personality and Social Psychology, 89*, 731–746.

Fraley, R., & Shaver, P. R. (2000). Adult romantic attachment: Theoretical developments, emerging controversies, and unanswered questions. *Review of General Psychology, 4*, 132–154.

Furman, W. (2002). The emerging field of adolescent romantic relationships. *Current Directions in Psychological Science, 11*, 177–180.

Gangestad, S. W., & Buss, D. M. (1993). Pathogen prevalence and human mate preferences. *Ethology and Sociobiology, 14*, 89–96.

Gangestad, S. W., Haselton, M. G., & Buss, D. M. (2006). Evolutionary foundations of cultural variation: Evoked culture and mate preferences. *Psychological Inquiry, 17*, 95–75.

Gangestad, S. W., & Simpson, J. A. (2000). The evolution of human mating: Trade-offs and strategic pluralism. *Behavioral and Brain Sciences, 23*, 573–644.

Gangestad, S. W., Simpson, J. A., Cousins, A. J., Garver-Apgar, C. E., & Christensen, P. (2004). Women's preferences for male behavioral displays change across the menstrual cycle. *Psychological Science, 15*, 203–206.

Gangestad, S. W., & Thornhill, R. (1998). Menstrual cycle variation in women's preferences for the scent of symmetrical men. *Proceedings of the Royal Society of London, Series B, 265*, 927–933.

Gangestad, S. W., & Thornhill, R. (2003). Fluctuating asymmetry, developmental instability, and fitness: Toward model-based interpretation. In M. Polak (Ed.), *Developmental instability: Causes and consequences* (pp. 62–80). Oxford: University Press.

Gangestad, S. W., Thornhill, R., & Garver-Apgar, C. E. (2005a). Adaptations to Ovulation. In D. M. Buss (Ed.), *The handbook of evolutionary psychology* (pp. 344–371). Hoboken, NJ: Wiley.

Gangestad, S. W., Thornhill, R., & Garver-Apgar, C. E. (2005b). Adaptations to ovulation: Implications for sexual and social behavior. *Current Directions in Psychological Science, 14*, 312–316.

Geary, D. C., Vigil, J., & Byrd-Craven, J. (2004). Evolution of human mate choice. *Journal of Sex Research, 41*, 27–42.

Gigerenzer, G., Todd, P. M., & the ABC Research Group (Eds.) (1999). *Simple heuristics that make us smart.* New York: Oxford University Press.

Gilbert, P., Price, J., & Allan, S. (1995). Social comparison, social attractiveness and evolution: How might they be related? *New Ideas in Psychology, 13*, 149–165.

Grammer, K., Fink, B., Juette, A., Ronzal, G., & Thornhill, R. (2002). Female faces and bodies: N-dimensional feature space and attractiveness. In G. Rhodes, & L. A. Zebrowitz (Eds.), *Facial attractiveness: Evolutionary, cognitive, and social perspectives* (pp. 91–125). Westport, CT: Ablex Publishing.

Grammer, K., Fink, B., Møller, A. P., & Manning, J. T. (2005). Physical attractiveness and health: Comment on Weeden and Sabini (2005). *Psychological Bulletin, 131*, 658–661.

Grammer, K., Fink, B., Møller, A. P., & Thornhill, R. (2003) Darwinian aesthetics: Sexual selection and the biology of beauty. *Biological Reviews, 78*, 385–407.

Gray, P. B., Campbell, B. C., Marlowe, F. W., Lipson, S. F., & Ellison, P. T. (2004a). Social variables predict between-subject but not day-to-day variation in the testosterone of U.S. men. *Psychoneuroendocrinology, 29*, 1153–1162.

Gray, P. B., Chapman, J. F., Burnham, T. C., McIntyre, M. H., Lipson, S. F., & Ellison, P. T. (2004b). Human male pair bonding and testosterone. *Human Nature, 15*, 119–131.

Gray, P. B., Kahlenberg, S. M., Barrett, E. S., Lipson, S. F., & Ellison, P. T. (2002). Marriage and fatherhood are associated with lower testosterone in males. *Evolution and Human Behavior, 23*, 193–201.

Greer, A. E., & Buss, D. M. (1994). Tactics for promoting sexual encounters. *Journal of Sex Research, 31*, 185–202.

Gross, M. R. (1996). Alternative reproductive strategies and tactics: Diversity within sexes. *Trends in Ecology and Evolution, 11*, 92–98.

Gutierres, S. E., Kenrick, D. T., & Partch, J. J. (1999). Beauty, dominance, and the mating game: Contrast effects in self-assessment reflect gender differences in mate selection. *Personality and Social Psychology Bulletin, 25*, 1126–1134.

Hagen, E. H. (2005). Controversial issues in evolutionary psychology. In D. M. Buss (Ed): *The handbook of evolutionary psychology* (pp. 145–173). Hoboken, NJ: John Wiley.

Halliday, T. R. (1983). The study of mate choice. In P. Bateson (Ed.), *Mate choice* (pp. 3–32). Cambridge: University Press.

Hammerstein, P., & Hagen, E. H. (2005). The second wave of evolutionary economics in biology. *Trends in Ecology and Evolution, 20*, 604–609.

Hamon, R. R., & Ingoldsby, B. B. (Eds.). (2003). *Mate selection across cultures.* Thousand Oaks, CA: Sage.

Hazan, C., & Diamond, L. M. (2000). The place of attachment in human mating. *Review of General Psychology, 4*, 186–204.

Helson, H. (1964). *Adaptation-level theory.* New York: Harper & Row.

Hill, S. E., & Reeve, H. (2004). Mating games: the evolution of human mating transactions. *Behavioral Ecology, 15*, 748–756.

Hunt, J., Bussiere, L. F., Jennions, M. D., & Brooks, R. (2004). What is genetic quality? *Trends in Ecology and Evolution, 19,* 329–333.

Hyde, J. S. (2005). The gender similarities hypothesis. *American Psychologist, 60,* 581–592.

Jasienska, G., Ziomkiewicz, A., Ellison, P. T., Lipson, S. F., & Thune, I. (2004). Large breasts and narrow waists indicate high reproductive potential in women. *Proceedings of the Royal Society of London, Series B, 271,* 1213–1217.

Jennions, M. D., & Petrie, M. (1997). Variation in mate choice and mating preferences: A review of causes and consequences. *Biological Reviews, 72,* 283–327.

Jennions, M. D., & Petrie, M. (2000). Why do females mate multiply? A review of the genetic benefits. *Biological Reviews, 75,* 21–64.

Jones, B., Little, A., Penton-Voak, I., Tiddeman, B., Burt, D., & Perrett, D. (2001). Facial symmetry and judgements of apparent health: Support for a "good genes" explanation of the attractiveness-symmetry relationship. *Evolution and Human Behavior, 22,* 417–429.

Jones, B. C., Little, A. C., Feinberg, D. R., Penton-Voak, I. S., Tiddeman, B. P., & Perrett, D. I. (2004). The relationship between shape symmetry and perceived skin condition in male facial attractiveness. *Evolution and Human Behavior, 25,* 24–30.

Kalmijn, M. (1998). Intermarriage and homogamy: Causes, patterns, trends. *Annual Review of Sociology, 24,* 395–421.

Kasperk, C., Helmboldt, A., Borcsok, I., Heuthe, S., Cloos, O., Niethard, F., & Ziegler, R. (1997). Skeletal sitedependent expression of the androgen receptor in human osteoblastic cell populations. *Calcified Tissue, 61,* 464–473.

Keller, M. C., & Miller, G. F. (2006). Resolving the paradox of common, harmful, heritable mental disorders: Which evolutionary genetic models work best? *Behavioral and Brain Sciences, 29,* 385–404.

Kelley, H. H., & Thibaut, J. W. (1978). *Interpersonal relations: A theory of interdependence.* New York: Wiley.

Kenrick, D. T., Groth, G. E., Trost, M. R., & Sadalla, E. K. (1993). Integrating evolutionary and social exchange perspectives on relationships: Effects of gender, self-appraisal, and involvement level on mate selection criteria. *Journal of Personality and Social Psychology, 64,* 951–969.

Kenrick, D. T., & Gutierres, S. E. (1980). Contrast effects and judgments of physical attractiveness: When beauty becomes a social problem. *Journal of Personality and Social Psychology, 38,* 131–140.

Kenrick, D. T., Gutierres, S. E., & Goldberg, L. L. (1989). Influence of popular erotica on judgments of strangers and mates. *Journal of Experimental Social Psychology, 25,* 159–167.

Kenrick, D. T., & Keefe, R. C. (1992). Age preferences in mates reflect sex differences in human reproductive strategies. *Behavioral and Brain Sciences, 15,* 75–133.

Kenrick, D. T., Neuberg, S. L., Zierk, K. L., & Krones, J. M. (1994). Evolution and social cognition: Contrast effects as a function of sex, dominance, and physical attractiveness. *Personality and Social Psychology Bulletin, 20,* 210–217.

Kenrick, D. T., Sadalla, E. K., Groth, G., & Trost, M. R. (1990). Evolution, traits, and the stages of human courtship: Qualifying the parental investment model. *Journal of Personality, 58,* 97–116.

Kirkpatrick, L. A., & Ellis, B. J. (2001). An evolutionary-psychological approach to self-esteem: Multiple domains and multiple functions. In G. Fletcher, & Clark, M. (Eds.), *The Blackwell handbook of social psychology, Vol. 2* (pp. 411–436). Oxford: Blackwell.

Kirkpatrick, L. A., & Ellis, B. J. (2006). What is the evolutionary significance of self-esteem? The Adaptive Functions of Self-Evaluative Psychological Mechanisms. In M. H. Kernis (Ed.), *Self-esteem: Issues and answers* (pp. 334–339). New York: Psychology Press.

Kokko, H., Brooks, R., Jennions, M. D., & Morley, J. (2003). The evolution of mate choice and mating biases. *Proceedings of the Royal Society of London, Series B, 270*, 653–664.

Kokko, H., & Jennions, M. (2003). It takes two to tango. *Trends in Ecology and Evolution, 18*, 103–104.

Kurzban, R., & Weeden, J. (2005). HurryDate: Mate preferences in action. *Evolution & Human Behavior, 26*, 227–244.

Landolt, M. A., Lalumiere, M. L., & Quinsey, V. L. (1995). Sex differences in intra-sex variations in human mating tactics: An evolutionary approach. *Ethology and Sociobiology, 16*, 3–23.

Langlois, J. H., Kalakanis, L., Rubenstein, A. J., Larson, A., Hallam, M., & Smoot, M. (2000). Maxims or myths of beauty? A meta-analytic and theoretical review. *Psychological Bulletin, 126*, 390–423.

Leary, M. R., & Baumeister, R. F. (2000). The nature and function of self-esteem: Sociometer theory. In M. P. Zanna (Ed.), *Advances in experimental social psychology* (Vol. 32, pp. 1–62). San Diego: Academic Press.

Leary, M. R., Tambor, E. S., Terdal, S. K., & Downs, D. L. (1995). Self-esteem as an interpersonal monitor: The sociometer hypothesis. *Journal of Personality and Social Psychology, 68*, 518–530.

Leitenberg, H., & Henning, K. (1995). Sexual fantasy. *Psychological Bulletin, 117*, 469–496.

Li, N. P., Bailey, J., Kenrick, D. T., & Linsenmeier, J. A. (2002). The necessities and luxuries of mate preferences: Testing the tradeoffs. *Journal of Personality and Social Psychology, 82*, 947–955.

Li, N. P., & Kenrick, D. T. (2006). Sex similarities and differences in preferences for short-term mates: What, whether, and why. *Journal of Personality and Social Psychology, 90*, 468–489.

Little, A. C., Jones, B. C., Penton-Voak, I. S., Burt, D. M., & Perrett, D. I. (2002). Partnership status and the temporal context of relationships influence human female preferences for sexual dimorphism in male face shape. *Proceedings of the Royal Society of London, Series B, 269*, 1095–1100.

Locke, J. L., & Bogin, B. (2006). Language and life history: A new perspective on the development and evolution of human language. *Behavioral and Brain Sciences, 29*, 259–280.

Low, B. S. (1990). Marriage systems and pathogen stress in human societies. *American Zoologist, 30*, 325–40.

Lykken, D. T., & Tellegen, A. (1993). Is human mating adventitious or the result of lawful choice? A twin study of mate selection. *Journal of Personality and Social Psychology, 65*, 56–68.

Manning, J. T., Scutt, D., Wilson, J., & Lewisjones, D. I. (1998). The ratio of 2nd to 4th digit length—a predictor of sperm numbers and concentrations of testosterone, luteinizing hormone and oestrogen. *Human Reproduction, 13*, 3000–3004.

Marlowe, F. W. (2004). Mate preferences among Hadza hunter-gatherers. *Human Nature, 15*, 365–376.

Marlowe, F. W., Apicella, C., & Reed, D. (2005). Men's preferences for women's profile waist-to-hip ratio in two societies. *Evolution and Human Behavior, 26*, 458–468.

Mascie-Taylor, C. G. (1989). Spouse similarity for IQ and personality and convergence. *Behavior Genetics, 19*, 223–227.

Mascie-Taylor, C. G. N., & Vandenberg, S. G. (1988). Assortative mating for IQ and personality due to propinquity and personal preference. *Behavior Genetics, 18*, 339–345.

Mata, R., Wilke, A., & Todd, P. M. (2005). Adding the missing link back into mate choice research. *Behavioral and Brain Sciences, 28*, 289.

Maynard Smith, J. (1987). Sexual selection: A classification of models. In J. Bradbury & M. B. Andersson (Eds.), *Sexual selection: Testing the alternatives* (pp. 96–118). Chichester: John Wiley.

Mead, G. H. (1934). *Mind, self, and society.* Chicago: University of Chicago Press.

Melamed, L., & Moss, M. K. (1975). The effect of context on ratings of attractiveness of photographs. *Journal of Psychology, 90*, 129–136.

Miller, G. F. (1997). Mate choice: From sexual cues to cognitive adaptations. In G. R. Bock & G. Cardew (Eds.), *Characterizing human psychological adaptations* (pp. 71–87). New York: Wiley.

Miller, G. F. (2000a). *The mating mind: How sexual choice shaped the evolution of human nature.* New York: Doubleday.

Miller, G. F. (2000b). Sexual selection for indicators of intelligence. In G. Bock, J. Goode, & K. Webb (Eds.), *The nature of intelligence* (pp. 260–275). New York: Wiley.

Miller, G. F., & Todd, P. M. (1998). Mate choice turns cognitive. *Trends in Cognitive Sciences, 2*, 190–198.

Miller, L. C. & Fishkin, S. A. (1997) On the dynamics of human bonding and reproductive success: Seeking windows on the adapted-for human environment interface. In J. A. Simpson & D. T. Kenrick (Eds.), *Evolutionary social psychology* (pp. 197–235). Mahwah, NJ: Lawrence Erlbaum Associates.

Mussweiler, T. (2003). Comparison processes in social judgment: Mechanisms and consequences. *Psychological Review, 110*, 472–489.

Nagoshi, C. T., Johnson, R. C., & Ahern, F. M. (1987). Phenotypic assortative mating vs. social homogamy among Japanese and Chinese parents in the Hawaii Family Study of Cognition. *Behavior Genetics, 17*, 477–485.

Nelson, L. D., & Morrison, E. L. (2005). The symptoms of resource scarcity: Judgments of food and finances influence preferences for potential partners. *Psychological Science, 16*, 167–173.

Noë, R., & Hammerstein, P. (1995). Biological markets. *Trends in Ecology and Evolution, 10*, 336–339.

Pawlowski, B. (1999). Loss of oestrus and concealed ovulation in human evolution: The case against the sexual-selection hypothesis. *Current Anthropology, 40*, 257–275.

Pawlowski, B., & Dunbar, R. I. M. (1999). Impact of market value on human mate choice decisions. *Proceedings of the Royal Society in London, Series B, 266,* 281–285.

Penke, L., & Denissen, J. J. A. (2006). *Adaptive sociometer contingencies and the allocation of reproductive effort in men.* Manuscript submitted for publication.

Penton-Voak, I. S., Jacobson, A., & Trivers, R. (2004). Populational differences in attractiveness judgments of male and female faces: Comparing British and Jamaican samples. *Evolution and Human Behavior, 25,* 355–370.

Phillips, K., Fulker, D. W., Carey, G., Nagoshi, C. T. (1988). Direct marital assortment for cognitive and personality variables. *Behavior Genetics, 18,* 347–356.

Plomin, R., DeFries, J. C., & Roberts, M. K. (1977). Assortative mating by unwed biological parents of adopted children. *Science, 196,* 449–450.

Pomiankowski, A. (1988). The evolution of female mate preferences for male genetic quality. *Oxford Survey of Evolutionary Biology, 5,* 136–184.

Puts, D. A. (2006). Cyclic variation in women's preferences for masculine traits: potential hormonal causes. *Human Nature, 17,* 114–127.

Regan, P. C. (1998a). What if you can't get what you want? Willingness to compromise ideal mate selection standards as a function of sex, mate value, and relationship context. *Personality and Social Psychology Bulletin, 24,* 1294–1303.

Regan, P. C. (1998b). Minimum mate selection standards as a function of perceived mate value, relationship context, and gender. *Journal of Psychology and Human Sexuality, 10,* 53–73.

Regan, P. C. (1999). Hormonal correlates and causes of sexual desire: A review. *Canadian Journal of Human Sexuality, 8,* 1–16.

Reynolds, C. A., Baker, L. A., & Pedersen, N. L. (2000). Multivariate models of mixed assortment: Phenotypic assortment and social homogamy for education and fluid ability. *Behavior Genetics, 30,* 455–476.

Rikowski, A., & Grammer, K. (1999). Human body odour, symmetry and attractiveness. *Proceedings of the Royal Society of London, Series B, 266,* 869–874.

Rhodes, G. (2006). The evolutionary psychology of facial beauty. *Annual Review of Psychology, 57,* 199–226.

Roberts, S., Little, A. C., Gosling, L., Perrett, D. I., Carter, V., Jones, B. C., et al. (2005). MHC-heterozygosity and human facial attractiveness. *Evolution and Human Behavior, 26,* 213–226.

Roney, J. R. (2005). *An alternative explanation for menstrual phase effects on women's psychology and behavior.* Paper presented at the annual meeting of the Human Behavior and Evolution Society, Austin, TX.

Rowe, L., & Houle, D. (1996). The lek paradox and the capture of genetic variance by condition dependent traits. *Proceedings of the Royal Society of London, Series B, 263,* 1415–1421.

Schmidt, F. L., & Hunter, J. (2004). General mental ability in the world of work: Occupational attainment and job performance. *Journal of Personality and Social Psychology, 86,* 162–173.

Schmitt, D. P. (2005a). Is short-term mating the result of insecure attachment? A test of competing evolutionary perspectives. *Personality and Social Psychology Bulletin, 31,* 747–768.

Schmitt, D. P. (2005b). Sociosexuality from Argentina to Zimbabwe: A 48-nation study of sex, culture, and strategies of human mating. *Behavioral and Brain Sciences, 28,* 247–275.

Schmitt, D. P., Alcalay, L., Allik, J., Ault, L., Austers, I., Bennett, K. L., et al. (2003). Universal sex differences in the desire for sexual variety: Tests from 52 nations, 6 continents, and 13 islands. *Journal of Personality and Social Psychology, 85,* 85–104.

Schmitt, D. P., Shackelford, T. K., & Buss, D. M. (2001). Are men really more 'oriented' toward short-term mating than women? A critical review of theory and research. *Psychology, Evolution and Gender, 3,* 211–239.

Shackelford, T. K., Schmitt, D. P., & Buss, D. M. (2005). Universal dimensions of human mate preferences. *Personality and Individual Differences, 39,* 447–458.

Shaner, A., Miller, G., & Mintz, J. (2004). Schizophrenia as one extreme of a sexually selected fitness indicator. *Schizophrenia Research, 70,* 101–109.

Simon, H. A. (1990). Invariants of human behavior. *Annual Review of Psychology, 41,* 1–19.

Simpson, J., & Oriña, M. (2003). Strategic pluralism and context-specific mate preferences in humans. In K. Sterelny & J. Fitness (Eds.), *From mating to mentality: Evaluating evolutionary psychology* (pp. 39–70). New York: Psychology Press.

Singh, D. (1993). Adaptive significance of female physical attractiveness: Role of waist-to-hip ratio. *Journal of Personality and Social Psychology, 65,* 293–307.

Srivastava, S., & Beer, J. S. (2005). How self-evaluations relate to being liked by others: Integrating sociometer and attachment perspectives. *Journal of Personality and Social Psychology, 89,* 966–977.

Swami, V., & Tovée, M. J. (2005). Male physical attractiveness in Britain and Malaysia: A cross-cultural study. *Body Image, 2,* 383–393.

Tambs, K., Sundet, J. M., & Berg, K. (1993). Correlations between identical twins and their spouses suggest social homogamy for intelligence in Norway. *Personality and Individual Differences, 14,* 279–281.

Thibaut, J. W., & Kelley, H. H. (1959). *The social psychology of groups.* New York: Wiley.

Thornhill, R., & Gangestad, S. W. (1999a). Facial attractiveness. *Trends in Cognitive Sciences, 3,* 452–460.

Thornhill, R., & Gangestad, S. W. (1999b). The scent of symmetry: A human sex pheromone that signals fitness? *Evolution and Human Behavior, 20,* 175–201.

Thornhill, R., & Gangestad, S. W. (2003). Do women have evolved adaptation for extra-pair copulation? In E. Voland, & Grammer, K. (Eds.), *Evolutionary aesthetics* (pp. 341–368). Berlin: Springer.

Thornhill, R., Gangestad, S. W., Miller, R., Scheyd, G., McCollough, J. K., & Franklin, M. (2003). Major histocompatibility complex genes, symmetry, and body scent attractiveness in men and women. *Behavioral Ecology, 14,* 668–678.

Thornhill, R., & Grammer, K. (1999). The body and face of woman: One ornament that signals quality? *Evolution and Human Behavior, 20,* 105–120.

Todd, P. M., & Billari, F. C. (2003). Population-wide marriage patterns produced by individual mate-search heuristics. In F. C. Billari & A. Prskawetz (Eds.), *Agent-based computational demography* (pp. 117–137). Berlin: Springer.

Todd, P. M., Billari, F. C., and Simão, J. (2005). Aggregate age-at-marriage patterns from individual mate-search heuristics. *Demography, 42,* 559–574.

Todd, P. M., Fasolo, B., & Lenton, A. P. (2004). *Testing patterns of mate preferences via actual choices.* Paper presented at the annual meeting of the Human Behavior and Evolution Society, Berlin, Germany.

Todd, P. M., & Miller, G. F. (1999). From pride and prejudice to persuasion: Satisficing in mate search. In G. Gigerenzer, P. M. Todd, and the ABC Research Group (Eds.), *Simple heuristics that make us smart* (pp. 287–308). New York: Oxford University Press.

Todd, P. M., Penke, L., Fasolo, B., & Lenton, A. P. (2006). *Cognitive processes underlying human mate choice reconsidered: Real choices differ from reported preferences.* Manuscript in preparation.

Tooby, J., Cosmides, L., & Barrett, H. C. (2005). Resolving the debate on innate ideas: Learnability constraints and the evolved interpenetration of motivational and conceptual functions. In P. Carruthers, S. Laurence and S. Stich (Eds.), *The innate mind: Structure and content* (pp. 305–337). Oxford: University Press.

Townsend, J. M. (1995). Sex without emotional involvement: An evolutionary interpretation of sex differences. *Archives of Sexual Behavior, 24,* 173–206.

Townsend, J. M., Kline, J., & Wasserman, T. H. (1995). Low-investment copulation: Sex differences in motivations and emotional reactions. *Ethology and Sociobiology, 16,* 25–51.

Trivers, R. L. (1972). Parental investment and sexual selection. In B. Campbell (Ed.), *Sexual selection and the descent of man* (pp. 136–179). Chicago, IL: Aldine-Atherton.

Vandenberg, S. G. (1972). Assortative mating, or who marries whom? *Behavior Genetics, 2,* 127–157.

Watkins, M. P., & Meredith, W. (1981). Spouse similarity in newlyweds with respect to specific cognitive abilities, socioeconomic status, and education. *Behavior Genetics, 11,* 1–21.

Watson, D., Klohnen, E. C., Casillas, A., Nus Simms, E., Haig, J., & Berry, D. S. (2004). Match makers and deal breakers: Analyses of assortative mating in newlywed couples. *Journal of Personality, 72,* 1029–1068.

Waynforth, D. (2001). Mate choice trade-offs and women's preference for physically attractive men. *Human Nature, 12,* 207–219.

Weaver, J. B., Masland, J. L., & Zillman, D. (1984). Effect of erotica on young men's aesthetic perception of their female sexual partners. *Perceptual and Motor Skills, 58,* 929–930.

Weeden, J., & Sabini, J. (2005). Physical attractiveness and health in Western societies: A review. *Psychological Bulletin, 131,* 635–653.

Wilson, T. D. (2002). *Strangers to ourselves: Discovering the adaptive unconscious.* Cambridge: Harvard University Press.

Wong, L. Y. (2003). Structural estimation of marriage models, *Journal of Labor Economics, 21,* 699–727.

Zahavi, A. (1975). Mate selection: A selection for a handicap. *Journal of Theoretical Biology, 53,* 205–214.

Zahavi, A., & Zahavi, A. (1997). *The handicap principle: A missing piece of Darwin's puzzle.* Oxford: Oxford University Press.

Zebrowitz, L. A., & Rhodes, G. (2004). Sensitivity to "bad genes" and the anomalous face overgeneralization effect: Cue validity, cue utilization, and accuracy in judging intelligence and health. *Journal of Nonverbal Behavior, 28,* 167–185.

Chapter 3

Mating Intelligence
in Personal Ads

Charlotte De Backer
University of Leicester

Johan Braeckman
Ghent University

Lili Farinpour
University of California, Santa Barbara

The ways we feel and act today during courtship have been shaped by sexual selection throughout human evolutionary history. Sexual selection shaped our desires and led to sex differences in what men and women find attractive in a potential mate (Buss, 2003). In their search for mates, women desire multiple traits in men (such as intelligence, ambition, and athleticism), and, similarly, men desire various traits in women (such as physical attractiveness and kindness). Therefore, popular aphorisms such as "Women want rich men" do not explain the entire picture (Graziano, Brothen, & Berscheid, 1997). In short, the qualities desired in potential mates are multi-faceted and complex—and also sexually differentiated. (see Buss, 2003). Importantly, sexual dimorphisms in mate preferences may not translate directly into different mating patterns between men and women, due to the constraints of mutual mate choice and a competitive mating market. Desires may often go unfulfilled, which is why sexual fantasy exists. For example, a young man might desire many new sex partners per day, but this desire cannot always be realized (Symons, 1979).

Personal advertisements are easily accessible and brief portraits of expressed desires in the mating market. Because individual advertisers must typically pay by the word for their ads, there is a significant financial incentive to be succinct. Thus, authors of such ads need to carefully consider what to put in and what to leave out. Because of this space limitation, it is reasonable to infer that individual advertisers mention only their most desired traits. Accordingly, the traits they request in personal ads can be seen as an ecologically valid answer to the question: "Please list the most important features you desire in a potential partner."

For many of the same reasons, personal ads provide important information when it comes to self-description in the mating market. As is the case for the *desired* traits, only an individual's most subjectively important assets can be described. Given their utility in providing information about both people's most-desired traits and the own traits that they think will be most appealing to potential mates, personal ads have great potential to shed light on issues of accuracy in mating intelligence. How good are members of each sex at knowing the preferences of the opposite sex? Thus, personal ads can supply rich, meaningful information to mating researchers (Greenless & McGrew, 1994).

Previous research on personal ads has mainly focused on sex differences in partner preferences. Such research has consistently confirmed males' interest in youth and physical attractiveness, and females' interest wealth, education, and other factors tied to resource-acquisition (e.g., Butler-Smith, Cameron, & Collins, 1998; Child, Low, McCormick, & Cocciarella, 1996; Davis, 1990; Deaux & Hanna, 1984; Feingold, 1992; Greenlees & McGrew, 1994; Hayes, 1995; Hirschman, 1987; Kenrick & Keefe, 1992; Rajecki, Bledsoe, & Rasmussen, 1991; Sprecher, Sullivan, & Hatfield, 1994; Thiessen, Young, & Burroughs, 1993; Wiederman, 1993; Willis & Carlson, 1993). Rather than presenting further evidence for these well-documented sex differences, this chapter examines how the sexes perform on estimating what the other sex desires. Do individuals understand accurately what their most desired traits are, and do they advertise these in their advertisements? Does each sex equally understand what the other sex wants in partners, or is one sex better than the other at doing this? Such cross-sex mind-reading abilities (see Haselton & Buss, 2000) must be a central component of human mating intelligence.

ARE YOU THE ONE? HUMAN MATING STRATEGIES

Before we discuss whether the sexes differ in the ability to know the mating desires of the opposite sex, we must review the typical sex differences in mating desires. In both long and short-term mating, mate-choice is finely structured and fairly choosy in both sexes. We all have certain idiosyncratic preferences, but there are also general differences across cultures in the traits that women and men desire in potential mates (Buss, 1989;

Buss, 1994; Buss & Schmitt, 1993; Symons, 1979). Some important sex differences in mating desires, which may be useful to consider in assessing the cross-sex mind-reading abilities of each sex, include preferences concerning relationship length, age of partner, physical traits, and stable psychological qualities, which we review in turn.

'til Death Do Us Part: Sex Differences in Preferred Relationship Length

One of the best-documented sex differences is that women often want longer sexual relationships than men do. Although monogamy has been important in human evolution (Miller & Fishkin, 1997), human monogamy may be best described as *serial monogamy*. Overlaid on our medium-term monogamous relationships are short-term flings, infidelities, and other short-term matings. We agree with Buss (1994) and Schmitt (Buss & Schmitt 1993) that both men and women have evolved specific mating strategies for both long-term and short-term mating.

However, one of the central claims in Buss and Schmitt's (1993) Sexual Strategy Theory (SST) is that, typically, men have a stronger desire for short-term mating, and women have a stronger desire for long-term mating. Because of differences in gamete production and parental investment, men have more advantages in mating with multiple partners. From a biological perspective, men are more likely to benefit genetically than women from short-term sexual strategies.

This sex difference in desired relationship length is supported by many studies. For instance, when questioning men and women about their sexual behavior and desires, Schmitt, Shackelford, and Buss (2001) confirmed that men expressed a stronger desire for short-term relations than women. They also concluded that men, more than women, have a strong desire for multiple sexual partners and that men require less time before consenting to sex. Schmitt (Schmitt et al., 2003), in cooperation with researchers from 10 major world regions (including North America, South America, Western Europe, Eastern Europe, Southern Europe, Middle East, Africa, Oceania, South/Southeast Asia, and East Asia) showed that these sex differences in preferred relationship length exist cross culturally. Their findings, based on a sample of more than 16,000 young adults, strongly supported the hypothesis that men have a stronger desire for more sexual partners and short-term sexual relations than women. Men not only show a greater desire than women do for a variety of sexual partners, men also require less time to elapse than women do before consenting to sexual intercourse, and men tend to more actively seek short-term mateships than women do (Schmitt et al., 2003, p. 101). This is why, around the world, both female and male prostitutes get the vast majority of their work from male clients (straight or gay).

Older Men and Younger Women: Sex Differences in Preferred Age

Age is an important discriminator in excluding people from our most-wanted potential-partners lists. Across cultures, people tend to seek partners of their own generation (Buss, 1989; Kenrick & Keefe, 1992). Within cohorts though, men usually prefer younger female partners over older female partners, while women prefer older male partners over younger male partners (Butler-Smith et al., 1998; Greenless & McGrew, 1994; Hayes, 1995; Matthews, 1999; Rajecki et al., 1991; Rasmussen et al., 1998; Sprecher et al., 1994; Wiederman, 1993; Willis & Carlson, 1993). As we will see in later sections, these age-related preferences may reflect preferences for certain physical traits (cues of youth and fertility) and cues of provisioning ability (cues of wealth and status).

Sizes Small and Tall: Sex Differences in Preferred Physical Partner Traits

When looking for potential partners, each sex tends to focus on specific physical traits that reveal important fitness-relevant information. Facial and body symmetry, for instance make both men and women more attractive, and such symmetry apparently signals health and genetic quality. Individuals with more symmetrical features are rated as more attractive, sexy, and healthy, and, on average, have more sexual partners than individuals with less symmetrical features (Gangestad & Thornhill, 1997; Grammer & Thornhill, 2003; Shackelford & Larsen, 1999; Thornhill & Gangstead, 1994).

Although men and women share a preference for symmetry in potential mates, their desires diverge regarding other physical features. Both in short and long-term mating, men pay more attention to cues (youth, health, breasts, buttocks, non-pregnant waist) that might advertise the current fertility and future reproductive value of potential female partners. However, some of those cues are rather unreliable, so men face the problem of estimating female fertility by integrating multiple physical and behavioural cues. For example, female ovulation is rather more concealed in humans than in other great apes that develop estral swellings, yet there are many cues available to males that would indicate a woman's current reproductive status, such as expressions of increased sexual desire (Regan, 1984), fluctuations in breast size (with bigger breast size during high fertility; Hussein et al., 1999), and sexually relevant behavioral shifts, such as dressing more revealingly (Grammar, 1987) and socializing more assertively (Chavanne & Gallup, 1998).

High levels of fertility and reproductive value correlate with indices of youth and health. Examples of proximate indicators that signal female youth and health (and, ultimately, fertility) include smooth skin, shiny hair, and neotenous facial features (Buss & Schmitt, 1993). What men regard as 'attractive' or 'beautiful' in potential partners corresponds strongly to such facial and bodily features.

In looking for mates, women also focus on physical attributes, but rather different ones. Whereas men focus on fertility cues, women focus on traits that correlate with status, dominance, power, and wealth. For instance, women prefer tall men over short men (Graziano, Brothen, & Berscheid, 1978; Hensley, 1994; Gillis & Avis, 1980; Jackson & Ervin, 1992; Peirce, 1996; Shepperd & Strathman, 1989). Male height correlates with status, power, access to resources, and ability to defend females and off-spring—all qualities that would yield benefits for potential offspring. In support of this hypothesis, many studies have found that people attribute more status and power to taller men than to shorter men (Dunbar, 1995; Harper, 2000; Muir, 2000; Murray, 2000).

Money Can Buy Love: Sex Differences in Preferred Wealth Status

A great deal of research has shown that women are choosier in picking part-ners who can offer resources and parental investment (e.g., Buss, 1994; Symons, 1979). This female preference reflects the fact that females are required to invest a great deal in offspring compared with males, due to the demands of internal gestation (pregnancy) and lactation (breast-feeding). Thus, females were under strong selection to favor long-term mating strategies that could deliver reliable bi-parental care to their offspring. Consequently, women, in general, desire higher-status men who are likely to be more reliable, successful provisioners and protectors. In modern societies, this status prefer-ence translates into a preference for wealth, education, stable employment, and conscientiousness—a preference for *dads* over *cads* as mates.

Although the general tendency for females to focus on status indica-tors in mate-selection exists across cultures, particular status indicators are often culturally specific. In pastoralist societies, male status may depend on having a vast herd of thousand-pound cattle, whereas in post-indus-trial societies, male status may depend on having a teeny-weeny cell phone. In Western consumerist cultures, status is strongly related to high income, and the resulting ownership of large houses, fast cars, and other conspicuous luxuries. Thus, males with high income levels are consis-tently rated more attractive as both long and short-term mates (Townsend & Levy, 1990a, b). The fact that job status and net worth tend to increase with age may partially account for women's preference for older men.

Preferred Mental Traits in the Domain of Mate-Selection

People also desire certain psychological traits in the mating market (e.g., Miller, 2000). When looking for mates, men and women pay careful attention to potential partners' mental traits such as intelligence, kindness, and sense of humor, with certain mental traits preferred over others. For example, consider sexual fidelity, a moral/personality trait valued by both men and women. Infidelity is an adaptive problem that confronts both men and women. Although much research has focused on sex differences in responses to infidelity (e.g., Buss, 2000), both sexes suffer significant fitness costs (sexually transmitted diseases, diverted resources, possible breakup) when a partner is unfaithful. So, both sexes have come to desire reliable, faithful, honest partners, and we assess potential mates quite carefully for these qualities.

Although men and women both desire honesty and reliability, males are a little more concerned to safeguard their paternity certainty (making sure they sired the children produced by their female partner), whereas females are a little more concerned to safeguard the flow of attention, support, and resources from their partners to themselves and their children. Research strongly supports these predications. For instance, women desire indicators not just of ability to acquire wealth, but of willingness to share wealth with themselves and their offspring (Buss, 1994, 1999; Buss & Schmitt, 1993). From a male's perspective, mating with reliable, faithful women can solve the paternity uncertainty issue, so, at least for long-term sexual relationships, men desire faithfulness, sexual loyalty, and chastity in women (Buss & Schmitt, 1993).

Intelligence is another highly desired mental trait. Intelligence, together with ambition, are traits that most often predict actual financial success in the later stages of life (Feingold, 1992). In a study across 37 cultures, Buss (1989) found that intelligence was the second most desired trait in a sexual partner for both sexes, and was even more important to women than to men. Much research is consistent with this finding that females favor male intelligence more than males favor female intelligence. For instance, Taylor et al. (2005) studied 900 men and women in their 50s whose IQs had been measured at age 11. These participants completed a battery of relationship outcome indices (e.g., questions concerning marital happiness, divorce, etc.), and male intelligence proved a better prediction of marital stability, longevity, and happiness than female intelligence did.

In his book *The Mating Mind*, Miller (2000) argues that several psychological qualities (e.g., artistic ability, sense of humor, selfless altruism, etc.) were shaped by sexual selection during human evolution. From his fitness indicator perspective, such qualities were *designed* (through selection) specifically to attract mates. He argued that creative intelligence is a key fitness indicator, since it often leads to outcomes that are costly in terms of time and energy (and neuronal capacity), such as the creation of large, ornamental sculptures. Miller argues that creativity may function like a peacock's tail by displaying one's overall genetic quality (as creativity likely results from multiple parts of the brain, reflecting quality levels of multiple genes and overall mutation load of a potential mate). Creative intelligence expressed, for example, in having a good sense of humor, is costly to produce and maintain. From this fitness-indicator perspective, such intelligence may qualify as a sexually selected trait. Further, since women are the choosier sex, Miller (2000) argues that women should focus especially on indices of creative intelligence in mate choice.

Sex and Lies

To meet the desires of potential mates, we often present ourselves as better than we really are. Both men and women use impression management (Bromley, 1993)—a nice way of saying deception—to impress their dates. Recent research suggests that these deceits tend to be sex-specific (Haselton et al., 2005). Haselton and Buss (2000; also Buss, 2003) have shown that men often display dishonestly high levels of willingness to commit, whereas women do not. However, to deceptively promise the fulfilment of male short-term sexual desires, women often falsely lead men to believe that they are interested in imminent sexual intercourse. In analyzing this kind of sexual deception from an evolutionary perspective, Buss (2003) argues that women can benefit by extracting resources from men through their apparent sexual availability. Further, such deception may simply increase a woman's desirability to men.

The Beauty of Personal Ads
(In the Eye of the Mating Researcher)

So far, we have focused mostly on the physical and psychological qualities desired by men and women, and sex-specific patterns of deception in courtship. Personal advertisements offer extraordinarily rich data that address each of these aspects of human mating. Clearly, the individual authors of such ads articulate the physical and psychological qualities that they most desire in potential mates. They typically describe their own traits as well, so we can analyze their self-presentation biases and deceptions.

Mating Intelligence as Accurate Cross-Sex Mind-Reading

In addition to allowing research on mating desires and courtship displays, analysis of personal ads can reveal people's degree of accuracy in cross-sex mind-reading—a key component of mating intelligence. Specifically, heterosexual personal ads provide sex-differentiated information about (a) the stated desires of each sex and (b) the stated traits offered by each sex, which presumably are traits that they think the other sex will desire. Given such data, we can ask whether each sex is, on average, *getting it* (i.e., knowing which qualities to display given the desires of the opposite sex).

METHOD

To investigate sex differences in the (a) traits desired in partners and (b) traits advertised by individuals, we did a content analysis of 800 personal advertisements that were published in various newspapers in Belgium. Readers of these newspapers come from different social classes, and form a heterogeneous group. (CIM, 2000). Each advertisement appeared in one of 13 Saturday editions of these newspapers between November 2000 and January 2001. We limited our sample to heterosexually oriented ads. Of the 800 advertisers, the majority (504, or 63 percent) were males (mean age = 44 years); 296 (37 percent) were females (mean age = 46.7 years). We coded the traits desired and offered in each ad in 9 categories: age, attractiveness, weight, height, wealth, ambition, intelligence, humor, and reliability. Obvious synonyms were collapsed into these categories (e.g., the Flemish or Dutch equivalents of "pretty," "hot," "handsome," "beautiful," etc. were all coded as describing "attractiveness").

The advertisements were coded by two independent coders. Inter-rater reliability was above .9 for the first 100 personal ads, for all variables—well above the usual threshold for psychology research (Hüttner et al., 1995). The results from one of the two coders were arbitrarily defined as the *correct* answers (a reasonable strategy in light of the high inter-coder reliability that we obtained).

RESULTS

The results were organized to address three general questions. First, we examined women's desires in potential mates. Next, we examined men's desires. Finally, we examined the degree to which each sex, on average, advertises the traits that are actually desired by the opposite sex.

Women's Desires

To analyze women's stated desires, we examined the percentage of the female ads that expressed desires for the specific qualities listed below.

A long-term mate

A moderate percentage (42.2 percent) of the 296 female advertisers expressed a desire for a particular relationship length. Of these, 23 percent preferred a short-term relationship and 77 percent preferred a long-term relationship. Most women who revealed their preferred relationship length clearly wanted a long-term commitment (see Table 3.1.).

An older man

Nearly all female advertisers (95.9 percent) expressed a preferred age for potential partners. Of these, most (40.2 percent) desired an older partner, or a same-aged partner (32.1 percent); only 23.6 percent wanted a younger partner. Thus, the great majority of women south potential mates who were older or about the same age as themselves.

A wealthy man

The next most-often mentioned trait was wealth. Almost half (48.6 percent) of the women expressed a wish for a wealthy man. No women wished for a poor man.

A reliable man

The next most popularly desired trait was reliability, with almost a quarter (23.6 percent) of female advertisers expressing a desire for this trait.

A handsome man

Also, almost a quarter (22.3 percent) of the female advertisers expressed a desire for a good-looking man.

An intelligent man

Twenty-two percent of female advertisers expressed a desire for an intelligent man.

A tall man

17.2 percent of female advertisers mentioned something about a preferred height. None expressed a desire for a short man. About a third of these (4.7 percent of the whole sample) explicitly preferred a taller man, and the remainder mentioned an exact preferred height, or a range of preferred heights.

A man with a good sense of humor

8.2 percent of women mentioned that humor was an important quality in a potential mate.

Weight and ambition

Two traits that were rarely mentioned were the physical trait 'weight,' and the psychological trait 'ambition.' Only 3.4 percent of the female advertisers mentioned something about preferred weight (usually for a slim man). Virtually no women (0.3 percent, or 1 out of 296) expressed a desire for ambition.

An overview of these results can be found in Figure 3–1 and Table 3.1.

Men's Desires

Long-term commitment

Half (49.9 percent) of all male advertisers mentioned something about a preferred relationship length. Of these, 76 percent reported seeking a

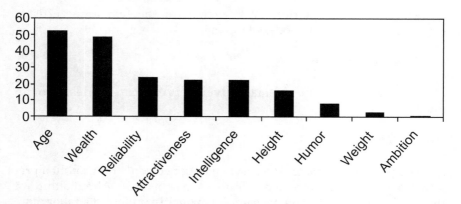

Ranking of male traits as asked for by female advertisers

FIGURE 3–1.   Ranking of male traits as asked for by female advertisers.

long-term relationship; 24 percent reported seeking a short-term relationship—a pattern quite similar to the women's desires

A younger woman

The feature of a potential mate that was mentioned most often by the male advertisers was age (mentioned by 81.1 percent of all male advertisers). Of these, most expressed a desire for younger partners (47.4 percent), followed by those who want a same-age partner (20.6 percent). Only 13.1 percent expressed a preference for an older female partner. These findings very much complement the pattern for female expressed desires, which generally favor older partners.

An attractive woman

The second most-often desired trait by male advertisers was physical attractiveness. Over a third (35.5 percent) mentioned wanting an attractive partner. Based on a chi-square goodness of fit, this percentage is significantly ($p < .001$) higher than the percentage (22.3 percent) of female advertisers who expressed a desire for a physical attractiveness.

A slim partner

Next to being generally attractive, the ideal female potential mate of these male advertisers is slim. Twenty-four percent of all male advertisers mentioned something about preferred weight, and a clear majority (94 percent of these) wanted a slim partner.

A wealthy woman

13.7 percent of all men expressed the desire for a wealthy partner. Consistent with past research on sex differences in the desire for wealth, this percentage was significantly ($p < .001$) lower than for females(48.6 percent seeking wealth).

A reliable woman

The top psychological trait that men desired was reliability. 12.5 percent of the male advertisers mentioned that they wanted a stable, reliable partner. This is significantly lower ($p < .001$) than the comparable percentage found in female's desires for this same trait (at 23.6 percent).

An intelligent partner

About one of ten (9.7 percent) male advertisers expressed a desire for an intelligent female mate—lower than the percentage as female advertisers desiring intelligence (22.0 percent).

Height, ambition, and humor

The other three traits that we examined in this study all had occurrence rates below 5 percent. The male advertisers clearly did not care much about a female mate's height (mentioned by only 3.8 percent), sense of humor (mentioned by 3.0 percent) or ambition (occurrence rate of 0.4 percent).

An overview of these results can be found in Figure 3–2 and Tables 3.1 and 3.2.

What does the best advertisement look like?

The current analysis yields some information about the ideal personal ad that could appeal to each sex. Given the limited space available in personal ads, an ideal ad might match the five or so qualities that are most-often sought by the opposite sex. For instance, a man's ad reflecting women's top desires might state:

> "I am a wealthy, reliable, mature man, with an intelligent mind and a pretty good body."

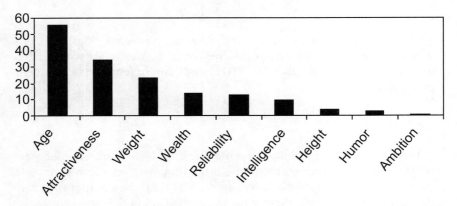

Ranking of female traits as asked for by male advertisers

FIGURE 3–2.   Ranking of female traits as asked for by male advertisers.

TABLE 3.1.
Sex Differences in Expression of Desired Partner Traits in 800 Belgian Personal Advertisements

Expressed Desires for Traits of Potential Mates			Sex Advertiser		
		I desire:	Male (% of N = 504)	Female (% of N = 296)	P value*
Relationship length		A short-term commitment	11.8	9.7	0.3601
		A long-term commitment	37.7	32.5	0.1389
Age		A younger partner	47.4	23.6	0.0000
		A same age partner	20.6	32.1	0.0003
		An older partner	13.1	40.2	0.0000
Physical traits	Attractiveness	A physically attractive partner	34.5	22.3	0.0003
	Weight	A slim partner	22.4	2.4	0.0000
		A normal weight partner	0	0	—
		A plump partner	0.6	0.0	0.1822
		An obese partner	0	0	—
		An athletic partner (%)	1.0	1.0	1.0000
	Height	A tall partner	0.2	4.7	0.0000
		A short partner	0	0	—
		A partner of "exact height"	3.6	12.5	0.0000
Mental traits		An ambitious partner	0.4	0.3	0.8204
		An intelligent partner	9.7	22.0	0.0000
		A humoristic partner	3.0	8.1	0.0013
		A reliable, trustable partner	12.5	23.6	0.0001
Status traits	Investment abilities	A wealthy partner	13.7	48.6	0.0000

* Computed with statistica significance tests for difference between two proportions.

An ideal ad for females looking for males that takes the current findings into account would look more like this:

"I am a young, attractive, slim woman, who is reliable and financially secure."

A MATING INTELLIGENCE ANALYSIS: HOW WELL DO MALE AND FEMALE ADVERTISERS KNOW THEIR OPPOSITE-SEX CLIENTS?

Our exploration of mating intelligence focuses on quantifying people's accuracy in cross-sex mind-reading. The current data set allows us to

TABLE 3.2.
Sex Differences in Self Descriptions in 800 Belgian Personal Advertisements

Self-Description in Personal Ads			Sex Advertiser		
		I am:	Male (% of N = 504)	Female (% of N = 296)	P value*
Age			82.5	80.7	
Physical traits	Attractiveness	Physical attractive	39.7	46.3	0.0683
	Weight	Slim	15.1	27.7	0.0000
		Normal weight	0.4	0.0	0.2763
		Plump	0.0	1.4	0.0079
		Obese	0.2	0.0	0.4416
		Build athletic	2.0	1.0	0.2812
	Height	Tall	3.8	3.4	0.7710
		Short	0.2	0.0	0.4416
		Giving "exact height"	29.6	15.9	0.0000
Mental traits		Ambitious	2.8	0.7	0.0420
		Intelligent	22.0	18.9	0.2977
		Humoristic	8.9	2.7	0.0007
		Reliable, trustable	24.4	15.9	0.0047
Status traits	Investment abilities	Wealthy	49.0	37.5	0.0016

* Computed with statistical significance tests for Difference between Two Proportions

calculate how often each sex advertises qualities that are actually desired by the opposite sex.

How Well Do Females Match Males' Actual Desires?

Age first

The top listed trait of female advertisers in their self-description is age. Most women (80.7 percent) mention their age, and they all mention their exact age without commenting whether they see this as 'young' or 'old.'

I am pretty

Next, almost half (46.3 percent) of all female advertisers described themselves as physically attractive.

I am wealthy

The third most-often mentioned trait of female advertisers was wealth. Many (37.5 percent) of the female advertisers describe themselves as prosperous, well-off, high-status, etc.

I am slim

Next, about a third (30.1 percent) of the women mentioned something about their weight; of these, 92 percent said that they were slim.

How tall I am

Roughly one-fifth (19.3 percent) of the women mentioned something about their height. Most of these (15.9 percent of the whole sample) gave their exact height, without commenting on whether they considered this *short* or *tall*.

Fewer focus on psychological traits

Female advertisers less often advertise their psychological traits than their physical qualities (age, attractiveness, slimness, height). About one-fifth (18.9 percent) of female advertisers described herself as being intelligent. This was followed by self-descriptions of being reliable (15.9 percent), having a good sense of humor (2.7 percent) and last, having ambition (0.7 percent).

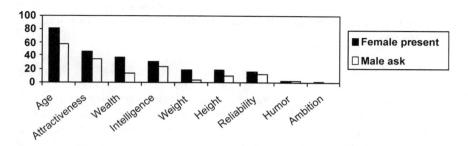

FIGURE 3–3.   How women present themselves in personal ads, in relation to what men desire.

What Female Advertisers Do Right . . . and Wrong

Female advertisers understand that males want to know about their age and physical attractiveness. These features explicitly desired by most males, and female advertisers showed good mating intelligence by including these features in their advertisements. However, females seemed to overestimate the importance that males attached to their economic status, height, and intelligence.

Figure 3–3 shows the ranking of self-descriptions by the female advertisers, and how they correspond to the expressed desires of the male advertisers.

How Male Advertisers Present Themselves

Age

Like the female advertisers, most (82.5 percent) male advertisers mentioned their specific age, without commenting on whether they consider themselves young or old.

I am wealthy

Half (49.0 percent) of male advertisers present themselves as being wealthy. This proportion is significantly ($p < .01$) larger than the proportion of female advertisers who described themselves as wealthy (37.5 percent).

I am handsome

39.7 percent of all male advertisers described themselves as 'handsome.' This percentage is not significantly different from the percentage of female advertisers describing themselves as 'pretty.' Apparently, both male and female advertisers thought that attractiveness was important to the other sex.

I am that tall or short

Fourth place in the ranking of males' self-descriptions is height. A third (29.6 percent) of male advertisers mentioned their exact height. A small number (3.8 percent) described themselves as being tall; only one described himself as short. A significantly ($p < .001$) higher percentage of male (29.6%) than female advertisers (19.3%) revealed their height.

How men present themselves in personal ads, in relation to what women desire

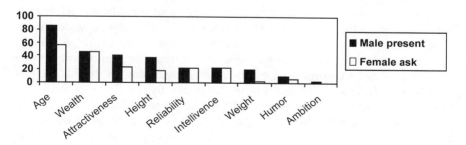

FIGURE 3–4.   How men present themselves in personal ads, in relation to what women desire.

I am reliable

Next, about a quarter (24.4 percent) of men describe themselves as reliable—a significantly higher ($p < .01$) proportion than for women (15.9 percent).

I am intelligent

A little over a fifth (22.0 percent) of the men mentioned their intelligence, about the same as the percentage of women who did (18.9 percent).

I am slim

17.7 percent of all male advertisers commented on their own weight. Most men (15.1 percent of the total sample) explicitly mentioned being slim. This is significantly ($p < .001$) lower than the percentage of female advertisers who describe themselves as slim (28.0 percent).

Humor and ambition

The two other mental traits we included in our analysis were rarely mentioned. 8.9 percent of the male advertisers said they had a good sense of humor. This is a significantly ($p < .001$) higher proportion than we found for the female advertisers (2.7 percent). Like the female advertisers, however, we hardly ever found self-descriptions about ambition. Only 2.8 percent of the men mentioned that they were ambitious.

What Male Advertisers Do Right . . . and Wrong

Just like female advertisers, male advertisers were generally aware of their two most important sex-specific assets—age and wealth—which match the two most often expressed desires of female advertisers. Male advertisers seemed overestimate the importance of their physical attractiveness, height and weight, which are all physical features. The proportion of male advertisers who commented on their own psychological traits, such as being reliable, intelligent, and funny, did generally match the percentages of female advertisers who expressed a desire for these traits.

Figure 3–4 shows the ranking of self-descriptions by the male advertisers, and how these rankings compare to the expressed desires of the female advertisers.

Sex Difference in Mating Intelligence: Overall Matching of Opposite-Sex Desires

Age is clearly a major criterion in the mating game—almost all males and females show desires for particular age ranges and they usually reveal their own age. Age is the most-mentioned trait for both men and women in the current data set. However, when examining the other traits included in this analysis, such cross-sex accuracy tends to drop a bit.

For the other eight traits we included in the analyses (attractiveness, weight, height, wealth, ambition, intelligence, humor, and reliability), we conducted an overall correlation of the percentage of times a trait is preferred (expressed desire) by one sex in relation to the percentage of times of times it is mentioned in the self-descriptions of the other sex. The Pearson correlation between what women want and what men advertise in their self-descriptions is .878 ($p = .004$, $N = 8$), while the correlation between what men want and what women advertise in their self-descriptions is .771 ($p = .025$, $N = 8$).

These correlations suggest that both sexes are very accurate in understanding the other's sexes preferences, but that men may be a little more accurate at determining what the other sex wants.

CONCLUSION

This chapter examined the content of personal ads to see how accurately men and women understand the preferences of the other sex. We coded the expressed preferences and self-descriptions of individual advertisers for of 800 personal ads placed in Belgian newspapers. We then compared the expressed preferences of each sex with the self-descriptions of the opposite sex.

Our general results are consistent with previous studies of personal ads. In looking at sex differences in expressed desires of relationship length, we did not find any differences; both our male and female advertisers most often expressed a desire for long-term commitment. This finding is consistent with some past findings (Willis & Carlson, 1993), but contradicts some other findings (Butler-Smith et al., 1998; Cameron & Collins, 1998; Wiederman, 1993) which found that more female than male advertisers display a desire for long-term commitment, and that more male than female advertisers display a desire for short-term commitment. This last finding is consistent with many evolutionary theories on human mating. However, personal ads might not be the best way to investigate preferences for relationship length. We agree with some authors (Butler-Smith et al., 1998; Hayes, 1995) who argue that individuals using personal ads are mainly seeking long-term relationships, because the slow communication between advertisers and responders is not well-suited to spontaneous, short-term mating. Alternately, the males may be lying (or adaptively self-deceiving) when 37.9 percent of them say they seek a long-term relationship, and only 12.0 percent of them say they seek a short-term relationship.

In examining the preferred ages of potential partners, we found that women more often desired older partners, and men more often desired younger partners, a result that agrees with previous studies (Butler-Smith et al., 1998; Greenless & McGrew, 1994; Hayes, 1995; Matthews, 1999; Rajecki et al, 1991; Rasmussen et al., 1998; Sprecher et al., 1994; Wiederman, 1993; Willis & Carlson, 1993). We found that both male and female advertisers almost always give their exact age, with no other comments ("young," "senescent") added concerning their age. By contrast, Pawlowski and Dunbar (1999) found that women mentioned their age in the personal ads less often than men. Age may be popular to ask for and reveal because it takes so few words, saving advertisers money ("SWF, 32" is cheaper to run than "Single white female, post-doctoral researcher in multivariate behavior genetics, divorced but still reasonably fertile").

In looking at advertiser's preferred physical traits and self-descriptions, we confirmed previous research showing that more male than female advertisers express a desire for a physically attractive mate, and that more female than male advertisers describe themselves as 'physical attractive' (e.g. Butler-Smith, Cameron, & Collins, 1998; Child, Low, McCormick, & Cocciarella, 1996; Davis, 1990; Feingold, 1992; Greenlees & McGrew, 1994; Hayes, 1995; Hirschman, 1987; Deaux & Hanna, 1984; Kenrick & Keefe, 1992; Rajecki, Bledsoe, & Rasmussen, 1991; Sprecher, Sullivan, & Hatfield, 1994; Thiessen, Young, & Burroughs, 1993; Wiederman, 1993; Willis & Carlson, 1993). Next, consistent with the studies of Thiessen et al. (1993) and Wilson and Carlson (1993), we also found that more male than female advertisers ask for a slim partner, and more female than male advertisers describe themselves as 'slim.'

While males more often express a preference regarding weight (slimness), females more often express a preference regarding height (tallness). This is not surprising, since male height is often linked to power and status (Dunbar, 1995), which are highly valued male traits. In previous studies of personal ads, more male than female advertisers reported their height (Epel et al., 1996; Willis & Carlson, 1993). Our results replicate this pattern. Further, our results showed that more female than male advertisers express a desire for tall partners—a finding that was not reported by these prior researchers.

With reference to sex differences in 'status' or 'investment abilities,' we examined the expressed desires and self-descriptions for financial status, which is a clear predictor of status in our Western societies. Several previous researchers (e.g., Butler-Smith, Cameron, & Collins, 1998; Child, Low, McCormick, & Cocciarella, 1996; Davis, 1990; Deaux & Hanna, 1984; Feingold, 1992; Greenlees & McGrew, 1994; Hayes, 1995; Hirschman, 1987; Kenrick & Keefe, 1992; Rajecki, Bledsoe, & Rasmussen, 1991; Sprecher, Sullivan, & Hatfield, 1994; Thiessen, Young, & Burroughs, 1993; Wiederman, 1993; Willis & Carlson, 1993) had already shown that, consistent with evolutionary arguments, more female than male advertisers desire a wealthy partner, and more male than female advertisers describe themselves as financial wealthy. Wiederman (1993), for instance, showed that male advertisers mention their financial wealth three times as often as female advertisers do, and that the percentage of female advertisers expressing a desire for financial wealth was ten times as large as the percentage of male advertisers expressing such as desire. Our results confirm that male wealth is still more important, even in prosperous, sexually egalitarian societies such as Belgium.

Last, we focused on mental traits that are highly desired in potential mates. Reliability, for instance, is valued in both male and female potential partners. However, consistent with some past findings (e.g., Wiederman, 1993), we found that more female than male advertisers express a desire for reliability in a partner. Further, both Wiederman's and the current results found that more male than female advertisers mention 'reliability' in their self-descriptions.

Another mental trait included in the current analysis is intelligence. Since intelligence can be perceived as a predictor of financial success, which as a signal of investment ability, it should be a valued trait, especially in females' preferences. Our results clearly show that more females than males express a desire for an intelligent partner. However, males and females commented equally often on their own intelligence.

A final mental trait examined was sense of humor, which may be considered a proxy for creative intelligence. In light of Miller's (2000) theory of creativity as a sexually selected trait, we predicted that humor expression was more desired by females in potential male mates than vice versa. Our results indeed show that more female than male advertisers desire potential mates with a good sense of humor. Further, we found that more male than female advertisers expressed this asset in their self descriptions. These findings are consistent with some prior research on the content of personal ads (Thiessen et al., 1993; Wiederman, 1993).

In addition to analyzing the state preferences and self-descriptions that male and female advertisers include in their personal ads, we also analyzed the accuracy of cross-sex mind-reading. Specifically, we investigated how well the male self-descriptions met the desired partner profiles of female advertisers, and vice versa. Our analyses suggest that males and females are, generally, very accurate in knowing the desires of the opposite sex, and in advertising their own qualities accordingly.

Further, the current analyses suggested that the self-descriptions of males matched the reported desires of females slightly better than vice versa, though this difference was not statistically significant. If these findings replicate, they may imply that mating intelligence in the domain of cross-sex mind-reading favors men over women. Such a pattern that would contradict the idea that women score better than men on virtually all empathizing tasks (Baron-Cohen, 2002, 2005) and other tasks that require the accurate interpretation of social and emotional stimuli (see Mayer, Salovey, & Caruso, 1999). More research is needed on this point, since mating is one of the few contexts where males may be highly motivated to use whatever Theory of Mind they have.

Several alternative explanations may explain why males seemed to show marginally higher cross-sex mind-reading ability in this personal ads study. Perhaps most-desired male traits (e.g., wealth, intelligence, reliability) are easier to fake and harder to evaluate at a glance than the most-desired female traits (e.g., youth, beauty, slimness). In general, men's desires for women revolve more around physical features, such as general physical attractiveness and body weight, while women's desires for men focus more on wealth and mental traits, as intelligence. So, females may have less latitude to use creative impression-management strategies in describing themselves. This would make it more difficult for females to describe themselves in a way that matches male desires than vice versa.

Alternatively, consider the fact that, across most contexts, females are notoriously more choosy in the mate-selection process compared with males (Trivers, 1972). This choosiness may put heavier pressure on males to understand the female mating mind than vice versa. Accordingly, men might have evolved better cross-sex mind-reading skills in the courtship domain. We are hopeful that future research will address both the reliability of and the causal mechanisms underlying this sex difference.

ACKNOWLEDGMENTS

We would like to thank Robin Dunbar, Donald Brown, Don Symons, Patrick Vyncke, Geoffrey Miller, and Glenn Geher for their comments on earlier drafts of this manuscript. We also wish to thank the Belgian American Educational Foundation for their support.

REFERENCES

Baron-Cohen, S. (2002). The extreme male brain theory of autism. *TRENDS in Cognitive Sciences, 6*(6), 248–254.

Baron-Cohen, S. (2005). Testing the extreme male brain (EMB) theory of autism: Let the data speak for themselves. *Cognitive Neuropsychiatry, 10*(1), 77–81.

Bromley, D. B. (1993). *Reputation, image, and impression management*. New York: John Wiley & Sons.

Buss, D. M. (1989). Sex differences in human mate preferences: evolutionary hypotheses tested in 37 cultures. *Behavioral and Brain Sciences, 12*, 1–49.

Buss, D. (1994). *The evolution of desire: Strategies of human mating*. New York: Basic Books.

Buss, D. (1999). *Evolutionary psychology: The new science of the mind*. Needham Heights: Allyn & Bacon.

Buss, D. M. (2000). *The dangerous passion: Why jealousy is as necessary as love or sex*. Bloomsbury.

Buss, D. M., & Schmitt, D. P. (1993). Sexual strategies theory: An evolutionary perspective on human mating. *Psychological Review, 100*(2), 204–232.

Butler-Smith, P., Cameron, S., & Collins, A. (1998). Gender differences in mate search effort: An exploratory economic analysis of personal advertisements. *Applied Economics, 30*, 1277–1285.

Cameron, S., & Collins, A. (1998). Sex differences in stipulated preferences in personal advertisements. *Psychological Reports, 82*(1), 119–123.

Chavanne, T. J., & Gallup, G. G., Jr. (1998). Variation in risk-taking behavior among female college students as a function of the menstrual cycle. *Evolution and Human Behavior 19*, 27–32.

Charman, T., Ruffman, T., & Clements, W. (2002). Is there a gender difference in false belief development? *Social Development, 11*(1), 1–10.

Child, M., Low, K. G., McCormick C., & Cocciarella, A. (1996). Personal advertisements of a male-to-female transsexuals, homosexual men, and heterosexuals, *Sex Roles, 34*(5–6), 447–455.

CIM. (2000). CIM bereiksindicators en bereikpercentage/ Profiel lezers laatste periode, Internet: *http://www/cim.be/card/audi/16/nl/audi.html*, Centrum voor Informatie over de Media.

Davis, S. (1990). Men as success objects and woman as sex objects: A study of personal advertisements, *Sex Roles, 23*(1–2), 43–50.

Deaux, K., & Hanna, R. (1984). Courtship in the personals column: The influence of gender and sexual orientation, *Sex roles, 11*(5–6), 363–375.

Dunbar, R. (1995). Are you lonesome tonight? *New Scientist*, February 11, 26–31.

Ellis, B. J., & Symons, D. (1990). Sex differences in sexual fantasy: An evolutionary approach. *The Journal of Sex Research, 27*, 527–555.

Epel, E. S., Spanakos, A., Kasl, G. J., &Bronwell, K. (1996). Body shape ideals across gender, sexual orientation, socioeconomic status, race, and age in personal advertisements. *International Journal of Eating Disorders, 19*(3), 265–273.

Etcoff, N. (1999). *Survival of the prettiest*. New York: Doubleday.

Faurie, C., Pontier, D., & Raymond, M. (2004). Student athletes claim to have more sexual partners than other students. *Evolution and Human Behavior, 25*, 1–8.

Feingold, A. (1992). Gender differences in mate selection preferences: A test of the parental investment model, *Psychological Bulletin, 112*(1), 125–139.

Furnham, A., McClelland, A., & Omer, L. (2003). A cross-cultural comparison of ratings of perceived fecundity and sexual attractiveness as a function of body weight and waist-to-hip ratio. *Psychology, Health & Medicine, 8*(2), 219–230.

Gangestad, S. W., & Thornhill, R. (1997). Human sexual selection and developmental stability. In J. A. Simpson & D. T. Kenrick (Eds.), *Evolutionary social psychology* (pp. 169–195). Mahwah, NJ: Lawrence Erlbaum Associates.

Gangestad, S.W., & Thornhill, R. (2003). Facial masculinity and fluctuating asymmetry. *Evolution and Human Behavior, 24*, 231–241.

Gillis, J. S., & Avis, W. E. (1980). The male-taller norm in mate selection. *Personality and Social Psychology Bulletin, 6*(3), 396–401.

Grammer, K., Jutte, A., & Fischmann, B. (1997). Der kampf der geschlecter und der krieg der signale. In B. Kanitscheider (Ed.) *Liebe, Lust und Leidenshcaft. Sexualitat im Spiegal der Wissenschaft*. Stuttgart: Hirzel.

Graziano, W., Brothen, T., & Berscheid, E. (1978). Height and attraction. Do men and women see eye-to-eye. *Journal of Personality, 46*(1), 128–145.

Graziano, W. G., Jensen-Campbell, L. A., Todd, M., & Finch, J. F. (1997). Interpersonal attraction from an evolutionary perspective: women's reactions to dominant and prosocial men. In: J. A. Simpson & D. T. Kenrick (Eds.), *Evolutionary social psychology* (pp. 141–168). Mahwah, NJ: Lawrence Erlbaum Associates

Greenlees, I. A., & McGrew, W. C. (1994). Sex and age differences in preferences and tactics of mate attraction: Analysis of published advertisements. *Ethology and Sociobiology, 15*(2), 59–72.

Hayes, A. F. (1995). Age preferences for same- and opposite-sex partners. *Journal of Social Psychology, 135*(2), 125–133.

Harper, B. (2000). Beauty, stature and the labour market: A British cohort study. *Oxford Bulletin of Economics and Statistics, 62*, 771–800.

Haselton, M. G., & Buss, D. M. (2000). Error management theory: A new perspective on biases in cross-sex mind reading. *Journal of Personality and Social Psychology, 78*, 81–91.

Haselton, M. G., Buss, D. M., Oubaid, V., & Angleitner, A. (2005). Sex, lies and strategic interference: The psychology of deception between the sexes. *Personality and Social Psychology Bulletin, 31*(1), 3–23.

Hensley, W. E. (1994). Height as a basis for interpersonal attraction. *Adolescence, 29*(114), 469–474.

Hirschman, E. (1987). People as products: Analysis of a complex marketing exchange. *Journal of Marketing, 51*(1), 98–108.

Hussain, Z., Roberts, N., Whitehouse, G. H., Garcia-Finana, M., & Percy, D. (1999). Estimation of breast volume and its variation during the menstrual cycle using MRI and stereology. *The British Journal of Radiology, 72,* 236–245.

Hüttner, H., Renckstorf, K., & Wester, F. (1995). *Onderzoekstypen in de communicatiewetenschap.* Houten/Diegem: Bohn Stafleu Van Loghum.

Jackson, L. A., &Ervin, K. S. (1992). Height stereotypes of women and men: The liabilities of shortness for both sexes. *Journal of Social Psychology, 132*(4), 433–445.

Jason, L. A., Moritsugu, J. N., & DePalma, D. M. (1992). Advertising as a strategy for meeting people. *Psychological Reports, 71,* 1311–1314.

Johnson, V. S., & Franklin, M. (1993). Is beauty in the eye of the beholder? *Ethology and Sociobiology, 14,* 183–199.

Kenrick, D., & Keefe, R. (1992). Age preferences in mates reflect sex differences in human reproductive strategies. *Behavioral and Brain Sciences, 15,* 75–133.

Mayer, J. D., Salovey, P., & Caruso, D. R. (1999). *MSCEIT Item Booklet (Research Version 1.1)* Toronto, ON:MHS Publishers

Matthews, T. D. (1999). A world wide web-based research project. *Teaching Psychology, 26*(3), 227–230.

Miller, G. (2000). *The mating mind. How sexual choice shaped the evolution of human nature.* London: William Heinemann.

Miller, L., and Fishkin, S. (1997). On the dynamics of human bonding and reproductive success. In J. Simpson & D. Kenrick (Eds.), *Evolutionary Social Psychology* (pp. 197–235). Mahwah, NJ: Lawrence Erlbaum Associates.

Muir, H. (2000). Height matters. It's official women look down their noses at short men. *Nature, 403,* 156.

Murray, J. E. (2000). Marital protection and marital selection: Evidence from a historical-prospective sample of American men. *Demography, 37*(4), 511–521.

Pawlowski, B., & Dunbar, R. I. (1999). Withholding age as a putative deception in mate search tactics. *Evolution and Human Behavior, 20*(1), 53–69.

Peirce, C. A. (1996). Body height and romantic attraction: A meta-analytic test of the male-taller norm. *Social Behavior and Personality, 24*(2), 143–149.

Rajecki, D. W., Bledsoe, S. B., & Rasmussen, J. L. (1991). Successful personal ads: Gender differences and similarities in offers, stipulation, and outcomes. *Basic and Applied Social Psychology, 12,* 457–469.

Rasmussen, J. L., Rajecki, D. W., Ebert, A., Lagler, K., Brewer, C., & Cochran, E. (1998). Age preferences in personal advertisements: Two life history strategies or one tactic? *Journal of Social and Personal Relationships, 15*(1), 77–89.

Schmitt, D. P., Shackelford, T. K., & Buss, D. M. (2001). Are men really more 'oriented' toward short-term mating than women? A critical review of theory and research. *Psychology, Evolution, and Gender, 3,* 211–239.

Schmitt, D. P., & 118 Members of the International Sexuality Description Project (2003). Universal sex differences in the desire for sexual variety: Tests from 52 nations, 6 continents, and 13 islands. *Journal of Personality and Social Psychology, 85*(1), 85–104.

Shackelford, T. K., & Larsen, R. J. (1999). Facial attractiveness and physical health. *Evolution and Human Behavior, 20,* 71–76.

Shepperd, J. A., & Strathman, A. J. (1989). Attractiveness and height: The role of stature in dating preference, frequency of dating, and perceptions of attractiveness. *Personality and Social Psychology Bulletin, 15*(4), 617–627.

Singh, D. (1993). Body shape and women's attractiveness: the critical role of the waist-to-hip ratio. *Human Nature, 4,* 297–321.

Singh, D. (1995). Female judgment of male attractiveness and desirability for relationships: Role of waist-to-hip ratio and financial status. *Journal of Personality and Social Psychology, 69*(6), 1089–1101.

Spiegel M. R. (1972). *Theory and problems of statistics. Schaum's Ouline series in Science.* Singapore: McGraw-Hill Book Company.

Sprecher, S., Sullivan, Q., & Hatfield, E. (1994). Mate selection preferences: gender differences examined in a national sample. *Journal of Personality and Social Psychology, 66*(6), 1074–1080.

Streeter, S. A., & McBurney, D. H. (2003). Waist-hip ratio and attractiveness: New evidence and a critique of "a critical test". *Evolution and Human Behavior, 24*(2), 88–98.

Symons. (1979). *The evolution of human sexuality.* Oxford: Oxford Press.

Taylor, M. D., Hart, C. L., Smith, G. D., Whalley, L. J., Hole, D. J., Wilson, V., & Deary, I. J. (2005). Childhood IQ and marriage by mid-life: The Scottish Mental Survey 1932 and the Midspan studies. *Personality and Individual Differences, 38*(7), 1621–1630.

Thiessen, D., Young, R., & Burroughs, R. (1994). Lonely hearts advertisements reflect sexually dimorphic mating strategies. *Ethology and Sociobiology, 14*(3), 209–229.

Torte, M. J., & Cornelissen, P. L. (2001). Female and male perceptions of female physical attractiveness in front-view and profile. *British Journal of Psychology 92*(2), 391–403.

Townsend, J. M., & Levy, G. D. (1990a). Effects of potential partner's physical attractiveness and socioeconomic status on sexuality and partner selection. *Archives of Sexual Behavior, 19,* 149–164.

Townsend, J. M., & Levy, G. D. (1990b). Effects of potential partner's costume and physical attractiveness on sexuality and partner selection. *Journal of Psychology, 124,* 371–389.

Trivers, R. (1972). Parental investment and sexual selection. In B. Campbell (Ed.), *Sexual selection and the descent of man* (pp. 136–179). Chicago: Aldine-Atherton.

Weisfield, G. E. (1993). The adaptive value of humor and laughter. *Ethology and Sociobiology, 14,* 141–169.

Wiederman, M. W. (1993). Evolved gender differences in mate preferences: evidence from personal advertisements. *Ethology and Sociobiology, 14*(5), 331–352.

Willis, F. N., & Carlson, R. A. (1993). Singles ads: Social class, and time. *Sex Roles, 29*(5–6), 387–404.

III

Strategic Flexibility in Mating Intelligence

Chapter 4

Intelligent Priorities: Adaptive Long- and Short-Term Mate Preferences

Norman P. Li
University of Texas at Austin

SEX SIMILARITIES AND DIFFERENCES IN SHORT-TERM MATES

Given that reproduction is at the heart of natural selection, mating decisions are of central adaptive significance. Human mating requires successful navigation of various adaptive issues (e.g., Buss & Schmitt, 1993), and, thus, selection likely has given rise to components of human intelligence that solve issues directly related to mating. There are many such issues, some of which are addressed in various sections of this book. In this chapter, I examine the problem of selecting partners for both long- and short-term relationships.

Men Care About Looks and Women Care About Status in Long-Term Mates

Studies conducted over several decades have consistently found that when considering long-term romantic (e.g., marriage) partners, men place higher importance on physical attractiveness than women do, and women value social status more than men do (e.g., Buss, 1989; Buss & Barnes, 1986; Harrison & Saeed, 1977; Hill, 1945; McGinnis, 1958; Sprecher, Sullivan, & Hatfield, 1994; Wiederman, 1993). The difference in preferences has been attributed by evolutionary psychologists to the different adaptive problems that men and women face in long-term partner selection. Because ancestral women tended to vary in their reproductive capacity, men likely evolved an attraction toward physical features that reveal sexual maturity and youth (Symons, 1979). As women age beyond their mid-20s, fertility drops, and decreases in estrogen cause noticeable changes in appearance. Lips become thinner and less colorful, hair loses luster and softness, skin wrinkles, muscle tone decreases, breasts and buttocks lose shape, and the waist expands. Thus, men are drawn to physical features such as full lips, soft hair, smooth skin, colorful cheeks, good muscle tone, a low waist-to-hip ratio, and secondary sexual characteristics including breasts and buttocks (e.g., Cant, 1981; Johnston & Franklin, 1993; Manning, Scutt, Whitehouse, & Leinster, 1997; Singh, 1993; Symons, 1979, 1995). The multi-billion-dollar cosmetics industry and the rapidly expanding cosmetic-surgery market reveal modern women's underlying awareness of decreasing mate value and the benefits of visually reversing the aging process.

In contrast to female fertility, male fertility presents less of an adaptive problem, as it declines more gradually over the lifespan, with many men capable of siring children into their 60s and 70s. However, modern and primitive men across all societies vary in their ability to generate resources (e.g., Betzig, 1986). Because ancestral men who were higher in status had better access to resources for offspring, women may have evolved to value social status in long-term mates (e.g., Buss & Schmitt, 1993).

But What About Other Desirable Characteristics?

Given that many characteristics may be important in maintaining long-term relationships (e.g., Barkow, 1989; Buss, 1989; Jensen-Campbell, Graziano, & West, 1995), a satisfying explanation of the mate-search process should take into account how physical attractiveness and status are regarded in relation to other desired traits. Do women pursue status and do men pursue physical attractiveness *at the exclusion of* other traits? Or, do women prefer status and do men prefer physical attractiveness equally *alongside* traits such as personality, creativity, or kindness? Relatedly, are traits other than attractiveness (to males) and status (to females) even more important? The desired traits that show the largest sex differences may not be the most-desired traits overall.

One clue can be found from a careful examination of the literature, which reveals that physical attractiveness and status are commonly rated as modest in importance, and are even ranked at the *bottom* of many trait lists designed to tap mating preferences. For example, a compilation of six mate-preference studies revealed the relative importance of 14 traits (Powers, 1971). "Good financial prospect" received an average rank of 9.5 from women (where 1 is most-important and 14 is least-important), versus 13.1 from men, and "favorable social status" received an average of 11.5

from women, versus 12.8 from men. "Good looks" received a mean rank of 12.0 from men, versus 13.3 from women. Thus, there are reliable sex differences in preferences for beauty and status, but their overall importance is very low. Similarly, when participants from 37 cultures rated the importance of various characteristics in potential marriage partners, predicted sex differences were found for the value of good looks, good financial prospect, and ambition-industriousness, yet neither sex considered them very important in an absolute sense (Buss, 1989). Thus, one might surmise that neither sex may be looking too hard for physical attractiveness or status in their partners, but, rather, that men desire status *even less* than women do, and women desire physical attractiveness *even less* than men do.

Tradeoffs

A key limitation is that prior studies tended to ask participants to rate desired characteristics one at a time, as if spouses could be selected from a mail-order catalog with customized, modular features. However, in long-term mating, both sexes are choosy, and this mutual mate choice means that everyone faces trade-offs. One's own mate value is always limited, so one cannot attract a committed partner who is at the maximum on every desired trait. Because actual potential mates possess bundles of desired traits, with different levels of each trait, and because those with higher trait levels are in greater demand, the selection of a high level of one trait often requires trading off against another trait. Thus, previous methods may have concealed the trade-offs normally made when selecting mates. In particular, subjects in previous studies could ignore their own mate-value limitations and act unrealistically choosy about every desired trait.

To date, some studies have tapped into mate-choice tradeoffs. Regan (1998) asked participants for acceptable percentile ranges on each of several characteristics. Cunningham, Druen, and Barbee (1997) offered choices of three different mates and found that windfall wealth was not as important as physical attractiveness or a desirable personality for both dating and marriage. Though this study provided an initial test of trade-offs, it offered only two states on each of three variables, and wealth obtained through luck does not signify status or resourcefulness as traditionally construed (e.g., lottery winners are not as respected as wealthy neurosurgeons). More recently, Fletcher, Tither, O'Loughlin, Friesen, and Overall (2004) offered participants choices between pairs of mates who were high on three factor-analyzed dimensions. For long-term mates, men preferred a partner who was higher on attractiveness/vitality, whereas women preferred status/resources and warmth/trustworthiness over attractiveness.

Priorities and Marginal Value

Though helpful in illuminating the tradeoffs inherent in mate choice, these studies did not investigate how traits are *prioritized* (Li, Bailey, Kenrick, & Linsenmeier, 2002). Surprisingly, this limitation even applies to surveys in which traits are ranked (e.g., Buss & Barnes, 1986, Study 2). For instance, consider the relative value of oxygen, water, and food. If one considers the amount of time, money, and effort typically spent pursuing these items, food may look the most valuable and oxygen the least valuable. Similarly, if asked to choose among high levels of each, one would likely forego excess oxygen in favor of extra food or water. However, a person will survive the least amount of time if deprived of oxygen, and drowning is much more aversive than thirst or hunger. Thus, a more complete account of the relative importance of these items should consider tradeoffs from the ground up: when deprived of all three, oxygen is most essential. Once a person has enough oxygen to breathe, attention then turns to water or food. All three are important, but they differ in their prioritization (Li & Kenrick, 2006).

To uncover priorities in mate preferences, it is helpful to apply a microeconomic framework (Li et al., 2002; Li & Kenrick, 2006). Microeconomics concerns the structure of individual consumer preferences and their aggregate effects on the relative prices of different goods and services. Here, there is an emphasis on costs and benefits as well as a distinction between *necessities* and *luxuries*. Necessities are goods or activities that receive initial priority, but *diminishing marginal returns* occur when the benefits that accrue from such items decrease as more units are obtained. For example, enough oxygen to breathe is a lot better than no oxygen, but extra ("marginal") oxygen is not much better than enough. Thus, oxygen has diminishing marginal returns. As marginal returns diminish for necessities, preferences shift toward other items (luxuries), which then offer greater marginal benefits. Relative to oxygen, food is a luxury. But then relative to food, a Maldives beach vacation is a luxury. Thus, when consumers have very little income, a large proportion of their expenditures tend to be on economic necessities such as electricity, rent, and basic food. However, as more of these are acquired, the benefits associated with acquiring even more of these items decrease. Thus, a smaller proportion of additional income will go toward these types of items, and a greater proportion gets spent on luxuries, including vacations and private education.

The fundamental concept of decreasing marginal benefits underlies not only consumer behavior, but more generally, how living organisms adaptively allocate effort across their alternatives. For example, in behavioral ecology, the marginal value theorem (Charnov, 1976) is used to explain animals' foraging patterns (e.g., Krebs & Davies, 1993). A forager stays at a particular patch of food until the value of moving on to the next patch outweighs the value of the current patch, which diminishes with further consumption.

From an evolutionary perspective, marginal value should be relevant to the mate-selection process. For men, mating with a non-fertile mate would be a reproductive dead end. Thus, when mating choices are constrained, men should prioritize fertility. To the extent that an ancestral woman's fertility was related to her observable physical features (Symons, 1979), men may have evolved to strongly desire at least a moderate level of physical attractiveness and apparent youthfulness in order to have a reasonable probability of fertility (Li et al., 2002). Indeed, an ancestral woman who is considered moderately attractive is likely able to reproduce (e.g., Singh & Young, 1995). Though more attractiveness is desirable, additional attractiveness is increasingly more difficult to obtain (given mutual mate choice and one's own limited mate value) and provides fewer additional benefits in terms of higher fertility. Thus, as greater attractiveness is obtained and its marginal value decreases, the relative value of other traits should increase, and other traits should be weighted more heavily as choices expand. In other words, trying to obtain an extremely attractive woman with little else to offer is likely less reproductively profitable than finding one who is moderately attractive and also has other positive traits, such as kindness. Nevertheless, looking first for kindness in a female mate makes less sense, because a kind but infertile mate is less reproductively viable than a fertile but selfish mate (Li et al., 2002).

Similarly, insofar as higher-status males could have better provisioned and protected their offspring in the evolutionary past (e.g., Buss, 2003), women may have evolved to prioritize male status before being concerned about other mate characteristics. A man with moderate status can likely generate a moderate but steady flow of resources and is reproductively a much better bet than a destitute loser. However, due to decreasing marginal value, a very high-status male may offer only a little improvement over a mid-status male in terms of offspring survival probabilities. Thus, it makes sense for women to first verify that a man has sufficient status/resources, and then to seek positive levels of other characteristics.

Testing the Tradeoffs in Long-Term Partners

To examine mate selection priorities, my colleagues and I devised a budget-allocation method and a mate-screening paradigm (Li et al., 2002). Under the budget-allocation method, men and women had three possible budgets of "mate dollars" with which they can "buy" different levels of different traits in a hypothetical long-term mate. For example, a woman with very high mate value, who is desired by many males, could be viewed as having many "mate dollars" to spend on selecting an ideal husband; a woman with very low mate value would have a much tighter budget. Whereas the high budget allowed subjects to "buy" high values on many desired traits, the low budget was very restrictive. Under the constraints of the low budget, men tended to spend the highest proportion of their budget on physical attractiveness, and women spent the highest proportion of their budget on status and resource-related characteristics (e.g., earning potential). As budgets increased, spending decreased on these traits but increased on others, such as creativity and intelligence. Put another way, both sexes tended to desire well-rounded mates when given the freedom to make such choices. But when push came to shove and choices were highly constrained, men prioritized some minimal level of physical attractiveness and women prioritized some minimal level of status. Both sexes also prioritized kindness.

In a mate-screening paradigm, subjects revealed their mate preferences not by allocating limited budgets across different desired traits for a single ideal mate, but by prioritizing the order in which they find out information about the different traits of potential mates. Heterosexual male and female subjects saw a sequence of potential mates portrayed on a computer screen—not in pictorial form, but in terms of numerical rankings on several desired traits (Li et al., 2002). These opposite-sex targets supposedly comprised a random subset of 100 individuals who were interviewed on a diverse campus street. Each of the 100 individuals were allegedly rated for their physical attractiveness, social status level, creativity, kindness, and liveliness. For each characteristic, those in the top third for their sex were categorized as 'above average' on that characteristic, those in the middle third for their sex were categorized 'average', and those in the bottom third were 'below average'. Participants had to decide whether each target was acceptable for a long-term relationship. For each opposite-sex target, buttons inscribed with each of the five characteristics (e.g. physical attractiveness) appeared alongside his or her name. Participants could find out a target's standing (above average, average, or below average) on each of the 5 characteristics by clicking the appropriate button, but were also told to uncover as little information as possible in order to make a reasonable decision one way or another. In effect, they were told to prioritize their information gathering. In this mate-screening paradigm, men most often inquired first about a potential long-term partner's physical attractiveness, and women most often inquired first about social level. For both sexes, kindness was a close second.

Further analyses involving hierarchical regression indicated that for both sexes, each of the five characteristics significantly affected the acceptability of opposite-sex targets for long-term relationships. This result is consistent with the idea that many characteristics are important for long-term relationships.

Also, when men were considering potential mates, the impact of physical attractiveness on the acceptability of a mate displayed a standard diminishing-marginal-returns pattern, whereby going from below average to average on physical attractiveness increased women's acceptability significantly more than going from average to above average did. Stated another way, being below average on physical attractiveness hurt a woman's desirability more than being above average on physical attractiveness helped. For women considering male marriage partners, the same diminishing-marginal-returns pattern was found for social status—going from below average social status to average increased men's acceptability more than going from average to above average did. No other traits displayed this diminishing-marginal-returns pattern. Thus, two different types of studies (budget-allocation and mate-screening) indicated that men tend to prioritize at least moderate physical attractiveness, and women prioritize at least moderate social status. Once these priorities are met, other traits are highly valued and are ideally sought after if given the opportunity to do so.

Interestingly, kindness was also highly prioritized by both sexes. Kindness may be indicative of one's willingness to share (Jensen-Campbell, Graziano, & West, 1995) and to look out for the interests of others (Li et al., 2002). A man's actual resource flow to a woman and her offspring can be viewed as the product of his ability to procure the resources (status) and his willingness to share its benefits (kindness). Similarly, a woman's effective reproductive value may depend not only on her underlying fertility, but also on her willingness to share her reproductive resources with a partner (i.e. to have sex). Thus, 'kindness' may be equally valued by both sexes, but may mean quite different things to each sex—females may consider a male's kindness to be his willingness to share attention and investment without demanding too much sex, whereas males may consider a female's kindness to be her willingness to have sex without demanding too much attention or investment. In addition, conflicts of interest occur between the sexes in many areas, especially those surrounding mating and parenting (see Buss, 2003). Thus, kindness also may be highly valued to ensure that one's partner holds one's interests at least as high as his or her own.

Short-Term Partners

For short-term mates (e.g., one-night stands), the adaptive problems are different. Because of the shorter time horizon, resources are less relevant. Instead, according to Strategic Pluralism Theory (Gangestad & Simpson, 2000), because pregnancy was always a possibility, women engaging in short-term mating may have had an adaptive need to identify partners with desirable heritable characteristics. According to this "good genes" theory (Thornhill & Gangestad, 1993), healthy genes and a strong immune system allow an individual to resist pathogens encountered during development. Susceptibility to pathogens can result in developmental instability, which results in deviations from bilateral facial and bodily symmetry. Because testosterone compromises the immune system, those men who simultaneously exhibit testosterone-rich features and a high degree of symmetry effectively advertise having genes that are resistant to local pathogens. Consistent with this idea, men who are considered physically attractive by women exhibit more facial masculinity (e.g., Johnston, Hagel, Franklin, Fink, & Grammer, 2001; Penton-Voak et al., 1999), muscularity (Frederick & Haselton, 2005), and bilateral symmetry (e.g., Scheib, Gangestad, & Thornhill, 1999; Thornhill & Gangestad, 1994). Symmetrical and masculine men have more sexual partners, are more desirable as affair partners (Gangestad & Thornhill, 1997b; Thornhill & Gangestad, 1994), and are especially preferred by women around the time of ovulation (e.g., Gangestad & Thornhill, 1998; Johnston et al., 2001; Penton-Voak et al., 1999). Though women find symmetrical men to be more attractive, women do not seem to be consciously aware of their focus on symmetry in the mate-selection process (Scheib et al., 1999). Rather, symmetry is correlated with masculinity and muscularity, which women consciously recognize as physically attractive. In ancestral environments, women who mated with men they found physically attractive during times of high fertility (near ovulation) may have accrued reproductive benefits by passing on good genes to offspring (Møller & Thornhill, 1998; Waynforth, 1998).

For men pursuing short-term sexual relationships, the issue of partner fertility is even more important than for men pursuing long-term relationships. So, men likely evolved to favor physical attractiveness and youthfulness especially in short-term partners. Indeed, studies have found that both sexes value physical attractiveness more in short-term mates than in long-term ones (e.g., Buunk et al., 2002; Fletcher et al., 2004; Regan, 1998; Regan & Berscheid, 1997).

Consistent with these theories, the reproductive benefits of short-term mating would be largely eliminated if a female was infertile or a male had undesirable heritable characteristics. Deficiencies along other dimensions (e.g., kindness, status) may not be as reproductively critical. To clear the key adaptive hurdles of infertility or poor gene quality, it makes sense for individuals considering a short-term partner to prioritize physical attractiveness as a necessity. That is, obtaining some baseline level of physical attractiveness should take precedence over obtaining other characteristics. However, once a moderate amount of physical attractiveness has been acquired, its relative value may decrease, and the reproductive benefits of further physical attractiveness may be outweighed by having positive levels of other traits.

To examine short-term mating priorities, we ran the budget-allocation and mate-screening programs on men and women considering one-night stands and affair partners (Li & Kenrick, 2006). When given an opportunity to purchase levels of various characteristics, both sexes tended to allocate the highest proportion of their constrained low mating budget to physical attractiveness. Men weighted physical attractiveness in their choices even more than women did, and more than men did for long-term mates. As budgets increased, however, both sexes allocated less of their mating budget toward physical attractiveness, and a greater proportion toward other traits, including creativity.

When screening short-term mates, both sexes inquired first about the physical attractiveness of opposite-sex targets before being concerned about creativity, social level, kindness, or liveliness. Once again, hierarchical regression showed that all traits influenced whether a target was acceptable as a short-term partner (except that women didn't care about creativity when screening short-term male mates). Physical attractiveness again showed the diminishing-marginal-returns pattern: for both sexes, an opposite-sex target going from below average to average on physical attractiveness increased the target's acceptability as a short-term partner more than if the target went from average to above average in attractiveness. That is, being below average on physical attractiveness hurt a target's acceptability more than being above average helped.

These results show that although many characteristics can affect the acceptability of a short-term mate, there is a clear prioritization of physical attractiveness by both men and women. The results also were consistent with men prioritizing fertility and women prioritizing good genes in short-term mating. However, at least two issues should be addressed. First, an alternative underlying motivation for women's short-term mating, according to Sexual Strategies Theory (Buss & Schmitt, 1993), is that by being open to short-term relationships, women can increase their options for long-term ones. They can solicit the interest of many men and use this wider net to evaluate potential long-term mates, or they may be able to turn short-term relationships into long-term ones. If women use short-term mating to assess or attain potential long-term relationships, then they should prioritize the same traits in short-term partners that they prioritize in long-term partners—status/resources and kindness (Li et al., 2002), and treat physical attractiveness as more of a luxury. Though our general results did not support this possibility, cluster analyses indicated that for a minority of women, their short-term choices mirrored their long-term choices, in which social status and kindness were prioritized (Li & Kenrick, 2006). A minority of men also specified short-term mates more like their long-term mates, putting less initial emphasis on physical attractiveness and more on kindness.

Second, how do we know that men prioritize physical attractiveness for fertility, whereas women prioritize it for good genes in short-term mates? Support for this interpretation comes from previous research on physical attractiveness as well as results in our studies. Specifically, the features that men find physically attractive tend to differ in meaningful ways from the ones that women find attractive. When asked what they find physically attractive, women specify features related to muscularity, strength, fitness, and masculinity (Li & Kenrick, 2006). As mentioned above, testosterone-mediated secondary sexual characteristics such as muscularity and facial masculinity are correlated with symmetry (Gangestad & Thornhill, 1997a; Scheib et al., 1999; Watson & Thornhill, 1994). Women particularly value such features (in addition to the scent of symmetrical men—see Gangestad & Thornhill, 1998) around the time of ovulation (e.g., Johnston et al., 2001; Penton-Voak et al., 1999). As a result, symmetrical and muscular men (but not women) have greater short-term mating success compared with their relatively asymmetrical and nonmuscular peers (e.g., Frederick & Haselton, 2005; Gangestad & Thornhill, 1997a; Thornhill & Gangestad, 1994). In light of these findings, women's prioritization of physical attractiveness in short-term partners is consistent with Strategic Pluralism Theory's assertion that women may be seeking genetic fitness in short-term partners (Gangestad & Simpson, 2000).

Further, evidence tends to support the contention that men prioritize physical attractiveness as a valid cue of fertility. Facial symmetry seems to be less important to men than to women in judgments of opposite-sex attractiveness (Shackelford & Larsen, 1997). Men factor breast symmetry into judgments of attractiveness, health, and desirability for long- and short-term relationships (e.g., Singh, 1994), and, tellingly, breast symmetry has been found to correlate with fertility (Manning et al., 1997; Møller, Soler, & Thornhill, 1995). In our studies, men indicated physical attraction toward features such as breasts and buttocks for both types of mates (Li & Kenrick, 2006), consistent with previous research suggesting that estrogen-influenced secondary sexual characteristics are attractive for purposes of identifying reproductively viable partners (e.g., Manning et al., 1997; Singh & Young, 1995). In other studies, men have indicated a preference toward a low waist-to-hip ratio, which is mediated by women's estrogen levels and is correlated with fertility and reproductive health (e.g., Singh, 1993, 2002; Zaastra et al., 1993). However, few studies have directly compared the current-fertility versus good-genes hypotheses for the same traits across both sexes; male symmetry, attractiveness, and muscularity may also correlate positively with sperm count and motility, and conversely, female breast and buttock size and symmetry are probably heritable, and genetically correlated with other fitness-related heritable traits.

Personalized Priorities

When it is adaptive to do so, psychological mechanisms may evolve to be sensitive to cues about the surrounding ecological and social environment (Tooby & Cosmides, 1990). One input that mate preferences may depend on is a person's own mate value, which profoundly influences which potential mates are likely to reciprocate one's sexual interest. Compared to those who are ignorant of their own mate value, those who are able to adjust mate preference standards according to their mate value can more readily avoid either having to settle for less rewarding relationships or facing costly rejection from more desirable partners (e.g., Berscheid, Dion, Walster, & Walster, 1971; Murstein, 1970). Also, non-equitable relationships (between partners of mismatched mate values) tend to provoke more negative emotions from both sides (Walster, Walster, & Traupmann, 1978) and are less stable (e.g., Hatfield, Utne, & Traupmann, 1979). Thus, it would be advantageous for people to be equipped to estimate their own mating desirability and to adjust their standards for mates accordingly.

If people regard certain traits in others as necessities that they prioritize but eventually shift away from, then one's own ability to offer those necessities (e.g. physical attractiveness or social status) may influence the set point at which one's own preference shifts occur. Thus, a physically attractive woman may require a higher level of resources in a long-term mate or physical attractiveness in a short-term mate before being concerned about other traits. In fact, this appears to be the case (Li, 2003). Analyzing the low-budget choices (where necessities are most apparent), I found that the independently rated physical attractiveness of a woman correlated positively with the amount of resources she purchased with her mate dollars for a long-term mate. This pattern was not found for male participants. These findings are consistent with data from actual marriages, which show that the best predictor of a husband's social status is the wife's physical attractiveness (Elder, 1969; Udry & Eckland, 1984). For short-term mates, the physical attractiveness of both male and female participants correlated positively with the level of physical attractiveness (but not resources) desired at the low budget (Li, 2003).

Thus, when searching for mates, people not only prioritize key traits according to mating context (long- versus short-term), but also seem to calibrate their demand for mating necessities according to their own value along dimensions valued by the opposite sex. Mate value is a relative concept and may itself depend on various other environmental variables (such as the local sex ratio). Some research has investigated which inputs influence one's mate value. For instance, Gutierres, Kenrick, and Partch (1999) found that people's judgments of their own mate value are affected by exposure to same-sex individuals who vary on criteria valued by the opposite sex. Specifically, viewing pictures of physically attractive women causes a woman to lower her self-perceived mate value, whereas attending to socially dominant men lowers a man's self-perceived mate value. Thus, one important determinant of mate value may be one's standing relative to one's competition on key traits prioritized by the other sex. Such adjustments are indicative of context-sensitive mate-value mechanisms, which may, in turn, feed into the setting of standards used in the mate-search process.

CONCLUSION

The budget-allocation and mate-screening paradigms reviewed in this chapter may be especially useful in understanding some apparent inconsistencies in human mating intelligence. They suggest that there may be minimal levels of certain key traits for mating to be reproductively worthwhile. Accordingly, mate search and mate choice may work best when people pre-consciously screen out all potential mates who do not meet certain minimum thresholds on the key traits (e.g. female youthfulness and attractiveness, male social status) or who even exceed one's mating budget (e.g., whose mate value vastly exceeds one's own). This may explain why high-mate-value New York women, when dining together surrounded by single waiters and bus-boys, complain that "There are no straight single men in Manhattan." They may not be literally correct, but they may be showing a high mating intelligence by commenting on the relative dearth of eligible (i.e., high-status) single men who appear on their mating radar. Conversely, the single bus-boys are probably saving a lot of courtship effort by not hitting on customers who are out of their league.

Men and women looking for mates, much like consumers shopping for goods or foragers looking for food, implicitly follow economic principles of marginal value, prioritizing key traits in their search for mates before looking at other traits. More generally, the findings reported on in this and other chapters in this volume are part of a growing body of literature that focuses on uncovering evolved psychological mechanisms specialized to solve various adaptive mating problems (e.g., Gangestad & Simpson, 2000; Haselton & Buss, 2000; Kenrick, Neuberg, Zierk, & Krones, 1994; Miller, 2000). Results thus far have helped to reveal the subtle structure of mate preferences, and will hopefully continue to contribute to a more extensive understanding of the nuances of mating intelligence.

REFERENCES

Barkow, J. (1989). *Darwin, sex, and status*. Toronto: University of Toronto Press.

Berscheid, E., Dion, K., Walster, E., & Walster, G W. (1971). Physical attractiveness and dating choice: A test of the matching hypothesis. *Journal of Experimental Social Psychology, 7*, 173–189.

Betzig, L. (1986). *Despotism and Differential Reproduction: A Darwinian View of History*. New York: Aldine de Gruyter.

Buss, D. M. (1989). Sex differences in human mate preferences: Evolutionary hypotheses tested in 37 cultures. *Behavioral & Brain Sciences, 12*, 1–49.

Buss, D. M. (2003). *The evolution of desire: Strategies of human mating* (Rev. Ed.). New York: Basic Books.

Buss, D. M. & Barnes, M. (1986). Preferences in human mate selection. *Journal of Personality and Social Psychology, 50*, 559–570.

Buss, D. M., & Schmitt, D. (1993). Sexual strategies theory: An evolutionary perspective on human mating. *Psychological Review, 100,* 204–232.

Buunk, B. P., Dijkstra, P., Fetchenhauer, D., & Kenrick, D. T. (2002). Age and gender differences in mate selection criteria for various involvement levels. *Personal Relationships, 9,* 271–278.

Cant, J. G. H. (1981). Hypothesis for the evolution of human breast and buttocks. *American Naturalist, 117,* 199–206.

Charnov, E. L. 1976. Optimal foraging: The marginal value theorem. *Theoretical Population Biology 9,* 129–136.

Cunningham, M. R., Druen, P. B., & Barbee, A. P. (1997). Angels, mentors, and friends. In J. A. Simpson & D. T. Kenrick (Eds.), *Evolutionary Social Psychology* (pp. 109–140). Mahwah, NJ: Lawrence Erlbaum Associates.

Elder, G. H., Jr. (1969). Appearance and education in marriage mobility. *American Sociological Review, 34,* 519–533.

Fletcher, G. J. O., Tither, J. M., O'Loughlin, C., Friesen, M., & Overall, N. (2004). Warm and homely or cold and beautiful? Sex differences in trading off traits in mate selection. *Personality & Social Psychology Bulletin, 30,* 659–672.

Frederick, D. A., & Haselton, M. G. (2005). *Male muscularity as a good-genes indicator: Evidence from men's self-reported sexual behaviors and women's preferences for muscularity.* Presented at the 18th annual meeting of the Human Behavior and Evolution Conference, Austin, TX.

Gangestad, S.W., & Simpson, J.A. (2000). The evolution of human mating: Trade-offs and strategic pluralism. *Behavioral and Brain Sciences, 23,* 573–587.

Gangestad, S. W., & Thornhill, R. (1997a). Human sexual selection and developmental stability. In J. A. Simpson & D. T. Kenrick (Eds.), *Evolutionary personality and social psychology* (pp. 169–195). Mahwah, NJ: Lawrence Earlbaum Associates.

Gangestad, S. W., & Thornhill, R. (1997b). The evolutionary psychology of extra-pair sex: The role of fluctuating asymmetry. *Evolution and Human Behavior, 18,* 69–88.

Gangestad, S. W., & Thornhill, R. (1998). Menstrual cycle variation in women's preferences for the scent of symmetrical men. *Proceedings of the Royal Society of London, B,* 927–933.

Harrison, A. A., & Saeed, L. (1977). Let's make a deal: An analysis of revelations and stipulations in lonely hearts advertisements. *Journal of Personality & Social Psychology, 35,* 257–264.

Gutierres, S. E., Kenrick, D. T., & Partch, J. J. (1999). Beauty, dominance, and the mating game: Contrast effects in self-assessment reflect gender differences in mate selection. *Personality and Social Psychology Bulletin, 25,* 1126–1134.

Harrison, A. A., & Saeed, L. (1977). Let's make a deal: An analysis of revelations and stipulations in lonely hearts advertisements. *Journal of Personality & Social Psychology, 35,* 257–264.

Haselton M. G., & Buss, D. M. (2000). Error management theory: A new perspective on biases in cross-sex mind reading. *Journal of Personality and Social Psychology, 78,* 81–91.

Hatfield, E., Utne, M. K., & Traupmann, J. (1979). Equity theory and intimate relationships. In R. L. Burgess & T. L. Huston (Eds.), *Social exchange in developing relationships* (pp. 99–133). New York: Academic Press.

Hill, R. (1945). Campus values in mate selection. *Journal of Home Economics, 37,* 554–558.

Jensen-Campbell, L. A., Graziano, W. G., & West, S. G. Dominance, prosocial orientation, and female preferences: Do nice guys really finish last? *Journal of Personality and Social Psychology, 68,* 427–440.

Johnston, V. S., & Franklin, M. (1993). Is beauty in the eye of the beholder? *Ethology and Sociobiology, 14,* 183–199.

Johnston, V. S., Hagel, R., Franklin, M., Fink, B., & Grammer, K. (2001). Male facial attractiveness: Evidence for hormone mediated adaptive design. *Evolution and Human Behavior, 21,* 251–267.

Kenrick, D. T., Neuberg, S. L., Zierk, K. L., & Krones, J. M. (1994). Evolution and social cognition: Contrast effects as a function of sex, dominance, and physical attractiveness. *Personality and Social Psychology Bulletin, 20,* 210–217.

Krebs, J. R., and N. B. Davies. (1993). *An introduction to behavioural ecology* (3rd ed.). London: Blackwell Scientific Publications.

Li, N. P. (2003). Short-term mate preference priorities: Necessities, luxuries, and comparisons to long-term mates (Doctoral dissertation, Arizona State University, 2003). *Dissertation Abstracts International, 64/03,* 1551.

Li, N. P., Bailey, J. M., Kenrick, D. T., & Linsenmeier, J. A. W. (2002). The necessities and luxuries of mate preferences: Testing the tradeoffs. *Journal of Personality and Social Psychology, 82,* 947–955.

Li, N. P., & Kenrick, D. T. (2006). Sex similarities and differences in preferences for short-term mates: What, whether, and why. *Journal of Personality and Social Psychology, 90,* 468–489.

Manning, J. T., Scutt, D., Whitehouse, G. H., & Leinster, S. J. (1997). Breast asymmetry and phenotypic quality in women. *Evolution and Human Behavior, 18,* 223–236.

McGinnis, R. (1958). Campus values in mate selection: A repeat study. *Social Forces, 36,* 368–373.

Miller, G. F. (2000). *The mating mind: How sexual choice shaped the evolution of human nature.* New York: Doubleday.

Møller, A. P., Soler, M., & Thornhill, R. (1995). Breast asymmetry, sexual selection, and human reproductive success. *Ethology and Sociobiology 16,* 207–219.

Møller, A. P., & Thornhill, R. (1998). Developmental stability and sexual selection: A meta-analysis. *American Naturalist, 151,* 174–192.

Murstein, B. (1970). Stimulus value role: A theory of marital choice. *Journal of Marriage & the Family, 32,* 465–481.

Penton-Voak, I. S., Perrett, D. I., Castles, D., Burt, M., Koyabashi, T., & Murray, L. (1999). Female preference for male faces changes cyclically. *Nature, 399,* 741–742.

Powers, E. A. (1971). Thirty years of research on ideal mate characteristics: What do we know? *International Journal of Sociology of the Family, 1,* 207–215.

Regan, P. C. (1998). What if you can't get what you want? Willingness to compromise ideal mate selection standards as a function of sex, mate value, and relationship context. *Personality and Social Psychology Bulletin, 24,* 1294–1303.

Regan, P. C., & Berscheid, E. (1997). Gender differences in characteristics desired in a potential sexual and marriage partner. *Journal of Psychology & Human Sexuality, 9,* 25–37.

Scheib, J. E., Gangestad, S. W., & Thornhill, R. (1999). Attractiveness, symmetry, and cues of good genes. *Proceedings of the Royal Society of London, B 266*, 1913–1917.

Shackelford, T. K., & Larsen, R. J. (1997). Facial asymmetry as an indicator of psychological, emotional, and physiological distress. *Journal of Personality and Social Psychology. 72*, 456–466.

Singh, D. (1993). Adaptive significance of female physical attractiveness: Role of waist-to-hip ratio. *Journal of Personality & Social Psychology, 65*, 293–307.

Singh, D. (1994). Female health, attractiveness, and desirability for relationships: Role of breast asymmetry and waist-to-hip ratio. *Ethology and Sociobiology, 16*, 465–481.

Singh, D. (2002). Female mate value at a glance: Relationship of waist-to-hip ratio to health, fecundity and attractiveness. *Neuroendocrinology Letters, 23*, 65–75.

Singh, D., & Young, R. K. (1995). Body weight, waist-to-hip ratio, breasts, and hips: Role in judgments of female attractiveness and desirability for relationships. *Ethology and Sociobiology, 16*, 483–507.

Sprecher, S., Sullivan, Q., & Hatfield, E. (1994). Mate selection preferences: Gender differences examined in a national sample. *Journal of Personality & Social Psychology, 66*, 1074–1080.

Symons, D. (1995). Beauty is in the adaptations of the beholder: The evolutionary psychology of human female sexual attractiveness. In P. R. Abramson, & S. D. Pinkerton, (Eds.), *Sexual nature, sexual culture* (pp. 80–118). Chicago: University of Chicago Press.

Thornhill, R., & Gangestad, S. W. (1993). Human facial beauty: Averageness, symmetry and parasite resistance. *Human Nature, 4*, 237–269.

Thornhill, R., & Gangestad, S. W. (1994). Fluctuating asymmetry and human sexual behavior. *Psychological Science, 5*, 297–302.

Tooby, J., & Cosmides, L. (1990). On the universality of human nature and the uniqueness of the individual: The role of genetics and adaptation. *Journal of Personality, 58*, 17–67.

Udry, J. R., & Eckland, B. K. (1984). The benefits of being attractive: Differential payoffs for men and women. *Psychological Reports, 54*, 47–56.

Walster, E., Walster, G. W., & Traupmann, J. (1978). Equity and premarital sex. *Journal of Personality and Social Psychology, 36*, 82–92.

Watson, P. J., & Thornhill, R. (1994). Fluctuating asymmetry and sexual selection. *Trends in Ecology and Evolution, 9*, 21–25.

Waynforth, D. (1998). Fluctuating asymmetry and human male life history traits in rural Belize. *Proceedings of the Royal Society of London, Series B, 265*, 1497–1501.

Wiederman, M. W. (1993). Evolved gender differences in mate preferences: Evidence from personal advertisements. *Ethology & Sociobiology, 13*, 331–352.

Zaastra, B. M., Seidell, J. C., Van Noord, P. A. H., Te Velde, E. R., Habbema, J. D. F., Vrieswijk, B., & Karbaat, J. (1993). Fat and female fecundity: Prospective study of effect of body fat distribution on conception rates. *British Medical Journal, 306*, 484–487.

Chapter 5

Personality, Mating Strategies, and Mating Intelligence

Daniel Nettle
Evolution and Behaviour Research Group, Division of Psychology, University of Newcastle

Helen Clegg
Psychology, University of Northampton

Mating intelligence can be defined as the set of cognitive abilities relevant to mating, courtship, and mate choice (Geher, Miller, & Murphy, this volume). As mating is such a crucial component of fitness, one would expect natural selection to have optimized the mental mechanisms that subserve strategies for selecting, understanding, and attracting mates. Yet, as differential psychologists have amply documented, there are abundant individual differences in sexual attitudes and behaviors. We will argue that much of this variation reflects stable personality dimensions. For example, Bailey and colleagues found substantial heritability for sexual promiscuity in a large-scale twin study (Bailey, Kirk, Zhu, Dunne, & Martin, 2000). Since these personality dimensions show substantial heritability (Bouchard & Loehlin, 2001), we must conclude that there is heritable variation in human mating-relevant cognitive mechanisms—and thus in mating strategies and perhaps mating intelligence.

Heritable variation is always of interest to the evolutionary scientist. Sometimes its presence suggests that a trait is affected by a very large number of genes, so variation can reveal general mutational load (see Keller, this volume; Miller, this volume). In other cases, heritable variation persists because of evolutionary trade-offs. A classic example is that an individual can grow a small body quickly or a large body slowly, so there is a trade-off between age of sexual maturity versus adult body size (Roff, 1992), which even affects human females (Nettle, 2002). The dilemma is whether to spend time growing bigger than one's competitors, or to start reproducing earlier than them; it is impossible to do both given the life-history constraints of growth. The optimal strategy depends very precisely on local ecological and demographic conditions. Selection may thus sometimes favor alleles that delay puberty in favor of larger adult body size, and sometimes, in slightly different environments, favor alleles of opposite effect. The net effect of such mixed selection pressures is often that heritable variation in both adult body size and juvenile growth rate is maintained in most wild populations. Some species, such as the pygmy swordtail, even have genetically distinct 'morphs' (discrete body types) that co-exist, such as large, slow-growing types, and small, sneaky-mating, fast-maturing types (Zimmerer & Kallman, 1989).

Applying such trade-off reasoning to humans, we can see how different mating strategies might persist over evolutionary time. In human mating, trade-offs arise mostly from issues of time-allocation and energy-allocation. The challenge of mating successfully can be decomposed into several sub-tasks. With limited time and energy, it is not possible to pursue all of these sub-tasks equally. For a species such as ours with highly dependent offspring that require sustained parental investment, there is an allocation-of-effort problem between parenting behaviours that nourish and protect existing offspring, versus mating behaviors that may lead to new offspring. This problem is most obvious for males, who can, often increase reproductive success by mate-switching. However, this problem also arises for females, who may have one child by an existing mate and be tempted by a better mate—but where mate-switching would disrupt the flow of parental effort from the existing mate. (This is no purely theoretical trade-off; it is very salient to married women with children who are considering divorce.) Also, females often face a trade-off between seeking genetic quality in a mate and seeking resources that will be invested reliably into the offspring—high-fitness males may be more likely to leave and cheat.

In this chapter, we review the evidence relating personality differences to mating strategies and mate preferences. We follow the widely accepted 'five-factor' approach to personality, which subsumes much of the stable variation between individuals into five broad dimensions (Costa & McCrae, 1992): openness, conscientiousness, extroversion, agreeableness, and neuroticism. We argue that individual differences in these five factors can be seen as variations in mating strategies that emphasize different routes to reproductive success. For example, Table 5.1. shows that all of the five personality dimensions except neuroticism have significant correlations (within at least one sex) with lifetime numbers of sexual

TABLE 5.1.
Correlations Between the Big Five Personality Dimensions and Self-Reported
Number of Sexual Partners in a General Population British Sample
(See Nettle, 2005, for Details).

	Whole Sample	*Men*	*Women*
Dimension	$n = 545$	$n = 203$	$n = 342$
Extraversion	0.27*	0.23*	0.29*
Neuroticism	0.05	0.10	0.02
Conscientiousness	−0.10*	−0.05	−0.13*
Agreeableness	−0.16*	−0.23*	−0.11*
Openness	0.06	0.00	0.11*

* $p < 0.05$

partners in a sample of 545 British adults (Nettle, 2005). Thus, openness, conscientiousness, extroversion, and agreeableness are not just relevant to modern school, work, and leisure—they have evolutionarily relevant mating implications. People also show clear preferences for certain personality traits in potential mates, and these shift adaptively according to the type of relationship sought (e.g., one-night-stand vs. marriage). We argue that such preferences make sense given the effects of partner personality traits on relationship outcomes, so these preferences may be well-designed to optimize various fitness benefits from various types of mating.

PERSONALITY FACTORS AND MATING STRATEGIES

The trade-offs involved in human mating seem to include the following:

1. Mate acquisition versus mate retention. How much energy should one invest in attracting new (perhaps higher-quality) mates, versus retaining existing ones?

2. Low versus high threshold for detecting mating-relevant threats. How much energy should one invest in detecting possible hazards, such as a mate's infidelity, loss of interest, loss of status or resources, loss of health, etc.?

3. Low versus high patience regarding future possible mating opportunities (discounting rate, in decision-theory terms). What is the optimal weighting of a present reproductive opportunity versus some future opportunity or cost, given that life is finite and uncertain?

4. Low versus high empathy regarding others' interests. What should be the relative weighting of the interests of significant others, versus one's own immediate advantage? Higher empathy should be

associated with higher patience, since the evolutionary payoff for attending to others' interests is presumably the benefits that they may render in the future.

5. Low versus high investment in costly, risky courtship signals. If human verbal and artistic creativity comprise a form of signalling behaviour whose main purpose is to attract mates (Miller, 2001), then a trade-off arises as to how much energy to invest in such signalling, given that it tends to be particularly costly in both time and effort.

This list has been contrived for the purposes of the chapter—and students of the five-factor personality model may have already guessed where we are headed—but each of these five trade-offs is evolutionarily plausible, and often arises within and across other species. It is unlikely that there is one globally optimal solution to any of them. Instead, the best strategy for an individual will depend on specific, local, transient conditions of the immediate environment, in relation to one's own genetic quality and phenotypic condition, relative to the population distribution of the current mating pool. Given such local fluctuations, we might expect that populations will tend to retain a spectrum of heritable mating-related phenotypes that reflect different points on these trade-off curves. The big five personality dimensions can be understood as capturing precisely such variation. For example, the mating implications of extraversion have been well-studied. More extraverted people tend to have more sexual partners (Eysenck, 1976; Heaven, Fitzpatrick, Craig, Kelly, & Sebar, 2000; Table 1), are more likely to terminate relationships (Nettle, 2005), and are more likely to have affairs (Nettle, 2005; Schmitt, 2004). Their gregariousness, positive mood, and high activity levels put them more often into social contexts full of potential mates; e.g., such that extraverted married women get more sexual invitations from other men (Schmitt & Buss, 2001).

If extraverts attract more potential mates, do they also enjoy higher reproductive success than introverts? If so, has there been consistent positive selection for extraversion? Our trade-off reasoning suggests not—if extraversion had mating benefits and no costs, we might all have evolved to be highly extraverted, and extraversion would no longer be variable or heritable across individuals. Indeed, extraversion does have costs: extraverts, through their risk-taking behaviors, suffer more accidents and hospitalizations (Nettle, 2005), and their promiscuity may undermine long-term relationships, reducing the parental investment available to their offspring. For example, extraverted women more often end up having their children raised with stepfathers (Nettle, 2005), who much more often neglect, abuse, and even kill their stepchildren (Daly & Wilson, 1985). Thus, extraverts may live fast and die young; introverts may live longer and stay married longer, to the benefit of their children. The continuing variability and heritability of the extraversion dimension suggests some kind of balance between such costs and benefits.

Neuroticism, the second of the big five traits, reflects one's threshold for feeling anxiety, concern, guilt, wariness, and depression. This can be interpreted as one's threshold for detecting biologically relevant threats, especially threats to one's social and sexual relationships. Highly neurotic people have hair-trigger threat-detectors—whether detecting threats from predators (e.g., snake phobias), pathogens (e.g., self-cleaning behaviors in obsessive-compulsive disorder), or sexual rivals (e.g., 'pathological' sexual jealousy). Often, such threats were very real and fitness-reducing under ancestral conditions, so many threat-detectors evolved to operate according to a 'smoke-detector' principle: better safe than sorry. Since failing to detect a real threat is so much more costly than over-reacting to an imagined threat, the optimal threshold for threat-detection may be quite low, so it produces many false positives but few false negatives (Haselton & Nettle, 2006; Nesse, 2005). For example, the human threshold for sexual jealousy is so low that it causes many relationship problems over imagined flirtations—but it may also prevent a few genuine cases of potential infidelity, cuckoldry, and desertion (Buss, 2000).

So far, it seems that a consistently low threat-detection threshold might be sensible. However, such a low threshold imposes many physiological, behavioural, and social costs. Frequently evoked alarm responses produce chronic stress, so those high in neuroticism are prone to many physical health problems, anxiety disorders, and major depressions (Neeleman, Sytema, & Wadsworth, 2002). More importantly in the context of mating intelligence, neurotic individuals undermine their own sexual relationships through relentless worry, suspicion, jealousy, and neediness. Neuroticism is the strongest (negative) predictor of a spouse's marital satisfaction, and of general relationship quality (Karney & Bradbury, 1997; Kelly & Conley, 1987). Thus, there is an interesting asymmetry, whereby it may be adaptive to have a moderate level of neuroticism oneself (to monitor possible threats), but to have a partner whose neuroticism is very low (to lower the frequency of false-positive over-reactions, and to lower the likelihood of them detecting one's own infidelities and mate-switching ambitions). This issue is discussed further in the next section.

So, although neuroticism seems like a bad thing, and high neuroticism undermines relationships (Karney & Bradbury, 1997) and physical and mental health (Neeleman et al., 2002), threat-detection systems exist for adaptive reasons, and often have adaptively low thresholds. As with other trade-offs, there are likely to be local, transient, population-sensitive variations in the trade-off between low and high threat-detection thresholds, so genetic variation in neuroticism is likely to persist. Indeed, major fitness threats are fairly rare and random, so it may be especially difficult for selection to optimize threat-detection thresholds, given the weakness of the fitness signal relative to the noise.

Conscientiousness, the third of the big five traits, reflects the common ground between responsibility, self-discipline, foresight, and sense of duty to self and others. Conscientious individuals weigh future costs and benefits relatively strongly against immediate ones. In decision-theory terms, their discounting rate is lower in slope and perhaps less hyperbolic in form: they show more patience and fewer preference-reversals. Less conscientious individuals favor immediate opportunities, with little regard for their future consequences. They are impulsive about pleasures and procrastinate about work. In mating, they are more promiscuous, more likely to be unfaithful, and more likely to have impulsive, unsafe sex under the influence of alcohol or drugs (Miller et al., 2004; Schmitt, 2004; Schmitt & Buss, 2000).

Thus, low conscientiousness tends to increase opportunistic short-term mating, but also increases the risk of sexually-transmitted diseases, violently jealous partners, and a bad sexual reputation. Very conscientious individuals may miss some sexual opportunities, but impose less stress on their relationships, social reputations, and immune systems. As with the other personality dimensions, the optimal weighting between present and future benefits will vary according to local factors such as social and ecological stability and life expectancy, so a spectrum of different phenotypes and genotypes can be maintained.

Agreeableness concerns empathy, trust, perspective-taking, gentleness, and consensus-seeking. It is closely related to conscientiousness both empirically (correlating about .35 in our data) and conceptually. However, the proximate mechanisms of the two dimensions seem different, with agreeableness based on empathy and the desire to please others (Nettle, in press), and conscientiousness based on responsibility and a sense of duty.

High agreeableness, like high conscientiousness, is associated with less infidelity, fewer sexual partners, and increased loyalty to mates (Schmitt, 2004; Schmitt & Buss, 2001; Table 1). Agreeable individuals tend to have harmonious relationships across all social domains, not just mating (Caprara, Barbaranelli, & Zimbardo, 1996; Heaven, 1996; Suls, Martin, & David, 1998). The costs of agreeableness may include missed sexual opportunities, as for conscientiousness, but also impaired status competition, because aggressiveness is the opposite of agreeableness. A study of male business executives found that agreeableness negatively predicted career success, with the nice guys finishing last in the competition for status and money (Boudreau, Boswell, & Judge, 2001). Given that males typically have more to gain from additional sexual partners and increased status, high agreeableness should be more costly for men than for women, and indeed, women consistently score around half a standard deviation higher than men on measures of agreeableness (Costa, Terraciano, & McCrae, 2001).

Openness to experience is the final big five trait to review. Openness concerns interest in culture, aesthetics, and diverse personal experiences. Typified by a fluid and metaphorical cognitive style, it predicts artistic creativity (McCrae & Costa, 1997). It is also associated with perceptual and cognitive distortions such as magical thinking and kinaesthetic hallucinations (Rawlings & Freeman, 1997), which are often found in successful artists and poets, as well as people with psychotic disorders (Nettle, 2006b). In a large sample of poets, artists, and control individuals, Nettle and Clegg (2006) found that these perceptual-cognitive distortions, which are typical of schizotypy, tend to predict creative output, which in turn predicts number of sexual partners.

Thus, openness to experience is a mixed blessing, associated with both psychosis (which is sexually unattractive) and creativity (which is sexually attractive). We interpret this finding in the light of Miller's theory that creativity acts as a mate-choice indicator (Miller, 2000, 2001, this volume), and that a schizotypal cognitive style may persist as a high-risk, high-gain mating strategy (Shaner, Miller, & Mintz, 2004). We suggest that overall genetic quality and phenotypic condition may tip the balance between openness increasing or decreasing reproductive success (Nettle & Clegg, 2006). Individuals in good condition can harness 'open' cognition to produce coherent, creative, interesting output (in language, art, music, or other domains), to attract mates and increase their social status and reproductive success. In individuals with poorer condition, the 'open' cognition becomes disorganized, incoherent, even psychotic—which repels mates and lowers reproductive success, among those afflicted with mental illnesses (see, e.g., Avila, Thaker, & Adami, 2001; Bassett, Bury, Hogkinson, & Honer, 1996). Thus, openness can have divergent reproductive outcomes, which, depending on one's overall genetic and phenotypic condition, can lead to high creativity, or to schizophrenia or depression (Nettle, 2006b; Nowakowska, Strong, Santosa, Wang, & Ketter, 2004). Individuals low in openness would have neither the mental-illness risks nor the reproductive rewards, so selection could maintain a diversity of types in the population at large (for a similar model, see Shaner, Miller, & Mintz, 2004, this volume).

In summary, each of the big five personality dimensions can be related to a trade-off in reproductive strategy. The trade-offs and associated dimensions and findings are summarised in Table 5.2. Precisely because these trade-offs offer no stable, universal optimum, selection can maintain a spectrum of heritable variation. In terms of mating intelligence, the existence of such a spectrum poses an interesting problem; what personality

TABLE 5.2.
Key Trade-Offs in Mating Strategies, the Associated Personality Dimensions, and Related Empirical Findings Concerning Their Benefits, Costs, and Mate Preferences. (For Elaboration and References, See Nettle, 2006a).

Trade-off	Associated Personality Dimension	Related Findings-Fitness Benefits	Related Findings-Fitness Costs	Related Findings-Preferences
Mate attraction versus retention	Extraversion	Increases social status, social network size, sexual partner numbers	Increases accident risk, infidelity, abandonment, exposure to step-parents,	High extraversion generally sought; more preferred by women and in short-term relationships
Threat detection	Neuroticism	Increases sensitivity to cues of infidelity or desertion	Reduces partner's satisfaction, increases stress, depression, and illness in self	Low neuroticism sought
Future discounting	Conscientiousness	Increases trust, fidelity, parental investment	Decreases opportunistic matings	High conscientiousness sought
Other's interests	Agreeableness	Increases in-pair cooperation, joint investment ability, sympathy, fidelity	Decreases opportunistic matings and status-seeking	High agreeableness sought
Creativity/ Signalling	Openness	Increases creativity & attractiveness	Increases vulnerability to mental illness	Successful signallers attractive, especially for short-term mating

phenotypes should one prefer given the range of possible mates given the wide range of possibilities likely to exist in the population. This issue is the subject of the next section.

MATE PREFERENCES

Many studies have shown that individuals have strong preferences about the personality traits that they desire in a partner (Buss et al., 1990; Buss

& Barnes, 1986; Goodwin, 1990; Kenrick, Groth, Trost, & Sadalla, 1993; Sprecher & Regan, 2002). Indeed, people generally rate dispositional qualities (e.g., intelligence, personality, moral virtues) in a possible mate as more important than situational variables (e.g., social status, wealth, family background), or physical attractiveness (Buss & Barnes, 1986). However, the preferred personality traits vary according to sex of partner sought and the type of relationship sought. Many of these preferences and preference differences may be interpretable within our trade-off framework.

The previous section highlighted a neglected issue in mating research: for many traits, it might be adaptive to seek different mental trait values in a partner than one has oneself. Key examples here are agreeableness and conscientiousness. Members of both sexes tend to seek cues of high agreeableness and conscientiousness in potential mates (Buss et al., 1990; Buss & Barnes, 1986; Goodwin, 1990). The desire for someone who is sympathetic and kind (high agreeableness) is one of the strongest and most consistent findings in mate-preference research. As discussed above, individuals with these qualities will weigh their partner's interests highly, and thus avoid opportunistic infidelity or desertion that would inflict distress on them. They will tend to invest in both their partner and the relationship for the long term. This constellation of behaviors is particularly valuable for women, who are seeking cues of post-reproductive investment, and who are particularly vulnerable to desertion. In Buss and Barnes' (1986) study, married women preferred cues of agreeableness and conscientiousness, such as honesty, dependability, kindness and understanding, even more strongly than married men did.

The optimal solution may be to seek a partner who is higher in agreeableness and conscientiousness than oneself. In fact, what drives levels of these dimensions up may be the chooser's insistence on such qualities in a potential mate. This would lead to strong selective pressure to be, or at least to appear as, high enough in the dimensions to attract partners, even at the cost of foregoing some mating opportunities of one's own. Several predictions follow from this idea. For example, early in courtship, men might be keen to behave in ways suggestive of agreeableness, such as caring for nephews or pets, and error management theory (Haselton & Nettle 2006) predicts that women in particular will be sceptical about such kindness-displays because of the high cost of being duped.

An asymmetry also exists for neuroticism. A highly neurotic partner will be insecurely attached, vigilant, potentially jealous, and will require powerful cues of commitment. It will be hard to keep such a partner happy—it may require very low neuroticism oneself. However, the optimal neuroticism level *for oneself* may be considerably higher, since one needs to be vigilant against infidelity and desertion. Once again, mate choice may favor low neuroticism, and conspicuous displays of emotional stability, but this may be counterbalanced by selection for sensitive threat-detection for one's own sake. Empirically, there is indeed a preference for low neuroticism (Botwin, Buss, & Shackelford, 1997; Buss & Barnes, 1986), and having a highly neurotic partner sharply reduces relationship satisfaction (Karney & Bradbury, 1997). Thus, we expect individuals in courtship-mode to hide their own neuroticism and exaggerate their emotional stability.

Most studies have found that people prefer high extraversion in a mate (Botwin et al., 1997; Buss & Barnes, 1986). Extraverted individuals will invest energy in gaining social status, building social networks, and thereby dominating local resources. Thus, extraverts are desirable mates. Given the heritability of this dimension, extraverts will also tend to produce socially popular, sexually desirable offspring. However, high extraversion strongly predicts infidelity, so choosing an extraverted mate exposes oneself to a higher risk of infidelity and abandonment. This leads to two possible predictions. One is that women might prefer higher extraversion in a male mate than men would prefer in a female, because female infidelity is costlier to a man (who may invest unwittingly in stepchildren) than to a woman. Moreover, the fitness payoffs for social status may have been higher for males than for females, giving women an additional incentive to favor extraversion more highly than men do. The second prediction is that extraversion should be more valued in short-term mating than in long-term mating. This is because possible future infidelity, the main reproductive cost of having an extraverted partner, does not matter so much in short-term relationships.

The evidence for the first prediction—that women favor extraverted mates more than men do—is mixed. In student samples, the extraversion preference seems equally strong in both sexes (Buss & Barnes, 1986; Goodwin, 1990). However, in samples of dating and newlywed couples (Botwin et al., 1997), and dating agency members (Goodwin, 1990), men prefer more introversion in their mates than women want in theirs, in line with our prediction. As for short-term versus long-term mating, Kenrick et al. (1993) found that highly extraverted men were more successful when seeking casual sex, but highly conscientious men were more successful when seeking a long-term relationship. Women always liked both extraversion and conscientiousness, but to different degrees in different types of relationships. Sprecher and Regan (2002) found that both sexes favor agreeableness and intelligence more highly when seeking a long-term mate, whereas the preference for an 'exciting personality' (a close approximation to extraversion) is slightly higher when seeking a short-term mate. These patterns fit our predictions: extraversion brings immediate social, material, and genetic rewards, so is valued more in short-term mating and in men, but may impose higher infidelity and desertion risks, so is valued less in long-term mating and in women.

Preference studies tend to report that high openness is attractive. However, openness is often conflated with intelligence in the descriptors used in these studies, and openness is objectively correlated with intelligence at the population level (Harris, 2004; Moutafi, Furnham, & Paltiel, 2005). Thus, it remains unclear whether people value openness apart from intelligence. Insofar as openness predicts creativity, Miller's (2001) fitness-indicator theory suggests that it should be sought, especially in short-term mates, since creativity displays mostly genetic quality rather than parental investment ability. Haselton and Miller (2006) found that women in the fertile phase of the menstrual cycle show stronger preferences for men who are described as creative, but here again, there is the confound problem in the descriptors: creativity could reflect either intelligence or openness.

Given the empirical relationship between openness and schizotypal cognition discussed earlier, we suggest that the preferences for openness should be modulated in a slightly complex way. Specifically, people should be strongly attracted to cues of openness combined with good phenotypic condition—signs that an open individual is genuinely creative rather than psychotic. Thus, successful poets, artists and innovators should be attractive. However, displaying 'disorganised' openness—weird beliefs, illogical thinking, bizarre behavior—would indicate low quality and should be sexually repulsive. Though no preference study so far has directly tested this idea, it is consistent with the results of the Haselton and Miller (2006) vignette study, the Nettle and Clegg (2006) study on the mating success of poets and artists, and the findings on the low reproductive success of psychiatric patients (Avila et al., 2001; Bassett et al., 1996).

CONCLUSION

We have argued that the big five personality traits are relevant to mating intelligence in two different ways. First, the big five reflect heritable individual differences in mating strategies to some extent (Schmitt & Buss, 2000)—variations that can be viewed as different 'set points' governing the allocation of effort between different components of mating effort, such as mate-acquisition versus mate-retention, costly signaling versus energy conservation, and so on. Thus, it would be accurate to say that the switching gear underlying mating-related decisions is calibrated differently in different people, with the five-factor framework useful in understanding these differences.

The second way that personality dimensions are relevant to mating intelligence is via mate-choice mechanisms. The existence of stable variation among humans creates strong selection on minds to detect cues of such variation and to use such information intelligently choosing one's mates (Buss, 1991). In the domain of mating intelligence, personality variation has created sets of preferences for qualities in potential mates that will reduce uncertainty both about the likely genetic quality of their off- spring, and about their likely parental investment after reproduction. Selection may also have created distinct abilities (a) to display certain types of personality cues, often somewhat deceptively, and (b) to see through the self-serving (and often deceptive) personality displays of others.

REFERENCES

Avila, M., Thaker, G., & Adami, H. (2001). Genetic epidemiology and schizophre- nia: A study of reproductive fitness. *Schizophrenia Research, 47*, 233–241.

Bailey, J. M., Kirk, K. M., Zhu, G., Dunne, M. P., & Martin, N. G. (2000). Do indi- vidual differences in sociosexuality represent genetic or environmentally- contingent strategies? Evidence from the Australian twin register. *Journal of Personality and Social Psychology, 78*, 537–545.

Bassett, A. S., Bury, A., Hogkinson, K. A., & Honer, W. G. (1996). Reproductive fit- ness in familial schizophrenia. *Schizophrenia Research, 21*, 151–160.

Botwin, M. D., Buss, D. M., & Shackelford, T. K. (1997). Personality and mate pref- erences: Five factors in mate selection and marital satisfaction. *Journal of Per- sonality, 65*, 107–136.

Bouchard, T. J., & Loehlin, J. C. (2001). Genes, evolution and personality. *Behavior Genetics, 31*, 243–273.

Boudreau, J. W., Boswell, W. R., & Judge, T. A. (2001). Effects of personality on exec- utive career success in the United States and Europe. *Journal of Vocational Behavior, 2001*, 53–58.

Buss, D. M. (1991). Evolutionary Personality Psychology. *Annual Review of Psy- chology, 42*, 459–491.

Buss, D. M. (2000). *The dangerous passion: Why jealousy is as necessary as love or sex.* New York: The Free Press.

Buss, D. M., Abbott, M., Angleitner, A., Asherian, A., Biaggio, A., & et al. (1990). International preferences in selecting mates. A study of 37 cultures. *Journal of Cross-Cultural Psychology, 21*, 5–47.

Buss, D. M., & Barnes, M. (1986). Preferences in human mate selection. *Journal of Personality and Social Psychology, 50*, 559–570.

Caprara, G. V., Barbaranelli, C., & Zimbardo, P. (1996). Understanding the com- plexity of human aggression: affective, cognitive and social dimensions of individual differences. *European Journal of Personality, 10*, 133–155.

Costa, R., & McCrae, R. (1992). Four ways five factors are basic. *Personality and Indi- vidual Differences, 135*, 653–665.

Costa, R., Terraciano, A., & McCrae, R. (2001). Gender differences in personality traits across cultures: Robust and surprising findings. *Journal of Personality and Social Psychology, 81*, 322–331.

Daly, M., & Wilson, M. (1985). Child abuse and other risks of not living with both parents. *Ethology and Sociobiology, 6*, 197–210.

Eysenck, H. J. (1976). *Sex and personality*. London: Open Books.

Geher, G, Miller, G. F., & Murphy, J. (this volume). Mating intelligence: Toward an evolutionarily informed construct. In G. Geher & G. F. Miller (Eds.), *Mating intelligence: Sex, relationships, and the mind's reproductive system*. Mahwah, NJ: Lawrence Erlbaum Associates.

Goodwin, R. (1990). Sex differences among partner preferences: Are the sexes really very similar. *Sex Roles, 23,* 501–513.

Harris, J. A. (2004). Measured intelligence, achievement, openness to experience, and creativity. *Personality and Individual Differences, 36,* 913–929.

Haselton, M. G., & Nettle, D. (2006). The paranoid optimist: An integrative evolutionary model of cognitive biases. *Personality and Social Psychology Review, 10,* 47–66.

Heaven, P. C. L., Fitzpatrick, J., Craig, F. L., Kelly, P., & Sebar, G. (2000). Five personality factors and sex: Preliminary findings. *Personality and Individual Differences, 28,* 1133–1141.

Heaven, P. L. (1996). Personality and self-reported delinquency: analysis of the 'big five' personality dimensions. *Personality and Individual Differences, 20,* 47–54.

Karney, B. R., & Bradbury, T. N. (1997). Neuroticism, marital interaction, and the trajectory of marital satisfaction. *Journal of Personality and Social Psychology, 72,* 1075–1092.

Kelly, E. L., & Conley, J. J. (1987). Personality and compatibility: A prospective analysis of marital stability and marital satisfaction. *Journal of Personality and Social Psychology, 52,* 27–40.

Kenrick, D. T., Groth, G. E., Trost, M. R., & Sadalla, E. K. (1993). Integrating evolutionary and social exchange perspectives on relationships: Effects of gender, self-appraisal, and involvement level on mate selection criteria. *Journal of Personality and Social Psychology, 64,* 951–969.

McCrae, R. R., & Costa, P. T. (1997). Conceptions and correlates of openness to experience. In S. Briggs (Ed.), *Handbook of Personality Psychology* (pp. 825–847). San Diego: Academic Press.

Miller, G. F. (2000). Mental traits as fitness indicators: Expanding evolutionary psychology's adaptationism. In P. Moller (Ed.), *Evolutionary Approaches to Human Reproductive Behavior.* New York.

Miller, G. F. (2001). Aesthetic fitness: How sexual selection shaped artistic virtuosity as a fitness indicator and aesthetic preference as mate choice criteria. *Bulletin of Psychology and the Arts, 2,* 20–25.

Miller, J. D., Lynam, D., Zimmerman, R. S., Logan, T. K., Leukefeld, C., & Clayton, R. (2004). The utility of the five factor model in understanding risky sexual behavior. *Personality and Individual Differences, 36,* 1611–1626.

Moutafi, J., Furnham, A., & Paltiel, L. (2005). Can personality factors predict intelligence? *Personality and Individual Differences, 38,* 1021–1033.

Neeleman, J., Sytema, S., & Wadsworth, M. (2002). Propensity to psychiatric and somatic ill-health: evidence from a birth cohort. *Psychological Medicine, 32,* 793–803.

Nesse, R. M. (2005). Natural selection and the regulation of defenses: A signal detection analysis of the smoke-detector problem. *Evolution and Human Behavior, 26,* 88–105.

Nettle, D. (2005). An evolutionary approach to the extraversion continuum. *Evolution and Human Behavior, 26*, 363–373.

Nettle, D. (2006a). The evolution of personality variation in humans and other animals. *American Psychologist, 61*, 622–631.

Nettle, D. (2006b). Schizotypy and mental health amongst poets, artists and mathematicians. *Journal of Research in Personality, 40*, 876–890.

Nettle, D., & Clegg, H. (2006). Schizotypy, creativity and mating success in humans. *Proceedings of the Royal Society of London Series B-Biological Sciences, 273*, 611–615.

Nettle, D. (in press). Empathising and systemising: What are they, and how far do they account for psychological sex differences? *British Journal of Psychology.*

Nowakowska, C., Strong, C. M., Santosa, S., Wang, P. W., & Ketter, T. A. (2004). Temperamental commonalities and differences in euthymic mood disorder patients, creative controls, and healthy controls. *Journal of Affective Disorders, 85*, 207–215.

Rawlings, D., & Freeman, J. L. (1997). Measuring paranoia/ suspiciousness. In G. Claridge (Ed.), *Schizotypy: Implications for illness and health* (pp. 38–60). Oxford: Oxford University Press.

Roff, D. A. (1992). *The evolution of life histories: Theory and analysis.* New York: Chapman and Hall.

Schmitt, D. P. (2004). The big five related to risky sexual behaviour across 10 world regions: Differential personality associations of sexual promiscuity and relationship infidelity. *European Journal of Personality, 18*, 301–319.

Schmitt, D. P., & Buss, D. M. (2000). Sexual dimensions of person description: Beyond or subsumed by the big five. *Journal of Research in Personality, 34*, 141–177.

Schmitt, D. P., & Buss, D. M. (2001). Human mate poaching: Tactics and temptations for infiltrating existing mateships. *Journal of Personality and Social Psychology, 80*, 894–917.

Shaner, A., Miller, G. F., & Mintz, J. (2004). Schizophrenia as one extreme of a sexually selected fitness indicator. *Schizophrenia Research, 70*, 101–109.

Sprecher, S., & Regan, P. C. (2002). Liking some things (in some people) more than others: Partner preferences in romantic relationships and friendships. *Journal of Social and Personal Relationships, 19*, 463–481.

Suls, J., Martin, R., & David, J. P. (1998). Person-environment fit and its limits: agreeableness, neuroticism, and emotional reactivity to interpersonal conflicts. *Personality and Social Psychology Bulletin, 24*, 88–98.

Zimmerer, E. J., & Kallman, K. D. (1989). Genetic basis for alternative reproductive tactics in the pygmy swordtail, *Xiphophorus nigrensis. Evolution, 43*, 1298–1307.

Chapter 6

Deception and Self-Deception as Strategies in Short- and Long-Term Mating

Maureen O'Sullivan
University of San Francisco

> . . . if you lived in a group, as humans have always done, persuading others of your own needs and interests would be fundamental to your well-being. Sometimes you had to use cunning. Clearly, you would be at your most convincing if you persuaded yourself first and did not even have to pretend to believe what you were saying. The kind of self-deluding individuals who tended to do this flourished, as did their genes. So it was we squabbled and scrapped, for our unique intelligence was always at the service of our special pleading and selective blindness to the weaknesses of our case. (McEwan, 1997, p. 112)

Mating intelligence, at first glance, seems oxymoronic, connoting, as it does, both heated passion and cool rationality. When in the throes of lust, most people would not describe their intensely focused, often frenzied activity as *intelligent*. Yet most modern-day theories of intelligence define this construct not as the ability to answer multiple-choice items on a paper-and-pencil test, but, rather, as the ability to adapt to a variety of environmental and social demands (Sternberg, 2000). Even within other species, the idea of a Machiavellian intelligence, in which social manipulation and cunning are used to achieve goals within one's group, has been extensively examined (Byrne & Whiten, 1988; Whiten & Byrne, 1997). In *The Mating Mind*, Geoffrey Miller (2000) explored the ways in which such social intelligence could be used to achieve reproductive success. And Buss's (2001) explication of the "cognitive biases and emotional wisdom" involved in sexual selection also pointed the way for understanding these stratagems as a kind of intelligence. The view of intelligence as the ability to adapt to environmental and social change raises the question of why such adaptation is necessary in mating. Isn't it all about biology? Well, no.

CHANGES SINCE 1960

The environment for both short and long-term mating in the United States has changed considerably in the last 45 years. Consider the age at first marriage. In 1960, the average age at first marriage was about 20 for women and 23 for men. In 2000, first marriages occurred on average at ages 25 and 27 for women and men, respectively (Popenoe & Whitehead, 2004). In 1960, divorce was far less common than it is today, when almost half of first marriages end. In 1960, fewer than five percent of people cohabited without marriage; nowadays, nearly 50 percent of people do so at some point in their lives (Bramlett & Mosher, 2002).

Clearly, the landscape of marriage and relationship-commitment has changed. Mating intelligence allows people to adapt to such changes. This chapter will explore the cognitive and emotional gyrations that women, and some men, go through in soliciting and maintaining romantic relationships. The uses of a wide variety of lies, deceptions, and self-deceptions which are often very like the "strategies" studied by evolutionary psychologists (e.g., Haselton and Buss, 2000) will be reviewed. This chapter will also consider the phenomenon of being "in love" that is an important aspect of mating in many cultures.

WHAT ARE LIES? WHAT IS SELF-DECEPTION?

Most definitions of lies require that a liar intentionally mislead another, without notification (Ekman, 2001). Obviously, for self-deception to "work," one aspect of the self cannot notify other parts of the self that misinformation is coming down the pike. Although the term "self-deception" is widely used, having been studied for many years (Adler, 1928), there is controversy about whether the concept makes any sense. Test constructors certainly assume it exists. Measures of social desirability (Marlowe & Crowne, 1960) are thought to assess both elements of impression management and self-deception. This view also underlies the development of the validity scales used in the MMPI, in which the L scale (to assess obvious lying) was differentiated from the K scale (to assess subtle deception and self-deception) (Lees-Haley, Iverson, Lange, Fox, & Allen, 2002). Also, clinicians who are comfortable with concepts such as repression and suppression have no difficulty believing that one part of the self can be unknown to another, through psychological processes both conscious and unconscious. On the other hand, writers such as Ekman (2001) suggest that the term 'self-deception' is poorly phrased and misleading, since to be deceived means to believe something that is not true. And how can one both know and not know at the same time?

Mele (2001) and Baumeister (1993) tackled this question and concluded that self-deception is one of the many self-serving tactics (Dunning, Heath & Suls, 2004) that most normal people use. In a related vein, Bargh, Gollwitzer, and Lee-Chai (2001) and Nisbett and Wilson (1977) have argued for the importance of what they term *non-conscious thought*, in which people are not consciously aware of what their behavior suggests they know. In experiments by these researchers, most of the demonstrations of non-conscious thought involve situations with little emotion. However, the model might also work as a generic template for knowing and not-knowing in situations that are more biologically important and psychologically charged, such as sex and romance.

Within the field of deception and romantic relationships, Kaplar and Gordon (2004) focused on differences in the perspectives of the lie-teller and the lie-receiver about the reasons for telling lies. Liars often describe their lies as "altruistic" (e.g., little white lies for their partner's peace of mind), whereas those lied to describe the lies more negatively. Discrepancies like this can be construed as a kind of self-deception by the liar. Kaplar and Gordon (2004) found many other substantial differences between perpetrators of lies and victims of lies regarding the nature of the lie, the liar, and the relationship. In all instances, the liar and the lie receiver disagreed about the liar's overall honesty, altruism, and other purported reasons for telling the lie, as well as the effect of the lie on the relationship. Those who were lied to also rated the lie as more serious than the lie teller did.

Only a few other studies have explicitly studied lies and deceptions in sexual relationships (e.g., Cole, 2001; Metts, 1989; Rowatt, Cunningham, & Druen, 1998; Miller, Mongeau, & Sleight, 1986; Peterson, 1996). Many researchers, however, discuss deceptive relationship behavior using less morally evaluative terms such as "bias," "disguises," "strategies," "inaccuracy" (Swann & Gill, 1997) and "implicit egotism" (Pelham, Carvallo & Jones, 2005). All these labels imply some degree of deception in behavior. So, regardless of whether they are called princes, toads, or frogs, this chapter presumes that all such behaviors can be considered lies, deceptions, or self-deceptions, and will review them as such.

ROMANTIC LOVE—HERE, THERE . . .
BUT EVERYWHERE?

Many domain-specific cognitive capacities have evolved to cope with particular adaptive problems—some environmental, some social, and some sexual (Barkow, Cosmides, & Tooby, 1992). The literature on romantic love analyzes some of these sexual adaptations from a subjective rather than a functional perspective, distinguishing romantic from maternal or fraternal love by the centrality of physical passion.

Although humans have always mated, the current cultural importance of the "in love" experience for long-term mating is notable. Although romantic love has existed throughout history and around the world (Jankowiak, 1995), its value was more obvious to those in the upper classes who had the leisure and money to pursue it. In many cultures, romantic love was seen as disruptive and transgressive, rather than as promoting successful marriage. For example, historians (Duby, 1988) often claim that in the European Middle Ages, only nobility actively sought romantic love, and such love was not expected with one's spouse, who was usually married for political and economic reasons. Romantic love was pursued with an unavailable love object—the king's wife, the husband's best friend. Solomon (1988) has argued that romantic love is almost entirely a cognitive construct, in that one thinks about the beloved constantly, and views him or her as unique, special, and qualitatively distinct—the love object is 'beyond comparison.' The state of being "in love" is usually triggered by at least some signs of being loved in return, so this also leads one to think of oneself as unique and special (Sprecher & Metts, 1999). Although granting that physical attraction is a core aspect of romantic love (even if not acted upon), Solomon argues that romantic love is more prevalent now than in earlier centuries because of several cultural changes. People now have more leisure time, sense of self, privacy, and economic freedom (Duby, 1988).

Even in the current era, there are marked cultural differences in expectations of the experience of being "in love." Although only 11 percent of American women and 19 percent of Japanese women said they would marry someone suitable with whom they were not in love, 41 percent of Russian women said they would (Sprecher, Aron, Hatfield, Cortese, Potapova, & Levitsky, 1994). In cultures with arranged marriages, the expected percentages of willingness to marry without love may be even higher.

WHAT IS ROMANTIC LOVE? COULD ONE FALL IN LOVE WITHOUT KNOWING WHAT IT WAS?

Although some researchers suggest that romantic love is a biologically based emotion (Gonzaga, Keltner, Londahl, & Sprull, 2001), it has a longer duration than the standard "basic emotions" such as anger, fear, and disgust. To be useful in long-term relationships such as parenting and marriage, romantic and maternal love need more staying power. Are they then really emotions? Or is it less confusing if they are distinguished from basic emotions, and acknowledged as more enduring types of "social" emotions? A defining aspect of romantic love is sexual attraction, whether acted on or not. In my view, lust is a motivation, like hunger and thirst, rather than an emotion like anger. One can have emotions about hunger and one can have emotions about lust, but that does not make lust or hunger an emotion, no matter how aroused one is by either. Like hunger, lust is a universal, a biological given, and is the *sine qua non* of romantic love. It need not be acted on. Celibates can be romantically in love, but love is not romantic if there is no lust. Another universal aspect of romantic love is likely to be negative affect—fear of loss, disappointment, and jealousy (Buss, 2000; Harris, 2003; O'Sullivan, 1996). The positive emotions of those "in love" are likely to be more culturally variable (O'Sullivan, 1999, 2001).

Solomon (1988) outlines, in impressive detail, the many factors involved in the cognitive construction of romantic love, but he addresses self-deception only obliquely. For most of history and in many parts of the world, even today, long-term mating occurs within a social network that provides economic, social, and psychological support for the couple. In more individualistic cultures, like the United States, social institutions such as marriage, which are partly biological and partly socially co structed, need more props to endure. The juggernaut of romantic love as the basis for long-term relationships is one such support. One needs the support of a social context that values romantic love within stable relationships, rather than viewing it as purely transgressive, inimical to traditional values, opposed to family stability, or separated from parental responsibilities. The development of this love-within-marriage idea exceeds the limits of this chapter, however. For our purposes, the important points are that, given a foundation of physical attraction: (1) romantic love requires many intricate cognitive and cultural elaborations, (2) many of these elaborations involve mismatches between beliefs and realities, i.e., adaptive self-deceptions.

For example, Murray and her colleagues (Murray, Holmes, Bellavia, Griffin, & Dolderman, 2002) demonstrated that people in enduring relationships saw their partners as more similar to themselves than they actually were. They termed this mismatch "egocentrism." Another name for it might be self-deception. Believing that one's partner is a soul mate allows one to feel understood, which leads to satisfaction in the relationship, which leads to its continuation.

"IN LOVE" = "FALSE BELIEFS"

In the parlance of everyday life, metaphors about the experience of being in love include: "losing your head" over someone, being "head over heels in love," "flying to the moon," "being nuts" about someone, being obsessed, and not being able to think about anything else. These metaphors communicate that clear analytical thinking is not a salient aspect of "falling in love" (Lakoff, 1987). They also suggest that people who are "in love" are not responsible for what they do. They are in the grip of an overwhelming emotional or hormonal or genetic storm. Such feelings are especially useful when trying to initiate a physically and emotionally intimate relationship with a stranger. A flood of hormones and a suspension of disbelief are both required to overcome the fearful apprehension and social distance that usually marks our interactions with unknown others.

Long-term relationships typically require agreement between the partners about their respective roles. Roles are complex, socially constructed, and socially reinforced behavior patterns; modern sociology is largely the study of social roles. For example, professional roles are highly ritualized in modern societies: lawyers do not lose their tempers and hit each other in court, doctors do not show disgust at bodily fluids and physical flaws, and hairdressers do not act bored with their customers' love lives. Such social roles involve sophisticated types of other-deception and self-deception, but the role is typically so over-learned through years of practice that such deception no longer requires conscious monitoring. Each profession's distinctive patterns of deception change gradually from learned tactics to internalized habits, so they start to feel natural after a while.

Likewise, the mastery of sexual roles within relationships is a crucial aspect of mating intelligence, and a major locus of self-deception. Maintaining the state of being "in love" may take considerable self-monitoring of emotions, selective attention to the lover's positive aspects and willful blindness to their negative one. Cultivating habits of empathy and cross-sex mind-reading, as well as knowing the stages that relationships can go through, are all aspects of mating intelligence.

DOMESTIC VIOLENCE AND SELF-DECEPTION

A pathological example of such sexual and romantic role expectations may be seen in recurring cases of domestic violence and marital infidelity. In a single year, serious violence occurred in 5 to 15 percent of married couples, and minor physical violence in 15 to 35 percent of them (Strauss, 1997). Higher incidences were reported among co-habiting, unmarried couples. And, most surprising, the initiator of the violence was as likely to be a woman as a man (Archer, 2000). When a man (or a woman) injures his or her partner in the United States, the ordinary understanding of this behavior is that the injurer is angry with the victim, and, at least at the moment of inflicting the injury, wishes to do harm. Only rarely is a single incident of physical aggression the stimulus for a relationship or marriage dissolution. When questioned about why they returned to the potentially harmful relationship, the victims, while often citing economic dependency and religious or cultural beliefs about commitment, will actually re-frame the abuse as evidence of the abuser's passionate love for them, or they will reinterpret events to blame themselves for provoking the injury (Shackelford, Goetz, Buss, Euler, & Hoier, 2005). This cognitive restructuring of the abusive relationship reflects an extreme case of making a silk purse out of a sow's ear.

Even in ordinary romantic relationships, something similar often occurs. To leave our family of origin, and the comfort of our role as someone's daughter or son, most of us must be propelled in some way. In cultures with arranged marriages, parents determine one's mate, and individual mate choice is not expected. If one is responsible for one's own choice (Solomon, 1988), compelling reasons must be sought to make the initial commitment and to continue to maintain it. If others make a choice for us, or it seems as though no choice is involved, then questions of the correctness of such a choice are irrelevant. In reassuring ourselves about the rightness of our romantic and marital choices, a little flawed assessment or self-deception may be psychologically helpful. When the commitment fails, or other options are sought, deception is almost always involved in the process. Although this self-deception is not as extreme as that seen in situations where abused partners re-frame their violent relationships, it is self-deception nonetheless.

UNFAITHFULNESS AND FOOLISHNESS

Estimates of infidelity in the United States range from 20 to 60 percent, even among married women (Glass & Wright, 1992). Unless the couple is in an "open" relationship, every infidelity involves lying, by omission if not commission. Most people are not very good at telling when others are lying (Malone & DePaulo, 2001) even if they are friends or lovers (Cole, 2001). Ekman (2001) has argued that one of the many reasons that people are poor lie detectors is that they unconsciously collude with the liar. Most people want to believe that others are telling them the truth. (Hence the willful gullibility of most consumers and voters.) In matters as grave as marital infidelity, many are highly motivated not to know the truth.

Another reason for "not knowing" was suggested by Geoffrey Miller (personal communication, January 30, 2006): "There may be an adaptive binary switch from total trust to total mistrust, with no fitness payoff for being in an in-between-state of semi-trust." Thus, a wife might suddenly reach a "tipping point" where she switches from trust to realization of a husband's infidelity. Such an on-off switch may be adaptive because what does one do if one suspects infidelity? Miller argued "In many situations, a prime function of mating intelligence may be to navigate these tipping points where there are fitness payoffs for being decisive one way or the other (e.g., . . . accuse them of infidelity or not; have an affair or not), and none for being indecisive."

Another aspect of deception in mating intelligence is the subtlety that is needed in negotiating some of these more Byzantine mating dances. Schmitt and Shackelford (2003) list twenty different tactics that can be used in "mate poaching" (acquiring a mate who is already in a relationship with someone else). Most of these are identical to non-poaching mating strategies, such as dressing attractively, displaying wealth, and showing interest in sex. However, the top ten "nifty" methods of mate poaching entail distinctive methods of deception to disguise the poaching both from the potential mate's partner and one's wider social network. Although called "disguises," such methods obviously depend upon lies.

Certainly, the adulterer lies in hiding his or her adultery, but it seems likely that the betrayed person (unconsciously) colludes with the adulterer in not reading the many clues that are later recalled and described as being overlooked. The partner who does not notice the available clues is probably deceiving himself at some level. When infidelity is uncovered, the wronged spouse, in retrospect, recalls many events that were odd, or suspicious, but dismissed at the time (Buss, 2000). This type of self-deception can sometimes allow an otherwise serviceable relationship to continue. Lies and self-deceptions, however, are not only involved in ending relationships, but also in starting them.

IMPRESSION MANAGEMENT IN SHORT-TERM MATING: THE CASE OF PHYSICAL ATTRACTIVENESS

Many evolutionary psychologists have studied people's strategies in a short-term mating (Buss, 1998). Many of these efforts involve enhancing physical appearance so that one seems maximally healthy—covering pimples, applying deodorant, decreasing dandruff and increasing hair volume and shine (Gangestad, 1993). Many cosmetic and surgical enhancements mimic the physiological changes that occur in sexual arousal. Lipstick and rouge simulate the heightened blood-flow to lips and cheeks that occurs in sexual arousal (Masters & Johnson, 1970); brassieres make breasts appear firmer, larger, more symmetrical and perky, mimicking the appearance of breasts at the age of peak fertility and during sexual arousal. High heels force the calf muscles into a flexion that simulates that of coitus. These are obvious deceptions practiced by women, with little attempt to conceal the artifice. With cosmetic changes such as Botox injections and face lifts, however, women often try to hide the fact that any "work" has been done. Men are also using more facials, cosmetics, hair styling, and cosmetic surgery. So, the efforts to advertise oneself as attractive, healthy and young are obvious in both sexes, with women, valued more highly for their physical appearance and youth, being more obviously motivated by such concerns.

IMPRESSION MANAGEMENT IN SHORT-TERM MATING: THE CASE OF EMOTIONAL CONTROL

Impression management requires not only the alteration of appearance, but also the management of one's emotions. Although most people are not able to completely control their emotional expressions, courtship, like courtesy, requires that a good faith effort be made. Lying about one's feelings is an important kind of deception, particularly in the early stages of courtship. Later on, the question of whether to say "I love you" when you may not be totally sure that you do, will arise. Often people feel pressured into declaiming an emotion, like love, that they are not sure they feel, because the other person has said it to them. Solomon (1988) describes being the first to say "I love you" as an aggressive act, because it demands a response. In addition to this kind of "in love" lie, people lie about other emotions: denying anger, exaggerating pleasure, squelching fear or sadness, and covering contempt, in trying to demonstrate what a charming, interesting mate they would be. Specifically, such courtship courtesy often exaggerates one's personality traits of agreeableness, extraversion, conscientiousness, and emotional stability. These traits often regress to one's heritable mean after marriage. That is, lovers often become more irritable, shy, slovenly, and neurotic after the relationship is secure. Such emotional management may not entirely be false advertising, however. Harker and Keltner (2001) found that the more intense the expression of positive affect in women's college graduation photos, the more successful their lives, including their marital state, twenty years later. Men's positive affectivity was not as predictive.

Another aspect of emotional regulation concerns the effort needed to handle the ubiquitous negative emotions (e.g., sexual frustration, disappointment, jealousy) occasioned in dating and mating (Ellis & Malamuth, 2000). Not every desired partner will accept one's overtures; most pairings will fail. Dating and mating, therefore, require the ability to overcome the negative feelings following actual rejection and the fear of future potential rejections (Ekman, 2003). Although sexual pleasure and procreative drive are a great help in motivating courtship behavior that is emotionally draining, the ability to manage emotions is another key part of mating intelligence. Haselton and her colleagues (Haselton, Buss, Oubaid, & Angleitner, 2005) have examined the role of emotion in responding to deception in short and long-term mating, but emotion and emotion-management can serve other roles in mating as well as in other aspects of life (Ekman, 2003).

FLIRTING

Another form of short-term mating behavior that involves a particular kind of deception is flirting. When one person flirts with another, there is a playful suggestion of potential sexual activity. Sometimes the flirting is foreplay, and the flirter is signaling his or her availability for sex (Abbey & Melby, 1986). Sometimes, however, the flirting is a game, a way to test one's desirability with no intention of actually engaging in intercourse. Phillips (1994, p. xii) wrote "Flirtation keeps things in play, and by doing so lets us get to know [potential lovers] in different ways. It allows us the fascination of what is unconvincing." In this passage, Phillips is turning the table, perhaps even flirting with the reader, suggesting that knowing something is false can be fascinating, whereas the unvarnished truth may be merely reassuring. Flirting is an enjoyable game for many, one which can gladden the hearts of both players. Sometimes, however, only one of the flirters is playing. In such cases, the deception is a source of anger, frustration, and humiliation for the flirter who is serious (Henningsen, 2004).

Although many elements of flirting behavior (light touch, close body position, displaying the body, eye gaze, open mouth (Simpson, Gangestad, & Biek, 1993)—mimic the biologically based behaviors that occur in actual foreplay (Grammer, 1991)—other elements of flirting are historically changeable, affected by, for instance, the fashions of contemporaneous celebrities. In the 1930s and 40s, smooth-shining hair (a sign of health) was sexually alluring; in the 1990s, tousled, unkempt hair (suggesting having just risen from bed) was the sign of a sexually interested woman. In the movies of the 30s and 40s, blowing cigarette smoke into the face of one's date was a clear statement of desire for greater intimacy. To do so in 2006 is a clear statement that one wishes to share one's increased chances of lung cancer. These cultural shifts suggest that, while most flirting behaviors are probably precursors of the "natural" activities that occur in sexual congress, our courtship tactics can be affected by cultural context. Styles or fashions in flirting can be observed. In order to be "in tune" with such changes, courtiers and courtesans must have social-emotional intelligence (or mating intelligence when used in the service of relationships).

Flirting fashions vary not only across time, but also across people. What might be considered lewd and lascivious by one potential mate could be viewed as loveable spontaneity by another. Adjusting one's flirting behavior for maximum effectiveness given the particular intended target is an important form of mating intelligence. In the movie *Black Widow*, Theresa Russell portrays a woman who totally changes her appearance, manner, personality and sexual preferences to woo a series of wealthy men who vary in age, interests and sexual appetites. Such mating intelligence may not be fully conscious, but it is also not fully spontaneous.

In her observational study of women's flirting in different situations, Moore (1985) observed that the level of flirting varied according to the context and that those women who flirted most attracted the most male attention. Miller (1997) has argued for the utility of unpredictability as a determinant of success in social situations among animals. By definition, variability should co-occur with unpredictability, so the flirting variability across situations, noted by Moore, as well as the success of flirting in attracting potential mates, both suggest that flirting fits the adaptive requirements of intelligent behavior.

But the deceptiveness of flirting is highly variable. For most people, flirting is a game with limited stakes, wherein they can find out about each other and determine whether they both wish to escalate the intimacy. Flirting is only rarely a case of lying, since a lie requires that its target not be notified of the intention to mislead (Ekman, 2001). In flirting, as in "bullshit" (Frankfurt, 2005), the stereotypy of the behavior provides notification that play, pretend, less-than-totally-honest behavior is occurring. As with bullshit, the communication is somewhat exaggerated. As with bullshit, at least two players are needed. One can flirt with danger, but flirting with one's self is not a sign of advanced mating intelligence.

FAKING ORGASM

Another form of mating-relevant deception is faking orgasm. Wiederman (1997) reported that more than half of the college women in his sample said they faked orgasm during intercourse. Although it is more difficult for men to do so, Levin (2004) suggests that the difficulty in detecting true orgasm leaves the door open for a wide variety of vocal, facial, and bodily responses that could be interpreted by both males and females as orgasm. The motivations for faking orgasm are as various as for any kind of lie—to please one's partner, to end the lovemaking, to be seen as a "hot" sexual partner, to do one's duty. A more subtle form of deception is involved in communicating how the orgasm is experienced. Just as there are "display rules" (Ekman & Friesen, 1969) for biologically based emotions, in which the expression of the emotion is exaggerated, minimized, disguised or suppressed differently in different cultures, so, too, partners can use different "display rules" to indicate the degree of their pleasure or displeasure with the orgasm they have (or have not) experienced.

When Meg Ryan in the movie, *When Harry Met Sally*, feigns a loud and boisterous orgasm in a restaurant, to prove to Billy Crystal how easy it is to do so, an older women a few tables away tells the waiter she wants to "have what she's having." The humor of this scene may come from her ordering an orgasm as though it were on the menu. But one aspect of the humor is the woman's age. Suppose the woman was not Rob Reiner's mother, but his sister. Would the scene be as funny? Humor allows us to deal with untoward aspects of life. For some people, the idea that an older woman wants a boisterous sex life is unexpected, and perhaps uncomfortable. Those emotions also contribute to the scene's humor. Another construction, coming at the situation from a totally different perspective, might be that in her generation such loud exuberance was reserved for food, not lovemaking. Recall that some Victorians believed that sex was for procreation not pleasure ("Lie back and think of England.") So the older woman, dressed in her dowdy coat and hat, may assume that Meg Ryan has ordered a particularly delectable entrée and simply wants the same.

ASKING FOR SEX

In his wonderfully nuanced book titled *Faking It*, William Miller (2003) discusses all kinds of deceptions (except, surprisingly, faking orgasm!). One of the deceptions he describes is the appropriate manner of soliciting sex. He points out that opening a conversation with an explicit, verbally stated request for sex is unlikely to be successful in educated or middle-class circles, but might be successful in other social contexts or classes. Learning how to ask for what one wants (as opposed to the more indirect flirting discussed above) clearly represents learned behavior. People of higher intelligence, by definition, learn better—more quickly, more deeply, more broadly. Each social environment has different norms for obtaining desired goals. Those with mating intelligence will learn how to ask and whom to ask to obtain the mating payoffs they want and need.

FRIENDS, NOT LOVERS

Another example of flawed self-assessment and reality-checking occurs in distinguishing sexual and friendship relationships. The question of cross-sex friendships has been studied from a variety of views (Werking, 1997). Most researchers find that although there are some truly platonic relationships, many cross-sex friendships involve some hidden sexual motives for one or both partners (Bleske-Rechek, & Buss, 2001). Self-deception is often involved in cross-sex friendships, particularly on the part of women, who frequently deny the sexuality underlying such relationships.

Among a group of 60 college students, 73 percent of women but only 47 percent of men said they believed that men and women could be "just friends" ($\chi^2(1) = 3.80$, $p = .05$; O'Sullivan, in preparation). This empirical discrepancy could be interpreted in different ways. Perhaps women are generally more optimistic and less realistic than men. However, studies of flawed self-assessment in non-mating domains (Dunning et al., 2004) do not reveal significant sex differences; only in questions about mating relationships does this sex difference emerge. The hypothesis that women show more flawed self-assessment in romantic reasoning than in other areas is somewhat supported by other data from the same study. When asked to list the positive and negative reasons for cross-sex friendships, (e.g., keep as a friend vs. be jealous when he dates someone else) although women agreed that platonic cross-sex friendships were possible by a two-to-one margin, women listed more negative reasons (mean = 1.81) than positive ones (mean = 1.69). Men on the other hand, who tended to think platonic cross-sex friendships were unlikely, listed more negative (1.63) than positive reasons (1.44). (A MANOVA of these findings was not significant, showing only a trend. But since this is a new line of research, the trend is suggestive and is being investigated in ongoing research.)

THE DARK SIDE OF SELF-DECEPTION: UNREQUITED LOVE

Self-deception can also be seen in cases of unrequited love, in which the rejected lover refuses to believe reality and, instead, continues to love someone who never loved them, or who no longer loves them. Baumeister and Wotman (1992) suggest that unrequited love often occurs when a more attractive partner rejects a less attractive would-be lover. The rejecter often claims no knowledge of a relationship—the unattractive would-be lover is below their mating radar. In such cases, self-deception on the part of the person rejected is clear. A version of this scenario occurs when a platonic relationship seems to be moving towards romance in the eyes of one person, but not in the eyes of the other. Self-deception in this case is more subtle, but extricating oneself without losing the friendship requires a very high level of mating intelligence. In any event, this is a use of self-deception that does not serve reproductive needs, at least in the short term, since it removes the unrequited lover from the plausible mating pool since time spent wooing an unwilling lover might be more economically spent courting an available one. But these psychological stratagems may serve as ego-enhancers to help maintain self-esteem and to dissipate the effects of a broken heart into gradual acceptance. Much like the emotional regulation described above, unrequited love may be a kind of self-deception that protects self-esteem in the short term, to allow re-entry into the mating game at a later time.

ROMANTIC LIES AND SELF-DECEPTION: A STUDYOF SEX-DIFFERENTIATED STRATEGIES REGARDING MATING-RELEVANT LIES

The study described in this section addresses the nature of lies to self and lies to potential partners in human mating. Previous research has not found sex differences in self-reported honesty (Paunomen, personal communication, 2003) or in honesty based on diary reports (DePaulo & Kashy, 1998). Given the different reproductive demands for men and women, however, it seem unlikely that these different sexual needs would not be reflected in different social strategies for initiating and maintaining mating relationships. Haselton and her colleagues (2005) examined sex differences in the emotional responses to lies of mating partners. In their Error Management Theory, Haselton and Buss (2000) predicted and found that men tended to overestimate sexual interest on the part of women, and that women tended to underestimate men's commitment. So clearly, there are differences in the mating strategies of men and women. Would those strategies also play out in the kinds of lies they told, or admitted telling?

Following Haselton and Buss, I did not think that one sex lied more than the other, but that they lied about different things. I predicted that men would be more likely to lie about resources and commitment, and that women would be more likely to lie about their fidelity and to lie in female-specific ways that would maintain the relationship.Fourteen kinds of lies were sampled (see Table 6.1.; further details are available from O'Sullivan, in preparation).

I predicted that men would be more likely to tell seven of the lies (listed in the top half of the table in bold print) and women would be more likely to tell the other seven (the bottom half of the table in italics). A sample of 95 college students (79 women and 16 men) was asked "Who is more likely to tell each kind of lie—men or women?" Students rated each statement on a scale from 1 to 8. For half the items, 1 was labeled "women" and 8 was labeled "men"; for the other half, 1 was labeled "men" and 8 was labeled "women." The two scales were alternated, every other item, but the scale values were standardized for Table 6.1. so that values between 1 and 4 reflect women being rated as more likely to tell that lie; values between 5 and 8 suggest that men were rated as more likely to tell that lie.

TABLE 6.1.
Average Ratings of the Likelihood of Women and Men Telling Lies

Statement	Mean	S.D.	Median	N	Predicted
lying about how much money they make or have	6.36	1.24	7	94	**
lying about having a sexually transmitted disease	5.97	1.44	6	94	**
lying about future plans, such as marriage	5.85	1.65	6	93	**
saying they are in love, when they are not	5.69	1.93	6	93	**
lying about the time they spend with their friends	5.48	1.69	6	92	**
lying about things in their past that their partner would not approve of	5.00	2.06	5.5	94	**
lying about flirting with or being interested in other people	4.47	1.98	4	89	X
lying about birth control	2.96	1.88	2.5	94	**
lying about how impressed they are by their partner's sexual anatomy or performance	3.00	1.70	3	94	**
exaggerating how attractive or intelligent they think their romantic partner is	4.33	2.20	4	95	**
lying about how impressed they are by their partner's body or figure	4.61	1.96	5	95	0
lying about their virginity	4.65	2,39	5	95	0
telling a lie to spare their romantic partner's feelings	4.81	2.03	5	95	0
telling a lie to avoid having their partner get angry with them	5.35	1.85	5	91	X

Men were predicted to be more likely to tell the first seven lies. Women were predicted to be more likely to tell the last seven lies (in italics).
Rating scale: 1= women most likely to tell this lie; 8 = men most likely to tell this lie; 4 = women slightly more likely to tell this lie; 5 = men slightly more likely to tell this lie.
Predicted column: ** = rating in predicted direction; 0 = no difference; X = rating in opposite direction, i.e., women predicted more likely, but men rated more likely to tell this lie.

As Table 6.1. indicates, men were rated as more likely to tell six of the seven lies they were predicted to tell (such as lying about how much money they have). The one exception was lying about flirting with or being interested in other people, where the median rating was 4, indicating that the subjects thought women were slightly more likely to tell this kind of lie. Women were rated as more likely to tell only three of the seven lies they were predicted to be more likely to tell (such as, *lying about how impressed they are by their partner's sexual anatomy or performance*). The subjects rated women and men as equally likely to lie about their virginity, to lie to spare their partner's feelings, and to lie about how impressed they were about their partner's body or figure. Men, not women, were rated as more likely to lie in order to avoid their partner's anger. These data present a picture of what young people think stereotypical men and women are likely to lie about. Of the 14 lies sampled, the college students agreed that men are more likely to tell eight of them. When asked to rate how likely they themselves are to tell such lies in their own romantic relationships, other students suggested a different view. Undergraduates ($N = 630$) in two different colleges were asked to rate, on a five-point scale, how likely they themselves were to tell each of the 14 lies described above. Table 6.2. gives the means and standard deviations of men's and women's ratings of the likelihood that they themselves would tell each of these lies and the corresponding t tests of the differences between the means.

As Table 6.2. shows, women rated themselves as significantly less likely to tell nine of these lies than men did. But even on the lies where the difference was not significant, the men's average rating was numerically higher than the women's. If one assigns a plus to each time the men's means are higher, and a minus when the women's means are lower, this run of 28 is highly significant ($Z = -4.815, p < .01$).

So, even though women and men agree that women are more likely to lie about birth control, flirting, and how impressed they are with their partner's sexual anatomy or performance, women report that they themselves are less likely to tell these kinds of lies than men do. In terms of deception, both men and women report lying about many aspects of romantic relationships. Some of these lies, such as lying about virginity and disease are more relevant in the early stages of mating. Others, such as avoiding anger, saying they are in love, plans about marriage, etc. are more relevant to maintaining longer-term relationships. So, out-right deception, in which one knows one is lying, is well documented in these data.

Less well established is the seeming self-deception of women versus men. Women see other women as lying about some aspects of relationships more than men do, but they rate their own likelihood of lying as less than that of men for all of the lies. As McEwan's quote at the start of this chapter suggests, believing your own lies is a powerful stratagem, since "leakage" of contrary emotion (Ekman & Friesen, 1969) is less likely.

TABLE 6.2.
Average Male and Female Ratings of "How Likely Are You to Tell This Lie?"

Statement	Male		Female		t	df	p
	Mean	SD	Mean	SD			
lying about how much money they make or have	2.37	(1.24)	1.95	(1.08)	4.556	632	.000
lying about having a sexually transmitted disease	1.41	(1.050)	1.29	(0.86)	1.454	632	ns
lying about future plans, such as marriage	2.38	(1.26)	2.00	(1.40)	4.121	630	.000
saying they are in love, when they are not	2.45	(1.42)	1.96	(1.25)	4.586	633	.000
lying about the time they spend with their friends	2.73	(1.43)	2.35	(1.32)	3.439	632	.001
lying about things in their past that their partner would not approve of	3.30	(1.41)	3.02	(1.38)	2.559	632	.011
lying about flirting with or being interested in other people	3.34	(1.40)	3.01	(1.33)	2.986	632	.003
lying about birth control	1.68	(1.17)	1.39	(0.87)	3.551	633	.000
lying about how impressed they are by their partner's sexual anatomy or performance	2.91	(1.27)	2.72	(1.19)	1.949	631	.052
exaggerating how attractive or intelligent they think their romantic partner is	3.15	(1.22)	3.04	(1.21)	1.144	630	ns
lying about how impressed they are by their partner's body or figure	2.68	(1.35)	2.37	(1.24)	2.986	631	.003
lying about their virginity	1.94	(1.37)	1.53	(1.06)	4.586	631	.000
telling a lie to spare their romantic partner's feelings	3.75	(1.11)	3.57	(1.23)	1.808	630	.000
telling a lie to avoid having their partner get angry with them	3.78	(1.34)	3.60	(1.35)	1.673	631	ns

Rating scale: 1 = not at all likely; 5 = extremely likely

Believing what you say means you will not fear being detected, or feel guilty about lying, since you are unaware that you are doing so (Ekman, 2001).

Gagne and Lydon (2004) have argued that the conflict between bias (self-deception in most instances) and accuracy in close relationships can be understood by clarifying when one needs to be accurate and when one can afford to have flawed perceptions of one's self and others. They argue that at key decision points in the relationship (e.g., whether to have sex, whether to get married), in what they term "epistemic-related relationship judgments," one needs accuracy, but in other aspects of the relationship where accuracy is less crucial and self-esteem issues are at stake, a little bias may serve a useful function.

"MEN TELL THE MOST LIES. WOMEN TELL THE BIGGEST LIES"

Chris Rock's (1999) joke fits these data quite well. Men not only thought that men would tell more of the lies surveyed than women would (8 out of 14), they also were significantly more likely to admit telling the lies themselves. Women, on the other hand, although thinking other women told some of these lies more than men, claimed that they themselves would tell fewer of them than men do. So, women tell the biggest lies because they lie to themselves.

Although deception and self-deception characterize many aspects of short and long-term mating for both men and women, there seems to be more evidence for self-deception as a mating strategy among women. Other evidence that speaks to women's greater malleability in the mating game is addressed by Baumeister and his colleagues (Baumeister, 2000; Baumeister, Catanese, & Vohs, 2001). They distinguish between the relatively constant sex drive in men, and the highly volatile, culturally malleable nature of erotic plasticity in women. They present many sources of data supporting a consistent level of sexual interest and performance in men throughout life. (Although there is a decrement with age, a highly sexed 18-year old male is likely to be a highly sexed 65-year old, relative to other same-aged males.) Women, on the other hand, show marked changes in their preferred sexual outlets throughout life: leaving or entering a homosexual lifestyle, for example, at much higher rates than men; having long periods of celibacy alternating with periods of intense sexual activity. Also, female immigrants show a much greater shift towards the sexual mores of their adopted countries than male immigrants, and their sexuality is more affected by education than men's is (Peplau, 2003). Using the term "self-deception" to describe such behavioral malleability may be over-reaching, but certainly some kind of cognitive work is necessary to make such major behavioral shifts.

Other evidence can be found in research on "sexual self-schemas" (people's cognitive representations of themselves as sexual beings). Andersen, Cyranowski, and Espindle (1999) report that a unidimensional scale is sufficient to describe most men's cognitive generalizations about their sexual selves. Men tend to give consistently positive, consistently negative or consistently neutral descriptions of their sexuality. Women, however, show several different patterns. Some women are consistently positive or negative, as men are, but other women are both strongly positive and strongly negative about aspects of their sexuality. So while some women may feel both 'hot' and proud of it, others feel 'hot' and guilty. A single continuum is inadequate to define most women's sense of their sexual selves. Women's understanding of their roles, including their sexual ones, seem to be more complicated than men's.

CONCLUSION

This chapter provided a brief description of some of the many ways in which deception and self-deception can occur in both short and long term mating. Recognizing these untruths, interpreting their meaning, and negotiating the relationships in which they occur, demands a high level of intelligence, a kind of ability that in non-mating situations might be called Machiavellian intelligence or social intelligence. In the context of sexual relationships, it is an important form of mating intelligence. I have provided some beginning data to suggest that self- deception is one of the highly intelligent (i.e., adaptive) strategies that people can use in their mating dance, and that in this regard women may be more light of foot than men.

REFERENCES

Abbey, A., & Melby, C. (1986). The effects of nonverbal cues on gender differences in perceptions of sexual intent. *Sex Roles, 15,* 282–298.

Adler, H. M. (1928). Deception and self-deception. *Journal of Abnormal and Social Psychology, 22,* 364–371.

Andersen, B. L., Cyranowski, J. M., & Espindle, D. (1999). Men's sexual self-schema. *Journal of Personality and Social Psychology, 76,* 645–661.

Archer, J. (2000). Sex differences in aggression between heterosexual partners: A meta-analytic review. *Psychological Bulletin, 126,* 651–680.

Bargh, J. A., Gollwitzer, P. M., & Lee-Chai, A. (2001). The automated will: Nonconscious activation and the pursuit of behavioral goals. *Journal of Personality and Social Psychology, 81,* 1010–1027.

Barkow, J., Cosmides, L., & Tooby, J. (Eds.) (1992). *The adapted mind.* New York: Oxford University Press.

Baumeister, R. F. (1993). Lying to yourself: The enigma of self-deception. In M. Lewis & C. Saarni (Eds.), *Lying and deception in everyday life* (pp. 166–183). New York: Guilford.

Baumeister, R. F. (2000). Gender differences in erotic plasticity. *Psychological Bulletin, 126,* 347–374.

Baumeister, R. F., Catanese, K. R., & Vohs, K. D. (2001). Is there a gender difference in strength of sex drive? *Personality and Social Psychology Review, 5,* 242–273.

Baumeister, R. F., & Wotman, S. R. (1992). *Breaking hearts: The two sides of unrequited love.* New York: The Guilford Press.

Bleske-Rechek, A. L., & Buss, D. M. (2001). Opposite-sex friendships: Sex differences and similarities in initiation, selection, and dissolution. *Personality and Social Psychology Bulletin, 27,* 1310–1323.

Bramlett, M. D., & Mosher, W. D. (2002). Cohabitation, marriage, divorce and remarriage in the United States. *Vital Health Statistics, 23,* 1–103. As cited in Miller, R. S., Perlman, D., & Brehm, S. S. (2004). *Intimate relationships (4th ed.).* Boston, MA: McGraw Hill.

Buss, D. M. (1998). The psychology of human mate selection: Exploring the complexity of the strategic repertoire. In C. Crawford & D. L. Krebs (Eds.) *Handbook of evolutionary psychology ideas, issues, and applications* (pp. 405–429). Mahwah, NJ: Lawrence Erlbaum Associates.

Buss, D. M. (2000). *The dangerous passion. Why jealousy is as necessary as love and sex.* New York: The Free Press.

Buss, D. M. (2001). Cognitive biases and emotional wisdom in the evolution of conflict between the sexes. *Current Directions in Psychological Science, 10,* 218–223.

Byrne, R., & Whiten, A. (Eds.) (1988). *Machiavellian intelligence social expertise and the evolution of intellect in monkeys, apes, and humans.* Oxford: Oxford University Press.

Cole, T. (2001). Lying to the one you love: The use of deception in romantic relationships. *Journal of Social and Personal Relationships, 18,* 107–129.

DePaulo, B. M., & Kashy, D. A. (1998). Everyday lies in close and casual relationships. *Journal of Personality and Social Psychology, 74,* 63–79.

Duby, G. (Ed.). (1988). *A history of private life II. Revelations of the medieval world.* Cambridge, MA: The Belknap Press of Harvard University Press.

Dunning, D., Heath, C., & Suls, J. M. (2004). Flawed self-assessment: Implications for health, education, and the workplace. *Psychological Science in the Public Interest, 5,* 69–106.

Ekman, P. (2001). *Telling lies: Clues to deceit in the marketplace, marriage, and politics* (3rd ed.). New York: W. W. Norton.

Ekman, P. (2003). *Emotions revealed.* New York: Henry Holt.

Ekman, P., & Friesen, W. V. (1969). The repertoire of nonverbal behavior: Categories, origins, usage, and coding. *Semiotica, 1,* 49–98.

Ellis, B. J., & Malamuth, N. M. (2000). Love and anger in romantic relationships: A discrete systems model. *Journal of Personality, 68,* 525–556.

Frankfurt, H. G. (2005). *On bullshit.* Princeton, NJ: Princeton University Press.

Gagne, F. M., & Lydon, J. E. (2004). Bias and accuracy in close relationships: An integrative review. *Personality and Social Psychology Review, 8,* 322–338.

Gangestad, W. W. (1993). Sexual selection and physical attractiveness: Implications for mating dynamics. *Human Nature, 4,* 205–235.

Glass, S. P., & Wright, T. L. (1992). Justification for extramarital relationships: The association between attitudes, behaviors, and gender. *Journal of Sex Research, 29,* 361–387.

Gonzage, G. C., Keltner, D., Londahl, E. A., & Sprull, M. D. (2001). Love and the commitment problem in romantic relations and friendships. *Journal of Personality and Social Psychology, 81,* 247–262.

Grammer, K. (1991). Strangers meet: Laughter and non-verbal signs of interest in opposite-sex encounters. *Journal of Nonverbal Behavior, 14,* 209–236.

Harker, L., & Keltner, D. (2001). Expressions of positive emotion in women's college yearbook pictures and their relationship to personality and life outcomes across adulthood. *Journal of Personality and Social Psychology, 80,* 112–124.

Harris, C. R. (2003). A review of sex differences in sexual jealousy, including self-report data, psycho physiological responses, interpersonal violence, and morbid jealousy. *Personality and Social Psychology Review, 7,* 102–128.

Haselton, M. G., & Buss, D. M. (2000). Error management theory: A new perspective on biases in cross-sex mind reading. *Journal of Personality and Social Psychology, 78,* 81–91.

Haselton, M. G., Buss, D. M., Oubaid, V., & Angleitner, A. (2005). Sex, lies, and strategic interference: The psychology of deception between the sexes. *Personality and Social Psychology Bulletin, 31,* 2–23.

Henningsen, D. D. (2004). Flirting with meaning: An examination of miscommunication in flirting interactions. *Sex Roles, 50,* 481–489.

Jankowiak, W. (Ed.) (1995). *Romantic passion A universal experience?* New York: Columbia University Press.

Kaplar, M. E., & Gordon, A. K. (2004). The enigma of altruistic lying: Perspective differences in what motivates and justifies lie telling within romantic relationships. *Personal Relationships, 11,* 489–507.

Lakoff, G. (1987). *Women, fire and dangerous things: What categories reveal about the mind.* Chicago, IL: University of Chicago Press.

Lees-Haley, P. R., Iverson, G. L., Lange, R. T., Fox, D. D., & Allen, L. M. (2002). Malingering in forensic neuropsychology: Daubert and the MMPI—2. *Journal of Forensic Neuropsychology, 3,* 167–203.

Levin, R. J. (2004). An orgasm is . . . Who defines what an orgasm is? *Sexual and Relationship Therapy, 19,* 101–107.

Malone, B. E., & DePaulo, B. M. (2001). Measuring sensitivity to deception. In J. A. Hall & F. J. Bernieri (Eds.), *Interpersonal sensitivity theory and measurement* (pp. 103–124). Mahwah, NJ: Lawrence Erlbaum Associates.

Marlowe, D., & Crowne, D. P. (1960). A new scale of social desirability independent of psychopathology. *Journal of Consulting Psychology, 24,* 349–354.

Masters, W. H., & Johnson, V. F. (1970). *Human sexual inadequacy.* Boston, MA: Little, Brown.

McEwan, I. (1997). *Enduring love.* New York: Nan Talese.

Mele, A. R. (2001). *Self-deception unmasked.* Princeton, NJ: Princeton University Press.

Metts, S. (1989). An exploratory investigation of deception in close interpersonal-relationships. *Journal of Social and Personal Relationships, 6,* 159–179.

Metts, S. (1989). An exploratory investigation of deception in close relationships. *Journal of Social Psychology, 6,* 159–178.

Miller, G. F. (1997). Protean primates: The evolution of adaptive unpredictability in competition and courtship. In A. Whiten & R. W. Byrne (Eds.), *Machiavellian intelligence II. Extensions and evaluations* (pp. 312–340). Cambridge: Cambridge University Press.

Miller G. F. (2000). *The mating mind: How sexual choice shaped the evolution of human nature.* New York: Doubleday & Co.

Miller, G. R., Mongeau, P. A., & Sleight, C. (1986). Fudging with friends and lying to lovers: Deceptive communication in personal relationships. *Journal of Social and Personal Relationships, 3,* 495–512.

Miller, W. I. (2003). *Faking it.* Cambridge: Cambridge University Press.

Moore, M. M. (1985). Nonverbal courtship patterns in women: Contexts and consequence. *Ethology and Sociobiology, 6,* 237–247.

Murray, S. A., Holmes, J. G., Bellavia, G., Griffin, D. W., & Dolderman, D. (2002). Kindred spirits? The benefits of egocentrism in close relationships. *Journal of Personality and Social Psychology, 82,* 563–581.

Nisbett, R. E., & Wilson, T. D. (1977). Telling more than we can know: Verbal reports on mental processes. *Psychological Review, 84,* 231–259.

O'Sullivan, M. (1996). *Negative emotion and romantic love.* Presented at the invited symposium on Mixed Emotions in Everyday life at the annual meeting of the American Psychological Society. San Francisco, CA.

O'Sullivan, M. (1999). *What is this thing called love?* Paper presented at the Cognitive Science Colloquium, San Sebastian, Spain.

O'Sullivan, M. (2001). *Deconstructing romantic love.* Poster presented at the annual meeting of the Society for Personality and Social Psychology. Los Angeles, CA.

O'Sullivan, M. (in preparation). *Love, lies and lust.*

Pelham, B. W., Carvallo, M. M., & Jones, J. T. (2005). Implicit egotism. *Current Directions in Psychological Science, 14,* 106–109.

Peplau, L. (2003). Human sexuality: How do men and women differ? *Current Directions in Psychological Science, 12,* 37–40.

Peterson, C. (1996). Deception in intimate relationships. *International Journal of Psychology, 31,* 279–288.

Phillips, A. (1994). *On flirtation.* Cambridge, MA: Harvard University Press.

Popenoe, D., & Whitehead, B. D. (2004). *The state of our unions, 2004.* Piscataway, NJ: The National Marriage Project. As cited in Miller, R. S., Perlman, D., & Brehm, S. S. (2004). *Intimate Relationships (4th ed.).* Boston, MA: McGraw Hill.

Rock, C. (2000). *Bigger and blacker.* HBO DVD of a 1999 live comedy performance.

Rowatt, W., Cunningham, M. R., & Druen, P. R. (1998). Deception to get a date. *Personality and Social Psychology Bulletin, 24,* 1228–1242.

Schmitt, D. P., & Shackelford, T. K. (2003). Nifty ways to leave your lover: The tactics people use to entice and disguise the process of human mate poaching. *Personality and Social Psychology Bulletin, 29,* 1018–1035.

Shackelford, T. K., Goetz, A. R., Buss, D. M., Euler, H. A., & Hoier, S. (2005). When we hurt the ones we love: Predicting violence against women from men's mate retention. *Personal Relationships, 12,* 447–463.

Simpson, J. S., Gangestad, S.W., & Biek, M. (1993). Personality and nonverbal social behavior: An ethological perspective on relationship initiation. *Journal of Experimental Social Psychology, 29,* 434–461.

Solomon, R. C. (1988). *About love: Reinventing romance for our time.* New York: Simon & Schuster.

Sprecher, S., Aron, A., Hatfield, E., Cortese, A., Potapova, F., &,Levitsky, A. (1994). Love: American style, Russian style, and Japanese style. *Personal Relationships, 1*, 349–369.

Sprecher, S., & Metts, S. (1999). Romantic beliefs: Their influence on relationships and patterns of change over time. *Journal of Social and Personal Relationships, 6*, 387–411.

Sternberg. R. J. (Ed.) (2000). *Handbook of intelligence*. Cambridge: Cambridge University Press.

Strauss, M. A. (1997). Physical assaults by women partners: A major social problem. In M. R. Walsh (Ed.), *Women, men & gender* (pp. 210–221). New Haven, CT: Yale University Press.

Swann, W. B., & Gill, M. J. (1997). Confidence and accuracy in person perception: Do we know what we think we know about our relationship partners? *Journal of Personality and Social Psychology, 73*, 747–757.

Werking, K. (1997). *We're just good friends: Women and men in nonromantic relationships*. New York: The Guilford Press.

Wiederman, M. W. (1997). Pretending orgasm during sexual intercourse: Correlates in a sample of young adult women. *Journal of Sex and Marital Therapy, 23*, 131–139.

Whiten, A., & Byrne, R. W. (Eds.) (1997). *Machiavellian intelligence II Extensions and evaluations* Cambridge: Cambridge University Press.

Chapter 7

How Having Children Affects Mating Psychology

Viviana A.Weekes-Shackelford,
Judy A. Easton, and Emily A. Stone
Florida Atlantic University

Human mating intelligence includes mating strategies that complement one's local ecological, social, and familial conditions. One major familial condition concerns the presence of offspring from prior matings. Does mating psychology change after an individual has a child? In particular, what are the effects of having children from prior mateships when it comes to our mating strategies? Past research on this topic has focused on the negative mating consequences (e.g., decreased mate value) and potential harm to offspring (e.g., step-parental abuse) for individuals with children from prior mateships. One goal of this chapter is to offer a provisional framework for continued research on the psychological intricacies of mating given children from previous relationships.

Throughout human evolutionary history, most sexually mature adults who were available in the mating market already had children from previous relationships. Thus, an individual with children was a typical and recurrent social feature of human evolution. This particular social feature was accompanied by a specific set of adaptive problems that likely played a role in the evolution of specific forms of Mating Intelligence—forms of MI that take into account the fitness costs and benefits associated with mating once an individual has children. Although we might expect differential psychological responses (e.g., changes in mate preferences) in each sex to the problems associated with the presence of children and securing or maintaining a mate, this chapter focuses on the psychological responses of females.

Human sexual psychology includes mechanisms for mate selection and for advertising the qualities or characteristics desired by others. These desired qualities, or mate preferences, have been shown to depend somewhat on whether an individual is pursuing a long-term mating strategy or a short-term mating strategy (see Buss, 2004; and Gangestad & Simpson, 2000, for reviews). Other contextual effects on mate preferences have been documented in both sexes. As we review in more detail below, a woman's ovulatory cycle status as well as her own current mate value influence her mate preferences (see Gangestad, Thornhill, & Garver-Apgar, 2005). We propose that having children from a previous relationship is another major contextual variable that should affect mate preferences in sex-specific ways. However, largely due to the fact that modern Western societies prescribe and facilitate a kind of monogamy that is likely not characteristic of ancestral mating patterns, modern researchers have tended to neglect the effects of children from prior mateships in their studies of human mating.

PREVIOUS RESEARCH ON CONTEXTUAL EFFECTS ON MATE PREFERENCES

Previous research shows that mate preferences vary as a function of several evolutionarily relevant contextual variables. For a woman, such contexts include her personal resources, whether she is pursuing a long-term or short-term relationship, her mate value, and her ovulatory-cycle status (e.g., Buss, 2004; Gangestad & Simpson, 2000; Gangestad et al., 2005). For a man, the relevant contextual variables include his social status, mate value, and short-term or long-term relationship desired (Buss, 2004). Ancestral humans who shifted their mate preferences across relevant contexts should have benefited from more reproductive opportunities than individuals who did not shift their mate preferences accordingly. Thus, it makes sense that evolutionary selection pressures would have selected mating mechanisms that were highly sensitive to such important contextual factors (This is why we have a context-sensitive Mating Intelligence, not just a context-ignorant 'Sex Drive').

Mate preferences shift depending on whether one is seeking a long-term or short-term relationship. This in turn probably depends on local ecological, social, and demographic variables, such as the local sex ratio of reproductive-aged men to reproductive-aged women (see Guttentag & Secord, 1983). In fact, research indicates that members of both sexes may have benefited ancestrally from a 'pluralistic' (flexible short- or long-term) mating strategy that changed in light of such local conditions (e.g., Buss & Schmitt, 1993; Gangestad & Simpson, 1990). We propose that mate preference shifts might also reflect pluralistic mating strategies after an individual has children. However, for men with children, there may be less variability in mate preferences when pursing a short-term mate relative to a long-term mate, perhaps because the costs associated with poor mate choice are less variable for men than for women (Buss, 2004; Trivers, 1972).

Women do not engage in short-term mating for the same reasons that men do. Accordingly, for women with children, adaptive switches between short and long-term mate preferences should follow different patterns than for men with children, because the costs and benefits are different. Women sometimes engage in short-term matings with extra-pair men while already in a long-term relationship (Buss, 2003; and see Greiling & Buss, 2000). Although this could be a costly to a woman, especially if the affair is discovered by her long-term partner, a woman could gain from these encounters if her extra-pair partner has something special to offer such as "good genes" or additional resources (see Greiling & Buss, 2000).

There is an asymmetry in the minimum obligatory parental investment (Trivers, 1972). A woman's minimal investment is the production of limited ova and the release of an ovum. When the ovum becomes fertilized the woman's investment heightens as she will now have to gestate the fetus for roughly nine months, birth the child, lactate for several years, and provision so as to ensure that the offspring reaches reproductive maturity. Contrasted with a woman's minimal investment, a man's minimal investment is the production of sperm (much smaller than female ovum). Because of this asymmetry, women risk greater costs than men for pursuing a short-term relationship or for having short-term sex. If already in a long-term relationship and discovered by a long-term partner, these costs to a woman may include being abandoned by her partner and thus losing access to any resources he may have invested in her and her offspring, being abused or killed by her partner, or suffering reputational damage from gossip (or her extra-pair partner; Daly & Wilson, 1988; Shackelford, Weekes-Shackelford, & Buss, 2003). These diverse costs may have provided selection pressures on female psychology to shift mate preferences when pursuing different mating strategies. Only when the benefits of short-term mating out-weigh these fitness costs might we see women seeking such opportunistic affairs with men displaying distinct qualities. Accordingly, previous research suggests that, when seeking a short-term mate, women prefer as partners men who can provide immediate resources (e.g., cash, or jewelry), for example, rather than men who have the potential for future resource acquisition (e.g., male medical students). Women also intensify their preference for physical attractiveness (a heritable trait) in a potential mate when they are seeking a short rather than long-term partner- a mate-preference shift that is consistent with the use of short-term casual sex as a means of obtaining "good genes" (Buss, 1998; Buss & Schmitt, 1993; Greiling & Buss, 2000; Schmitt & Buss, 1996).

Another important context variable concerns ovulatory-cycle status. It may have benefited ancestral women to prefer physically attractive men— especially when they were ovulating and seeking short-term mates (see Gangestad et al., 2005). Women are not generally aware of when they are ovulating and, accordingly, such shifts in mate preferences are not expected to result from conscious awareness of fertility. However, previous research indicates that women show stronger preferences for physically attractive short-term male partners when they are ovulating versus not ovulating, and when they are seeking short-term versus long-term partners, even without conscious awareness of ovulation (Gangestad & Cousins, 2001; Gangestad, Simpson, Cousins, Garver-Apgar, & Christensen, 2004; Gangestad & Simpson, 2000; Gangestad et al., 2005).

Men and women probably do not experience contextual shifts in their mate preferences in the same manner. Men's fertility, for example, does not vary as dramatically or cyclically as women's fertility does (men's ability to produce viable sperm and, thus impregnate a woman, is not dependent on a 28-day cycle, whereas women's likelihood of becoming pregnant is dependent on a 28-day cycle); therefore men's mate preferences should not shift much from day to day. Male sexual psychology may be more sensitive than women's to a different context, however: one's relative position in the local status hierarchy. Although men generally prefer youth and physical attractiveness in both long-term and short-term partners (Buss, 1989), the number of prospective partners with whom a man might establish a long-term or short-term relationship is limited; not all men can mate with all women as sexual partners, for example. Because women prefer as long-term partners men who have large amounts of resources, men with great power and high levels of status would potentially have access to more women, and to women of higher mate value (Buss, 2003). If men with less power or status did not lower their preference standards, they may not be able to acquire a mate at all, short-term or long-term. Accordingly, it would have benefited ancestral men to shift their mate preferences according to their current status and power relative to local men.

Historical evidence confirms that men with large amounts of power were able to obtain sexual access to, and even form long-term mateships with, larger numbers of younger, more attractive women than men with less power. Betzig (1986; 1992), for example, reports that kings and despots often managed to retain propriety harems of attractive, young women; predictably replacing aging women with younger, more attractive women. Every member of such harems would make for one less young, attractive woman available to the non-ruling men. In modern times, men with higher occupational status and greater access to resources, such as sports stars or movie stars, often marry younger, more attractive women than do men with lesser occupational status or access to resources (Buss, 2004; Perusse, 1994).

There may be other contexts in which it would have benefited ancestral men and women to shift their mate preferences. For example, individuals may shift their preferences according to self-assessments of their own mate value, or relative attractiveness as a mate in the local mating pool (see Penke, Todd, Lenton, and Fasolo, this volume). Those who perceive themselves as having relatively low mate value may lower their mate preference standards, to increase the chances of securing or being selected as a mate (Buss, 2003; Landolt, Lalumiere, & Quinsey, 1995).

We propose that as the presence of children from a previous mateship was a recurrent context encountered throughout human evolutionary history, so having vs. not having kids seems a likely candidate for the kind of contextual variable that influences mating decisions. Thus, men and women with children may have evolved specific forms of Mating Intelligence to optimize their success in the mating game. We turn next to this context, which is the focus of the remainder of this chapter.

PAIR BONDING AND DISSOLUTION

Pair-bonding between a male and a female is found in many species (Alcock, 2004; Buss, 2004). Human marriage can be characterized as a pair bond. Formal marriage unions between men and women exist cross culturally (Buss 1985; Buss & Schmitt, 1993). Other types of pair bonding in humans can be described as cohabiting and dating relationships. Whether a relationship is characterized as a marriage, cohabitation, or dating, pair-bonding has been a recurrent aspect of mating behavior in many species, including humans. However, pair-bonds sometimes dissolve. Divorce in humans has been documented cross culturally (Betzig, 1989). While the leading causes of divorce include infertility, infidelity, and death across disparate cultures (see Betzig, 1989), sex differences in parental investment play a pivotal role in the dissolution of a relationship.

The context of mating and parenting provides the setting for the expression of this differential investment between men and women. Because women are the more investing sex, women are more discriminating than are men about their mate choices, in both short-term and long-term relationships (Buss, 1993). Women must consider not only a prospective mate's physical characteristics, but also (especially in a long-term context) his ability and willingness to invest in her and any potential offspring (Bjorklund, 2002; Buss, 2004). Men, on the other hand, are the less investing sex and, therefore less discriminating about individuals with whom they will mate, especially in the short-term context. The characteristics that men take into consideration, perhaps especially in the long-term context, provide cues to a woman's current and future reproductive potential, such as her physical attractiveness and youthfulness (see Buss, 1989, 2004).

DIVORCE, REMARRIAGE, AND THE ADAPTIVE PROBLEMS OF CHILDREN FROM A PREVIOUS MATESHIP

Given that the sexes differ in their reproductive psychology (and the manifestations thereof), there is a sexual conflict of interest in all relationships (Campbell, 2002). This conflict can lead relationships to dissolve—a common situation in over one hundred cultures that have been studied (see Betzig, 1989). Given that (a) 'serial monogamy' (having one committed relationship after another) is the most common mating system in humans (Buss, 2003; Smith, 1984), and (b) marriage and divorce are practiced cross culturally, it is reasonable to assume that re-mating (or remarriage) was a recurrent phenomenon throughout evolutionary history.

Ancestral women who re-mated after the death or desertion of a long-term partner might have thereby recovered access to some of the social, economic, and political support that they lost after the previous break-up. If a child was produced in a previous union, re-mating may be prudent, since the mother needs to recover resources and garner future resources for herself and her offspring. In a national study on the effects of divorce, Hoffman and Duncan (1988) found that in the year following a divorce, women suffered an average 30 percent decrease in income. In contrast, men had 10 percent to 15 percent more income. Upon the death or desertion of a father, detriment to a mother may also come in the form of child mortality. Research on the Ache of Paraguay indicates that children were frequently killed (or that they starved or died accidentally) after the death of their father (Hill & Hurtado, 1996). Further, roughly 63 percent of the Ache children were reported to have a secondary father (i.e., the mother had re-mated). This suggests that, by re-mating, mothers are not only seeking to replace lost resources; they are also seeking to increase the chances of offspring survival. Accordingly, remarriage is common among pre-industrial cultures (Broude & Greene, 1983; Frayser, 1985), suggesting that humans may have evolved psychological adaptations to respond to this mating contingency. Indeed, several evolutionary theories of human mating have postulated that humans are designed to marry, divorce, and remarry every four to seven years (Fisher, 1992). According to Hetherington (2002), in 1998 the remarriage rate in the United States was equal to the rate of first marriage. Furthermore, research by Wineberg and McCarthy (1998) indicates that 27 percent of all married couples in the United States include one spouse who was previously married, and half the families include at least one child from the previous union.

Over historical time and evolutionary time, women more than men were likely to have functioned as single parents due to spousal death, divorce, or desertion (Shackelford, Weekes-Shackelford, & Schmitt, 2005). Remarriage may be one solution whereby a woman with children may regain access to lost resources for herself and her child.

But remarriage that includes children from a previous mateship presents a set of new adaptive problems for the woman and her children, in the form of finding a suitable stepfather who will not abuse or kill her children (also known as *filicide*). Previous research indicates that the single best predictor of child abuse is living with a step-parent (Daly & Wilson, 1988), even after controlling for potential confounds such as socioeconomic status (see also Daly & Wilson, 1985, 1988, 1998).

Daly and Wilson (1988) investigated the risk of filicide by stepparents and by genetic parents. In an American sample, they found that children less than 2 years of age living with one stepparent and one genetic parent are 100 times more likely to be killed than are children living with two genetic parents. These results were replicated using a Canadian database of homicides (Daly & Wilson, 1988). This increased risk of abuse and filicide by stepparents has been documented across diverse cultures (see Bjorklund & Pellegrini, 2002, and Daly & Wilson, 1988, 1998). Therefore, we expect women to be sensitive to characteristics in a potential stepfather that might signal good parenting towards her children, which in turn would mean a decreased likelihood of abuse or murder.

SOME EXPECTED FINDINGS

We expect that women with children from a previous mateship who are seeking a new mate may shift their specific mate preferences (see Table 7.1.). For example, women with children from prior mateships might place greater importance on finding a partner who is willing to invest in the woman and her current or future children. Women's preferences for a man who displays a willingness to invest in her and her children, perhaps by being dependable and demonstrating positive interactions with children, probably helped to solve the adaptive problem of securing a mate and resources after the dissolution of a previous relationship.

We also expect that women with children from a previous mateship, relative to women without children, will place more importance on finding a new mate who displays good parenting skills. Demonstrating good parenting skills may indicate that a potential stepfather will not be abusive toward a woman's children. Men who are emotionally stable and kind may possess the characteristics suggestive of good parenting skills, and will likely be a stable figure who is able to confer social skills on the woman's children. Women may use a man's willingness to invest and his

TABLE 7.1.
Predicted Mate Preferences for Women with Children Seeking a Subsequent Mateship

Adaptive Problems Associated With This Context	Relevant Evolved Mate Preference	Predicted Change for Women with Children
Finding mate who is:		
Able to invest	Financial resources & ambition	− − −+++
Willing to invest in self & current/future children	Dependability & positive interactions w/children	++++++
Able to protect self & children	Size & strength	− − − − − −
Show (s) good parenting skills	Emotional stability & kindness	++++++
Social/parentally compatible	Similar personalities & values	++++++
Healthy	Attractiveness	− − − − − −

++++++   Preferences will increase in importance
− − − − − − Preferences will decrease in importance
− − −+++   Theoretical arguments can be made for an increase or decrease of importance in these mate preferences.

display of good parenting skills as indicators of his actual investment and his actual parenting ability, especially if he already has children who have survived to reproductive age. Thus, while women in general seem to seek men who display signs of interest and efficacy in parenting, women with children from prior mateships likely emphasize such features even more.

We also hypothesize that women with children from a previous mateship might lower the relative importance they place on other characteristics. Women with children, relative to women without children, for example, might place less importance on a man's cues to good health (e.g., physical attractiveness) and perhaps especially, his physical size, strength, and prowess. Preferences for a prospective partner's physical size, strength, and prowess are expected to be less important for women with children from a previous partner, relative to women without children from a previous partner, because these characteristics might be perceived as a cue to likely physical abuse to the woman and her children. These mate preference shifts by women with children might therefore represent a solution to the increased risk of abuse and murder by a stepparent (Daly & Wilson, 1988; Weekes-Shackelford & Shackelford, 2004). A decreased emphasis on a partner's heritable physical attractiveness might also be expected because it may be more beneficial for women with children to trade-off good genes for a man's greater parental investment (e.g., Gangestad & Simpson, 2000).

Men have a finite amount of time and energy, and an increase in mating effort necessitates a decrease in parenting effort (hence, the trade-off). Accordingly, men who are more symmetrical on bilateral traits (an indication of developmental stability and good genes), obtain more extra-pair sexual partners as well as more sexual partners over a lifetime, relative to less symmetrical men (Gangestad & Simpson, 2000). This suggests that more symmetrical (high quality) men may be trading-off some amount of parenting effort in favor of sustained mating effort. And because more symmetrical men are generally more attractive than less symmetrical men, we expect that women with children, relative to women without children, will place less importance on the characteristic of physical attractiveness relative to other women. Men with good genes generally pursue more short-term mating opportunities, and thus tend to be less willing to invest parentally in children, perhaps especially children sired by other men.

Finally, we hypothesize shifts in preferences for a man's ability to materially invest in a woman and her children. However, this could go either way. It is possible that the desire for a man's ability to invest will increase. A woman may prefer a man who is not only willing to invest in her but who is also actually able to provide the resources. This preference may be intensified for women who bring with them children from previous mateships, as a woman with children may require a greater resource investment from her partner than a woman without children. However, a women's preference for this investment ability might also decrease given her lower overall mate value. A woman with children from a previous mateship (relative to women without children from a previous mateship), who is already disadvantaged on the mating market, may therefore trade immediate investment for other characteristics or traits in a prospective mate that might be more important. These other characteristics may include those which signal that the prospective mate is likely to treat her children from a previous mateship with reasonable care, and might include, for example, a potential mate's emotional stability. In sum, we expect that women with children from a previous mateship will shift their mate preferences to solve specific adaptive problems associated with this context.

CONCLUSION

This chapter began with the argument that ancestral men and women often had children from a previous mateship when they were seeking to establish a new mateship. We reviewed previous research indicating that other contextual factors, such as ovulatory cycle status and own mate value influence preferences for characteristics in a potential mate. We then argued that, because the presence of a child from a previous mateship presents a different set of adaptive problems than those present when there is no child from a previous mateship, men and women with children from prior mateships, relative to others in the mating market, may show different mate preferences. Furthermore, we argued that these shifts in preferences follow an adaptive logic. In this chapter, we focused on women's mate preference shifts, and provided illustrations of the rationale for the particular mate preference shifts by highlighting how the context of remarriage may have contributed to the evolution of mate preferences. We hope that the framework presented here helps guide future empirical work in addressing the nature of mating preferences as a function of having children from prior mateships.

The point of the work described in this volume is to integrate traditions in psychology that underlie the interface between human intelligence and mating. The ideas included in our chapter speak directly to this interface in terms of species-typical psychological mechanisms. Generally, we argue that a core part of our mating intelligence pertains to our ability to shift our mating preferences and decisions vis-à-vis evolutionarily relevant contextual factors. Specifically, we posit that the presence of children from a prior mateship is exactly the kind of factor that our minds should be sensitive to when making mating-relevant decisions. Evidence of contextually sensitive psychological mechanisms suggests that our mating psychology has an extremely intelligent basis. Such contextually sensitive processes may be conceptualized as a core component of human mating intelligence.

ACKNOWLEDGMENTS

The authors thank Glenn Geher, Geoffrey Miller, and Todd K. Shackelford for helpful comments, suggestions, and discussions.

REFERENCES

Alcock, J. (2001). *Animal behavior* (7th ed.). Sunderland, MA: Sinauer Associates.

Baker, R. R., & Bellis, M. A. (1995). *Human sperm competition.* Chapman & Hall: London

Betzig, L. L. (1986*). Despotism and differential reproduction: A Darwinian view of history.* Hawthorne, NY: Aldine.

Betzig, L. (1989). Causes of conjugal dissolution: A cross-cultural study. *Current Anthropology, 30,* 654–676.

Betzig, L. L. (1992). Roman polygyny. *Ethology and Sociobiology, 13,* 309–349.

Bjorklund, D. F., & Pellegrini, A. D. (2002). *The origins of human nature: Evolutionary developmental psychology.* Washington, DC: APA Books.

Broude, G. J., & Greene, S. J. (1976). Cross-cultural codes on husband-wife relationships. *Ethnology, 22,* 263–280.

Buss, D. M. (1985). Human mate selection. *American Scientist, 73,* 47–51.

Buss, D. M. (1989). Sex differences in human mate preferences: Evolutionary hypotheses tested in 37 cultures. *Behavioral and Brain Sciences, 12,* 1–49.

Buss, D. M. (1998). Sexual strategies theory: Historical origins and current status. *The Journal of Sex Research, 35,* 19–31.

Buss, D. M. (2003). *The evolution of desire: Strategies of human mating* (Rev. ed.). New York: Basic Books.

Buss, D. M. (2004). *Evolutionary psychology* (2nd ed.). Boston: Allyn & Bacon.

Buss, D. M., & Schmitt, D. P. (1993). Sexual strategies theory: An evolutionary perspective on human mating. *Psychological Review, 100,* 204–232.

Buss, D. M., & Schmitt, D. P. (1993). Sexual strategies theory: An evolutionary perspective on human mating. *Psychological Review, 100,* 204–232.

Campbell, A. (2002). *A mind of her own: The evolutionary psychology of women.* Oxford: Oxford University Press.

Daly, M., & Wilson, M. (1985). Child abuse and other risks of not living with both parents. *Ethology and Sociobiology, 6,* 197–210.

Daly, M., & Wilson, M. (1988). *Homicide.* Hawthorne, NY: Aldine de Gruyter.

Daly, M., & Wilson, M. I. (1994). Some differential attributes of lethal assaults on small children by stepfathers versus genetic fathers. *Ethology and Sociobiology, 15,* 207–217.

Daly, M., & Wilson, M. (1998). *The truth about Cinderella.* London: Weidenfeld & Nicolson.

Fisher, H. E. (1992). *Anatomy of love: The natural history of monogamy, adultery, and divorce.* New York: Norton.

Frayser, S. (1985). *Varieties of sexual experience: An anthropological perspective.* New Haven, CT: HRAF Press.

Gangestad, S. W., & Cousins, A. J. (2001). Adaptive design, female mate preferences, and shifts across the menstrual cycle. *Annual Review of Sex Research, 12,* 145–186.

Gangestad, S. W., & Simpson, J. A. (1990). Toward an evolutionary history of female sociosexual variation. [Special issue: Biological foundations of personality: Evolution, behavioral genetics, and psychophysiology.] *Journal of Personality, 58,* 69–96.

Gangestad, S. W., & Simpson, J. A. (2000). The evolution of human mating: Trade-offs and strategic pluralism. *Behavioral and Brain Sciences, 23,* 573–644.

Gangestad, S. W., Simpson, J. A., Cousins, A. J., Garver-Apgar, C. E., & Christensen, P. N. (2004). Women's preferences for male behavioral displays change across the menstrual cycle. *Psychological Science, 15,* 203–207.

Gangestad, S. W., Thornhill, R., & Garver-Apgar, C. E. (2005). Adaptations to ovulation. In David M. Buss (Ed.), *The handbook of evolutionary psychology* (pp. 344–371). Hoboken, NJ: John Wiley & Sons, Inc.

Greiling, H., & Buss, D. M. (2000). Women's sexual strategies: The hidden dimension of extra-pair mating. *Personality and Individual Differences, 28,* 929–963.

Guttentag, M., & Secord, P. F. (1983). *Too many women? The sex ratio question.* Beverly Hill, CA: Sage.

Hamilton, W. D. (1964). The genetical evolution of social behavior. I and II. *Journal of Theoretical Biology, 7,* 1–52.

Hetherington, E. M., & Kelly, J. (2002). *For better or worse: Divorce reconsidered.* New York: Norton.

Hill, K., & Hurtado. A. M. (1996). *Ache life History.* New York. Aldine de Grutyer.

Hoffman, S. D., & Duncan, G. J. (1988). What are the economic consequences of divorce? *Demography, 25,* 641–645.

Landolt, M. A., Lalumiere, M. L., & Quinsey, V. L. (1995). Sex differences in intra-sex variations in human mating tactics: An evolutionary approach. *Ethology and Sociobiology, 16,* 3–23.

Penke, L., Todd, P. M., Lenton, A. P., & Fasolo, B. (this volume). How self-related cognitions can guide human mating decisions. In G. Geher, & G. F. Miller (Eds.), *Mating intelligence: Sex, relationships, and the mind's reproductive system.* Mahwah, NJ: Lawrence Erlbaum Associates.

Perusse, D. (1994). Mate choice in modern societies: Testing evolutionary hypotheses with behavioral data. *Human Nature, 5,* 255–278.

Schmitt, D. P., & Buss, D. M. (1996). Strategic self-promotion and competitor derogation: Sex and context effects on the perceived effectiveness of mate attraction tactics. *Journal of Personality & Social Psychology, 70,* 1185–1204.

Shackelford, T. K., Weekes-Shackelford, V. A., & Buss, D. M. (2003). Wife killings committed in the context of a lovers triangle. *Basic and Applied Social Psychology, 25,* 137–143.

Shackelford, T. K., Weekes-Shackelford, V. A., & Schmitt, D. P. (2005). An evolutionary perspective on why some men refuse or reduce their child support payments. *Basic and Applied Psychology, 27,* 297–306.

Smith, R. L. (1984). Human sperm competition. In R.L. Smith (Ed.), *Sperm competition and the evolution of animal mating systems* (pp. 601–659). New York: Academic Press.

Trivers, R. (1972). Parental investment and sexual selection. In B. Campbell (Ed.), *Sexual selection and the descent of man* (pp. 136–179). Chicago: Aldine-Atherton.

Weekes-Shackelford, V. A., & Shackelford, T. K. (2004). Methods of filicide: Stepparents and genetic parents kill differently. *Violence and Victims, 19,* 75–81.

Wineberg, H., & McCarthy, J. (1998). Living arrangements after divorce: Cohabitation versus remarriage. *Journal of Divorce and Remarriage 29,* 131–146.

Mental Fitness Indicators
and Mating Intelligence

Chapter 9

The Role of Mutations in Human Mating

Matthew C. Keller
University of Colorado, Boulder

Evolutionary theory is the central organizing principle in the life sciences. Like other theoretical pillars in science, its value comes not only from its ability to explain existing observations according to a set of lawful principles, but also from its ability to test those explanations with new predictions. Given that there is no competing scientific explanation for complex biological design, and that human behavior is undoubtedly guided by mechanisms that are biologically complex, the question is not *whether* evolution has shaped the brain mechanisms that underlie human behavior, but rather *how* it has done so. This is not to say that everything that evolutionary psychologists have hypothesized to date is correct; the merit of these hypotheses will continue to become clearer as more data accumulate. Rather, the point is that evolutionary approaches will be central to the scientific understanding of human behavior, and indeed have already proven their scientific worth by stimulating the formation of testable and novel hypotheses in psychology (Buss, 2005).

To date, evolutionary psychologists have been focused mainly on one central aspect of evolutionary theory: adaptationism, or species-typical design features that aided ancestral fitness. There is, however, another central aspect of evolutionary theory that has been much-neglected so far in evolutionary psychology: understanding the causes and consequences of genetic variation within our species. This division between the study of adaptation and the study of genetic variation is not unique to psychology. At the beginning of the 20th century, until such luminaries as Ronald Fisher, Sewell Wright, and J. B. S. Haldane showed otherwise, many scientists believed that Mendelian principles of heredity conflicted with

173

the theory of natural selection (Bowler, 1989). Although the apparent conflicts between genetics and natural selection seem antiquated today, biology departments are often still divided between those studying genetics
(typically at the molecular level) and those studying adaptation (typically
at the organismic level).

The reason for the scientific divide between natural selection and
genetics is not purely historical, however. The specific principles used to
understand genetic differences are related but distinct from those used to
understand genetic similarities (i.e., species-typical design features). It is
no great surprise, then, that psychologists interested in adaptation have
largely ignored evolutionary genetics. More surprising is the fact that
behavioral geneticists and other psychologists interested in individual differences, with a few exceptions (Bailey, 2000; Eaves, Martin, Heath, Hewitt,
& Neale, 1990; Gangestad & Yeo, 1997; Miller, 2000), have only rarely considered genetic variation in the light of evolutionary genetics.

Evolutionary psychology is missing an important piece of the puzzle
by neglecting evolutionary genetics. In this chapter, I argue that evolutionary genetics, especially new evidence on the role that mutations play
in the evolutionary process, is fundamental to understanding individual
differences in behavior (e.g., variation in intelligence, personality, attractiveness, status, and courtship abilities as assessed in mate choice), as well
as those species-typical adaptations that track such individual differences
(e.g., mate choice systems). Thus, evolutionary-genetic principles also help
to distinguish between different conceptualizations of Mating Intelligence
(MI). Finally, insofar as a theoretical approach demonstrates its worth by
making testable predictions, I conclude with two illustrations of how a
mutational hypothesis of individual differences can make novel predictions regarding MI.

ON MUTATIONS AND BEING HUMAN

Errors are inherent to life. Despite my best intentions, it is likely that a
few grammatical or spelling errors have found their way into this chapter. But this chapter has only 7,300 words and 49,000 characters. If, instead,
I were to write a tome of, say, 12.5 million words and 75 million characters (about 25,000 pages long—like the 25,000 genes in the human
genome), not even careful writing and a full team of meticulous editors
could successfully keep the work mistake-free. The probability of mistakes
per event can be vanishingly small, but across enough events, mistakes
become inevitable. Along with natural selection, this simple principle of
probability is at the core of the evolutionary process.

Mutations are errors introduced into the structure of DNA, such as
substitution of the original base-pair (A, C, G, or T) for another (called a
point mutation), alterations in base-pair numbers (such as deletions or
insertions), or larger changes in base-pair organization at the chromosomal

level (such as translocations, inversions, or duplications). In this chapter, I focus only on point mutations (hereafter, simply *mutations*) because these are the most common (Nachman & Crowell, 2000) and best understood. Mutations most often occur during the replication of DNA prior to cell division, although the probability that a mutation occurs during the replication of any given base-pair of DNA is low and remarkably consistent across eukaryotic life-forms: about two errors per billion base-pair copying event (Keightley & Eyre-Walker, 2000). This low error rate is a testament to billions of years of intense selection for fidelity in gene duplication, and for correction of those errors that happen to occur. Most DNA errors arise in non-germline cells, and are of little evolutionary interest because they are not transmitted to offspring (although they can result in diseases, such as cancer). However, central to the evolutionary process are those mutations that occur in sperm or egg cells, and that are then transferred to the fertilized ovum and, eventually, to every cell in the offspring's body, including the offspring's own germline cells.

Although the probability of a mutation per base pair per meiosis (cell division) is miniscule, human germline cells go through tens to hundreds of meiotic events before becoming an egg or a sperm. For each of these meiotic events, about 75 million evolutionarily important base pairs in or around the 25,000 genes (out of 3 billion base pairs overall in human genome) must be replicated. As with errors in the 25,000 page tome described above, the probability of an offspring inheriting a new mutation becomes quite high across the entire genome—current estimates are that around four in every five human offspring inherit one or more new mutations that affect the phenotype.[1] These mutations almost always harm fitness for the same reason that random changes to a computer's circuitry would almost always harm performance: entropy erodes functional complexity (Ridley, 2000).

---

[1] By comparing the sequences of chimpanzee and human protein-coding DNA, Eyre-Walker and Keightley (1999) deduced the substitution rate at neutral and non-neutral human DNA sites. They used this to estimate that about two new deleterious mutations arise on average per human per generation. Their estimate of the number of protein-coding genes in humans (60,000) has turned out to be too high, but they also did not account for mutations in regulatory (non-coding) regions of the genome, and about as much DNA in this region is evolutionarily constrained between species (Keightley & Gaffney, 2003). Accounting for both factors, it is likely that the deleterious mutation rate in the human lineage is slightly lower than two ($\sim$1.67) per individual per generation. If these mutations occur independently of one another, their frequency distribution per individual per generation should be described by a Poisson process, with mean = variance = λ = 1.67. Therefore, the probability of being born with no *new* mutations is ($e^{-\lambda} \lambda^{-0} /0! = .189$, or about one in five. All these estimates are likely to be somewhat conservative because they do not include deletions or insertions (which are rare).

Thus, most people reading this chapter carry one or more new mutations that impair fitness, that pervade every cell in the body, and that arose in a parent's germline cell but did not affect the parent's other cells. Sometimes these mutations are catastrophic to the phenotype, causing, for example, skull malformation and digit fusion (Apert's syndrome) or short-limbed dwarfism (Achondroplasia). But most new, deleterious mutations have minor, perhaps unnoticeable, phenotypic effects, such as causing one to be a little less bright, attractive, or athletic. These mutations are nevertheless significant evolutionarily, and most are destined to become extinct at some point in the future, although it may take a while for selection to eliminate them. For example, a mutation causing a 1 percent reduction in fitness (e.g., a 1 percent reduction in number of surviving offspring) will persist, on average, for about 10 generations and pass through about 100 different bodies (in multiple coexisting copies) in a large population before going extinct (García-Dorado, Caballero, & Crow, 2003). Because of this time-lag between a mutation's origin and its elimination, every population at any given time carries an encrustation of slightly old, slightly deleterious mutations. As a result, offspring do not just inherit a couple of new deleterious mutations; they also inherit from their parents an average of 500 (and perhaps many more) older, very slightly deleterious mutations in all of their cells (Fay, Wyckoff, & Wu, 2001). Humans and other animals with large genomes and long generational intervals are awash with deleterious mutations.

How might these mutations affect the phenotype? Clearly they do not usually result in Mendelian catastrophes. Elsewhere, Geoffrey Miller and I (Keller & Miller, 2006) have proposed that much of the genetic variation underlying the liability to mental disorders may be a consequence of mutations that undermine the adaptive brain mechanisms responsible for normal human behaviors. In that paper we presented several empirical observations supporting the view that mutations are important in the genetic etiology of mental disorders: (1) the apparent fitness costs of mental disorders (as manifest in reduced social and sexual success, at least in modern environments), (2) the very small effect sizes of those few susceptibility alleles that have been found to predict mental disorders so far in gene-mapping studies (suggesting that many mutations, rather than a few major genes maintained by selection, account for most mental disorder risk), (3) the increased risk of mental disorders with genetic inbreeding (which reveals the full effect of many, partially recessive, but deleterious mutations), and (4) the increased risk of mental disorders with paternal but not maternal age (the number of mutations in sperm but not eggs increases as parents age). These observations are exactly what would be predicted if most susceptibility alleles for mental disorders are actually harmful mutations that have not yet been removed by natural selection. Further, these observations are hard to reconcile with other mechanisms of genetic variation, such as balancing selection, which can favor a diversity of strategies in a population, but which tends to orchestrate their development through genes that show large effect sizes, equal average fitness, no inbreeding depression, and no paternal age effects.

Mental disorders are merely the tip of the iceberg. Individual differences in nearly every phenotype studied are related, to various degrees, to differences in peoples' genes. That is, nearly every phenotypic trait studied so far is heritable to some degree (Plomin, DeFries, McClearn, & McGuffin, 2001). We suggest that much of this genetic variation, especially in traits related to fitness, may be maladaptive—an inevitable consequence of the hundreds of individually minor deleterious mutations that everyone harbors to different degrees.

However, the idea that deleterious mutations have much impact on traits related to fitness seems to fly in the face of canonical evolutionary thought. The traditional view before about 1990 was that mutations might be common enough in traits that are peripherally related to fitness, but that natural selection should ensure that they play little role in traits strongly related to fitness. As discussed in the next section, this common-sense expectation has turned out to be wrong—wrong enough to have misguided mate-choice research for many decades. Because mating intelligence is so strongly related to fitness (reproductive success), a better understanding of the evolutionary genetics of mutation may be crucial to developing a better understanding the role of human intelligence in mate attraction and mate choice.

MUTATIONS AND GENETIC VARIATION IN FITNESS-RELATED TRAITS

Alleles are the different variants (versions of DNA sequences) at genetic loci (genes positioned on chromosomes), and are the cause of genetic variation in phenotypes. Although geneticists often reserve the term *mutations* for genetic variants with frequencies below 1 percent and *alleles* for genetic variants with frequencies over 1 percent, all alleles came into existence originally as mutation events. Thus, in this chapter, *allele* will be used as the generic term, irrespective of frequency. A single allele will have an *average*, or additive effect, on some phenotype, across all of its likely genetic contexts (all other possible alleles at other loci). Because this additive effect does not depend on specific combinations of alleles, it tends to be shared between parent and offspring. The additive genetic variation of a trait in a population, V_A, is roughly the cumulative variation of all these average effects across all alleles affecting the trait (Falconer & Mackay, 1996). One of the longest-standing expectations in evolutionary genetics, often called "Fisher's Fundamental Theorem," has been the idea that strong selection should drive the fittest alleles (those with the most fitness-positive additive effects) to "fixation" (100 percent prevalence), and should drive all less fit alleles to extinction (0 percent prevalence), causing the V_A of fitness-related traits (those that are under strong selection) to approach zero (Fisher, 1930; Haldane, 1932; Kimura, 1958). This occurs because any locus with a single allele fixated at 100 percent prevalence will show no locus-level genetic variation, so will contribute nothing to trait-level genetic variation. Thus, Fisher's Fundamental Theorem implied that the V_A of fitness-related traits should be very low. Empirical data initially seemed to confirm these expectations: traits that are highly relevant to fitness, such as fecundity and lifespan, had lower heritabilities (a rough index of V_A, see below) than traits less related to fitness, such as body size (Roff & Mousseau, 1987).

The expectation of minimal V_A in traits related to fitness did create some problems of its own, however. For example, what good would it do for females to choose males based on some sexually selected trait, such as long tails or deep croaks, when no genetic benefits of female choice are apparent? One common explanation for female choice—that females receive better genes by choosing males who are exceptional on these traits—relies on male traits that honestly advertise genetic *differences* in fitness. Yet how could genetic differences in fitness exist, given that fitness should be under maximal selection pressure, and should thereby show minimal amounts of V_A? This quandary became known as the "lek paradox" (Andersson, 1994; Borgia, 1979; Kirkpatrick & Ryan, 1991).

A lek is a congregation of males in certain species who compete and display for females during breeding season. It was seen as paradoxical that females in such species should care at all about choosing one male over another given that persistent female choice should erode genetic variation in male genetic quality. A common response to the paradox was to simply refute the idea that females were selecting for good genes at all: for decades, many biologists expected 'good genes' mate choice to be irrelevant, and focused on the material benefits of choosing high-quality mates—greater nuptial gifts, parental investment, survival, fertility, and so forth. But for many species, especially lekking species where females receive no material benefit or parental aid, such practical benefits of female choice could not be found (Andersson, 1994).

The crisis came to a head when biologists such as Houle (1992), Charlesworth (1987), and Price (1991) realized that fitness-related traits might not have low V_A after all—that premature conclusion may have been an artifact of how scientists were comparing different traits' genetic variation. V_A is measured in (squared) units of whatever metric is used to measure a trait. Clearly one cannot directly compare the V_A of two traits measured on two different scales, such as the V_A of height in squared centimeters versus the V_A in squared number of offspring. To make these variances comparable (to remove their scale-dependence), V_A has traditionally been standardized by dividing it by the total phenotypic variation. The resulting measure, called narrow-sense heritability, is the proportion of phenotypic variation that is due to additive genetic effects. Heritability is used so often as an index of V_A that it is easy to forget that dividing genetic variance by total phenotypic variance is just one possible way to remove scale-dependence. Specifically, narrow-sense heritability might be misleadingly low, not because the absolute V_A is low, but because the total phenotypic variation is high (due to cumulative random effects in development and life-success), as it often is for traits highly related to fitness. For example, achieved fecundity—actual number of offspring produced by a particular organism—depends not just on genetic quality, but on luck in surviving and reproducing; whereas leg length or brain size depends relatively less on luck. Another technique for removing scale dependence, and one that is not confounded by the total phenotypic variation, is to divide a trait's variation (or technically, its standard deviation) by its mean. This metric is called the "coefficient of variation." It is usually expressed as a percentage, so coefficients of variation (CVs) can range from 0 percent to 100 percent (if a trait's standard deviation equals its mean) to more than 100 percent. Traits that vary more across individuals within a species show higher CVs; for example, the CV of human brain volume is about 8 percent, whereas the CV of male human penis volume is about 37 percent, and the CV of female human breast volume is about 62 percent (Miller & Penke, in press).

Neither heritability nor CV is a perfect index of genetic variation: trait heritabilities are lower when trait development is more influenced by random events, and CVs are lower when trait sizes are measured as lengths rather than areas or volumes (Lande, 1977). However, Houle (1992) gave good reasons to believe that CV is often more informative. When traits were investigated using this new metric of V_A, a remarkable observation emerged: *the coefficient of additive genetic variation of fitness-related traits (such as fecundity or survival) was about five times higher than it was for traits less related to fitness (morphological traits such as bristle number or weight)* (Houle, 1992)—the opposite of what Fisher's Fundamental Theorem seemed to predict. Houle's observation, along with the paradox of the lek, created a real theoretical crisis in evolutionary genetics throughout the 1990s, the ramifications of which are only now beginning to seep into the consciousness of evolutionary psychology and the study of human mate choice.

Why would traits under the strongest selection have the highest mean-standardized V_A? It now appears that one of the most important factors affecting any traits' V_A is the *number of loci that influence the trait*, because many loci provide a larger 'target size' for mutations (Houle, 1998; Houle, Morikawa, & Lynch, 1996). Mutations tend to disrupt the functioning of more highly polygenic traits (those influenced by many genetic loci, such as traits closely related to fitness—survival ability, sexual attractiveness, and achieved reproductive success), whereas they have less effect on simpler traits that depend on fewer loci, and that influence fitness less directly. At the same time, natural selection works to reduce the genetic variation introduced by these mutations. The end result is a balance between mutation and selection, and an equilibrium number of mutations that degrade the functioning of—and cause V_A in—every conceivable trait.

Fitness traits tend to be highly polygenic because they require the proper functioning of so many other subsidiary, 'upstream' processes (Charlesworth, 1987; Houle, 1992, 1998; Price & Schluter, 1991)—one cannot produce offspring, for instance, without first producing antibodies to fight infection, neural circuitry to feel appropriate motivations, hormones to time maturation, and so forth. Thousands of 'upstream' traits must function together to build a body capable of surviving, finding a mate, and reproducing. Indeed, the mutational target size of "fitness" is, by definition, every gene in the genome that has any fitness effect. Among the most compelling pieces of evidence for the idea that mutations are the culprit behind the high mean-standardized in fitness traits are the high, positive correlations in fruit flies between a) the estimated number of loci influencing traits, b) traits' coefficients of additive genetic variation, and c) the amount of V_A that mutations contribute to traits per generation (Houle, 1998). (At the level of basic evolutionary genetics, fruit flies are surprisingly good proxies for humans, though they have only about 14,000 genes compared to our 25,000).

Thus, fitness-related traits show high levels of V_A—not because selection favors this variation and not because selection fails to work against it—but rather because selection fights against a constant mutational headwind that replenishes genetic variation in highly polygenic traits. This explanation also clarifies why fitness-related traits have relatively low heritabilities: downstream, fitness-related traits tend to be influenced by many sources of variation: not just V_A, but also non-additive genetic variation (dominance and epistatic genetic variation, which concern interactions between alleles at a genetic locus or across loci), random environmental effects, and random developmental errors. Because natural selection can reduce V_A at a much faster rate than it can reduce these other sources of variation (Fisher, 1930; Merilä & Sheldon, 1999), the ratio of V_A to the total phenotypic variation (V_A + non-additive genetic variation + environmental variation) tends to be low in fitness-related traits—which is why they show low heritability but high CVs.

MUTATIONS AND SEX

Under mutation-selection balance, certain individuals have a low *mutation load* (i.e., possess relatively few mutations and/or possess mutations that tend to have lower average effects), while other individuals have a higher mutational load. Individuals who have a low load of mutations will tend to have mechanisms less degraded by harmful mutations, and so will tend to have higher fitness over evolutionary time, while those with more mutations will tend to have lower fitness. Such genetic variation in fitness is a prerequisite to all 'good genes' theories of mate selection, including those in evolutionary psychology. Evolutionary processes besides mutation-selection that maintain genetic variation in populations—such as balancing selection or drift plus recurrent neutral mutations—imply that alternative alleles have *equal* fitness, when averaged across all the genomes and environments in which those alleles could find themselves (Keller & Miller, 2006). In other words, balancing selection and neutral drift produce fitness-neutral genetic variation, but they cannot produce fitness-correlated V_A (i.e., heritable variation in good genes). Aside from finding genes that complement one's own (e.g., mating with the right species, avoiding genetic inbreeding), there is no genetic advantage in choosing mates if there is no fitness-correlated V_A—given balancing selection or neutral drift, any randomly chosen mate would have about equally fit genes on average. Thus, the only plausible origin for V_A in fitness-related traits, such as sexually selected traits, is mutation-selection balance.

A mutation-selection explanation for V_A in fitness also neatly resolves the lek paradox: if sexually selected traits are highly correlated with fitness ("index handicaps") or are costly in 'fitness currency' ("strategic handicaps"), then any process that maintains V_A in fitness (i.e., mutation-selection) must also maintain V_A in the sexually selected traits that reflect fitness. Indeed, persistent sexual selection on any arbitrary trait should eventually cause that trait to correlate with fitness and, hence, to become more highly polygenic (Rowe & Houle, 1996). That is, sexual selection tends to make sexually attractive traits more fitness-sensitive, more dependent on many genes, and more reliable indicators of overall mutation load and genetic quality.

To illustrate why this should be, consider what would occur if, over evolutionary time, females were most attracted to males with the longest fingers. As finger length increased, this trait would become increasingly costly (dealing with foot-long fingers would be a tough thing to do!). Selection would favor contingent adaptations that allow expression of the costly trait only to the degree that it pays off in fitness currency. For example, if males didn't care for finger length in female mates, then females would receive none of the sexual benefits but all of the survival costs of expressing their exaggerated-finger-length genes. In this case, selection would favor an adaptation that turns exaggerated-finger-length genes on or off depending upon whether the genes are in male or female bodies. In other words, sexual selection for a trait in only one sex should lead to sexual dimorphism, which is widely observed in nature (Darwin, 1871).

For the same reason that sexual selection leads to differences in the expression of sexual traits *between* sexes, it should also lead to differences in the expression of sexual traits *within* a sex, depending upon each individual's genetic quality (low mutation load) and phenotypic condition (overall health). Continuing with the example of sexual selection for finger length, males whose fingers are too long given their condition would have lower survival: if they had many mutations, poorly-functioning brains, and poor hand-eye coordination, they would often get their fingers cut, crushed, and burned, and they wouldn't be able to hunt or fight effectively with such handicaps. On the other hand, males with few mutations, smarter brains, and better coordination would suffer fewer survival costs and would enjoy higher reproductive benefits from their super-sexy fingers. These differential costs and benefits of finger-length should lead selection to favor a contingent (condition-dependent) adaptation: males should grow the longest fingers possible *given* their own condition. Once such contingent mechanisms are universal, the fittest males—those least degraded by harmful mutations—would be best able to bear the costs of developing long, ornamental, self-handicapping fingers; low-fitness males would grow shorter, more practical fingers. Finger length, even if the trait were originally controlled by only a small number of genes, would become an honest signal of condition; the mutational target size of finger length increases from the genes originally only devoted to finger length, before sexual selection, to all the fitness-related genes in the genome, after sexual selection.

The end result of sexual selection is a species where an initially arbitrary trait comes to be correlated with individual mutation load, condition, and fitness. This is an interesting evolutionary property, because it suggests that whatever the origins for sexual selection preferences, be they due to Fisherian runaway, to random sensory bias, or because they genuinely reflect genetic quality from the beginning (for discussion of the possible origins of sexual selection traits, see Andersson, 1994), they will eventually become good ways to distinguish mates based upon genetic quality/mutation load (Kirkpatrick & Ryan, 1991; Rowe & Houle, 1996).

MUTATIONS AND MATING INTELLIGENCE

The relationship between mutations and sexual selection, discussed above, is relevant to different ways of thinking about mating intelligence (MI). Geher, Miller, and Murphy (this volume) identified several ways that MI can be conceptualized; here, I will discuss three broad categories of MI that are related, but not identical, to those made by Geher et al. None of these three conceptualizations is 'correct,' of course, but the evolutionary-genetics principles explored above suggest that different types of mating intelligence require different types of evolutionary explanation, fulfill different adaptive functions, and may benefit from different names. One potential conceptualization of MI concerns *mating preferences*—qualities that people find attractive in mates. Understanding human mating preferences has been one of the major interests of evolutionary psychologists, as a glance through any evolutionary psychology journal or textbook would indicate (e.g., Buss, 2004). Different types of mating preferences probably serve somewhat different functions—some may help secure mates willing and able to commit material resources, some may help secure behaviorally compatible mates, and, as detailed above, some may help select mates of high genetic quality (Buss, 1999). Cues of genetic quality may be favored, for example, by mate preferences for intelligence and artistic ability (Miller, 2000), symmetrical faces and bodies (Gangestad & Thornhill, 1999b), athleticism (Buss & Schmitt, 1993), body shape (Singh, 1993), dancing ability (Brown et al., 2005), and facial features associated with sex-hormones (Thornhill & Gangestad, 1999).

A different conceptualization of MI concerns *mating abilities*—individual differences in those traits that people find attractive—which have been the central focus of the current chapter so far. For example, how successful are different people at attracting desirable mates? Reflecting the long standing divide between evolutionary genetics and adaptationism discussed at the beginning of this chapter, the study of mating abilities mainly concerns individual differences, while the study of mating preferences mainly concerns species-typical design. The two concepts are inherently related, of course—some species-typical mating preferences have evolved in order to track individual differences in mating ability—but their evolutionary origins and adaptive functions nevertheless require quite different types of explanations.

To simplify somewhat, we should expect much more fitness-related genetic variation in mating abilities than in mating preferences[2]. This is

---

[2]This is not to say that mating preferences should necessarily be less heritable than mating abilities. Not only is heritability a poor way to compare the levels of genetic variation between traits, as discussed above, but the scaling of the genetic variation must take into account its fitness effects. Specifically, the prediction is that genetic variation in mating preferences should be unrelated to fitness, while the genetic variation in mating abilities should be related to fitness. This could be easily tested if the correct data set exists: mating abilities should share high genetic correlations with each other and with other traits known to be related to fitness, while mating preferences should not.

because mating preferences should have evolved toward those preferences that are best at discriminating between good mates, but there is no reason to believe that the genetic bases of such preferences would be any more polygenic than any other evolved preference or behavior. An evolved rule that says, "Be attracted to the longest fingers," is under selection for a *single* preference, and those alleles that code for such a preference should become fixed in the population, leading to little fitness-relevant genetic variation in the preference. Similarly, we do not expect much genetic variance in food preferences: sweet, salty, fatty tastes (indicating ancestrally scarce nutrients) are universally attractive, whereas bitter tastes (indicating plant toxins) and rancid tastes (indicating bacterial spoilage) are universally unattractive.

By contrast, mating abilities have been under open-ended, directional (more-is-better) selection for a long time, and they have become correlated with fitness, and hence highly polygenic, for the reasons outlined above. Mating abilities will show high levels of fitness-related genetic variation, and thereby will reliably reveal the different genetic qualities of different potential mates, despite being under intense selection. Most of this genetic variation in mating abilities should be due to deleterious mutations. At the genetic level, intelligent or beautiful people do not so much have genes that cause them to be intelligent or beautiful as they lack the genes (mutations) that would make them unintelligent or unattractive.

A final conceptualization of MI concerns *individual differences in people's understandings of human mating preferences.* For example, how well do different people understand that females tend to be more interested than males in a partner's status? Note that this conceptualization of MI does not concern how well people understand or 'mind read' potential mates, which may well be related to mating abilities. Rather, it concerns how well peoples' conscious, reported beliefs about mating preferences correspond to some evidence-based standard.

It is difficult to form evolutionary predictions about this understanding-of-mating-preferences conceptualization of MI. Much in the same way that people can maximize their reproductive success without having a conscious desire for offspring, there is no necessary connection between people's mating behavior and people's conscious beliefs about human mating preferences. Perhaps those with the best understanding of species-typical mating preferences had higher fitness, but this does not seem self-evident. A reproductively successful male could be motivated to acquire status, resources, and so forth, and yet may report a lower-than-average awareness that women find such traits desirous. Indeed, high mate-value individuals may have less understanding of how mating preferences work, because they rarely have to work very hard to attract mates or confront difficult trade-offs themselves. Moreover, if an accurate understanding of mating preferences were indeed under selection, it should show very little fitness-related genetic variation, for much the same reasons that mating preferences themselves should show little fitness-related genetic variation: such an understanding would be under strong selection, yet should be no more polygenic than any other evolved preference.

To complicate matters, there may be a lot of adaptive self-deception about mating preferences. I suspect that most of the genetic variation in people's understandings of human mating preferences is related to intelligence and personality variables (extraversion, agreeableness, etc.), while most of the modern environmental variation is related to incidental factors such as mating experience, parental and peer influences, socio-political attitudes, education, exposure to popular science, and so forth. For these reasons, I believe that evolutionary predictions of this final conceptualization of MI are not straight-forward.

PREDICTIONS ABOUT MATING INTELLIGENCE

In this section, I briefly put forward two predictions about different conceptualizations of MI, the first concerned with mating preferences, and the second with mating abilities.

Females May Have a Fitness Advantage in Mating With Younger Males, Whose Sperm Is Less Likely To Carry New, Harmful Mutations.

Female humans are born with their full supply of 400 or so eggs, and these eggs have gone through only 23 replications, a number which does not change as females age. By contrast, males continue to produce sperm throughout life. At age 15, sperm cells have gone through about 35 chromosomal replications, increasing to 380 by age 30, and 840 by age 50 (Crow, 2000). The probability of germ-line mutations increases with paternal age because each chromosomal replication carries a small chance of a copying error (mutation). Consistent with this point, higher paternal, but not maternal, age is associated with lower intelligence as well as many Mendelian disorders and common mental disorders (Crow, 2000). For unknown reasons, greater maternal age is associated with a higher probability of major chromosomal abnormalities (such as Down syndrome and other trisomies), but these events are very rare compared to new mutations.

Although both women and men carry the same number of old, slightly deleterious mutations, the vast majority of mutations that exist in the population were introduced by male sperm from older fathers. The proportion of existing mutations in the population that come from males could be quantified with better information on the relationships among age, fertility, and mutation rate. The key question regarding female preferences is: how much would individual female fitness suffer over evolutionary time by having offspring with older males?

One approach is to estimate the cumulative harmfulness of new mutations per generation (which females might avoid in their offspring by mating with young males) relative to the cumulative harmfulness of old mutations per generation (which females might avoid in their offspring by mating with attractive, intelligent males). New mutations in a fathers' sperm cells will be phenotypically expressed only in the fathers' offspring and descendents; these new mutations are not phenotypically expressed in the fathers themselves, and so do not reduce a males' mating ability. The only way that females can assess the chance that a male will pass on a new mutation to her offspring is based on cues of male age.

Although old mutations are over a hundred times more common, new mutations tend to be more deleterious, since the old mutations that persist after generations of selection must have had relatively small fitness costs. Recent, albeit tentative, results suggest that about 20 percent of new, deleterious mutations have effects large enough to be detectable in mutation-accumulation experiments, and these detectable mutations reduce fitness by an average of about 5 percent (García-Dorado, López-Fanjul, & Caballero, 2004). On the other hand, evolutionary genetic theory predicts that most old mutations should reduce fitness by between 0.00005 percent and 0.05 percent. Under the simplifying assumptions that undetectable new mutations have the same fitness effects as old mutations, and that old mutations reduce fitness by an average of, say, 0.0025 percent, then a given new mutation is on average 400 times more deleterious to fitness than a given old mutation. Because people harbor perhaps 500+ old mutations in their genome (Fay et al., 2001), and inherit 1–2 new mutations (Eyre-Walker & Keightley, 1999), this calculation suggests that, in terms of female fitness, it is about equally important to prefer a younger male, who is less likely to pass on new mutations, as it is to prefer a high-quality male, who is less likely to pass on older mutations. The prediction that cues of youth and of genetic quality are about equally important to human females is highly speculative at this point, and could easily be wrong. While it is based upon a number of assumptions that are likely to be fairly accurate (the hominid deleterious mutation rate; the number of old, deleterious mutations per human; the average effect size of new, detectable mutations), it is also based upon some assumptions by the author that are little more than educated guesses (the average effect of old mutations; the average effect of new, undetectable mutations). Several complications, such as the non-linear acceleration in rates of paternal mutations with age (Crow, 2000), were also unaccounted for; it seems likely that below a certain age (perhaps around 35–40), the chance of a new mutation in male germline cells is still quite low, and females have little to worry about. Thus, women may not show a preference for extreme male youth so much as an aversion to extreme male age.

The goal of this exercise was to illustrate how evolutionary-genetic theory, given empirical data from seemingly distant fields, can make new, quantifiable predictions relevant to human mate choice and mating intelligence. This exercise also shows the types of data that would be relevant in rigorously assessing the relative importance of old mutation load (affecting male mating ability) versus new mutation load (signaled by male age). Such data are increasingly available using modern genetic techniques, and more accurate estimates than the ones presented here will probably be available in a few years.

If better modeling does predict that females have an important fitness advantage in mating with younger males, it would seem to go against the standard evolutionary psychology view that males prefer youth while females do not. It is true that many females end up in long-term relationships with high-resource, older men, but this might only reflect that female reproductive success depends on many variables and trade-offs (e.g., protection and provisioning from older, higher-status males versus the increased chance of mutations in offspring that come from mating with such males). This hypothesis suggests that (a) relative to females in relationships with younger males, females in relationships with older males may be more likely to have or desire extramarital affairs, (b) these affairs would tend to be with younger males, and (c) this tendency to seek out younger males might peak when females are at peak fertility in their menstrual cycles. Indeed, women do seem to have adaptations for seeking good-genes extra-pair partners at peak fertility (Haselton & Gangestad, 2006). Researchers might also study how cues of older male age may override cues of male genetic quality in female mate choice. This could then be compared to estimates of how harmful new versus old mutations are in females' mates. If these numbers agreed, it would support the hypothesis that paternal age is a factor in female mate-choice, and the view that mutations have been crucial in sexual selection.

The Alleles That Affect Mating Abilities Will Be Numerous, of Small Effect, and Difficult To Find.

Whereas the first prediction concerned mating preferences, this second prediction concerns mating abilities. Furthermore, whereas the first prediction was very sensitive to quantitative assumptions about which little is definitively known, this second prediction is fairly robust and reliable. As described previously, the genetic variation in mating abilities should be due to old and new mutations at many genes (Rowe & Houle, 1996).

Because mutations can occur anywhere along a locus, the coding portion of which is typically around 1,500 base pairs long, mutation-selection has created many different, lineage-specific deleterious alleles. The frequency distributions of alleles/mutations at such loci should be extremely skewed, such that besides the most common, adaptive allele, no single maladaptive allele should have a frequency greater than about 5 percent (Pritchard, 2001), and usually, its frequency should be much lower. These factors—many loci, and many different, lineage-specific alleles at each locus—work against current methods of gene detection using linkage and especially association studies (Terwilliger & Weiss, 1998; Weiss & Clark, 2002; Wright & Hastie, 2001). A mutation-selection hypothesis predicts slow progress in finding genes related to mating abilities.

If, as argued by Miller (2000), intelligence is a mating ability, the slow progress in finding specific genes associated with intelligence is consistent with this expectation; several likely IQ genes have been found, but none explain much of the population variation in IQ (e.g., less than 1 percent; Butcher et al., 2005), despite very large studies designed to find such genes. Indeed, a mutational hypothesis suggests that gene-mapping studies on mating abilities may be misconceived. Rather than a small number of alleles "for" intelligence, there may be many thousands of different alleles (mutations) "for" unintelligence. We should predict similarly slow progress in detecting genes that affect other potential mating abilities, such as physical attractiveness, fluctuating asymmetry, musical ability, sense of humor, and athleticism.

CONCLUSION

I end the chapter by extending an analogy introduced at the beginning of the chapter. Imagine a world in which everyone inherits two virtually identical books of code, one from mother and one from father (representing two sets of chromosomes). Each codebook contains 75 million characters (representing evolutionarily important, phenotypically expressed base pairs), 25,000 pages (genes and their surrounding regulatory regions), and 23 chapters of various length (chromosomes). The purpose of the two codebooks together is to create an intricate, self-directed machine (an individual), and on each page of each book is a section of code for assembling one aspect of the machine (some part of an adaptation). Both codebooks, in combination, average about 500+ old copying errors committed by some great, great, great . . . grandparent (probably grand-father), as well as one or two newer errors, committed by the mother or, more likely, the father, when they were putting these codebooks together. Some people's codebooks have more errors, and some have fewer, and these errors are only rarely on the same pages (much less the same characters!) between different codebooks. No-one knows exactly where these errors lie in any given codebook, although they degrade the performance of each machine to various degrees.

Now imagine a great tournament, in which every machine is unleashed into a grand playing field. Machines that function the best were created from the most error-free codebooks and have the highest probability of surviving. As is the custom in this imaginary world, people pass on one complete codebook to each of their children, and each new codebook is a carefully aligned pastiche of the codebooks from father and mother. Well-functioning machines are critically important, and so a core concern is to find a mate with codebooks that have the fewest and least harmful errors. To this end, machines are designed to ask other machines to do extraordinarily difficult and complicated actions to reveal how many errors exist in their codebooks. Machines with the fewest codebook errors perform the best at such tasks (show the best mating abilities), and are the most attractive (according to mate preferences for codebook quality). The best-performing machines tend to pair up with the other best-performing machines, while the worst pair up with the worst. In this way, the population-level variation in codebook errors is greatly magnified; some codes have very few errors and make well-functioning machines, while others are so riddled with errors that they have difficulty functioning at all.

This analogy is fanciful, but it illustrates the situation that humans and other long-lived species find themselves in. Humans have evolved under intense mutational pressure; sexual selection from both sexes has been a way that our ancestors have managed this pressure. As evolutionary psychologists such as Miller (1998, 2000) and Gangestad (1997, 1999a, 2000) have hypothesized, it is likely that those traits which make up an 'attractive' mate are precisely those traits that have been under sexual selection because they reveal the mutation load that each person carries. Physical attractiveness, intelligence, athleticism, social charm, artistic abilities . . . all these may be attractive because they are difficult to develop and display well, and they thereby reflect an individual's mutational load. Those innate aspects of mating intelligence that make us attracted to certain types of people have been designed through millions of years of natural selection to make it likely that our offspring can keep one step ahead of the mutational beast that forever chases us.

ACKNOWLEDGMENTS

Thanks to Paul Andrews and the editors, Glenn Geher and Geoffrey Miller, for helpful comments and guidance.

REFERENCES

Andersson, M. (1994). *Sexual selection*. Princeton, NJ: Princeton University Press.

Bailey, J. M. (2000). How can psychological adaptations be heritable? In G. R. Bock, J. A. Goode, & K. Webb (Eds.), *The nature of intelligence* (pp. 171–179). West Sussex, UK: Wiley & Sons.

Borgia, G. (1979). Sexual selection and the evolution of mating systems. In M. S. Blum & N. A. Blum (Eds.), *Sexual selection and reproductive competition in insects* (pp. 19–80). New York: Academic Press.

Bowler, P. J. (1989). *Evolution: The history of an idea* (revised ed.). Berkeley: University of California Press.

Buss, D. M. (1999). *Evolutionary psychology: The new science of the mind*. Boston: Allyn & Bacon.

Buss, D. M. (Ed.). (2005). *The handbook of evolutionary psychology*. Hoboken, NJ: Wiley & Sons.

Buss, D. M., & Schmitt, D. P. (1993). Sexual strategies theory: An evolutionary perspective on human mating. *Psychological Review, 100,* 204–232.

Charlesworth, B. (1987). The heritability of fitness. In J. W. Bradbury & M. B. Andersson (Eds.), *Sexual selection: Testing the alternatives* (pp. 21–40). London, UK: Wiley & Sons.

Crow, J. F. (2000). The origins, patterns, and impliciations of human spontaneous mutation. *Nature Reviews Genetics, 1,* 40–47.

Darwin, C. (1871). *The descent of man, and selection in relation to sex*. London: Murray.

Eaves, L. J., Martin, N. G., Heath, A. C., Hewitt, J. K., & Neale, M. C. (1990). Personality and reproductive fitness. *Behavior Genetics, 20,* 563–568.

Eyre-Walker, A., & Keightley, P. D. (1999). High genomic deleterious mutation rates in hominids. *Nature, 397,* 344–347.

Falconer, D. S., & Mackay, T. F. C. (1996). *Introduction to quantitative genetics* (4th ed.). Harlow, Essex, UK: Addison Wesley Longman.

Fay, J. C., Wyckoff, G. J., & Wu, C. (2001). Positive and negative selection on the human genome. *Genetics, 158,* 1227–1234.

Fisher, R. A. (1930). *The genetical theory of natural selection*. Oxford: Clarendon Press.

Gangestad, S. W., & Simpson, J. A. (2000). The evolution of human mating: Trade-offs and strategic pluralism. *Behavioral and Brain Sciences, 23,* 573–644.

Gangestad, S. W., & Thornhill, R. (1999a). Facial attractiveness. *Trends in Cognitive Science, 3,* 452–460.

Gangestad, S. W., & Thornhill, R. (1999b). Individual differences in developmental precision and fluctuating asymmetry: A model and its implications. *Journal of Evolutionary Biology, 12,* 402–416.

Gangestad, S. W., & Yeo, R. W. (1997). Behavioral genetic variation, adaptation and maladaptation: An evolutionary perspective. *Trends in Cognitive Science, 1,* 103–108.

García-Dorado, A., Caballero, A., & Crow, J. F. (2003). On the persistence and pervasiveness of a new mutation. *Evolution, 57,* 2644–2646.

García-Dorado, A., López-Fanjul, C., & Caballero, A. (2004). Rates and effects of deleterious mutations and their evolutionary consequences. In A. Moya & E. Font (Eds.), *Evolution: From molecules to ecosystems*. Oxford: Oxford University Press.

Geher, G., Miller, G. F., & Murphy, J. W. (this volume). Mating intelligence: Toward an evolutionarily informed construct. In G. Geher (Ed.), *Mating Intelligence: Sex, Relationships, and The Mind's Reproductive System*. Mahwah, NJ: Lawrence Erlbaum Associates.

Haldane, J. B. S. (1932). *The causes of evolution*. Princeton, N.J.: Princeton University Press.

Haselton, M. G., & Gangestad, S. W. (2006). Conditional expression of women's desires and men's mate guarding across the ovulatory cycle. *Hormones and Behavior, 49*, 506–518.

Houle, D. (1992). Comparing evolvability and variability of quantitative traits. *Genetics, 130*, 195–205.

Houle, D. (1998). How should we explain variation in the genetic variance of traits? *Genetica, 102*, 241–253.

Houle, D., Morikawa, B., & Lynch, M. (1996). Comparing mutational variabilities. *Genetics, 143*, 1467–1483.

Keightley, P. D., & Eyre-Walker, A. (2000). Deleterious mutations and the evolution of sex. *Science, 290*, 331–333.

Keightley, P. D., & Gaffney, D. J. (2003). Functional constraints and frequency of deleterious mutations in noncoding DNA of rodents. *Proceedings of the National Academy of Sciences, 100*, 13402–13406.

Keller, M. C., & Miller, G. (2006). Resolving the paradox of common, harmful, heritable mental disorders: Which evolutionary genetic models work best? *Behavioral and Brain Sciences, 29*, 385–452.

Kimura, M. (1958). On the change of population fitness by natural selection. *Heredity, 12*, 145–167.

Kirkpatrick, M., & Ryan, M. J. (1991). The evolution of mating preferences and the paradox of the lek. *Nature, 350*, 33–38.

Lande, R. (1977). On comparing coefficients of variation. *Systematic Zoology, 26*, 214–217.

Merilä, J., & Sheldon, B. C. (1999). Genetic architecture of fitness and nonfitness traits: Empirical patterns and development of ideas. *Heredity, 83*, 103–109.

Miller, G. (2000). *The mating mind*. New York: Doubleday.

Miller, G., & Todd, P. M. (1998). Mate choice turns cognitive. *Trends in Cognitive Science, 2*, 190–198.

Nachman, M. W., & Crowell, S. L. (2000). Estimate of the mutation rate per nucleotide in humans. *Genetics, 156*, 297–304.

Plomin, R., DeFries, J. C., McClearn, G. E., & McGuffin, P. (2001). *Behavioral genetics* (4th ed.). New York: Worth Publishers.

Price, T., & Schluter, D. (1991). On the low heritability of life-history traits. *Evolution, 45*, 853–861.

Pritchard, J. K. (2001). Are rare variants responsible for susceptibility to complex diseases? *American Journal of Human Genetics, 69*, 124–137.

Ridley, M. (2000). *Mendel's demon: Gene justice and the complexity of life*. London: Orion.

Roff, D. A., & Mousseau, T. A. (1987). Quantitative genetics and fitness. *Heredity, 58*, 103–118.

Rowe, L., & Houle, D. (1996). The lek paradox and the capture of genetic variance by condition dependent traits. *Proceedings of the Royal Society of London, Series B, 263*, 1415–1421.

Singh, D. (1993). Adaptive significance of waist-to-hip ratio and female physical attractiveness. *Journal of Personality and Social Psychology, 65*, 293–307.

Terwilliger, J. D., & Weiss, K. M. (1998). Linkage disequilibrium mapping of complex disease: Fantasy or reality? *Current Opinion in Biotechnology, 9*, 578–594.

Thornhill, R., & Gangestad, S. W. (1999). Facial attractiveness. *Trends in Cognitive Science, 3*, 452–460.

Weiss, K. M., & Clark, A. G. (2002). Linkage disequilibrium and the mapping of complex human traits. *Trends in Genetics, 18*, 19–24.

Wright, A. F., & Hastie, N. D. (2001). Complex genetic diseases: Controversy over the Croesus code. *Genome Biology, 2*, 1–8.

Chapter 9

Mental Disorders as Catastrophic Failures of Mating Intelligence

Andrew Shaner
University of California, Los Angeles and
the Veterans Affairs Greater Los Angeles
Healthcare System

Geoffrey Miller
University of New Mexico

Jim Mintz
University of California, Los Angeles and
the Veterans Affairs Greater Los Angeles
Healthcare System

Some animals attract mates by displaying indices of genetic quality known as *sexually selected fitness indicators* (Andersson, 1994). Peacocks, for example, vibrate their showy tails as peahens hunt for the male with the biggest tail. That's because his big tail indicates that he has the genes most likely to produce high fitness in her offspring. Similarly, some human mental abilities, such as language, music, dance, art, and humor, may function as fitness indicators—the human equivalents of peacock tails (Miller, 2000). If so, those mental abilities must vary greatly in quality and that variation must include low-fitness, unattractive extremes—the human equivalents of small peacock tails. Why? Because fitness indicators can be used for mate selection only if some beaus have high-quality attractive versions and others don't; the more a trait varies across individuals, the more it can be used to select the fittest mate.

Our thesis is that some human mental disorders represent the low-fitness extremes of traits that evolved, at least in part, as sexually selected fitness indicators. In this chapter, we explore that proposition and some of its ramifications. Specifically, we'll discuss schizophrenia as a catastrophic failure of mating intelligence (as manifest in courtship ability), and anti-schizophrenia stigmatization as a possibly adaptive form of mating intelligence (as manifest in mate choice). Then, we'll explore whether fitness-indicator theory may apply to other mental disorders, including severe anxiety, depression, and mania, and whether they can be considered break-downs in mating intelligence. Finally, we'll discuss how fitness indicators arising outside the mating context may explain other mental disorders such as autism.

SCHIZOPHRENIA AS AN EVOLUTIONARY PARADOX

Schizophrenia strikes about 1 percent of people worldwide, producing delusions, hallucinations, disorganized speech, bizarre behavior, and emotional blunting. Typically beginning in late adolescence or early adulthood, it often leads to social isolation and severe lifelong disability (American Psychiatric Association, 2000). Schizophrenia is an evolutionary paradox (reviewed in Brune, 2004) as it markedly reduces reproductive success (Haukka, Suvisaari, & Lonnqvist, 2003) *and* is highly heritable (e.g., Cardno et al., 1999). So why hasn't selection eliminated the responsible genes? How can it persist at such a high prevalence—far in excess of the rate possible from a single deleterious mutation (Wilson, 1997)?

One possibility, originally suggested by Julian Huxley, Ernst Mayr, and colleagues (1964), and recently reviewed in detail (Brune, 2004), is that the same genes that cause schizophrenia in some people produce advantages in their relatives. These hidden adaptive benefits might enhance survival and reproduction, offset the evolutionary disadvantage of schizophrenia, and thereby perpetuate the responsible genes within the gene pool. However, no survival benefits have been confirmed in relatives, and while some studies have found that relatives of schizophrenics have more children than expected, other larger studies have not (reviewed in Haukka et al., 2003). Moreover, behavior-genetic modeling shows that schizophrenia is not due to a single gene or even just a few genes, as one might expect from a hidden-benefits model (Keller & Miller, 2006; Riley & McGuffin, 2000). Decades of schizophrenia gene-hunting through linkage and association studies have also failed to find any major-risk genes. Consequently, investigators have concluded that schizophrenia is probably due to many genes, each accounting for a small percentage of cases (McDonald & Murphy, 2003).

This polygenic model leads to a second (and widely accepted) explanation for the persistence of schizophrenia. If schizophrenia is sufficiently polygenic, that is, if alleles (genetic differences) at many loci (chromosomal locations) are involved in its etiology, and if the penetrance (power to cause schizophrenia) of these susceptibility alleles is low, then new mutations could maintain an overall frequency of susceptibility alleles at a level sufficient to produce schizophrenia in one percent of the population (see Pritchard, 2001).

But why would *so many* genes predispose individuals to schizophrenia? Why would human mental functioning be so vulnerable to mutations at so many loci? A partial answer is that the brain systems that fail in schizophrenia are unusually vulnerable to "developmental instability" (DI). When manifest in body growth, DI results in right-left asymmetries and minor physical anomalies; when manifest in brain development, DI results in abnormal lateralization, unusual brain anatomy, lower intelligence, and psychopathology (Prokosch, Yeo, & Miller, 2005; Yeo, Gangestad, Edgar, & Thoma, 1999).

But traits needed for survival tend to develop reliably despite mutations and environmental hazards (Pomiankowski & Moller, 1995; Rowe & Houle, 1996). Why would human mental functioning be an exception? The answer may be that the brain systems which go awry in schizophrenia evolved not because they increase the odds of survival, but because they are useful in sexual courtship and competition. They increase the odds of mating, and they thereby enhance reproductive success. In other words, if a well-functioning brain is an attractive human characteristic that affects mate choice, schizophrenia may be evolutionarily analogous to a small, dull peacock's tail. More technically, it may be the low-fitness, unsuccessful extreme of a sexually selected fitness indicator that evolved in humans by mutual mate choice (Shaner, Miller, & Mintz, 2004).

That single sentence, if true, would explain many puzzling and otherwise apparently unrelated facts about schizophrenia, including why it begins in adolescence and early adulthood, why it reduces reproductive success, why it is highly heritable, why the genes underlying it are so hard to find, why it's worse in males, why it's associated with environmental hazards and abnormal brain development, why dopamine blockers are therapeutic, and even why affected individuals are so socially stigmatized.

Moreover, the hypothesis leads to some surprising and testable predictions. One, for example, is that genetic and environmental causes of schizophrenia will number in the hundreds or thousands, each accounting for no more than a few percent of cases. Another prediction is that the responsible genes will comprise a wide variety of fitness-reducing mutations that remain lineage-specific (localized in particular populations), and therefore will not replicate well across populations. A third prediction is that drugs which reduce courtship behaviors in animals (e.g., a drug that stops peacocks from displaying their tails to peahens) may improve schizophrenia in humans.

To explain our hypothesis, we'll first review how sexually selected traits may serve as fitness indicators. Next, we'll explain how schizophrenia can be viewed as the unattractive extreme of such a trait. Finally, we'll show how this view can have so much explanatory and predictive power.

SEXUALLY SELECTED FITNESS INDICATORS

Darwin argued that traits which improve survival are more likely than others to be passed on to offspring, and that this selection process could account for the evolution of new adaptations and new species (Darwin, 1859). But he was troubled by the large number of traits that have no survival value or that might even impair survival—traits such as peacock tails, elk antlers, and human music. He suggested that they evolved for a different purpose—acquiring mates (Darwin, 1871). He wrote:

> All animals present individual differences, and as man can modify his domesticated birds by selecting the individuals which appear to him the most beautiful, so the habitual or even occasional preference by the female of the more attractive males would almost certainly lead to their modification; and such modification might in the course of time be augmented to almost any extent, compatible with the existence of the species. (pp. 750–751)

Traits that improved mating success, he argued, also stood a better chance of being passed on to offspring, and this process could account for the evolution of new species. Darwin discussed two mechanisms of sexual selection: "Contests" between males over females, which favor "weapons" such as elk antlers, and "mate choice" by females, which favors male "ornaments" such as peacock tails. More recently, biologists have identified additional sexual-selection mechanisms including endurance rivalry, scramble competition, and sperm competition (Andersson, 1994).

What makes a trait attractive to potential mates? Darwin didn't know, but subsequent evolutionary theorists have suggested several possibilities (which can act simultaneously). Traits may become attractive because they advertise health, fertility, vigor, longevity, parenting ability, optimal genetic distance, good genes, and/or simply the prospect of passing on attractiveness itself (Andersson, 1994).

How can an ornament, such as a peacock's tail, advertise genetic quality or fitness? If healthier birds tend to grow brighter feathers, then the brightness of feathers would indicate fitness (Fisher, 1915). Moreover, the offspring of females who prefer brighter feathers would inherit the father's genes for better fitness and the mother's genes for preferring bright feathers. Across generations, the increasing co-occurrence within individuals of the preference genes and the fitness genes would lead to a powerful positive-feedback process that could fuel the rapid evolution of brighter feathers—a process termed "runaway sexual selection" (Fisher, 1930).

Why would healthier birds have brighter feathers or bigger tails? One possibility is a mechanism called "the handicap principle" (Zahavi, 1975). A peacock's tail takes considerable energy to grow, maintain, and display. This cost could make it a reliable indicator of fitness, because only the fittest peacocks can afford the energy necessary to grow large and colorful tails. As a result, peahens would evolve a preference for the extravagant extreme. The handicap principle and several related mechanisms produce extravagant traits in theoretical models (Andersson, 1994; Hasson, 1989; Michod & Hasson, 1990)—even in monogamous species (Hooper & Miller, submitted). Moreover, empirical work has shown that some sexually selected traits bear the three hallmarks of fitness indicators (Andersson, 1994): (1) they vary greatly in size, loudness, complexity, or other qualities across individuals; (2) that variance correlates with underlying fitness and condition; and (3) potential mates prefer the high-fitness extreme.

But this leads to another question—why don't all peacocks have big, beautiful tails? Tails vary greatly in size and complexity, and that variation is somewhat heritable. However, in a group of peafowl, the one or two peacocks with the most elaborate tails sire virtually all the offspring (Petrie, Halliday, & Sanders, 1991). Why don't the genes for big tails proliferate and why don't the genes for less elaborate tails disappear? This question is called "the paradox of the lek" (Kirkpatrick & Ryan, 1991)—a lek being the clearing in which male birds display their ornaments as females inspect and choose—not unlike a singles bar. Recently, several investigators have suggested a common potential resolution of the "lek paradox" (Houle & Kondrashov, 2002; Kotiaho, Simmons, & Tomkins, 2001; Michod & Hasson, 1990; Pomiankowski & Moller, 1995; Rowe & Houle, 1996). This resolution, discussed subsequently, is at the heart of the explanatory and predictive power of our hypothesis regarding schizophrenia.

THE LEK PARADOX RESOLVED

The resolution requires a distinction between "good" and "bad" genes. "Good genes" are those versions of genes ("alleles") best suited to an animal's current ecological niche, and to the rest of its species-typical genome. Individuals with "good genes" grow better bodies and brains, find more food, resist more parasites, avoid more predators, survive longer, and, thereby, leave more offspring. However, to reproduce, they must make sperm or ova. In that process, they must copy DNA, and DNA cannot be copied perfectly. Copying errors produce new versions of genes that are (almost always) less well-suited to the niche. These altered genes are called *fitness-reducing mutations* or "bad genes." They reduce the chances that offspring will survive and reproduce. In every generation, copying errors supply new "bad genes." For example, the average human child has two to four new harmful mutations that neither parent had (Eyre-Walker & Keightley, 1999). Selection immediately removes fatal mutations, and quickly removes very harmful mutations. Mildly harmful mutations, however, can persist for many generations. A mutation causing a 1 percent reduction in fitness will persist in the population for 100 generations, on average (Falconer, 1996). The balance between mutation and selection leads to an equilibrium frequency of "bad genes" in a population (Keller & Miller, 2006). For example, the average human carries 500 to 2,000 old mutations inherited from his or her ancestors—mutations that have not yet been eliminated by selection (Fay, Wyckoff, & Wu, 2001; Sunyaev et al., 2001). The number and type of "bad genes" (referred to, in composite, as "mutation load") varies across individuals and is responsible for most of the heritable variation in fitness (Houle & Kondrashov, 2002; Michod & Hasson, 1990; Rowe & Houle, 1996).

Mutation load reduces fitness and is the key to resolving the lek paradox. In panel "a" of Figure 9–1, we've modeled variation in fitness as a normal distribution with a mean of 50 and standard deviation of 10. Panel "b" shows a hypothetical relationship between fitness and the ultimate attractiveness of a sexually selected trait. Panel "c" shows the result of applying the function in "b" to the distribution in "a." For now, apply the figure to the attractiveness of peacock tails. Ignore the dashed lines in panels "b" and "c" as well as the reference to schizophrenia in panel "c."

Imagine that we could pick out the peacock embryos lucky enough to have been conceived with very few "bad genes" (i.e., a low mutation load) and therefore high fitness, say "75" on the fitness scale in panels "a" and "b." These embryos have "good genes" for precise cell migration, efficient feeding, parasite resistance, predator evasion, and any other process that can ultimately affect tail size. Thus, embryos with "good genes" for general fitness tend to develop into adult peacocks with very large and elaborate tails at about "7" on the attractiveness scale.

However, most peacock embryos contain some "bad genes" and end up with somewhat smaller, less elaborate tails. A few peacock embryos at the low-fitness extreme of the distribution contain more than their share of bad genes. Imagine we could pick out embryos with a fitness score of "35." The "bad genes" in these embryos are so numerous or so severe that they interfere with several of the hundreds of developmental processes that can

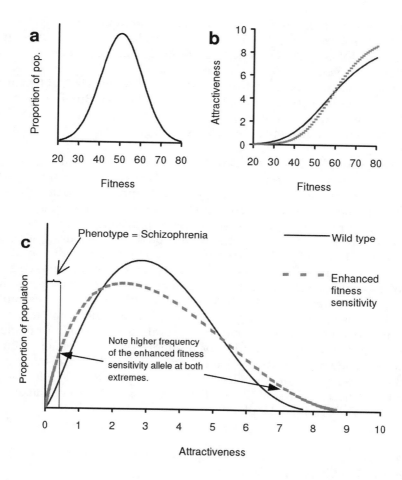

Figure 9–1.   Hypothetical relationships among fitness, the attractiveness of an indicator trait, and the prevalence of schizophrenia.
a. Fitness (i.e., genetic quality) in the general population as a simple normal distribution displayed as T-scores with mean set at 50 and SD = 10. **b.** Attractiveness (on an arbitrary scale from zero to 10) expressed as two similar sigmiodal functions of fitness. **c.** Attractiveness in the general population. This is the result of applying the functions in "b" to the distribution in "a." We assumed that half the population has the wild type indicator and half have the enhanced fitness sensitivity indicator. Arbitrary parameters were set for both functions to illustrate how the "enhanced-sensitivity" function could produce greater proportions of the population at both the attractive and unattractive extremes. We chose a threshold that defines an unattractive extreme (which we hypothesize is identical to schizophrenia) containing one percent of the total population. In this illustration, that one percent comprises about one quarter percent with the wild type indicator and three quarters percent with the enhanced-sensitivity indicator.

affect tail size. By impairing anything from embryonic cell migration to adult feather preening, they disrupt tail development or maintenance enough that these peacocks tend to grow small, dull tails, at less than "1" on the attractiveness scale.

Thus, the tail's sensitivity to fitness converts otherwise subtle variation in fitness into obvious variation in attractiveness. But, if only those peacocks with the most attractive tails get to mate, why are there any offspring with unattractive tails in the next generation? This is the lek paradox.

The answer may lie in the new "bad genes" that arise during the formation of ova and (especially) sperm. The risk of a copying error in any one gene is very low. But so many genes influence tail size that there is high risk that at least one is copied incorrectly in each gamete. This is especially a problem in males, since sperm production involves many more cell-copying events than egg production does in females. For example, mature human females carry eggs that have gone through only about 20 DNA replications, whereas age-30 males carry sperm that have gone through about 380 DNA replications, and age-50 males carry sperm that have gone through about 840 DNA-replications (Crow, 2000). Thus, mutation load rises rapidly with paternal age, but not maternal age. This onslaught of new mutations in every generation—especially from older males—restores the distribution of heritable fitness in panel "a" and ensures a wide range of tail sizes, including small, dull ones, in every generation. This is a potential resolution of the "lek paradox."(Houle & Kondrashov, 2002; Kotiaho et al., 2001; Michod & Hasson, 1990; Pomiankowski & Moller, 1995; Rowe & Houle, 1996).

FITNESS INDICATORS IN ANIMALS INCLUDING HUMANS

Sexually selected fitness indicators have been found in a wide range of species. Many are bodily traits like the peacock's tail (Petrie, 1994). Others are behavioral (Andersson, 1994). For example, in several bird species, females prefer males with louder, more complex, and more numerous songs, and these measures correlate with various indices of fitness including nestling development (Nowicki, Hasselquist, Bensch, & Peters, 2000), immune function (Garamszegi, Moller, & Erritzoe, 2003), and longevity (Forstmeier, Kempenaers, Meyer, & Leisler, 2002).

Even insects use behavioral fitness indicators. At one point during fruit fly courtship, the female turns to face her pursuing suitor. He vibrates his wings in a characteristic pattern called "wing song." This vibrational song varies greatly among males within a population. It also varies between geographically separated populations of the same species (Pail-lette, Bizat, & Joly, 1997)—as does human song. If the female likes her suitor's song, she allows him to mount her. If she doesn't like the song, she vibrates her wings in a characteristic rejection sound that is exactly the same all over the world. In *Drosophila montana*, females prefer a higher-frequency song (which requires faster, more energetic movements of the male's wings), and song frequency correlates with the survival rate of the male's progeny from egg to adulthood (Hoikkala, Aspi, & Suvanto, 1998).

When female choice predominates, indicators evolve in males only. However, when there is mutual choice, as exists in many socially monogamous birds and primates, indicators can evolve in both sexes (Andersson, 1994). For example, both male and female crested auklets sport a crest of feathers above their beaks, and both males and females prefer mates with larger crests (Jones & Hunter, 1993).

Are any human traits sexually selected? Recent evidence suggests that several human body traits may have evolved as fitness indicators through mate choice, including long head hair, expressive faces, everted lips, and hairless skin (Miller, 2000). Also, female choice has increased male height, upper-body muscularity, and facial masculinity (Perrett, May, & Yoshikawa, 1994), and male choice has increased female breast, hip, and buttock size (Etcoff, 1999). Thus, the mate-choice preferences contained within the brains of each sex in our species likely shaped the bodies of the opposite sex.

Of course, people looking for mates focus on far more than bodily traits. In courtship we play, dance, sing, embrace, and, most of all, we talk (and we talk *a lot*). On average, it takes about three months of frequent sex before a couple conceives its first child. Assume they talk just two hours per day at the typical rate of three words per second. In the three months before conceiving a child, they will exchange about a million words each—enough to fill six 500-page books (Miller, 2000).

What is the point of all this talk? One possibility is that courtship talk serves to reveal the quality of our genes. Not only can mate choice sculpt the bodies of the opposite sex, it can also influence the evolution of their brains and behavior. Preferences in the brains of women may have molded the brain structures underlying male verbal courtship behavior. Similarly, preferences in the brains of men may have affected female verbal courtship (Miller, 2000).

The idea that the human brain has played an active role in its own evolution is not new. Darwin (1871) argued that once the brain of any animal evolved the powers of mate choice, love, jealousy, and the appreciation of beauty, these would cause the brains of the opposite sex to evolve such mental traits as courage, pugnacity and perseverance, as well as bodily traits including size and strength, musical organs, bright colors, and ornaments.

Building on Darwin's insight, Miller (2000c) proposed that many human mental and behavioral abilities, such as language, music, humor and art—and the brain systems that support them—may have evolved as fitness indicators through mutual mate choice. For example, suppose that in our hominid ancestors, the brain systems responsible for primitive language were already somewhat sensitive to the fitness of the individual in which they develop. This might have been so because the necessary brain systems were sufficiently complex or energetically demanding that only hominids with the best genes for general fitness could grow those brain systems well. If so, then those who preferred verbally skilled mates would have secured better genes (with fewer mutations) for their offspring. Moreover, their offspring would inherit their parents' genes both for verbal skill and for preferring verbally skilled mates. The increasing correlation of these three kinds of genes—general fitness, indicator, and mate preference—would result in the rapid evolution of language as a fitness indicator. However, the process is not restricted to verbal skill. Any skill with some initial fitness-sensitivity could become the focus of mate choice and evolve, by this mechanism, into a far more elaborate fitness indicator. This reasoning sets the stage for our argument that schizophrenia represents a set of courtship mechanisms gone badly awry.

SCHIZOPHRENIA AS THE LOW FITNESS EXTREME OF A FITNESS INDICATOR

Suppose that every human embryo carries genetic instructions to grow and maintain complex brain systems for a particular set of courtship behaviors. For the moment, don't worry about exactly what those behaviors are. Just imagine that the brain systems needed to produce the behaviors are so complex or demanding of energy that their development and function are highly sensitive to overall genetic quality and environmental hazards. They grow correctly and perform best in the few individuals whose genes and environments are far above average. All others grow the systems with errors. The severity of errors depends on overall genetic quality and exposure to environmental hazards. This leads to great variation in the construction of the brain systems and great variation in their effectiveness during courtship—variation that correlates with underlying fitness.

At one extreme, those with high fitness and favorable environmental conditions develop and maintain the systems well, and display a highly effective version of this courtship behavior. They will show high mating intelligence, construed as display ability and behavioral attractiveness. The vast majority—who carry some fitness-reducing mutations or encounter some environmental hazards—develop the systems with some errors, and display less effective versions of the behavior. An average mutation load leads to an average-quality fitness indicator. Those with high mutation loads and poor environments develop more fundamental errors in the brain systems that function as fitness indicators. They display an ineffective, unattractive version of this courtship behavior—very low mating intelligence and behavioral attractiveness. In 1 percent of the population, developmental errors are so severe that the brain systems produce the symptoms of schizophrenia rather than behaviors recognizable as courtship.

Note that we use the word "attractive" in the technical evolutionary-biology sense. It means "having the power to attract" mates, and not necessarily "pleasing or charming" in an aesthetic or moral sense. Indeed, by this definition, "attractive" behaviors could be deceptive or manipulative. Similarly, we use "unattractive" to mean lacking the power to attract mates; it does not mean undeserving of attention, concern, and care.

Now return to Figure 9–1 and apply it, not to peacock tails, but to the human courtship behaviors that go awry in schizophrenia. Imagine that we could pick out those human embryos with a fitness score of "75" (panel "a"). As their brains develop (both before and after birth), these embryos have the "good genes" needed to ensure precise cell migration, differentiation, synaptogenesis, and programmed cell death, despite environmental threats to these processes such as malnutrition, hypoxia, and infection. As a result, their brain systems for our presumed "particular set of courtship behaviors" develop well and produce, on average, a highly attractive version of the behaviors—around "7" on the attractiveness scale (which could also be interpreted as a 'mating intelligence' scale).

Now imagine we could pick out human embryos with a fitness score of "35." As they attempt to grow these complex and fitness-sensitive brain systems, their "bad genes" interfere with crucial developmental processes. As adults, their aberrant brain systems perform these courtship behaviors poorly, and they score, on average, less than "1" on the attractiveness scale. In some, the behavior is so disrupted that it no longer resembles courtship and, instead, shows the characteristic symptoms of schizophrenia. "Bad genes," thus, may be responsible for the persistence of schizophrenia, just as they are responsible for the persistence of small, dull peacock tails.

Further, our hypothesis suggests a second kind of gene (in addition to fitness-reducing mutations or "bad genes"), which could also increase the risk for schizophrenia. Ornaments may evolve through the successive accumulation of genes that increase fitness sensitivity (Hasson, 1989; Pomiankowski & Moller, 1995; Rowe & Houle, 1996). Suppose that this applies to the evolution of the brain systems that go awry in schizophrenia. If such genes persist, then some families and lineages will show higher fitness-sensitivity than others. They may produce more geniuses (individuals with very high-quality mental fitness indicators), but also more individuals with schizophrenia (individuals with very low-quality mental fitness indicators). This is not necessarily because their overall average fitness is higher or lower than average, but because they have alleles that increase neuro-developmental risk-seeking. They go for broke. Sometimes, this pays off with astonishing creativity or brilliance, but sometimes it leads to disastrous psychosis. Albert Einstein, John Nash, and James B. Watson all got the Nobel Prize, and they all had sons with severe schizophrenia.

WHAT COURTSHIP ABILITIES GO WRONG IN SCHIZOPHRENIA?

The question is difficult to answer. Biologists usually analyze fitness indicators starting from the attractive extreme, observing that individuals with the brightest feathers or loudest calls attract the most mates. In contrast, our theorizing begins at the other extreme, with reports that schizophrenia markedly reduces marriage rates and reproduction (reviewed in Haukka et al., 2003). We speculate that the symptoms of schizophrenia (including delusions, disorganized speech, blunted affect, poor sense of humor, and social awkwardness) reduce reproductive success by impairing courtship ability—by undermining mating intelligence. If so, what is the normal mental adaptation that goes wrong in schizophrenia?

One possibility is creative verbal courtship. The behavioral symptoms of schizophrenia might be extremely aberrant versions of uniquely human verbal courtship behaviors. By "verbal courtship" we mean more than successful pick-up lines by males to attract females. Instead, we imagine a complex verbal "dance" of mutual mate choice and display, in which each potential mate tries to talk in ways that will be interesting and attractive, given the other's beliefs, desires, interests, and attitudes. This requires fluent coordination among many psychological adaptations, including those for listening, perspective-taking, personality-assessment, planning, and talking. These brain systems are probably very complex and their development may therefore be vulnerable to mutations at many loci, and to a wide range of environmental hazards.

Return to Figure 9–1 once more and imagine that the x-axis of panel "c" represents the attractiveness of verbal courtship. Embryos drawn from the high-fitness extreme can correctly develop the complex brain systems needed for successful verbal courtship. Suppose that, as adults, these complex brain systems can generate many possible conversational gambits and critique, practice, and improve the gambits using an evolving model of the potential mate's mind. The end results include interesting utterances, enjoyable conversation, high mating intelligence, and ultimately, high mating success.

Good conversation requires rapid, semi-conscious planning of one's utterances, including internal self-criticism. Disrupted development might impair the effectiveness and accuracy of this process of internal critique. The internal-utterance critic might fail to appreciate which ideas others will believe and what sequence of ideas others will be able to follow. This could explain why the speech of people with schizophrenia usually contains delusions and is often disorganized. If this internal-utterance critic develops aberrantly, so it connects too strongly to auditory systems, it might be experienced as derogatory auditory hallucinations. For example, many people with schizophrenia hear an insulting voice commenting disdainfully on their thoughts and behaviors. Often, this internal voice is experienced as older, higher-status, and better-educated (Nayani & David, 1996).

Language abnormalities are common in schizophrenia (reviewed in Covington et al., 2005), and people with schizophrenia have deficits in verbal humor, and in the ability to represent the beliefs, thoughts and intentions of other people (reviewed in Brune, 2005). However, schizophrenia tends to disrupt many other courtship-related skills in addition to verbal courtship. So, some of its symptoms may reflect low-fitness extremes of other fitness indicators. These may include (1) capacities for musical rhythm and dance (schizophrenia impairs sense of rhythm and motor coordination (reviewed in Boks, Russo, Knegtering, & van den Bosch, 2000)), (2) capacities for humor (schizophrenia impairs sense of humor, wit, and joke-production ability), (3) capacities for happy socializing (schizophrenia leads to social withdrawal, flat affect, and anhedonia), and (4) capacities for empathic Theory of Mind (schizophrenia impairs perspective-taking accuracy, increases paranoia, and increases selfishness and narcissism). Thus, in many ways, schizophrenia is the mirror-image of mating intelligence—it is what happens when many courtship abilities go amiss in parallel.

SEXUAL RIVALRY AND SCHIZOPHRENIA

To illustrate our hypothesis, we have focused on mate choice. However, some sexually selected traits evolved both as weapons *and* ornaments. For example, elk with the biggest antlers win contests over females (Berglund, Bisazza, & Pilastro, 1996). In addition, females prefer males with larger antlers (Fiske, Rintamaki Pekka, & Karvonen, 1998). Suppose human language evolved for both contests and courtship. Those who could model the minds of potential mates and produce more attractive verbal gambits could have used the same brain systems to model the minds of sexual rivals and produce more intimidating verbal gambits (Miller, 2000). For example, a low mutation load might allow individuals to develop complex brain systems that enable them to detect sexual rivals, subconsciously generate many possible intimidating gambits, and subconsciously critique, practice, and improve the gambits using a constantly updated model of the rival's mind. The end result is successful intimidation and high mating success. Disrupted development might lead to inaccurate detection of rivals—expressed as persecutory delusions and insulting or threatening auditory hallucinations. This may explain why the typical auditory hallucination in schizophrenia—a short, obscene, coarse, or sexually toned insult (Nayani & David, 1996)—closely resembles a derogatory remark to or about a sexual rival (Buss & Dedden, 1990). Disrupted development might also lead to poor attempts at intimidation—expressed as grandiose delusions, which, in this context, can be viewed as overly obvious bragging. Thus, schizophrenia may represent severely impaired mating intelligence in both the domains of inter-sexual attraction and intra-sexual rivalry.

THE CONTINUUM OF PSYCHOSIS AND CONTINUOUS VARIATION IN INDICATOR QUALITY

One of the implications of our hypothesis is that schizophrenia is not so discrete a condition as one might suppose. Across individuals, sexually selected fitness indicators vary greatly and continuously in size, color intensity, loudness, pitch, etc. One peacock in a population must have the smallest tail, but several more have tails nearly as small. This may explain why the symptoms of schizophrenia appear to lie on the same continuum with the experiences of people in general (diagnosed with a mental disorder or not) (Strauss, 1969).

For example, several disorders known in composite as the *schizophrenia spectrum* are genetically linked to schizophrenia (Parnas et al., 1993). The most-studied is schizotypal personality disorder (SPD), which includes multiple oddities of perception, thought, emotion and behavior, but not psychotic symptoms (American Psychiatric Association, 2000). Compared with the general population, SPD is five times more common among the close relatives of people with schizophrenia (Kendler et al., 1993; Parnas et al., 1993). If the SPD phenotype lies adjacent to schizophrenia, near the unattractive extreme of the same indicator trait (see Figure 9–1), this would explain several facts about SPD including its association with developmental abnormalities similar to those found in schizophrenia (e.g., Takahashi et al., 2004), and its frequent improvement with dopamine antagonists (Koenigsberg et al., 2003).

In addition, a surprisingly large number of individuals without mental disorders have experienced hallucinations and delusions (Eaton, Romanoski, Anthony, & Nestadt, 1991; Strauss, 1969). In one study (van Os, Hanssen, Bijl, & Ravelli, 2000), non-mentally-ill people who reported these symptoms resembled those with schizophrenia in that they were more likely to be young, single, city dwellers with less education, poorer quality of life, and blunting of affect. In another study, delusions and hallucinations were common among patients attending a medical care clinic (even among those with no psychiatric treatment history) (Verdoux et al., 1998). These symptoms were most common in people 18 to 29 years old, and became less common with increasing age. This age distribution resembles the distribution of schizophrenia's age at onset (Hafner, Maurer, Loffler, & Riecher-Rossler, 1993), and suggests a shared mechanism. That mechanism could be the development of the sexually selected fitness indicator we propose.

EXPLANATORY AND PREDICTIVE POWER OF THE FITNESS INDICATOR MODEL

All of our explanations and predictions depend on seven generic properties of sexually selected fitness indicators. Moreover, it doesn't matter whether the relevant fitness indicator is verbal courtship, verbal intimidation, sense of humor, or rhythmic dance, because our basic explanations and predictions apply to the low-fitness extreme of *any* sexually selected fitness indicator. They apply not only to schizophrenia but also to small dull peacock tails, and low-frequency wing song in fruit flies. If our predictions hold up to empirical scrutiny, then further research will clarify which fitness indicators go awry in schizophrenia.

1. Indicators are displayed during courtship.

This leads to the general prediction that anything which stimulates courtship will precipitate or worsen schizophrenia. Peahens can't see that a peacock has a small, dull tail until the peacock matures, courts peahens, and unfurls its tail. So, if schizophrenia is analogous to a small tail, it should not be apparent to others until the age at which courtship and sexual competition usually begin, and when mating intelligence becomes important. This may explain schizophrenia's typical onset in adolescence and early adulthood. Although neurodevelopmental precursors of schizophrenia appear long before puberty (Woods, 1998), schizophrenia itself is rare before puberty, and most cases begin between the ages of 15 and 26 (Hafner et al., 1993)—a time of peak mating effort in those without schizophrenia.

Of course, other maturational hypotheses are consistent with adolescent onset. Ours, however, leads to several specific predictions. First, because the age at onset of courtship varies across populations, we predict that the average age of onset of schizophrenia will be correlated across different human groups (e.g., sexes, ethnic groups, races, and birth cohorts) with the average age at which courtship begins. For example, if courtship begins 3 years earlier in one ethnic group than another (e.g., as indexed by mean age at first kiss or first sexual intercourse), we predict that schizophrenia will also begin 3 years earlier in that ethnic group. Note that it does not matter whether the difference in age at onset of courtship is due to genes or culture or both—the prediction still holds.

Second, the lifetime course of schizophrenia symptoms should parallel age-specific changes in mating effort in the general population. Symptoms should peak in severity at the age of peak mating effort, and often spontaneously remit as mating effort declines in the 40s and 50s. Likewise, having children in a stable, supportive, sexual relationship should often reduce symptom intensity, as mating effort gives way to parenting effort.

Third, situations that stimulate courtship and sexual competition in normal individuals (for example, dating, falling in love, being derogated by a sexual rival, getting divorced) should precipitate or worsen schizophrenia. Sexual interest in a potential mate, coupled with being verbally derogated by a sexual rival, should be a particularly powerful trigger for a psychotic 'first break.' More subtle forms of sexual competition (e.g., for wealth and status) should also precipitate or exacerbate symptoms of schizophrenia. Such social stimulation of courtship and sexual competition might explain the high rate of schizophrenia among immigrants (Cantor-Graae & Selten, 2005) and city dwellers (Marcelis, Navarro-Mateu, Murray, Selten, & van Os, 1998). Racial and ethnic discrimination might force immigrants to compete harder for wealth and status (a form of sexual competition), while cities might function as vast leks, providing frequent encounters with both potential mates and sexual rivals.

Fourth, drugs that block courtship should improve schizophrenia. If we are correct that schizophrenic behaviors are dysfunctional versions of courtship behaviors, then drugs that increase or decrease courtship behaviors in normal individuals should have the same effect on schizophrenic behaviors. For example, in a wide range of species including crabs, birds, rats, flies, monkeys and humans, dopaminergic drugs alter courtship. Dopamine agonists, like amphetamine, stimulate courtship, while antagonists, like haloperidol, inhibit courtship (Chang et al., 2005; Melis & Argiolas, 1995; Wood, 1995). Consistent with our prediction, dopamine agonists, like amphetamine, worsen schizophrenia, while dopamine antagonists, like haloperidol, improve it (Kahn, 1995). This suggests that other drugs which reduce courtship behaviors may prove therapeutic for schizophrenia. Investigators could find them by developing animal models of courtship and searching for drugs that block courtship but leave other behaviors unaffected. For example, drugs that specifically block the recently discovered ultrasonic courtship song of male mice (Holy & Guo, 2005) may also reduce the symptoms of schizophrenia.

2. Indicators affect the probability of mating.

As the unattractive extreme of a fitness indicator, schizophrenia should impair the ability to attract and retain mates. This notion could explain reduced rates of marriage (15–73 percent of normal) and reproduction (30–70 percent of normal) among individuals with schizophrenia (reviewed in Haverkamp, Propping, & Hilger, 1982). The reduced rate of reproduction among those with schizophrenia is probably due to failure to attract a mate, rather than physiological infertility, because those who do marry report nearly normal numbers of children (Nanko & Moridaira, 1993).

3. Indicators show predictable sex differences.

Even in socially monogamous species like humans, males show higher reproductive skew and higher variation in reproductive success. Compared with females, a higher proportion of males attract multiple mates, and a higher proportion of males attract no mates. Thus, males are subject to somewhat stronger sexual selection, and they court and compete earlier, more frequently, and more intensely (Andersson, 1994; Miller, 2000). This may explain why schizophrenia begins earlier and is more often severe in males (Jablensky, 2000)—despite minimal sex differences in schizophrenia's overall prevalence. The genetic, hormonal, and neurophysiological sex differences that accelerate and amplify male mating effort also amplify any abnormality, such as schizophrenia, which represents the unattractive extreme of the indicator.

4. The development of indicators is sensitive to fitness and condition.

This quality of fitness indicators permits them to perform their main evolutionary function—to convert otherwise subtle variation in genetic fitness into obvious variation in attractiveness, and thereby to make it easier for the opposite sex to choose high-quality mates. This may explain several facts about schizophrenia. (1) Abnormal brain development is common (Woods, 1998; Yeo et al., 1999) because fitness indicators reveal poor fitness through disordered development. (2) Polygenic inheritance underlies schizophrenia (McDonald & Murphy, 2003; Tsuang, Stone, & Faraone, 2001) because an indicator must have a large "mutational target" in the genome (see Keller, this volume). That is, it must be sensitive to many loci to adequately reflect overall heritable fitness (Houle, 1998; Houle & Kondrashov, 2002). (3) Schizophrenia is associated with environmental hazards such as prenatal exposure to infection (e.g., Brown et al., 2004), famine (e.g., St. Clair et al., 2005), and hypoxia (Cannon et al., 2002), because the environmental sensitivity of fitness indicators amplifies their ability to reveal bad genes. (4) Compared with those in the general population, people with schizophrenia have a higher rate of death (at all ages)—mostly from a wide range of physical illnesses, not just suicide and drug abuse (e.g., Osby, Correia, Brandt, Ekbom, & Sparen, 2000)—because the same "bad genes" that reduce fitness and cause physical illnesses also disrupt the fitness indicator and cause schizophrenia.

More speculatively, the idea of fitness-sensitivity offers an additional and complementary explanation (see prediction one, above) for the high rate of schizophrenia among immigrants and city dwellers—sensitivity to fitness and condition favors locally adapted individuals. Theoretically, peacocks living in the environment to which their ancestors adapted should grow larger, more attractive tails than immigrant peacocks whose ancestors were better-adapted to a different environment. That's because the fitness distribution for the immigrant population (in their new environment) is shifted lower (to the left in Figure 9–1, panel a). Indeed, the females of several species prefer locally adapted males, and simulations show that the local condition-dependence of sexually selected traits could account for the evolution of such preferences (Proulx, 2001; Reinhold, 2004).

Afro-Caribbean immigrants to the U.K. and the Netherlands are physiologically adapted to the pathogens, parasites, toxins, and other ecological challenges of their homelands, more so than they are to the ecological challenges of Northern Europe. During development (both before and after birth), they encounter environmental hazards to which their immune systems and other development-stabilizing systems are not adapted. These hazards impair condition and thereby interfere with development of the relevant brain systems. This might account for their unusually high rate of schizophrenia.

The same logic may explain why those born in cities develop schizophrenia at a higher rate than those born in rural environments. Compared with rural environments, cities may contain new and rapidly changing environmental hazards (e.g., more virulent pathogens and nastier neurotoxins). If so, the fitness distribution for those born in cities would be shifted lower (to the left in Figure 9–1, panel "a"), thereby increasing the proportion with schizophrenia.

5. "Bad genes" cause most of the heritable variation in the attractiveness of indicators.

As we showed earlier, embryos with the most "bad genes" are the most likely to grow small tails or, according to our hypothesis, develop schizophrenia. Thus, we predict that most of the genes responsible for schizophrenia will be mutations that reduce general fitness (e.g., by impairing embryonic cell migration or immunity). Because they reduce fitness, they are evolutionarily transient (selection removes them eventually), and they can't spread widely across human populations (Keller & Miller, 2006) Instead, they remain lineage-specific until they are ultimately removed. Such "bad genes" may explain why schizophrenia persists at such a high prevalence, and why, despite its high heritability, decades of gene-hunting have found so few susceptibility alleles that replicate across populations (McDonald & Murphy, 2003; Tsuang et al., 2001).

6. Genes may increase the fitness-sensitivity of indicators.

This prediction concerns a second type of susceptibility gene that should replicate better across populations. Evolutionary biologists have proposed that extravagant traits evolved through the successive accumulation of genes that increase fitness sensitivity (Hasson, 1989; Pomiankowski & Moller, 1995; Rowe & Houle, 1996). That is, the preference of ancestral pea-hens for the peacock with the biggest tail favored genes that produced larger tails in high-fitness peacocks, even at the cost of smaller tails in low-fitness peacocks. A series of such genes spread throughout the population (i.e., went to fixation) such that modern peacock tails are large and highly sensitive to fitness.

Suppose that a given courtship trait underlying schizophrenia evolved in the same manner. Such a courtship trait (perhaps verbal courtship) would have become increasingly elaborate and fitness-sensitive, until further increases imposed a net disadvantage. If this limit were identical in all human populations, then there would be no genetic differences affecting fitness sensitivity. All of the variation in the courtship trait and in the rate of schizophrenia would arise from differences in genetic quality (i.e., "bad genes," mutation load) and exposure to environmental hazards.

However, the optimal degree of fitness sensitivity depends on factors that differ between human populations, and that continue to change within populations. For example, higher rates of polygyny and/or extra-pair copulations ("infidelity") lead to more intense sexual competition, which would favor higher fitness-sensitivity. The rates of polygyny and infidelity have probably varied geographically and temporally across human evolution. So, different modern human populations may include different proportions of higher fitness-sensitivity alleles (that were favored by more intense sexual competition), and lower fitness-sensitivity alleles (that were favored by less intense sexual competition as occurs in monogamy). These fitness-sensitivity alleles are further mixed by migration and mating between groups.

Alleles for higher fitness-sensitivity would produce more successful courtship among the few with high overall fitness, at the expense of even less successful courtship, and an increased rate of schizophrenia, among less fit individuals. The dashed curve in Figure 9–1 labeled "enhanced fitness-sensitivity allele," in panels "b" and "c" shows the effect of such an allele on the relationship between fitness and attractiveness and on the distribution of attractiveness. Such sensitivity-boosting alleles would be more common among people with schizophrenia and in their relatives. This allows us to make several predictions.

First, compared with the general population, the relatives should show higher variance in the relevant courtship trait, such as verbal-courtship ability. They should also show higher variance in the anatomical and neurophysiological bases (or endophenotypes (Cadenhead & Braff, 2002)) for that trait. Second, they should show higher variance in observer-rated sexual charisma, psychological attractiveness, and mating success. In some populations, the increased variance will result in a net increase in reproductive success among relatives, but this depends on whether the current rates of polygyny and infidelity are high enough to favor enhanced fitness-sensitivity alleles. This may explain the higher-than-average reproduction rates sometimes observed in unaffected relatives of schizophrenics (reviewed in Haukka et al., 2003), and in those with mild schizotypy (Nettle & Clegg, 2006). Third, we should find a higher prevalence of schizophrenia, especially among males, in historically polygynous populations with high reproductive skew, in which increased sexual competition would have favored enhanced fitness-sensitivity alleles.

To find such genes, investigators should begin with endophenotypes (quantifiable aspects of brain structure and physiology) that (1) are abnormal in schizophrenia, (2) have the highest variance in the general population, (3) have even higher variance among the relatives of schizophrenics, and (4) are plausibly related to mating intelligence. More specifically, investigators should focus on endophenotypes that have a high coefficient of additive genetic variation, indicating that many mutation-vulnerable loci are responsible for the phenotypic variation (Houle, 1992; Miller & Penke, 2007).

7. Mate preferences co-evolve with the indicator.

Well-developed versions of an indicator trait are perceived as sexually attractive, and poorly developed versions of the trait are perceived as sexually unattractive (Andersson, 1994; Kokko, Brooks, Jennions Michael, & Morley, 2003). If schizophrenia is the unattractive extreme of an indicator, this would explain why people with schizophrenia suffer so much stigmatization across cultures (Dickerson, Sommerville, Origoni, Ringel, & Parente, 2002). This view also predicts that anti-schizophrenia bias should increase after puberty (when mate-choice systems mature), and should be more severe in females (who are typically choosier about their sexual partners), especially when females are ovulating (when it is most important to focus on indicators of "good genes") (Gangestad, Thornhill, & Garver, 2002; Penton-Voak et al., 1999). Thus, the stigmatization of the mentally ill could be viewed as an adaptive component of mating intelligence, in the form of discriminative mate choice. Such stigmatization, like that of the physically handicapped or mentally retarded, may be morally unwarranted, politically undesirable, and socially oppressive—but it may have a hidden adaptive logic that explains its pervasiveness as part of human nature.

APPLICATIONS TO OTHER MENTAL DISORDERS

Are any other mental disorders analogous to small, dull peacock tails?

One possibility concerns emotional instability (Costa et al., 1992), a basic component of many psychological disorders. Emotional stability likely requires complex and energetically demanding brain systems to 'stay cool' (coordinate adaptive behavior without losing focus) while simultaneously detecting, analyzing, and responding to a wide range of challenges (especially the challenges of courtship and sexual competition). Such brain systems might be sensitive to fitness, such that coolness or emotional stability would vary according to mutation load. A preference for mates with this ability (as documented in 62 cultures by Schmitt et al., 2004) could have fueled the evolution of calm self-control as a fitness indicator. At one extreme, those with high fitness (low mutation load) might grow these brain systems well and appear cool under the most stressful situations (think James Bond). At the other extreme, in those with low fitness, a wide range of fitness-reducing mutations might interfere with the development of these brain systems such that individuals appeared much more anxious in a much wider variety of situations (think Woody Allen). That is, they would appear neurotic. Indeed, neuroticism is another name for the low extreme of emotional stability, which is one of the 'Big Five' personality traits (Costa, McCrea, & Psychological Assessment Resources Inc., 1992). Extreme neuroticism is seen in generalized anxiety disorder and in many phobias. From this point of view, coolness evolved through sexual selection to advertise that we are not neurotic, and are likely to have better genes. A similar case could be made for depression as the unattractive extreme of happiness as a sexually selected fitness indicator.

But do any mental disorders other than schizophrenia behave as we expect of the unattractive extremes of fitness indicators? To address this question, we believe it is useful to consider particular disorders *vis à vis* the seven generic properties of fitness indicators described above. Many common mental disorders meet the criteria for heritability, prevalence, and stigmatization, but less is known about mating success, sex differences, age profiles, and paternal age effects. For instance, bipolar disorder meets some of the criteria. It begins in adolescence and early adulthood (Costello et al., 2002), affects about one percent of the population (Bauer & Pfennig, 2005), is highly heritable (Kieseppa, Partonen, Haukka, Kaprio, & Lonnqvist, 2004), and depends on many genes (Kennedy, Farrer, Andreasen, Mayeux, & St. George-Hyslop, 2003) However, its effect on lifetime reproductive success is largely unknown. Indeed, those with bipolar could be viewed as implementing the risk-seeking strategy by cycling between high-mating-intelligence states (mild mania) and low-mating-intelligence states (depression) within their life-times. If the reproductive payoffs of occasional mania out-weigh the reproductive costs of depression, bipolar disorder can persist evolutionarily. The difference between bipolar and 'normal' individuals may be that bipolar people have endogenously driven mania cycles, whereas 'normal' individuals have more context-sensitive mania states of high mating intelligence, which they call 'being in love.'

If other mental disorders are the low-fitness extremes of fitness indicators, this may explain why people with one mental disorder often have another mental disorder, far more often than would be expected by chance. Indeed, our hypothesis predicts three sources of co-morbidity: overlapping "mutational targets," overlapping environmental risk factors, and the power of sexual selection to concentrate "bad genes" in an unlucky minority of the population. An indicator's "mutational target" comprises all the genetic loci that can potentially affect the trait's quality (see Keller, this volume) (Keller & Miller, 2006). Suppose the mutational targets of two fitness-indicator traits overlap, such that some of the mutant alleles that disrupt one indicator also disrupt the other. This would increase the odds that an individual carrying those mutant alleles develops both disorders. Comorbidity could also arise if two different fitness indicators share sensitivity to the same environmental risk factors, such as prenatal infection, birth trauma, starvation, head injury, or social isolation.

A third reason for the high co-morbidity of mental disorders is that sexual selection leads to assortative mating, which aggregates "bad genes" in a subset of the population (J. F. Crow & Kimura, 1979). If both height and intelligence are preferred by both sexes, then genes for height and intelligence will tend to end up in the lucky offspring of highly desired parents—but genes for being short and simple will also end up together, in the unlucky offspring of less-desired parents (see Kanazawa & Kovar, 2004). To the extent that mental disorders are associated with fitness-reducing alleles that are avoided in mate choice, they too will aggregate in the lower-fitness offspring of less-desirable parents. This is true even without overlapping mutational targets or shared environmental sensitivities. This effect may be augmented if "bad genes" also undermine mating intelligence construed as mate-choice accuracy—so that individuals with mental disorders are less sexually discriminating (i.e., less biased, more accepting) against others with mental disorders.

A corollary of these explanations for comorbidity is that individual mental disorders may be our way of lumping together several conditions that co-occur more frequently than not. For example, schizophrenia symptoms form natural groups or clusters often labeled "positive," "negative," and "disorganized" (Arndt, Alliger, & Andreasen, 1991). These natural groups may represent the unattractive extremes of different sexually selected fitness indicators. In this view, the unattractive extremes often appear in the same individuals because the relevant mutational targets and environmental sensitivities overlap extensively, and because "bad genes" are concentrated in a subset of the population. Because the unattractive extremes are more likely to occur together than separately, they appear to be a syndrome—one that Bleuler (1911) labeled 'schizophrenia.' This is important because it suggests the possibility that various symptoms occur together in schizophrenia, not because they share any proximate causes or common endophenotyopes, but because they share an ultimate cause—sexual selection for fitness indicators.

PARENTAL SELECTION AND CHILDHOOD MENTAL DISORDERS

Sexual selection is not the only form of directional selection that can produce fitness indicators. In many species, siblings must compete for scarce parental resources. At the same time, parents must allocate scarce resources to those offspring most likely to survive and reproduce. This conflict has produced a vast array of bodily and behavioral traits in both parents and offspring (reviewed extensively in Mock & Parker, 1997). In some species, offspring have evolved traits that advertise fitness and thereby attract parental care and feeding. For example, healthy barn swallow nestlings beg for food with wide-open mouths (or gapes) colored bright red. The color fades to dull yellow when nestlings are sick because they must divert the crucial carotenoid pigments to immune function instead of gape color. Thus, gape color serves as a fitness indicator, and parents preferentially feed nestlings with bright red gapes (Saino et al., 2000). In North American coots, bright orange filaments cover the heads of chicks, only to be shed just before fledging. Experimental manipulation of the filaments shows that they attract parental feeding and may serve as a fitness indicator (Lyon, Eadie, & Hamilton, 1994).

Could any childhood-onset mental disorders be the equivalent of dull gapes in barn swallow nestlings or dull filaments in coot chicks? One possibility is autism. Suppose that the ability of very young children to charm their parents—through language, facial expression, creative play, and coordinated social interaction—evolved as a parentally selected fitness indicator (Miller, 2000, pp. 216–217). More articulate, expressive, playful, and socially engaged children would give a reliable warranty of their genetic and phenotypic quality, so would solicit higher parental investment. Young children would vary greatly in their ability to charm parents and that variation would correlate with underlying fitness. Autism could represent the least charming, low-fitness extreme of this variation—accounting not only for the typical symptoms of autism, but also for the extreme frustration and alienation experienced by parents of autistic children.

Such a view would lead to explanations and predictions much like those regarding schizophrenia, since the evolutionary mechanism is quite similar, except that parents rather than mates make the selection. Evolutionary biologists have discovered many other adaptations for sibling rivalry and for allocating parental resources that might help explain the behavior of human children and their parents. The approach might even lead to a subsequent book entitled "Parenting Intelligence."

CONCLUSION

Many animals, including humans, prefer mates with better-quality genes. This preference appears to have driven the evolution of bodily and behavioral displays of fitness known as sexually selected fitness indicators. Both the preference for fitness and the corresponding behavioral displays of fitness can be viewed as important components of mating intelligence. If so, then the evolutionary biology of fitness indicators may lead to a deeper understanding of human mating intelligence. Here we have argued that any behaviors which evolved as sexually selected fitness indicators will have low-fitness, unattractive, or unsuccessful extremes that may correspond to mental disorders. Just as pathology illuminates physiology, these low extremes of mating intelligence can illuminate the high extremes and the normal variation.

As an example, we have discussed schizophrenia. Because we focused on fitness-indicator theory, our hypothesis differs from previous evolutionary hypotheses regarding schizophrenia in several ways. First, it does not propose that schizophrenia itself is adaptive, or that the responsible genes produce consistent fitness benefits among the relatives. Second, our model does not propose that schizophrenia arises from any typical etiology—any small set of predictable defects in genes, neurodevelopment, or neurophysiology. Rather, it predicts that most of the responsible genes will be a large number of fitness-reducing mutations with a wide range of harmful effects on development, physiology, immunity, and other vital processes. Third, our model at this stage does not predict exactly which brain systems—which forms of mating intelligence—go awry in schizophrenia, only that they will be brain systems required for sexual attraction of mates and/or sexual competition against rivals. Verbal courtship is one possibility, but none of our explanations or predictions hinge on whether the indicator trait is verbal courtship or something else.

Even without specifying the relevant courtship trait, our hypothesis explains many key features of schizophrenia, including onset in adolescence and early adulthood, greater severity and earlier age at onset in males, reduced reproductive rate, substantial heritability, polygenic basis, the failure of psychiatric genetics to find replicable risk alleles of major effect size, frequent developmental abnormalities, increased mortality, association with prenatal environmental hazards, the treatment efficacy of dopamine antagonists, and cross-culturally severe social stigmatization. It also leads to some surprising and testable predictions.

Our hypothesis also resolves the evolutionary paradox that has baffled schizophrenia researchers for decades: its persistence across generations and cultures despite impairing both survival and reproduction and despite its substantial heritability (which should have allowed selection to eliminate it). The attractive extreme of any fitness indicator is attractive precisely because its development is so easily disrupted by fitness-reducing mutations and environmental hazards. For this reason, every fitness indicator must also include a low-fitness, unattractive extreme.

If, as we propose, schizophrenia is the unattractive extreme of a fitness indicator, then schizophrenia persists as an inevitable and distinctively human side effect of sexual selection for some distinctively human mode of courtship, probably involving language and social cognition. Our hypothesis also suggests the possibility that other mental disorders (e.g., depression and anxiety disorders) are low-fitness extremes of fitness indicators, and it lays out the criteria for empirically addressing this idea. If other disorders meet these criteria, such a pattern would explain the high comorbidity of mental disorders.

We are not the first to consider sexual selection in schizophrenia. Both Crow (1995) and Randall (1998) proposed roles for sexual selection, but neither addressed its effects on the genetic and phenotypic variance of sexually selected traits. Consequently, Crow postulated a single-gene model, and Randall proposed that females perpetuate susceptibility alleles by reproducing before illness onset. Neither model is plausible given evolutionary genetics and ancestral reproduction patterns (see Keller, this volume; Keller & Miller, 2006). We may be the first to use fitness-indicator theory to explain the evolutionary origins, genetic basis, and characteristic symptoms of schizophrenia. In the context of this book, schizophrenia and other mental disorders are not just clinical curiosities; they reveal the awesome adaptive complexity of mating intelligence in normal individuals by showing how many ways it can go wrong in the unlucky few.

REFERENCES

American Psychiatric Association. (2000). *Diagnostic and statistical manual of mental disorders : DSM-IV-TR* (4th, text revision. ed.). Washington, DC: American Psychiatric Association.

Andersson, M. (1994). *Monographs in behavior and ecology: sexual selection.* Princeton, NJ: Princeton University Press.

Arndt, S., Alliger, R. J., & Andreasen, N. C. (1991). The distinction of positive and negative symptoms. The failure of a two-dimensional model. *British Journal of Psychiatry, 158,* 317–322.

Bauer, M., & Pfennig, A. (2005). Epidemiology of bipolar disorders. *Epilepsia, 46 Suppl 4,* 8–13.

Berglund, A., Bisazza, A., & Pilastro, A. (1996). Armaments and ornaments: An evolutionary explanation of traits of dual utility. *Biological Journal of the Linnean Society, 58*(4), 385–399.

Bleuler, E. (1911). Dementia Praecox oder gruppe der schizophrenien. In G. Aschaffenburg (Ed.), *Handbuch der psychiatrie.* Leipzig und Wien: Franz Deuticke.

Boks, M. P. M., Russo, S., Knegtering, R., & van den Bosch, R. J. (2000). The specificity of neurological signs in schizophrenia: a review. *Schizophrenia Research, 43*(2–3), 109–116.

Brown, A. S., Begg, M. D., Gravenstein, S., Schaefer, C. A., Wyatt, R. J., Bresnahan, M., et al. (2004). Serologic evidence of prenatal influenza in the etiology of schizophrenia. *Archives of General Psychiatry, 61*(8), 774–780.

Brune, M. (2004). Schizophrenia—an evolutionary enigma? *Neuroscience & Biobehavioral Reviews, 28*(1), 41–53.

Brune, M. (2005). "Theory of Mind" in Schizophrenia: A Review of the Literature. *Schizophrenia Bulletin, 31*(1), 21–42.

Buss, D. M., & Dedden, L. A. (1990). Derogation of competitors. *Journal of Social and Personal Relationships, 7,* 395–422.

Cadenhead, K. S., & Braff, D. L. (2002). Endophenotyping schizotypy: a prelude to genetic studies within the schizophrenia spectrum. *Schizophrenia Research, 54*(1–2), 47–57.

Cannon, T. D., van Erp, T. G., Rosso, I. M., Huttunen, M., Lonnqvist, J., Pirkola, T., et al. (2002). Fetal hypoxia and structural brain abnormalities in schizophrenic patients, their siblings, and controls. *Archives of General Psychiatry, 59*(1), 35–41.

Cantor-Graae, E., & Selten, J. P. (2005). Schizophrenia and migration: a meta-analysis and review. *American Journal of Psychiatry, 162*(1), 12–24.

Cardno, A. G., Marshall, E. J., Coid, B., Macdonald, A. M., Ribchester, T. R., Davies, N. J., et al. (1999). Heritability estimates for psychotic disorders: the Maudsley twin psychosis series. *Archives of Psychiatry, 56*(2), 162–168.

Chang, H. Y., Grygoruk, A., Brooks, E. S., Ackerson, L. C., Maidment, N. T., Bainton, R. J., and Krantz, D. E. (2005). Overexpression of the Drosophila vesicular monoamine transporter increases motor activity and courtship but decreases the behavioral response to cocaine. *Molecular Psychiatry, 11*(1), 99–113.

Costa, P. T., McCrea, R. R., & Psychological Assessment Resources Inc. (1992). *Revised NEO Personality Inventory (NEO PI-R) and NEO Five-Factor Inventory (NEO-FFI)*. Odessa, Fla. (P.O. Box 998, Odessa 33556): Psychological Assessment Resources.

Costello, E. J., Pine, D. S., Hammen, C., March, J. S., Plotsky, P. M., Weissman, M. M., et al. (2002). Development and natural history of mood disorders. *Biological Psychiatry, 52*(6), 529–542.

Covington, M. A., He, C., Brown, C., Naci, L., McClain, J. T., Fjordbak, B. S., et al. (2005). Schizophrenia and the structure of language: the linguist's view. *Schizophrenia Research, 77*(1), 85–98.

Crow, J. F. (2000). The origins, patterns and implications of human spontaneous mutation. *Nature Reviews Genetics, 1*(1), 40–47.

Crow, J. F., & Kimura, M. (1979). Efficiency of Truncation Selection. *Proceedings of the National Academy of Sciences of the United States of America, 76*(1), 396–399.

Crow, T. J. (1995). A Darwinian approach to the origins of psychosis. *British Journal of Psychiatry, 167*(1), 12–25.

Darwin, C. (1859). *On the origin of species by means of natural selection*. London: J. Murray.

Darwin, C. (1871). *The descent of man, and selection in relation to sex*. London: J. Murray.

Dickerson, F. B., Sommerville, J., Origoni, A. E., Ringel, N. B., & Parente, F. (2002). Experiences of stigma among outpatients with schizophrenia. *Schizophrenia Bulletin, 28*(1), 143–155.

Eaton, W. W., Romanoski, A., Anthony, J. C., & Nestadt, G. (1991). Screening for psychosis in the general population with a self-report interview. *Journal of Nervous & Mental Disease, 179*(11), 689–693.

Etcoff, N. L. (1999). *Survival of the prettiest: The science of beauty*. New York: Doubleday.

Eyre-Walker, A., & Keightley, P. D. (1999). High genomic deleterious mutation rates in hominids. *Nature, 397*(6717), 344–347.

Falconer, D. S. (1996). *Introduction to quantitative genetics* (4th edition). New York: Longman/Wiley.

Fay, J. C., Wyckoff, G. J., & Wu, C. I. (2001). Positive and negative selection on the human genome. *Genetics, 158*(3), 1227–1234.

Fisher, R. A. (1915). The evolution of sexual preference. *Eugenics Review, 7*, 184–192.

Fisher, R. A. (1930). *The genetical theory of natural selection*. Oxford: Clarendon Press.

Fiske, P., Rintamaki Pekka, T., & Karvonen, E. (1998). Mating success in lekking males: A meta-analysis. *Behavioral Ecology, 9*(4), 328–338.

Forstmeier, W., Kempenaers, B., Meyer, A., & Leisler, B. (2002). A novel song parameter correlates with extra-pair paternity and reflects male longevity. *Proceedings of the Royal Society of London, Biological Science, 269*(1499), 1479–1485.

Gangestad, S. W., Thornhill, R., & Garver, C. E. (2002). Changes in women's sexual interests and their partners' mate-retention tactics across the menstrual
cycle: evidence for shifting conflicts of interest. *Proceedings of the Royal Society
of London, Biological Science, 269*(1494), 975–982.

Garamszegi, L. Z., Moller, A. P., & Erritzoe, J. (2003). The evolution of immune
defense and song complexity in birds. *Evolution, [print] 57*(4), 905–912.

Hafner, H., Maurer, K., Loffler, W., & Riecher-Rossler, A. (1993). The influence of
age and sex on the onset and early course of schizophrenia. *British Journal of
Psychiatry, 162,* 80–86.

Hasson, O. (1989). Amplifiers and the handicap principle in sexual selection: A
different emphasis. *Proceedings of the Royal Society of London, Biological Science,
235*(1281), 383–406.

Haukka, J., Suvisaari, J., & Lonnqvist, J. (2003). Fertility of patients with schizophrenia, their siblings, and the general population: a cohort study from 1950
to 1959 in Finland. *American Journal of Psychiatry, 160*(3), 460–463.

Haverkamp, F., Propping, P., & Hilger, T. (1982). Is there an increase of reproductive rates in schizophrenics? I. Critical review of the literature. *Archiv für Psychiatrie und Nervenkrankheiten, 232*(5), 439–450.

Hoikkala, A., Aspi, J., & Suvanto, L. (1998). Male courtship song frequency as an
indicator of male genetic quality in an insect species, *Drosophila montana.
Proceedings of the Royal Society of London, Biological Science, 265*(1395), 503–508.

Holy, T. E., & Guo, Z. (2005). Ultrasonic Songs of Male Mice. *PLoS Biology, 3*(12).

Hooper, P., & Miller, G. F. (Submitted). Mutual mate choice can drive ornament
evolution even under perfect monogamy. *Proceedings of the Royal Society of
London, Biological Science.*

Houle, D. (1992). Comparing evolvability and variability of quantitative traits.
Genetics, 130(1), 195–204.

Houle, D. (1998). How should we explain variation in the genetic variance of traits?
Genetica (Dordrecht), 102–103(0), 241–253.

Houle, D., & Kondrashov, A. S. (2002). Coevolution of costly mate choice and
condition-dependent display of good genes. *Proceedings of the Royal Society of
London, Biological Science, 269*(1486), 97–104.

Huxley, J., Mayr, E., Osmond, H., & Hoffer, A. (1964). Schizophrenia as a genetic
morphism. *Nature, 204,* 220–221.

Jablensky, A. (2000). Epidemiology of schizophrenia: the global burden of disease and
disability. *European Archives of Psychiatry and Clinical Neuroscience, 250*(6), 274–285.

Jones, I. L., & Hunter, F. M. (1993). Mutual sexual selection in a monogamous
seabird. *Nature, 362*(6417), 238–239.

Kahn, R. S. a. D., K.L. (1995). New Developments in Dopamine and Schizophrenia. In F. E. B. a. D. J. Kupfer (Ed.), *Psychopharmacology: The fourth generation of
progress* (pp. 1193–1203.). New York: Raven Press, Ltd.

Kanazawa, S., & Kovar, J. L. (2004). Why beautiful people are more intelligent.
Intelligence, 32(3), 227–243.

Keller, M., & Miller, G. F. (2006). Resolving the paradox of common, harmful, heritable mental disorders: Which evolutionary genetic models best? *Behavioral
and Brain Sciences, 29*(4), 385–452.

Kendler, K. S., McGuire, M., Gruenberg, A. M., O'Hare, A., Spellman, M., & Walsh, D. (1993). The Roscommon family study. III. Schizophrenia-related personality disorders in relatives. *Archives of General Psychiatry, 50*(10), 781–788.

Kennedy, J. L., Farrer, L. A., Andreasen, N. C., Mayeux, R., & St. George-Hyslop, P. (2003). The genetics of adult-onset neuropsychiatric disease: complexities and conundra? *Science, 302*(5646), 822–826.

Kieseppa, T., Partonen, T., Haukka, J., Kaprio, J., & Lonnqvist, J. (2004). High concordance of bipolar I disorder in a nationwide sample of twins. *American Journal of Psychiatry, 161*(10), 1814–1821.

Kirkpatrick, M., & Ryan, M. J. (1991). The evolution of mating preferences and the paradox of the lek. *Nature, 350*(6313), 33–38.

Koenigsberg, H. W., Reynolds, D., Goodman, M., New, A. S., Mitropoulou, V., Trestman, R. L., et al. (2003). Risperidone in the treatment of schizotypal personality disorder. *Journal of Clinical Psychiatry, 64*(6), 628–634.

Kokko, H., Brooks, R., Jennions Michael, D., & Morley, J. (2003). The evolution of mate choice and mating biases. *Proceedings of the Royal Society of London, Biological Science, [print] 270*(1515), 653–664.

Kotiaho, J. S., Simmons, L. W., & Tomkins, J. L. (2001). Towards a resolution of the lek paradox. *Nature, 410*(6829), 684–686.

Lyon, B. E., Eadie, J. M., & Hamilton, L. D. (1994). Parental choice selects for ornamental plumage in American coot chicks. *Nature, 371*(6494), 240–243.

Marcelis, M., Navarro-Mateu, F., Murray, R., Selten, J. P., & van Os, J. (1998). Urbanization and psychosis: A study of 1942–1978 birth cohort in the Netherlands. *Psychological Medicine, 28*(4), 871–879.

McDonald, C., & Murphy, K. C. (2003). The new genetics of schizophrenia. *Psychiatric Clinics of North America, 26*(1), 41–63.

Melis, M. R., & Argiolas, A. (1995). Dopamine and sexual behavior. *Neuroscience & Biobehavioral Reviews, 19*(1), 19–38.

Michod, R. E., & Hasson, O. (1990). On the evolution of reliable indicators of fitness. *American Naturalist, 135*(6), 788–808.

Miller, G. F. (2000). *The mating mind: How sexual choice shaped the evolution of human nature* (1st ed.). New York: Doubleday.

Miller, G. F., & Penke, L. (2007). The evolution of human intelligence and the coefficient of additive genetic variance in human brain size. *Intelligence, 35*(2), 97–114.

Mock, D. W., & Parker, G. A. (1997). *The evolution of sibling rivalry.* New York: Oxford University Press.

Nanko, S., & Moridaira, J. (1993). Reproductive rates in schizophrenic outpatients. *Acta Psychiatrica Scandinavica, 87*(6), 400–404.

Nayani, T. H., & David, A. S. (1996). The auditory hallucination: a phenomenological survey. *Psychological Medicine, 26*(1), 177–189.

Nettle, D., & Clegg, H. (2006). Schizotypy, creativity and mating success in humans. *Proceedings of the Royal Society of London, Biological Science, 273*(1586): 611–615.

Nowicki, S., Hasselquist, D., Bensch, S., & Peters, S. (2000). Nestling growth and song repertoire size in great reed warblers: Evidence for song learning as an indicator mechanism in mate choice. *Proceedings of the Royal Society of London, Biological Science, 267*(1460), 2419–2424.

Osby, U., Correia, N., Brandt, L., Ekbom, A., & Sparen, P. (2000). Mortality and causes of death in schizophrenia in Stockholm county, Sweden. *Schizophrenia Research, 45*(1–2), 21–28.

Paillette, M., Bizat, N., & Joly, D. (1997). Differentiation of dialects and courtship strategies in allopatric populations of Drosophila teissieri. *Journal of Insect Physiology, 43*(9), 809–814.

Parnas, J., Cannon, T. D., Jacobsen, B., Schulsinger, H., Schulsinger, F., & Mednick, S. A. (1993). Lifetime DSM-III-R diagnostic outcomes in the offspring of schizophrenic mothers. Results from the Copenhagen High-Risk Study. *Archives of General Psychiatry, 50*(9), 707–714.

Penton-Voak, I. S., Perrett, D. I., Castles, D. L., Kobayashi, T., Burt, D. M., Murray, L. K., et al. (1999). Menstrual cycle alters face preference. *Nature, 399,* 741–742.

Perrett, D. I., May, K. A., & Yoshikawa, S. (1994). Facial shape and judgments of female attractiveness. *Nature, 368*(6468), 239–242.

Petrie, M. (1994). Improved growth and survival of offspring of peacocks with more elaborative trains. *Nature, 371*(6498), 598–599.

Petrie, M., Halliday, T., & Sanders, C. (1991). Peahens Prefer Peacocks with Elaborate Trains. *Animal Behaviour, 41*(2), 323–332.

Pomiankowski, A., & Moller, A. P. (1995). A resolution of the lek paradox. *Proceedings of the Royal Society of London, Biological Science, 260*(1357), 21–29.

Pritchard, J. K. (2001). Are rare variants responsible for susceptibility to complex diseases? *American Journal of Human Genetics, 69*(1), 124–137.

Prokosch, M. D., Yeo, R. A., & Miller, G. F. (2005). Intelligence tests with higher g-loadings show higher correlations with body symmetry: Evidence for a general fitness factor mediated by developmental stability. *Intelligence, 33*(2), 203–213.

Proulx, S. R. (2001). Female choice via indicator traits easily evolves in the face of recombination and migration. *Evolution, 55*(12), 2401–2411.

Randall, P. L. (1998). Schizophrenia as a consequence of brain evolution. *Schizophrenia Research, 30*(2), 143–148.

Reinhold, K. (2004). Modeling a version of the good-genes hypothesis: female choice of locally adapted males. *Organisms Diversity & Evolution, 4*(3), 157–163.

Riley, B. P., & McGuffin, P. (2000). Linkage and associated studies of schizophrenia. *American Journal of Medical Genetics, 97*(1), 23–44

Rowe, L., & Houle, D. (1996). The lek paradox and the capture of genetic variance by condition dependent traits. *Proceedings of the Royal Society of London, Biological Science, 263*(1375), 1415–1421.

Saino, N., Ninni, P., Calza, S., Martinelli, R., De Bernardi, F., & Moller, A. P. (2000). Better red than dead: Carotenoid-based mouth coloration reveals infection in barn swallow nestlings. *Proceedings of the Royal Society of London, Biological Science, 267*(1438), 57–61.

Schmitt, D. P., Alcalay, L., Allensworth, M., Allik, J., Ault, L., Austers, I., et al. (2004). Patterns and Universals of Adult Romantic Attachment Across 62 Cultural Regions: Are Models of Self and of Other Pancultural Constructs? *Journal of Cross-Cultural Psychology, 35*(4), 367–402.

Shaner, A., Miller, G., & Mintz, J. (2004). Schizophrenia as one extreme of a sexually selected fitness indicator. *Schizophrenia Research, 70*(1), 101–109.

St. Clair, D., Xu, M., Wang, P., Yu, Y., Fang, Y., Zhang, F., et al. (2005). Rates of adult schizophrenia following prenatal exposure to the Chinese famine of 1959–1961. *Journal of the American Medical Association, 294*(5), 557–562.

Strauss, J. S. (1969). Hallucinations and delusions as points on continua function: rating scale evidence. *Archives of General Psychiatry, 21*(5), 581–586.

Sunyaev, S., Ramensky, V., Koch, I., Lathe, W., III, Kondrashov, A. S., & Bork, P. (2001). Prediction of deleterious human alleles. *Human Molecular Genetics, 10*(6), 591–597.

Takahashi, T., Suzuki, M., Zhou, S. Y., Hagino, H., Kawasaki, Y., Yamashita, I., et al. (2004). Lack of normal gender differences of the perigenual cingulate gyrus in schizophrenia spectrum disorders. A magnetic resonance imaging study. *European Archives of Psychiatry & Clinical Neuroscience, 254*(5), 273–280.

Tsuang, M. T., Stone, W. S., & Faraone, S. V. (2001). Genes, environment and schizophrenia. *British Journal of Psychiatry, 178*(Suppl 40), S18–24.

van Os, J., Hanssen, M., Bijl, R. V., & Ravelli, A. (2000). Strauss (1969) revisited: a psychosis continuum in the general population? *Schizophrenia Research, 45*(1–2), 11–20.

Verdoux, H., van Os, J., Maurice-Tison, S., Gay, B., Salamon, R., & Bourgeois, M. (1998). Is early adulthood a critical developmental stage for psychosis proneness? A survey of delusional ideation in normal subjects. *Schizophrenia Research, 29*(3), 247–254.

Wilson, D. R. (1997). Evolutionary epidemiology: Darwinian theory in the service of medicine and psychiatry. In S. Baron-Cohen (Ed.), *The maladapted mind: classic readings in evolutionary psychopathology* (pp. 39–55). Hove, East Sussex, UK: Psychology Press.

Wood, D. E. (1995). Neuromodulation of rhythmic motor patterns in the blue crab Callinectes sapidus by amines and the peptide proctolin. *Journal of Comparative Physiology A Sensory Neural and Behavioral Physiology, 177*(3), 335–349.

Woods, B. T. (1998). Is schizophrenia a progressive neurodevelopmental disorder? Toward a unitary pathogenetic mechanism. *American Journal of Psychiatry, 155*(12), 1661–1670.

Yeo, R. A., Gangestad, S. W., Edgar, C., & Thoma, R. (1999). The evolutionary genetic underpinnings of schizophrenia: the developmental instability model. *Schizophrenia Research, 39*(3), 197–206.

Zahavi, A. (1975). Mate selection a selection for a handicap. *Journal of Theoretical Biology, 53*(1), 205–214.

V

Mating Intelligence and Other Individual Differences

Chapter 10

The Role of Creativity and Humor in Human Mate Selection

Scott Barry Kaufman
Yale University

Aaron Kozbelt
*Brooklyn College of the City
University of New York*

Melanie L. Bromley
California State University, San Bernardino

Geoffrey F. Miller
University of New Mexico

Let's face it: most people think humor is sexy. One need not scour countless scientific journal articles to reach this conclusion. Open your favorite newspaper or magazine to the "Personals" section and you are bound to see plenty of people looking for a "good sense of humor" in a potential mate. Alternatively, do an impromptu pilot study and ask the next 10 people you meet how high humor ranks on their lists of important mate characteristics; you will likely obtain similar results.

Research has confirmed that a good sense of humor is an important human mate preference worldwide (Asia: Toro-Morn & Sprecher, 2003; Europe: Todosijevik, Snezana, & Arancic, 2003; North America: Regan & Joshi, 2002). When people are asked to rate the importance of various traits for romantic relationships, a good sense of humor is consistently at or near the top of their lists (Hansen, 1977; Hewitt, 1958; Goodwin, 1990; Smith,

Waldorf, & Trembath, 1990), sometimes outranking physical attractiveness (Sprecher & Regan, 2002; Toro-Morn & Sprecher, 2003). There is also evidence that the preference for funniness may be stronger in seeking romantic partners than in seeking platonic friends (Sprecher & Regan, 2002). Further, the preference for humor seems to increase with the duration of the relationship: we seem to value humor especially in long-term mates (Kenrick, Sadalla, Groth, & Trost, 1990).

Taken together, these findings suggest that any discussion of mating intelligence will not be complete unless the topic of humor is brought to the table. But what is humor? Is it a unitary construct or a constellation of separate components or abilities? How is humor related to intelligence, creativity, and other factors potentially related to mating intelligence and genetic fitness? Are there sex differences in humor production and appreciation that might illuminate the nature of mating intelligence? Answering these questions is no simple matter. To explore the relevance of humor to mating intelligence, one must tackle these issues and examine humor's relationship to other psychological constructs that have been linked to mating success, such as intelligence and creativity.

Other chapters in this volume have addressed the relationship between general intelligence and mating intelligence (see Kanazawa, this volume) and the relationship between creativity and mating intelligence (see Nettle and Clegg, this volume). The terms "intelligence" and "creativity" are very broad, however. In this chapter, we argue that humor is a particular manifestation and indicator of both intelligence and creativity. A major aim of this review is to convey the complexities and subtleties of humor as played out in human mating while emphasizing the multidimensionality of the humor construct and its important links to mating intelligence. Toward this goal, we will first examine some candidate selection pressures that may have shaped the evolution of humor as a psychological adaptation. With that foundation in place, we will examine the psychometric perspective, detailing attempts to measure humor, creativity, intelligence, and their inter-relations. Finally, we will examine the evidence linking humor to mating intelligence, and suggest some future research directions.

POTENTIAL SELECTION PRESSURES
FOR THE EVOLUTION OF HUMOR

Natural Selection

The central mechanism for the evolution of humor is Darwinian natural selection (Darwin, 1859), which may be defined as the differential reproduction of genes by virtue of their effects on heritable design features of the organism. For natural selection to occur, there must be heritable variation for a given trait or behavior, and that variation must lead to differential survival and reproductive payoffs.

However, there are many different forms of natural selection at many different levels, including gene-level selection, individual-level survival selection, individual-level sexual selection, kin selection, and group selection. Evidence from archaeology, anthropology, and ethnography suggests that individual-level survival ('natural selection proper', in the survival-of-the-fittest sense) has played a key role in the acceleration of creative inventions and innovations. These heritable characteristics or adaptations could improve ones' survival and inclusive fitness. This would give the individual a better chance of making a genetic contribution to subsequent generations, thereby initiating the process of genotypic change within their population (Andrews, Gangestad, & Matthews, 2002). For instance, hunting dangerous prey, a potentially fatal task, required our ancestors to creatively find ways to reduce their risk. They did so by fashioning weapons out of stones and later developing projectiles such as spears, to reduce their risks of being killed. Thanks to their ability to make something novel and useful, they reaped the benefits of their ingenuity and so did their children and kin (Berger & Trinkaus, 1995; Cattelain, 1997). The cognitive abilities for planning and remembering important ecological facts may have been extended into capacities for art, story-telling, and humor (Carroll, 1995; Gabora, 2003; McBrearty & Brooks, 2000). These marks of cleverness and progressive ingenuity likely reflect the phylogenetic development of human cognitive capacities, and represent prime examples of the impact of evolution and adaptation on our species.

So how does humor fit into this picture? One possible clue that humor evolved through natural selection is that humor is ubiquitous among *Homo sapiens*. All *Homo sapiens* have the capacity to respond to humor by laughing or smiling. There is even evidence that laughter and smiles are universally recognized and labeled as positive signals of emotional expression (Caron, 2002). Human responses to humorous stimuli (e.g., tickling) appear in infants at about 4 months of age, and their participation in humorous activities (e.g., Peek-a-boo) can be seen in infants as early as 6 months (Shultz, 1976; Sroufe & Waters, 1976). This is preceded by the occurrence of spontaneous laughter, which is one of the first vocalizations that human infants make, usually around 1 to 6 months old (MacNeilage, 1997; Sroufe & Waters, 1976; Sroufe & Wunsch, 1972). The smiles and laughter associated with pleasure have even been reported in congenitally deaf and blind children (Eibl-Eibesfeldt, 1970). This evidence has quite reasonably led many researchers to suggest that humans are genetically predisposed to produce and perceive humor (Caron, 2002; Provine, 2000).

However, such universals do not necessarily implicate survival-selection as an explanation. Although universality may imply that humor was favored by selection, and suggests that an evolutionary approach to humor is appropriate, the universality of a trait gives little information about the particular selection pressures that may have favored it. Indeed, the "survival value" of a good sense of humor is not immediately obvious. Sexual selection also seems important, insofar as both sexes across cultures desire humor in prospective mates (Buss & Barnes, 1986; Feingold, 1981, 1992; Goodwin, 1990). One interesting possibility is that natural selection drives mainly the more applied or technological aspects of creativity, like advances in science and engineering, whereas sexual selection drives more ornamental or aesthetic aspects of creativity, including art, music, dance, and humor (Feist, 2001). Technical-applied creativity aims for a practical, veridical understanding of the world; it has clear survival benefits and probably emerged 2 to 3 million years ago with the origins of stone tool making. In contrast, aesthetic-ornamental creativity has no clear survival value and appears to have originated much later; indeed, some archaeologists have argued that it may be no more than 40,000 to 60,000 years old.

Social Bonding

One possible explanation for the existence of humor as a species-typical human capacity concerns its ability to promote social bonding and cohesion. This may confer an advantage on the individual humor producer or appreciator, through an implicit form of group selection. Humor's ability to provoke delight and to influence the thoughts and emotions of the listener give the humor-producer some clear social benefits within a particular social context, even when the humor seems sort of stupid outside that context. For instance, Provine (1996, 2000) has found that the vast majority of laughter in natural settings is triggered by apparently banal remarks like "Look, it's Andre" or "I'll see you guys later." Outside their immediate social context, these do not seem very witty or funny at all. However, laughing at such remarks can function "to ease social tensions, to indicate friendly intent, and to strengthen social bonds" (McGhee, 1979, p. 103). Moreover, some have argued that humor has more to do with social "good-heartedness" (Storey, 2002, p. 320) than with creative "wit" (at least in the United States, but perhaps not in Britain!). Indeed, in marital relationships, humor appears to promote intimacy, belonging, and cohesiveness, rather than hilarity (Ziv, 1988a). So whether in multi-person groups or dyads, one could argue that humor's playfulness provides a socially binding force which, under ancestral conditions, would have promoted the individual or inclusive fitness of the person expressing it (Caron, 2002).

Although humor might function in these ways, this social-bonding view has a few problems. First, its reliance on an implicit form of group selection needs to be clarified and made more evolutionarily reputable.

Using humor to altruistically 'promote social bonds' within a group is not an evolutionarily stable strategy if defectors can reap the benefits of the social cohesion without paying the costs of being funny. Second, this theory cannot explain why humor sometimes fails—if it always benefited both producer and receiver, by promoting social cohesion between them, why would jokes ever fall flat? Third, this theory cannot explain the sexual attractiveness of humor, including sex differences in its production and reception, and its importance in both attracting short-term mates and in sustaining long-term relationships. Is the universal preference for humor in mates due solely to a desire for intimacy and belonging? Is there nothing sexy about humor?

Sexual Selection

Besides survival selection and group selection, Darwin's theory of sexual selection (Darwin, 1871) represents another potential mechanism for the evolution of humor. Sexual selection theory proposes that, within most species, one sex (usually females) invests more in parenting, and therefore is more restricted in how many offspring they can conceive. Consequentially, members of this higher-investing sex should be more selective when choosing a mate, because they must seek maximum quality in offspring to compensate for the severe limit on quantity that they face. This phenomenon of mate choice results in competition by the less-discriminate sex for the attention of the more-discriminate sex. In all mammals, including humans, this leads to males competing for female attention.

This sexual selection process is very distinct from survival selection, which is largely the competition to gain ecological resources and to avoid predators and parasites. Sexual selection theory suggests that there is a competition to mate with individuals who exhibit traits such as humor that are (in theory) metabolically expensive to produce, hard to maintain, and not easily counterfeited, because these qualities will be the most reliable indicators of genetic fitness. In recent years, Miller (1998; 2000a; 2000b; 2000c; 2001) has developed and popularized the most elaborated version of this theory. Miller suggests that sexual selection has played a much greater role than natural selection in shaping the most distinctively human aspects of our minds, including creativity and humor. He contends that creative and comedic behaviors are the results of complex psychological adaptations whose primary functions were to attract mates, yielding reproductive rather than survival benefits.

Because females are typically choosier than males (at least in short-term mating), males and females tend to use different reproductive strategies. *Intrasexual competition* is the competition for mates by driving away, intimidating, derogating, or killing one's same-sex rivals. Because males experience much higher variance in reproductive success, they are under much stronger selection to compete in risky, aggressive ways against their rivals. Such intrasexual competition resembles 'survival of the fittest,' in some respects (desperation, aggression, dominance), but its mechanisms allow for displays that are not just based on physical strength or endurance. One can become the alpha male, or "top dog", not just through brute force, but through humor—especially humorous derogation of sexual rivals (Buss, 1988). Many males will cut down a competitor by making fun of his most important sexually-selected traits, such as his allegedly inferior levels of kindness ("wife-beating psycho"), intelligence ("clodpate saphead"), physical attractiveness ("pencil-dick dwarf"), or wealth and status ("Yo, your would-be pimped-out ride is more illin' than killin' ").

Such competitor-derogation parallels one of the oldest explanations for the origins of humor, the "superiority theory" (Morreall, 1987). Philosophers such as Plato, Aristotle, and Hobbes suggested that since humans are naturally competitive, humor emerged as an expression of our pleasure in being the victor. That is, we laugh because we are not the losers—at least not this time. Along these lines, Ludocivi (1933) described laughter as a symbolic baring of the teeth, and makes comparisons to other animals in which teeth-baring is a clear sign of aggressive intent. If a jest against a rival succeeds, it displays social dominance that could translate into sexual success. In hunter-gatherer societies, social dominance, control of resources, and mating success are tightly correlated. For this reason, males might use humor to display their social dominance, to deter sexual rivals, and to position themselves as desirable mates (Buss, 1994).

Females also exercise their intrasexual competition skills—they may derogate the sexually-selected traits of a female rival, such as her inferior levels of moral virtue ("skanky coke-head slut") or physical attractiveness ("wattle-necked hippo-ass freak"). However, they aren't likely to use the same tactics that males use, because female social status and reproductive success tends to be more influenced by social networking skill than by physical or symbolic dominance (Silk, Alberts, & Altmann, 2003). Thus humorous derogation of other females isn't likely to be an effective means of intrasexual competition, because local males might actually favor "skanky coke-head sluts" (at least as short-term mates), and they might easily see that one's rival does not have a "wattle-neck" or a "hippo-ass." To promote her social status, a woman is more likely to use cooperation and kindness, rather than to display social dominance via humor. Rucas, Gurven, Kaplan, Winking, Gangestad, and Crespo (2006) argue that in tribal communities more representative of human ancestral conditions, a woman's social status depends heavily on her desirability as a friend and peer, and having a good sense of humor does not much influence this desirability.

However, sexual selection is not restricted to intrasexual competition, where males clash on an open battlefield of wits and direct one-upmanship.

Attracting the other sex, through physical and behavioral displays, is just as important (Buss, 1998). For traits to remain sexually attractive across many generations, they must be reliable indicators of reproductive fitness. Consequently, such signals tend to be costly to produce, hard to maintain, and highly sensitive to the presence of genetic mutations. Miller (1998, 2000a, 200b, 2000c, 2001) noted that cultural displays of human creativity (including humor) satisfy these requirements. Perhaps in mate choice then, the production of humor is a valuable index of genetic fitness (Bressler, 2005), since high-quality humor cannot be easily "faked." Indeed, Miller (1998) argued that most cultural displays (i.e., painting, poetry, architecture, etc.) are the results of male efforts to broadcast courtship displays to multiple female recipients. For example, males produce significantly more art, music, and literature than women, and the majority of this work is produced when men are between the ages of 20 and 35, at the peak age of mating effort (Miller, 1998). Some of this sex difference is surely due to historical and social differences in opportunities for being creative, and it is much more likely to reflect a sex difference in display motivation than in cognitive ability: men are not brighter than women; they are just more desperate to show off in colossally narcissistic ways that might attract sexual interest.

Some evidence suggests that Miller's theory of sex-differentiated mating effort extends to humor production in courtship. Hay (2000) argued, based on historical sources, that humor in courtship has been much more rarely produced by females than by males. Kotthoff (2000) likewise reported evidence that males were more likely than females to produce verbal humor in informal social situations. Although quality of humor is probably a better index of genetic fitness than quantity (since quality is harder to fake, [Bressler, 2005]), the more frequent attempts by males to be funny suggest that their humor-production abilities were under stronger sexual selection.

Summary of Selection Pressures for Humor

In sum, several plausible mechanisms have been proposed to explain the evolution of humor: social bonding (group selection), intrasexual selection (humorous derogation of sexual rivals), and intersexual selection (mate choice for humor as a fitness indicator). Of particular relevance to mating intelligence are the sexual selection models, since they make the most specific empirical predictions concerning humor's relationships to other hypothesized mental fitness indicators, such as creativity and intelligence. However, up to now, the discussion of these constructs (humor, creativity, and intelligence) has been rather vague. The rest of this chapter aims to define each construct more specifically, evaluate the psychometric rela-

tionships between these constructs, and use this framework to comparatively assess the potential mechanisms for the evolution of humor.

THE PSYCHOMETRIC PERSPECTIVE

In most discussions of the evolution of humor, words such as "intelligence," "creativity," and "creative intelligence" are frequently used. In
fact, they are often used interchangeably with "humor." However, do
these terms really correspond to the same thing? Alternatively, does each
of these constructs reflect a distinct, unitary ability? Researchers have
spent over a century trying to measure intelligence and another half
century trying to measure creativity; only rarely have they considered
the evolutionary origins, adaptive functions, and genetic correlations
between these constructs. Our bet here is that the psychometrics of intelligence, creativity, and humor can illuminate their evolutionary history,
and vice-versa.

Creativity

What is creativity? Early Greek philosophers thought it was a mystical
inspiration from the seven muses (Rothenberg & Hausman, 1976). Freud
viewed creativity as resulting from the tension between conscious reality
and unconscious drives (Freud, 1908/1959). More recently, Greenberg
(2004) described creativity as involving "both the process and product of
unprecedented or novel perception, thoughts, or actions by which an
organism or group of organisms copes with present or potential changes in
the composition and structure of its environment" (p. 310). Though Greenberg's definition sounds appealingly general, it really only posits survival
payoffs for creativity ('coping with the environment'), and it ignores
potential sexual payoffs. Likewise, there is a general consensus now that
'creative' things must be both novel and useful (Kaufman, in press; Mayer,
1999). Since this utility criterion is typically understood in economic, technological, or scientific terms, it frames genuine creativity as something that
must have survival payoffs—with a patentable innovation as the premier
example of a creative product. Verbal humor in courtship tends to get
overlooked as a creative activity, because its novelty need only be local
(new to the listener, rather than the patent office), and its utility need only
be reproductive (arousing to the listener, rather than contributing to economic growth).

Researchers have tried to measure domain-general creative abilities by
assuming that divergent thinking—the ability to form unique associations
and connections—is fundamental to creative behavior. Divergent thinking
tests usually ask people to generate new ideas or uses for a particular

object, such as a brick. The most frequently used measure of creativity is the Torrance Test of Creative Thinking (1974), which is scored along the dimensions of originality, fluency, flexibility, and elaboration. Other divergent-thinking measures of creativity were developed by Guilford (1959), Getzels and Jackson (1962), and Wallach and Kogan (1965). Critics have emphasized that creativity depends not just on divergent thinking, but also on problem identification (before divergent thinking) and solution evaluation (after divergent thinking) (Plucker & Renzulli, 1999).

Experts have also extolled the need to distinguish expert-level creativity from everyday "garden variety" creativity (Kaufman & Baer, 2002; Kaufman, in press; Csikszentmihalyi, 1998). To attain greatness in any field, it takes about ten years just to reach the level of competence necessary to make a contribution (Hayes, 1989). Very few individuals have the time and resources to become an expert in multiple domains, so data on the domain specificity of genius-level creativity are limited. Though many fine art-works or epic poems represent spectacular achievements, it is in the everyday forms of human creativity, such as courtship humor, that we find the conspicuous individual differences that make psychological adaptations for creativity such relevant, reliable, and sexually attractive indicators of genetic fitness.

When we describe someone as "creative" we usually imply a rather generic predisposition towards creativity across many domains. However, being creative in one field (such as music) does not necessitate creativity in another field (such as painting). Evidence for domain-specificity comes from studies of creative performance in which a population-representative sample of participants create more than one thing (such as poems, stories, mathematical puzzles, collages and drawings), and each artifact is judged for creativity by appropriate experts (for validation of this consensual assessment technique, see Amabile, 1982). The correlations among the creativity ratings of products made by the same person in these studies have been quite low, especially when academic ability (a proxy for general intelligence) is controlled for (Baer, 1991; 1993; 1994; Conti, Coon, & Amabile, 1996; Han, 2000; Runco, 1989). Since the amount of shared variance across a wide variety of tasks is often less than 5 percent (Baer, 1993), some have argued that "creativity" is not a general factor that works across domains (Baer, 1998).

Other researchers have found that both domain-specific and domain-general processes play roles in everyday creativity. Sternberg and Lubart (1991) asked 63 university students to create various kinds of products (in domains of writing, art, advertising, and science) that could be reliably rated for their creativity. In the writing domain, they were given story titles and asked to compose a short story based on that title. In the art domain, they were asked to produce art drawings with titles such as "The Beginning of Time." In the advertising domain, they were asked to produce verbal advertisements for a list of products. In the science domain, they were asked to solve problems such as how one might detect extraterrestrial aliens living on earth who are trying to escape detection. Participants created two products in each domain.

Sternberg and Lubart (1991) found, first, that the following resources were needed for creativity: intelligence, knowledge, motivation, appropriate thinking styles, appropriate personality traits, and the environment. Two main types of intelligence that seemed especially important for creativity were the ability to redefine problems and the ability to think insightfully. Domain-specific knowledge seems important for expert-level creativity, since without knowledge of the field, it is hard to judge which problems are the important ones to solve, and hard to judge when one has found an adequate solution. Not just the *ability* to think creativity but the *desire* to think creativity (motivation) also seemed crucial to creative production. The thinking styles most relevant to creativity seem to be the 'legislative' style (enjoying formulating problems and creating new ways of seeing things) and the 'global' thinking style (seeing the big picture and think "outside the box"). The personality traits that seemed most conducive to creativity were tolerance of ambiguity, willingness to grow, sensible risk-taking (which would now be lumped together as 'openness' in the Big Five system), willingness to surmount obstacles and persevere ('conscientiousness'), and a belief in oneself ('emotional stability'). The last component of the Sternberg and Lubart (1991) model is the environment, which sets the context for creativity and gives feedback about the quality of one's creativity (e.g., for humor to be deemed creative, people in one's environment need to find the joke funny). People in every culture have a sense of humor in some form, but they may differ in what they actually find funny (e.g., cross-dressing comedian Eddie Izzard may be considered hilarious in London, but baffling, surreal, and alarming in Dallas). Sternberg and Lubart (1991) suggest that a creative product or idea is the result of these many interacting processes, not all of which are cognitive abilities, and not all of which are under our control. They also found that creativity is relatively domain-specific: correlations of individuals' creativity ratings across domains were fairly low. Lastly, they found that correlations between their measures of creativity and traditional tests of intelligence tended to be higher when the intelligence test items required innovative thinking.

In summary, creative ability can either be expressed at the expert level or the more common, everyday level. The type of humor valued in mating studies is likely to be at the everyday level of creativity—a preference for a light-hearted, amusing mate, not a professional stand-up comedian. Even though everyday creativity depends on both domain-general traits (e.g., intelligence, openness, divergent thinking) and domain-specific expertise, creativity research so far suggests that creativity is surprisingly domain-specific. Therefore, the ability to produce humor in a creative, witty fashion may be a unique ability, rather uncorrelated with other forms of creativity. Indeed, professional humorists seem to have developed a substantial body of humor knowledge which they employ when creating humor (Siegler, 2004). It is also important to realize that the reception of humor and creativity at the everyday level is the result of many interacting processes, some of which (e.g., listener mood and cultural background) are out of our control and may not reflect innate talent.

Intelligence

What is intelligence? Most intelligence researchers accept a hierarchical model of intelligence, with a unitary g factor at the top, and subordinate factors corresponding to more specific cognitive abilities (Jensen, 1998; Detterman, 2002; Gottfredson, 2002; Kyllonen, 2002; Petrill, 2002), a common factor underlying diverse cognitive abilities. Others emphasize lower-order factors corresponding to distinct cognitive abilities (e.g., Gardner, 1983, 1999; Sternberg, 1997, 2000). The debate is not a new one. At the turn of the 20th century, Charles Spearman (1904) argued for a general factor of human intelligence, whereas Louis Thurstone (1938) believed that the general factor was less important than the careful measurement of its components, which he thought included (a) Verbal comprehension (ability to understand spoken and written language), (b) Verbal fluency (ability to talk and write fluently), (c) Number (ability to do fast arithmetic), (d) Perceptual Speed (ability to visually recognize numbers and letters quickly), (e) Inductive reasoning (generalizing from specific cases to general principles), (f) Spatial visualization (imagining objects and their transformations), and (g) Memory (encoding and retrieving information). It is important to note here that Thurstone found a statistical distinction between verbal comprehension and verbal fluency, partially supporting his multi-dimensional model of intelligence, as well as suggesting that humor comprehension and production may involve separate processes.

The debate between Spearman and Thurstone could not be reconciled on purely theoretical grounds, but accumulating evidence supported hierarchical factor models of intelligence, with more general intelligence abilities at the top, and various 'group factors' (specific forms of intelligence) underneath. Two hierarchical theories that have had the most influence on modern intelligence research are the Cattell-Horn model and Carroll's theory of cognitive abilities.

Early versions of the Cattell-Horn theory proposed that general intelligence has two major parts: fluid intelligence (gf) and crystallized intelligence (gc) (Horn & Cattell, 1966). Fluid intelligence reflects the efficient online functioning of the central nervous system (e.g., solving new abstract reasoning problems); whereas crystallized intelligence reflects individually acquired knowledge, learned skills, and culture-specific content (e.g., composing symphonies, writing scientific papers).

The more recent model that dominates current intelligence research is Carroll's Three-Stratum theory (Carroll, 1993). Carroll proposed this model after an extensive analysis of more than 460 data sets from the psychometric literature. In Carroll's model, Stratum I reflects highly specialized skills (e.g., proof-reading manuscripts, understanding topographic maps, fixing bicycles), Stratum II reflects somewhat broader abilities (e.g., verbal intelligence, spatial reasoning, perceptual-motor performance), and Stratum III has only one ability, the g factor, that allegedly underlies all aspects of intellectual activity. Carroll's model differs from the Cattell-Horn model in positing this superordinate g factor, and by assigning 'crystallized' abilities to lower strata.

Recently, Carroll's model and the Horn-Cattell model have been synthesized into the Cattell-Horn-Carroll (CHC) theory (Flanagan & Harrison, 2005). Even though the CHC model still incorporates a g factor, its main emphasis is on the measurement of middle-stratum factors. The CHC theory has been influential in developing a variety of IQ tests, including the fifth edition of the Stanford-Binet (Roid, 2004), the second edition of the Kaufman Assessment Battery for Children (KABC–II; Kaufman, et al., 2005), and the third edition of the Woodcock-Johnson Cognitive Abilities Assessment (WJ III; Mather, et al., 2001).

Other contemporary researchers have emphasized the domain-specificity of intelligence. Howard Gardner (1983) introduced a 'Multiple Intelligences' model that included 7 distinct cognitive abilities: linguistic, logical-mathematical, spatial, musical, bodily-kinesthetic, interpersonal, and intrapersonal. Although Gardner has never demonstrated that his proposed intelligences are statistically independent, unloaded on the g factor, or irreconcilable with the Carroll hierarchical model, his model has profoundly influenced educational psychology. It also led others to propose additional possible intelligences, such as emotional intelligence, social intelligence, spiritual intelligence, existential intelligence, and now of course, mating intelligence.

Robert Sternberg (1997, 2000) also argues for looking "beyond g". He emphasizes *successful intelligence*—the ability to achieve success in life by capitalizing on cognitive strengths and correcting or compensating for cognitive weaknesses, in order to adapt to, shape, and select environments, through a balance of analytical, creative, and practical abilities. According to Sternberg, analytical intelligence is required to solve problems and to judge the quality of ideas, creative intelligence is required to formulate good problems and solutions, and practical intelligence is needed to use the ideas and analysis in an effective way in one's everyday life. As with the survival-oriented models of creativity as novelty plus utility, Sternberg's work emphasizes practical, economic, and social forms of success, rather than sexual attractiveness. Although Sternberg's theory has received the criticism that analytical, creative, and practical forms of intelligence are uncorrelated, unloaded on g, or anything other than mid-stratum 'group factors' (Brody, 2003; Gottredson, 2003), Sternberg and his collaborators have recently displayed evidence suggesting that these three forms of intelligence are at least partially distinct (Cianciola et al., 2006; Sternberg & The Rainbow Project Collaborators, 2006), further lending support to the need to distinguish the construct of intelligence from the construct of creativity.

Regardless of these theoretical debates, almost all intelligence researchers agree that verbal intelligence is, at the very least, a distinctive 'group factor' or mid-stratum ability: it is highly correlated with the g factor (general intelligence), but is statistically distinguishable from other group factors. It seems sensible that verbal intelligence is an important contributor to humor ability, which depends on general intelligence, and which will be correlated with many other desirable forms of cognitive ability. Thus, a good sense of humor may reveal good general intelligence, especially good verbal intelligence.

Relationship Between Intelligence and Creativity

What is the relationship between intelligence and creativity? Even though some researchers argue that intelligence and creativity are basically the same construct and depend upon the same cognitive processes (Weisberg, 1993), the more common view is that creativity and intelligence are overlapping, although not identical, constructs (Sternberg & O'Hara, 2000).

Several robust findings are consistent with this partial-overlap view of intelligence and creativity. First, when publicly recognizable 'creative' people such as successful artists, novelists, scientists, and engineers are studied, they tend to show IQs above 120 (Barron, 1963; Cox, 1926; Roe, 1952, 1972). This does not mean that people below IQ 120 are incapable of everyday-level creative behavior, but that they may be less likely to achieve expert-level creativity. Second, some evidence suggests that there is *threshold effect* (Barron, 1963, 1969), such that extra intelligence above IQ 120 does not much increase the likelihood of highly creative output (Sternberg, 2000). If there is an IQ 120 threshold for expert-level creativity, other personality factors such as conscientiousness, openness to experience, and emotional stability may become more important above that level. Also, in some fields such as getting elected to political leadership positions, very high intelligence and creativity may be detrimental, since they make candidates incomprehensible to the average (IQ 100) voter (Simonton, 1985).

However, a recent study challenged this threshold effect hypothesis, finding that even above IQ 120, intelligence remains highly predictive of occupational success and creative achievement (Lubinski et al., 2006). Here, creative achievement was defined much more stringently, e.g., as having achieved a tenured full professorship in a top-50 U.S. university by age 35. There may have been ceiling effects in previous creativity tests that reduced the correlation between intelligence and creativity at the upper end of the distribution.

Also, most of the support for the threshold hypothesis comes from comparisons of intelligence-creativity correlations within average-IQ versus high-IQ groups. To overcome the problem of restricted range among the high IQ groups, a recent study equated the variances of an average IQ group and a high IQ group (Sligh, Conners, & Roskos-Ewoldsen, 2005), and asked college students to complete some traditional tests of intelligence and the Finke Creative Invention Task (FCIT, Finke, 1990), which is based on the GenePlore model of creative cognition (Finke, Ward, & Smith, 1992). The FCIT requires participants to generate (the 'Gene' part of the model) a form (by drawing a picture) that combines three specified shapes (e.g., cone, square, set of wheels), and then interpret or explore (the 'Plore' part of the model) the invention as something meaningful within a particular category (e.g., transportation, toys, games). They found that crystallized intelligence displayed a threshold effect in predicting 'creative cognition' performance: crystallized g and creativity were more highly correlated in lower IQ individuals than in higher-IQ individuals. However, fluid intelligence showed the opposite pattern: fluid g and creativity were more highly correlated in higher-IQ individuals than in lower-IQ individuals.

Therefore, Sligh et al.'s (2005) findings suggest that the threshold effect seems to hold only for some creativity measures and some intelligence measures. This may help explain why studies find highly variable relationships between IQ and creativity, ranging from weakly positive to strongly positive (Baron & Harrington, 1981; Flescher, 1963; Getzels & Jackson, 1962; Guilford, 1967; Herr, Moore, & Hasen, 1965; Torrance, 1962, 1975; Wallach & Kogan, 1965). For instance, Anne Roe (1952, 1972) estimated the IQs of the highly creative scientists in her sample to range between 121 and 194, depending on whether the IQ test was verbal, spatial, or mathematical. Also, general intelligence may play less of a role in evolutionarily ancient domains of creativity such as art and music, than in evolutionarily novel domains such as mathematics and science (Kanazawa, this volume; McNemar, 1964). Thus, if humor is evolutionarily ancient, it may be a more reliable indicator of verbal creativity than of general intelligence. Further research is needed on this point.

Taken together, the research suggests a substantial overlap (but not identity) between intelligence and creativity. Consequently, verbal intelligence and verbal creativity may also be partially distinct. The implication for humor is that a reasonably high global IQ or even verbal IQ may be necessary, but not sufficient, for exceptional humor production ability.

Humor

Up to this point, we've mentioned humor several times, without describing in detail what we mean by it. Like creativity and intelligence, humor is a complex construct that eludes a unified description or definition (Ruch, 1998). Hundreds of studies have examined the psychological nature of humor (Roeckelein, 2002), but surprisingly few have conceptualized humor as an individual-differences skill or trait (Martin, 1998).

However, humor seems most relevant to mating intelligence when it is construed as a 'trait' in the psychometric and genetic sense—a stable, possibly heritable individual differences dimension that may be genetically correlated with other desirable traits, and which thereby might function as a fitness indicator. Also, as in other evolutionary analyses of animal signaling systems, 'sense of humor' is easiest to analyze when a clear distinction is made between humor production (trait display by a signaler) and humor appreciation (trait assessment by a receiver).

So far, there is vastly more work on humor appreciation than on humor production. Humor production refers to the ability to generate new instances of humor or to amuse others (Köhler & Ruch, 1996; Koppel & Sechrest, 1970). Humor production can take many forms, but most research (and our focus) has been on verbal humor, such as creating funny cartoon captions, which are then rated by judges (e.g., Derks & Hervas, 1988; Feingold & Mazzella, 1993; Kozbelt & Nishioka, in press); Siegler, 2004). Verbal humor is probably the most common form of humor production in natural situations, and is thus the most likely form of humor for selection to have acted upon (Bressler, 2005). Verbal humor may also show the clearest links to other known fitness indicators such as intelligence and creativity, especially when the *quality* of achieved humor (not just quantity of attempted humor) is taken into account.

By contrast, humor comprehension is the process of understanding or "getting" a joke, which involves requires language processing, reasoning, mental flexibility, and working memory (Shammi & Stuss, 2003), as well as problem solving (Shultz, 1972; Suls, 1972). Humor comprehension is typically assessed using multiple-choice questions where participants must correctly interpret a cartoon's meaning (e.g., Couturier, Mansfield, & Gallagher, 1981; Kozbelt & Nishioka (in press); Wierzbicki & Young, 1978). Individual differences in humor comprehension may constitute an objectively assessable trait (much like reading comprehension), and may be fairly correlated with intelligence, creativity, and cultural knowledge.

Finally, humor appreciation is the experience of finding something amusing. It is typically operationalized by the intensity and duration of the "mirth response," including smiling and laughing, or subjective funniness ratings given in response to humorous stimuli (Goldstein, 1970;

Sheehy-Skeffington, 1977)—measures which cannot really be scored as correct or incorrect. Since individual differences in humor appreciation may reflect arbitrary, personality-based differences in thresholds for finding things funny, humor appreciation may not reflect an underlying skill or ability in the way that humor production and comprehension do (Galloway, 1994; Wierzbicki & Young, 1978). On the other hand, extremely low thresholds for mirth responses are often taken as symptoms of mental illness (as when individuals with schizophrenia or mania laugh to themselves), as are extremely high thresholds (as in depression or autism). Moreover, if humor appreciation functions as part of the human mate choice system, there should be an optimal degree of responsiveness (maximum accuracy, minimal bias, and a moderate threshold) that helps receivers distinguish truly funny suitors from unfunny suitors. Indeed, an optimal humor appreciation system would comprehend many more attempts at humor than it actually finds amusing—it should 'get' many more jokes than it genuinely laughs at, just as a peahen can perceive many more peacock tails than she finds attractive. Thus, humor appreciation may be an important part of mate choice, just as humor production is an important part of courtship effort (Bressler, 2005; Grammar & Eibl-Eibesfeldt, 1990).

What are the psychometric relationships between humor production, comprehension, and appreciation? This question is not easy to answer, for several reasons. First, much research on individual differences in humor production, comprehension, and appreciation is plagued with methodological shortcomings, and does not meet standard psychometric criteria of reliability and validity (see critiques by Köhler & Ruch, 1996; Sheehy-Skeffington, 1977; Thorson & Powell, 1993a, 1993b). Also, few researchers have made clear distinctions between production, comprehension, and appreciation, and almost never have these traits been measured systematically in the same participants. Finally, compared to comprehension and appreciation, few investigations have examined the quality of humor production: Rockelein's (2002) comprehensive humor bibliography of psychological research on humor, running to nearly 600 pages, includes only a few pages on humor production.

Nevertheless, some psychometric evidence suggests positive correlations between humor production, comprehension, and appreciation. Least surprisingly, comprehension seems to correlate positively with appreciation (Kozbelt & Nishioka, in press); Wierzbicki & Young, 1978). In a study of neuropsychiatric participants, Byrne (1956) found a positive correlation between humor comprehension (the ability to distinguish between hostile and non-hostile cartoons), and humor appreciation (actually finding hostile cartoons amusing). However, this effect held only after controlling for the confounding variable of intelligence, which likely contributes to humor comprehension but not appreciation (see below). Also, in a study of children aged 10 to 14, Masten (1986) found no correlation between comprehension and self-reported verbal funniness ratings, but did find a positive correlation between comprehension and observed 'facial mirth response' (smiling, laughing). Thus, while more research is needed to resolve this point, the data thus far suggest at least a mild positive association between humor appreciation and comprehension.

Evidence for a relationship between humor production and appreciation is far more tenuous. For instance, Köhler and Ruch (1996) found only very low positive correlations between humor appreciation and production, as measured by peer-rated performance criteria (rather than self-reported humor initiation). According to the researchers, this indicates that "those who rate jokes and cartoons as funny are not necessarily . . . able to produce many or funny punch lines; and vice versa, the wit may equally well be a person who appreciates humor or who dislikes the humor of others" (p. 18). Koppel and Sechrest (1970) found a slight positive correlation between humor appreciation and production but concluded they are largely separate constructs. Consistent with this, Kozbelt and Nishioka (in press) found no relationship between participants' funniness ratings of cartoons and the rated funniness of captions created by the same participants. Masten (1986) observed no correlation between the quality of humor production and funniness ratings but she did observe a positive correlation between humor production and mirth response. Finally, Thorson and Powell (1993a, 1993b) found in a factor analysis study that self-reported humor production items loaded onto a separate factor than self-reported humor appreciation items.

Thus, there is some evidence that the association between humor production and appreciation is quite low. From a sexual signaling viewpoint, this is not surprising. If very funny individuals tend to be more intelligent and creative, they will have higher 'mate value' (desirability to the other sex), so they can afford to be choosier about their partners—i.e., their threshold for finding others funny will be quite high, and it will take a lot to amuse them. Thus, the very funny may seem mirthless, while those who laugh easily may have low standards, low mate value, and low humor production ability. Without understanding the distinctive functions of humor production versus appreciation, it is very hard to make sensible predictions about their likely relationship as individual-differences variables.

The strongest relationship is between humor production and humor comprehension. It makes sense that these two should be related, insofar as it would be hard to tell a funny story that was beyond one's understanding (Attardo, 1994; Feingold, 1983). The available empirical evidence largely supports this view. For instance, Feingold and Mazzella (1993) found a positive correlation between the peer-rated quality of participants' humor production (cartoon captioning and repartee generation) abilities and their humor comprehension (joke knowledge and joke reasoning) abilities. Kozbelt and Nishioka (in press) also found a positive correlation between the peer-rated quality of humor production and comprehension, as measured by the ability to detect "latent content" (Freud, 1905/1960) that was either matched or mismatched to a particular cartoon.

Thus, humor production, comprehension, and appreciation can be conceptually, functionally, and psychometrically distinguished. Humor comprehension is positively correlated with both production and appreciation, but appreciation and production show little association—nor should they, from a sexual-signaling viewpoint. Thus, while people do show stable individual differences in humor appreciation (e.g., Köhler & Ruch, 1996; Koppel & Sechrest, 1970), these individual differences do not necessarily represent an underlying ability (Wierzbicki & Young, 1978). Humor appreciation (mirthfulness) may instead represent a type of mate-choice threshold that tacitly incorporates one's knowledge of one's own mate value and likely success in a competitive mating market. The sexually desperate should laugh at almost everything; the sexually choosy should be very hard to amuse.

Relationship Between Humor and Verbal Intelligence

If humor production and comprehension abilities are a good reliable index of genetic fitness, then they should be positively correlated with characteristics such as intelligence, creativity, and physical attractiveness. A view of humor comprehension as incongruity-resolution or problem-solving implies a close association between humor, creativity, and intelligence (Martin, 1998). However, studies on the relationship between intelligence and humor, broadly defined, have yielded equivocal results (Galloway, 1994; Holt & Willard-Holt, 1995). Distinguishing between humor production, comprehension, and appreciation clarifies the results and reinforces the view that production and comprehension are fitness-related abilities, while humor appreciation is not.

For instance, evidence suggests a minimal relationship between humor appreciation and intelligence. Koppel and Sechrest (1970) and Landis and Ross (1933) found no significant correlations between humor appreciation and SAT scores. Byrne (1956) studied neuropsychiatric participants and found no relationship between estimated IQ and the extent to which a set of hostile cartoons were found funny. Ziv and Gadish (1990) found that gifted adolescents showed a bimodal distribution of self-reported humor appreciation: some showed high mirthfulness, while others seemed mirthless. Cunningham (1962) studied high school girls and found a significant negative correlation between IQ (as measured by the Thurstone Test of Mental Alertness) and humor appreciation (mirthfulness)—as we might expect if IQ correlates positively with mate value and choosiness. Indeed, in the few studies reporting positive associations between humor appreciation and intelligence, there are almost always confounding factors, such as participant conscientiousness and motivation (Masten, 1986), subjectively assessing participants' humor appreciation via interviews (Weissberg & Springer, 1961), or using unusual types of stimuli to assess humor appreciation. As an illustration of the latter, Feingold (1983) reported no correlation between IQ and humor appreciation (measured as self-reported interest in the films of Mel Brooks and Woody Allen) in "dull" (IQ < 104) participants, but a significant positive correlation in brighter (IQ > 104) participants. Here again, humor 'appreciation' of such films demands a certain level of humor comprehension, which should be more intelligence-related.

In contrast, positive correlations have often been found between intelligence and humor comprehension. This is not surprising: the Stanford-Binet intelligence test includes items on 'comprehension of absurdities' that function as a good measure of general intelligence (Ziv & Gadish, 1990). Along these lines, Feingold (1983; Feingold & Mazzella, 1991, 1993) found that verbal intelligence was positively correlated with humor and comprehension. Wierzbicki and Young (1978) observed a positive correlation between humor comprehension and IQ, estimated by the Vocabulary subtest of the WAIS, in a sample of college males. Developmental investigations (Bird, 1925; Couturier, Mansfield, & Gallagher, 1981; Masten, 1986; Owens & Hogan, 1983; Schwager, 1983) have yielded similar results. Finally, two dissertation studies (Jaffe, 1995; Schaier, 1975) found that among the elderly, humor appreciation increases with age, but humor comprehension decreases with age—effects which might be attributed to declines in fluid intelligence.

Finally, evidence concerning the correlations between intelligence and humor production ability is rather meager, largely due to the scarcity of studies on humor production. In understanding the role of humor in mating intelligence, this dearth of evidence is unfortunate, since production is the aspect of humor most relevant for testing the predictions of sexual selection theory. However, the evidence that does exist is consistent with Miller's view. For instance, Feingold and Mazzella (1993) found a reliable positive correlation between verbal ability, measured by a multiple-choice test of word knowledge, and the quality of humor production, measured by ratings given by two judges to cartoon captions and repartee statements. Likewise, Koppel and Sechrest (1970), in a study of college fraternity brothers, found a small but reliable correlation between SAT scores and humor production ability, measured by peer ratings of newly devised cartoon captions. Finally, Masten (1986) found substantial positive correlations between both IQ and academic achievement and humor production, measured by ratings given by two judges to cartoon captions.

Since research to date has investigated only a few issues related to these constructs, much remains to be examined. However, the preliminary pattern of relationships between intelligence and three aspects of humor (production, comprehension, and appreciation) is largely consistent with the predictions of a sexual selection account: both humor production and comprehension seem positively correlated with intelligence, and thus may represent a cue to genetic fitness. In contrast, humor appreciation, which is more like a mate choice threshold than a courtship display, does not seem related to intelligence. Clearly, more research is necessary to resolve these relations, especially regarding the link between humor production and intelligence.

Relationship Between Humor and Creativity

In studying the links between intelligence and humor, at least psychometrics provides good, reliable, valid measures of intelligence. Studying the links between creativity and humor is trickier, because creativity and humor are both more difficult to operationalize (Humke & Schaefer, 1996; Murdock & Ganim, 1993). Most of this creativity-humor research measures creativity in quite domain-general ways, and does not clearly distinguish between humor production, comprehension, and appreciation. Ziv (1988b) noted that creativity may seem spuriously linked to humor if creativity is operationalized in rather vague ways, such as 'divergent thinking' (Guilford, 1959), or the 'fluency, flexibility, originality, and elaboration of thought' (e.g., Wallach & Kogan, 1965). Conceptually, humor production and creativity share many components (such as playfulness, risk-taking, and loose associations), as do humor comprehension and creativity (such as incongruity-resolution, and insight—Koestler, 1964; Kuhlman, 1984; Rouff, 1975). Along these lines, Murdock and Ganim's (1993) content analysis of definitions and theories of humor suggested that humor and creativity are closely related, and that humor production is basically a subset of creativity. If this is right, then creativity should be positively correlated with both humor production and humor comprehension, just as intelligence seems to be. What, then, is the evidence regarding the psychometric relations between creativity and these aspects of humor?

As with intelligence, there is evidence for only a slight relationship between creativity and humor appreciation. Treadwell (1970), studying college students, found no relationship between self-reported humor appreciation and three paper-and-pencil tests of creative thinking: the Remote Associates Test, Gestalt transformations, and Need for Novelty scales from the Thematic Apperception Test. Schoel and Busse (1971) found no creativity difference (as assessed by two paper-and-pencil creativity tasks) between a group of 'funny' students (as selected by their teachers) and a control group of average students. However, the criteria for selecting humorous students included items such as "appreciates the ludicrous" (p. 34), and the authors concluded that their null result may reflect their selection criteria, which conflated humor appreciation and humor production. Similarly, two dissertations have found no relationship between humor appreciation and creativity among first graders (Gilbert, 1977) or high school students (Townsend, 1982).

Psychometric evidence on the relationship between humor comprehension and creativity is rather scant, but several studies suggest a positive relationship. Rouff (1973, 1975) found that creativity and humor comprehension were positively correlated among undergraduates, and argued that they have a common basis in the ability to find hidden connections between apparently disparate concepts. Gilbert (1977) also found a positive relationship between humor comprehension and creativity among first graders, in contrast to a negligible correlation between humor appreciation and creativity. Moreover, "reflective" children had the greatest humor comprehension and demonstrated the most creativity.

Finally, as with humor comprehension, few studies have measured humor production in relationship to creativity, but the evidence so far suggests a positive correlation. Treadwell (1970) found positive correlations between the quality of humor production and three paper-and-pencil measures of creativity. Smith and White (1965), studying U.S. Air Force personnel, observed a positive association between wit and creativity. Townsend (1982) found quantity of humor positively predicted creative thinking in high school students. Finally, Brodzinsky and Rubien (1976) found that creativity was positively related to humor production; they also observed that men generated funnier captions than women for sexual and aggressive cartoons, but not for neutral stimuli. The scarcity of studies on links between creativity and humor comprehension or production seems more symptomatic of the lack of attention paid to distinct aspects of humor than of intrinsically weak relationships between the constructs: other investigations examining the association between creativity and humor (broadly defined) have generally found positive relationships between the two. For instance, Fabrizi and Pollio (1987) found correlations between teacher and peer ratings of the humor of 11th graders and these students' originality and elaboration scores on the Torrance Test of Creative Thinking (in contrast to null findings with 7th graders). Several investigations (Humke & Schaefer, 1996; Kovács, 1999) have found positive relationships between paper-and-pencil creativity measures and scores on Thorson and Powell's (1993a, 1993b) Multidimensional Sense of Humor Scale, though this research did not clearly distinguish the four factors of the scale (humor production, humor and coping, humor appreciation, and attitudes toward humor). Finally, Ziv (1976, 1988b) described some studies showing that humor training is effective at enhancing creativity in adolescents.

In sum, despite limited empirical evidence, creativity seems to have positive relationships with both humor comprehension and production, but not with appreciation. This pattern echoes that found between intelligence and humor (Galloway, 1994). Since creativity is also at least partially related to IQ, the prospects are good for understanding intelligence, creativity, and humor in a more integrated way, as closely related fitness indicators and likely products of sexual selection.

EVIDENCE FOR HUMOR AS AN IMPORTANT COMPONENT OF MATING INTELLIGENCE

Although the available psychometric evidence seems consistent with a sexual selection understanding of the nature and functions of humor, one might object that the evidence is fairly indirect. For instance, psychometric methods of measuring intelligence, creativity, and humor often seem artificial and ecologically invalid (Babad, 1974), particularly compared to whatever role these constructs may have played in the EEA (Storey, 2002). Moreover, one might argue that there is, so far, no evidence of increased sexual attractiveness or increased reproductive success from intelligence, creativity, or humor in a natural-fertility population (e.g., hunter-gatherers who do not use contraception)—which might be the best test of Miller's theory. Perhaps humor, intelligence, and creativity evolved via natural selection for survival benefits somehow, and people simply prefer to socialize with others who are funny, smart, and creative, rather than humorless, dull, and unimaginative. Moreover, socializing with intelligent, funny people would allow one to benefit from their superior mental traits when new adaptive problems face one's social group. In this view, the main role of humor in survival is facilitating adaptive social bonding and problem-solving, rather than acting as a fitness indicator in sexual selection. Is there anything specifically sexual about the function (rather than content) of humor, which could resolve this issue?

One approach is to examine sex differences in humor production that could reveal a mating function, and that would not be predicted by a sex-blind social-bonding theory. Specifically, if humor functions as a fitness indicator, and if females are generally choosier than males, then males should invest more effort in humor production, and females should show more overt humor appreciation (to encourage male courtship attempts), accompanied by a more discriminating covert humor appreciation (to distinguish which men are truly amusing). Until recently, little research has focused on sex differences in this way (Galloway, 1994). However, some recent research suggests that while men and women both say they like a "good sense of humor," they mean different things by that: men prefer women who appreciate their humor, while women prefer men who make them laugh (Bressler, Martin, & Balshine, 2006). This is consistent with Provine's (2000) analysis of over 3,000 singles ads, in which women were more likely to offer good humor appreciation, whereas men were more likely to offer good humor production ability. Furthermore, Bressler and Balshine (2006) found that women rated humorous men as better potential partners, and as more friendly, fun, and popular. Women did not show any such preference for humorous women as potential friends. Additionally, a man's view of other men's or women's personality attributes was uninfluenced by how funny such others were.

This is consistent with the sex differences in humor production discussed earlier (Hay, 2000; Kotthoff, 2000), and with some experimental studies suggesting sex differences in humor appreciation. If overt humor appreciation is indicated by laughter, then females demonstrate significantly more such appreciation than males (Chapell, Batten, Brown, Gonzalez, Herquet, Massar, & Pedroche, 2002; McAdams, Jackson, & Kirshnit, 1984). Further, this sex difference seems to begin in early childhood (Chapman & Foot, 1976). This sex difference in humor appreciation seems to reflect real-world differences in sexual choosiness: Grammer and Eibl-Eibesfeldt (1990) found that synchronized laughter during spontaneous male/female conversations predicted mutual initial attraction—but the amount of laughter the woman produced was most predictive of mutual interest in actually dating. Thus, both sexes treat the woman's laughter as an index of humor appreciation and mate choice.

Further evidence for such sex differences comes from recent fMRI research examining the brain's response to humorous cartoons (Azim, Mobbs, Booil, Menon, & Reiss, 2005). In this study, participants viewed a series of cartoons, pressed a button if they found each cartoon funny, and then rated the humor value of each cartoon. Members of both sexes found about 80 percent of the cartoons funny and showed no reliable difference in funniness ratings or response time. However, women showed more activation in left prefrontal cortex than men (suggesting deeper verbal analysis of the cartoons), and in the nucleus accumbens (the brain's reward center, suggesting that they derived more pleasure from the humor). Finally, women were faster to rate low-humor cartoons as unfunny. Such results suggest that women may process humor more deeply, derive more pleasure from successful humor, and reject unsuccessful humor more quickly—signs that their humor appreciation may be more discriminating than that of men. Thus, males show higher mating intelligence in the sense of humor production ability, but females may show higher mating intelligence in the sense of humor appreciation—as the fitness indicator theory of humor would suggest.

Finally, some of the most provocative evidence for humor as a fitness indicator comes from research on shifts in women's mate preferences across the menstrual cycle (Haselton & Miller, 2006; Miller, 2003). The logic here is that human females have concealed ovulation that allows only a brief window of time when fertilization can occur. While mating that brings material benefits (food, protection, paternal investment) would have benefits that extend throughout the cycle, traits that are good gene indicators (e.g., creativity or humor, as hypothesized by Miller) should be more valued just before ovulation, when fertilization is most likely to occur (Gangestad, Simpson, Cousins, Garver-Apgar, & Christensen, 2004). Only at peak fertility can a male mate's good genes be passed on to off-spring, so at peak fertility women should women pay attention to "good genes" indicators. If creativity and humor are good gene indicators, they should become more attractive to women during peak fertility, just before ovulation. Women using hormonal contraception such as the Pill (which suppresses ovulation) do not experience the associated hormonal or psy-chological changes, and so should not show a mid-cycle preference shift.

From this argument Haselton and Miller (2006) made some predic-tions about women's mating preferences. First, higher fertility should lead women to favor male creativity more highly relative to male wealth—but only for short-term mating preferences. Preferences for long-term partners (who should stick around for many ovulatory cycles) should not be so dependent on immediate fertility fluctuations, so should have little effect on the desirability for creativity (good genes) versus wealth (good dad/provider). To test this hypothesis, Haselton and Miller asked partici-pants to read pairs of vignettes about potential male mates: descriptions of a creative but poor artist versus a non-creative but rich artist and a creative but poor businessman versus a non-creative but rich businessman. The vignettes explicitly portrayed the creativity as a natural (and presumably heritable) trait, whereas the wealth was portrayed as due to luck (artistic fashion or a windfall inheritance). Haselton and Miller (2006) confirmed their predictions: higher fertility increased the relative desirability of poor but creative men, but only for short-term mating, not for long-term mating.

Some preliminary evidence also suggests that such ovulatory cycle effects influence female attraction to humor itself. As in the Haselton and Miller study, Miller and Caruthers (2003) had 206 female participants read vignettes about potential male mates who were described as showing dif-ferent levels of humor-production ability (good, average, or bad). Women then rated a number of personality and cognitive traits for each male, and rated his attractiveness as a potential short-term and long-term mate. Three results are worth noting here. First, men described as having higher humor production ability were rated as significantly more socially sensi-tive, adaptable, extroverted, exciting, happy, and able to play well with kids (all $p < .01$), and as more intelligent, kind, tall, healthy, masculine, and muscular (all $p < .05$). Women seemed to be viewing humor production ability as a reliable cue of many other desirable fitness-related traits. Second, among naturally-cycling women (not using the Pill), female fertility significantly increased the short-term attractiveness of men with high humor-production ability ($r = +.20, p = .028, N = 124$), but had no effect on these men's long-term attractiveness ($r = -.11$, n.s., $N = 128$). There were no fertility effects on attraction to men with medium or low humor-production ability, and no cycle effects for women using hormonal contraception. Finally, among women in steady sexual relationships ($N = 105$), the rated humor-production ability of their current male partner significantly predicted their general relationship satisfaction ($r = +.73, p < .001$), their expected relationship length ($r = +.47, p < .001$), and their expected future likelihood of having children together ($r = +.41, p < .001$). Thus, male humor production ability seems important both as a 'good genes' indicator in attracting women for short-term mating, and for retaining women in long-term relationships. These preliminary results are consistent with the fitness indicator view of humor, but they need replication in other labs, ideally with larger samples of naturally-cycling women, more accurate physiological measures of fertility status, and more ecologically valid ways of displaying potential male mates who differ in humor production ability.

   In sum, mounting evidence supports the view that sexual selection favored the evolution of humor production ability as a fitness indicator, and humor appreciation ability as a mate choice mechanism. In particular, males and females value different aspects of humor in potential mates (females like funny males, and males like appreciative females), female and male brains respond to humor differently (females process linguistic aspects of humor more efficiently and show greater activation in reward centers), and females near peak fertility are especially attracted to males who display creativity and humor. These sex differences and cycle shifts build upon the basic psychometric distinctions between humor production, comprehension, and appreciation, which are related to each other and to intelligence and creativity in ways that are also consistent with sexual selection theory and fitness indicator theory. Since mating intelligence consists of the cognitive arsenal used to attract and retain mates, the findings so far suggest that humor, as an indicator of both creativity and intelligence, is an important part of that arsenal.

CONCLUSION

The scientific study of humor and its relationship to mating intelligence is no laughing matter. The available evidence paints a coherent but still somewhat vague picture of the relationships among sexual selection, humor, intelligence, and creativity. Far more empirical research will be needed to clarify the psychometric and functional relationships among these constructs, their role in mate attraction and intra-sexual rivalry, and their evaluation by mate choice mechanisms. Here, we propose a few directions for future research.

One clear direction is simply to clarify the basic psychometric relationships within and between the constructs of humor, creativity, and intelligence, paying closer attention to the distinctions between production, comprehension, and appreciation, and making more explicit ties to evolutionary theory. Doing so would bolster confidence in the validity of the apparent positive correlations among humor production, comprehension, intelligence, and creativity. It might also lead to discovery of positive correlations between humor appreciation (in the sense of accurate discrimination, not mindless hilarity), and other person-perception abilities, such as the capacities to judge intelligence, creativity, and personality traits accurately.

While some research has addressed sex differences in "sense of humor" (e.g., Bressler, 2005; Bressler & Balshine, 2006; Bressler, Martin, & Balshine, 2006; Brodzinsky & Rubien, 1976), a great deal of further work remains to be done, using more sophisticated sexual selection models that can predict specific, functional sex differences in humor production, comprehension, and appreciation. A high priority should be given to replicating the provisional results showing ovulatory cycle effects on women's preferences for male creativity and humor production ability (Haselton & Miller, 2006; Miller & Caruthers, 2003).

Research also suggests that sex-differentiated mate preferences can be understood more clearly by distinguishing between short-term and long-term mating strategies (Buss, 2000). This distinction may be especially important in understanding mate preferences for humor (Stewart, Stinnett, & Rosenfeld, 2000). Future research should try to understand humor's distinctive roles in initial attraction, serious courtship, relationship formation, mate retention, and deterrence of sexual rivals. Assortative mating for humor ability may be especially important to study, since it can quickly amplify the heritable genetic variation in humor ability. Assortative mating may even exist for specific types and modes of humor (Murstein, & Brust, 1985; Priest & Thein, 2003). Future research should also elucidate the conditions in which the desire for humor is expressed (short term relationship vs. long term relationship) and the reasons why the desire is expressed (good genes vs. good parents vs. social bonding) for both males and females.

Another direction for future research involves examining the natural patterns of genetic covariation between humor production ability and other fitness-related traits such as body symmetry, physical attractiveness, physical health, and mental health. For example, the fitness indicator theory of humor predicts a positive genetic (but not necessarily phenotypic) correlation between humor production ability and physical attractiveness among males. A low correlation could suggest that humor is not a very reliable good genes indicator, or that there are strong genetic or phenotypic trade-offs between growing efficient brain systems for humor production and growing an attractive body. Several studies (Bressler, 2005; Bressler & Balshine, 2006; Bressler, Martin, & Balshine, 2006; Lundy, Tan, & Cunningham, 1998) have manipulated humor and physical attractiveness as independent variables, with interesting results. For instance, Lundy et al. (1998) manipulated both humor (using interview transcripts containing humorous self-deprecating responses) and physical attractiveness (using photographs) and found that men who expressed humor were rated as more desirable than nonhumorous individuals for a serious relationship and marriage, but only when the men were physically attractive. However, there seem to be no studies so far that examine the correlation between humor production ability and physical attractiveness in a broad population-representative sample, using double-blind ratings of humor and attractiveness (to avoid 'halo effects' whereby an attractive person's humor tends to be judged more generously—see, e.g., Lundy et al., 1998). Such a halo effect might partly explain the dissociation sometimes observed between psychometric assessments of humor ability versus peer or self ratings of humorousness (e.g., Köhler & Ruch, 1996; Koppel & Sechrest, 1970).

Another possibility is that humor self-report questionnaires do not accurately capture individual differences in humor production ability in ecologically valid, socially complex settings (Babad, 1974). Of course, the standard psychometric approaches to measuring creativity and intelligence also may not be ecologically valid when applied to the mating domain. Many convergent lines of evidence, using different research methods, stimuli, and tasks, will be needed to clarify the place of humor in the overall structure of human phenotypic traits and genetic differences.

An additional complication concerns the possibility that humor production may have evolved as an 'alternative mating strategy'—a compensatory strategy pursued by those who lack more obvious fitness indicators such as physical attractiveness or social status (Bressler, 2005). Thus, even if humor and physical attractiveness are positively correlated at the genetic level (as good genes indicators), they might be negatively correlated at the phenotypic level (given trade-offs between alternative mating strategies). If humor, creativity, and intelligence were perfectly positively correlated, there would be no need to assess them separately as fitness indicators: one trait would suffice for mate choice. If these are modestly inter-correlated, then there may be scope for mate choice to use 'improper linear models' (Dawes, 1979) or 'fast and frugal heuristics' (Gigerenzer & Todd, 1999), whereby a set of correlated variables are assessed independently then integrated using some rough-and-ready heuristic to make a judgment (in this case, about a mate's likely genetic fitness). Only by measuring these constructs more precisely, distinguishing between produc-

tion, comprehension, and appreciation, assessing their genetic and phenotypic inter-correlations, and studying the discriminatory mechanisms
adapted to judge them, will we learn whether sexual selection is indeed
responsible for their evolution as distinctively human forms of mating
intelligence.

REFERENCES

Amabile, T. M. (1982). Social psychology of creativity: A consensual assessment
    technique. *Journal of Personality and Social Psychology, 43*, 997–1013.
Andrews, P. W., Gangestad, S. W., & Matthews, D. (2002). Adaptationism—How to
    carry out an exaptationist program. *Behavioral and Brain Sciences, 25*, 504–553;
    discussion.
Apte, M. L. (1985). *Humor and laughter: An anthropological approach.* Ithaca, NY: Cor-
    nell University Press.
Attardo, S. (1994). *Linguistic theories of humor.* New York: Mouton de Gruyter.
Azim, E., Mobbs, D., Booil, J., Menon, V., & Reiss, A. L. (2005). Sex differences in
    brain activation elicited by humor. *Proceedings of the National Academy of Sci-
    ences of the United States of America, 102*, 16496–16501.
Babad, E. (1974). A multi-method approach to the assessment of humor: A critical
    look at humor tests. *Journal of Personality, 42*, 618–631.
Baer, J. (1991). Generality of creativity across performance domains. *Creativity
    Research Journal, 4*, 23–29.
Baer, J. (1993). *Divergent thinking and creativity: A task-specific approach.* Hillsdale, NJ:
    Lawrence Erlbaum Associates.
Baer, J. (1994). Divergent thinking is not a general trait: A multi-domain training
    experiment. *Creativity Research Journal, 7*, 35–46.
Baer, J. (1998). The case for domain-specificity of creativity. *Creativity Research Jour-
    nal, 11*, 173–177.
Barber, N. (1995). The evolutionary psychology of physical attractiveness: Sexual
    selection and human morphology. *Ethology and Sociobiology, 16*, 395–424.
Barron, F. (1963). *Creativity and psychological health.* Princeton, NJ: D. Van Nostrand.
Barron, F. (1969). *Creative person and creative process.* New York: Holt, Rinehart &
    Winston.
Barron, F., & Harrington, D. M. (1981). Creativity, intelligence, and personality.
    Annual Review of Psychology, 32, 439–476.
Bird, G. (1925). An objective humor test for children. *Psychological Bulletin, 22*,
    137–138.
Bressler, E. R. (2005). *Humor and human courtship: Testing predictions from sexual selec-
    tion theory.* Unpublished doctoral dissertation, McMaster University.
Bressler, E. R., & Balshine, S. (2006). The influence of humor on desirability. *Evolu-
    tion and Human Behavior, 27*, 29–39.
Bressler, E. R., Martin, R. A., & Balshine, S. (2006). Production and appreciation of
    humor as sexually selected traits. *Evolution and Human Behavior, 27*, 121–130.
Brody, N. (2003). Construct validation of the Sternberg Triarchic Abilities Test:
    Comment and reanalysis. *Intelligence, 31*, 319–329.

Brodzinsky, D., & Rubien, J. (1976). Humor production as a function of sex of subject, creativity, and cartoon content. *Journal of Consulting and Clinical Psychology, 44,* 597–600.

Buss, D. M. (1988). The evolution of human intrasexual competition: Tactics of mate attraction. *Journal of Personality & Social Psychology, 54,* 616–628.

Buss, D. M. (1994). *The evolution of desire: Strategies of human mating.* New York: Basic Books.

Buss, D. M. (2000). Desires in human mating. In D. LeCroy & P. Moller (Eds.), *Evolutionary perspectives on human reproductive behavior* (pp. 39–49). New York: New York Academy of Sciences.

Buss, D. M., & Barnes, M. (1986). Preferences in human mate selection. *Journal of Personality and Social Psychology, 50,* 559–570.

Byrne, D. (1956). The relationship between humor and the expression of hostility. *Journal of Abnormal and Social Psychology, 53,* 84–89.

Carroll, J. (1995). *Evolution and literary theory.* Columbia, MO: University of Missouri Press.

Carroll, J. (2004). *Literary Darwinism: Evolution, human nature, and literature.* New York: Routledge.

Carroll, J. B. (1993). *Human cognitive abilities: A survey of factor-analytic studies.* New York: Cambridge University Press.

Caron, J. E. (2002). From ethology to aesthetics: Evolution as a theoretical paradigm for research on laughter, humor, and other comic phenomena. *Humor: International Journal of Humor Research, 15,* 245–281.

Chapell, M., Batten, M., Brown, J., Gonzalez, E., Herquet, G., Massar, C., & Pedroche, B. (2002). Frequency of public laughter in relation to sex, age, ethnicity, and social context. *Perceptual and Motor Skills, 95,* 746.

Chapman, A. J., & Foot, H. C. (1976). *Humor and laughter: Theory, research, and applications.* London: Wiley.

Cianciola, A. T., Grigorenko, E. L., Jarvin, L., Guillermo, G., Drebot, M. E., & Sternberg, R. J. (2006). Practical intelligence and tacit knowledge: Advancements in the measurement of developing expertise. *Learning and Individual Differences, 16,* 235–252.

Conti, R., Coon, H., & Amabile, T. M. (1996). Evidence to support the componential model of creativity: Secondary analyses of three studies. *Creativity Research Journal, 9,* 385–389.

Couturier, L. C., Mansfield, R. S., & Gallagher, J. M. (1981). Relationships between humor, formal operational ability, and creativity in eighth graders. *Journal of Genetic Psychology, 139,* 221–226.

Cox, C.M. (1926). *The early mental traits of three hundred geniuses.* Stanford, CA: Stanford University Press.

Csikszentmihalyi, M. (1998). Reflections on the field. *Roeper Review, 21,* 80–81.

Cunningham, A. (1962). Relation of sense of humor to intelligence. *Journal of Social Psychology, 57,* 143–147.

Darwin, C. R. (1859). *On the origin of species.* London: John Murray.

Darwin, C. R. (1871). *The descent of man and selection in relation to sex.* London: John Murray.

Dawes, R. M. (1979). The robust beauty of improper linear models. *American Psychologist, 34,* 571–582.

Derks, P., & Hervas, D. (1988). Creativity in humor production: Quantity and quality in divergent thinking. *Bulletin of the Psychonomic Society, 26,* 37–39.

Detterman, D. K. (2002). General intelligence: Cognitive and biological explanations. In R. J. Sternberg & E. L. Grigorenko (Eds.), *The general factor of intelligence: How general is it?* (pp. 223–243). Mahwah, NJ: Lawrence Erlbaum Associates.

Eibl-Eibesfeldt, I. (1970). *The expressive behaviour of the deaf and blind born.* London: Academic Press.

Fabrizi, M. S., & Pollio, H. R. (1987). Are funny teenagers creative? *Psychological Reports, 61,* 757–761.

Feingold, A. (1981). Testing equity as an explanation for romantic couples "mismatched" on physical attractiveness. *Psychological Reports, 49,* 247–250.

Feingold, A. (1983). Measuring humor perception: Revision and construct validation of the Humor Perceptiveness Test. *Perceptual and Motor Skills, 56,* 159–166.

Feingold, A. (1992). Gender differences in mate selection preferences: a test of the parental investment model. *Psychological Bulletin, 112,* 125–139.

Feingold, A., & Mazzella, R. (1991). Psychometric intelligence and verbal humor ability. *Personality and Individual Differences, 12,* 427–435.

Feingold, A., & Mazzella, R. (1993). Preliminary validation of a multidimensional model of wittiness. *Journal of Personality, 61,* 439–456.

Feist, G. J. (2001). Natural and sexual selection in the evolution of creativity. *Bulletin of Psychology and the Arts, 2,* 11–16.

Finke, R. A. (1990). *Creative imagery: Discoveries as inventions in visualization.* Hillsdale, NJ: Lawrence Erlbaum Associates.

Finke, R. A., Ward, T. B., & Smith, S. M. (1992). *Creative cognition: Theory, research, and application.* Cambridge: MIT Press.

Flanagan, D. P., & Harrison, P. L. (2005). *Contemporary intellectual assessment: Theories, tests, and issues* (2nd edition). New York: Guilford Press.

Flescher, I. (1963). Anxiety and achievement of intellectually gifted and creatively gifted children. *Journal of Psychology, 56,* 251–268.

Freud, S. (1905/1960). Jokes and their relation to the unconscious. In J. Strachey (ed. and trans.), *The Standard Edition of the Complete Psychological Works of Sigmund Freud,* Vol. 8. London: Hogarth Press.

Freud, S. (1908/1959). *The relation of the poet to day-dreaming.* In E. Jones (Ed.), Collected Papers (Vol. 4, pp. 173–183). New York: Basic Books. (J. Riviere, trans.).

Gabora, L. (2003, July 31-August 2). *Cultural focus: A cognitive explanation for the cultural transition of the Middle/Upper Paleolithic.* Paper presented at the Proceedings of the 25th Annual Meeting of the Cognitive Science Society, Boston MA.

Galloway, G. (1994). Psychological studies of the relationship of sense of humor to creativity and intelligence: A review. *European Journal for High Ability, 5,* 133–144.

Gangestad, S. W., Simpson, J. A., Cousins, A. J., Garver-Apgar, C. E., & Christensen, P. N. (2004). Women's preferences for male behavioral displays change across the menstrual cycle. *Psychological Science, 15,* 203–207.

Gardner, H. (1983). *Frames of mind: The theory of multiple intelligences.* New York: Basic Books.

Gardner, H. (1999). *Intelligence reframed: Multiple intelligences for the 21st century.* New York: Basic Books.

Getzels, J. W., & Jackson, P. W. (1962). *Creativity and intelligence: Explorations with gifted students.* New York: John Wiley & Sons.

Gigerenzer, G., & Todd, P. M. (1999). Fast and frugal heuristics: The adaptive toolbox. G. Gigerenzer & P. M. Todd (Eds.), *Simple heuristics that make us smart* (pp. 3–34). New York: Oxford University Press.

Gilbert, C. (1977). *Humor, creativity, conceptual tempo, and IQ in first grade children.* Unpublished doctoral dissertation, University of Oregon.

Goldstein, J. H. (1970). Humor appreciation and time to respond. *Psychological Reports, 27,* 445–446.

Goodwin, R. (1990). Sex differences among partner preferences: Are the sexes really very similar? *Sex Roles, 23,* 501–513.

Gottredson, L. S. (2002). g: Highly general and highly practical. In R. J. Sternberg & E. L. Grigorenko (Eds.), *The general factor of intelligence: How general is it?* (pp. 331–380). Mahwah, NJ: Lawrence Erlbaum Associates.

Gottfredson, L. S. (2003). Dissecting practical intelligence theory: Its claims and evidence. *Intelligence, 31,* 343–397.

Grammer, K., & Eibl-Eibesfeldt, I. (1990). *The ritualisation of laughter.* Bochum: Brockmeyer.

Greenberg, N. (2004). The beast at play: The neuroethology of creativity. In R. Clements & L. Fiorentino (Eds.), *The child's right to play: A global approach* (pp. 309–327). Westport, CT: Praeger Press.

Guilford, J. P. (1959). Three faces of intellect. *American Psychologist, 14,* 469–479.

Guilford, J. P. (1967). *The nature of human intelligence.* New York: McGraw-Hill.

Han, K. S. (2000). Varieties of creativity: Investigating the domain-specificity of creativity in young children. *Dissertation Abstracts International Section A: Humanities and Social Sciences, 61,* 1796.

Hansen, S. L. (1977). Dating choices of high school students. *The Family Coordinator, 26,* 133–138.

Haselton, M. G., & Miller, G. F. (in press). Women's fertility across the cycle increases the short-term attractiveness of creative intelligence compared to wealth. *Human Nature.*

Hay, J. (2000). Functions of humor in the conversations of men and women. *Journal of Pragmatics, 32,* 709–742.

Hayes, J. R. (1989). Cognitive processes in creativity. In J.A. Glover, R.R. Ronning, & C. R. Reynolds (Eds.), *Handbook of Creativity* (pp. 135–146). New York: Plenum Press.

Herr, E. L., Moore, G. D., & Hasen, J. S. (1965). Creativity, intelligence, and values: A study of relationships. *Exceptional Children, 32,* 114–115.

Hewitt, L. E. (1958). Student perceptions of traits desired in themselves as dating and marriage partners. *Marriage and Family Living, Nov.,* 344–349.

Holt, D. G., & Willard-Holt, C. (1995). An exploration of the relationship between humor and giftedness in students. *Humor: International Journal of Humor Research, 8,* 257–271.

Horn, J. L., & Cattell, R. B. (1966). Refinement and test of the theory of fluid and crystallized general intelligences. *Journal of Educational Psychology, 57,* 253–270.

Kotthoff, H. (2000). Gender and joking: On the complexities of women's image politics in humorous narratives. *Journal of Pragmatics, 32*, 55–80.

Humke, C., & Schaefer, C. E. (1996). Sense of humor and creativity. *Perceptual and Motor Skills, 82*, 544–546.

Jaffe, J. (1995). *Age-related changes in creation and appreciation of humor in the elderly.* Unpublished doctoral dissertation, California School of Professional Psychology, San Diego.

Jensen, A. R. (1998). *The 'g' factor: The science of mental ability.* Westport, CT: Preager.

Kanazawa, S. (this volume). The independence of mating intelligence and general intelligence. In G. Geher & G. F. Miller (Eds.), *Mating intelligence: Sex, relationships, and the mind's reproductive system.* Mahwah, NJ: Lawrence Erlbaum Associates.

Kaufman, A. S., Lichtenberger, E. O., Fletcher-Janzen, E., & Kaufman, N. L. (2005). *Essentials of KABC-II Assessment.* New York: Wiley.

Kaufman, J. C., & Baer, J. (2002). Could Steven Spielberg manage the Yankees?: Creative thinking in different domains. *The Korean Journal of Thinking & Problem Solving, 12*, 5–14.

Kaufman, S. B. (in press). *Creativity.* To appear in Encyclopedia of Special Education (2nd ed.). New York: Wiley.

Kenrick, D. T., Sadalla, E. K., Groth, G., & Trost, M. R. (1990). Evolution, traits, and the stages of the parental investment model. *Journal of Personality, 58*, 97–117.

Koestler, A. (1964). *The act of creation.* New York: Dell.

Köhler, G., & Ruch, W. (1996). Sources of variance in current sense of humor inventories: How much substance, how much method variance? *Humor: International Journal of Humor Research, 9*, 363–397.

Koppel, M. A., & Sechrest, L. (1970). A multitrait-multimethod matrix analysis of sense and humor. *Educational and Psychological Measurement, 30*, 77–85.

Kovács, T. (1999). Creativity and humor. *Psychológia a Patopsychológia Dietata, 34*, 346–350.

Kozbelt, A., & Nishioka, K. (in press). Humor comprehension, humor production, and insight: An exploratory study. *Humor: International Journal of Humor Research.*

Kuhlman, T. L. (1984). *Humor and psychotherapy.* Homewood, IL: Dorsey.

Kyllonen, P. C. (2002). g: Knowledge, speed, strategies, or working-memory capacity? A systems perspective. In R. J. Sternberg & E. L. Grigorenko (Eds.), *The general factor of intelligence: How general is it?* (pp. 415–445). Mahwah, NJ: Lawrence Erlbaum Associates.

Landis, C., & Ross, W. (1933). Humor and its relation to other personality traits. *Journal of Social Psychology, 4*, 156–175.

Lubinski, D., Benbow, C. P., Webb, R. M., & Bleske-Rechek, A. (2006). Tracking exceptional human capital over two decades. *Psychological Science, 17*, 194–199.

Ludovici, A. (1933). *The secret of laughter.* New York: Viking.

Lundy, D. E., Tan, J., & Cunningham, M. R. (1998). Heterosexual romantic preferences: The importance of humor and physical attractiveness for different types of relationships. *Personal Relationships, 5*, 311–325.

MacNeilage, P. F. (1997). *Acquisition of speech.* Blackwell.

Martin, R. A. (1998). Approaches to the senses of humor: A historical review. In W. Ruch (Ed.), *The sense of Humor: Explorations of a personality characteristic* (pp. 15–60). Berlin: Walter de Gruyter & Co.

Masten, A.S. (1986). Humor and competence in school-aged children. *Child Development, 57,* 461–473.

Mather, N., Wendling, B. J., & Woodcock, R. W. (2001). *Essentials of WJ III tests of achievement assessment.* New York: Wiley.

Mayer, R. E. (1999). Fifty years of creativity research. In R. J. Sternberg (Ed.), *Handbook of creativity* (pp. 449–460). New York: Cambridge University Press.

McAdams, D. P., Jackson, R. J., & Kirshnit, C. (1984). Looking, laughing, and smiling in dyads as a function of intimacy motivation and reciprocity. *Journal of Personality, 52,* 261–273.

McBrearty, S., & Brooks, A. S. (2000). The revolution that wasn't: A new interpretation of the origin of modern human behavior. *Journal of Human Evolution, 39,* 453–563.

McGhee, P. E. (1979). *Humor: Its origin and development.* San Francisco: Freeman.

McNemar, Q. (1964). Lost: Our intelligences? Why? *American Psychologist, 19,* 871–882.

Miller, G. F. (1998). How mate choice shaped human nature: A review of sexual selection and human evolution. In C.B. Crawford & Krebs, D.L. (Eds.), *Handbook of evolutionary psychology: Ideas, issues, and applications* (pp. 87–129). Mahwah, NJ: Lawrence Erlbaum Associates.

Miller, G. F. (2000a). *The mating mind.* New York: Random House.

Miller, G. F. (2000b). Mental traits as fitness indicators: Expanding evolutionary psychology's adaptationism. In LeCroy, D., & Moller, P. (Eds.), *Evolutionary perspectives on human reproductive behavior* (pp. 62–74). New York: New York Academy of Sciences.

Miller, G. F. (2000c). Sexual selection for indicators of intelligence. *Novartis Foundation Symposium, 233,* 260–270; discussion 270–280.

Miller, G. F. (2001). Aesthetic fitness: How sexual selection shaped artistic virtuosity as a fitness indicator and aesthetic preferences as mate choice criteria. *Bulletin of Psychology and the Arts, 2,* 20–25.

Miller, G. F., & Caruthers, D. (2003). *A great sense of humor is a good genes indicator: Ovulatory cycle effects on the sexual attractiveness of male humor ability.* Paper presented at the Human Behavior and Evolution Society 15th Annual Meeting, Nebraska.

Morreall, J., *personal communication.*

Morreall, J. (1987). *The philosophy of laughter and humor.* Albany: State University of New York Press.

Murdock, M., & Ganim, R. (1993). Creativity and humor: Integration and incongruity. *Journal of Creative Behavior, 27,* 57–70.

Murstein, B., & Brust, R. (1985). Humor and interpersonal attraction. *Journal of Personality Assessment, 49,* 637–640.

Nettle, D., & Clegg, H. (this volume). Personality, mating strategies, and mating intelligence. In G. Geher & G. F. Miller (Eds.), *Mating intelligence: Sex, relationships, and the mind's reproductive system.* Mahwah, NJ: Lawrence Erlbaum Associates.

Owens, H. M., & Hogan, J. D. (1983). Development of humor in children: Roles of incongruity, resolution, and operational thinking. *Psychological Reports, 53,* 477–478.

Petrill, S. A. (2002). The case for general intelligence: A behavioral genetic perspective. In R. J. Sternberg & E. L. Grigorenko (Eds.), *The general factor of intelligence: How general is it?* (pp. 281–298). Mahwah, NJ: Lawrence Erlbaum Associates.

Plucker, J. A., & Renzulli, J. S. (1999). Psychometric approaches to the study of human creativity. In R. J. Sternberg (Ed.), *Handbook of creativity* (pp. 35–62). New York: Cambridge University Press.

Priest, R. F., & Thein, M. T. (2003). Humor appreciation in marriage: Spousal similarity, assortative mating, and disaffection. *Humor: International Journal of Humor Research, 16,* 63–78.

Provine, R. R. (1996). Laughter. *American Scientist, 84,* 38–45.

Provine, R. R. (2000). *Laughter: A Scientific Investigation.* New York: Viking.

Regan, P. C., & Joshi, A. (2003). Ideal partner preferences among adolescents. *Social Behavior and Personality, 31,* 13–20.

Roe, A. (1952). *The making of a scientist.* New York: Dodd, Mead.

Roe, A. (1972). Patterns of productivity of scientists. *Science, 176,* 940–941.

Roeckelein, J. E. (2002). *The psychology of humor: A reference guide and annotated bibliography.* Westport, CT: Greenwood Press.

Roid, G. H., & Barram, R. A. (2004). *Essentials of Stanford-Binet intelligence scales (SB5) assessment.* New York: Wiley.

Rothenberg, A., & Hausman, C. R. (Eds.). (1976). *The creativity question.* Durham, NC: Duke University Press.

Rouff, L. L. (1973). *The relation of personality and cognitive structure to humor appreciation.* Unpublished doctoral dissertation, Bryn Mawr College.

Rouff, L. L. (1975). Creativity and sense of humor. *Psychological Reports, 37,* 1022.

Rucas, S. L., Gurven, M., Kaplan, H., Winking, J., Gangestad, S., & Crespo, M. (2006). Female intrasexual competition and reputational effects on attractiveness among the Tsimane of Bolivia. *Evolution and Human Behavior, 27,* 40–52.

Ruch, W. (1998). *The sense of humor: Explorations of a personality characteristic.* Berlin: Walter de Gruyter.

Runco, M. A. (1989). The creativity of children's art. *Child Study Journal, 19,* 177–190.

Schaier, A. (1975). *Humor appreciation and comprehension in the elderly.* Unpublished doctoral dissertation, Purdue University.

Schoel, D., & Busse, T. (1971). Humor and creative abilities. *Psychological Reports, 29,* 34.

Schwager, I. (1983). *The relationship between operational level and children's comprehension, appreciation, and memory for cognitive humor.* Unpublished doctoral dissertation, City University of New York.

Shammi, P., & Stuss, D. T. (2003). The effects of normal ageing on humor appreciation. *Journal of the International Neuropsychological Society, 9,* 855–863.

Sheehy-Skeffington, A. (1977). The measurement of humor appreciation. In A. J. Chapman & H. C. Foot (Eds.), *It's a funny thing, humor* (pp. 447–449). Oxford: Pergamon Press.

Shultz, T. R. (1972). The role of incongruity and resolution in children's appreciation of cartoon humor. *Journal of Experimental Child Psychology, 13,* 117–125.

Shultz, T. R. (1976). *A cognitive-developmental analysis of humour*. New York: Wiley.

Siegler, J. N. (2004). *Funny you asked: Re-representation and the cognitive processes involved in creating humor*. Unpublished doctoral dissertation, University of Wisconsin.

Simonton, D. K. (1985). Intelligence and personal influence in groups: Four non-linear models. *Psychological Review, 92*, 532–547.

Silk, J. B., Alberts, S. C., & Altmann, J. (2003). Social Bonds of Female Baboons Enhance Infant Survival. *Science, 302*, 1231–1234.

Sligh, A. C., Conners, F. A., & Roskos-Ewoldsen, B. (2005). Relation of creativity to fluid and crystallized intelligence. *Journal of Creative Behavior, 39*, 123–136.

Smith, E. E., & White, H. L. (1965). Wit, creativity, and sarcasm. *Journal of Applied Psychology, 49*, 131–134.

Smith, J. E., Waldorf, V. A., & Trembath, D. L. (1990). "Single white male looking for thin, very attractive . . .," *Sex Roles, 23*, 675–685.

Spearman, C. (1904). "General intelligence," objectively determined and measured. *American Journal of Psychology, 15*, 201–293.

Sroufe, L. A., & Waters, E. (1976). The ontogenesis of smiling and laughter: A perspective on the organization of development in infancy. *Psychological Review, 83*, 173–189.

Sroufe, L. A., & Wunsch, J. P. (1972). The development of laughter in the first year of life. *Child Development, 43*, 1326–1344.

Sternberg, R. J. (1997). *Successful intelligence*. New York: Plume.

Sternberg, R. J. (2000). The theory of successful intelligence. *Gifted Education International, 15*, 4–21.

Sternberg, R. J., & Lubart, T. I. (1991). An investment theory of creativity and its development. *Human Development, 34*, 1–31.

Sternberg, R. J., & O'Hara, L. A. (2000). Intelligence and creativity. In R. J. Sternberg (Ed.), *Handbook of intelligence* (pp. 611–631). New York: Cambridge University Press.

Sternberg, R. J., & The Rainbow Project Collaborators (2006). The Rainbow Project: Enhancing the SAT through assessments of analytical, practical and creative skills. *Intelligence, 34*, 321–350.

Stewart, S., Stinnett, H., & Rosenfeld, L. B. (2000). Sex differences in desired characteristics of short-term and long-term relationship partners. *Journal of Social and Personal Relationships, 17*, 843–853.

Storey, R. (2002). Humor and sexual selection. *Human Nature, 14*, 319–336.

Suls, J. M. (1972). A two-stage model for the appreciation of jokes and cartoons: An information processing analysis. In J. Goldstein & P. McGhee (Eds.), *Psychology of Humor* (pp. 41–45). New York: Academic Press.

Thorson, J. A., & Powell, F. C. (1993a). Development and validation of a multidimensional sense of humor scale. *Journal of Clinical Psychology, 49*, 13–23.

Thorson, J. A., & Powell, F. C. (1993b). Sense of humor and dimensions of personality. *Journal of Clinical Psychology, 49*, 799–809.

Thurstone, L. M. (1938). *Primary mental abilities*. Chicago: University of Chicago Press.

Todosijevic, B., Snezana, L., & Arancic, A. (2003). Mate selection criteria: A trait desirability assessment study of sex differences in Serbia. *Evolutionary Psychology, 1*, 116–126.

Toro-Morn, M., & Sprecher, S. (2003). A cross-cultural comparison of mate preferences among University students; The United States versus the People's Republic of China (PRC). *Journal of Comparative Family Studies, 34*, 151–170.

Torrance, E. P. (1962). *Guiding creative talent.* Englewood Cliffs, NJ: Prentice-Hall.

Torrance, E. P. (1974). *Torrance tests of creative thinking.* Lexington, MA: Personnel Press.

Torrance, E. P. (1975). Creativity research in education: Still alive. In I. A. Taylor & J. W. Getzels (Eds.), *Perspectives in creativity* (pp. 278–296). Chicago: Aldine.

Townsend, J. (1982). *Relationships among humor creative thinking abilities, race, sex, and socioeconomic factors of advantagedness and disadvantagedness of a selected sample of high school students.* Unpublished doctoral dissertation, University of Georgia.

Treadwell, Y. (1970). Humor and creativity. *Psychological Reports, 26,* 55–58.

Wallach, M., & Kogan, N. (1965). *Modes of thinking in young children.* New York: Holt, Rinehart, & Winston.

Weisberg, R. W. (1993). *Creativity: Beyond the myth of genius.* New York: Freeman.

Weissberg, P. S., & Springer, K. J. (1961). Environmental factors in creative function. *Archives of General Psychiatry, 5,* 554–564.

Wierzbicki, M., & Young, R. D. (1978). The relation of intelligence and task difficulty to appreciation of humor. *The Journal of General Psychology, 99,* 25–32.

Ziv, A. (1976). Facilitating effects of humor on creativity. *Journal of Educational Psychology, 68,* 318–322.

Ziv, A. (1988a). Humor's role in married life. *Humor: International Journal of Humor Research, 1,* 223–229.

Ziv, A. (1988b). Using humor to develop creative thinking. *Journal of Children in Contemporary Society, 20,* 99–116.

Ziv, A., & Gadish, O. (1990). Humor and giftedness. *Journal for the Education of the Gifted, 13,* 332–345.

Chapter 11

Emotional Intelligence, Relationship Quality, and Partner Selection

James J. Casey
Yale University

James Garrett
Columbia University

Marc A. Brackett and Susan Rivers
Yale University

For over a century, researchers have been trying to understand whether people favor similarity in sexual partners, and what determines satisfaction in sexual relationships (Galton, 1869; Mowrer, 1935). Emotions are at the very core of human interaction and relationships; thus, it is no surprise that relationship researchers have begun to investigate the role of the emotion-related skills that comprise emotional intelligence (EI; Mayer & Salovey, 1997). Accumulating evidence suggests that EI, which includes the abilities to perceive emotion, use emotion to facilitate thought, understand emotion, and manage emotion, is important for both relationship satisfaction and partner selection (Brackett, Warner, & Bosco, 2005; Brackett et al., 2006; Carstensen, Gottman, & Levenson, 1995; Carton, Kessler, & Pape, 1999; Fitness, 2001a).

We argue that EI allows for easier navigation through the emotionally intense situations that characterize romantic relationships. Indeed, members of couples in which both partners score high on a performance test of EI tend to be happier and more satisfied with their relationships than members of couples in which both partners score low (Brackett et al., 2005, 2006). In examining how each of these emotion abilities is relevant to romantic relationships, we explore the ways in which EI is related closely to Mating Intelligence (MI; Geher, Miller, & Murphy, this volume). MI refers to the abilities to understand a potential mate's emotional expressions, intentions, and preferences and to modulate and express one's own emotions effectively during courtship. For example, the ability to perceive facial and verbal cues of sexual interest in a potential mate are crucial aspects of both EI and MI. Likewise, EI and MI both would promote the ability to exhibit attractive emotions (happiness, confidence, kindness) and to suppress displays of unattractive emotions (irritability, shame, envy) during courtship. Similarly, the ability to assess people's emotional sincerity would be important in distinguishing whether flattery during courtship is honest or empty—whether "I love you" means "I want a life of monogamous bliss and babies with you" or "I want to sexually exploit you tonight."

In this chapter, we use the theory of EI (Mayer & Salovey, 1997) as a guiding framework to examine emotion-related skills in mating. First, we discuss the theory of EI and its measurement. We review Mayer and Salovey's four-part theory of EI and briefly present their performance-based measure of EI, the Mayer-Salovey-Caruso Emotional Intelligence Test (MSCEIT, 2002). Second, we review the link between EI and sexual relationship quality and satisfaction. Here, we examine studies measuring EI in couples and its relation to intimacy and conflict. Third, we present research on the role that EI may play in partner selection, and whether couple similarity in EI is due to initial assortative mating or trait convergence during a relationship. Finally, we offer suggestions for future research on the interface between mating, intelligence, and emotions in short-term and long-term sexual relationships. This final section also considers how future MI research can be informed by existing EI research.

EMOTIONAL INTELLIGENCE

The Ability Model of EI

In Western society, emotions have long been seen as disruptive to rational thought and biasing accurate cognitive assessments of the environment (Damasio, 1994). This belief has roots as early as Ancient Greece (Aeschylus, 458 BCE/1984). In more recent centuries, emotions are believed to be adaptive, serving important roles in motivation, learning, decision-making, and social communication, and conveying information about people's thoughts, intentions, and behaviors (e.g., Darwin, 1872; Ekman, 1973; Keltner & Haidt, 2001). For example, anger, which generally occurs when a goal is obstructed, increases heart rate and produces faster movement. These physiological responses enable one to react quickly and powerfully to the cause of the anger. EI is consistent with this functional view of emotion. From an EI perspective, neither emotion nor rationality is sufficient on its own; rather, emotion and rationality together allow for the greatest effectiveness in day-to-day life (Salovey & Mayer, 1990). In the words of Tomkins (1962), "Reason without affect would be impotent, affect without reason would be blind" (p. 112).

The term "emotional intelligence" was introduced in 1990. Salovey and Mayer's (1990) initial analysis of the literature regarding emotion-related skills led them to define EI as "the ability to monitor one's own and others' feelings and emotions, to discriminate among them, and to use this information to guide one's thinking and actions" (p. 189). Since then, Mayer and Salovey (1997) have refined the term, and now define EI with a four-part model including the abilities to: (1) perceive emotion; (2) use emotion to facilitate cognitive processes and adaptive action; (3) understand emotion and emotional information; and (4) regulate or manage emotions in oneself and others. Unlike general intelligence (e.g., analytical reasoning ability), which is most often associated with "cold" cognitive processes, EI operates through "hot" cognitive-emotional processes that concern things of personal, social, and often evolutionary importance (Abelson, 1963; Metcalfe & Mischel, 1999). What follows is a brief summary of the four emotion-related skills that comprise EI; more detailed presentations can be found elsewhere (e.g., Brackett & Salovey, 2004; Mayer & Salovey, 1997; Mayer, Salovey, & Caruso, 2004).

Perception of emotion is the ability to discern emotions in oneself and others (i.e., facial expressions, tone of voice), as well as in human artifacts such as stories, music, and works of art. People who are aware of their own and others' emotions gain a lot of information about themselves and those around them, as emotions are highly indicative of people's perceptions, judgments, motivations, and intentions. In contrast, those who do not recognize their own and others' emotions don't have access to this useful information. The accurate perception of emotion is the foundation of EI; without this ability, one cannot use the other three EI skills effectively (Salovey, Mayer, & Caruso, 2002).

Use of emotion involves the ability to evoke and generate task-relevant emotions in oneself and in others in order to focus attention, enhance cognitive processes, and improve memory. This skill is based on the knowledge that different emotions promote different cognitive styles that may be better suited to different tasks. Happiness, for example, fosters creativity and more optimistic thinking, while sadness leads to more pessimistic and detail-oriented thinking (Fredrickson, 1998; Mayer, Gaschke, Braverman, & Evans, 1992). Thus, each of these emotions may be useful in certain circumstances. Proficiency in this use-of-emotion domain depends on the ability to generate different emotions in different contexts in order to improve the effectiveness of thought or behavior (Salovey et al., 2002).

Understanding of emotion concerns insight into the causes and consequences of emotions, such as understanding that people typically feel sadness after experiencing some loss and feel happiness after experiencing some gain. This skill also involves understanding how emotions blend together and change over time in given situations. For example, if a source of frustration is not removed, the frustration is likely to turn to anger, and eventually to fury. In addition, understanding emotion includes the size of one's emotional vocabulary. Someone with a large emotional vocabulary, for example, would probably be able to define "elation" and distinguish it from "love." Having a large emotional vocabulary lets one articulate one's emotions clearly.

Management of emotion refers to the ability to adaptively regulate one's own emotions and those of others in the service of achieving behavioral goals. Research shows that some emotion-management techniques work better than others (see Thayer, Newman, & McCain, 1994). Thus, this skill involves both knowing the most effective emotion-management techniques for a given situation, and having the expertise to execute them appropriately (Salovey et al., 2002). Adaptive emotion management does not necessarily entail ignoring or suppressing emotion. Even "negative" emotions such as sadness, anger, and guilt can have positive fitness payoffs in certain contexts. Displays of intense grief, for example, may signal to others that the grieving person needs company to help build new social bonds or strengthen existing ones as he or she has lost someone dear, as well as social support to work through the situation.

Measuring EI as a Set of Abilities

There are two general methods used to measure EI: self-report inventories and performance tests. Self-report inventories ask participants to rate themselves on several dimensions of EI, and often on several unrelated qualities such as optimism and motivation, as well (Bar-On, 1997; Petrides & Furnham, 2003; Schutte et al., 1998). Those that measure abilities other than the four we discuss in this paper—perceiving emotion, using emotion to facilitate thought, understanding emotion, and managing emotion— generally do so because they are operating under a different model of EI. There are several problems with self-report inventories: most importantly, they correlate poorly with performance measures of EI and correlate highly with existing measures of established indices of personality (Brackett & Mayer, 2003; Brackett, Rivers, Shiffman, Lerner, & Salovey, in press; see also Brackett & Geher, 2006).

Performance measures assess EI with tasks that require participants to solve emotion-laden problems. The predominant performance measure of EI is the Mayer Salovey Caruso Emotional Intelligence Test (MSCEIT;

Mayer, Salovey, Caruso, & Sitarenios, 2002). On the MSCEIT, some answers are objectively better than others. Correct answers are determined by reference to normative or expert samples. Consensus scores reflect the proportion of people in the normative sample (over 5,000 people from North America) who endorsed each MSCEIT test item alternative. Expert norms were obtained from a sample of twenty-one members of the International Society for Research on Emotions (ISRE). The reliability, validity, and other psychometric properties of the MSCEIT have been established by multiple studies (Brackett & Salovey, 2004; Mayer et al., 2004; Mayer, Salovey, & Caruso, 2002).

The MSCEIT measures EI using two separate tasks for each of the four domains. *Perception of emotion* is measured by having respondents rate the emotions present in (a) photographs of people's faces and (b) landscapes and abstract pictures. *Use of emotion* is measured by having respondents (a) call up emotions in themselves in order to recognize unusual sensory descriptions of emotions (such as "cool" or "purple") and (b) report how useful various emotions would be while completing certain tasks. *Understanding of emotion* is measured by having respondents (a) recognize how simple emotions combine to form more complex emotions and (b) select the emotion that is most likely to occur when another emotion becomes stronger or weaker. Finally, *management of emotion* is measured by having respondents read emotionally provocative vignettes and then rate the effectiveness of different emotion-regulation strategies in (a) private situations and (b) interpersonal situations (Mayer et al., 2002).

Emotional Intelligence and Relationship Quality and Satisfaction

There is some evidence that emotional competencies are related to satisfaction in sexual relationships. For example, couples who experienced positive emotions together and who were emotionally stable reported more satisfying relationships (Gottman, 1982; Kelly & Conley, 1987; Russell & Wells, 1994). Two initial studies suggest that EI is related to relationship quality and satisfaction (Brackett et al., 2005, 2006). In these studies, relationship quality was operationalized as the extent to which one feels: (1) that one's partner provides social support; (2) that one is "positive, important, and secure" in the relationship; and (3) that the relationship is not conflicted or ambivalent (see Pierce, Sarason, & Sarason, 1991). Relationship satisfaction was measured with a scale adapted from the Satisfaction with Life Scale (Diener, Emmons, Larsen, & Griffin, 1985), and included items such as "The conditions of my relationship are excellent." In both studies, couples in which both partners scored high on the MSCEIT reported greater relationship satisfaction and relationship quality.

How EI contributes to relationship quality and satisfaction is still unknown. The four branches of EI (perceiving, using, understanding, and managing emotions) may simply add up to promote good relationships, or they may contribute in different ways to relationship quality and satisfaction. For example, perceiving emotion may help individuals to accurately interpret the nonverbal emotion cues conveyed by their partners. Using emotion to facilitate thought could allow individuals to generate the emotions their partners feel in order to "put themselves in their shoes." Understanding emotion may help individuals to clearly articulate their feelings and predict their partners' emotions in a given situation. Finally, managing emotions could help individuals resolve conflicts while maintaining the emotional well-being of their partners and themselves. In the next section we review literature supporting the view that each domain of EI contributes to relationship satisfaction. As only two studies have examined the relationship between EI, as measured by the MSCEIT, and relationship satisfaction, we instead look at studies that measure the relationship between several EI-related abilities and relationships and infer the potential influence of EI from them.

Perception of Emotion

Accurate perception of emotion appears to be related to relationship quality and satisfaction. Among college students, self-rated relationship quality was positively correlated with their ability to detect happiness, sadness, anger, and fear in photographs of strangers' faces and in audio recordings of people speaking (Carton et al., 1999). Similarly, among married couples, self-rated ability to identify and communicate one's own emotions was related to relationship satisfaction and security; conversely, partners of individuals who reported difficulty in identifying and communicating their emotions reported lower relationship satisfaction (Cordova, Gee, & Warren, 2005). While promising, these results should be interpreted with care, as Cordova et al. used self-ratings rather than objective measures to assess emotion-identification abilities. People whose skill in a certain domain is below average often greatly overestimate their skill in that domain, perhaps because the knowledge necessary to be above average also is necessary to accurately judge one's ability (Dunning, Johnson, Erlinger, & Kruger, 2003). This is particularly true in the domain of EI (Brackett, Rivers, Shiffman, Lerner, & Salovey, 2006).

The link between perception of emotion and relationship satisfaction may be complex and reciprocal. It may be that accurate emotion perception promotes satisfaction or that satisfaction makes accurate emotion perception more bearable. For example, Kahn (1970) asked satisfied and unsatisfied married couples to interpret the emotional meaning underlying ambiguous statements. Husbands and wives in the study read innocuous sentences (e.g., "Didn't we have chicken a few nights ago?") in one of three ways: as an expression of irritation (i.e., 'The *same* meal again?'), curiosity (i.e., 'I can't remember what we had; can you?'), or elation (i.e., 'I love chicken and am excited we're having it again!'). Before beginning, each participant reported which of the three meanings they were most and least likely to express in their relationship; the researchers used this information to make each participant express an equal number of positively endorsed, negatively endorsed, and neutrally endorsed interpretations. Spouses in satisfied relationships could better select which meaning their partners were trying to convey. Those in unsatisfied relationships could not.

In another study, 21 married couples were videotaped while interacting (Gottman & Porterfield, 1981). The couples then were tested for their ability to send and receive nonverbal emotion-laden messages during the interaction. The better the husbands could "read" their wives' emotions from nonverbal cues, the happier both partners were with their relationship. To determine if the wives in the unsatisfied couples were just poor senders of emotion cues, Gottman and Porterfield (1981) recruited a second group of couples to watch the videotaped interactions and rate the nonverbal cues. The men in this second group were much better at understanding the emotional cues of the videotaped women than their own husbands were. There are at least three possible explanations for this. First, it may be that husbands low in EI dismiss their wives as overly emotional, ignore their nonverbal cues, and thereby create relationship problems (Rubin, 1978). Second, relationship problems may lead husbands to withdraw emotionally from marriages, reducing their emotion-reading ability and motivation (Kahn, 1970). Or third, husbands with generally low mate value may also have low EI, and be unsatisfying to their wives for other reasons.

Use of Emotion to Facilitate Thinking

Little research has been done on the ability to use emotion to facilitate useful styles of thought in sexual relationships. Many psychologists, however, have studied more domain-general influences of emotion on cognition. We can make some educated guesses from these studies about how relationship satisfaction may be influenced by each partner's ability to generate emotions that promote adaptive styles of reasoning, judgment, and decision-making.

Depending on the domain, task, and emotion, emotions can increase or decrease the ability to think clearly, quickly, and adaptively. The induction of positive emotion sometimes makes people better at decision-making, in domains ranging from medical diagnosis to car-purchasing (Isen, 2001). On the other hand, somber, somewhat depressed affect can promote careful analytical thinking and more accurate, risk-averse decision-making (Ambady & Gray, 2002; Clore et al., 2001; Forgas, 1998;

Gasper, 2004; Schwarz & Bless, 1991). For example, Forgas (1998) found that sad-induced participants were less likely to commit the fundamental attribution error, that is, that they more accurately judged how much influence external-situational and internal-dispositional factors had on someone's behavior, while subjects who felt neutral emotions or happiness tended to overemphasize internal-dispositional factors. These differences in decision-making occur in part because happiness promotes "top-down" processing (for example, basing judgments on scripts and stereotypes) and attention to the big picture, while sadness promotes "bottom-up" processing (basing judgments on new, immediately relevant information) and attention to details (see Gasper, 2004). The intensity of the emotions in question affects cognition, as well. Gasper (2004) found that stronger emotions reduced response time in certain emotion-specific tasks: the sadder participants were, the more quickly they responded to small details in a pattern-matching exercise; the happier participants were, the more quickly they responded to broader differences. Such emotion-cognition interactions are especially important in sexual relationships, which often require joint decisions and may result in disagreements. Spiro (1983) found that 88% of 179 couples had recently disagreed over a major household purchase, such as a piece of furniture. EI may reduce the severity and frequency of such disagreements by helping each partner understand how the other person's decision-making style may be influenced by their current general mood or specific emotions. EI also may help couples coordinate adaptive shifts in mood and emotion during a joint decision process, so they can examine their options from different viewpoints, using different cognitive styles.

Emotions also affect the memories that people retrieve when they think of someone or something. Happiness generates more positive memories than negative ones, and anger and sadness generate more negative memories. Forgas and Bower (1987) induced either a positive or a negative emotion in 52 undergraduates by giving them a very high or a very low score on a fake test. The students then read descriptions of four characters, each of whom had twenty positive characteristics and twenty negative characteristics. The students who felt induced positive emotion remembered more positive characteristics than negative characteristics, while the induced negative emotion group remembered more negative characteristics than positive characteristics. This phenomenon of mood-congruent memory helps explains why irritated and angry people in close relationships have such ease remembering their partner's bad traits, errors, and betrayals, and such difficulty remembering their good traits. (The phrase, "Why did I ever marry him?" comes to mind.) In this situation, the emotionally intelligent person who understands mood-congruent memory effects may pause, take a few deep breaths, and think of something to feel happier.

This can help more positive memories to surface, allowing the person to remember all the care and support they have shared over the years.

Understanding of Emotion

The third branch of EI, understanding of emotion, includes one's ability to consciously recognize and verbally articulate one's own emotions so the emotions can be discussed openly. Such open communication of emotions is important in relationships. Couples who are satisfied with their relationships are more likely to communicate in a "contactful" style, that is, to speak directly about their emotions with their partners (Cieslak, 1986). A critical aspect of such open emotional communication is one's emotional vocabulary—having the words and concepts to describe emotions with precision and nuance (like Henry James, rather than Homer Simpson).

Emotional clarity, the ability to recognize, acknowledge, categorize, understand, and reason about one's own emotions, is related closely to understanding emotion. For example, Fitness (2001b) showed that emotional clarity was related to partners' ability to forgive each other after a transgression (such as an infidelity). Ninety married and 70 divorced men and women described an offense in their marriage and whether it was forgiven. Participants also took the Trait Meta Mood Scale, a self-report measure of one's attention to feelings, clarity of feelings, and ability to repair bad moods (Salovey, Mayer, Goldman, Turvey, & Palfai, 1995). High emotional clarity was related to likelihood of forgiveness, no matter how happy each partner had been before the offense, how grave the offense was, or how hurt they had been by the offense. Emotional clarity may have helped wronged individuals understand both the sincerity of their partners' apologies and their own long-term interests in continuing the relationship. Emotional clarity was also related to marital happiness in this study, perhaps due to higher forgiveness rates, higher mutual understanding of emotions, or other factors. As emotional clarity is tested with a self-report measure, however, the results of this study should be interpreted with some caution; self-reports often do not reflect actual behavior (see Brackett et al., in press).

Management of Emotion

There is substantial evidence that the fourth domain of EI, management of emotion, is related to relationship quality. The inhibition of potentially harmful emotional behaviors (insulting, ranting, ignoring) is essential in defusing potentially explosive situations. One study of 123 couples showed that those who responded constructively to a negative situation (e.g., averting a potential argument by talking calmly and listening to the other's point of view) felt greater relationship satisfaction than couples that responded destructively to such situations (Rusbult, Bissonnette, Arriaga, & Cox, 1998). Constructive behaviors are acts that validate one's partner, such as talking out problems, acknowledging and validating a partner's feelings, and offering emotional support. Destructive behaviors, on the other hand, dismiss or reject a partner's concerns, emotions, and interests, perhaps by belittling or by 'stonewalling' (silently refusing to acknowledge a problem). If a partner does not help enough with household chores, for example, a destructive reaction might be to call the partner a "lazy sexist idiot," or to beat him senseless with a mop. This would probably hurt the other's feelings, damage the relationship, and fail to solve the problem. A more effective way of managing one's emotions in the same situation would be to stop, acknowledge one's anger, and inhibit an angry destructive response. This may mean anticipating the harmful effects of verbal or physical abuse and planning to talk through the issue calmly later that evening.

Being open to different emotions, another aspect of emotion management, also appears to be important to relationship satisfaction. Inhibiting destructive behaviors and remaining open to different emotions are not contradictory goals, as destructive actions and not the emotions themselves are to be inhibited. Indeed, anger can motivate a couple to discuss and solve a problem in their relationship; the trick is to channel the emotion to this purpose without letting it lead to petty or mean behavior. If one inhibits the anger itself instead of remaining open to it, the problem will probably be unresolved and the bottled-up anger may build. A self-report study of 238 married couples found that individuals who ignored or stifled emotions felt less relationship satisfaction, while couples who expressed positive and negative emotions constructively reported greater relationship satisfaction (Feeney, 1999). Adaptive emotion management in relationships requires much more than the blanket inhibition of emotions. Indeed, couples in emotionally expressive marriages tend to report greater relationship satisfaction (Huston & Houts, 1998).

Emotionally Intelligent Mating

The old saying, "Birds of a feather flock together" rings true for almost all human traits. Human beings tend to be similar to their long-term partners. Recent research suggests that intra-couple concordance, that is, similarity between partners, may occur with EI just as it does with age, religiosity, attitudes, verbal intelligence, political orientation, personality, and values (Botwin, Buss, & Shackelford 1997; Luo & Klohnen, 2005; Watson et al., 2004). This may be because everyone tries to attract the highest-quality partner they can, such that in a competitive mating market with mutual mate choice, everyone tends to form relationships with partners of similar mate value—an explanation of intra-couple concordance called "assortative mating." Assortative mating may occur at the level of specific trait matching (such that very bright people only marry very bright people), or at the level of overall mate value (such that very bright people sometimes marry very beautiful or very rich but rather stupid people). Alternatively, people in long-term committed relationships may be alike because they "converge," becoming more similar over time as they live together and mutually adapt.

Some evidence suggests that intra-couple concordance occurs for EI, but may be modified by relationship length. For example, Brackett et al. (2006) found a significant correlation in EI ($r = .38$) between partners in 100 long-term couples from an English community sample. Another study found lower partner similarity in EI for couples in earlier stages of their relationships (Brackett et al., 2005). Thus, consistent with previous research on showing that married couples are more likely than dating couples to engage in assortative mating with regard to other individual characteristics (Keller, Thiessen, & Young, 1996), individuals may be more likely to select mates based on EI similarity in long-term rather than in short-term relationships. Selecting a mate using EI may be especially important given that serious emotional crises are more likely to arise in long-term relationships (due to both their greater longevity and their more frequent association with children, mortgages, career trade-offs, in-laws, and other major stressors). As the importance of emotion-related skills becomes recognized, high-EI individuals may come to appreciate the benefits of a partner with similarly high EI and relationships with EI-disparate partners may end earlier than relationships with EI-similar partners.

Assortative Mating

Intra-couple EI concordance may be explained by what evolutionary psychologists refer to as "assortative mating for maximum affordable mate value" (Buss, 1985). In other words, individuals may try to form relationships with the most valuable mate—one that is the most attractive, intelligent and virtuous mate who is willing to be part of the relationship (Buss, 1985; Woolbright, Greene, & Rapp, 1990). Certain traits, especially high conscientiousness, emotional stability, and physical attractiveness, tend to be desired in a mate, regardless of one's own characteristics (Botwin et al., 1997; Figueredo et al., 2004). Although many desire maximally conscientious, stable, and beautiful mates, few people are desirable enough themselves to attract such a super-mate. In a competitive mating market with mutual mate choice, everyone ends up with the best mate they can "afford," given their own mate value.

According to this perspective, EI may be concordant within couples not because low-EI people actually prefer low-EI mates, but because high-EI people are attracted to each other, form relationships, and reject low-EI mates. This leaves those with lower-EI no choice but to mate with each other.

This hypothesis could apply to each of the four EI skills, since they are all desirable in relationships. It would be useful to mate with someone who could perceive emotions well, because such a mate could, for example, detect the early signs of sadness and quickly comfort a sad partner or child. Using emotions to facilitate thought would allow one partner to feel the emotions the other partner was feeling, thereby putting himself in his partner's emotional shoes, which would help him understand his partner's thinking and behavior better. Understanding emotions well would help partners foresee how their emotions might progress in a tense situation, so they could avoid arguments and reach more constructive solutions. Managing emotions well would help individuals inhibit their own aggression or moodiness and help them promote positive emotions and good moods in their partners. Because all of these skills are important to successful romantic relationships, it seems advantageous to select the most emotionally intelligent partners possible. In doing so, people mate with partners whose emotional abilities are similar to their own.

Mate choice for EI seems likely given that EI could so powerfully promote good long-term relationships with efficient social coordination and joint parenting. According to evolutionary psychologists, human females generally value long-term relationships more than males do (Buss, 1998). Because EI is related to relationship satisfaction (Brackett et al., 2005, 2006), and satisfying relationships tend to last longer and are more valuable to women, women may have evolved to prefer high-EI partners even more than men do. High EI partners may also offer survival benefits: satisfying relationships provide social support that can promote physical and psychological well-being, buffer individuals from stress, and inhibit the progression of some diseases (Uchino, 2004; Bolger, Zuckerman, & Kessler, 2000; Leserman et al., 2000; Wills, 1997).

People may prefer mates with high EI because high EI may (unconsciously) reveal good genetic quality that could be passed along to offspring. If EI is correlated at the phenotypic level with important heritable cognitive traits (such as general intelligence), personality traits (such as emotional stability), and mental health, then EI may also be genetically correlated with these traits. That is, it may depend on overlapping sets of genes. If so, then EI can function as an indicator of general genetic quality. For example, many heritable mental disorders (such as schizophrenia, depression, bipolar, autism, anxiety disorders, and psychopathy) tend to reduce all four components of EI (emotion perception, understanding, management, and thought-facilitation). Therefore, high EI could act as a sort of neurogenetic warranty that reliably advertises mental health, and freedom from these disorders.

Convergence

Another possible explanation for intra-couple EI concordance is convergence: perhaps partners become more similar in EI abilities because they spend so much time together and learn from each other (Schooley, 1936). Convergence does not seem to occur for basic personality traits (Caspi, Herbener, & Ozer, 1992), but it does seem to explain why partners become more similar in self-esteem, dependency, attachment style, and the strength of positive and negative emotions felt when talking about good days and bad days, respectively (Anderson, Keltner, & John, 2003; Melamed, 1994; Schafer & Keith, 2002). Convergence also seems to affect more malleable traits such as eating patterns, alcohol consumption, and social activity (Bove, Sobal, & Rauschenbach, 2003; Price & Vendenberg, 1980). At least some EI skills are malleable. For example, the ability to read emotions from facial expressions can be improved with training (Grinspan, Hemphill, & Nowicki, 2003), as can one's verbal understanding of emotion (Pons, Harris, & Doudin, 2002). Perhaps the strongest evidence that EI skills can be learned is the success of Dialectical Behavior Therapy (DBT). A core element of DBT is emotion-regulation-skills training, which includes identification and labeling of emotions, increasing tolerance of negative affect, effective emotional expression, and behavioral management of high-stress conflict (Linehan, Cochran, & Kehrer, 2001). Insofar as long-term sexual relationships constitute a sort of never-ending mutual DBT, partners may learn EI skills from each other, and may converge in overall EI.

Separation of Low-EI Pairs

A final hypothesis regarding intra-couple EI concordance is that higher average EI scores lead to longer-lasting relationships, and that as the low-EI couples separate, a bias toward the long-lasting high-EI couples develops. Couples who can manage their emotions and who evoke more frequent positive interactions may stay together, whereas relationships full of anger, yelling, and fighting may not last. This may explain why there is a marginally stronger intra-couple EI correlation in long-term than in short-term relationships (Brackett et al., 2005, 2006). In other words, a type of "natural selection" may occur, such that high-EI couples are more likely to stay together—a sort of "survival of the fittest relationship."

The importance of average EI plays out in the selection of one's partner. For example, a low-EI person could benefit from seeking a high-EI partner. This would yield higher relationship satisfaction and longevity, and, if convergence applies, an increase in one's own EI. However, high-EI people may be even more aware (being high-EI) that low-EI partners make for less satisfying, shorter relationships. So, high-EI people may avoid low-EI mates even more strongly than low-EI people are attracted to high-EI mates. Recognizing the advantages and disadvantages of a partner's EI level may help in selecting the optimal partner.

Implications for Mating Intelligence

Not surprisingly, EI and MI overlap in some ways. All four branches of EI (i.e., the perception, use, understanding, and management of emotion) are useful for finding a sexual partner and forming a relationship. Because the skills involved in EI and MI are related, even the tests for these abilities are similar. Geher's method of measuring MI is modeled after the performance measure of EI, the MSCEIT (Mayer et al., 2002). For example, males taking the MI test are asked to identify which of three personal ads was written by the man who was rated the best potential husband by the most women. Unlike self-report instruments, performance tests have objectively correct and incorrect answers, thereby allowing for more precise and accurate measurement. Moreover, people tend not to be accurate at reporting their EI (Brackett et al., in press). Self-reports of mating intelligence also are likely to be fairly inaccurate and biased; most individuals rate their own sense of humor and creativity (major components of MI) as above average.

Although there are many conceptual similarities between EI and MI, and between their respective measures, they probably differ in their relation to couple satisfaction and intra-couple concordance. Current research shows that the most satisfied long-term couples, for example, are those in which both partners have high EI, while the least satisfied couples are those in which both partners have low EI; couples with one partner high and one partner low in EI have satisfaction between the extremes (Brackett et al., 2006). The high-EI partner's abilities to empathize and manage emotions can somewhat compensate for the other partner's EI deficit. In terms of MI, however, it may be better for partners to have very similar levels (even both low) than to have a mismatched pair. A relationship between a mating-genius and a mating-moron may be quite unstable: the high-MI partner will lose interest in the low-MI partner, and could easily attract other potential mates. If the partners have about equal MI, though, they will be able to maintain the others' interest to a similar extent. This benefit of MI-similarity and the potential risks of MI-dissimilarity make intra-couple concordance seem even more likely for MI than it is for EI.

CONCLUSION

To date, only two studies have examined EI skills in couples using the MSCEIT. In one study with undergraduates in new relationships, couples with one high-EI partner reported relationship quality as high as couples with two high-EI partners (Brackett et al., 2005). These results suggest a threshold effect for EI, that is, that some minimum level of EI in one partner allows for optimal EI-moderated relationship quality for both partners. However, in a second study with couples in their mid-20s who were in longer-term relationships, EI showed an additive effect, such that couples with two high-EI partners reported higher relationship satisfaction than couples with one high-EI partner, who in turn reported higher satisfaction than couples with two low-EI partners (Brackett et al., 2006). Thus, EI seems to become more valued and more related to satisfaction in longer-term relationships.

More research is needed to examine the link between EI and relationship quality using additional performance measures of EI and couples from more diverse populations. The EI of older couples, non-Caucasian couples, and homosexual couples, for example, has been examined less than that of young, white, heterosexual couples. Studying the EI of these populations with performance measures and other means (e.g., experiments manipulating each partner's emotions) would give a broader view of the role of EI in relationships.

The specific mechanisms of EI-moderated relationship satisfaction need further investigation as well. Research is needed to clarify how different components of EI correlate with relationship satisfaction and duration. Although all four branches of EI seem to influence relationship satisfaction, some may be more important in relationships than others. The differences between EI and MI in relationship satisfaction also need further research. Perhaps MI is important mostly early in courtship (fuelling initial sexual attraction) and EI is important mostly later in long-term relationships (sustaining efficient cooperation, managing conflict, and increasing relationship length and quality). Or perhaps MI and EI both play important and inter-related roles at every stage of human sexual relationships. The link between relationship satisfaction and partner similarity in EI and MI, too, should be investigated further. High EI may matter more than similar EI, while the opposite may be true of MI.

The possible reasons underlying partner similarity in EI also is an understudied domain. Individuals within couples correlate positively on their EI scores, but it remains unclear what proportion of this pattern is due to assortative mating (individual preferences for maximum EI in partners), relationship selection effects (longer-lasting relationships when couples have similar EI scores), or EI convergence effects. Longitudinal studies of couples could better distinguish assortative mating from relationship selection and convergence effects. For example, studies of newlyweds would be informative, since such couples have already chosen their mate and survived initial courtship, but may not have been together long enough for their EI to have converged. Behavior genetics research on the heritabilities of EI and MI and whether they are genetically correlated with general intelligence, personality traits, mental health, and each other would inform research on partner similarity, as well. The malleability and learnability of EI and MI also need further investigation: to what extent are they stable, recalcitrant traits versus teachable skills? If partner similarity and discrepancy affect relationship quality and satisfaction, as seems to be the case, research in these areas will improve our understanding of what makes for a good relationship.

REFERENCES

Aeschylus (458 BCE/1984). *The Eumenides* (R. Lattimore, Trans.). Chicago: University of Chicago Press. (Original work written 458 BCE).

Abelson, R. P. (1963). Computer simulation of "hot cognitions." In S. Tomkins & S. Messick (Eds.), *Computer simulation of personality* (pp. 277–298). New York: Wiley.

Ambady, N. & Gray, H. M. (2002). On being sad and mistaken: Mood effects on the accuracy of thin-slice judgments. *Journal of Personality and Social Psychology, 83,* 947–961.

Anderson, C., Keltner, D., & John, O. P. (2003). Emotional convergence in close relationships. *Journal of Personality and Social Psychology, 84,* 1054–1068.

Bar-On, R. (1997). *Bar-On Emotional Quotient Inventory (EQ-I): A test of emotional intelligence.* Toronto: Multi-Health Systems.

Bolger, N., Zuckerman, A., & Kessler, R. C. (2000). Invisible support and adjustment to stress. *Journal of Personality and Social Psychology, 79,* 953–961.

Botwin, M. D., Buss, D. M., & Shackelford, T. K. (1997). Personality and mate preferences: Five factors in mate selection and marital satisfaction. *Journal of Personality, 65,* 107–136.

Bove, C. F., Sobal, J., & Rauschenbach, B. S. (2003). Food choices among newly married couples: Convergence, conflict, individualism, and projects. *Appetite, 40,* 25–41.

Brackett, M. A., & Geher, G. (2006). Measuring emotional intelligence: Paradigmatic diversity and common ground. In J. Ciarrochi, J. P. Forgas, & J. D. Mayer (Eds.), *Emotional intelligence and everyday life* (pp. 27–50). New York: Psychology Press.

Brackett, M. A., Lord, H., Casey, J., Cox, A., Gaines, S. O., & Salovey, P. (2006). *Emotional intelligence and relationship quality among heterosexual couples.* Unpublished data, Yale University.

Brackett, M. A., & Mayer, J. D. (2003). Convergent, discriminant, and incremental validity of competing measures of emotional intelligence. *Personality and Social Psychology Bulletin, 29,* 1–12.

Brackett, M. A., Rivers, S. E., Shiffman, S., Lerner, N., & Salovey, P. (2006). Relating emotional abilities to social functioning: A comparison of performance and self-report measures of emotional intelligence. *Journal of Personality and Social Psychology, 91,* 780–795.

Brackett, M. A., & Salovey, P. (2004). Measuring emotional intelligence as a mental ability with the Mayer-Salovey-Caruso Emotional Intelligence Test. In. G.

Geher (Ed.), *Measurement of emotional intelligence* (pp. 179–194). Hauppauge, NY: Nova Science Publishers.

Brackett, M. A., Warner, R. M., & Bosco, J. S. (2005). Emotional intelligence and relationship quality among couples. *Personal Relationships, 12,* 197–212.

Buss, D. M. (1985). Human mate selection. *American Scientist, 73,* 47–51.

Buss, D. M. (1998). Sexual strategies theory: Historical origins and current status. *Journal of Sex Research, 35,* 19–31.

Carstensen, L. L., Gottman, J. M., & Levenson, R. W. (1995). Emotional behavior in long-term marriage. *Psychology and Aging, 10,* 140–149.

Carton, J. S., Kessler, E. A., & Pape, C. L. (1999). Nonverbal decoding skills and relationship well-being in adults. *Journal of Nonverbal Behavior, 23,* 91–100.

Caspi, A., Herbener, E. S., & Ozer, D. J. (1992). Shared experiences and the similarity of personalities: A longitudinal study of married couples. *Journal of Personality and Social Psychology, 62,* 281–291.

Cieslak, K. (1986). Mutual communication and marital success. *Polish Psychological Bulletin, 17*(3–4), 177–182.

Clore, G. L., Wyer, R. S., Dienes, B., Gasper, K., Gohm, C., & Isbell, L. (2001). Affective feelings as feedback: Some cognitive consequences. In L. L. Martin & G. L. Clore (Eds.), *Theories and mood and cognition: A user's guide* (pp. 27–62). Mahwah, NJ: Lawrence Erlbaum Associates.

Cordova, J. V., Gee, C. B., & Warren, L. Z. (2005). Emotional skillfulness in marriage: Intimacy as a mediator of the relationship between emotional skillfulness and marital satisfaction. *Journal of Social and Clinical Psychology, 24,* 218–235.

Damasio, A. R. (1994). *Descartes' error: Emotion, reason, and the human brain.* New York: Putnam.

Darwin, C. (1872). General principles of expression—concluded. In *The expression of emotion in man and animals* (Chap. 3). Retrieved October 13, 2005 from http://www.netlibrary.com/Reader/

Diener, E., Emmons, R. A., Larsen, R. J., & Griffin, S. (1985). The satisfaction with life scale. *Journal of Personality Assessment, 49,* 71–75.

Dunning, D., Johnson, K., Ehrlinger, J., & Kruger, J. (2003). Why people fail to recognize their own incompetence. *Current Directions in Psychological Science, 12,* 83–87.

Ekman, P. (1973). Universal facial expressions in emotion. *Studia Psychologica, 15,* 140–147.

Feeney, J. A. (1999). Adult attachment, emotional control, and marital satisfaction. *Personal Relationships, 6,* 169–185.

Figueredo, A. J., Sefcek, J. A., Vasquez, G., Brumbach, B. H., King, J. E., & Jacobs, W. J. (2005). Evolutionary personality psychology. In D. M. Buss (Ed.), *The handbook of evolutionary psychology* (pp. 851–877). Hoboken, NJ: John Wiley and Sons, Inc.

Fitness, J. (2001a). Emotional intelligence and intimate relationships. In J. Ciarrochi, J. Forgas, & J. Mayer (Eds.), *Emotional intelligence in everyday life: A scientific inquiry* (pp. 98–112). New York: Psychology Press.

Fitness, J. (2001b). Betrayal, rejection, revenge, and forgiveness: An interpersonal script approach. In M. Leary (Ed.), *Interpersonal rejection.* New York: Oxford University Press.

Forgas, J. P. (1998). On being happy and mistaken: Mood effects on the fundamental attribution error. *Journal of Personality and Social Psychology, 75,* 318–331.

Forgas, J. P., & Bower, G. H. (1987). Mood effects on personal perception judgments. *Journal of Personality and Social Psychology, 53,* 53–60.

Fredrickson, B. L. (1998). What good are positive emotions? *Review of General Psychology, 2,* 300–319.

Galton, F. (1869). *Hereditary genius.* New York: Macmillan Co.

Gasper, K. (2004). Do you see what I see? Affect and visual information processing. *Cognition and Emotion, 18,* 405–421.

Gottman, J. (1982). Emotional responsiveness in marital conversations. *Journal of Communication, 32,* 108–120.

Gottman, J. M., & Porterfield, A. L. (1981). Communicative competence in the nonverbal behavior of married couples. *Journal of Marriage and the Family, 43(4),* 817–824.

Grinspan, D., Hemphill, A., & Nowicki, S. (2003). Improving the ability of elementary school-age children to identify emotion in facial expression. *Journal of Genetic Psychology, 164,* 88–100.

Huston, T. L., & Houts, R. M. (1998). The psychological infrastructure of courtship and marriage: The role of personality and compatibility in romantic relationships. In T. N. Bradbury (Ed.), *The developmental course of marital dysfunction* (pp. 114–151). Cambridge: Cambridge University Press.

Isen, A. M. (2001). An influence of positive affect on decision making in complex situations: Theoretical issues with practical implications. *Journal of Consumer Psychology, 11,* 75–85.

Kahn, M. (1970). Nonverbal communication and marital satisfaction. *Family Process, 9,* 449–456.

Keller, M., Thiessen, D., & Young, R. K. (1996). Mate assortment in dating and married couples. *Personality and Individual Differences, 21,* 217–221.

Kelly, E. L., & Conley, J. J. (1987). Personality and compatibility: A prospective analysis of marital stability and marital satisfaction. *Journal of Personality and Social Psychology, 52,* 27–40.

Keltner, D., & Haidt, J. (2001). Social functions of emotions. In T. J. Mayne & G. A. Bonanno (Eds.), *Emotions: Current issues and future directions.* (pp. 192–213). New York: Guilford Press.

Leserman, J., Petitto, J. M., Gu, H., Gaynes, B. N., Barroso, J., Golden, R. N., et al. (2000). Impact of stressful life events, depression, social support, coping, and cortisol on progression to AIDS. *American Journal of Psychiatry, 157,* 1221–1228.

Linehan, M. M., Cochran, B. N., & Kehrer, C. A. (2001). Dialectical behavior therapy for borderline personality disorder. In D. H. Barlow (Ed.), *Clinical handbook of psychological disorders: A step-by-step treatment manual* (3rd ed., pp. 470–522). New York: Guilford Press.

Luo, S., & Klohnen, E. C. (2005). Assortative mating and marital quality in newlyweds: A couple-centered approach. *Journal of Personality and Social Psychology, 88,* 304–326.

Luteijn, F. (1994). Personality and the quality of an intimate relationship. *European Journal of Psychological Assessment, 10,* 220–223.

Manuck, S. B., Flory, J. D., Robert, E. F., Dent, K. M., Mann, J. J., & Muldoon, M. F. (1999). Aggression and anger-related traits associated with a polymorphism of the tryptophan hydroxylase gene. *Biological Psychiatry, 45,* 603–614.

Mayer, J. D., Gaschke, Y. N., Braverman, D. L., & Evans, T. W. (1992). Mood-congruent judgment is a general effect. *Journal of Personality and Social Psychology, 63,* 119–132.

Mayer, J. D., & Salovey, P. (1997). What is emotional intelligence? In P. Salovey & D. Sluyter (Eds.), *Emotional development and emotional intelligence: Educational implications* (pp. 3–31). New York: Basic Books

Mayer, J. D., & Salovey, P. (2002). The positive psychology of emotional intelligence. In C. R. Snyder & S. J. Lopez (Eds.), *Handbook of positive psychology* (pp. 159–171). New York: Oxford University Press.

Mayer, J. D., Salovey, P., & Caruso, D. (2002). *MSCEIT technical manual.* Toronto: Multi Health Systems.

Mayer, J. D., Salovey, P., & Caruso, D. (2004). Emotional intelligence: Theory, findings, and implications. *Psychological Inquiry, 15,* 197–215.

Mayer, J. D., Salovey, P., Caruso, D., & Sitarenios, G. (2003). Measuring emotional intelligence with the MSCEIT V2.0. *Emotion, 3,* 97–105.

Melamed, T. (1994). Partner's similarity over time: The moderating effect of relationship status. *Personality and Individual Differences, 16,* 641–644.

Metcalfe, J., & Mischel, W. (1999). A hot/cool-system analysis of delay of gratification: Dynamics of will power. *Psychological Review, 106,* 3–19.

Mowrer, H. R. (1935). *Personality adjustment and domestic discord.* New York: American Book Co.

Petrides, K.V., & Furnham, A. (2003). Trait emotional intelligence: Behavioural validation in two studies of emotion recognition and reactivity to mood induction. *European Journal of Personality, 17,* 39–57.

Pierce, G. R., Sarason, I. G., & Sarason, B. R. (1991). General and relationship-based perceptions of social support: Are two constructs better than one? *Journal of Personality and Social Psychology, 61,* 1028–1039.

Pons, F., Harris, P. L., & Doudin, P. (2002). Teaching emotional understanding. *European Journal of Psychology of Education, 17,* 293–304.

Price, R. A., & Vandenberg, S. G. (1980). Spouse similarity in American and Swedish couples. *Behavior Genetics, 10,* 59–71.

Rubin, L. B. (1978). *Worlds of pain.* New York: Basic Books.

Rusbult, C. E., Bissonnette, V. L., Arriaga, X. B., & Cox, C. L. (1998). Accommodation processes during the early years of marriage. In T. N. Bradbury (Ed.), *The developmental course of marital dysfunction* (pp. 74–113). Cambridge: Cambridge University Press.

Rushton, J. P. (1989). Genetic similarity, human altruism, and group selection. *Behavioral and Brain Sciences, 12,* 503–559.

Russell, R. J. H., & Wells, P. A. (1994). Predictors of happiness in married couples. *Personality and Individual Differences, 17,* 313–321.

Salovey, P., & Mayer, J. D. (1990). Emotional intelligence. *Imagination, Cognition, and Personality, 9,* 185–211.

Salovey, P., Mayer, J. D., & Caruso, D. (2002). The positive psychology of emotional intelligence. In C. R. Snyder & S. J. Lopez (Eds.), *The handbook of positive psychology* (pp. 159–171). New York: Oxford University Press.

Salovey, P., Mayer, J. D., Goldman, S. L., Turvey, C., & Palfai, T. P. (1995). Emotional attention, clarity, and repair: Exploring emotional intelligence using the trait meta-mood scale. In J. W. Pennebaker (Ed.), *Emotion, disclosure, and health* (pp. 125–154). Washington, DC: American Psychological Association.

Schafer, R. B., & Keith, P. M. (2002). Self-esteem agreement in the marital relationship. *Journal of Social Psychology, 132,* 5–9.

Schooley, M. (1936). Personality resemblances among married couples. *Journal of Abnormal and Social Psychology, 36,* 340–347.

Schutte, N. S., Malouff, J. M., Hall, L. E., Haggerty, D. J., Cooper, J. T., Golden, C. J., & Dornheim, L. (1998). Development and validation of a measure of emotional intelligence. *Personality and Individual Differences, 25,* 167–177.

Schwarz, N., & Bless, H. (1991). Happy and mindless, but sad and smart? The impact of affective states on analytic reasoning. In J. P. Forgas (Ed.), *Emotion and social judgment* (pp. 55–72). New York: Pergamon.

Solomon, R. L. (1980). The opponent process theory of acquired motivation: The cost of pleasure and the benefits of pain. *American Psychologist, 35,* 691–712.

Spiro, R. L. (1983). Persuasion in family decision-making. *Journal of Consumer Research, 9,* 393–402.

Spuhler, J. N. (1968). Assortative mating with respect to physical characteristics. *Eugenics Quarterly, 15,* 128–140.

Thayer, R. E., Newman, J. R., & McCain, T. M. (1994). Self-regulating of mood: Strategies for changing a bad mood, raising energy, and reducing tension. *Journal of Personality and Social Psychology, 67,* 910–925.

Tomkins, S. S. (1962). *Affect, imagery, and consciousness: Vol. I. The positive affects.* New York: Springer.

Uchino, B. N. (2004). *Social support and physical health.* New Haven, CT: Yale University Press.

Watson, D., Klohnen, E. C., Casillas, A., Simms, E. N., Haig, J., & Berry, D. S. (2004). Match makers and deal breakers: Analyses of assortative mating in newlywed couples. *Journal of Personality, 72,* 1029–1068.

Wills, T. A. (1997). Social support and health. In A. Baum, S. Newman, J. Weinman, R. West, & C. McManus (Eds.) *Cambridge handbook of psychology, health and medicine* (pp. 168–171). Cambridge: Cambridge University Press.

Woolbright, L. L., Greene, E. J., & Rapp, G. C. (1990). Density-dependent mate searching strategies of male woodfrogs. *Animal Behavior, 40.* 135–142.

Chapter 12

Mating Intelligence and General Intelligence as Independent Constructs

Satoshi Kanazawa

London School of Economics and Political Science

Mating intelligence is the latest in a series of new variants of intelligence, including constructs such as "emotional intelligence" (Gardner, 1995; Salovey & Mayer, 1990), "social intelligence" (Marlowe, 1986), and Gardner's (1983) notion of "multiple intelligences," which includes "linguistic intelligence," "logical-mathematical intelligence," "bodily-kinesthetic intelligence," "spatial intelligence," "musical intelligence," "interpersonal intelligence," and "intrapersonal intelligence." Intelligence, in its original definition (Spearman, 1904), referred to purely cognitive abilities of logic and reasoning; I personally would have preferred to keep it that way. However, the tide appears to have turned against my purist position, as implied by the nature and the contents of the current volume. So, in line with the other contributors in this volume and its main theme, I use the phrase "mating intelligence" to mean the constellation of abilities and skills of humans to seek, select, and retain mates, and provide joint parental investment into the offspring with their mates.

Although the definition of mating intelligence adopted by Geher, Miller, and Murphy (this volume) includes the word "cognitive," I seek to demonstrate in this chapter that mating success has very little to do with cognitive abilities. I will, instead, argue that mating intelligence defined as such is entirely independent of general intelligence, a purely cognitive ability to think and reason. I will rely on a recent evolutionary psychological theory of the nature and evolution of general intelligence (Kanazawa, 2004a) that views it as largely independent of other evolved psychological mechanisms. I will also specify the likely conditions under which general intelligence and mating intelligence intersect.

THE EVOLUTION OF GENERAL INTELLIGENCE FROM AN EVOLUTIONARY PSYCHOLOGICAL PERSPECTIVE[1]

The concept of general intelligence poses a theoretical problem for evolutionary psychology. One of the basic tenets of evolutionary psychology is that the human mind consists of many evolved psychological mechanisms or adaptations (Tooby & Cosmides, 1992). There is a distinct psychological mechanism or mechanisms for each adaptive problem of survival or reproduction. Psychological mechanisms are designed to solve specific adaptive problems in a specific domains of life; they are domain-specific.

Therein lies the problem for evolutionary psychology posed by the concept and ubiquitous importance of general intelligence (the g factor).[2] No intelligence researchers deny the existence and importance of general intelligence, and, as its name implies, its importance is not limited to one or a few specific areas of life. General intelligence is important for individual performance in virtually every sphere of modern life (Gordon, 1997; Gottfredson, 1997; Herrnstein & Murray, 1994). If the human mind consists of domain-specific evolved psychological mechanisms, as evolutionary psychologists contend, how then does evolutionary psychology explain the existence and importance of general intelligence?

The co-founders of modern evolutionary psychology, Leda Cosmides and John Tooby, have already attempted to explain the evolution of general intelligence from an evolutionary psychological perspective. They first make a distinction between *dedicated intelligence* and *improvisational intelligence*. "Dedicated intelligence refers to the ability of a computational system to solve a predefined, target set of problems. Improvisational intelli-

---

[1]The following sections draw on Kanazawa (2004a). Copyright © 2004 by the American Psychological Association. Adapted with permission.

[2]In my 2004 *Psychological Review* article (Kanazawa, 2004a), I use the phrases "general intelligence" and "the g factor" synonymously and interchangeably. Technically, however, the g factor is a latent variable which emerges in a factor analysis of various cognitive ("IQ") tests. What I mean by "general intelligence," however, is the ability to think and reason, deductively or inductively, think abstractly, use analogies, synthesize information, and apply knowledge to new domains (see below). They are therefore not exact synonyms. My theory is about general intelligence as an evolved psychological mechanism, and not at all about the g as the latent variable in a factor analysis. I thank Geoffrey F. Miller for pointing this out to me.

gence refers to the ability of a computational system to improvise solutions to novel problems" (Cosmides & Tooby, 2002, p. 146). In essence, what they call dedicated intelligence here corresponds to what they and other evolutionary psychologists refer to as a domain-specific evolved psychological mechanism, and what they call improvisational intelligence here is what psychometricians call general intelligence.

Although their definitions are very clear, their explanation for how general intelligence evolved is not quite as explicit. They argue that general intelligence evolved as an emergent property of a collection of psychological mechanisms. "Cognitive specializations, each narrow in their domain of application, *can be bundled together in a way* that widens the range of inputs or domains that can be successfully handled" (Cosmides & Tooby, 2002, pp. 177–178, emphasis added). Exactly how the domain-specific psychological mechanisms can be bundled together to produce domain-general intelligence is not clear, however. "Large amounts of knowledge are embodied in intelligent, domain-specific inference systems, but these systems were designed to be triggered by stimuli in the world. This knowledge could be unlocked and used for many purposes, however, *if a way could be found* to activate these systems in the absence of the triggering stimuli—that is, if the inference system could be activated by imagining a stimulus situation that is not actually occurring: a counterfactual" (Cosmides & Tooby, 2002, p. 182; emphasis added). They do not explicate how this *way* could be found; so far they have provided only a partial, preliminary description of how this might work (Cosmides & Tooby, 2000).

Figure 12–1a presents the schematic representation of my interpretation of Cosmides and Tooby's view of general intelligence. The inner circle represents the human brain. In accordance with the prevailing assumption of evolutionary psychology, the brain consists of domain-specific evolved psychological mechanisms, such as the cheater detection mechanism (Cosmides, 1989), the language acquisition device (LAD) (Pinker, 1994), the Theory of Mind module (ToMM) (Baron-Cohen, Leslie, & Frith, 1985), and discriminative parental solicitude (Daly & Wilson, 1987). There are a large number of other evolved psychological mechanisms that evolutionary psychologists have identified, and there are probably even more that they have not yet catalogued. Mating intelligence may be conceived of as one such evolved psychological mechanism (or a small collection of them). Each psychological mechanism can solve adaptive problems in its own domain but nowhere else; that is why Cosmides and Tooby (2002) call it *dedicated* intelligence. The cheater detection mechanism can only help actors decide who has violated social contracts; it does not help them acquire their native language, decide which of their children should receive a relatively higher proportion of parental resources, or indeed select and retain their mates.

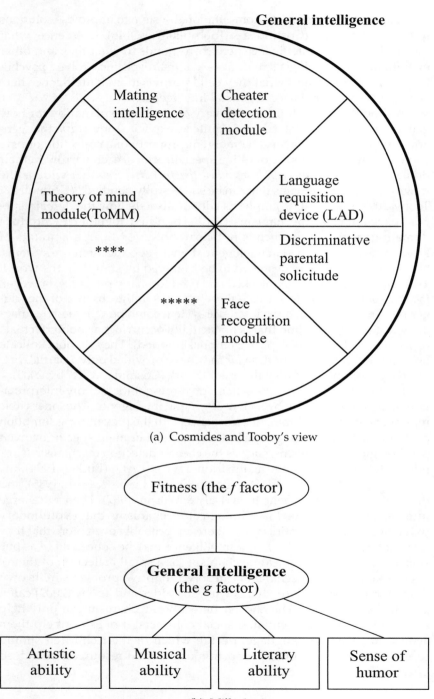

(a) Cosmides and Tooby's view

(b) Miller's view

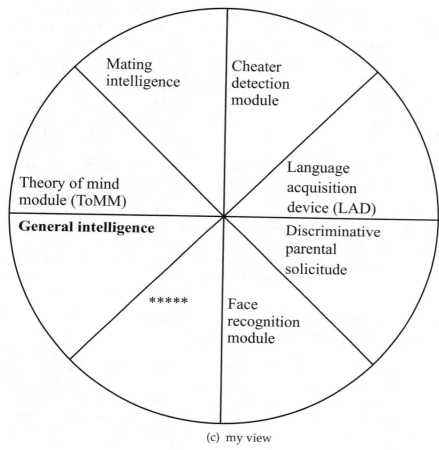

(c) my view

Figure 12–1.   Three alternative explanations for the evolution of general intelligence.

According to Cosmides and Tooby (2002), domain-general general intelligence emerges as a function of the bundle of domain-specific evolved psychological mechanisms. I designate this bundle as an outer circle encompassing all of the evolved psychological mechanisms. Its domain of application covers the sum total of all the domains of the psychological mechanisms which form its foundation. It is therefore domain-general.

Apart from the absence in their writing of exactly *how* general intelligence evolves, one of the most unsatisfying aspects of Cosmides and Tooby's (2000, 2002) explanation of the evolution of general intelligence is that it is not an adaptation selected for by evolutionary forces. It is instead an exaptation, which first appears as an emergent property of all the adaptations (psychological mechanisms) and then acquires its function later

(Buss, Haselton, Shackelford, Bleske, & Wakefield, 1998). An exaptation is "a feature, now useful to an organism, that did not arise as an adaptation for its present role, but was subsequently co-opted for its current function" (Gould, 1991, p. 43). It seems unlikely that something as important, crucial, and empirically robust as general intelligence was not selected by evolutionary forces or *designed* for its current functions.

Another, potentially more damaging problem with Cosmides and Tooby's theory is the fact that the domain of general intelligence appears limited to the sum total of all evolutionarily familiar domains (see Figure 12–1a), for which dedicated psychological mechanisms exist, *but nothing else*. If general intelligence receives its input from the underlying evolved psychological mechanisms, then it should be applicable to all domains which existed during evolutionary history, but not to entirely evolutionarily novel domains. Cosmides and Tooby's theory therefore does not explain why more intelligent individuals are better than less intelligent individuals at calculus, auto mechanics, string theory, Raven's Progressive Matrices, piloting an airplane, or any other task for which there are not plausible counterparts during evolutionary history.[3]

GENERAL INTELLIGENCE AS AN INDICATOR OF UNDERLYING FITNESS

Geoffrey F. Miller (2000a, 2000b, this volume) presents an alternative view of general intelligence. He first posits the existence of a general fitness factor, which he calls the f factor, and which reflects an individual's genetic quality and developmental health. Since such genetic quality is highly heritable and offspring of individuals with higher fitness will also be fit,

---

[3]In support of Cosmides and Tooby's view, Geoffrey F. Miller asks why it is that we tend to need evolutionarily familiar metaphors and analogies whenever we think about evolutionarily novel problems. For example, we need a 3-D imagery for the 11-D M-theory in string theory, or we need a Theory of Mind analogy in the artificial intelligence research in robotics. If general intelligence was designed to deal with evolutionarily novel problems, as I argue (see below), why can intelligent string theorists and AI researchers not use their general intelligence to solve their theoretical problems without invoking evolutionarily familiar metaphors and analogies?

My response is that: 1) only extremely intelligent individuals engage in string theory or AI research; and 2) the brains of even the most intelligent individuals are still constrained by their evolutionary limitations of the sorts outlined in Kanazawa (2004b). Extremely intelligent individuals can engage in string theory or AI research with the aid of evolutionarily familiar metaphors and analogies; less intelligent individual cannot do so even with such metaphors and analogies.

individuals seek out mates with higher fitness. Miller then argues that general intelligence (the g factor) is a reliable indicator of general fitness (the f factor); in factor analysis, the f factor will be superordinate to the g factor, just as the g factor is superordinate to specific cognitive tasks. Because general intelligence highly correlates with (or loads heavily on) general fitness, individuals should also seek out mates who have high general intelligence. General intelligence therefore evolves via sexual selection in the same way that general fitness does.

Miller then posits that many activities that are unique to humans, such as art, music, story-telling, or humor, are signals of general intelligence; those who possess high general intelligence will on average also possess high levels of artistic, musical, narrative, and comic abilities. Individuals will then seek out mates who possess such abilities, because they are first-order indicators of general intelligence, and second-order indicators of general fitness. Miller's theory can simultaneously explain both men's tendency toward cultural displays (showing off their abilities and prowess in various areas) (Miller, 1998, 1999) and women's tendency to be attracted to and mate with men who possess such abilities (Haselton & Miller, 2006). By choosing to mate with men who show greater artistic, musical, narrative, and comic abilities, women are in essence mating with men with greater general intelligence and thus greater general fitness and genetic quality.

Figure 12–1b presents a schematic view of Miller's theory of general intelligence. While Miller's view is very different from Cosmides and Tooby's (presented in Figure 12–1a), they share one feature in common: a significant functional overlap and positive correlation between general intelligence and mating intelligence. In fact, Miller would predict a much higher correlation between general intelligence and mating success than Cosmides and Tooby would. For Cosmides and Tooby, mating intelligence is but one of many evolved psychological mechanisms which form the foundations of general intelligence. For Miller, the primary function of general intelligence is to signal the underlying level of genetic quality and to attract mates. As Geher et al. (Chapter 1, this volume) put it, for Miller, "all human intelligence is mating intelligence."

GENERAL INTELLIGENCE AS A DOMAIN-SPECIFIC ADAPTATION

I completely share Cosmides and Tooby's (2002) view on the evolution of dedicated intelligence. There were recurring adaptive problems in the environment of evolutionary adaptedness (EEA), the solution of which enhanced individuals' inclusive fitness. Evolution by natural and sexual selection has therefore equipped humans (and other organisms) with domain-specific psychological mechanisms to solve these problems in given domains of life. This is why we have an innate ability to be sensitive to potential cheaters in social exchange (Cosmides, 1989; Yamagishi, Tanida, Mashima, Shimoma, & Kanazawa, 2003); why all developmentally normal human children can acquire any natural human language with relative ease (Pinker, 1994) and develop Theory of Mind which allows them to understand the beliefs and desires of others (Baron-Cohen et al., 1985); and why parents can unconsciously favor some offspring whose reproductive prospects are greater, at the cost of others whose reproductive prospects are gloomier (Daly & Wilson, 1987). I agree with Cosmides and Tooby's multimodular view of the human mind (sometimes known as the "massive modularity hypothesis") and the existence of every single module they posit, *except for one.*

The Pleistocene Epoch (about 1.6 million to 10,000 years ago), during which humans evolved, was a period of extraordinary constancy and continuity in the lifestyle of our ancestors. They were hunter-gatherers on the African savanna all their lives. Their grandparents were hunter-gatherers on the African savanna all their lives. Their grandchildren were hunter-gatherers on the African savanna all their lives. It is against this backdrop of extreme stability that all of our adaptations evolved, because, for instance, those who had a taste for sweet and fatty food during the Pleistocene lived longer and reproduced more successfully, by acquiring more calories (Barash, 1982, pp. 144–147), or those who preferred certain landscape for their habitat lived longer and reproduced more successfully, by avoiding potential predators in hiding (Orians & Heerwagen, 1992). The evolution of psychological mechanisms assumes a relatively stable environment in which only some fitness-relevant parameters change; solutions cannot evolve in the form of psychological mechanisms if the problems keep changing in many ways at once. The fact that we have so many evolved psychological mechanisms is testimony to extraordinary stability of the EEA.

Because adaptive problems in the EEA remained more or less the same generation after generation, our evolved psychological mechanisms were sufficient to solve them. In a sense, our ancestors did not have to *think* in the EEA. They did not have to think, for instance, what was good to eat. All they had to do was eat and keep eating what tasted good to them (sweet and fatty foods that contained high calories), and they lived long and remained healthy. People who preferred the wrong kind of food died off before leaving too many offspring, and we did not inherit our psychological mechanisms from them. Or, more central to the theme of this volume, our ancestors did not have to think who would make great mates. All they had to do was mate with those they found attractive (in other words, rely on their innate mating intelligence), and whoever they chose made sufficiently good mates and provided sufficient parental investment into their joint offspring. People who preferred the wrong kind of mates did not leave many surviving offspring, and we did not inherit our psychological mechanisms from them. All the adaptive problems were anticipated by our evolved psychological mechanisms, which then provided their solutions. In a sense, evolution did all the thinking for us, anticipated all the adaptive problems, and equipped us with the right solutions in the form of evolved psychological mechanisms, the execution of which would have solved the problems in the context of the EEA, so that we did not have to think for ourselves.

Even in the extreme stability and constancy of the EEA, however, there were a few novel, nonrecurrent[4] problems on occasion. By definition, we do not have prepared solutions in the form of evolved psychological mechanisms for novel problems. As a result, many of our potential ancestors undoubtedly perished because they could not solve these novel problems. Solutions to such problems require improvisational intelligence—the ability to think and reason, deductively or inductively, think abstractly, use analogies, synthesize information, and apply knowledge to new domains. In other words, the solution of novel problems requires *general intelligence*. An individual whose brain consists entirely of dedicated intelligences (domain-specific psychological adaptations) cannot solve novel problems, and, in the worst-case scenario, they may die because of their inability to solve such problems. It therefore follows that, if novel problems arose frequently enough in the EEA, then any genetic mutation that equips its carrier to think and reason better about the evolutionary novelty would be favored by selection, and could evolve as a domain-specific adaptation for solving novel problems. Novelty would become its domain of application; general intelligence evolves as a domain-specific adaptation for the domain of evolutionary novelty. From this perspective, "general intelligence" is nothing but another domain-specific evolved psychological mechanism (see Figure 12–1c).

Examples of novel adaptive problems during evolutionary history may have included:

1. The lightning has struck the tree near the camp and set it on fire. The fire is now spreading to the dry underbrush. What should I do? How

---

[4]If the problem was novel but recurring from then on (which thus ceases to be novel), then there would eventually be an evolved psychological mechanism specifically to deal with them. General intelligence would not be necessary to solve such problems.

could I stop the spread of the fire? How could I and my family escape it? (Since lightning never strikes the same place twice, this is guaranteed to be a nonrecurrent problem.)

2. We are in the middle of the severest drought in a hundred years. Nuts and berries at our normal places of gathering, which are usually plentiful, are not growing at all, and animals are scarce as well. We are running out of food because none of our normal sources of food are working. What else can we eat? What else is safe to eat? How else can we procure food?

3. A flash flood has caused the river to swell to several times its normal width, and I am trapped on one side of it while my entire band is on the other side. It is imperative that I rejoin them soon. How could I cross the rapid river? Should I walk across it? Or should I construct some sort of buoyant vehicle to use to get across it? If so, what kind of material should I use? Wood? Stones?

I hasten to add that the extreme constancy and continuity of the EEA necessitates that these novel problems did not occur very frequently, and dedicated intelligence was sufficient to solve a vast majority of problems in the EEA. In clear contrast to modern life, what psychometricians today call general intelligence was not important in solving most problems in the EEA. But it was sufficiently important to have evolved.

From my perspective, general intelligence has become so universally important in modern life (Gordon, 1997; Gottfredson, 1997; Herrnstein & Murray, 1994) precisely because characteristics of modern life for most humans are almost entirely evolutionarily novel. Virtually every physical object around us today in our *physical* environment (books, computers, telephones, television, automobiles, houses, etc.) is evolutionarily novel, even though much of our *social* environment (other people and our relationships with them) has remained the same. Our evolved psychological mechanisms, adapted to the EEA, should not be able to interact effectively with many of the physical objects around us today (Kanazawa, 2002, 2004b, 2006a), and our evolved psychological mechanisms are therefore useless in solving most of our daily problems, except when they deal with other people and our relationships with them. We need general intelligence to program TiVo but not to make friends and influence colleagues. Even in the social area, however, evolutionarily novel inventions, such as effective contraception, socially imposed monogamy, and criminal laws regarding the age of consent, foil the operations of our evolved psychological mechanisms. General intelligence has become so pervasively important in our lives only because we have created and live in an evolutionarily novel world.

THE INDEPENDENCE OF MATING INTELLIGENCE AND GENERAL INTELLIGENCE

The three theories—Cosmides and Tooby's (2000, 2002) theory of the evolution of general intelligence as an emergent exaptation, Miller's (2000a, 200b, Chapter 15, this volume) theory of general intelligence as an indicator of genetic quality, and my theory of general intelligence as a domain-specific adaptation for evolutionarily novel problems—lead to different empirical predictions, especially concerning the relationship between mating intelligence and general intelligence (as is discussed at length in Chapter 1 this volume). Because Cosmides and Tooby argue that general intelligence emerges from, and is built on the foundation of, the "bundle" of evolved psychological mechanisms, their theory implies a positive correlation across individuals between general intelligence and the efficiency of any evolved psychological mechanism at its foundation, including mating intelligence (Figure 12–1a). "Improvisational intelligence does not appear to be an autonomous ability, disconnected from the rest of the architecture and not relying on any other computational or information resources. On the contrary. Not only does it depend on a base of dedicated intelligences but it also must be supplied with a dense accumulation of information relevant to the situation being faced" (Cosmides & Tooby, 2002, p. 179). In other words, Cosmides and Tooby's theory would predict that individuals with high IQs (as a measure of general intelligence) would also have greater ability to detect cheaters in exchange situations, acquire native language, infer others' intentions correctly, and, most importantly for our current purposes, select better mates and retain them. Because general intelligence in this theory depends on so many domain-specific adaptations, we might expect relatively modest positive correlations between general intelligence and any particular domain-specific ability.

The positive correlation between general intelligence and mating success is predicted to be much greater in Miller's (2000a, 2000b, Chapter 15, this volume) theory. General intelligence in this view is a reliable indicator of underlying genetic quality (the *f* factor), and individuals prefer to mate with others who exhibit signs of higher general intelligence, such as great artistic, musical, narrative, and comic talent. The primary function of general intelligence in Miller's view is to signal the individual's genetic quality and thus mate value. *Both Cosmides and Tooby's theory and Miller's theory would therefore predict that individuals with greater general intelligence would also have greater mating intelligence.*

In sharp contrast, my theory would predict complete independence of general intelligence from all the other evolved psychological mechanisms in the brain. I would not expect those who are good at recognizing faces to be better at allocating parental resources among their children. Similarly, I would not expect individuals with high general intelligence to be necessarily better at either, or any other, evolutionarily familiar task. *My theory would predict that individuals with greater general intelligence would not have greater mating intelligence, except in areas where the execution of mating intelligence requires evolutionarily novel stimuli.*

General Intelligence, Mating, and Parenting

Mating and parenting are eminently evolutionarily familiar domains of life. Despite the cumbersome interventions of modern inventions (condoms, sperm banks, *Playboy*), we still mate, pretty much the same way as our ancestors did a million years ago. Sexual courtship today still involves initial visual attraction, verbal and physical interaction, mutual mate choice based on social status, physical attractiveness, and moral character as clues to good genes and parental abilities, foreplay, copulation, positive or negative reaction to the mate choice by friends and family, etc. And we still have children as they did then. Children today, as then, are raised by pair-bonded couples, single mothers and her kin, biological mothers and stepfathers, etc. If general intelligence and mating intelligence are truly independent, as my theory predicts, then general intelligence should have no relationship to individuals' likelihood of mating and parenting, that is, the quality and quantity of mates and offspring. In contrast, Cosmides and Tooby, and Miller, would predict that general intelligence and the likelihood of successful mating and parenting should be related.

Herrnstein and Murray (1994) compile a comprehensive list of life outcomes that are affected by general intelligence. From schooling to employment to crime and welfare dependency to civility and citizenship, not only do more intelligent individuals achieve more desirable outcomes, but general intelligence almost always has a linear positive relationship with the desirability of the outcome.

Marriage and parenting are among the very few exceptions to this pattern in their comprehensive review of American life. In fact, "very bright" individuals (with IQs above 125, at or above the 95th percentile of the IQ distribution) are the *least* likely to marry of all the cognitive classes. Only 67 percent of these "very bright" white Americans marry before the age of 30, whereas between 72 percent and 81 percent of those in other cognitive classes marry before 30 (Herrnstein & Murray, 1994, pp. 168–172). The mean age of first marriage among the very bright whites is 25.4, whereas that among the "very dull" (with IQs below 75) is 21.3 and that among the "dull" (with IQs between 75 and 90) is 21.5.

General intelligence therefore does not seem to confer advantages to marriage, one significant adaptive problem which mating intelligence should be designed to solve. Two caveats are in order, however. First, being unmarried is not necessarily the same as being unmated, especially in a liberal western nation like the United States. Second, these results, and those which follow, do not necessarily mean that highly intelligent individuals are less efficacious in achieving their goals, because very bright people may not *want* to get married or have children. This, however, is precisely my point. If very bright individuals are efficacious in achieving their personal goals of *not* getting married and *not* having children, then it means that their mating intelligence is not functioning efficiently. To say that some (very bright) individuals do not want to get married or have children is analogous to saying that some (very dull) individuals do not want to receive higher education or hold a lucrative, prestigious occupation. Some individuals do not want to solve evolutionarily novel problems of doing well in school and making a lot of money in a capitalist economy because their general intelligence does not function very efficiently. Some individuals do not want to solve evolutionarily familiar problems of finding mates and having children because their mating intelligence does not function very efficiently. Herrnstein and Murray's analysis shows that highly intelligent individuals are less efficacious in pursuing the Darwinian end of reproductive success, for which human beings (as well as other living organisms) *and their mating intelligence* are designed.

The pattern is similar in parenting. General intelligence does not confer advantages in giving birth to healthy babies. Five percent of white babies born to "very bright" mothers suffer from low birth weight, compared to 1.6 percent of those born to merely "bright" mothers (with IQs between 110 and 125) and 3.2 of those born to "normal" mothers (with IQs between 90 and 110). Only those born to "dull" mothers (7.2 percent) and "very dull" mothers (5.7 percent) fare worse (Herrnstein & Murray, 1994, pp. 213–218).

The lack of IQ advantage continues later in the childhood. "Very bright" mothers are more likely to have children who are behind in motor and social development or have the worst behavioral problems. Ten percent of children born to "very bright" white mothers are in the bottom decile of the motor and social development index, compared to five percent of those born to "bright" mothers and six percent of those born to "normal" mothers. Similarly, 11 percent of children born to "very bright" mothers find themselves in the bottom decile of the behavioral problems index, compared to six percent of those born to "bright" mothers and 10 percent of those born to "normal" mothers (Herrnstein & Murray, 1994, pp. 225–229).

Now since "very bright" white women marry later, and thus give birth to their babies at an older age (compared with other mothers), perhaps some of these physical and behavioral problems of their children may be attributable to their older maternal age at birth, or higher mutation load in male sperm due to higher paternal age (Crow, 2003). Once again, this is precisely my point. From a purely biological perspective, marrying, and giving birth to their children, at an older age, is a distinct indication of low mating intelligence, just like leaving school at a younger age or holding low-wage dead-end jobs is a distinct indication of low general intelligence. The lack of advantage of general intelligence in the area of marriage and parenting is stark in the context of Herrnstein and Murray's comprehensive survey of its undeniably clear advantage everywhere else in modern American life. This exception is so puzzling that it has led Herrnstein and Murray to muse "Can Mothers Be Too Smart for Their Own Good?" (1994, p. 216).

This is not to argue, however, that intelligent people are not better mates or parents in general today. Intelligent individuals *do* make better mates and parents in some ways in the current (evolutionarily novel) environment. For one thing, more intelligent individuals universally attain more desirable outcomes in all evolutionarily novel domains, such as education, economy, criminal justice, even health and longevity in contemporary society (Kanazawa, 2006b). One need go no farther than to recall the news story from several years ago of an illiterate teenage mother whose baby died of dehydration because the mother could not read the instructions for how to make the baby formula and instead fed the dry powder to the baby as is, without first dissolving it in water. Note, however, that this tragedy happened precisely because it involved written instructions for making a baby formula—an evolutionarily novel stimulus about an evolutionarily novel product. My contention is that even this mother may have done fine raising her children in the EEA, where childrearing most likely did not require general intelligence. In the EEA, everyone was illiterate.

In a recent paper, Lubinski et al. (2006) present summary findings from the longitudinal study of "Talent Search" participants, who are selected before the age of 13 on the basis of exceptionally high SAT scores in the top .01 percent for their age (SAT-Q $\geq$ 700 or SAT-V $\geq$ 630). They therefore have IQs above 155. Lubinski et al.'s (2006) sample contains 286 men and 94 women twenty years after they have been identified by the Talent Search. Their mean age in 2003–2004 is 33.6.

Consistent with their exceptionally high general intelligence, these Talent Search participants have attained extraordinary achievements in such evolutionarily novel arenas as education and employment. More than half of them (51.7 percent of men and 54.3 percent of women) have earned a doctorate (Ph.D., M.D. or J.D.), compared to the population baseline in the United States of 1 percent. An additional 5.3 percent have earned an MBA, all but one of them in the top 10 U.S. programs. Nearly half (45.8 percent) of them are university professors, engineers, or scientists; an additional 13.6 percent are in medicine and law. More than a fifth (21.7 percent) of those in tenure-track positions in the top 50 U.S.

universities are already full professors in their early thirties. More than a third of the men and about a fifth of the women earn more than $100,000 a year. 17.8 percent of men and 4.3 percent of women have earned patents, compared to the adult population baseline of 1 percent.

Yet in stark contrast, and mirroring the findings from the National Longitudinal Survey of Youth, these men and women of exceptional intelligence do not attain great reproductive success. 64.9 percent of men and 69.0 percent of women remain childless at age 33, compared to the population average of 26.4 percent for the age group 30–34. The majority of parents only have one child. As a result, the mean number of children is .61 for men and .44 for women, compared to the population average of 1.59 for women in ages 30–34. Despite their extraordinarily high general intelligence, these men and women seem to have far below average mating intelligence.

My analysis of the General Social Surveys (GSS) replicates Herrnstein and Murray's analysis of the National Longitudinal Survey of Youth. The GSS measures verbal intelligence of its respondents by asking them to select a synonym for a word out of five candidates, in a manner similar to the questions in the Verbal section of the Graduate Record Examination (GRE). Each respondent answers 10 of these questions, and their total score thus varies from 0 to 10. I use the total number of correct responses as a crude measure of verbal intelligence.

Not surprisingly, this measure of verbal intelligence positively correlates with two measures of achievement in evolutionarily novel domains: formal schooling and earnings. Table 12.1. shows that, controlling for age, the measure of verbal intelligence correlates .53 with formal schooling and .19 with earnings (both $ps < .05$). These statistics confirm the importance of general intelligence in everyday life in the current environment (Gordon, 1997; Gottfredson 1997; Herrnstein & Murray, 1994).

In sharp contrast, intelligence does not seem to confer much advantage in the evolutionarily familiar domains of mating and parenting. The total number of children the GSS respondent has ever had is negatively correlated with verbal intelligence ($r = -.12, p < .05$). The more intelligent they are, the fewer children they have. Since the number of children is a significant (albeit not the sole) determinant of inclusive fitness (because the quality of children matters as much as their quantity), this finding suggests that intelligent people have lower inclusive fitness than less intelligent people, suggesting a negative correlation between verbal intelligence (as a measure of general intelligence) and mating intelligence. This is the essence of what Vining (1986) calls the "central theoretical problem of human sociobiology," which I have attempted to solve elsewhere (Kanazawa, 2003, 2004a, 2005).

Consistent with Herrnstein and Murray (1994), my analysis of the GSS data shows that intelligent people are no more likely to get married. The

TABLE 12.1.

The Effect of General Intelligence in Evolutionarily Novel and Familiar
Domains (General Social Survey 1972–2000)

	r	p	n
Evolutionarily novel domains			
Formal schooling	.5272	<.001	20,188
Income	.1924	<.001	12,977
Evolutionarily familiar domains			
Total number of children	−.1207	<.001	20,177
Ever married	.0040	ns	20,188
Currently married	.0554	<.001	20,188
controlling for income	−.0073	ns	12,964
Lifetime number of sex partners	.0283	<.05	8,324
Men	.0263	ns	3,533
Women	.0894	<.001	4,788
Number of sex partners in last 5 years	−.0378	<.01	6,930
Men	−.0261	ns	2,974
Women	−.0398	<.05	3,953
Number of sex partners in last 12 months	−.0371	<.001	9,554
Men	−.0597	<.001	4,095
Women	−.0052	ns	5,456

Note. r's are partial correlation coefficients, controlling for age.

partial correlation between verbal intelligence and whether they have ever
been married, controlling for age, is nil ($r = .0040$, *ns*). The partial correlation between verbal intelligence and whether they are *currently* married
is small but statistically significantly positive ($r = .06$, $p < .05$). However,
even this significant correlation is spurious, produced by the fact that more
intelligent people make more money, and people who make more money
are less likely to divorce. Once I control for income, the same partial correlation becomes nil as well ($r = −.01$, *ns*).

General intelligence does not seem to confer advantages in finding
mates, either. The GSS measures the lifetime number of heterosexual partners that the respondent has had with the following question: "Now thinking about the time since your 18th birthday (including the past 12 months)
how many male [female] partners have you had sex with?" While the correlation between verbal intelligence and the lifetime number of sex partners since 18 is significantly positive, the magnitude of correlation is very
small ($r = .03$, $p < .05$). Further, the correlation between verbal intelligence
and the number of sex partners either in the last five years or in the last
12 months is significantly negative ($r = −.04$ for both). The more intelligent
an American is, the fewer mates he or she has *recently* had, once again,

strongly suggesting a negative correlation between general intelligence and mating intelligence, although, just as in the case of children, one has to take into consideration the *quality* as well as the *quantity* of sexual partners.

Now, of course, due to the sexual asymmetry in the reproductive biology (Trivers, 1972), "the number of sex partners" has a vastly different meaning for men and women. While men can linearly increase their reproductive success with the number of women that they have sexual access to, there is no clear reproductive advantage to women for having sex with a large number of men. In this context, it is very interesting to note that it is intelligent *women*, not intelligent men, who acquire a large number of sex partners in their lifetimes. The partial correlation between verbal intelligence and the lifetime number of sex partners, controlling for age, is strongly positive among women ($r = .09$, $p < .05$, $n = 4,788$), but nonsignificant among men ($r = .03$, ns, $n = 3,533$). It appears that intelligent men cannot use their greater intelligence to acquire more mates and increase their reproductive success, and intelligent women use their intelligence to acquire more mates when doing so does not increase their reproductive success.[5] The former finding seems to contradict Miller's (2000a, 2000b, Chapter 15, this volume) contention that general intelligence is a fitness indicator among males, at least in the context of the evolutionarily novel environment from which the GSS data come.

All the empirical data presented above, from my analysis of the GSS data, Lubinski et al.'s (2006) analysis of the Talent Search participants, and Herrnstein and Murray's (1994) analysis of the National Longitudinal Survey of Youth, support my prediction that general intelligence is an advantage only in evolutionarily novel domains of life (such as formal schooling and earnings), and not in evolutionarily familiar domains of mating, marriage, and parenting. The data suggest the independence of (or even negative correlation between) general intelligence and mating intelligence, and are inconsistent with both Cosmides and Tooby's (2002) contention that general intelligence emerges from and thus highly correlates with domain-specific psychological mechanisms, and with Miller's (2000a, 2000b, Chapter 15, this volume) contention that general intelligence is a reliable indicator of genetic quality and thus mating success.

However, I hasten to add that all the empirical data come from one society only (the United States). They are therefore not ideal in testing propositions about universal human nature, such as those derived from all

---

[5]Technically, I do not know if intelligent women are really *using* their intelligence to attract mates. More intelligent women are physically more attractive on average than less intelligent women (Kanazawa & Kovar, 2004), so that may be the reason why they have a larger number of mates. The only thing I can say for sure is that more intelligent women report having had more sexual partners in their lifetimes than less intelligent women.

three competing evolutionary psychological theories under consideration here. Evolutionary psychological theories should ideally be tested with large cross-cultural data (Buss, 1989; Schmitt, 2003).

WHEN MATING INTELLIGENCE ENCOUNTERS EVOLUTIONARY NOVELTY: AN EXCEPTION WHICH PROVES THE RULE

My theory of the evolution of general intelligence predicts the independence of mating intelligence from general intelligence, and, as discussed above, the available empirical data support this prediction. However, this prediction assumes that mating and parenting are evolutionarily familiar, that we find and keep our mates and reproduce children pretty much as our ancestors did in the EEA. This is true for most aspects of mating and parenting. However, my theory would also predict that, in the few areas where mating intelligence interacts with evolutionarily novel stimuli, then it would *not* be independent of general intelligence, and more intelligent individuals *will* perform better as mates and parents than less intelligent individuals.

One significant evolutionarily novel factor in mating and parenting in the current environment is contraception. In the EEA, our ancestors probably mated all the time, with pregnancy and lactation (lactational amenorrhea) serving as the only natural means of contraception. As a result, our ancestors invariably produced a larger number of offspring than we do today, but many of them died in infancy due to infectious diseases, malnutrition, and other natural causes (including predation by humans and other animals). The average number of offspring surviving to sexual maturity in the EEA might not have been much larger than it is today. So while mating and parenting are evolutionarily familiar, voluntary control of fertility through contraception (such as condoms or the pill) is evolutionarily novel. Thus my theory of the evolution of general intelligence would predict that *more intelligent individuals are better able to control their fertility voluntarily through artificial means of contraception than less intelligent individuals.*

Several empirical implications follow from this prediction. First, general intelligence is positively correlated with social class (Kanazawa & Kovar, 2004, pp. 232–234). In the GSS data, the means of the verbal intelligence scores monotonically increase with self-reported social class: 4.68 for lower class ($n = 1,021$), 5.59 for working class ($n = 9,206$), 6.47 for middle class ($n = 9,268$), and 6.69 for upper class ($n = 643$). There is moderate correlation between social class and verbal intelligence ($F_{(3,20134)} = 426.59$, $p < .05$, $\eta = .2445$, $r = .2396$). If the negative correlation between social class and fertility ("the central theoretical problem of human sociobiology"; see Table 12.1.) results from lower-class individuals' difficulty (due to their lower general intelligence) in using contraception effectively (Kanazawa, 2004a), then social class should *not* be related to how many children individuals *desire* or *plan* to have, only with how many children they *actually end up having*. While lower-class individuals may in fact have a larger number of children, they should not necessarily want a larger number of children than individuals in middle or upper classes.

Second, if less intelligent individuals have a larger number of children as a result of their difficulty in using contraception, then their fertility should be a more direct function of sexual activity than that of more intelligent individuals. For instance, the number of sex partners (as a measure of sexual activity) should be more strongly related to the number of children among less intelligent individuals than among more intelligent individuals. General intelligence and the number of sex partners should have a significant interaction effect on the number of children.

Of course, due to the sexual asymmetry in reproductive biology, it is easier for men to increase their reproductive success with the number of sexual partners than it is for women. If a man has 100 sex partners in a year, he can potentially produce 100 children (or more, if there are multiple births). In sharp contrast, if a woman has 100 sex partners in a year, she can still only produce one child at the end of the year (barring a multiple birth). So the interaction effect between general intelligence and the number of sex partners on the number of children should be stronger among men than among women.

The analysis of the GSS data confirm all of these empirical implications. In two surveys (in 1988 and 1994), the GSS asks its respondents the following question: "All in all, what do you think is the ideal number of children for a family to have?" I use the respondents' response to this question as an admittedly somewhat crude measure of their desired number of children. Equation (1) in Table 12.2 confirms the existence of "the central theoretical problem of human sociobiology." Controlling for age, race, sex, years of formal schooling, whether the respondent has ever been married, and religion, social class has a strongly negative relationship with the number of children. Net of the effects of these demographic variables, lower-class individuals have a statistically larger number of children than the middle- and upper-class individuals.

In sharp contrast, Equation (2) shows that, controlling for the same demographic variables, social class has absolutely no relationship with the number of *desired* children. The data presented in Table 12.2 therefore suggests that lower-class individuals have more children than middle- and upper-class individuals *even though they do not desire or plan to*. Combined with the negative correlation between social class and verbal intelligence, this is consistent with the prediction that less intelligent individuals have

TABLE 12.2.
Effects of Social Class on the Number of Children and the
Desired Number of Children

	(1) Number of Children	(2) Number of Desired Children
Social class	−.0809****	−.0050
	(.0132)	(.0303)
Age	.0197****	.0052****
	(.0005)	(.0012)
Race (1 = black)	.5555****	.2923****
	(.0240)	(.0584)
Sex (1 = male)	−.1096****	.0041
	(.0162)	(.0367)
Education	−.0787****	−.0321****
	(.0028)	(.0066)
Ever married (1 = yes)	1.6274****	−.0933
	(.0223)	(.0493)
Religion		
Catholic	.2806****	.3249****
	(.0311)	(.0718)
Protestant	.1521****	.1472*
	(.0288)	(.0672)
Jewish	−.0092	−.0049
	(.0616)	(.1580)
Other	−.0254	.3516**
	(.0615)	(.1159)
Constant	.7661	2.5988
	(.0562)	(.1284)
R^2	.2673	.0457
Number of cases	38,687	2,618

Note. Main entries are unstandardized regression coefficients.
Numbers in parentheses are standard errors.

* $p < .05$ ** $p < .01$ *** $p < .001$ **** $p < .0001$

TABLE 12.3.
INTERACTIVE EFFECTS OF INTELLIGENCE AND LIFETIME NUMBER
OF SEX PARTNERS ON THE NUMBER OF CHILDREN
Number of Children

	(1) *All Respondents*	*(2)* *Men*	*(3)* *Women*
Lifetime number of sex partners	.0043 (.0023)	.0054* (.0023)	.0163 (.0119)
Verbal intelligence	−.0241** (.0091)	−.0152 (.0130)	−.0175 (.0135)
Interaction	−.0009** (.0003)	−.0011** (.0003)	−.0030 (.0017)
Age	.0244**** (.0010)	.0286**** (.0015)	.0214**** (.0014)
Race (1 = black)	.6139**** (.0771)	.4825**** (.0495)	.6425**** (.0652)
Sex (1 = male)	−.1566**** (.0321)	—	—
Education	−.0611**** (.0063)	−.0342**** (.0086)	−.0894**** (.0090)
Ever married (1 = yes)	1.4147**** (.0403)	1.4919**** (.0549)	1.3181**** (.0582)
Religion			
Catholic	.2102*** (.0545)	.2414*** (.0704)	.1528 (.0830)
Protestant	.0348 (.0499)	.0662 (.0634)	−.0218 (.0769)
Jewish	−.0720 (.1135)	.0253 (.1520)	−.1768 (.1651)
Other	−.0314 (.1043)	−.0045 (.1357)	−.1033 (.1562)
Constant	.5310 (.1017)	−.2979 (.1337)	1.1320 (.1535)
R^2	.3031	.3655	.2543
Number of cases	8,252	3,500	4,752

Note. Main entries are unstandardized regression coefficients.
Numbers in parentheses are standard errors.

* $p < .05$ ** $p < .01$ *** $p < .001$ **** $p < .0001$

greater difficulty in using evolutionarily novel contraception to control their fertility voluntarily.

Equation (1) in Table 12.3 shows that, controlling for the same demographic variables as in Table 12.2, verbal intelligence has a significantly negative main effect on the number of children. More importantly, the interaction effect between the lifetime number of sex partners and verbal intelligence is significantly *negative*. Consistent with the prediction above, the positive effect of the lifetime number of sex partners on the number of children becomes significantly weaker as the respondent's verbal intelligence increases. In other words, the number of children is a stronger function of the lifetime number of sex partners among the less intelligent than among the more intelligent.

Figure 12–2 presents the partial effect of the lifetime number of sex partners on the number of children separately for less and more intelligent individuals. The residual plot in Figure 12–2(a) presents the partial relationship among the respondents whose verbal intelligence is below the median of 6. The scatterplot shows that the relationship is nonsignificantly positive (standardized beta = .0261, *ns*). Figure 12–2(b) shows that the

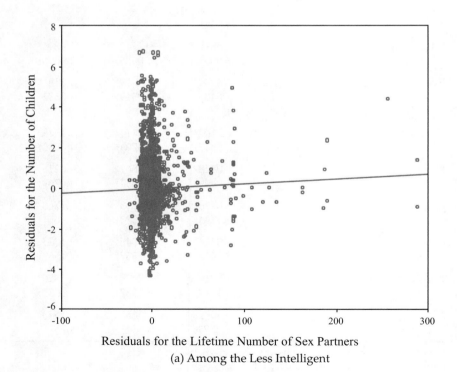

Residuals for the Lifetime Number of Sex Partners

(a) Among the Less Intelligent

Figure 12–2.   Partial Effect of the Lifetime Number of Sex Partners on the Number of Children Among Respondents.

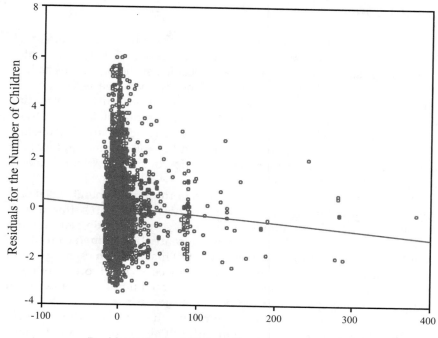

Residuals for the Lifetime Number of Sex Partner
(b) Among the More Intelligent

Figure 12–2.   (*Continued*)

same partial relationship among the respondents whose verbal intelligence is above the median is significantly *negative* (standardized beta = −.0396, $p < .05$). Among the more intelligent, the more sex partners they have in their lifetime, the *fewer* children they have. This pattern is weak but consistent with the prediction that general intelligence allows individuals to deal with evolutionarily novel stimuli of modern contraception more efficiently.

Finally, Table 12.3, Columns (2) and (3), re-estimate the model presented in Column (1) separately for men and women. Column (2) shows that the interaction effect between the lifetime number of sex partners and verbal intelligence among men remains significantly negative as in the sample of all respondents. In contrast, the same interaction effect is not significant among women. The sexually dimorphic pattern in the significance of the interaction effect between the lifetime number of sex partners and verbal intelligence on the number of children is consistent with the prediction derived from my theory of the evolution of general intelligence as a domain-specific adaptation for solving evolutionarily novel problems.

CONCLUSION

A new evolutionary psychological theory of the evolution of general intelligence (Kanazawa, 2004a) proposes that what is now called general intelligence originally evolved as a domain-specific psychological mechanism to solve evolutionarily novel problems. The theory suggests that general intelligence is independent of all other adaptations, including mating intelligence. From the perspective of this theory, more intelligent individuals should be no better at solving problems for which mating intelligence is designed, such as problems of finding and keeping mates and making parental investment, *except* when the solution of such problems requires evolutionarily novel stimuli.

Consistent with this prediction, the data from the General Social Surveys (GSS) show that more intelligent individuals are no better at such evolutionarily familiar mating tasks as finding mates, getting and staying married, and having children. In fact, more intelligent men cannot use their intelligence to attract a larger number of mates, when doing so could significantly increase their reproductive success, and more intelligent women do use their intelligence to attract a large number of mates, when doing so cannot increase their reproductive success.

In a perfect example of an exception which proves the rule, the GSS data also show that more intelligent individuals are better at voluntary control of fertility because it requires evolutionarily novel means of contraception in the current environment. Lower-class individuals, who have lower average intelligence than middle- or upper-class individuals, have more children even though they do not desire to, and the number of children is a more direct function of sexual activities (measured by the lifetime number of sex partners) among the less intelligent than among the more intelligent. In fact, among the more intelligent, the partial relationship between the lifetime number of sex partners and the number of children is significantly negative; the more sex partners they have, the fewer children they have. The analysis of the GSS data supports the theory of the evolution of general intelligence as a domain-specific adaptation for evolutionary novelty. The analyses presented here suggest that mating success is hardly related to general intelligence. These findings may call into question the utility of the concept of mating intelligence.

ACKNOWLEDGMENTS

I thank the volume editors and Rosalind Arden for their constructive comments and suggestions on earlier drafts.

REFERENCES

Barash, D. P. (1982). *Sociobiology and behavior* (2nd ed.). New York: Elsevier.

Baron-Cohen, S., Leslie, A., & Frith, U. (1985). Does the autistic child have a 'theory of mind'? *Cognition, 21,* 37–46.

Buss, D. M. (1989). Sex differences in human mate preferences: Evolutionary hypotheses tested in 37 cultures. *Behavioral and Brain Sciences, 12,* 1–49.

Buss, D. M., Haselton, M. G., Shackelford, T. K., Bleske, A. L., & Wakefield, J. C. (1998). Adaptations, exaptations, and spandrels. *American Psychologist, 53,* 533–548.

Cosmides, L. (1989). The logic of social exchange: Has natural selection shaped how humans reason? Studies with the Wason selection task. *Cognition, 31,* 187–276.

Cosmides, L., & Tooby, J. (2000). Consider the source: The evolution of adaptations for decoupling and metarepresentation. In Sperber, D. (ed.), *Metarepresentations: A multidisciplinary perspective* (pp. 53–115). Oxford: Oxford University Press.

Cosmides, L., & Tooby, J. (2002). Unraveling the enigma of human intelligence: Evolutionary psychology and the multimodular mind. In R. J. Sternberg & J. C. Kaufman (eds.), *The Evolution of intelligence* (pp. 145–198). Mahwah, NJ: Lawrence Erlbaum Associates.

Crow, J. F. (2003). There's something curious about paternal-age effects. *Science, 301,* 606–607.

Daly, M., & Wilson, M. (1987). The Darwinian psychology of discriminative parental solicitude. *Nebraska Symposium on Motivation, 35,* 91–144.

Gardner, H. (1983). *Frames of mind: The theory of multiple intelligences.* New York: Basic Books.

Goleman, D. (1995). *Emotional intelligence.* New York: Bantam.

Gordon, R. A. (1997). Everyday life as an intelligence test: Effects of intelligence and intelligence contexts. *Intelligence, 24,* 203–320.

Gottfredson, L. S. (1997). Why *g* matters: The complexity of everyday life. *Intelligence, 24,* 79–132.

Gould. S. J. (1991). Exaptation: A crucial tool for evolutionary psychology. *Journal of Social Issues, 46,* 43–65.

Haselton, M. G., & Miller, G. F. (2006). Women's fertility across the cycle increases the short-term attractiveness of creative intelligence compared to wealth. *Human Nature, 17,* 50–73.

Herrnstein, R. J., & Murray, C. (1994). *The bell curve: Intelligence and class structure in American life.* New York: Free Press.

Kanazawa, S. (2002). Bowling with our imaginary friends. *Evolution and Human Behavior, 23,* 167–171.

Kanazawa, S. (2003). Can evolutionary psychology explain reproductive behavior in the contemporary United States? *Sociological Quarterly, 44,* 291–302.

Kanazawa, S. (2004a). General intelligence as a domain-specific adaptation. *Psychological Review, 111,* 512–523.

Kanazawa, S. (2004b). The Savanna Principle. *Managerial and Decision Economics, 25*, 41–54.

Kanazawa, S. (2005). An empirical test of a possible solution to "the central theoretical problem of human sociobiology." *Journal of Cultural and Evolutionary Psychology, 3*, 249–260.

Kanazawa, S. (2006a). Why the less intelligent may enjoy television more than the more intelligent. *Journal of Cultural and Evolutionary Psychology, 4*, Forthcoming.

Kanazawa, S. (2006b). Mind the gap . . . in intelligence: Reexamining the relationship between inequality and health. *British Journal of Health Psychology, 11*, 623–642.

Kanazawa, S., & Kovar, J. L. (2004). Why beautiful people are more intelligent. *Intelligence, 32*, 227–243.

Lubinski, D., Benbow, C. P., Webb, R. M., & Bleske-Rechek, A. (2006). Tracking exceptional human capital over two decades. *Psychological Science, 17*, 194–199.

Marlowe, Jr., H. A. (1986). Social intelligence: Evidence for multidimensionality and construct independence. *Journal of Educational Psychology, 78*, 52–58.

Miller, G. F. (1998). How mate choice shaped human nature: A review of sexual selection and human evolution. In C. Crawford & D. L. Krebs (Eds.). *Handbook of Evolutionary Psychology: Ideas, Issues, and Applications* (pp. 87–129). Mahwah, NJ: Lawrence Erlbaum Associates.

Miller, G. F. (1999). Sexual selection for cultural displays. In R. Dunbar, C. Knight, & C. Power (Eds.). *The evolution of culture* (pp. 71–91). New Brunswick, NJ: Rutgers University Press.

Miller, G. F. (2000a). *The mating mind: How sexual choice shaped the evolution of human nature.* New York: Doubleday.

Miller, G. F. (2000b). Sexual selection for indicators of intelligence. In G. Bock, J. Goode, & K. Webb (eds.), *The nature of intelligence* (pp. 260–275). New York: Wiley.

Orians, G. H., & Heerwagen, J. H. (1992). Evolved Responses to Landscapes. In J. H. Barkow, L. Cosmides, & J. Tooby (eds.), *The adapted mind: Evolutionary psychology and the generation of culture* (pp. 555–579). New York: Oxford University Press.

Pinker, S. (1994). *The language instinct.* New York: Morrow.

Salovey, P., & Mayer, J. D. (1990). Emotional intelligence. *Imagination, Cognition and Personality 9*, 557–568.

Schmitt, D. P. (2003). Universal sex differences in the desire for sexual variety: Tests from 52 nations, 6 continents, and 13 islands. *Journal of Personality and Social Psychology, 85*, 85–104.

Spearman, C. (1904). "General intelligence" objectively determined and measured. *American Journal of Psychology, 15*, 201–293.

Tooby, J., & Cosmides, L. (1992). Psychological foundations of culture. In Barkow, J, Cosmides, L., & Tooby, J (eds.), *The adapted mind: Evolutionary psychology and the generation of culture* (pp. 19–136). New York: Oxford University Press.

Trivers, R. L. (1972). Parental investment and sexual selection. In B. Campbell, (ed.), *Sexual selection and the descent of man 1871–1971* (pp. 136–179). Chicago: Aldine.

Vining, D. R., Jr. (1986). Social versus reproductive success: The central theoretical problem of human sociobiology. *Behavioral and Brain Sciences, 9,* 167–216.

Yamagishi, T., Tanida, S., Mashima, R., Shimoma, E., & Kanazawa, S. (2003). You can judge a book by its cover: Evidence that cheaters may look different from cooperators. *Evolution and Human Behavior, 24,* 290–301.

VI

The Ecological Context of Mating Intelligence

Chapter 13

Brain Size, Intelligence, and Paleoclimatic Variation

Jessica Ash and Gordon G. Gallup, Jr.
State University of New York at Albany

Contrary to what many people have been taught, evolution has nothing to do with the survival of the fittest. It is not a question of whether you live or die. The key to evolution is reproduction. Whereas all organisms eventually die, not all organisms reproduce. Further, among those that do reproduce, some leave more descendants than others.

Evolution implies change, and those changes are driven by gradual variations in the composition of a gene pool over time. From an evolutionary perspective, organisms do not compete among themselves for scarce resources or survival. Rather, they compete for genetic representation in subsequent generations. You could be the fittest person imaginable in terms of strength, intelligence, disease resistance, and vitality, but if you fail to reproduce (or to facilitate the reproduction of kin with your shared genes), your contribution to the future of the human gene pool is zero. For anything to evolve it has to affect the probability of passing on your genes.

Sex is the final common path for all evolutionary change, and fitness can only be defined in terms of reproduction. As a consequence, what is or is not adaptive has to be measured in terms of its impact on reproduction. An adaptive trait is one that confers a reproductive advantage, a neutral trait has no reproductive consequences, while a maladaptive trait detracts from the likelihood of passing on one's genes.

According to this reasoning, the giraffe's neck is really a reproductive appendage. It is tempting to think of the giraffe's neck as a survival device that enabled giraffes to more effectively compete among one another for scarce food resources. That is, as giraffes became relatively plentiful under

313

ancestral conditions, they began to deplete the leaves on trees that were within easy reach, and, as a consequence, those with longer necks had access to more food. However, in such a scenario, giraffes were not just competing among one another for food or survival; they were ultimately competing with each other to produce descendants. Access to food simply affects the likelihood with which genes are passed on to subsequent generations (see Miller's [2000] theory that higher-order mental qualities in humans are also 'reproductive appendages').

Thus, the name of the game when it comes to evolution is not obtaining food or other resources—it is reproduction. Which came first, the chicken or the egg? From an evolutionary perspective the egg did. A chicken is merely an egg's way of producing another egg. The chicken is just a transient reproductive superstructure that provides for the perpetuation of genes.

BRAIN SIZE AND INTELLIGENCE

Like every other organ, brains evolved primarily because (directly or indirectly) they conferred a reproductive advantage. Across most of human evolutionary history, brains got bigger and bigger. This suggests that people with larger brains behaved in ways that allowed them to leave more descendents. In other words, there was differential reproduction based on cranial capacity, and genes that coded for big brains became more prevalent because big brains (for many possible reasons) increased the likelihood of reproductive success. Although the particular selection pressures for larger brains continue to be debated [they're a matter for further research, not conjecture] larger-brained individuals must have had some set of reproductive advantages.

In the context of this volume on mating intelligence, and in light of our reasoning about the reproductive advantages of larger brains, we can ask whether big brains make a difference when it comes to intelligence. Research on modern humans shows that head circumference (as an imperfect and indirect measure of brain size) is significantly and consistently correlated with performance on standardized IQ tests. Across a number of studies that include people of different ages and ethnic backgrounds, as head size increases, so does IQ (for a review, see Rushton & Ankney, 1996). The average correlation between head size and IQ test scores is about .20. Nguyen and McDaniel (2000), for example, report correlations from .17 to .26 for three different head size measures.

A growing number of recent and more sophisticated studies of brain size based on magnetic resonance imaging (MRI) also find that brain size and IQ are related, with most correlations in the range of .40 (Andreasen, Flaum, Swayze, O'Leary, Alliger, Cohen, Ehrhardt, & Yuh, 1993; Egan,

Chiswick, Santosh, Naidu, Rimmington, & Best, 1994; Egan, Wickett, & Vernon, 1995; Gignac, Vernon, & Wickett, 2003; Harvey, Persaud, Ron, Baker, & Murray, 1994; Kareken, Gur, Mozley, Mozley, Saykin, & Shtasel, 1995; Posthuma, De Geus, Baare, Pol, Kahn, & Boomsma, 2002; Raz, Torres, Spencer, Millman, Baertschi, & Sarpel, 1993; Reiss, Abrams, Singer, Ross, & Denckla, 1996; Wickett, & Vernon, 1994; Wickett, Vernon, & Lee, 2000; Willerman, Schultz, Rutledge, & Bigler, 1991). Applying corrections for restriction of range and attenuation to these studies, Wickett, Vernon, and Lee (2000) conclude that the correlation between brain volume, as measured by MRI, and IQ is actually closer to .50. In light of such findings, the evidence among contemporary humans shows that big brains make a considerable difference when it comes to performance on IQ tests.

A further question is whether higher intelligence is associated with higher indices of reproductive success. A recent review of the literature concerning the predictive value of IQ shows that, almost without exception, as IQ test scores increase, so do educational achievement, job performance, and annual income (Sternberg, Grigorenko, & Bundy, 2001). These correlations are in the range of .2 to .6. Moreover, Gottfredson (1997) has shown that when it comes to occupational success, the predictive validity of general intelligence is higher for more complex jobs. Other things being equal, people with better jobs and higher incomes are not only in a better position to provision and care for their children, they may also be able to attract higher quality mates.

One reason why big brains predict intelligence concerns the relationship between brain size, neuronal number, and synaptic connections. Other things being equal, as brain size increases, so do the number of neurons and the number of synaptic connections. Simply speaking, a neuron is like an electronic switch: it can either fire (i.e., *be on*) or not. Using this digital-processing-system metaphor, it follows that the number of computations that the brain can apply to environmental input increases exponentially as the number of neurons increase. The fact that cortical interneurons often show a graded response rather than an all-or-none action potential means that increases in number of neurons actually magnify the computational power of the brain even more, through the more nuanced summation of graded potentials.

Some simple mathematics can illustrate this point. Today, the typical human has a brain of about 1200 cubic centimeters. There are about 20 billion neocortical neurons in the human brain (Drachman, 2005). Therefore, each cubic centimeter of brain tissue contains about 16.7 million neurons, and nearly a trillion synapses (Drachman, 2005). As such, an increase of as little as thirty or forty cubic centimeters, which is only about 3 percent of total brain volume, amounts to over half a billion brain cells. Clearly, differences of a couple hundred million brain cells, and a corresponding increase in the number of synaptic connections among neurons, would

create the potential for more complex/sophisticated information processing. From an evolutionary perspective, this raises the question: how
exactly did bigger brains with more computational power yield reproductive benefits to ancestral humans?

PALEOCLIMATE DYNAMICS AND BRAIN EVOLUTION

Bigger brains may have, among other things, evolved to cope with the
more unpredictable environments caused by increased paleoclimatic variation and decreased temperatures (Ash & Gallup, in press). In other words,
short-term and long-term environmental variability created variable habitats that led to new adaptive problems. Among humans, these new problems may have favored behavioral plasticity as a means of promoting survival and reproduction in unpredictable settings (Potts, 1998a, 1998b, 2001).

As shown in Figures 13–1 and 13–2, two prominent features characterize climatic conditions during human evolution. First, there is overall
global cooling and drying. Second, there are periodic fluctuations in temperature that have increased in amplitude over the past 6 million years,
driving ever-larger climate changes across time (see Potts, 1998a for a
review). According to the variability-selection hypothesis, evolutionary
change through natural selection is driven mostly by environmental fluctuations rather than environmental constants (Potts, 2001). This hypothesis maintains that continuous variation in environmental conditions drove
continuous variation in survival and reproductive challenges, which
favored genetic capacities for adaptive flexibility. Larger brains and better
cognition, for example, may have increased ancestral human abilities to
respond in innovative ways to the ambiguity inherent in uncertain environmental situations. In other words, bigger brains buffered our bodies
from ever-changing environments.

In this chapter we present data that bear on whether changes in
absolute and relative brain size in *Homo* taxa were related to changes in
global temperature, as measured by oxygen isotope ratios and paleo-sea-
surface temperatures as a means of reconstructing past climates (Bradley,
1999). These measures can be used to reveal both climate patterns over
the entire Earth and seasonal change in specific regions.

PALEOCLIMATE INDICES

Oxygen isotope analyses (denoted by the symbol $\delta^{18}O$) depend on heavy-
weight and light-weight oxygen in water (NASA, online). Light-weight
oxygen-16 contains 8 protons and 8 neutrons, and is the most common
isotope found in nature, followed by much lesser amounts of heavy-

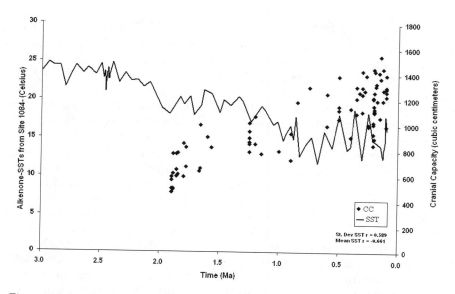

Figure 13–1. Sea-surface temperature record from Site 1084 compared with hominid cranial capacity across time.

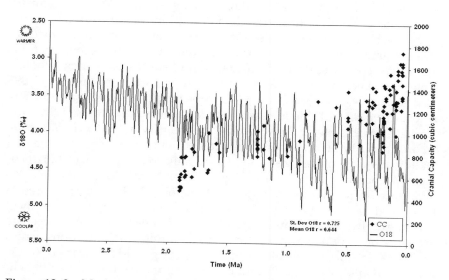

Figure 13–2 Marine oxygen isotope records from Sites 677 and 846 compared with hominid cranial capacity across time.

weight oxygen—18, with 8 protons and 10 neutrons. The ratio of these two types of oxygen in water varies depending on air temperature, the total amount of ice in the world, and the amount of local precipitation—all important aspects of climate. By determining how the ratio of heavy-to-light oxygen in marine sediments, ice cores, and fossilized shells of animals and plants is different from an accepted standard, scientists can learn something about climate variation that has occurred across time. Oxygen isotope data for our study were derived from Ocean Drilling Program (ODP) Site 677 (Shackleton, Berger, & Peltier, 1990) and ODP Site 846 (Shackleton, Hall, & Pate, 1995), both located in the East Pacific. Together, these locations provide the best available high-resolution data for the Pliocene and Lower Pleistocene time periods when human evolution took place (Shackleton, 1995). The oxygen isotope record from Site 677 is available for the interval 0.34–1.811 Ma, and from Site 846 for the interval 1.811–8.35 Ma, with sampling intervals from both sites recorded every 3,000 years. Although oxygen isotope analyses represent an important source of paleoclimatic data, there are several variables (e.g., salinity of the ocean, temperature skew from fossilized shells), that can affect the validity of temperature estimates derived from this technique. Still, oxygen isotope analyses continue to offer fundamental information about global ice volume variations.

To get a more complete picture of past climates, paleo sea-surface temperature data were also used in our analyses. Paleo-sea surface temperature (SST) data from Marlow, Lange, Wefer, and Rosell-Melé (2000) were obtained by a well-developed biomarker technique called the *ketone-unsaturation* index, which is based on the long—chain alkenone chemistry of minute phytoplankton. This data-collection method is a somewhat more reliable biomarker of paleotemperature change compared to oxygen-isotope data (Bradley, 1999). For the current study, SST reconstructions were derived from Site 1084 off the coast of southwest Africa, where a well-preserved and continuous sedimentary record from 4.6 Ma to 0.093 Ma is found (Marlow et al., 2000). While the temporal resolution of the SST record from Site 1084 is low, with average measurements < 50kyr, the strengths of this methodology and the similarity of the oxygen isotope record from Site 1084 to that of the global ice volume record are the two main reasons for using these data. Specifically, Marlow et al. (2000) documented a nearly synchronous timing of isotopic variations from Site 1084 and those from other locations across the globe. Such a pattern suggests that the data from this site are not restricted to changes in the local oceanography of the South Atlantic, but instead represent accurate accounts of climatic variation for many hominid fossil locations across the globe. In sum, these paleoclimatic sources provide a means of tracking glacial and interglacial periods to determine if either millennial climatic variations (i.e., fluctuations in climate across thousands of years) or the climatic trend (i.e., cooling over longer time-scales) is associated with human brain evolution.

CLIMATE VARIATION AND FOSSILIZED SKULLS

Climatic variation was defined as the standard deviation of the climatic parameter (i.e., either SST or $\delta^{18}O$ measurements) 200,000 years before the age of each cranium used in our analyses. For example, a cranium dated 1.7 million years ago (Ma) was viewed as a product of 200,000 years of environmental variation *prior* to that date. So, for this cranium, the standard deviation of SSTs or $\delta^{18}O$ measurements would be calculated from 1.9–1.7 Ma. A 200 kyr (kiloyear) time frame was used because the variability-selection hypothesis predicts that large episodic shifts in adaptive settings occurred over about 100–200 kyr scales, exceeding the scale of seasonal or lifetime fluctuations (see Potts, 1998a). However, to preclude a statistical artifact of 200 kyr periods, and to determine whether climatic variation provided greater selective pressure over shorter intervals of time, we also examined the standard deviation of $\delta^{18}O$ and SST measurements over 100 kyr periods for each cranium as well.

To evaluate whether the overall cooling trend or the consistent effects of the environment affected brain evolution, climatic consistency was operationally defined as the mean of the climatic parameter for 200 kyr and 100 kyr periods prior to the age of each cranium. To estimate brain size during human evolution, gross cranial-capacity measurements (cc) were used as a basis for inferring the evolution of general cognitive abilities in hominids. A total of 109 crania from the *Homo* genus, including *Homo habilis, Homo ergaster, Homo erectus, Homo heidelbergensis, Homo neanderthalensis,* and archaic *Homo sapiens* were selected because their antiquity could be dated with reasonable accuracy, and their endocranial capacity could be reasonably measured. These populations encompass a large time span of human evolutionary history across diverse and varying natural environments beginning with the Plio Pleistocene epoch (deMenocal & Bloemendal, 1995). Thus, they offer an ideal sample for studying the effects of climatic variation on brain evolution. Table 13.1. lists the individual crania used in our analyses and the references for the data we used. The age and cranial capacity (cc) of most crania were obtained from an archival database (De Miguel & Henneberg, 2001), which listed all estimates of cranial capacity for fossil hominids in the Pliocene and Pleistocene found in the literature up to April 2000. If the cc or date for any particular cranium had been revised/updated in more recent literature, then recent estimates were assumed to be more accurate and were used in our study.

TABLE 13.1.
Fossil Information

Legend for taxa:

ahs: *Archaic Homo sapiens*	h: *Homo*
hant: *Homo antecessor*	he: *Homo erectus*
hher: *Homo ergaster*	hh: *Homo habilis*
hhei: *Homo heidelbergensis*	hn: *Neandertal*

No	Fossil	Taxon	CC		Date	
1	SK 47 (adult)	early h	595.000	a	1.900	a
2	Stw 53	early h	570.000	a	1.900	a
3	SK 847	h, hh/he	507.000	a	1.900	a
4	SK 27	h	475.000	a	1.900	a
5	KNM-ER 1470 (Koobi Fora)	hher	776.000	a	1.890	a
6	KNM-ER 3732 (Koobi Fora)	hher	622.500	a	1.890	a
7	KNM-ER 1813 (Koobi Fora)	hh	506.333	a	1.890	a
8	Omo L894-1	h	500.000	a	1.890	a
9	Dmansi 2280	hh	775.000	b	1.860	b
10	Dmansi 2282	hh	650.000	b	1.860	b
11	Dmansi 2700	hh	600.000	c	1.860	b
12	KNM-ER 1590 (Koobi Fora)	hr	782.500	a	1.850	a
13	KNM-ER 1805 (Koobi Fora)	hh	616.000	a	1.850	a
14	Modjokerto (adult)	he	855.000	a	1.800	a
15	OH 24 (Olduvai)	hh	597.000	d	1.800	a
16	KNM-ER 3733 (Koobi Fora)	hher	825.400	a	1.780	a
17	OH 7 (adult) (Olduvai)	hh	674.000	a	1.780	a
18	OH 16 (adult) (Olduvai)	hh	639.200	a	1.670	a
19	Sangiran 4	he	856.000	a	1.660	a
20	OH 13 (adult) (Olduvai)	hh	662.286	a	1.660	a
21	Sangiran 31	he	1000.000	a	1.660	a
22	KNM-WT 15000 (adult) (Nariokotome)	he	904.500	a	1.600	a
23	KNM-ER 3883 (Koobi Fora)	hher	825.667	a	1.570	a
24	Sangiran 12	he	951.000	a	1.250	e
25	Sangiran 3 (adult)	he	900.000	a	1.250	e
26	Sangiran 10	he	868.600	a	1.250	e
27	Sangiran 9	he	856.000	a	1.250	e
28	Sangiran 2	he	792.571	a	1.250	e
29	Sangiran 17	he	1020.000	a	1.250	e
30	OH 9 (Olduvai)	he	1070.500	a	1.200	a
31	Gongwangling 1	he	779.000	a	1.150	a
32	Buia	he	800.000	a	1.000	a
33	Trinil 2	he	940.000	a	0.900	a
34	Ceprano	hhei	1185.000	a	0.850	k
35	OH 12 (Olduvai)	he	732.330	a	0.840	a
36	Ternifine	ahs	1300.000	a	0.750	a

(continued)

TABLE 13.1—Continued

No	Fossil	Taxon	CC		Date	
37	Bodo	hhei	1250.000	f	0.600	f
38	Nanjing	he	1000.000	c	0.600	c
39	Atapuerca 4 (AT 600)	hant	1390.000	a	0.500	g
40	Atapuerca 6 (11–14 year old)	hant	1153.333	a	0.500	g
41	Atapuerca 5 (AT 700)	hant	1125.000	a	0.500	g
42	Sambungmacan 1	he	1056.333	a	0.500	a
43	Salé 1	he	911.000	a	0.400	a
44	Araho 21	hhei	1138.667	a	0.400	a
45	Broken hill 1 (Kabwe)	hhei	1310.000	a	0.350	a
46	Saldanha 1 (Elandsfontein)	hhei	1216.667	a	0.350	a
47	Yunxian	he	1100.000	a	0.350	a
48	Ndutu 1	ahs	1100.000	a	0.350	a
49	Petralona 1	hhei	1266.556	a	0.325	a
50	Reilingn	hhei	1432.000	a	0.300	a
51	Swanscombe 1	hhei	1305.000	a	0.300	a
52	Narmada 1	he	1249.333	a	0.300	a
53	Steinheim 1	hhei	1111.192	a	0.300	a
54	Florisbad 1	ahs	1280.000	a	0.279	h
55	KNM-ER 3884	ahs	1400.000	a	0.270	a
56	Ngawi	he	1000.000	c	0.250	c
57	Hexian	he	1012.500	a	0.250	a
58	Zhoukoudian (III)	he	937.500	a	0.210	i
59	Zhoukoudian (VI)	he	850.000	a	0.210	i
60	Zhoukoudian L1 (X)	he	1225.000	a	0.210	i
61	Zhoukoudian h3 (V)	he	1220.000	a	0.210	i
62	Zhoukoudian D1 (II)	he	1030.000	a	0.210	i
63	Zhoukoudian L3 (XII)	he	1030.000	a	0.210	i
64	Zhoukoudian L2 (XI)	he	1015.000	a	0.210	i
65	Dali 1	ahs	1160.000	a	0.205	a
66	Ehrinhsdorf 9	hhei	1450.000	a	0.203	a
67	Sambungmacan 3	he	900.000	a	0.200	a
68	Solo 5, Ngandong V	he	1266.167	a	0.200	a
69	Solo 9, Ngandong IX	he	1135.000	a	0.200	a
70	Solo 1, Ngandong I	he	1121.429	a	0.200	a
71	Solo 6, Ngandong VI	he	1115.714	a	0.200	a
72	Solo 10, Ngandong X	he	1109.000	a	0.200	a
73	Omo 2	ahs	1432.500	a	0.195	j
74	Jinniushan	he	1316.667	a	0.187	a
75	Vértesszöllös 2	ahs	1334.571	a	0.186	a
76	Biache	hhei	1200.000	a	0.178	a
77	Fontéchevade 2	hn	1420.000	a	0.160	a
78	La Chaise	hn	1065.000	a	0.151	a
79	Singa 1	hn	1550.000	a	0.150	a

(continued)

TABLE 13.1—Continued

No	Fossil	Taxon	CC		Date	
80	KNM-ES-11693 (Eliye Springs)	ahs	1375.000	a	0.150	a
81	Jebel Irhoud 2	hn	1400.000	l	0.140	a
82	Jebel Irhoud 1	hn	1305.000	l	0.140	a
83	Krapina - D	hn	1450.000	a	0.130	a
84	Krapina 3	hn	1200.000	a	0.130	a
85	Ngaloba	ahs	1283.500	a	0.125	a
86	Daka (BOU VP-2/66)	he	995.000	c	0.100	c
87	Saccopastore 2	hn	1295.000	a	0.100	a
88	Tabun C1	hn	1270.500	a	0.100	a
89	Saccopastore 1	hn	1234.333	a	0.100	a
90	Skhul 9	hn	1587.333	a	0.090	a
91	Skhul 4	hn	1554.500	a	0.090	a
92	Skhul 5	hn	1499.500	a	0.090	a
93	Skhul 2	hn	1300.000	a	0.090	a
94	La Ferrassie 1	hn	1650.200	a	0.068	a
95	Teshik-Tash (adult)	hn	1581.000	a	0.060	a
96	Gibraltar 1 (Forbes' Quarry)	hn	1226.750	a	0.060	a
97	Monte Circeo I	hn	1551.000	a	0.055	a
98	Amud 1	hn	1745.000	a	0.051	a
99	Shanidar 1	hn	1650.000	a	0.050	a
100	La Chapelle-aux-Saints	hn	1626.000	a	0.050	a
101	Shanidar 5	hn	1550.000	a	0.050	a
102	Spy 2	hn	1487.400	a	0.050	a
103	Spy 1	hn	1457.500	a	0.050	a
104	La Quina 5	hn	1345.250	a	0.050	a
105	Neandertal 1	hn	1337.750	a	0.050	a
106	Ganovce 1	hn	1320.000	a	0.050	a
107	Le Moustier 1	hn	1486.200	a	0.040	a
108	Galilee	ahs	1400.000	a	0.040	a
109	Eyasi	ahs	1235.000	a	0.035	a

References:

a. De Miguel, C., and M. Henneberg   2001
   Variation in hominid brain size: how much
   is due to method? *Homo* 52:2-56

b. Lee, S-H.   2005
   Brief communication: Is variation in the cranial capacity
   of the Dmansi sample too high to be from a single species?
   American Journal of Physical Anthropology 127:263–266.

c. Lee, S-H and M. H. Wolpoff   2003
   The pattern of evolution in Pleistocene
   human brain size. *Paleobiology* 29:186–196.

(continued)

TABLE 13.1—Continued

d.	Tobias, P. V. Olduvai gorge, Vol.4: *The Skulls, Endocasts and Teeth of homo habilis*. Cambridge: Cambridge University Press	1991
e.	Larick, R., R.L. Ciochon, Y. Zaim, Sudijono, Suminto, Y. Rizal, F. Aziz, M. Reahan, and M. Heizler Early Pleistocene 40Ar/39Ar ahes for Bapang Formation hominids, Central Jawa, Indonesia. *Proceedings of the National Academy of Sciences* 98: 4866–4871.	2001
f.	Conroy, H.C., Weber, H., Seidler, H., Recheis, W., zur Nedden, D. and J. H. Mariam Endocranial capacity of the Bodo cranium determined from three-dimensional computed tomography. *American Journal of Physical Anthropology* 113:111–118.	2000
g.	Bischoff, J. L. and D. D. Shamp The Sima de los Huesos hominids date to beyond U/Th equilibrium (> 350 kyr) and perhaps to 400-500 kyr: New radiometric dates. *Journal of Archaeological Science* 30:275–280.	2003
h.	Kunman, K., Inbar, M, and R. J. Clark Palaeoenvironments and cultural sequence of the Florisbad Middle Stone Age hominid site, South Africa. *Journal of Archaeological Science* 26:1409–1425.	1999
i.	Shen, G., Cheng, H., and R. L. Edwards Mass spectrometric U-series dating of New Cavt at Zhoukoudian, China. *Journal of Anthropological Science* 31:337–342.	2004
j.	McDougall, I., Brown, F. H., and J. G. Fleagle Stratigraphic placement of modern humans from Kibish, Ethiopia. *Nature* 433:733–735.	2005
k.	Bruner, E. and G. Manzi CT-based description and phyletic evaluation of the archaic human calvarium from Ceprano, Italy. *Anatatomical Record* 285A:643–658.	2005
l.	Holloway, R. L., Broadfield, D. C., and M. S. Yuan eds. The human fossil record: *Brain endocasts–the paleoneurological evidence*. New Jersey: John Wiley & Sons Inc.	2004

An encephalization quotient (EQ) for hominids, providing an index of brain size relative to body size, was also used to circumvent the problems of interpreting absolute brain volume in the face of corresponding variation in body size. However, the methods used to estimate encephalization quotients are also somewhat problematic because they rely on postcranial (below-the-head) remains to estimate body size, and these are often poorly preserved in the prehistoric record and/or difficult to match with the right crania. Taking into account these difficulties, Rightmire (2004) determined EQ data for *Homo* specimens by estimating body size based on the orbital height of the cranium, a known reliable predictor of body mass (Aiello & Wood, 1994). EQ data for 15 crania included from the aforementioned populations were included in our analyses.

To illustrate the findings, Figure 13–1 displays the brain size (cc) data overlaid with one type of climate record (the SST data), while Figure 13–2 displays the brain size (cc) data overlaid with the other type of climate record (the $\delta^{18}O$ data). Both figures reveal prolonged and gradual cooling across time. In Figure 13–1, from 2.0 to 1.4 Ma, there is an apparent pause in the cooling trend. However, this phase is associated with an increase in brain-size variability. A rapid decline in SST is noticeable beginning at 1.4 Ma followed by a transition at 0.6 Ma to fluctuating SSTs similar to the 100 kyr glacial-interglacial cycles (Marlow et al., 2000). Brain size shows a marked increase beginning with heightened SST variability between 2.0 and 1.4 Ma, followed by what appears to be a stasis in the brain size trend from 1.4 to ∼ 0.6 Ma. Then, as SST variability peaks in amplitude, brain size reaches its highest values, with marked variation. In Figure 13–2, deviations in the trend toward cooler temperatures are more apparent due to the greater resolution of the sampling interval of $\delta^{18}O$ measurements. The range of $\delta^{18}O$ extremes grows larger over time with concomitant increases in brain sizes beginning at time intervals similar to those in the SST record.

To examine how environmental changes may influence brain size increases, correlation coefficients were calculated with climatic means and standard deviations of the environmental measures ($\delta^{18}O$ or SST) serving as separate independent variables and brain size (endocranial capacity) serving as the dependent variable in each 200 kya time-period. Spearman's rank-order correlations were used because the variables showed skew, heteroscedasticity, and other distributional problems (Cohen, Cohen, West, & Aiken, 2003).

The analyses can be summarized as follows. First, climatic variation measured in 100 kyr intervals rather than 200 kyr intervals accounted for the greatest amount of variance in brain size(r (109) = .725, $p < .01$, $R^2 =$ 52.5 percent), compared to mean cooling trend shown by oxygen isotope records ($r(109) = .644$, $p < .01$, $R^2 = 41.4$ percent). Figures 13–3 and 13–4 depict the scatterplot of the correlations with the $\delta^{18}O$ data. For the SST data, the data follow a pattern in which climatic variation accounts for about the same amount of variance in cc ($r(89) = .589$, $p < .01$, $R^2 = 35$

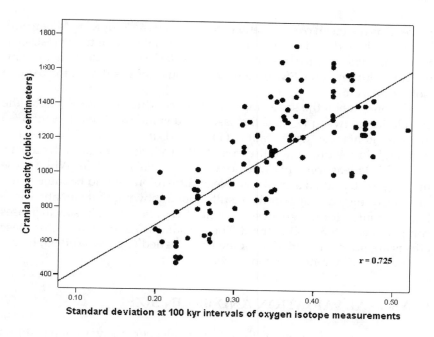

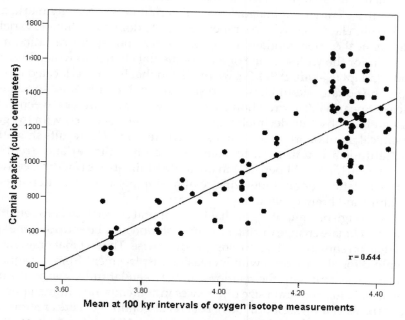

Figure 13–3   Cranial capacity as a function of standard deviations of oxygen isotope measurements at 100,000 year intervals.

percent) as the mean overall trend ($r(89) = -.661, p < .01, R^2 = 44$ percent). Note that the reduced sample size for the SST data is due to the restricted time range available for this period (i.e., 3.0–.093 Ma). In addition, the temporal resolution of the SST data is not as consistent as that of the oxygen isotope analyses.

Second, when the same analyses were conducted with EQ data, the correlation between EQ and the associated standard deviations of $\delta^{18}O$ measurements was significant ($r(14) = .731, p < .05, R^2 = 54$ percent). Although in the predicted direction, the correlation based on the means of the $\delta^{18}O$ measurements was not ($r(14) = .493, p = .073$). While these findings are based on a small sample and therefore should be interpreted cautiously, they do support the results above showing that climatic variation accounted for the greatest amount of variance in brain size increases compared with the cooling trend. The EQ data also demonstrate that these effects are not confounded, as some have argued (e.g., Vrba, 1995) by climate driven differences in body size.

SEASONAL VARIATION AND BRAIN SIZE

These analyses only examine the effect of paleoclimatic variation on brain size across *time*. To investigate environmental dynamics across *space*, we conducted a separate analysis that considered the site locations from which these crania originated. Seasonal variation is especially marked in mid to high latitudes, where temperature is the dominant climatic variable (deMenocal & Bloemendale, 1995). Moreover, short-term variation may account for the widest range of environmental change to which humans had to adapt (Calvin, 1996). So, we predicted that hominids located farther from the equator would have correspondingly larger brains. To test this idea, a Spearman's correlation coefficient was calculated between brain size and the absolute decimal degrees of latitude associated with the geographical point of origin of each fossilized cranium. The results show that site latitude accounts for a substantial amount of the variance ($r(109) = .478, p < .01, R^2 = 23$ percent) in absolute brain size, providing convergent validation for an underlying relationship between variation in temperature and brain evolution.

Although one might argue that the temporal correlation between brain size and climate change during human evolution may be spurious, the spatial data on equatorial distance suggest otherwise. The fact that brain size in hominid fossils increases with increasing displacement from the equator is also consistent with the relationship between latitude, seasonal variation in climate, and brain size differences in contemporary human populations (Beals, Smith, & Dodd, 1984). Beals et al. conducted a linear regression using degrees of latitude as the predictor for 122 contemporary ethnic populations based on a sample size of 20,000 individuals, and found a 2.5 cm^3 increase in brain size for every degree of latitude displacement from the equator. Following their precedent, we found an 8.27 cm^3 increase in brain volume among our sample of fossilized crania for every degree of equatorial distance ($sr_i^2 = 0.453$ $t(108) = 5.306, p < .05$).

BIG BRAINS AND ENVIRONMENTAL CHANGE

Although these data are (by necessity) correlational, it is clear that Plio-Pleistocene hominids confronted more environmental variation at diverse temporal and spatial scales, embedded in an overall trend toward cooler, more arid conditions. The evolution of humans may have been influenced (directly or indirectly) by these ever colder, more erratic climatic conditions. One evolutionary response to these trends, with environmental variability possibly providing the greatest selective force, may have been bigger and more complex brains to promote survival and reproduction in a variety of challenging habitats.

Consistent with the suggestion by Rushton and Jensen (2005), it seems reasonable to suppose that increases in brain size were associated with more sophisticated cognitive functioning and behavioral flexibility needed to adapt to various environmental conditions. This conclusion is supported by many studies showing that MRI-measured brain sizes substantially predict scores on standardized IQ tests within modern humans (see McDaniel (2005) for a recent meta-analysis). Individual lobe volume and aggregate gray and white matter volumes also correlate with IQ (Andreasen et al., 1993; Posthuma et al., 2002). Thus, there is substantial evidence supporting the use of brain size as a proxy for intelligence.

Problems posed by cooling and seasonal variation in temperature have been solved by most affected species through a series of physical and physiological adaptations, such as metabolic and thermoregulatory mechanisms, energy stores in the form of fat deposits, down, fur, and subcutaneous layers of fat to prevent heat loss, hibernation during extended periods of reduced temperature, and migration as a means of avoiding seasonal variation extremes. In stark contrast with other species, humans were able to exploit areas that were appreciably displaced from the equator through the development of cognitive/intellectual innovations. An increased reliance on hunting and meat eating undoubtedly put a premium on intricate patterns of cooperative hunting and the development of more sophisticated weapons. Related pressures for the need to develop improved clothing and shelter, along with mastering the use of fire, may have further accelerated the development of the cognitive/intellectual skills needed to compete for scarce resources and successfully reproduce in colder climates.

In addition to the question of *why* larger brains evolved, an equally important question concerns *how* larger brains are maintained, since brains are costly in energetic terms. Even though human brains account for only about 2 percent of body weight, they consume over a third of the daily caloric intake. As a consequence, brains generate a lot of heat, and, like computers, they have to be cooled in order to operate efficiently and effectively. The problem of dissipating heat from the brain may have been a physiological constraint on human brain size. One intriguing approach to the brain-cooling problem is the radiator hypothesis, which posits that an intricate system of tiny emissary veins evolved to selectively cool the human brain when it got too hot (Falk & Gage, 1997). This brain-cooling network became more extensive with brain expansion from gracile australopithecines to *Homo sapiens* (Falk, 1990). In modern humans, the diploic veins in the cranium seem to help cool the brain, and larger skulls tend to have a more extensive diploic system than smaller skulls (Hershkovitz et al., 1999). In addition, diploic vein patterns appear to be more intricate in humans compared with nonhuman primates.

The importance of effective brain cooling may also be related to the correlation between brain size and distance from the equator, since more extreme latitudes are associated with more exaggerated oscillations between hot and cold (Crowley & North, 1991). Human abilities to survive higher latitudes, colder climates, and wider seasonal fluctuations were probably helped by the use of fire, clothing, and shelter, which all require intelligence. For evidence that the growing use of fire in Northern Europe impacted human evolution, the ability to tolerate inhaling some of the toxic byproducts of combustion varies in contemporary populations of humans as a function of their former reliance on fire as a means of staying warm, see Platek, Gallup, and Fryer (2002).

SEASONALITY AND MEAT EATING

Life under higher-latitude conditions would also require an increased reliance on meat eating, since high-latitude plants have evolved to flourish only during warmer seasons. In winter most plants die or become dormant. Thus, edible biomass at high latitudes tends to be stored in the bodies of large, well-insulated animals, which can be killed only through cooperative hunting with effective weapons.

Meat eating, in this context, has some interesting cognitive implications. In particular, the means by which members of different species acquire food (e.g., predation vs. foraging) generally determine the amount of time spent looking for food. Differences in these foraging strategies may relate to an operant conditioning paradigm referred to as *free* versus *earned* food (e.g., Neuringer, 1969). After first training rats to press a lever for food and then providing rats with a choice between the resumption of bar pressing for food or simply eating food that was made freely available, rats show a preference for bar pressing. This phenomenon, typified by animals working for food under conditions in which food is otherwise available, has been termed *contrafreeloading* (see Inglis, Forkman, & Lazarus, 1997 for a review). Contrafreeloading is well-documented and has been demonstrated in a variety of different species, including rats (Jensen, 1963), pigeons (Neuringer, 1969), and even monkeys (Anderson & Chamove, 1984). A notable exception to this pattern of results is found among domestic cats. Cats opt to freeload rather than work for food (Koffer & Coulson, 1971).

One way to think about these differences is in terms of how well contrafreeloading, or the lack thereof, maps onto the natural history of the species in question. Animals that contrafreeload (such as rats, pigeons, and monkeys) forage for their food, and typically find and eat small amounts of food intermittently. Because food is often scarce, foraging is a very time-consuming, almost endless preoccupation. In contrast, cats and many other predators that track and kill large prey often eat large amounts of food on a single occasion. Upon killing prey, some predators gorge themselves on the carcass and do not resume hunting for several days. In other words, because the caloric intake per meal is so much greater, predation and meat eating have the potential to create a lot of spare time. Consider a pride of lions sleeping and languishing around for extended periods following a kill. Unlike rodents and birds, prototypical predators can often afford to be lazy.

Meat eating, therefore, can lead to free time that can be spent on more creative, abstract, and intellectually challenging activities. In between meals, organisms that eat meat (and are self-aware) have the luxury of being able to reflect on themselves and pursue a variety of increasingly abstract problem solving activities. Big brains are a necessary but not sufficient condition for intelligence. Whether big brains translate into instances of intelligent behavior depends on how they are used. Those with big brains that rise to the occasion can use the free time that results from meat-eating to pursue more intellectually productive and challenging activities.

BIG BRAINS AND MATING INTELLIGENCE

What do big brains have to do with mating intelligence? We tend to side with Miller (2000) on the question of mating intelligence (see also Geher, Miller, and Murphy's introductory chapter in this volume). All selection is sexual selection in the sense that sex is the only means by which genes find their way from one generation to the next. Selection is represented by a correlation between genotype and reproductive success. If the correlation is positive, there will be selection for the trait and it will become relatively prevalent. If the correlation is negative, the trait will be selected against. For any phenotypic trait to evolve, it has to confer, directly or indirectly, a reproductive advantage. With that in mind, mating intelligence could be viewed as the evolution of behavioral, cognitive, and interpersonal strategies that increase the likelihood of attracting high-quality mates and leaving high quality descendents.

For example, because of pregnancy and lactation, females must invest much more time and energy in reproduction and child rearing than men. However, because human infants are so altricial (helpless at birth and parent-dependent over extended periods of time), successful child rearing also required the assistance of the father. As a consequence, during the early phases of courtship, females were probably selected to make judicious decisions among prospective mates, and to take into account their ability to care for, protect, and provide for the female and her prospective children. In addition to strength and stamina, competition among males for the scarce resources needed to sustain females and children could have favored the development of a variety of intellectual skills associated with hunting, such as effective weapon-development, tracking skills, and an appreciation for behavioral propensities of the prey (being a good hunter often requires being a good animal psychologist). By the same token, females needed to distinguish between males that were willing to make genuine, long-term commitments and those who deliberately feigned commitments to get sex (i.e., "I love you, so let's go to bed"). Selective pressure for making subtle, fine-grained distinctions among prospective mates based on their fitness indicators, commitment, honesty, and love could have been a major selection pressure for bigger and more complex brains. For a more extended discussion of the evolution of mental state attribution (as relevant to discerning commitment and honesty in mates) see Gallup (2006).

Likewise, the possibility of human males being duped into investing in offspring sired by other males due to female infidelity (i.e., being cuckolded), probably shaped a variety of sophisticated paternal-assurance tactics and nonparternity-detection mechanisms in men. For example, we have shown that males invest preferentially in infants whose facial features resemble their own (Platek, Critton, Burch, Frederick, Myers, & Gallup, 2003). For a detailed categorization of the many different evolved paternal-assurance strategies see Gallup and Burch (2006).

Another aspect of mating intelligence concerns mate choice for partner intelligence. In an unpublished study (Gallup & Suarez, 1983), we asked several hundred college students to respond to two open-ended questions: "What psychological characteristics of members of the opposite sex do you find most sexually attractive?" and "What physical characteristics of members of the opposite sex do you find most sexually attractive?" In response to the first question, females mentioned intelligence more often than any other trait. If female mate choice puts a premium on intelligence, women might have been the cutting-edge selective pressure that favored our bigger and bigger brains. Indeed, in competing for scarce resources and mating opportunities during human evolution, intellectual prowess probably became as important as physical prowess. Clearly, females who favored pair bonds with intelligent mates probably received better care and produced more surviving children than those who were indifferent to their mate's intelligence.

CONCLUSION

The evidence provided in this chapter is consistent with the argument that climatic variability and unpredictability provided critical contexts for brain expansion in hominids. Larger brains provided more phenotypic plasticity for survival and reproduction under variable conditions, and thereby decoupled our species from reliance on any single habitat (Potts, 2001). Combined with the fact that a significant amount of the variance in brain size among the skulls in our sample can be explained by latitude, these data suggest that colder more variable climates were important in the evolution of large human brains. Nothing else that has ever been suggested as promoting cranial expansion among hominids even comes close to climate in explaining as much of the variance in cranial capacity. Recall, for example, that oxygen isotope analyses of temperature variation at 100 kyr intervals accounted for an astounding 52.5% of the observed variance in cranial capacity (see Figure 13–3).

Our view is similar to Kanazawa (2004) concerning the role of general intelligence in adapting to evolutionarily novel problems, especially those that were driven by novel climate and ecological conditions. Among humans, picking mates with better climate-coping abilities may have developed into an increasingly more important form of selection over the past several million years. Modern courtship displays that show off capacities for surviving in harsh environments (e.g., becoming a deep sea diver, astronaut, ice skater, mountaineer, skier, sailor, ice climber, explorer) could illustrate the convergence of natural selection (through climatic harshness and variability favoring intelligence) and sexual selection (through mate choice favoring intelligence). Indeed, one might even speculate that harsher climates promoted more socially monogamous mating due to the thermal benefits couples derived from each other while sleeping together.

In closing, it is tempting to comment on a peculiar irony of our findings. If the trend toward colder and more variable climates was a factor in prompting the development of bigger human brains, the recent and dra-

matic reversal of this trend toward global warming has interesting implications. As a consequence of our growing reliance on fossil fuels, we
appear to be in the process of reversing the conditions that may have lead
to the development of our big brains in the first place.

ACKNOWLEDGMENTS

We thank the editors, Glenn Geher and Geoffrey Miller for many helpful
suggestions and ideas about the issues presented in this chapter.

REFERENCES

Ash, J. A. & Gallup, G. G. (in press). Paleoclimatic variation and brain expansion
    during human evolution. *Human Nature.*
Aiello, L. C., & Wood, B. A. (1994). Cranial variables as predictors of hominid body
    mass. *American Journal of Physical Anthropology, 95,* 409–426.
Anderson, J. R., & Chamove, A. S. (1984). Allowing captive primates to forage. In
    Standards in laboratory animal management, part 2 (pp. 253–256). Potters Bar:
    Universities Federation for Animal Welfare.
Andreasen, N. C., Flaum, M., Swayze, V., II, O'Leary, D. S., Alliger, R., Cohen, G.,
    Ehrhardt, J., & Yuh, W. T. C. (1993). Intelligence and brain structure in normal
    individuals. *American Journal of Psychiatry, 150,* 130–134.
Barton, R. A., & Harvey, P. H. (2000). Mosaic evolution of brain structure in mam-
    mals. *Nature, 405,* 1055–1058.
Beals, K. L., Smith, C. L., & Dodd, S. M. (1984). Brain size, cranial morphology,
    climate and time machines. *Current Anthropology, 25,* 301–330.
Bradley, R. S. (1999). *Paleoclimatology: Reconstructing climates of the quaternary* (2nd
    Ed.). San Diego: Academic Press.
Calvin, W. H. (1996). *How brains think.* New York: Basic Books.
Cohen, J., Cohen, P., West, S. G., & Aiken, L. S. (2003). *Applied multiple regression/
    correlation analysis foe the behavioral sciences* (3rd ed.). Mahwah, NJ: Lawrence
    Erlbaum Associates.
Crowley, T. J., & North, G. R. (1991). *Paleoclimatology.* New York: Oxford University
    Press.
deMenocal, P. B., & Bloemendal, J. (1995). Plio-Pleistocene subtropical African cli-
    mate variability and the paleoenvironment of hominid evolution: A combined
    data-model approach. In: E. Vrba, G. Denton, L. Burckle, & T. Partridge (Eds.),
    Paleoclimate and evolution with emphasis on human origins (pp. 262–288). New
    Haven, CT: Yale University Press.
Demiguel, C., & Henneberg, M. (2001). Variation in hominid brain size: How much
    is due to method? *Homo, 52,* 3–58.
Drachman, D. A. (2005). Do we have brain to spare? *Neurology, 64,* 2004–2005.
Egan, V., Chiswick, A., Santosh, C., Naidu, K., Rimmington, J. E., & Best, J. J. K.
    (1994). Size isn't everything: A study of brain volume, intelligence and audi-
    tory evoked potentials. *Personality and Individual Differences, 17,* 357–367.

Egan, V., Wickett, J. C., & Vernon, P. A. (1995). Brain size and intelligence: Erratum, addendum, and correction. *Personality and Individual Differences, 19,* 113–315.

Falk, D. (1990). Brain evolution in Homo—The radiator theory. *Behavioral and Brain Science, 13,* 333–343.

Falk, D., & Gage, T. B. (1997). Flushing the radiator? A reply to Braga & Boesch. *Journal of Human Evolution, 33,* 495–502.

Gallup, G. G., Jr., & Suarez, S. D. (1983). Unpublished data.

Gallup, G. G., Jr. (1998). Can animals empathize? Yes. *Scientific American, 9,* 66–71.

Gallup, G. G., Jr., & Burch, R. L. (2006). The semen displacement hypothesis: Semen hydraulics and the intra-pair copulation proclivity model of female infidelity. In S. Platek & T. Shackelford (Eds.), *Female Infidelity and Paternal Uncertainty.* Cambridge: Cambridge University Press.

Gignac, G. E., Vernon, P. A., & Wickett, J. C. (2003). Factors influencing the relationship between brain size and intelligence. In H. Nyborg (Ed.). *The scientific study of general intelligence: Tribute to Arthur R. Jensen.* Oxford: Pergamon.

Harvey, I., Persaud, R., Ron, M. A., Baker, G., & Murray, R. M. (1994). Volumetric MRI measurements in bipolars compared with schizophrenics and healthy controls. *Psychological Medicine, 24,* 689–699.

Hershkovitz, I., Greenwald, C., Rothschild, B. M., Latimer, B., Dutour, O., Jellema, L. M., et al. (1999). The elusive diploic veins: Anthropological and anatomical perspective. *American Journal of Physical Anthropology, 108,* 345–358.

Inglis, I. R., Forkman, B., & Lazarus, J. (1997). Free food or earned food: A review and fuzzy model of contrafreeloading. *Animal Behaviour, 53,* 1171–1191.

Jensen, E. D. (1963). Preference for bar pressing over free-loading as a function of the number of unrewarded presses. *Journal of Experimental Psychology, 65,* 451–454.

Kaas, J. H., & Collins, C. E. (2001). Evolving ideas of brain evolution. *Nature, 411,* 141–142.

Kanazawa, S. (2004). General intelligence as a domain-specific adaptation. *Psychological Review, 111,* 512–523.

Kareken, D. A., Gur, R. C., Mozley, P. D., Mozley, L. H., Saykin, A. J., Shtasel, D. L., & Gur, R. E. (1995). Cognitive functioning and neuroanatomic volume measures in schizophrenia. *Neuropsychology, 9,* 211–219.

Koffer, K., & Coulson, G. (1971). Feline indolence: cats prefer free to response-produced food. *Psychonomic Science, 24,* 41–42.

Marlow, J. R., Lange, C. B., Wefer, G., & Rosell-Melé, A. (2000). Upwelling intensification as part of the Pliocene-Pleistocene climate transition. *Science, 290,* 2288–2291.

McDaniel, M. A. (2005). Big-brained people are smarter: A meta-analysis of the relationship between in vivo brain volume and intelligence. *Intelligence, 33,* 337–346.

Miller, G. F. (2000). Sexual section for indicators of intelligence. In G. Bock, J. Goode, & K. Webb (Eds.), *The nature of intelligence* (pp. 260–275). Hoboken, NJ: Wiley.

NASA Earth Observatory: Paleoclimatology (n.d.). Retrieved August, 2004, from http://earthobservatory.nasa.gov/Study/Paleoclimatology_OxygenBalance/oxygen_balance.html

Neuringer, A. J. (1969). Animals respond for food in the presence of free food. *Science, 166,* 399–401.

Nguyen, N. T., & McDaniel, M. A. (2000). *Brain size and intelligence: A meta-analysis.* Paper presented at the First Annual Conference of the International Society of Intelligence Research, Cleveland, OH.

Platek, S. M., Gallup, G. G., Jr., & Fryer, B. D. (2002). The fireside hypothesis: Was there differential selection for resistance to lung disease during human evolution? *Medical Hypotheses, 58,* 1–5.

Platek, S. M., Critton, S. R., Burch, R. L., Frederick, D. A., Myers, T. S., & Gallup, G. G., Jr. (2003). How much resemblance is enough? Determination of a just noticeable difference at which male reactions towards children's faces change from indifferent to positive. *Evolution and Human Behavior, 23,* 81–87.

Posthuma, D., De Geus, E. J. C., Baare, W. F. C., Pol, H. E. H., Kahn, R. S., Boomsma, D. I. (2002). The association between brain volume and intelligence is of genetic origin. *Nature Neuroscience, 5,* 83–84.

Potts, R. (1998a). Environmental hypotheses of hominid evolution. *Yearbook of Physical Anthropology, 41,* 93–136.

Potts, R. (1998b). Variability selection in hominid evolution. *Evolutionary Anthropology, 7,* 81–96.

Potts, R. (2001). Complexity and adaptability in human evolution. In: M. Goodman & A. S. Moffat (Eds.) *Probing human origins,* (pp. 33–58). Cambridge: American Academy of Arts and Sciences.

Raz, N., Torres, I. J., Spencer, W. D., Millman, D., Baertschi, J. C., & Sarpel, G. (1993). Neuroanatomical correlates of age-sensitive and age-invariant cognitive abilities: An in vivo MRI investigation. *Intelligence, 17,* 407–422.

Reiss, A. L., Abrams, M. T., Singer, H. S., Ross, J. L., & Denckla, M. B. (1996). Brain development, gender and IQ in children. A volumetric imaging study. *Brain, 119,* 1763–1774.

Rightmire, G. P. (2004). Brain size and encephalization in early to mid-Pleistocene *Homo. American Journal of Physical Anthropology, 124,* 109–123.

Rushton, J. P., & Ankey, C. D. (1996). Brain size and cognitive ability: Correlations with age, sex, social class, and race. *Psychonomic Bulletin and Review, 3,* 21–36.

Rushton, J. P., & Jensen, A. R. (2005). Thirty years of research on race differences in cognitive ability. *Psychology, Public Policy, and Law, 11,* 235–294.

Shackleton, N. J., Berger, A., & Peltier, W. R. (1990). An alternative astronomical calibration of the lower Pleistocene timescale based on ODP Site 677. *Transactions of the Royal Society of Edinburgh, Earth Science, 81,* 251–261.

Shackleton, N. J. (1995). New data on the evolution of Pliocene climate variability. In E. Vrba, G. H. Denton, T. C. Partridge, & L. H. Burckle (Eds.) *Paleoclimate and evolution with emphasis on human origins,* (pp. 242–248). New Haven, CT: Yale University Press.

Shackleton, N. J., Hall, M. A., & Pate, D. (1995). Pliocene stable isotope stratigraphy of Site 846. In N. G. Pisias, L. A. Janacek, A. Palmer-Julson, & T. H. Van Andel (Eds.) *Proceedings of the ocean drilling program, scientific results*: Vol. 138 (pp. 337–355). College Stanation: Ocean Drilling Program.

Sternberg R., Grigorenko E., & Bundy D. (2001). The predictive value of IQ. *Merrill-Palmer Quarterly, 47,* 1–41.

Vrba, E. S. (1995). The fossil record of African antelopes in relation to human evolution and paleoclimate. In E. S. Vrba, G. H. Denton, T. C. Partridge, & L. H.

Buckle (Eds.), *Paleoclimate and evolution, with emphasis on human origins.* New Haven, CT: Yale University Press.

Wickett, J. C., & Vernon, P. A. (1994). Peripheral nerve conduction velocity, reaction time, and intelligence: An attempt to replicate Vernon and Mori (1992). *Intelligence, 18,* 127–131.

Wickett, J. C., Vernon, P. A., & Lee, D. H. (2000). Relationships between factors of intelligence and brain volume. *Personality and Individual Differences, 29,* 1095–1122.

Willerman, L., Schultz, R., Rutledge, J. N., & Bigler, E. D. (1991). In vivo brain size and intelligence. *Intelligence, 15,* 223–228.

Chapter 14

Ecological Constraints on Mating Tactics

Aurelio José Figueredo, Barbara H. Brumbach,
Daniel N. Jones, Jon A. Sefcek,
Geneva Vásquez, and W. Jake Jacobs
University of Arizona

Mating tactics do not exist in a vacuum. Rather, they develop within specific environmental contexts. Such contextual influences can be conceptualized as a series of concentric circles around the individual, as in Bronfenbrenner's (1979) ecological model of behavioral development, that are hierarchically nested within each other like a set of Russian dolls. Bronfenbrenner placed behavioral development within an ecological perspective by combining principles from sociology and developmental psychology. Within Bronfenbrenner's theoretical framework, relationships between individuals and their environments are viewed as *mutually shaping*, in that they systematically interact with one another. He proposed four interlocking systems that purportedly shape early individual development: (1) *the micro-system*, which includes the individual's interactions with family and community (e.g., home, neighborhood); (2) *the meso-system*, which includes interrelationships among the various social settings within which the individual must function (e.g., schools, day-care centers); (3) *the exo-system*, which includes external forces upon which the individual has no direct control but which indirectly influence the individual (e.g., school boards, social service agencies, and planning commissions); and (4) *the macro-system*, which includes forces at the sociocultural level that provide the broad ideological and organizational patterns within which the lower levels of interaction play out. Although the Bronfenbrenner model was designed for understanding the forces governing child development, we may use a similar model to contextualize the adaptive significance of mating tactics within an ecological framework. Such ecological forces may be expected to inform and constrain the development of specific mating tactics. We propose that any evolutionarily meaningful conceptualization of Mating Intelligence must encompass an interactive engagement of the individual with those critical environmental contingencies. Mating Intelligence is partly intelligence about the socio-ecological context of mating.

Evolutionary theory also accommodates the role of environmental factors in the development and expression of behavior, but the general expectation is that such factors should elicit an evolved adaptive response from the organism, and not just an arbitrary "shaping," if they were reliably present in the evolutionary history of the species (e.g., Cosmides & Tooby, 1992). The essential difference from the Standard Social Science Model (*SSSM*) approach to such environmental influences is that evolutionary theory views the organismic responses as *strategic* and not randomly or passively reactive. This perspective does not deny the occasional existence of pathological and maladaptive responses, but predicts that they should be fairly rare within reasonably natural environments. However, although reaction to environmental factors is offered as a causal explanation by *SSSM* theories, these theories frequently fail to explain why a specific reaction to these influences would be functionally appropriate. For example, if father-absence predicts younger puberty and onset of sexual behavior among daughters, then *SSSM* theory might posit that father-absence leads girls to react to their existential loss by seeking a surrogate father-figure in the form of a boyfriend, but would not explain why that represents a fitness-promoting strategy, whereas the evolutionary developmental theory at least tries to identify some fitness benefits to reactive puberty-timing (e.g., Belsky, Steinberg, & Draper, 1991).

We should carefully delimit what is and what is not implied by the concept of a *strategic* response in evolutionary psychology. What distinguishes evolutionary thinking from the *SSSM* approach is the explicit consideration of the ultimate consequences of the organism's reactions for survival and reproduction. Thus, although an environmental stimulus might elicit a response from the organism, the nature of the response will be naturally selected based upon its effect on the environment, especially its effect on the fate of one's genes within that environment. Therefore, a truly ecological theory is not merely one that posits environmental explanations of behavior. Ecology is the study of the organism's *interactive and reciprocal relationship* with its environment, including other organisms. *Evolutionary* ecology goes further to analyze how this interaction might be *fitness-promoting*. The organism's response to its environment therefore has to make adaptive sense in order to be favored by natural selection over evolutionary time. Furthermore, evolutionary psychology demands that when one proposes an evolved adaptive mechanism, one does not merely posit an unspecified influence but instead identifies the operating characteristics of the proposed psychological mechanism in terms of specific *inputs* and *outputs* of the specialized subsystem.

The evolutionary-theoretical framework that we will be using to contextualize mating tactics is called Life History Theory. Life History Theory is a selectionist theory, based on evolutionary theory, which explains the coordinated allocation of bioenergetic and material resources to survival and reproduction across an individual's life-span. The theory describes variation in life-history strategy as a continuum from *r-selected* to *K-selected* allocation of resources. The theory characterizes K-selected species (e.g., humans, whales, elephants) as preferentially allocating bioenergetic resources to Somatic Effort (the continued survival of the organism) over Reproductive Effort (the production of new organisms), whereas r-selected species (e.g., cockroaches, mice, rabbits) preferentially allocate these same resources to Reproductive Effort over Somatic Effort. Of course, all organisms must invest in both Somatic and Reproductive Effort to survive and reproduce, because the latter is not possible without the former, but the difference between these two general classes of behavioral strategies lies in relative emphasis. Moreover, the theory suggests that when allocating Reproductive Effort, K-selected species preferentially allocate resources to Parental Effort (the survival of offspring) and Nepotistic Effort (the survival of kin) over Mating Effort (obtaining and retaining sexual partners) whereas r-selected species preferentially allocate resources to Mating Effort over both Parental Effort and Nepotistic Effort.

These fundamental allocations would necessarily inform and constrain the behavioral evolution and development of alternative mating tactics. That is because mating tactics need to be coordinated with a variety of related life-history traits for the allocation of resources among these fitness-enhancing activities to be optimal. Uncoordinated life-history traits, although perhaps individually efficacious, will inevitably create strategic interference with each other. For example, risky, impulsive courtship displays (a form of Mating Effort) might interfere with slow, careful body growth (a form of Somatic Effort), because early death tends to prevent further growth. Coordinated life-history traits, including appropriate mating tactics, should instead comprise a coherent reproductive strategy.

Life History Theory predicts that many human psychosocial traits will accumulate in adaptively coordinated ways, combining into intertwined functional composites or clusters that represent coadapted reproductive strategies (Figueredo, Vásquez, Brumbach, Schneider, Sefcek, et al., 2006). The core psychological characteristics clustering toward the low end of the "Differential K" continuum (a term used in relation to individual differences in levels of K-selected strategy among humans) entail a focus on short-term gains at the expense of long-term costs, numerous mates, and little parental investment. Within modern society, these low-K characteristics could manifest as impulsivity, short-term thinking, promiscuity, low female parental investment, little or no male parental investment, little social support, disregard for social rules, and extensive risk-taking. The core psychological characteristics at the high end of the Differential K continuum entail long-term considerations, selective mating, and high parental investment. Within modern society, these high-K characteristics could manifest as long-term thinking, monogamy, extensive parental investment, substantial social support structures, adherence to social rules (e.g., cooperation, altruism), and careful consideration of risks.

Our research group at the University of Arizona has recently documented large and reliable individual differences in a wide array of correlated life-history traits (Figueredo, Vásquez, Brumbach, Sefcek, Kirsner, & Jacobs, 2005; Figueredo, Vásquez, Brumbach, & Schneider, 2007, 2004; Figueredo, Vásquez, Brumbach, Schneider, Sefcek, Tal, Hill, Wenner, & Jacobs, 2006). This cluster of coordinated life-history traits, which we have called the "K-Factor," has a high heritability. A behavioral-genetic comparison of Monozygotic and Dizygotic twins revealed a heritability coefficient for the K-Factor of .65, yet this figure still permits a considerable amount of ecological flexibility during individual development (Figueredo, Vásquez, Brumbach, & Schneider, 2004). Thus, at the level of both behavioral evolution by natural selection and behavioral development by biologically prepared learning, life-history strategy is expected to be exquisitely responsive to the ambient ecology of the organism.

We propose that although life-history strategies are somewhat heritable, ecological factors can adaptively shape the life-history strategy of individuals. The life-history strategy of an individual, with its optimal allocations of bioenergetic and material resources to the various components of Somatic and Reproductive Effort, in turn adaptively shapes the selection of mating tactics. This shaping occurs by the complementary mechanisms of: (1) behavioral evolution by means of natural and sexual selection, and (2) behavioral development by means of biologically prepared learning (Figueredo, Hammond, & McKiernan, 2006). Furthermore, we propose that a hierarchy of environmental factors, from long-term evolutionary ecological conditions (e.g., climate), to immediate social contingencies (e.g., sex ratio within a local community), to family context during development (e.g. strong or weak kin support), to transient situations which the organism may encounter (e.g., spontaneous mating opportunities), shape individual life-history strategies in theoretically specifiable ways. We will therefore be proposing a hierarchy of specific ecological inputs and outputs of the proximate mechanisms presumed to be regulating life-history strategy. Life-history strategy will, in turn, be conceptualized as the primary organizing principle behind the evolution and development of mating tactics. Ecology will therefore constrain mating tactics through the mediating mechanism of life-history strategy. Evolutionary psychological theory conceives of the human mind as a product of the natural and sexual selective pressures that have acted over evolutionary time (see Geary, 2005; Figueredo, Hammond, & McKiernan, 2006). These natural and sexual selective pressures include the hierarchy of ecological constraints which we outline in this chapter. Thus, the emerging SUNY New Paltz model of Mating Intelligence presented in this volume should explicitly incorporate responsiveness to these ecological constraints on mating tactics as an essential operating characteristic of the dedicated and domain-specific mechanisms of Mating Intelligence.

Whereas the *SSSM* presumes that humans somehow possess an undirected and generalized sensitivity to the environment, Evolutionary Psychology instead expects that directed and adaptively appropriate responses to specific cues will be biologically prepared (Figueredo, Hammond, & McKiernan, 2006). Thus, a critic may doubt that the higher sociocultural levels of the Bronfenbrenner model are relevant to Evolutionary Psychology under the presumption that the supposed Pleistocene "Environment of Evolutionary Adaptedness" of humans contained no higher level of social organization than the simple hunter-gatherer band (e.g., Cosmides, Tooby, & Barkow, 1992). On the other hand, there is indirect archaeological and ethnographic evidence indicating that, at least since the late Pleistocene, most hunter-gatherer societies have probably possessed tribal-scale institutions among distant relatives that are substantially more complex than that of the small band, and have thus evolved behavioral-genetic "tribal instincts" as an adaptation to this higher level of social organization (Richerson & Boyd, 1998, 1999, 2001a, 2001b).

In addition, many Darwinian anthropologists and molecular geneticists maintain that human evolution did not end with the close of the Pleistocene, but instead continued well into the Holocene (e.g., Irons, 1998; Hrdy, 1999; Evans, Gilbert, Mekel-Bobrov, Vallender, Anderson, Vaez-Azizi, Tishkoff, Hudson, & Lahn, 2005; Mekel-Bobrov, Gilbert, Evans, Vallender, Anderson, Hudson, Tishkoff, & Lahn, 2005). The 10,000 years or more since the inception of agriculture have been more than enough time for gene-culture co-evolution to produce physiological and behavioral genetic adaptations to the dramatically altered conditions of existence (Irons, 1998; Lumsden & Wilson, 1981). Evidence for such continuing gene-culture co-evolution includes the finding that the geographic patterns of variation in the first principal component of gene frequencies for the six most important milk proteins in native European cattle breeds correlated with both the locations of European Neolithic cattle farming sites (−.75) and with the frequency of genes for lactose tolerance (−.59) in modern Europeans, the distribution of cattle farming sites being correlated (.73) with the lactase persistence gene frequencies (Beja-Pereiral et al.,

2003). Similarly, the spread of genes for sickle-cell anemia was correlated with the spread of the malaria parasite, its mosquito vectors, and ultimately with the clearing of patches of rainforest for the cultivation of yams in Africa (Durham, 1992; Coluzzi, 1999).

Given the massive changes in both morphology and behavior that have occurred in virtually all of our domesticated plants and animals in exactly the same time period (Palumbi, 2001), it is hard to believe that gene-culture co-evolution did not produce any significant changes in humans during the Holocene (Lumsden & Wilson, 1981). Arguably, these domesticates changed our "Adaptively Relevant Environments" (Irons, 1988) as much as we changed theirs. There is substantial molecular genetic evidence for massive population expansions and migrations during the Holocene over many large areas of the world, typically correlated with innovations in and intensification of food production (Cavalli-Sforza, Menozzi, & Piazza, 1993, 1994). It is therefore unreasonable to imagine that behavioral genetic changes in our mental adaptations to the more densely populated and complex societies produced by agriculture did not also occur during that period. Thus, the higher sociocultural levels of the Bronfenbrenner model are indeed relevant to the evolutionary psychology of mating intelligence.

THE EVOLUTIONARY ECOLOGICAL LEVEL

Although the Bronfenbrenner model only describes events occurring within developmental time, we will also consider changes occurring over evolutionary time (Figueredo, Hammond, & McKiernan, 2006). *Evolutionary* behavioral ecology addresses how the ecology affects the long-term evolution of behavior in entire populations, and not just the behavioral development of organisms within their individual lifetimes. Both physical and cultural ecology influence mating systems over evolutionary time. Physical ecology is referring to the material environment and cultural ecology is referring to the social environment.

Humans adapt to different ecological niches. The physical environment may vary in topography, climate, and ecology, which will influence types of subsistence methods (ways of getting food) humans adopt (Diamond, 1999). We propose that differences in physical ecology and subsistence economies will influence cultural ecology. For example, a cultural ecology is less likely to have extreme stratification among individuals based on wealth when it is difficult to maintain and hold resources in that physical ecology. Cultural ecologies vary across groups. Variation between cultures can exist because of variation in the physical ecology. Consequently, cultural variability may influence the variability in mating systems by means of differential life-history strategies. For example, oppressive patriarchal cultures may severely limit female mate choice, shifting the adaptive costs and benefits of different mating strategies. Depending on characteristics of the physical ecology, some cultural practices, traditions, and norms will enhance inclusive fitness better than others. Thus, differences in physical ecologies and subsistence methods influence cultural ecologies that, in turn, influence general mating systems.

During human evolution, it is likely that physical and cultural ecological conditions varied and that human mating systems may have been accordingly variable. We suggest that Mating Intelligence is best viewed within the broader context of physical and cultural ecologies. We predict that humans make systematic changes in mating systems based on the current ecology as a way to optimize the coordination of life-history strategies—specifically in relation to reproductive effort being differentially allocated between mating effort and parental effort. Groups must develop cultures that find the right balance between good-genes mate choice and high investment parenting. When the future is uncertain, it may be a better strategy to focus on mating effort (e.g., more offspring with higher genotypic diversity), as opposed to, when the future is certain it may be a better strategy to focus on parental effort (e.g., few offspring with lower genotypic diversity). An illustrative change in physical ecological conditions will provide a preliminary test of the hypothesized causal relations among physical and cultural ecology and mating systems.

One example of a major change in physical ecology is the shift in subsistence patterns brought on by the agricultural revolution. The onset of intensive agriculture had profound effects on the physical ecology of humans. Humans changed from having a somewhat nomadic lifestyle to one that was more sedentary. Since food production was typically focused on one or two staple crops, there was less variability in the diet. In addition, there was an increase in infectious disease due to increased population size and living in close proximity to domesticated animals. (Cavalli-Sforza, Menozzi, & Piazza, 1994; Diamond, 1999). During our evolutionary history, some physical ecologies contained resources that could be controlled by individuals, and some did not. For example, farmland can be defended by either groups or individuals. Such defense is only adaptive when the benefits of holding the land out-weigh the costs of defending it—which is usually true for societies whose subsistence relied on anything from small-scale horticulture to intensive agriculture. Some of the world's ecological niches will be more conducive to this type of farming (Cavalli-Sforza, Menozzi, & Piazza, 1994; Diamond, 1999).

We will first discuss two types of cultural ecologies, matrilineal and patrilineal societies, which are related to the ability to hold and control resources. Matrilineal and patrilineal cultures will first be discussed in the context of pre-agricultural subsistence economies. Then we will discuss the changes that happen in post-agricultural societies.

There are physical ecologies that *are not* conducive to individuals holding resources. Hunting and gathering societies represent good examples of such societies. Since land and animals cannot be passed on to offspring in these societies, it is likely that social status, rather than material resources, will be the primary competitive advantage to be passed down. In such societies where holding resources is difficult, it may not matter very much whether social status is passed down through female or male lines (Hrdy, 1999). For example, social status is passed down matrilineally (through the female line) in many nonhuman primates.

Societies in which it is hard for individuals to hold material resources tend to be more egalitarian, since there is less of an economic basis for social stratification. Consequently, the mating system is likely to support female mate choice of male qualities such as charisma or health, rather than resource-holding potential (wealth). These mating practices are conducive to a matrilineal social structure in which social status and resources are passed along the female line. Although status and resources can be passed directly from mother to daughter, in humans that transfer of resources is usually made more indirectly through the female line. For example, transfer can be made to the mother's brother's or sisters' sons (Gaulin, 1997; Hrdy, 1999; Warner, Lee, & Lee, 1986). Since there is less direct male investment in females' offspring, there is less need for the mother to ensure the husband's paternity of the children. Consequently, in matrilineal societies, females tend to have more sexual freedom. For example, the Canela, a matrilineal group in Brazil, follow this pattern. They live in an unpredictable and resource-scarce environment in which the male mortality rate is high. When a Canela woman finds that she is pregnant, she may try to have sexual relations with several men (usually of high status) other than the husband, presumably to confuse paternity. Each male lover is less likely to kill, abuse, or neglect her child, since he may be the father. In this way, the mother may secure investment and protection from several men, rather than gambling on investment exclusively from a single mate who is likely to die young. During traditional Canela marriage ceremonies, the couple is reminded to stay together until all of their children have grown up, to tolerate each other's affairs, and to remember that the welfare and survival of the child is more important than the man controlling the wife's sexuality (Hrdy, 1999).

In contrast, other physical ecologies *are* conducive to individuals holding resources. Societies that practiced small-scale horticulture, or had other resources (such as grazing lands or domesticated animals) that could be held, are examples of societies that predate the emergence of intensive agriculture. If there is potential for holding material resources, it tends to be the men doing the controlling. This results in mating systems where males have intense intra-sexual competition for resources, and consequently, are likely to have male stratification in status based on ability to hold and control economic resources (Ellis, 2001; Hrdy, 1997; Smuts, 1995).

This type of society tends to encourage female mate-choice based on male resource holding potential and wealth. Because females should want these resources passed to their offspring, they should try to ensure the husband's paternity certainty regarding the children. Consequently, the mating system will likely have high paternal investment, and resources will almost invariably pass down the male lineage, in a patrilineal pattern (Hrdy, 1997; Smuts, 1995). In these societies, female chastity is valued and females are punished much more heavily for infidelity. For example, the Maya in Mexico and Central America reinforce norms of female fidelity and ensure paternity certainty through religious doctrine. Women are fearful of going out unchaperoned at night because they risk being harmed by the demon H'ık'al. In one variation of this myth, the demon captures women who have not followed the menstruation rules or who have behaved immodestly, rapes them, and then the women die from giving perpetual birth (Hrdy 1997, 1999).

The impact that the agricultural revolution had on cultural ecologies and ultimately on mating systems can be considered a natural experiment. After the introduction of intensive agriculture, there would have been definite property (e.g., farm land and domestic animals) to pass on to offspring (Diamond, 1999). If a society had originally been *patrilineal*, then this change may have accentuated the properties of the existing system. For example, there were even bigger winners and losers because there was even more property that could be controlled by an individual, leading to even greater male stratification. The population would have increased, there would have been more specialization in jobs, and there would have been more complex religious and political organization. Ultimately however, since the mating system was originally based on small-scale resource holding potential and female choice of the most wealthy males, the system would have stayed basically the same, if more extreme. For example, even stricter rules about female chastity and adultery would have developed (cf., Wemple, 1981).

The agricultural revolution, however, would have had a very different impact on societies that were originally *matrilineal*. Since matrilineal systems can exist when there are not resources to hold and pass down to offspring, intensive agriculture would have produced major changes. The strategic cultural change would have been to adopt patriliny and the mating strategies associated with *that* social structure. In fact, as soon as intensive agriculture is introduced to a matrilineal society, it invariably changes to a patrilineal society (Hrdy, 1999).

Mating tactics should differ between patrilineal groups and matrilineal groups. Consequently, what is an "intelligent" or adaptive mating tactic in one social structure may not be in the other. There are two ways that adaptive mating tactics might arise from different types of social structure. First, there could have been gene-culture co-evolution, in which humans were genetically flexible with their social structure before the agricultural revolution but became more genetically canalized toward patriliny with the onset of large-scale agriculture. Individuals might become evolution-arily predisposed towards mating strategies that work best in patrilineal societies (i.e., males competing for high status and resources, females act-ing in ways to ensure paternity certainty). An alternative scenario, how-ever, is that humans evolved more developmental sensitivity to the inter-related set of environmental cues that signal monopolizable resources, patriliny, wealth-based social status, female choice for paternal invest-ment, and male concern with paternity. In the latter scenario, Mating Intel-ligence would include an individual's ability to properly assess the envi-ronment and employ the mating tactics best suited to the current social structure.

THE SOCIETAL LEVEL

The societal level is comprised of many sociocultural constraints including social customs, morals, norms, values, and laws, which affect individu-als, but which they cannot individually control (Brofenbrenner, 1979). From an adaptationist perspective, this may be considered one of the more abstract, larger-scale psychological components of the *adaptive landscape,* or set of selective forces which act upon individuals. This system itself is composed of a hierarchical assortment of subsystems, in which specific values or norms may apply only in certain sub-populations. For example, Western culture varies from country to country, city to city, street to street, and house to house. As such, behavior that is seen as "dysfunctional" within one cultural niche may be functional within a different cultural niche. For example, beating a rival to death may boost one's reputation and mating success in a criminal gang, but would raise eye-brows in most faculty meetings.

The importance of this system can be illustrated by considering behav-ioral norms in relation to the concept of "mental disorder". Some current estimates suggest that approximately 50 percent of Americans will be diagnosed with a mental disorder at least once in their lifetime. Such a high prevalence of maladaptive behavior is surprising from an adapta-tionist standpoint, leading researchers such as Wakefield (1992) and Nesse (1999) to propose that such "disorders" may have yielded some hidden adaptive benefits under ancestral conditions. In this view, the mismatch between prehistoric small-group living and modern urban living causes previously adaptive strategies (e.g., depression, schizotypy, phobias) to appear maladaptive.

This mismatch perspective might illuminate the personality "disorder" of psychopathy. Behaviorally, psychopaths are egocentric and grandiose, ruthlessly goal-directed, Machiavellian and dominant, insensitive to risk, impulsive, and lacking in basic social emotions. Mealey (1995) offered a general evolutionary account of this suite of behaviors, arguing that it is an adaptive strategy in which there may be a continuum of heritable psychopathic mating tactics, ranging from hard-wired, empathy-blind rapists to morally flexible opportunists. This perspective is supported by evidence suggesting "deficiencies" in psychopaths' brain systems governing empathy, fear, and startle responses (Blair, 2003; Patrick, 1994), and "abnormal" brain activation patterns in facial-emotion-recognition tasks (Gordon, Baird, & End, 2004). On the other hand, psychopaths show lower levels of fluctuating asymmetry, a standard marker of "developmental instability" or maladaptedness (Lalumiere, Harris, & Rice, 2001), as compared to non-psychopathic criminals. We argue that not only are many psychopathic traits (e.g., Machiavellianism) adaptive (Wilson, Near, & Miller, 1996), but following Mealey, we suggest that they collectively represent a coherent reproductive strategy—one of intraspecific social parasitism and sexual exploitation. Within certain socio-cultural niches, psychopathic strategies may increase reproductive success, particularly when psychopaths' decreased startle, fear, empathy, and remorse would make them more effective at using coercive tactics (e.g., cheating, stealing, raping, and killing). Thus, the degree of psychopathic behavior may reflect the degree of biological preparedness (the genetic "push" given the right environment), for that strategy that is inherited by any given individual (Figueredo, 1995).

Yet, do these behaviors really represent a functionally adaptive strategy? Universally, psychopathic behaviors are considered morally repulsive, and psychopaths are considered *cheaters* in every sense of the word. Psychopathy clashes with prevailing sociocultural standards of behavior as codified in criminal law (e.g., there is a 20–70 percent prevalence rate of psychopathy in U.S. prisons, making psychopathy nearly synonymous with criminality). Hare (1993) reports that features of real psychopaths include promiscuity, philandering, multiple marriages over their lifetime, and multiple children with multiple partners. Each of these tendencies can increase reproductive success relative to non-cheaters within the same population. Further, currently incarcerated psychopaths may just be the ones that were not adept enough at their strategy to get away with such behaviors. This perspective leads us to what we term the *harmful function model* of psychopathy; essentially, psychopaths suffer from an *ethical pathology* (Wiebe, 2004), which is socially harmful to everyone else, but

which may be adaptively functional, subjectively enjoyable, and reproductively successful for the individual.

In this view, it is the societal context of psychopathic behavior that is
the problem. Ultimately, what is moral or adaptive from the standpoint
of "society" may be different from what is adaptively functional for certain
individuals. A five-year prison term for a five-minute rape may not sound
like a rationally desirable outcome, but it is an outcome that evolution
might favor, as part of a psychopathic mating strategy, under certain conditions. Thus, we may view the problem of psychopathy as one of conflict between different reproductive strategies, perhaps existing in a frequency-dependent dynamic equilibrium. The interests ascribed by social
scientists to "society" as a whole are nothing more than those of the dominant reproductive life history strategy, which stand in conflict with those
of the psychopathic "cheaters."

Miller (2004, personal communication) has offered a cultural analogy
to illustrate this principle of context-specificity. When playing violent
"first-person shooter" computer games, such as Half-Life 2 and Grand
Theft Auto, we adopt the role of a psychopath, for fun. We become insensitive to the true costs of risky behavior (we get multiple 'lives'), we don't
worry about police retribution for impulsivity, there is no moral ambiguity about our mission, we become egocentric and grandiose about who
we are and what our goal is, and we feel nothing for our "victims." While
computer-gamers become temporarily psychopathic in the game context,
this behavior does not seem to generalize to the real world—it is an enter-
taining form of self-inflicted, transient psychopathy. Real psychopaths
simply bring the same gaming mind-set into their real social and sexual
interactions.

We may therefore align ourselves with Wakefield's (1992) *harmful dysfunction model* of human mental disorders, yet focus on the ever-changing
modern environment rather than on differences between the Pleistocene
and today. This perspective fits perfectly into the Brofenbrenner framework because it construes "functionality" as biology working under particular sociocultural constraints. The human environment has changed
dramatically over the Holocene (the last 10,000 years). From agriculture
to agri-business, and bronze-age industry to industrial revolutions, many
aspects of modern life never existed before. Over the past 300–500 years
alone, we switched from small pre-industrial farming towns to post-indus-
trial technological mega-cities, and from semi-arranged patriarchal marriages to speed dating. Psychopaths flourish in mega-cities with speed dating. Given that such psychopath-conducive environments probably did
not exist in previous human evolutionary history, psychopathy itself may
be a newly emerging adaptation associated with an increasingly complex
society. A strong version of our hypothesis would predict that, if molecular behavior genetics finds alleles that predict psychopathy, those alleles

will be only several hundred to a few thousand years old (no more ancient than the socio-cultural conditions that favor opportunistic, coercive mating strategies), and have been spreading rapidly. Also, the partially facultative (developmentally flexible) nature of psychopathy (at least for "secondary psychopaths") suggests that Mating Intelligence mechanisms would necessarily involve an evolved sensitivity to socio-cultural cues (e.g. mobility, anonymity, gullibility) that predict when psychopathy will pay.

THE FAMILIAL LEVEL

Human family structures influence our mating strategies and are unique in many respects, including the unprecedented number of years of investment that we devote to our offspring. One cause of this investment is that our offspring, who are among the most altricial, or helpless, within the animal kingdom, would perish before the age of reproductive maturity without high investment. However, viewed from an evolutionary standpoint, the helplessness of human infants reveals our generally K-selected life-history strategy. Furthermore, the helplessness of babies is intimately connected to a large suite of other traits that are typical of our species, but not very common among other animals, including our longevity, large brains, maternal milk production, and paternal investment. The necessity for parental investment, inherent in K-selected life-history strategies, constrains the human allocation of mating effort, especially for high-investing mothers and fathers. Because we assume that the average person possesses a limited amount of resources, including time, those people who invest heavily into the survival and growth of their children will tend to have less time for finding and investing in additional mating opportunities, including extra-pair copulations.

A favored explanation for the extended developmental period of humans, in the emerging field of evolutionary developmental psychology, is that humans need a long childhood to learn the social skills necessary to navigate through the complexities of human groups (cf., Ellis & Bjorklund, 2005). The development of mating intelligence may be central to this process, since courtship, sexual competition, and mate choice must be among the most complex social tasks that a human will ever face.

Although there are countless ways in which families seem to influence human mating tactics, in this section we will focus on only two. The first will be the way that fathers influence the mating tactics of daughters. Although paternal investment is not required to ensure a child's survival in some human societies, the average amount of paternal investment in offspring is remarkable—humans are the only species of primate that invests extensive paternal care while living in groups that include complex multi-male coalitions (Flinn & Ward, 2005). Again, this is likely due to the altricial nature of our offspring. However, these observations beg the question: What happens when fathers don't invest? While boys experience a variety of correlates of father absence, such as increased delinquency, aggression, and other indicators of high mating effort, one of the most widely studied aspects of familial influence on mating strategies is the effect of father absence on daughters (Draper & Belsky, 1990).

Belsky, Steinberg, and Draper (1991) offered an evolutionary theory of socialization based on a previous theory of father absence proposed by Draper and Harpending (1982). They posited that several features of the family environment during the first seven years of life, including father absence, could set daughters on a developmental trajectory toward early puberty and sexual behavior, because the familial micro-environment serves as a litmus test of the social macro-environment in which girls will find themselves. In particular, if one's own father was absent and uninvesting, then perhaps other males in the local mating market will act similarly, and it would be prudent not to count on them as long-term providers. This leads to the development of an appropriate (more r-selected) life-history strategy for the macro-environment, which leads to adoption of the optimal (more short-term) mating strategy given the socio-ecological conditions. Familial stressors associated with low paternal investment are correlated with a variety of physical and psychological outcomes among daughters, including early menarche, initiation of sexual activity, and age at first birth; higher incidence of affective disorders; and greater likelihood of reproductive system cancers and obesity (Ellis, 2004). These all comprise elements of lower-K (high mating effort, high fertility) life-history strategies.

Certain revisions of Belsky et al.'s (1991) evolutionary socialization model have challenged the view that all daughters are equally prone to the specified outcomes. These theories, including Belsky's (2005) revision (suggesting differential susceptibility to environmental influence), have stressed the importance of genetic contributions to the development of an individual's life history strategy and the likelihood of father absence. In a twin study, Figueredo, Vásquez, Brumbach, and Schneider (2004) found that life history strategy, as measured by many indicators (including father absence), is highly heritable. Furthermore, studies find that the behavioral outcomes in daughters (e.g., precocious sexuality) are much smaller if the father absence is due to accidental death (which is less likely to reflect heritable personality and life-history traits) than if the father absence is due to divorce or abandonment (which is more likely to reflect heritable personality and life-history traits) (cf., Krohn & Bogan, 2001). Adding further weight to theory that genetic factors play a role in the correlation between father absence and sexual strategy outcomes, Comings et al. (2002) found that a variant X-linked androgen receptor gene seemed to predispose fathers to absence from their children and predispose daughters to precocious sexuality and other outcomes described by Belsky et al. (1991). Thus, recent evidence suggests that the typical familial ecology in which one's ancestors evolved may exert a great deal of influence upon an individual's adoption of a sexual strategy. However, the fact that a person's family history, in the broadest sense, influences his or her sexual behavior does not negate the necessity for environmental input, and none of the lines of evidence regarding genetic influence upon life history strategy have suggested that genes are responsible for all of the variance in a person's sexual strategy. Instead, to unite the two perspectives described above, it seems that father absence, and its mating-strategy correlates, is a condition that some individuals are more biologically prepared for than others. Father absence, especially for some individuals, serves as trigger for early sexual maturity, early mating behavior, and lower expectations regarding paternal investment.

The two decades of life that human females often experience after menopause also influence our mating decisions (Hrdy, 1999). Although the longevity of post-menopausal women may have arisen to allow mothers to survive long enough to see their lastborn child reach adulthood, research indicates an additional benefit of the post-menopausal phase. Maternal grandmothers often use their later years to increase their inclusive fitness by channeling resources to their children and grandchildren. Hawkes et al. (1998) found that, compared to primate species in which females do not experience a long post-menopausal phase, human females can breed faster, with more closely spaced offspring. In many hunter-gather societies grandmothers provide more food to children than do young mothers (cf., Hrdy, 1999). A recent census suggests that roughly four million grandmothers are the primary caretakers of their grandchildren in the United States. (Hrdy, 1999). It is likely that the mothers whose children are being reared by grandmothers are capitalizing on their assistance to practice lower-K life history strategies while increasing the survival rates of their offspring. Hrdy (1999) even suggested that female teenagers who think their mothers will help them in caring for offspring are more likely to get pregnant than girls who think their mothers would not offer childcare assistance. If this is indeed the case, it seems to be an example of Mating Intelligence at work in the adoption of an alternative reproductive strategy. As with male psychopathy, what looks like a pathology at first glance (teen pregnancy) may turn out to have a hidden adaptive logic.

The facts above suggest that, while some people may be more easily influenced by certain environmental cues, almost all people can use a wide array of cues to adjust their mating behaviors to their socio-ecological context. Due to conditions experienced by their ancestors, some individuals may be more prepared to respond to scarcity of resources as a cue to adopt a lower-K strategy while others may be more prepared to respond to familial cues. For example, throughout much of human history, it is likely that girls who were raised in father-absent conditions were likely to find, once they reached adulthood, that other men within their social group were also unwilling to invest in long-term partners or children. However, because of gene-culture evolution and both sexes' susceptibility to environmental influences, the same girls were also likely to live in social groups in which women, namely mothers and daughters, lived in close proximity to one another and invested in each other's offspring. By investing in the offspring of their daughters, and channeling investment into their offspring from their own mothers, women in this social situation might attain equal fitness to women in societies in which men invest heavily into their own children. Although the two situations represent different strategies, both are examples of Mating Intelligence at work.

THE INDIVIDUAL LEVEL

Individuals who pursue varied reproductive strategies may have certain intra-psychic processes (e.g., obedience to authority, conformity, tolerance for dissonance) which aid in achieving reproductive success. Such intra-psychic processes may serve immediate functions such as staying out of trouble, facilitating good peer relations, and avoiding inconsistency among behavioral tactics. However, the benefits of such processes may depend strongly on the environment and the life-history strategy of the individual. Stable environments which favor higher-K life-history strategies are likely to select for individuals who favor a stable social structure, invest in kin and social networks, learn from their relatives and friends, and benefit from consistent behavior. As a result, individuals with higher-K life-history strategies should be more obedient to authority, conform more to social norms, and maintain higher consistency in cognitions. In contrast, unstable environments favoring lower-K life-history strategies may select for individuals who are high in Machiavellianism, antisocial tendencies, and opportunistic and random behaviors. As a result, individuals with lower-K life-history strategies should be less obedient to authority, conform less, and have lower consistency in beliefs and behaviors. Thus we hypothesize that certain intra-psychic processes are ultimately the result of the selective pressures placed upon individuals given a specific ecological niche and based upon their life-history strategy.

The Theory of Cognitive Dissonance (Festinger, 1957) is a good example of an intra-psychic process which is likely to have evolved as a means of maintaining a cohesive life-history strategy. Cognitive Dissonance theory states that when an individual has two competing cognitions, such as freely advocating a position one is opposed to, the individual will be motivated to reduce the discomfort (dissonance) associated with the discrepancy of the cognitions. Furthermore, individuals will avoid situations likely to create a discrepancy between cognitions. Festinger (1957) also noted that individuals are likely to differ with respect to their tolerance for dissonance.

We propose that such differences in tolerance for dissonance are likely to hinge upon the reproductive costs and benefits of behavioral consistency for a given individual. For example, individuals with a higher-K life-history strategy are likely to invest in their careers, relationships, and children, and be long-term planners. Behaving inconsistently with one's moral beliefs or social commitments (e.g., quitting a job, cheating on a partner) might impose serious reproductive costs (e.g., loss of a job, partner, or friends) in the long run. Thus, the discomfort of dissonance would lead an individual with a higher-K life-history strategy to avoid inconsistency, proximately to avoid the associated discomfort, but ultimately to save the individual from such reproductive costs. Additionally, if he or she did make a change (e.g., new partner, new job), the individual with a higher-K life-history strategy is likely to adapt by changing their beliefs (e.g., "I hated that job") to match the new situation and restore consistency. Likewise, if the new behavior or situation is destructive, consistency can also be restored by changing the inconsistent behavior or by vowing never to behave in such an inconsistent way again (e.g., "I'll never cheat again"). In situations where ephemeral changes or inconsistencies are likely to be short-lived, such individuals are likely to use dissonance reduction strategies such as self-affirmation or trivialization, which would reduce the discomfort of dissonance while still maintaining a strong internal need for consistency, maintaining overall integrity.

Conversely, individuals with a lower-K life-history strategy may have fewer consistency needs. Since uncertain environments favor opportunistic over planned (higher-K) behaviors, consistency may be undesirable. As a result, individuals who pursue lower-K life-history strategy are not likely to benefit from consistency, resulting in reduced inhibitions and a reduced need to rationalize behavior. For example, individuals who are not constrained by consistency can behave in ways that suit them best in the short term, and while consistency may pay off eventually, low-K individuals are not interested in long-term payoffs. These life-history strategies may further play out in moral domains, as outlined in Kohlberg's (1969) stages of moral development. Low-K individuals might benefit from developing simpler, short-term moral values such that they only avoid punishment and gain rewards. To progress beyond such simple rules to viewing others' perspectives may only be adaptive within stable and long-term social relationships, which high-K individuals are better suited for.

Cognitive consistency, beyond its role in maintaining a cohesive reproductive strategy, is also likely to create a perception of integrity in the consistent individual, because she does what she says and says what she does.
Thus, higher-K individuals are also likely to prize integrity and consistency as
desirable traits in a partner, which, in addition to being desirable, may
themselves create consistency, predictability, and comfort in social interactions, and may also signal things like long-term pair-bonding, fidelity, and
parental investment.

The attributions (internal vs. external) that individuals make based
on positive or negative outcomes comprise an important dimension in
how an individual interprets his or her environment (Heider, 1958). Further, one's attribution style is another intra-psychic process that may be
related to life-history strategy. For example, an individual who decides to
go to college but fails, can make an internal attribution (e.g., "I am not
smart enough for college") or an external attribution (e.g., "the professors
didn't like me") for the failure outcome. An individual who makes an
external attribution regarding college failure might attempt to try a different college, since he or she may think they will succeed if future professors are more agreeable. In contrast, an individual who makes an internal attribution regarding college failure is likely to skip any future college
attempts. Individuals who pursue higher-K life-history strategies benefit
from long-term planning, learning from their mistakes, and thinking in
terms of the long run. Therefore, it is likely that individuals with a higher-
K life-history strategy will make more accurate attributions whether they
be internal or external regarding both their successes and failures.
Although such accurate attributions may at times be unpleasant, they have
the potential for a long-term pay off by allowing the individual to adjust
and learn from past situations. Because higher-K life-history strategies
are often pursued in the context of long-term stable environments, accurate attributions, even if self-effacing at times, are likely to pay off over
time. Thus, by acknowledging one's own limitations by making internal
attributions to failure when necessary could help avoid bad long-term
outcomes, which may result in higher-K individuals experiencing tempo-
rary depression or negative affect in the face of failure. Internal attributions for success would provoke approaching situations where one's abilities are rewarded, and would lead to more favorable future outcomes and
increased positive affect for higher-K individuals. Likewise, however,
external attributions to success, when appropriate, may keep an individual from pursuing a behavior that may have paid off once, but is not likely
to pay off over time. Moreover, attribution style may also be a strong mating indicator in the sense that, over time, accurate attributions may create
the perception of maturity and self-awareness, which would be an attractive quality for those seeking a long-term partner, whereas "passing the

buck" (e.g., inappropriate external attributions to failure) may pay off in the short term, but eventually foster a negative image of immaturity and narcissism in the minds of other group members.

Individuals with a lower-K life-history strategy are likely to benefit from a preponderance of self-enhancing attributions rather than accurate ones (i.e., mostly external attributions for failure and internal attributions for success). Consistently denying failure and accepting success may create the positive self-perception and confidence necessary for short-term opportunistic behaviors, even though such behavior may be seen as hypocritical and self-serving over the longer term. Since individuals who pursue lower-K life-history strategies live in unstable environments and try to mate with more people, changing one's behavior (due to any internal attribution for failure) may be maladaptive, as such behavior may be adaptive later in the ever-changing environment, or when encountering a new person. For example, a lower-K person may approach a prospective partner in a certain way and get rejected. If he or she attributes the rejection to their approach tactic, he or she might fail to use that tactic again, even though it may work in a different situation with a different person. A lower-K life-history strategist benefits from opportunistic behavior as well, thus, making any internal attributions for failure might discourage future opportunistic behavior. Furthermore, the positive benefit of self-accuracy over time is not likely to pay-off for lower-K individuals, since they are only interested in the short-term.

We propose that intra-psychic processes such as obedience to authority, conformity, cognitive dissonance, and attributional style have evolved to serve individuals based upon their particular ecological niches and life-history strategies. However, differences in life-history strategy may interact with other individual difference variables to limit the utility of these intra-psychic mechanisms. For example, individuals who are high in self-monitoring (Synder, 1974) and who pursue higher-K life-history strategies may have unique intra-psychic processes aimed at maximizing reproductive success, such as higher tolerance for dissonance (Geher et al., 2005). Thus, an individual may pursue a generally high-K life-history strategy but also opportunistically exploit certain short-term opportunities, without cognitive dissonance. Such an adaptively hypocritical individual might better exploit short-term opportunities while presenting minimal risk to more important long-term investments, thereby maximizing reproductive potential when the ecology would favor such an approach.

In sum, we hypothesize that the ultimate objective of pursuing a cohesive life-history strategy will lead to more specific proximate mechanisms such as a need for consistency, obedience to authority, conformity, and attributional style, which have generally favored the survival and reproduction of individuals.

THE SITUATIONAL LEVEL

Surprisingly little theoretical work has tried to categorize fitness-relevant situations. In this section, we address that shortcoming, focusing on social situations that influence the mating tactics exhibited by adult humans.

An individual's immediate environment offers 'affordances' (Gibson, 1979) or 'stimulus support' (Tolman, 1932) that constrain an individual's behavioral options. The relevant affordances in mating situations include the: (1) potential mates, (2) sexual rivals, (3) other socially relevant individuals (e.g., mates' and rivals' friends and families), and (4) mating strategies available to the individual.

Any mating situation consists of adaptive problems encountered during intrasexual or intersexual cooperation and conflict and the extant mating strategies of the target individual. The adaptive problems that an individual faces in a mating situation logically fall into several distinct classes (aside from those generated by individual differences in the mating strategies of the particular cooperators or competitors involved). Each of these distinct classes calls for a corresponding set of distinct mating tactics. Four distinct classes of sexual cooperation are: Male-Male intrasexual cooperation (MM+); Female-Female intrasexual cooperation (FF+); Male-Female intersexual cooperation (MF+); and Female-Male intersexual cooperation (FM+). Four distinct classes of sexual conflict are: Male-Male intrasexual conflict (MM−); Female-Female intrasexual conflict (FF−); Male-Female intersexual conflict (MF−); and Female-Male intersexual conflict (FM−). Each of these classes can be further subdivided into long-term and short-term mating contexts. Furthermore, any specific situation might involve a complex combination of cooperation and conflict (a 'mixed-motive game' in game theory terms) among the interacting individuals. For the moment, we will describe just the four basic classes of sexual conflict—the basic modes of strategic interference among different individuals' reproductive interests.

Females are the limiting resource for male reproduction because any male that attracts more than one mate does so at the expense of other males within the same mating market. To the extent that these two conditions hold, the logical distinction drawn above will also hold in the natural environment; distinct sets (and thereby classes) of adaptive problems are marked empirically by these four forms of intraspecific sexual conflict.

The first situation involves Male-Female intersexual conflict (MF−). Here, we expect the female to set the adaptive problems—the male must convince the female that his genetic material or parental investment potential is the best available to that female. Under these circumstances, we expect the male to exhibit fitness displays related to the female's apparent preferences, such as displays of athletic prowess, risk taking, humor, resources, honesty, fidelity, and the like. These may be honest or dishonest displays.

A second situation involves Female-Male intersexual conflict (FM-). Here, we expect the male to set the adaptive problems—the female must convince the male that, if he is to invest, *her* genetic material or parental investment potential is the best available to that male. Under these circumstances, we expect the female to exhibit fitness displays related to the male's apparent preferences, displays that maximize indicators of fecundity such as hip to waist ratio, clear skin, shiny hair, sexual interest as well as humor, honesty, fidelity, and the like. These may be honest or dishonest displays. This fact sets a second set of adaptive problems for the female: She must detect dishonest displays. Hence, we expect the female to 'interview' the male, examining the honesty of his display.

A third situation involves Male-Male intrasexual conflict (MM-). Here, we expect the competing male to set the primary adaptive problems. Assuming that females can observe the outcome of MM-, the male's adaptive problem is to achieve higher status than other males, which will attract the largest quantity or quality of female mates. Thus, males should pursue strategies that advance his relative status or dominance in the male community. He may use some of the same strategies that he uses in MF-, such as resource or fitness-indicator displays, but he may also use aggressive strategies specific to male-male competition.

A fourth situation involves Female-Female intrasexual conflict (FF-). Here, we expect the competing female to set the primary adaptive problems. Assuming that the genetic quality of males varies, the adaptive problem for the female is to attract and retain the best possible male genes in the face of competition from other females. Under these circumstances, we expect the female to display her reproductive potential to its best advantage (e.g., fertility, maternal care ability), and to denigrate the reproductive potential of her rivals.

The diversity of these situations and individual differences related to them (see e.g., Shoda & Mischel, 1995), would impose selection for the abilities to discriminate among them, to assess the relevant adaptive problems (e.g., to "mind read" the intentions of others; see Baron-Cohen, 1997, 2003), and to adjust behavioral tactics appropriately. In addition, we expect behavioral tactics to be adaptively modulated by subjective estimates of one's own mate value and mating strategies relative to that of rivals and potential mates. Thus, adaptive mating behavior should be controlled through both immediate environmental contingencies *and* evolved 'behavioral rules' (rule governance; e.g., Baum, 2005; Catania, 1990; Hayes, 1989).

Hence, adaptive mating tactics should take into account (1) the class of mating situation (MF-, FM-, MM-, or FF-), (2) the relative mate values and mating strategies of each potential mate and rivals, (3) one's available fitness indicators and competitive tactics, (4) instinctive or learned estimates of the costs, benefits, and risks of different indicators and tactics given the mating situation, relative mate values, and different mating strategies of each relevant individual. Given that situations tend to repeat themselves and that relative mate values and mating tactics tend to remain stable, the organism, at maturity, produces distinct and individually unique behavioral signatures (e.g., Mischel, Shoda, & Mendoza-Denton, 2002; Shoda & Smith, 2004). Furthermore, dispositional traits such as life-history strategies will moderate how an organism responds to different situations, generating a spectrum of behavioral signatures that match individual differences in strategic objectives. For example, the choice of long-term or short-term mating tactics will be partially influenced by the individual's overall life-history strategy.

The most immediate level of an organism's ecology is the set of transient social situations encountered, each of which set the occasion for specific actions—or behavioral tactics—to occur (Mischel, 1968; Skinner, 1938). These tactics either work or don't, given the situation; those that work tend to be repeated when the organism re-encounters the situation; those that don't tend to drop out of the organism's behavioral repertoire (Baum, 2005). Tendencies to retain and reproduce 'successful' behavioral tactics generate individually distinct, situation-contingent behavioral signatures, which one can use to predict future behavior (e.g., Schmajuk, Lamoureaux, & Holland, 1998; Shoda & Mischel, 1995).

Hence, we predict that behavioral strategies, acquired in a specific situation through selective mechanisms such as those described above, generalize to those situations falling within the same taxonomic class. The specific tactics used in each situation, however, will depend upon the perceived affordances present in that situation (e.g., Gibson, 1974).

Consider, for example, that males typically learn appropriate intersexual behavior. The family (parents and perhaps siblings) is the foundational source of training for social and sexual behavior in the home. Peer groups, however, are the foundational source of training for social and sexual behavior outside of the home (see Harris, 1995, 1998, 2005 for extensive reviews). Now consider such behavior outside of the home.

For most humans, especially in ancestral hunter-gatherer societies, there are no special training and no special schools. Instead, individuals in local peer groups dictate the contingencies, which shape social and sexual behavior in any given situation. If both same sex and opposite sex peers respond well to first attempts, the male learns and continues the appropriate behavior. If the male doesn't get it right the first few times, he may well withdraw into shyness, insecurities, inferiority feelings, simply give up, or, if options are available, seek other peer groups.

In short, males receive extensive training in the form of modeled examples, verbal rules, and immediate social and sexual consequences for appropriate and inappropriate behavior (see Baum, 2005 for an extended review of these principles), both in their home environment and in their extended social environment. Conversely, sexually coercive males have been shown to use "Macho" tactics, more suited to intermale competition (MM−), in their courtship of females (Lalumiere et al., 1996). Thus, resorting to sexually coercive tactics may result from a failure to discriminate between different classes of mating situation.

As these examples illustrate, structured experience supports discrimination, shaping, and continued practice of social skills in each of main sexual situations (MF, FM, MM, or FF) we described. Thus, any adaptive, dedicated, domain-specific Mating Intelligence should take into account these distinct mating situations, their associated cues, and the selective contingencies inherent to them.

CONCLUSION

We have reviewed a hierarchy of nested environmental levels (the evolutionary-ecological, the societal, the familial, the individual, and the situational) in which both physical and social ecology constrain mating tactics. These ecological contexts shape, but do not dictate, which particular mating tactics are optimal. Other individual differences (such as biologically prepared life-history strategy, genetic quality, phenotypic condition, available resources, and reproductive history) are also expected to influence mating tactics. For example, young, healthy, child-less individuals can afford to invest heavily in mating effort, even if they are genetically predisposed towards high parental effort once children arrive. A dedicated, domain-specific psychological mechanism of Mating Intelligence should be specifically adapted to detect and respond to external cues regarding the appropriateness of mating tactics within each specific ecological context. So, mating tactics should not be studied in a vacuum, as in some oversimplified game theory models and much evolutionary psychological research. Instead, Mating Intelligence should be contextualized within the surrounding physical and social ecology, so reproductive costs and benefits of different mating tactics can be adequately assessed. Further research on the nature and functions of Mating Intelligence should explicitly consider the complex ecological and situational variables that constrain mating tactics.

REFERENCES

Baron-Cohen, S. (1997). *Mindblindness: An essay on autism and theory of mind.* Cambridge, MA: MIT Press.

Baron-Cohen, S. (2004). *The essential difference: The truth about the male and female brain.* London: Penguin.

Baum, W. M. (2005). *Understanding behaviorism* (2nd Edition). Malden, MA: Blackwell Publishing.

Beja-Pereiral, A., Luikart, G., England, P. R., Bradley, D. G., Jann, O. C., Bertorelle, G., Chamberlain, A. T., Nunes, T. P., Metodiev, S., Ferrand, N., & Erhardt, G. (2003). Gene-culture co-evolution between cattle milk protein genes and human lactase genes. *Nature Genetics, 35*(4), 1–3.

Belsky, J. (2005). Differential susceptibility to rearing influence. In B. J. Ellis & D. F. Bjorklund (Eds.), *Origins of the social mind: Evolutionary psychology and child development* (pp. 19–44). New York: The Guilford Press.

Belsky, J., Steinberg, L., & Draper, P. (1991). Childhood experience, interpersonal development, and reproductive strategy: An evolutionary theory of socialization. *Child Development, 62,* 647–670.

Blair, R. J. R. (2003). Neurobiological basis of psychopathy. *British Journal of Psychiatry, 102,* 5–7.

Bronfenbrenner, U. (1979). *The ecology of human development: Experiments by nature and design.* Cambridge, MA: Harvard University Press.

Catania, A. C., Matthews, B. A., & Shimoff, E .H. (1990). Properties of rule-governed behaviour and their implications. In D. E. Blackman & H. Lejeune (Eds.), *Behaviour analysis in theory and practice: Contributions and controversies* (pp. 215–230). Hillsdale, NJ: Lawrence Erlbaum Associates.

Cavalli-Sforza, L L., Menozzi, P., & Piazza, A. (1993). Demic expansions and human evolution. *Science, 259,* 639–646.

Cavalli-Sforza, L. L., Menozzi, P., & Piazza, A. (1994). *The history and geography of human genes.* Princeton, NJ: Princeton University Press.

Cavalli-Sforza, L. L., Menozzi, P., and Piazza, A. (1994). *The history and geography of human genes.* Princeton, NJ: Princeton University Press.

Coluzzi, M. (1999). The clay feet of the malaria giant and its African roots: Hypotheses and inferences about origin, spread and control of *Plasmodium falciparum. Parassitologia, 41,* 277–283.

Comings, D. E., Muhleman, D., Johnson, J. P., & MacMurray, J. P. (2002). Parent-daughter transmission of the androgen receptor gene as an explanation of the effect of father absence on age of menarche. *Child Development, 73*(4), 1046–1051.

Cosmides, L., Tooby, J., & Barkow, J. H. (1992). Introduction: Evolutionary psychology and conceptual integration. In Barkow, J. H., Cosmides, L., & Tooby, J., (Eds), *The adapted mind: Evolutionary psychology and the generation of culture* (pp. 3–15). Oxford: Oxford University Press.

Diamond, J. (1999). *Guns, germs, and steel: The fates of human societies.* New York: W. W. Norton & Company.

Draper, P., & Belsky, J. (1990). Personality development in evolutionary perspective. *Journal of Personality, 58,* 141–160.

Draper, P., & Harpending, H. (1982). Father absence and reproductive strategy: An evolutionary perspective. *Journal of Anthropological Research, 38,* 255–273.

Durham, W. H. (1992). *Co-evolution: Genes, culture, and human diversity.* Stanford: Stanford University Press.

Ellis, B. J. (2004). Timing of pubertal maturation in girls: An integrated life history approach. *Psychological Bulletin, 130*, 920–958.

Ellis, L. (2001). The biosocial female choice theory of social stratification. *Social Biology, 48*, 297–319.

Evans, P. D., Gilbert, S. L., Mekel-Bobrov, N., Vallender, E .J., Anderson, J. R., Vaez-Azizi, L .M., Tishkoff, S. A., Hudson, R. R., & Lahn, B. T. (2005). Microcephalin, a gene regulating brain size, continues to evolve adaptively in humans. *Science, 309*(5741), 1717–1720.

Festinger, L. (1957). *A theory of cognitive dissonance*. Stanford: Stanford University Press.

Figueredo, A. J. (1995). The epigenesis of sociopathy. *Behavioral and Brain Sciences, 18*(3), 556–557.

Figueredo, A. J., Hammond, K. R., & McKiernan, E. C. (2006). A Brunswikian evolutionary developmental theory of preparedness and plasticity. *Intelligence, 34*(2), 211–227.

Figueredo, A. J., Vásquez, G., Brumbach, B. H., & Schneider, S. M. R. (2004). The heritability of life history strategy: The K-factor, covitality, and personality. *Social Biology, 51*, 121–143.

Figueredo, A. J., Vásquez, G., Brumbach, B. H., & Schneider, S. M. R. (2007). The K-factor, covitality, and personality: A psychometric test of life history theory. *Human Nature, 18*(1), 47–73.

Figueredo, A .J., Vásquez, G., Brumbach, B. H., Schneider, S. M. R., Sefcek, J. A., Tal, I. R., Hill, D., Wenner, C. J., & Jacobs, W. J. (2006). Consilience and life history theory: From genes to brain to reproductive strategy. *Developmental Review, 26*, 243–275.

Figueredo, A. J., Vásquez, G., Brumbach, B. H., Sefcek, J. A., Kirsner, B. R., & Jacobs, W. J. (2005). The K-Factor: Individual differences in life history strategy. *Personality and Individual Differences, 39*(8), 1349–1360.

Flinn, M. V. & Ward, C. V. (2005). Ontogeny and evolution of the social child. In B. J. Ellis & D. F. Bjorklund (Eds.), *Origins of the social mind: Evolutionary psychology and child development* (pp. 19–44). New York: The Guilford Press.

Geary, D. C. (2005). *The origin of mind: Evolution of brain, cognition, and general intelligence*. Washington, DC: American Psychological Association Press.

Geher, G., Bloodworth, R., Mason, J., Stoaks, C., Downey, H., Renstrom, K. L., & Romero, J. (2005). Motivational underpinnings of romantic partner perceptions: Psychological and physiological evidence. *Journal of Social and Personal Relationships, 22*, 255–281.

Gibson, J. J. (1974). *Perception of the visual world*. Westport, CT: Greenwood Press.

Gibson, J. J. (1979). *The ecological approach to visual perception*. Boston. Houghton Mifflin Company

Gordon, H. L., Baird, A. A., & End, A. (2004). Functional differences among those high and low on a trait measure of psychopathy. *Biological Psychiatry, 56*(7), 516–521.

Hare, R. D. (1993). *Without conscience: The disturbing world of the psychopaths among us*. New York: Guilford Press.

Harris, J. R. (1995). Where is the child's environment? A group socialization theory of development. *Psychological Review, 102*, 458–489.

Harris, J. R. (1998). *The nurture assumption: Why children turn out the way they do.* New York: Free Press.

Harris, J. R. (2005). Social behavior and personality development: The role of experiences with siblings and with peers. In B. J. Ellis & D. F. Bjorklund (Eds). *Origins of the social mind: Evolutionary psychology and child development* (pp. 245–270). New York: Guilford Press.

Harris, J. R. (2006). *No two alike: Human nature and human individuality.* New York: W. W. Norton.

Hawkes, K., O'Connell, J. F., Blurton-Jones, N. G., Alvarez, H., & Charnov, E. L. (1998). Grandmothering, menopause, and the evolution of human life histories. *Proceedings of the National Academy of Science, 95,* 1336–1339.

Hayes, S. C. (1989). *Rule governed behavior: Cognition, contingencies, and instructional control.* New York: Plenum Press.

Heider, F. (1958). *The psychology of interpersonal relations.* New York: Wiley.

Hrdy, S. B. (1997). Raising Darwin's consciousness: female sexuality and the prehominid origins of patriarchy. *Human Nature, 8,* 1–49.

Hrdy, S. B. (1999). *Mother nature: Maternal instincts and how they shape the human species.* New York: Ballantine Books.

Irons, W. (1998). Adaptively relevant environments versus the environment of evolutionary adaptedness. *Evolutionary Anthropology, 6*(6), 194–204.

Kohlberg, L. (1969). Stage and sequence: The cognitive-developmental approach to socialization. In D.S. Goslin (Ed.), *Handbook of socialization theory and research* (pp. 347–480). Chicago: Rand McNally.

Krohn, F. B., Bogan, Z. (2001). The effects absent fathers have on female development and college attendance. *College Student Journal, 35*(4), 598–608.

Lalumiere, M. L., Chalmers, L. J., Quinsey, V. L., & Seto, M. C. (1996). A test of the mate deprivation hypothesis of sexual coercion. *Ethology and Sociobiology, 17*(5), 299–318.

Lalumiere, M. L., Harris, G. T., & Rice, M. E. (2001). Psychopathy and developmental instability. *Evolution and Human Behavior, 22,* 75–92.

Lumsden, C. J., & Wilson, E. O. (1981). *Genes, mind, and culture: The co-evolutionary process.* Cambridge, MA: Harvard University Press.

Mealey, L. (1995). The sociobiology of sociopathy: An integrated evolutionary model. *Behavioral & Brain Sciences, 8* (3), 523–599.

Mekel-Bobrov, N., Gilbert, S. L., Evans, P. D., Vallender, E. J., Anderson, J. R., Hudson, R. R., Tishkoff, S. A., & Lahn, B. T. (2005). Ongoing adaptive evolution of ASPM, a brain size determinant in Homo sapiens. *Science, 309*(5741), 1720–1722.

Miller, G. F. (2004). Personal communication.

Mischel, W. (1968). *Personality and assessment.* New York: John Wiley & Sons.

Mischel, W., & Shoda, Y. (1995). A cognitive-affective system theory of personality: Reconceptualizing situations, dispositions, dynamics, and invariance in personality structure. *Psychological Review, 102,* 246–268.

Mischel, W., Shoda, Y., & Mendoza-Denton, R. (2002). Situation-behavior profiles as a locus of consistency in personality. *Current Directions in Psychological Science, 11,* 50–54.

Nesse, R. M. (1999). What Darwinian medicine offers psychiatry. In Trevathan, W. R., McKenna, J. J., & Smith, E. O. (Eds.) *Evolutionary medicine* (pp. 351–372). New York: Oxford University Press.

Palumbi, S. R. (2001). *The evolution explosion: How humans cause rapid evolutionary change*. New York: W. W. Norton & Company.

Patrick, C. J. (1994). Emotion and psychopathy: Some startling new insights. *Psychophysiology. 31*, 319–330.

Richerson, P. J., & Boyd., R. (1998). The evolution of human ultra-sociality. In I. Eibl-Eibesfeldt and F. K. Salter (eds.), *Indoctrinability, ideology and warfare* (pp. 71–96). New York: Berghahn Books.

Richerson, P. J., & Boyd., R. (1999). Complex societies: the evolutionary origins of a crude superorganism. *Human Nature, 10*, 253–289.

Richerson, P. J., & Boyd., R. (2001a). Institutional evolution in the Holocene: the rise of complex societies. In W. G. Runciman (Ed.), *The origin of human social institutions* (pp. 197–204). Proceedings of the British Academy 110.

Richerson, P. J., & Boyd., R. (2001b). The evolution of subjective commitment to groups: A tribal instincts hypothesis. In R. M. Nesse (Ed.), *The Evolution and the capacity for subjective commitment* (pp. 186–220). New York, NY: Russell Sage.

Schmajuk, N. A., Lamoureux, J. A., & Holland, P. C. (1998). Occasion setting: A neural network approach. *Psychological Review, 105*, 3–32.

Shoda, Y., & Smith, R. E. (2004) Conceptualizing personality as a cognitive-affective processing system: A framework for models of maladaptive behavior patterns and change. *Behavior Therapy, 35*, 147–165.

Skinner, B. F. (1938). *The behavior of organisms: An experimental analysis*. Oxford: Appleton-Century.

Smuts, B. (1995). The evolutionary origins of patriarchy. *Human Nature, 6*, 1–34.

Snyder, M. (1974). Self-monitoring of expressive behavior. *Journal of Personality and Social Psychology, 30*, 526–537.

Tolman, E. C. (1932). *Purposive behavior in animals and men*. New York: Appleton-Century.

Trivers, R. L. (1972). Parental investment and sexual selection. In B. Campbell (Ed.), *Sexual selection and the descent of man, 1871–1971* (pp. 136–179). Chicago: Aldine.

Wakefield, J. C. (1992). The concept of mental disorder: On the boundary between biological facts and social values. *American Psychologist, 47*(3), 373–388.

Warner, R. L., Lee, G. R., & Lee, J. (1986). Social organization, spousal resources, and marital power: a cross-cultural study. *Journal of Marriage and the Family, 48*, 121–128.

Wemple, S. F. (1981). *Women in Frankish society: marriage and the cloister 500 to 900*. Philadelphia: University of Pennsylvania Press.

Wiebe, R. P. (2004). Psychopathy and sexual coercion: A Darwinian analysis. *Counseling and Clinical Psychology Journal, 1*(1), 24–41.

Wilson, D. S., Near, D., & Miller, R. R. (1996). Machiavellianism: A synthesis of the evolutionary and psychological literatures. *Psychological Bulletin, 119*(2), 285–299.

VII

Conclusions

Chapter 15

Mating Intelligence: Frequently Asked Questions

Geoffrey Miller
University of New Mexico

Mating Intelligence (MI) is the whole set of human psychological adaptations for sexual reproduction—for making babies, but not for raising them (which would be Parenting Intelligence, presumably). MI includes mental capacities for courtship and display; for sexual competition and rivalry; for relationship-formation, commitment, coordination, and termination; for flirtation, foreplay, and copulation; for mate-search, mate-choice, mate-guarding, and mate-switching; and for many other behavioral capacities that bring mainly reproductive payoffs (Miller, 2000a). Each of these capacities cuts across traditional psychological distinctions between perception, cognition, emotion, motivation, learning, memory, planning, intelligence, and personality.

WHAT FORMS DOES MI TAKE?

There is a major distinction within MI theory between 'mental fitness indicators' and 'mating mechanisms.' Mental fitness indicators are psychological adaptations that have evolved through mate choice to advertise one's phenotypic and genetic quality to potential mates. They should typically show large individual differences, high heritabilities, substantial correlations with other indices of fitness (e.g., general intelligence, body symmetry, physical health, mental health, longevity, fertility), and a high degree of sexual attractiveness, especially in serious, long-term relationships (Miller, 2000a, b; Miller & Todd, 1998). Examples of mental fitness indicators would include the perceptual, cognitive, emotional, and behavioral capacities for:

- Language: sustaining interesting conversations and telling memorable stories during courtship (Dunbar, Marriot, & Duncan, 1997; Miller, 2000a; Shaner, Miller, & Mintz, 2004);
- Humor: producing amusing verbal and non-verbal behaviors (Bressler & Balshine, 2006; Bressler, Martin, & Balshine, 2006; Gervais & Wilson, 2005; Weisfeld, 2006);
- Art: producing creative, skilled works of ornamental or representational art (Haselton & Miller, 2006; Miller, 2001; Nettle & Clegg, 2006);
- Music: e.g., entraining and producing complex rhythms when drumming or dancing (Bachner-Melman et al., 2005; Brown et al., 2005; Miller, 2000c; Sluming & Manning, 2000);
- Morality: displaying attractive moral virtues such as kindness, honesty, heroism, humility, or gift-giving; (Farthing, 2005; Kelly & Dunbar, 2001; Miller, 2007; Sozou & Seymour, 2005);
- Ideology: creating novel world-views; debating arcane details of religious and political ideologies with sexual rivals (Kanazawa, 2000; Miller, 1996; Tybur, Miller, & Gangestad, in press);
- Drug use: taking psychoactive drugs that boost subjective mate value (Newlin, 2002) and mental fitness indicator functioning (Sullivan & Hagen, 2002), but that would provoke mental illness if one were genetically vulnerable (Diamond, 1992; see Arseneault et al., 2004; Svenningsson et al., 2003);
- Foreplay: orchestrating manual, oral, and genital contact that is sexually arousing to a lover (Haavio-Mannila & Kontula, 1997; S. Miller & Byers, 2004; Puts & Dawood, 2006).

The study of mental fitness indicators is most closely allied with current psychological research on individual differences: intelligence, personality, behavior genetics, clinical psychology, creativity, and ideological attitudes. Its theoretical foundation is a branch of evolutionary biology called costly signaling theory (Bird & Smith, 2005; Cronk, 2005; Miller, 2000a).

On the other hand, most other aspects of MI should take the form of reliable 'mating mechanisms'—psychological adaptations that evolved through broader forms of sexual selection to understand, judge, and influence potential sexual partners and rivals. They should typically show smaller individual differences, lower heritabilities, lower correlations with indexes of fitness, and a lower degree of direct sexual attractiveness. When they do show individual differences, these may often reflect different mating strategies rather than differences in general phenotypic quality (e.g., Figueredo et al., 2006; Gangestad & Simpson, 2000; Nettle, 2005; Shackelford, Schmitt, & Buss, 2005). Examples of such mating mechanisms would include the perceptual, cognitive, emotional, and behavioral capacities for:

- Mate search: finding potential mates, and accurately assessing their age, sex, relationship status, and parental status (Todd & Miller, 1999);
- Mate choice: judging the physical and psychological attractiveness of potential mates (Miller, 2000a);
- Self-assessment: learning one's own mate value (see Ben Hamida, Mineka, & Bailey, 1998; Kirkpatrick & Ellis, 2001);
- Mating acculturation: learning the ecological, cultural, social, and demographic constraints governing the local mating market;
- Learning about sex differences in typical behavior patterns and preferences, both cross-cultural universals (e.g., Archer, 2004; Schmitt, 2003, 2005) and culture-specific adaptations to local ecologies and ideologies (e.g., Gangestad & Buss, 1993; Marlowe, 2003; Moore et al., 2006),
- Mind-reading: understanding the beliefs and desires of potential mates, current mates, sexual rivals, and their interested friends and family members (e.g., Haselton & Buss, 2000; Thomas & Fletcher, 2003);
- Strategic mating: adopting appropriate mating strategies given one's mate value, the local mating market, and specific potential mates; adaptively switching mating strategies when circumstances change (e.g., when mates, rivals, children, or friends get pregnant, change social status, get sick, die); derogating and deterring sexual rivals and stalkers (see Gangestad & Simpson, 2000);
- Mating emotions: developing infatuations, falling in love, forming romantic attachments, and feeling jealousy;
- Short-term mating: managing short-term affairs, infidelities, jealousies, and break-ups.

Mating mechanisms tend to be human universals—reliably developing legacies of prehistoric mating patterns. The study of mating mechanisms is most closely allied with current psychological research in evolutionary psychology, human sexuality, intimate relationships, Theory of Mind, social cognition, social neuroscience, person perception, emotions, decision making, and self-esteem.

IS MI A WAY TO DESCRIBE HUMAN UNIVERSALS OR INDIVIDUAL DIFFERENCES?

Both—as outlined above. MI has two aspects that make it a bit confusing at first. There is a universal aspect: MI as a set of species-typical adaptations—the human sexuality part of human nature that we have in common—which we call 'mating mechanisms.' Then there is an individual-differences aspect: MI as a set of individual differences—the differences in attractiveness, personality, intelligence, sexual strategies, and mate preferences that we find so salient and gossip-worthy in others, and such a source of high or low self-esteem in ourselves. MI's universality means that all normal adult humans have some basic capacities for flirting, conversing, being funny, telling stories, choosing mates, and falling in love. MI's variability means that some people are much better at these things than others. Thus, MI includes both human universals (as studied by evolutionary psychology) and individual differences (as studied by psychometrics, behavior genetics, personality psychology, and clinical psychology).

DOES MI EXPLAIN EVERYTHING DISTINCTIVE ABOUT HUMANS?

No, it mainly concerns mental capacities that are displayed in courtship, used in mate choice, used in cross-sex mind-reading, and that guide context-sensitive sexual strategies. It is less relevant to research on human capacities that have more obvious survival and social payoffs, such as finding food, navigating through space, avoiding predators and pathogens, caring for offspring, helping kin, making friends, coordinating group behavior, and sustaining social norms (see Buss, 2005). There are probably hundreds of human psychological adaptations that evolved without much influence from mate choice. MI is just a subset of the human mind's capacities (albeit an evolutionarily central and emotionally momentous subset).

IS MI DISTINCTIVELY HUMAN?

No, almost all multi-cellular, sexually-reproducing species would be expected to have evolved complex psychological adaptations for courtship, mate choice, sexual rivalry, and so forth (Kokko et al., 2002). However, certain advanced capacities for understanding the beliefs and desires of the opposite sex would presumably require Theory of Mind, and may be more limited across species. Also, certain advanced courtship tactics (e.g., sarcasm, lingerie—see Jorgensen, 1996; Storr, 2002) may be limited to humans. In fact, it makes sense that evolutionary forces would have shaped species such that the nature of fitness-indicators and mating mechanisms tend to be relatively species-specific (Verzijden, Lachlan, & Servedio, 2005; Via, 2001).

WHICH PEOPLE EMBODY MI IN THE FORM OF MENTAL FITNESS INDICATORS?

Most mythological figures and popular culture celebrities who are known for more than just their looks exemplify some form of mating intelligence—specifically in the form of mental fitness indicators—which is why we're interested in them (see Brune, 2001; McCutcheon, Lange, & Houran, 2002).

Mythological figures exemplifying various forms of MI mental fitness indicators include the Greek gods Aphrodite, Apollo, Athena, and Dionysus, the Hindu gods Krishna, Lakshmi, and Sarasvati, and the *Arabian Nights* narrator Scheherezade. Even in monotheistic religions, superhuman levels of MI (e.g., empathy, creativity, general knowledge) are often ascribed to the deity, although such charismatic traits would seem more useful in a polytheistic mixed-sex pantheon.

Western historical exemplars of MI mental fitness indicators would include Abelard and Heloise, Shakespeare, Casanova, Mozart, Jane Austen, Pablo Picasso, Jimi Hendrix, and Germaine Greer (see Miller, 2000a). With regard to contemporary celebrities, different people will think of different professional exemplars for each domain of courtship. My personal MI icons happen to include artists Cindy Sherman and Andy Goldsworthy, musicians Tori Amos and Andre Benjamin, comedians Sarah Silverman and Eddie Izzard, novelists Mary Gaitskill and Chuck Palahniuk, and actors Tilda Swinton and Denzel Washington. Since celebrity is transient and faddish, each of these names will sound poignantly out-dated within a few years. Also, the winner-take-all nature of celebrity and the economic division of labor lead to the fact that that most celebrities are known for only one form of MI, giving the false impression that there are ferocious trade-offs between different forms of MI. I suspect that Tori Amos could learn to do film-acting better than most humans could, and that Denzel Washington could learn to sing and play piano better than most humans could, but they have little to gain and much to lose by trying to do so publicly (see Amos & Powers, 2005).

People who do not embody the mental-fitness aspects of MI typically do not usually become famous, except through physical appearance, sports ability, family background, crime, or blind luck. Super-models, football stars, British royalty, serial killers, and lottery winners may achieve notoriety, but do not often embody MI's signature fitness-display features, and therefore are not usually respected for their deeper personal qualities.

WHICH PEOPLE EMBODY MI IN THE FORM OF MATING MECHANISMS?

Although reliable mating mechanisms (such as the ability to accurately judge prevailing sex ratios in a local mating market) show smaller individual differences than mental fitness indicators, some people still show exemplary efficiency, accuracy, and strategic intelligence in their mate choice, cross-sex mind-reading, and relationship-management skills. I know a few friends, family members, therapists, and colleagues who excel at these things, but you haven't heard of them, so you'll need to think of your own list. Most such people are respected and envied within their small social circle, but never achieve public notoriety, because they are mostly average in their physical and mental fitness indicators.

Also, some people are much better able to articulate how these reliable mating mechanisms work, through their novels, plays, or films. To gain insight into these aspects of MI, it helps a lot to read pre-modern playwrights and novelists who thought about courtship and character, love and money, passion and convention, before literature became all alienated and self-referential—novelists such as Jane Austen, Gustave Flaubert, George Eliot, Anthony Trollope, Charles Dickins, Henry James, and Edith Wharton. A few more contemporary writers also have good MI insights—John Updike, Martin Amis, Salman Rushdie, Anne Tyler, Ian McEwan, and Margaret Atwood. Whenever one of my bright young Ph.D. students gets overly conceited and thinks they understand everything about human mating, I recommend stepping back from the science, reading a good novel, and remembering how large a gap remains between the behavioral phenomena portrayed in literary fiction, and psychology's ability to explain those phenomena.

HOW DOES MI RELATE TO OTHER SOCIAL ADAPTATIONS?

In our highly social species, we often do collective mate-attraction (e.g., through coordinated music) and collective mate choice (e.g., through collaborative gossip). Thus, MI can also include the signaling systems for exchanging and understanding mating-relevant information. For example, MI would include the capacities for seeking advice from friends about how to stay faithful and committed to one's relationship, or how to extricate oneself from the relationship, depending on its prospective costs and benefits. Thus, MI includes not just courtship adaptations and mate-choice adaptations for forming one's own sexual relationships, but social-insight and social-persuasion adaptations for following and influencing the courtship behaviors and mate choices of others.

HOW DOES GENERAL INTELLIGENCE RELATE TO MI IN THE FORM OF MENTAL FITNESS INDICATORS?

General intelligence (a.k.a. IQ, general cognitive ability, the g factor) is the best-established, most predictive, most heritable mental trait ever found in psychology (Jensen, 1998; Plomin et al., 2003). Whether measured with a formal IQ test or assessed through informal conversation, intelligence predicts objective performance and learning ability across all important life-domains that show reliable individual differences (Deary, 2000; Gottfredson, 1997, 2003; Lubinski, 2000). Thus, it is very likely to predict individual differences in the mental fitness indicator components of MI as well.

Evolutionary psychology often misunderstands general intelligence as if it were a rather implausible psychological adaptation in its own right. It is misconstrued as a specific mental organ, module, brain area, or faculty—yet one that is fairly general-purpose (Kanazawa, 2004). However, it is not viewed that way by most intelligence researchers. Instead, they view general intelligence as an individual-differences construct—like the constructs 'health,' 'beauty,' or 'status.' Health is not a bodily organ; it is a latent variable that emerges when one factor-analyzes the functional efficiencies of many different organs. Because good genes, diet, and exercise tend to produce good hearts, lungs, and antibodies, the vital efficiencies of circulatory, pulmonary, and immune systems tend to positively correlate, yielding a general 'health' factor. Likewise, beauty is not a single sexual ornament like a peacock's tail; it is a latent variable that emerges when one factor-analyzes the attractiveness of many different sexual ornaments throughout the face and body (Thornhill & Grammer, 1999). Similarly, general intelligence is not a mental organ, but a latent variable that emerges when one factor-analyzes the functional efficiencies of many different, mostly domain-specific mental organs (Carroll, 1993).

General intelligence seems to be a pretty good index of genetic quality, phenotypic condition, and mate value, since it is positively correlated with:

- Genetic outbreeding (which would mask harmful mutations) (Mingroni, 2004);

- Physical health and longevity (Anstey et al., 2004; Gottfredson, 2004; Rushton, 2004; Whalley & Deary, 2001);
- Body symmetry (Bates, 2004; Prokosch et al., 2004)
- Physical attractiveness (Kanazawa & Kovar, 2004; Zebrowitz et al., 2002);
- Mental health (Cannon et al., 2002; Walker et al., 2002);
- Brain size (McDaniel, 2005; Miller & Penke, 2007; Posthuma et al., 2002; Thoma et al., 2005);
- Creativity (Kuncel, Hezlett, & Ones, 2004; Rindennann & Neubauer, 2004);
- Leadership ability (Judge, Colbert, & Ilies, 2004);
- Emotional intelligence (Ciarrochi, Chan, & Caputi, 2000; Mayer, Caruso, & Salovey, 1999; Schulte, Ree, & Carretta, 2004; Van Rooy & Viswesvaran, 2004);

Thus, many mental fitness indicators are likely to function as good-genes indicators by virtue of working as indicators of general intelligence (Miller, 2000b). That is, a simple model would be:

good genes → big, bright brains → general intelligence → specific mental fitness indicators

A more complex model would reflect the positive effects of both general intelligence and certain personality traits (e.g., agreeableness, extroversion, and openness to experience) on social and emotional intelligence, and their effects on courtship abilities.

HOW DOES GENERAL INTELLIGENCE RELATE TO MI IN THE FORM OF MATING MECHANISMS?

If general intelligence indexes the neurodevelopmental stability of brain growth and brain functioning in general, it may also be modestly predictive of individual differences in the functional efficiency of mating mechanisms. That is, brighter people may be better not just at courtship displays, but also at mating mechanisms such as mate choice, cross-sex mind-reading, relationship management, learning their own mate value, detecting infidelities, and so forth. This has a couple of implications for MI research. First, we should be routinely measuring the intelligence of all of our participants in research on mate choice, cross-sex social attribution, etc., to see how g-loaded each of these abilities really is. We don't necessarily need to give the full 36-item Raven's Advanced Progressive Matrices test; it may be sufficient to ask students to self-report SAT scores, ACT scores, and college grades. Second, if these capacities do have substantial g-loadings, we should realize that mating research conducted on bright college sophomores is not likely to generalize very well to other humans. Likewise, marital therapies developed for professional couples may not work very well for working-class clients.

WHAT BRAIN AREAS ARE INVOLVED IN MI?

We don't know yet. Cognitive neuroscience arose in the late 1980s to find brain areas for perceptual and abstract cognitive abilities; social neuroscience arose in the late 1990s to identify brain areas for face recognition, person perception, and social attribution. There is almost no research so far in 'sexual neuroscience' on brain areas for mate choice and courtship. Neuroscientists are only beginning to identify the brain areas most related to heritable general intelligence, verbal intelligence, and social intelligence (e.g., Posthuma et al., 2003).

The main areas likely to be relevant to MI, based on what we know so far from cognitive and social neuroscience, are the:

- Prefrontal area of the cerebral cortex: for social and sexual behavior, Theory of Mind, perspective-taking, emotional intelligence, motivation, creativity, flexible problem solving, verbal humor appreciation
- Premotor and motor areas of frontal cortex: for spontaneous behavior, learning skilled tasks, complex movement initiation and control, facial expression, language production (Broca's area)
- Temporal lobes: for language comprehension (Wernicke's area), long-term memory
- Parietal lobes: for multi-modal sensory integration, and probably some highly g-loaded functions
- Cerebellum (esp. neocerebellum): for coordination and learning of complex voluntary movements
- Basal ganglia (striatum, globus pallidus, subthalamic nucleus, substantia nigra): for complex motor coordination and learning

Brain areas likely to be less important for MI are the:

- Occipital lobes: mostly for vision
- Diencephalon (thalamus, pineal, hypothalamus, pituitary, infundibulum, mammary bodies): for sensory integration, homeostasis, thirst, hunger, circadian rhythms, emotions, learning, memory, hormone regulation

- Midbrain (tectum, periaqueductal gray, red nucleus): for head and eye movements, coordinating breathing and circulation
- Limbic system (amygdala, hippocampus, cingulated gyrus, fornix, septal nuclei): for motivating key survival and reproductive behaviors, but not usually for controlling advanced courtship or mate choice abilities
- Brainstem (pons, medulla, inferior olive, pyramid): for arousal, balance, heart beat, breathing, swallowing, digestion, sleep

Emerging cognitive neuroscience work is identifying the brain areas most closely associated with general intelligence, such as lateral and medial prefrontal cortex and posterior parietal cortex (e.g., Colom et al., 2006; Gong et al., 2005; Gray et al., 2003; Haier et al., 2004; Lee et al., 2006). These cortical areas will probably underlie many MI systems, especially mental fitness indicators. As would be predicted from a fitness indicator perspective, these g-loaded areas also tend to be the areas that show the highest heritability in size and functional efficiency (Toga & Thompson, 2005; Winterer et al., 2005).

Such work is progressing rapidly, and might benefit from focusing more on cognitive tasks that are both highly g-loaded and highly relevant to courtship, mate choice, and cross-sex mind-reading. Also, an MI perspective might illuminate some of the dramatic sex differences that are being found in these highly g-related cortical areas (e.g., Haier et al., 2005; Jung et al., 2005; Schmithorst & Holland, 2006).

WHAT IS THE GENETIC BASIS OF HUMAN MI?

We don't know yet. The genetic basis of individual differences in mental fitness indicators is probably related to mutation load (see Keller, this volume). This should result in substantial heritability (and fairly high coefficients of additive genetic variance) in most such indicators (see Miller & Penke, 2007). For example, there is strong evidence of substantial heritability in human intelligence, creativity, and personality traits.

The genetic basis of our species-typical MI capacities must have evolved in the last 5–6 million years since our lineage split from the common ancestor of chimpanzees and bonobos. Results of the Human Genome Project (Collins & McKusick, 2001) compared to the Chimpanzee Genome Project (Olson & Varki, 2003) show that about 1.2 percent of our 3 billion DNA base pairs are different from those of chimpanzees (Ebersberger et al., 2002). Specifically, human-chimpanzee divergence involved at least 35 million single-nucleotide changes, 5 million insertion/deletion events, and significant chromosomal rearrangements (Mikkelsen et al., 2005), plus large segmental duplication events (Cheng et al., 2005), major shifts in the hot-spots for genetic recombination (Ptak et al., 2005), changes in gene promotor region activity patterns (Heissig et al., 2005), and more rapid changes in genes underlying brain development in humans than in chimpanzees (Khaitovich et al., 2005). Thus, it is highly misleading to repeat the 30-year-old claim that "chimpanzees are 98 percent genetically identical to humans," which implies that the evolved genetic and mental differences are trivial.

Further clarification of the genetic basis of distinctively human MI should follow from sequencing the Neanderthal genome, which diverged from humans about 300,000 years ago (Dalton, 2006; Hublin & Paabo, 2006; Krings et al., 1997). As with most differences between mammalian species, the distinctively human forms of MI are likely to result not so much from differences in basic structural genes that code for proteins, and that tend to be highly evolutionarily conserved, but from differences in genomic cis-regulatory elements that coordinate gene expression during development (Ochoa-Espinosa & Small, 2006; Stathopoulos & Levine, 2005).

CAN AN INDIVIDUAL'S MI BE INCREASED?

Boosting MI in the form of optimizing mating mechanisms is probably the major adaptive function of the human life-history stage known as adolescence, through gaining experience of sexual attraction, mate choice, and rivalry before the reproductive stakes get very high. In modern societies, boosting mental fitness indicators is probably also a major function of 'extra-curricular activities' by children and adolescents (e.g., art, music, athletics), and of higher education itself (especially a classical liberal arts education). For young adults, whole genres of magazines (e.g., for men: *Esquire, FHM, Maxim*; for women: *Cosmopolitan, Glamour, Marie Claire*) are devoted to boosting MI by increasing one's physical and psychological attractiveness, and revealing the 'secret' beliefs and desires of the other sex. For mature adults, maintaining one's MI (e.g., in order to stay at least marginally interesting to a spouse) is probably a major function of keeping up with news and current affairs, and of reading discussable novels and quotable non-fiction. Boosting MI is also, of course, the main point of couple's therapy, and of much individual psycho-therapy. Further research is needed to determine how well such putatively MI-boosting goods and services actually work.

Young males seem especially motivated to boost their MI through gaining sexual experience in dating and relationships, and paying for seduction seminars and dating mentors (see Strauss, 2005). Boosting MI may also be a major (though often unconscious) goal of ingesting 'smart drugs' (e.g., Ginkgo biloba, Ma-huang, DMEA, GHB, Hydergine, Piracetam, Aniracetam, Minaprine, Oxiracetam, phenylalanine, choline) and psychoactive drugs (e.g., caffeine, nicotine, Ecstasy, marijuana, cocaine, LSD)—though evidence for their effectiveness is mixed at best.

An individual's maximum attainable MI may be constrained by their general intelligence, social intelligence, and emotional intelligence, but few individuals seem to get anywhere near their limit, since they're too busy working and raising children.

ARE THERE AGE DIFFERENCES IN MI?

Most adaptations mature only when they are needed in the life-history of the organism. We expect MI to mature only after puberty, as humans grow towards sexual maturity. Compared to most capacities studied by developmental psychologists, MI capacities may be among the last-maturing cognitive and emotional capacities in the human behavioral repertoire.

The mental fitness indicator components of MI are predicted to be especially costly, complex, vulnerable to disruption, and correlated with general phenotypic quality. For these reasons, we might expect the fluency, efficiency, and quality of mental fitness indicators that depend upon quick, spontaneous cognitive processing to peak in young adulthood, at the peak of mating effort. This is indeed when 'fluid g' (general intelligence in the form of novel problem-solving) peaks, and when creative output is highest in poetry, comedy, mathematics, music composition, and artistic innovation. However, for mental fitness indicators that depend more heavily upon slowly-acquired skills and knowledge ('crystallized g'), we expect a later peak, as in literature, science, politics, and architecture.

The mating mechanisms of MI may show a more gradual, monotonic increase with age, compared with the fitness indicators of MI. Indeed, the wisdom that comes with advancing age is in no small part wisdom about human sexual relationships. For example, the mate choices made by teenagers often seem appallingly stupid to their parents. In part, this is because teenagers seem overly influenced by the traits that are easiest to assess: physical attractiveness and status among peers. Parents have decades more experience in assessing the harder-to-discern traits, such as intelligence, conscientiousness, agreeableness, and emotional stability, and they better understand the benefits of these traits, not just in marriage, but even in the short-term relationships that teenagers prefer. As another example, cross-sex mind-reading probably continues to improve throughout life, until senescence. The mind of the opposite sex is an exotic dark continent at age 15, a partly-explored colony at age 35, and an over-familiar garden at age 55. Moreover, in a species where adults live long past their reproductive prime and exert considerable influence over the mate choices and sexual relationships of their children and grand-children, there may have been strong selection pressures to maintain high MI well into old age.

For these reasons, future MI research should include a much broader age-spectrum of participants in research. If we want to do protocol analysis of mate choice by true experts, we must consult people who have lived for 60 years, not just 6 years, past puberty.

ARE THERE SEX DIFFERENCES IN MI?

If evolution shaped psychological sex differences anywhere in the human mind, we should expect them most prominently in MI abilities, since MI is most closely associated with reproduction, and sex differences arise most prominently in reproductive strategies.

We should expect that these sex differences will sometimes be big, and sometimes small. They will probably be big when the adaptive problems faced by the sexes are very different (e.g., males face paternity uncertainty but females don't; females have ovulatory cycles but males don't). They will probably be small when the adaptive problems faced by the sexes are very similar (e.g., both sexes need to be able to comprehend language in courtship, and to do certain kinds of cross-sex mind-reading).

The patterning of sex differences may be quite different for different components of MI. In the domain of mental fitness indicators, mutual mate choice may result in sexual similarity in the basic cognitive capacities for many courtship displays (e.g., language, humor, art), but higher variance in male reproductive success may have driven higher male motivation, risk-taking, and status-seeking in the drive to display such capacities publicly, to multiple potential mates (Miller, 2000a).

In the domain of mate choice, both sexes should be capable of high accuracy in assessing each other's physical and mental traits, but males may take longer in a relationship to bother reaching this level of accuracy, since females have high incentives to be choosy about both short-term and long-term partners, whereas males only have incentives to be choosy about long-term partners. In the domain of self-evaluation mechanisms for assessing one's own mate value, both sexes should show reasonable accuracy at learning about their physical and psychological attractiveness, but males may be under stronger sexual selection to act confident and cocky, so they may show more of a disjunction between subjective mate value and public behavior.

In the domain of cross-sex mind-reading, both sexes should be pretty good at understanding each other's beliefs and desires, except for the many situations in which there are fitness benefits to having blind spots, empathy deficits, adaptive self-deceptions, willful ignorance, and plausible deniability; these situations are likely to be sex-differentiated, so cross-sex mind-reading abilities will probably show some sex differences that look peculiar until they are investigated from an adaptationist perspective (Haselton & Buss, 2000)

Thus, the MI perspective can lead to finely nuanced, theoretically derived, testable hypotheses about sex differences in human mating psychology.

WHAT FIELDS NEED TO BE BETTER INTEGRATED INTO MI RESEARCH?

- Evolutionary biology, including new developments in sexual selection theory, costly signaling theory, mutual mate choice, and MI across species.
- Genetics, including evolutionary, behavioral, molecular, and neurodevelopmental genetics; the heritability of MI components and their genetic correlations with other traits; heritable individual differences in mating strategies; etc.
- Biological anthropology, including cross-cultural adaptationist studies of mating, courtship, and intimate relationships in small-scale societies.
- Many areas of psychology, including adolescent and young-adult development, social cognition, person perception, intelligence research, personality research, judgment and decision-making, emotion and motivation, and intimate relationships research.
- Linguistics, especially naturalistic observations on conversational pragmatics and sociolinguistics.
- Sex research, women's studies, and science-friendly feminism.
- The fine arts and humanities, including quantitative studies of the role of MI in art, comedy, dance, literature, music, philosophy, and theater.

WHAT FIELDS COULD BE MOST INFLUENCED BY ADVANCES IN MI RESEARCH?

- Medicine: the roles of MI, sexual competition, and fitness indicators in comorbidity, senescence, stress, exercise, and health psychology, sexually-transmitted infections, drug and alcohol use, and risky behavior.
- Psychiatry and clinical psychology, including the role of MI disorders and alternative mating strategies in psychopathology.

- Economics: the roles of MI and sexual competition in work, leisure, competition, bargaining, experimental game theory, and behavioral finance.
- Marketing: the roles of MI and mating effort in consumption, advertising, branding, and product design.
- Political science: the roles of MI and ideological display in political attitudes, beliefs, preferences, activism, hierarchies, and power.
- Sociology: the roles of MI, mating effort, and sexual competition in wealth, status, education, gender, marriage, family, ethnic relations, social capital, and culture.
- Education: improved ways to cultivate MI-based skills in language, art, music, drama, etc., and to harness benign sexual competition more effectively in learning evolutionarily novel, counter-intuitive skills in math and science.
- Criminology and law: the roles of MI, sexual competition, and mate choice in aggressive, anti-social, risk-seeking, sexual-coercive, and deceptive behavior.

SHOULD WE WORRY THAT MI FITNESS-INDICATOR THEORY SOUNDS LIKE EUGENICS?

MI research on mate choice for 'good genes' indicators, including mental fitness indicators, has some parallels to themes in the early 20th century eugenics movement (Carlson, 2001; Lynn, 2001). Both are concerned with genetic quality, mutation load, offspring health, and the dynamics of mating markets (Miller, 2003). However, the differences are significant:

	MI research	Eugenics
Nature	Descriptive science	Prescriptive policy
Basis of mate choice:	Unconscious, individual	Connscious, socially engineered
Goal:	Healthy relationships and offspring	Genetically purified population
Traits valued:	All forms of MI	Socially economically useful
Political orientation:	None in particular	Totalitarian (fascist, socialist)
Current human evolution:	Naturally favors good genes	Unnaturally favors bad genes

Basically, MI research supposes that most humans unconsciously favor fitness indicators and good genes, and have been doing so for hundreds of thousands of years, driving human evolution in extraordinarily interesting directions. By contrast, eugenics supposes that most humans have always made stupid, dysgenic mate choices, and therefore need remedial guidance from "genetically enlightened" social activists. The more adaptive complexity we discover in human mate choice and courtship adaptations, the less relevant eugenics should seem.

HOW DOES MI RELATE TO PSYCHIATRY AND CLINICAL PSYCHOLOGY?

Some mental disorders such as schizophrenia and depression may represent the low-fitness extremes of mental fitness indicators such as verbal courtship ability (Shaner, Miller, & Mintz, 2004), aesthetic creativity (Nettle, 2001; Nettle & Clegg, 2006), and subjective well-being.

Other mental disorders may represent harmful dysfunctions in mating mechanisms, especially those concerned with mate choice, self-assessment of mate value, cross-sex mind-reading, strategic mating, and management of mating-related emotions. Disorders characterized by adolescent and early-adulthood onset are especially likely to reflect MI dysfunctions, insofar as MI capacities would mature only after puberty (Shaner, Miller, & Mintz, 2004).

Some sexual disorders represent dysfunctional mate choice systems that drive sexual attraction to the wrong age (pedophilia directed at the sexually immature), the wrong species (bestiality/zoophilia directed at non-human animals), the wrong state of living (necrophilia directed at dead people), or the wrong state of animacy (fetishism directed at inanimate objects) (see Freund & Seto, 1998). Within this context, homosexuality might be classed as sexual attraction to the wrong sex (with respect to evolutionarily viable offspring-production—see below). Other sexual disorders (e.g., exhibitionism, frotteurism, voyeurism, erotomania) probably reflect overactive, inappropriately modulated courtship tactics that may have been ancestrally common among other social primates, but that are now beyond our cultural norms (see Brune, 2001; Sheets-Johnstone, 1990).

However, many sexual 'dysfunctions' may not really be disorders when considered from an MI perspective. If a woman experiences low sexual interest (sexual aversion disorder, female sexual arousal disorder), vaginal resistance or pain (vaginismus, dyspareunia), or lack of orgasm (female orgasmic disorder), these may reflect adaptive mate choice mechanisms that reject low-fitness or low-commitment mates—even if those mates are socially validated (e.g., husbands, boyfriends) as 'appropriate' (see Reissing, Binik, & Khalife, 1999). For example, a man who seems 'nice', but who lacks compelling mental fitness indicators, foreplay skills, and copulatory courtship abilities, may not provoke orgasm—and that may be the right adaptive response, to inhibit reproduction and pair-bonding with an inferior mate (Shackelford, Pound, & Goetz, 2005; Shackelford, Weekes-Shackelford, et al., 2000; Thornhill, Gangestad, & Comer, 1995). Sometimes these disorders generalize across all sexual partners, but often they do not.

Some mental disorders seem to reflect faulty mechanisms for self-assessing mate value. The eating disorders anorexia and bulimia are often associated with body image distortions (e.g., body dysmorphic disorder) in which someone thinks they are much fatter than the other sex, or same-sex rivals, would find attractive. This results in runaway sexual competition for thinness (Abed, 1998; Faer et al., 2005). This could also be seen as a failure of cross-sex mind-reading (e.g., assuming that men want ultra-skinny super-models, when they actually prefer women with normal gynoid fat distributions that indicate higher fertility—see Furnham, Petrides, & Constantinides, 2005).

Moods disorders such as dysthymia and major depression may also reflect dysfunctions in mechanisms for self-assessing mate value. They are often triggered by sexual rejection, relationship stress or failure, or a sense of being trapped in the wrong relationship (Gilbert & Allan, 1998; Nesse, 2000). They often provoke low sexual self-esteem (subjective mate value), reduced libido, withdrawal from the mating market, and anxieties about socio-sexual interaction. Such responses may be adaptive for a limited time after a mating set-back, but when they become chronic and driven by endogenous cycles rather than external circumstances, they seem dysfunctional (Nesse, 2000). Alternatively, some mood disorders and hypochondria may reflect unconscious tactics to extort higher support, commitment, and care from a reluctant mate (Hagen, 2002; Watson & Andrews, 2002).

Almost all personality disorders seem to reflect MI dysfunctions in some way—or perhaps they are adaptive, alternative mating strategies. Narcissistic personality disorder, which is much more common in males, leads to over-active display of physical and mental fitness indicators, driven by a sense of grandiosity, a need for admiration, and a sense of social and sexual entitlement (Baumeister, Catanese, & Wallace, 2002; Wallace & Baumeister, 2002). It is often associated with over-estimating one's mate value, including one's intelligence, attractiveness, social status, and sexual popularity. It also drives intense envy and animosity towards sexual rivals who threaten one's relative status. It typically leads to a lot of short-term, impulsive mating, and lower long-term commitment (Campbell & Foster, 2002). Of course, it may be a form of adaptive MI, insofar as some narcissistic males achieve very high short-term mating success. Bipolar disorder can also lead to very high short-term mating success in the manic phases, when individuals invest huge energy into physical and mental fitness indicators (Brody, 2001; Nettle, 2001).

Similarly, antisocial personality disorder (psychopathy) is much more common in males, and leads to a wide variety of exploitative, opportunis-

tic, or coercive short-term mating tactics, ranging from deceptive seduction to forcible rape (Charles & Egan, 2005; Lalumiere & Quinsey, 1996). It
combines heightened cross-sex mind-reading (better abilities to understand, deceive, and manipulate potential mates), with reduced cross-sex
sympathy (no interest in their suffering). Psychopaths, like narcissists,
often achieve very high short-term mating success, until they are ostracized, imprisoned, or lynched. This mating-focused view of psychopathy
contrasts with the traditional evolutionary psychology view that it is a
generally exploitative social strategy for deception, betrayal, and free-
riding (Mealey, 1995; Wilson, Near, & Miller, 1996).

By contrast, borderline personality disorder is much more common
in females, and seems to reflect several MI dysfunctions, including
reduced subjective mate value (low self-esteem), impulsive short-term
mating (promiscuity), and highly unstable assessments of sexual partners'
commitment levels, moral virtues, and personality traits (Liotti, 2002;
Moeller et al., 2001). Women with borderline tend to cycle between pre-
maturely intense attachment to male sexual partners, and premature rejection of partners who do not reciprocate such attachment immediately
(Aaronson et al., 2006). Thus, borderline seems in involve dysfunctions in
cross-sex mind-reading, managing mating-related emotions (lust, love,
jealousy), mating mechanisms for assessing own mate value, and the
strategic modulation of attachment and commitment levels.

Of course, many other mental disorders seem much less related to
mating and MI, and much more related to dysfunctions of psychological
adaptations for survival (e.g., snake phobias, obsessive-compulsive disorder, post-traumatic stress disorder, pyromania, hypochondriasis) and for
general social living (e.g., agoraphobia, generalized anxiety disorder, dis-
sociative disorders, intermittent explosive disorder, kleptomania) (see
Cosmides & Tooby, 1999). Nevertheless, an MI perspective may lead to
new ways of diagnosing, categorizing, and treating many mental illnesses,
and for understand sex differences in mental disorder prevalence rates and
symptom patterns.

WHAT ABOUT HOMOSEXUALITY?

From a strictly evolutionary-functional viewpoint, homosexuality represents a significant MI malfunction, insofar as it drives sexual attraction to
same-sex potential mates who cannot produce offspring with oneself. This
is why it has proven so very difficult to explain the existence of heritable
homosexual preferences in a small percentage of men and women. The
best evolutionary explanations so far seem to view homosexuality as a

maladaptive byproduct of X-chromosome alleles that evolved through sexually antagonistic co-evolution to increase female fecundity (Camperio-Ciani, Corna, & Capilucci, 2004).

This is not to say that there is anything morally, politically, or spiritually wrong with homosexuality, or that it should be classed as a mental disorder. Indeed, homosexuality could be viewed in some respects as the triumph of the individual's mating intelligence over the gonads' evolutionary interests. This is because homosexuality eliminates much of the sexual conflict that characterizes heterosexual courtship and relationships (Kurdek, 2005). Mind-reading becomes easier when one's mate is the same sex. Coordinating sexual strategies becomes easier when one's mate has the same preferences with regard to short-term versus long-term mating, promiscuity versus commitment, and spontaneous intercourse versus leisurely foreplay (Ekstrand et al., 1999; Mackey, Diemer, & O'Brien, 2000). Sexual dysfunctions and frustrations become less likely when mates understand each other's bodies as well as they understand their own. Sexual rivalry becomes easier to undercut when one's rival is the same sex as one's lover, and therefore seducible. Sexual coercion is harder to use and easier to avoid when one's mates have bodies more closely matched in size and strength. Thus, homosexuality solves a lot of MI problems with a peremptory elegance.

For all these reasons, MI research should include a lot more studies of gay men and lesbians. They make highly informative comparison groups in many ways. For example, suppose one studies domestic conflict in heterosexual married couples, and finds that many husbands think their wives nag them too much, and many wives think that husbands shirk their domestic duties too often. We can't tell to what extent each sex's view is accurate, because each sex's behavior is conflated with the other sex's reaction. Now, if we found that gay men also think their partners nag them too much, we might suspect that the aversion to nagging is a special case of general male irritability, rather than a righteous defense against female obsessiveness. Whenever we expect sex differences and/or sexual conflicts of interest, MI research should strive to include gay men and lesbians in every multi-study research program, if not in every study.

IS MI RESEARCH IDEOLOGICALLY PERNICIOUS IN ANY OTHER WAYS?

No, but it makes some folks really uncomfortable, until they come to terms with human sexuality—their own, their mates', their rivals', and their children's (see Miller, 2003).

ARE THE FAQ ANSWERS IN THIS CHAPTER
INTENDED TO BE AUTHORITATIVE?

Absolutely not. These are my personal hunches at the moment, as of August 2006, and they do not necessarily reflect the views of any other contributors to this book. If the MI research program is empirically and theoretically successful—if it surprises us, like good science should—I may well change my mind in the future about many of these issues.

REFERENCES

Aaronson, C. J., Bender, D. S., Skodol, A. E., & Gunderson, J. G. (2006). Comparison of attachment styles in borderline personality disorder and obsessive-compulsive personality disorder. *Psychiatric Quarterly, 77*(1), 69–80.

Abed, R. T. (1998). The sexual competition hypothesis for eating disorders. *British Journal of Medical Psychology, 71*(4), 525–547.

Amos, T., & Powers, A. (2005). *Piece by piece.* New York: Broadway.

Anstey, K. J., Windsor, T. D., Jorm, A. F., Christensen, H., & Rodgers, B. (2004). Association of pulmonary function with cognitive performance in early, middle, and late adulthood. *Gerontology, 50*(4), 230–234.

Archer, J. (2004). Sex differences in aggression in real-world settings: A meta-analytic review. *Review of General Psychology, 8*(4), 291–322.

Arseneault, L., Cannon, M., Witton, J., & Murray, R. M. (2004). Causal association between cannabis and psychosis: Examination of the evidence. *British Journal of Psychiatry, 184*, 110–117.

Bachner-Melman, R., Dina, C., Zohar, A. H., et al. (2005). AVPR1a and SLC6A4 gene polymorphisms are associated with creative dance performance. *PLOS Genetics, 1*(3), 394–403.

Bates, T. (2004). Fluctuating asymmetry, schizophrenia, and intelligence. *Australian Journal of Psychology, 56*(S), 105.

Baumeister, R. F., Catanese, K. R., & Wallace, H. M. (2002). Conquest by force: A narcissistic reactance theory of rape and sexual coercion. *Review of General Psychology, 6*(1), 92–135.

Ben Hamida, S., Mineka, S., & Bailey, J. M. (1998). Sex differences in perceived controllability of mate value: An evolutionary perspective. *Journal of Personality and Social Psychology, 75*(4), 953–966.

Bird, R. B., & Smith, E. A. (2005). Signaling theory, strategic interaction, and symbolic capital. *Current Anthropology, 46*(2), 221–248.

Bressler, E. R., & Balshine, S. (2006). The influence of humor on desirability. *Evolution and Human Behavior, 27*(1), 29–39.

Bressler, E. R., Martin, R. A., & Balshine, S. (2006). Production and appreciation of humor as sexually selected traits. *Evolution and Human Behavior, 27*(2), 121–130.

Brody, J. F. (2001). Evolutionary recasting: ADHD, mania, and its variants. *Journal of Affective Disorders, 65*(2), 197–215.

Brown, W. M., Cronk, L., Grochow, K., Jacobson, A., Liu, C. K., Popovic, Z., & Trivers, R. (2005). Dance reveals symmetry especially in young men. *Nature, 438*(7071), 1148–1150.

Brune, M. (2001). De Clerambault's syndrome (erotomania) in an evolutionary perspective. *Evolution and Human Behavior, 22*(6), 409–415.

Buss, D. M. (Ed.). (2005). *The handbook of evolutionary psychology.* Hoboken, NJ: John Wiley.

Cannon, M., Caspi, A., Moffitt, T. E., Harrington, H., Taylor, A., Murray, R. M., & Poulton, R. (2002). Evidence for early-childhood, pan-developmental impairment specific to schizophreniform disorder: Results from a longitudinal birth cohort. *Archives of General Psychiatry, 59*(5), 449–456.

Carlson, E. A. (2001). *The unfit: A history of a bad idea.* Cold Spring Harbor Laboratory Press.

Camperio-Ciani, A., Corna, F., & Capilucci, C. (2004). Evidence for maternally inherited factors favouring male homosexuality and promoting female fecundity. *Proceedings of the Royal Society of London B, 271*(1554), 2217–2221.

Campbell, W. K., & Foster, C. A. (2002). Narcissism and commitment in romantic relationships: An investment model analysis. *Personality and Social Psychology Bulletin, 28*(4), 484–495.

Carroll, J. (1993). *Human cognitive abilities: A survey of the factor-analytic literature.* Cambridge: Cambridge University Press.

Charles, K. E., & Egan, V. (2005). Mating effort correlates with self-reported delinquency in a normal adolescent sample. *Personality and Individual Differences, 38*(5), 1035–1045.

Cheng, Z., Venture, M., She, X. W., et al. (2005). A genome-wide comparison of recent chimpanzee and human segmental duplications. *Nature, 437*(7055), 88–93.

Ciarrochi, J. V., Chan, A. Y. C., & Caputi, P. (2000). A critical evaluation of the emotional intelligence construct. *Personality and Individual Differences, 28*(3), 539–561.

Collins, F. S., & McKusick, V. A. (2001). Implications of the Human Genome Project for medical science. *Journal of the American Medical Association, 285*(5), 540–544.

Colom, R., Jung, R. E., & Haier, R. J. (2006). Distributed brain sites for the g-factor of intelligence. *NeuroImage, 31*(3), 1359–1365.

Cosmides, L., & Tooby, J. (1999). Toward an evolutionary taxonomy of treatable conditions. *Journal of Abnormal Psychology, 108*(3), 453–464.

Cronk, L. (2005). The application of animal signaling theory to human phenomena: some thoughts and clarifications. *Social Science Information, 44*(4), 603–620.

Dalton, R. (2006). Neanderthal DNA yields to genome foray. *Nature, 441*(7091), 260–261.

Deary, I. (2000). *Looking down on human intelligence.* Oxford: Oxford University Press.

Deary, I. J., Thorpe, G., Wilson, V., Starr, J. M., & Whalley, L. J. (2003). Population sex differences in IQ at age 11: The Scottish Mental Survey 1932. *Intelligence, 31*(6), 533–542.

Diamond, J. (1992). *The third chimpanzee: The evolution and future of the human animal.* New York: Harper Perennial.

Dunbar, R. I. M., Marriot, A., & Duncan, N. D. C. (1997). Human conversational behavior. *Human Nature, 8*(3), 231–346.

Ebersberger, I., Metzler, D., Schwarz, C., & Paabo, S. (2002). Genomewide comparison of DNA sequences between humans and chimpanzees. *American Journal of Human Genetics, 70*(6), 1490–1497.

Ekstrand, M. L., Stall, R. D., Paul, J. P., Osmond, D. H., & Coates, T. J. (1999). Gay men report high rates of unprotected anal sex with partners of unknown or discordant HIV status. *AIDS, 13*(12), 1525–1533.

Faer, L. M., Hendricks, A., Abed, R. T., & Figueredo, A. J. (2005). The evolutionary psychology of eating disorders: Female competition for mates or for status? *Psychology and Psychotherapy: Theory, Research, and Practice, 78*(3), 397–417.

Farthing, G. W. (2005). Attitudes toward heroic and nonheroic physical risk takers as mates and as friends. *Evolution and Human Behavior, 26*(2), 171–185.

Figueredo, A. J., Vasquez, G., Brumbach, B. H., Schneider, S. M. R., Sefcek, J. A., Tal, I. R., Hill, D., Wenner, C. J., & Jacobs, W. J. (2006). Consilience and life History theory: From genes to brain to reproductive strategy. *Developmental Review, 26*(2), 243–275.

Freund, K., & Seto, M. C. (1998). Preferential rape in the theory of courtship disorder. *Archives of Sexual Behavior, 27*(5), 433–443.

Furnham, A., Petrides, K. V., & Constantinides, A. (2005). The effects of body mass index and waist-to-hip ratio on ratings of female attractiveness, fecundity, and health. *Personality and Individual Differences, 38*(8), 1823–1834.

Gangestad, S. W., & Buss, D. M. (1993). Pathogen prevalence and human mate preferences. *Ethology and Sociobiology, 14*(2), 89–96.

Gangestad, S. W., & Simpson, J. A. (2000). The evolution of human mating: Trade-offs and strategic pluralism. *Behavioral and Brain Sciences, 23*(4), 573–644.

Gervais, M., & Wilson, D. S. (2005). The evolution and functions of laughter and humor: A synthetic approach. *Quarterly Review of Biology, 80*(4), 395–430.

Gilbert, P., & Allan, S. (1998). The role of defeat and entrapment (arrested flight) in depression: An exploration of the evolutionary view. *Psychological Medicine, 28*(3), 585–598.

Gong, Q. Y., Sluming, V., Mayes, A., Keller, S., Barrick, T., Cezayirli, E., & Roberts, N. (2005). Voxel-based morphometry and stereology provide convergent evidence of the importance of medial prefrontal cortex for fluid intelligence in healthy adults. *NeuroImage, 25*(4), 1175–1186.

Gottfredson, L. S. (1997). Why *g* matters: The complexity of everyday life. *Intelligence, 24*(1), 79–132.

Gottfredson, L. S. (2003). Dissecting practical intelligence theory: Its claims and evidence. *Intelligence, 31*(4), 343–397.

Gottfredson, L. S. (2004). Intelligence: Is it the epidemiologists' elusive "fundamental cause" of social class inequalities in health? *Journal of Personality and Social Psychology, 86*(1), 174–199.

Gray, J. R., Chabris, C. F., & Braver, T. S. (2003). Neural mechanisms of general fluid intelligence. *Nature Neuroscience, 6*(3), 316–322

Haavio-Mannila, E., & Kontula, O. (1997). Correlates of increased sexual satisfaction. *Archives of Sexual Behavior, 26*(4), 399–419.

Hagen, E. H. (2002). Depression as bargaining: The case postpartum. *Evolution and Human Behavior, 23*(5), 323–336.

Haier, R. J., Jung, R. E., Yeo, R. A., Head, K., & Alkire, M. T. (2004). Structural brain variation and general intelligence. *NeuroImage, 23*(1), 425–433.

Haier, R. J., Jung, R. E., Yeo, R. A., Head, K., & Alkire, M. T. (2005). The neuroanatomy of general intelligence: Sex matters. *NeuroImage, 25*(1), 320–327.

Haselton, M. G., & Buss, D. M. (2000). Error management theory: A new perspective on biases in cross-sex mind reading. *Journal of Personality and Social Psychology, 78*(1), 81–91.

Haselton, M., & Miller, G. F. (2006). Women's fertility across the cycle increases the short-term attractiveness of creative intelligence compared to wealth. *Human Nature, 17*(1), 50–73.

Heissig, F., Krause, J., Bryk, J., et al. (2005). Functional analysis of human and chimpanzee promoters. *Genome Biology, 6*(7), R57.

Hublin, J. J., & Paabo, S. (2006). Neanderthals. *Current Biology, 16*(4), R113-R114.

Jensen, A. (1998). *The g factor: The science of mental ability.* London: Praeger.

Jorgensen, J. (1996). The functions of sarcastic irony in speech. *Journal of Pragmatics, 26*(5), 613–634.

Judge, T. A., Colbert, A. E., & Ilies, R. (2004). Intelligence and leadership: A quantitative review and test of theoretical propositions. *Journal of Applied Psychology, 89*(3), 542–552.

Jung, R. E., Haier, R. J., Yeo, R. A., Rowland, L. M., Petropoulos, H., Levine, A. S., Sibbitt, W. L., & Brooks, W. M. (2005). Sex differences in N-acetylaspartate correlates of general intelligence: An H—1-MRS study of normal human brain. *NeuroImage, 26*(3), 965–972.

Kanazawa, S. (2000). Scientific discoveries as cultural displays: a farther test of Miller's courtship model. *Evolution and Human Behavior, 21*(5), 317–321.

Kanazawa, S. (2004). General intelligence as a domain-specific adaptation. *Psychological Review, 111,* 512–523.

Kanazawa, S., & Kovar, J. L. (2004). Why beautiful people are more intelligent. *Intelligence, 32,* 227–243.

Kelly, S., & Dunbar, R. I. M. (2001). Who dares, wins—Heroism versus altruism in women's mate choice. *Human Nature, 12*(2), 89–105.

Khaitovich, P., Hellmann, I., Enard, W., Nowick, K., Leinweber, M., Franz, H., Weiss, G., Lachmann, M., & Paabo, S. (2005). Parallel patterns of evolution in the genomes and transcriptomes of humans and chimpanzees. *Science, 309*(5742), 1850–1854.

Kirkpatrick, L. A., & Ellis, B. J. (2001). An evolutionary-psychological approach to self-esteem: Multiple domains and multiple functions. In G. J. O. Fletcher & M. S. Clark (Eds.), *Blackwell handbook of social psychology: Interpersonal processes* (pp. 411–436). Oxford: Blackwell.

Kokko, H., Brooks, R., McNamara, J. M., & Houston, A. I. (2002). The sexual selection continuum. *Proceedings of the Royal Society of London B, 269*(1498), 1331–1340.

Krings, M., Stone, A., Schmitz, R. W., Krainitzki, H., Stoneking, M., & Paabo, S. (1997). Neandertal DNA sequences and the origin of modern humans. *Cell, 90*(1), 19–30.

Kuncel, N. R., Hezlett, S. A., & Ones, D. S. (2004). Academic performance, career potential, creativity, and job performance: Can one construct predict them all? *Journal of Personality and Social Psychology, 86*(1), 148–161.

Kurdek, L. A. (2005). What do we know about gay and lesbian couples? *Current Directions in Psychological Science, 14*(5), 251–254.

Lalumiere, M. L., & Quinsey, V. L. (1996). Sexual deviance, antisociality, mating effort, and the use of sexually coercive behaviors. *Personality & Individual Differences, 21*(1), 33–48.

Lee, K. H., Choi, Y. Y., Gray, J. R., Cho, S. H., Chae, J. H., Lee, S., & Kim, K. (2006). Neural correlates of superior intelligence: Stronger recruitment of posterior parietal cortex. *NeuroImage, 29*(2), 578–586.

Liotti, G. (2002). The inner schema of borderline states and its correction during psychotherapy: a cognitive-evolutionary approach. *Journal of Cognitive Psychotherapy, 16*(3), 349–366.

Lubinski, D. (2000). Scientific and social significance of assessing individual differences: "Sinking shafts at a few critical points". *Annual Review of Psychology, 51*, 405–444.

Lynn, R. (2001). *Eugenics: A reassessment*. New York: Praeger.

Mackey, R. A., Diemer, M. A., & O'Brien, B. A. (2000). Psychological intimacy in the lasting relationships of heterosexual and same-gender couples. *Sex Roles, 43*(3–4), 201–227.

Marlowe, F. W. (2003). The mating system of foragers in the standard cross-cultural sample. *Cross-Cultural Research, 37*(3), 282–306.

Mayer, J. D., Caruso, D. R., & Salovey, P. (1999). Emotional intelligence meets traditional standards for an intelligence. *Intelligence, 27*(4), 267–298.

McCutcheon, L. E., Lange, R., & Houran, J. (2002). Conceptualization and measurement of celebrity worship. *British Journal of Psychology, 93*(1), 67–87.

McDaniel, M. A., (2005). Big-brained people are smarter: A meta-analysis of the relationship between in vivo brain volume and intelligence. *Intelligence, 33*(4), 337–346.

Mealey, L. (1995). The sociobiology of sociopathy: An integrated evolutionary model. *Behavioral and Brain Sciences, 18*, 523–541.

Mikkelsen, T. S., Hillier, L. W., Eichler, E. E., et al. (2005). Initial sequence of the chimpanzee genome and comparison with the human genome. *Nature, 437*(7055), 69–87.

Miller, G. F. (1996). Political peacocks. *Demos Quarterly, 10* (Special issue on evolutionary psychology), 9–11.

Miller, G. F. (2000a). *The mating mind: How sexual choice shaped the evolution of human nature*. New York: Doubleday.

Miller, G. F. (2000b). Sexual selection for indicators of intelligence. In G. Bock, J. Goode, & K. Webb (Eds.), *The nature of intelligence* (pp. 260–275). Novartis Foundation Symposium 233. New York: John Wiley.

Miller, G. F. (2000c). Mental traits as fitness indicators: Expanding evolutionary psychology's adaptationism. In D. LeCroy & P. Moller (Eds.), *Evolutionary perspectives on human reproductive behavior (Annals of the New York Academy of Sciences, (Volume 907)* pp. 62–74.

Miller, G. F. (2001). Aesthetic fitness: How sexual selection shaped artistic virtuosity as a fitness indicator and aesthetic preferences as mate choice criteria. *Bulletin of Psychology and the Arts 2*(1), 20–25.

Miller, G. F. (2003). Fear of fitness indicators: How to deal with our ideological anxieties about the role of sexual selection in the origins of human culture. In

Being human: Proceedings of a conference sponsored by the Royal Society of New Zealand (pp. 65–79). Wellington: Royal Society of New Zealand, Miscellaneous series 63.

Miller, G. F. (2007). Sexual selection for moral virtues. *Quarterly Review Biology, 82*(2), 97–125.

Miller, G. F., & Penke, L. (in press). *The evolution of human intelligence and the coefficient of additive genetic variance in human brain size.*

Miller, S. A., & Byers, E. S. (2004). Actual and desired duration of foreplay and intercourse: Discordance and misperceptions within heterosexual couples. *Journal of Sex Research, 41*(3), 301–309.

Mingroni, M. A. (2004). The secular rise in IQ: Giving heterosis a closer look. *Intelligence, 32*(1), 65–83.

Moeller, F. G., Barratt, E. S., Dougherty, D. M., Schmitz, J. M., & Swann, A. C. (2001). Psychiatric aspects of impulsivity. *American Journal of Psychiatry, 158*(11), 1783–1793.

Moore, F. R., Cassidy, C., Smith, M. J. L., & Perrett, D. I. (2006). The effects of female control of resources on sex-differentiated mate preferences. *Evolution and Human Behavior, 27*(3), 193–205.

Nesse, R. M. (2000). Is depression an adaptation? *Archives of General Psychiatry, 57*(1), 14–20.

Nettle, D. (2001). *Strong imagination: Madness, creativity and human nature.* Oxford: Oxford University Press.

Nettle, D. (2005). An evolutionary approach to the extraversion continuum. *Evolution and Human Behavior, 26*(4), 363–373.

Nettle, D., & Clegg, H. (2006). Schizotypy, creativity and mating success in humans. *Proceedings of the Royal Society of London B, 273*(1586), 611–615.

Newlin, D. B. (2002). The self-perceived survival ability and reproductive fitness (SPFit) theory of substance use disorders. *Addiction, 97,* 427–445.

Ochoa-Espinosa, A., & Small, S. (2006). Developmental mechanisms and cis-regulatory codes. *Current Opinion in Genetics & Development, 16*(2), 165–170.

Olson, M. V., & Varki, A. (2003). Sequencing the chimpanzee genome: Insights into human evolution and disease. *Nature Reviews Genetics, 4*(1), 20–28.

Plomin, R., DeFreis, J. C., McClearn, G. E., & McGuffin, P. (2003). *Behavior genetics* (4th Ed.). New York: Worth Publishers.

Postuma, D., Baare, W. F. C., Hulshoff Pol, H. E., Kahn, R. S., Boomsma, D. I., & De Geus, E. J. C. (2003). Genetic correlations between brain volumes and the WAIS-III dimensions of verbal comprehension, working memory, perceptual organization, and processing speed. *Twin Research, 6*(2), 131–139.

Posthuma, D., De Geus, E.J. C., Baaré, W. F. C., Pol, H. E. H., Kahn, R. S., & Boomsma, D. I. (2002). The association between brain volume and intelligence is of genetic origin. *Nature Neuroscience, 5,* 83–84.

Prokosch, M. D., Yeo, R. A., & Miller, G. F. (2005). Intelligence tests with higher g-loadings show higher correlations with body symmetry: Evidence for a general fitness factor mediated by developmental stability. *Intelligence, 33*(2), 203–213.

Ptak, S. E., Hinds, D. A., Koehler, K., Nickel, B., Patil, N., Ballinger, D. G., Przeworski, M., Frazer, K. A., & Paabo, S. (2005). Fine-scale recombination patterns differ between chimpanzees and humans. *Nature Genetics, 37*(4), 429–434.

Puts, D. A., & Dawood, K. (2006). The evolution of female orgasm: Adaptation or byproduct? *Twin Research and Human Genetics, 9*(3), 467–472.

Reissing, E. D., Binik, Y. M., & Khalife, S. (1999). Does vaginismus exist? A critical review of the literature. *Journal of Nervous and Mental Disease, 187*(5), 261–274.

Rindennann, H., & Neubauer, A. C. (2004). Processing speed, intelligence, creativity, and school performance: Testing of causal hypotheses using structural equation models. *Intelligence, 32*(6), 573–589.

Rushton, J. P. (2004). Placing intelligence into an evolutionary framework, or how *g* fits into the r-K matrix of life-history traits including longevity. *Intelligence, 32*(4), 321–328.

Schulte, M. J., Ree, M. J., & Carretta, T. R. (2004). Emotional intelligence: Not much more than *g* and personality. *Personality and Individual Differences, 37*(5), 1059–1068.

Schmitt, D. P. (2003). Universal sex differences in the desire for sexual variety: Tests from 52 nations, 6 continents, and 13 islands. *Journal of Personality and Social Psychology, 85*(1), 85–104.

Schmitt, D. P. (2005). Sociosexuality from Argentina to Zimbabwe: A 48-nation study of sex, culture, and strategies of human mating. *Behavioral and Brain Sciences, 28*(2), 247–311.

Shackelford, T. K., Schmitt, D. P., & Buss, D. M. (2005). Universal dimensions of human mate preferences. *Personality and Individual Differences, 39*(2), 447–458.

Shackelford, T. K., Pound, N., & Goetz, A. T. (2005). Psychological and physiological adaptations to sperm competition in humans. *Review of General Psychology, 9*(3), 228–248.

Shackelford, T. K., Weekes-Shackelford, V. A., LeBlanc, G. J., Bleske, A. L., Euler, H. A., & Hoier, S. (2000). Female coital orgasm and male attractiveness. *Human Nature, 11*(3), 299–306.

Shaner, A., Miller, G. F., & Mintz, J. (2004). Schizophrenia as one extreme of a sexually selected fitness indicator. *Schizophrenia Research, 70*(1), 101–109.

Sheets-Johnstone, M. (1990). Hominid bipedality and sexual selection theory. *Evolutionary Theory, 9*(1), 57–70.

Sluming, V. A., & Manning, J. T. (2000). Second to fourth digit ratio in elite musicians: Evidence for musical ability as an honest signal of male fitness. *Evolution and Human Behavior, 21*(1), 1–9.

Sozou, P. D., & Seymour, R. M. (2005). Costly but worthless gifts facilitate courtship. *Proceedings of the Royal Society of London B, 272*(1575), 1877–1884.

Stathopoulos, A., & Levine, M. (2005). Genomic regulatory networks and animal development. *Development Cell, 9*(4), 449–462.

Storr, M. (2002). Classy lingerie. *Feminist Review, 71*, 18–36.

Strauss, N. (2005). *The game: Penetrating the secret society of pick-up artists.* New York: Regan Books.

Sullivan, R. J., & Hagen, E. H. (2002). Psychotropic substance-seeking: Evolutionary pathology or adaptation? *Addiction, 97*, 389–400.

Svenningsson, P., Tzavara, E. T., Carruthers, R., et al. (2003). Diverse psychotomimetics act through a common signaling pathway. *Science, 302*(5649), 1412–1415.

Thoma, R. J., Yeo, R. A., Gangestad, S. W., Halgren, E., Sanchez, N. M., & Lewine, J. D. (2005). Cortical volume and developmental instability are independent predictors of general intellectual ability. *Intelligence, 33*, 27–38.

Thomas, G., & Fletcher, G. J. O. (2003). Mind-reading accuracy in intimate relationships: Assessing the roles of the relationship, the target, and the judge. *Journal of Personality and Social Psychology, 85*(6), 1079–1094.

Thornhill, R., Gangestad, S. W., & Comer, R. (1995). Human female orgasm and mate fluctuating asymmetry. *Animal Behavior, 50*(6), 1601–1615.

Thornhill, R., & Grammer, K. (1999). The body and face of woman: One ornament that signals quality? *Evolution and Human Behavior, 20*(2), 105–120.

Todd, P.M., & Miller, G. F. (1999). From pride and prejudice to persuasion: Satisficing in mate search. In G. Gigerenzer & P. Todd. (Eds.), *Simple heuristics that make us smart* (pp. 286–308). Oxford: Oxford University Press.

Tybur, J. M., Miller, G. F., & Gangestad, S. W. (in press). Testing the controversy: An empirical examination of adaptationists' attitudes towards politics and science. *Human Nature.*

Van Rooy, D. L., & Viswesvaran, C. (2004). Emotional intelligence: A meta-analytic investigation of predictive validity and nomological net. *Journal of Vocational Behavior, 65*(1), 71–95.

Verzijden, M. N., Lachlan, R. F., & Servedio, M. R. (2005). Female mate-choice behavior and sympatric speciation. *Evolution, 59*(10), 2097–2108.

Via, S. (2001). Sympatric speciation in animals: The ugly duckling grows up. *Trends in Ecology & Evolution, 17*(7), 381–390.

Walker, N. P., McConville, P. M., Hunter, D., Deary, I. J., & Whalley, L. J. (2002). Childhood mental ability and lifetime psychiatric contact: A 66-year follow-up study of the 1932 Scottish Mental Ability Survey. *Intelligence, 30*(3), 233–245.

Wallace, H. M., & Baumeister, R. F. (2002). The performance of narcissists rises and falls with perceived opportunity for glory. *Journal of Personality and Social Psychology, 82*(5), 819–834.

Watson, P. J., & Andrews, P. W. (2002). Toward a revised evolutionary adaptationist analysis of depression: The social navigation hypothesis. *Journal of Affective Disorders, 72*, 1–14.

Weisfeld, G. E. (2006). Humor appreciation as an adaptive esthetic emotion. *Humor: The International Journal of Humor Research, 19*(1), 1–26.

Whalley, L. J., & Deary, I. J. (2001). Longitudinal cohort study of childhood IQ and survival up to age 76. *British Medical Journal, 322*(7290), 819.

Winterer, G., Hariri, A. R., Goldman, D., & Weinberger, D. R. (2005). Neuroimaging and human genetics. *International Review of Neurobiology, 67*, 325–383.

Wilson, D. S., Near, D., & Miller, R. R. (1996). Machiavellianism: A synthesis of the evolutionary and psychological literatures. *Psychological Bulletin, 119*(2), 285–299.

Zebrowitz, L. A., Hall, J. A., Murphy, N. A., & Rhodes, G. (2002). Looking smart and looking good: Facial cues to intelligence and their origins. *Personality and Social Psychology Bulletin, 28*(2), 238–249.

Zebrowitz, L. A., & Montepare, J. (2006). The ecological approach to person perception: Evolutionary roots and contemporary offshoots. In M. Schaller, J. A. Simpson, & D. T. Kenrick (Eds.), *Evolution and social psychology* (pp. 81–113). New York: Psychology Press.

Chapter 16

Mating Intelligence: An Integrative Model and Future Research Directions

Glenn Geher and Michael A. Camargo
State University of New York at New Paltz

Stephen D. O'Rourke
The College of New Rochelle

In conceiving of mating intelligence (MI) as the whole set of cognitive processes tied to mating-relevant outcomes, it becomes clear that we are talking about a very broad domain of psychology, and a major portion of human nature. Accordingly, the MI construct can usefully guide future research only insofar as we can develop a clear, systematic, evidence-based model of MI's main components, including their evolutionary origins, adaptive functions, design features, and inter-relationships. In light of the variegated perspectives on MI presented in this volume, this chapter describes such a provisional model.

DOMAINS OF MATING INTELLIGENCE

What domains comprise MI? To the extent that MI encompasses all the cognitive processes that bear upon mating-relevant outcomes, MI potentially relates to all elements of human mating psychology. Major psychological domains of human mating would include at least the following:

1. *courtship display mechanisms,* including behavioral displays of physical qualities such as strength, virility, fertility, and athleticism, and

395

similar displays of psychological qualities ('mental fitness indicators') such as kindness, creativity, intelligence, resourcefulness, status, humor, and mental health (e.g., the chapters in this volume by
Kaufman, Kozbelt, Bromley, & Miller; Keller; Nettle & Clegg; Shaner,
Miller, & Mintz);

2. *mate-choice mechanisms* for evaluating and choosing among potential
sexual partners, based on integrating diverse physical and behavioral cues of mate value, whether directly observed (e.g., chapters
by Li and Penke, Todd, Lenton, & Fasolo, this volume) or reported by
others (see De Backer, Braeckman, & Farinpour, this volume);

3. *self-evaluation mechanisms* for assessing one's own mate value, attractiveness, mating intelligence, and capacity for sexual competition
(see Penke et al., this volume);

4. *mechanisms for making context-sensitive decisions about mating strategies,*
including:

   (a) whether to pursue short-term or long-term relationships
   (Weekes-Shackelford, Easton, & Stone, this volume),
   (b) whether to pursue honest or deceptive courtship (O'Sullivan,
   this volume),
   (c) seeking good parent or good genes traits (Miller, this volume),
   (d) adopting mate-attraction or rival-intimidation tactics (Kaufman
   et al., this volume)
   (e) evaluating the local mating market's current ecological, social,
   cultural, and demographic features (Ash & Gallup; Figueredo,
   Brumbach, Jones, Sefcek, Vasquez, & Jacobs, this volume), and
   (f) evaluating one's own mate value in relation to the mate value
   distribution of potential mates in the local mating market (Penke
   et al., this volume);

5. *cross-sex mind-reading mechanisms* for understanding and influencing
the behavior of potential mates, and of their friends, families, and
children (De Backer et al.; O'Sullivan, this volume);

6. *same-sex mind-reading mechanisms* for understanding and influencing
the behavior of potential sexual rivals, and of their friends, families,
and allies (Kaufman et al., this volume).

Although future MI research is sure to uncover other fundamental
domains of MI, these six domains capture much of what we mean to this
construct. A model based on these domains should serve as a useful foundation for further MI research.

FIXED VERSUS VARIABLE COMPONENTS
OF MATING INTELLIGENCE

Two competing ideas can be advanced regarding the nature of the elements of MI. One suggests that the elements of MI are best treated as ancestrally shaped adaptations, which should vary little among individuals and, thus, be relatively fixed within the population (see Kanazawa, this volume). The other view argues that the elements of MI are best conceptualized as prototypical fitness indicators and, thus, should have a discernable heritable component, should be strongly related to other fitness indicators, and should show a great deal of variability within the population (see Miller, 2000). However, our position is that this debate over the nature of MI need not be characterized as an "either/or" proposition. The integrated model presented here suggests that some elements of MI are likely best described by the 'fixed within the population' adaptation model, whereas other elements may be best conceptualized as fitness indicators.

Some elements of MI—especially the courtship display mechanisms—should be highly variable and heritable, because they evolved as fitness indicators (Keller, Miller, Nettle, Shaner et al., this volume). Such mental fitness indicators should reflect an individual's overall phenotypic quality and/or genetic quality. In conceiving of these qualities as *fitness indicators*, we see them as valued in mate choice *partly* because genetic quality reveals a low mutation load, so predicts good offspring. Thus, such qualities may have survival benefits separate from their benefits to offspring as fitness indicators, but their nature is conceptualized as having evolved partly due to their utility in helping potential mates discriminate among different partners with genotypes that vary in quality. As such, the quality of these indicators should correlate positively with each other, with general intelligence, and with physical health, fertility, and attractiveness.

Other elements of MI, however, that either do not serve a courtship-signaling function at all, or that do not have such signaling as a primary purpose, likely do not behave as would be expected of fitness indictors. Rather, these other elements of MI should be human universals—tightly optimized adaptations shared by all normal, sexually mature men and/or women (Kanazawa; Miller, this volume). Although we might expect large individual differences in capacities for attracting mates through the display of intelligence, creativity, or humor, we might expect much smaller differences in mate choice mechanisms, self-evaluation mechanisms, decision-making mechanisms regarding mating strategies, and cross-sex and same-sex mind-reading abilities. The functional efficiency of these mechanisms should show much lower positive correlations with each other, with general intelligence, with rated psychological attractiveness, with physical health, or with achieved reproductive success.

For instance, consider the cognitive abilities for satisficing in sequential mate search (Penke et al., this volume), including the process of setting an optimal aspiration level for potential mates based on feedback about one's own mate value. This process does not primarily serve to advertise one's own fitness to potential mates. These cognitive abilities are unlikely to have originated as fitness indicators in their own right. In principle, the mechanism for setting an aspiration level could be a human universal, with low variance and low heritability, and a functional efficiency that is not very correlated with general intelligence or genetic quality.

The output of the mechanism—one's aspiration level itself—could come to be perceived as a fitness indicator of sorts. For example, a person with a long and successful mating history is likely to set a high aspirational level for potential mates. That trait of being "choosy" could well become a valid attractiveness cue to others. However, our concern here in modeling MI is more focused on the mechanism itself and people's ability to optimally set a satisficing threshold. This ability should demonstrate less inter-individual variability compared with abilities that are more clearly tied to fitness advertisement. Further, such a satisficing ability may demonstrate less heritability compared with abilities that are more defensibly characterized as fitness indicators.

The MI model presented here (see Figure 16–1) suggests that many elements of MI can be dichotomized into high-variability fitness indicators versus low-variability mating adaptations. This distinction may point to a reconciliation between the models of MI proposed by Miller (2000b) and by Kanazawa (2004). In short, perhaps the fitness-indicator elements of MI are strongly and reliably related to general intelligence (g), as suggested by Miller (2000), whereas the other, more universal elements of MI are best conceptualized as ancestral adaptations with low g-loadings (consistent with Kanazawa's (2004) approach). In a subsequent section on future MI research, we discuss potential research that could shed light on this aspect of our integrative model.

RELATEDNESS TO GENERAL INTELLIGENCE (g)

Given the prominent place of general intelligence (the g factor) in the psychological literature on individual differences, any human attribute hypothesized as comprising a sort of intelligence should show some positive and reliable relationship with g (Mayer, Caruso, & Salovey, 2000). Our model suggests that different elements of MI should vary in their g-loadings. In light of recent work suggesting that g may directly reflect phenotypic and genetic quality (Prokosch, Yeo, & Miller, 2005), we might expect higher g-loadings among the courtship-display abilities than among the

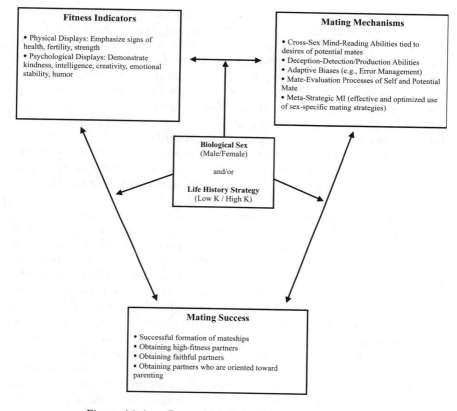

Figure 16–1.   General Model of Mating Intelligence.

universal mating adaptations (for mate choice, self-evaluation, strategic decision-making in mating, and cross-sex and same-sex mind-reading). Future tests of this prediction should clarify the relationships between mating intelligence and general intelligence.

THE MODERATING EFFECTS OF SEX AND LIFE-HISTORY STRATEGY

A coherent, unified theory of MI needs to take into account variables such as sex and life-history strategy (see Figueredo et al., this volume) that have been demonstrated to influence mating behaviors across cultures. The most relevant such variables will be fundamental traits (such as being male or female) that have pervasive influences across all aspects of mate search, mate choice, courtship, sexual rivalry, relationship formation, mate retention, and reproduction.

Sex differences in human mating outcomes are so well-documented (both in this volume and in other publications), that, regardless of one's theoretical orientation, any serious scientific research on human mating must address sex differences. In terms of the two general classes of MI constructs included in our model, for instance, males and females have been found to differ in the quality and quantity of different courtship display behaviors (e.g., humor; see Kaufman et al., this volume), with males often *producing* a larger quantity of such displays, and females often *discriminating* more accurately the quality of such displays (see Miller, 2000a). Further, a great deal of research demonstrates that the sexes differ in their general mating strategies, with males using short-term, opportunistic, and coercive strategies more often than females (see Buss, 2003).

In the light of a unified framework for understanding MI, then, biological sex must be seen as a major moderating variable (see Figures 16–2 and 16–3). In terms of courtship-display components of MI, we expect sex differences in the cognitive processes underlying both the production and perception of such signals. Specifically, we predict that male humans will show higher means and variances in the quantities, qualities, costs, and risks of their courtship displays, just as Darwin (1871) observed for males of most species. Conversely, we expect that female humans will show higher accuracies, lower biases, higher reliabilities, and higher validities in their judgments of courtship displays by the opposite sex, just as Darwin (1871) observed for females of most species. Regarding courtship displays, MI among males will primarily be evidenced through proficiency in signal production, while MI among females will primarily be evidenced through signal detection and judgment.

We also predict important sex differences in other components of MI apart from courtship display. For example, males should generally be more adept at short-term mating strategies, whereas females should be more adept at long-term mating strategies. Thus, males may be better at judging whether a female is interested in casual sex, whereas females may be better at screening out males who feign commitment in hopes of obtaining sexual relations (see Figures 16–2 and 16–3).

Life-history strategy (Figueredo, Vasquez, & Brumbach, 2005) concerns the hierarchy of fundamental biological trade-offs of time, energy, resources, and risk. At the most general level, there are trade-offs between 'somatic effort' (growth, survival) and 'reproductive effort' (mating, parenting). Within reproductive effort, there are trade-offs between trying to produce new offspring (mating) versus investing in existing offspring (parenting). In the sphere of mating, there are trade-offs between trying to attract new mates (courtship effort) versus trying to retain an existing mate (mate retention effort). Within courtship effort, there are

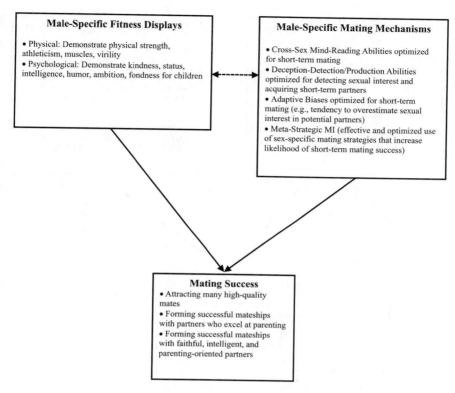

Figure 16–2.   A Model of Mating Intelligence for Males.

trade-offs between focusing all energy on one potential mate (falling in love) versus spreading effort across several potential mates (playing the field).

Different species, sexes, and individuals tend to adopt different 'life-history strategy' at each of these levels, which correspond to different points on these trade-off curves. At the psychological level, a life-history strategy can be viewed as a super-ordinate personality variable that incorporates both domain-general personality traits (e.g., emotional stability/neuroticism, extraversion/introversion; see Nettle & Clegg, this volume) and mating-specific aspects of social and sexual behavior (such as adult attachment style—Zeifman & Hazan, 1997). In Figueredo et al.'s conception of life-history strategy (this volume), individuals differ in the time and energy they allocate to survival versus mating, depending on the predictability of the environment. If ecological conditions are generally unstable (making life expectancy short), it makes more sense to focus on fast,

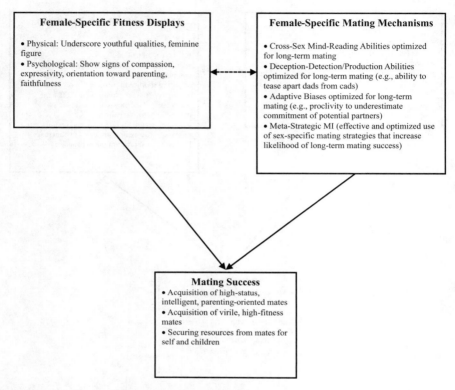

Figure 16–3.   A Model of Mating Intelligence for Females.

opportunistic mating and reproduction (live fast, die young—the 'low K' strategy). Under more stable, low-risk, resource-rich conditions, it makes more sense to grow slowly, mate carefully, and parent conscientiously (live long and prosper—the 'high K' strategy).

This low-K (fast, reckless) versus high-K (slow, careful) life-history dimension is exactly the kind of unifying, evolutionarily informed, big-picture construct that warrants inclusion in a general model of MI. Just as biological sex has important theoretical ramifications for both the courtship-display and mating-adaptation elements of MI, life-history strategy probably does too (see Figures 16–4 and 16–5).

In terms of the courtship-display elements of MI, life-history strategy may influence the kinds of signals one emits in courtship and the kinds of signals that one prefers from a potential mate. We predict that explic-itly sexual signals (e.g., provocative clothing, dance movements, double entendres) should be produced more often by individuals with a relatively

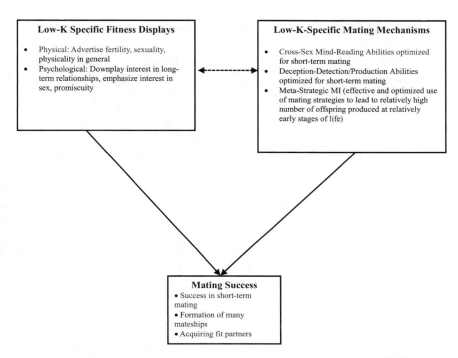

Figure 16–4.   A Model of Mating Intelligence for Individuals With Low-K (Fast) Life-History Strategy.

fast (low-K) life-history strategy and, likewise, such signals should be more attractive to other low-K individuals. In terms of mating mechanisms, we predict that relatively fast (low-K) individuals should possess cognitive mechanisms better optimized for short-term, opportunistic mating with multiple partners, and for lower parental investment in each offspring, whereas relatively slow (high-K) individuals should possess cognitive mechanisms better optimized for long-term, committed mating with fewer high-quality partners, and for high parental investment in each offspring.

Importantly, sex and life-history strategy should have somewhat similar effects on mating intelligence, with males most similar to the low-K strategy, and females most similar to the high-K strategy. Accordingly, research inspired by this model could benefit from delineating the extent to which sex and life-history strategy explain unique variance within the mating domain, by measuring these factors simultaneously in correlational and experimental studies.

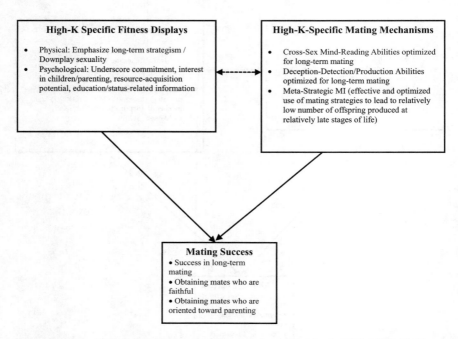

Figure 16–5.   A Model of Mating Intelligence for Individuals With High-K (Slow) Life-History Strategy.

SUMMARY OF OUR INTEGRATED MODEL OF MATING INTELLIGENCE

Our model (see Figures 16–1 through 16–5) suggests that MI can be broken into two basic classes of constructs: those primarily focused on courtship-displays (fitness indicators) and those that are not (what we refer to as mating mechanisms). Courtship-display components of MI are predicted to behave very much like other sexually selected traits, demonstrating high inter-individual variability and heritability, showing sex differences in means and variances for both production and discrimination of such displays, and being inter-correlated with other indices of genetic fitness (such as general intelligence, physical health, and mental health). Mating mechanisms (such as the ability to accurately know if a potential mate is a long-term strategist and is relatively dependable) are predicted to behave more like other species-typical adaptations, showing less variability and heritability among individuals, and being less inter-correlated with indices of genetic fitness (see Figure 16–1).

However, even the reliable mating mechanisms may show some variability due to frequency-dependent selection, which can maintain different strategic forms of an adaptation in a population over evolutionary time.

For instance, while many males may possess cognitive processes optimized for short-term mating success, others may possess mechanisms more optimized for long-term mating—mechanisms that may be rarer, more attractive, and hence more effective when there is a local excess of short-term strategists (see Geher, Derieg, & Downey, 2004).

As with all constructs in mating psychology, it is important to incorporate biological sex as a major variable that pervades all elements of mating. Our model suggests that the psychometric structure of MI varies between the sexes (see Figures 16–2 and 16–3). Intelligence tied to courtship displays may be sex-differentiated such that male intelligence is more strongly focused on producing displays and female intelligence may be more focused on judging the quality of displays. Further, the mating mechanisms are also likely to be sex-differentiated. Finally, we believe that life-history strategy is an important superordinate individual-differences construct that predicts individual differences in MI (see Figures 16–4 and 16–5).

PROPOSED RESEARCH ON IMPORTANT QUESTIONS RELATED TO MATING INTELLIGENCE

Our integrative model of MI is broad and multi-faceted, identifying several new confluences between *mating* and *intelligence*. Accordingly, the ideas integrated into this volume provide myriad fertile ideas for future researchers. Some of the core hypotheses and research directions inspired by this volume are presented here, in a list intended to be provocative rather than exhaustive.

THE RELATIONSHIP BETWEEN SUCCESSFUL MATING AND INTELLIGENCE: KANAZAWA VERSUS MILLER (OR "HBES 2006 REVISITED")

In one of the more memorable presentations at the 18th meeting of the Human Behavior and Evolution Society conference in Philadelphia (2006), Satoshi Kanazawa argued that general intelligence is both theoretically and empirically unrelated to human reproductive success. One of the slides in his presentation explicitly pointed out the conflicts between his perspective and that of Geoffrey Miller, who argues that general intelligence is a major fitness indicator that was selected because it increased the sexual attractiveness of our ancestors.

Future research on MI should address this apparent conflict between Kanazawa's (2004) and Miller's (2000) theses. The discrepancy is basically this: Miller argues that the centrality of g in human psychology reflects its centrality as a fitness indicator shaped by mate choice throughout prehistory. Thus, he conceptualizes g as a subordinate factor that underlies a general biological 'fitness factor' that represents general phenotypic and genetic quality. As such, he argues that g should be moderately related to other indices of phenotypic quality (such as body symmetry, physical health, longevity, fertility, and mental health). Miller, his colleagues, and others have found modest all-positive correlations between g and these variables (Prokosch et al., 2005). On the other hand, Kanazawa conceives of g as a psychological adaptation in its own right that evolved fairly recently to cope with evolutionarily novel ecological challenges, and that therefore should be unrelated to sexual attractiveness or reproductive success in modern societies. His data are consistent with his ideas (see Kanazawa, 2004).

It may be useful to consider the nuanced differences between these approaches. Simply, Miller predicts *a positive correlation* between g and indices of general biological fitness whereas Kanazawa predicts *no correlation* between g and contemporary mating success. These predictions differ in the particular constructs thought to relate to g. In support of his position, Kanazawa reviews substantial evidence that g does not predict mating success (e.g. numbers of sexual partners, numbers of offspring) in modern societies. We may be able to resolve the discrepancy as follows: In ancestral times, g probably correlated with both biological fitness *and* mating success (including quality and quantity of mates and offspring). However, under evolutionarily novel modern conditions (e.g., with contraception and society-imposed monogamy standards), some evidence suggests that individuals higher in g are having fewer children than individuals who are lower in g (see Kanazawa, this volume). This pattern likely pertains to the fact that individuals higher in g are generally more capable of obtaining and using birth control effectively—not necessarily because they are less capable of attracting high-quality mates than others. Thus, highly g-loaded forms of MI might still be fulfilling their evolved adaptive purpose—attracting interest from many high-quality partners. This may explain Kanazawa's observations that g does not predict reproductive success *in modern contexts*.

This suggested resolution of Miller's and Kanazawa's frameworks could be tested through cross-cultural research. Specifically, researchers could examine relationships between MI, mating success, and reproductive success in natural-fertility populations (without contraception or 'Western' lifestyles), such as the Ache of Paraguay, the Tsimane of Bolivia, or the Hadza of Tanzania. In such samples, g might positively predict the quality and/or quantity of mates, offspring, and grand-offspring. If so, the apparent discrepancy between Kanazawa's and Miller's theories would represent a classic case of 'mismatch' between ancestral and modern conditions.

Another important feature of MI to consider in future research would be the distinction between courtship-display and non-courtship display domains. Miller's (2000) theory regarding the evolution of higher-order human mental qualities focuses on such qualities as having been shaped for courtship-display. Such qualities are predicted to load onto a general fitness factor and, thus, are predicted to inter-correlate with other fitness indicators. However, the mating mechanisms of MI in our model (elements of MI that are not for courtship display) should not act as fitness indicators and should be less related to other fitness indicators (such as g). Thus, this model makes clear predictions regarding the inter-relationships between g, different domains of MI, and reproductive success in natural-fertility populations. In such populations, we predict that g would be positively related to both courtship-display elements of MI and reproductive success (consistent with Miller's perspective), while g would be *less* related to the efficiency of mating mechanisms (such as detecting mating-relevant lies by potential mates)—though these mating mechanisms may still predict reproductive success.

THE PSYCHOMETRIC VALIDATION OF MATING INTELLIGENCE

The mating mechanisms in our model may be inter-related much like the abilities that underlie emotional intelligence (see Mayer et al., 2000). The Mayer/Salovey/Caruso ability-based model of emotional intelligence suggests that there are four basic facets of emotional intelligence, which are somewhat inter-related and mildly g-loaded. Specifically, they argue that the main elements of emotional intelligence are the abilities to identify emotions, assimilate emotion into thought, understand emotions, and manage emotions (in one's self and others). While emotional intelligence has provoked much skepticism within academic circles (see Matthews, Zeidner, & Roberts, 2004), the Mayer/Salovey/Caruso four-pronged model has generally been considered the most theoretically and empirically defensible of the different models that do exist (see Casey et al., this volume).

This framework may prove to be a useful model for understanding MI. Just as emotional intelligence may have basic inter-related components that underlie it (such as the identifying-emotion ability), MI may also have basic elements (including the abilities presented in Figure 16–1, such as the ability to accurately assess one's own mate value) which may be inter-related and, ultimately, may be found to comprise a distinct set of mating-relevant cognitive abilities. Given the important distinction between courtship-display and mating-mechanism elements of MI, such a model would need to treat these domains separately, possibly predicting no (or little) correlation between courtship-display and mating-mechanism domains of MI.

The kind of psychometric work that has been done to validate the ability-based model of emotional intelligence (see Mayer & Geher, 1996; Brackett et al., 2003) could also be used to validate our model of MI. In addition to such basic psychometric qualities such as internal reliability of measuring instruments, etc., such work would need to demonstrate (a) that different elements of MI are inter-related, (b) that they are somewhat related to g, (c) that they are not redundant with well-established personality traits such as the Big Five (Costa & McCrae, 1992), and (d) that abilities which comprise MI are, indeed, predictive of mating success (such as the abilities to attract, choose, court, and retain high-quality sexual partners, and to deter sexual rivals and infidelities). Such psychometric work will be crucial in determining whether MI is a useful individual-differences construct within psychology writ large. Further, given that emotional intelligence is predictive of success in intimate relationships (see Casey et al., this volume), research on the interface between emotional intelligence and MI could be both theoretically and practically valuable.

MATING INTELLIGENCE AND STRATEGIC PLURALISM

One of the core insights of modern evolutionary psychology concerns strategic pluralism (see Buss & Schmitt, 1993; Simpson & Gangestad, 2000), the observation that a variety of strategic behavioral patterns can often co-exist within a population, with each such pattern promoting reproductive success through its own distinctive methods (e.g., Geher et al., 2004). For example, the different sexes may represent different strategies that achieve equal average reproductive success, but through quite different channels, which is why a balanced sex ratio has evolved. Likewise, being extraverted makes it easier to meet new mates but imposes higher social and physical risks, so a balance of extroversion and introversion can persist in human populations (Nettle, 2005).

Human mating strategies comprise the central behavioral domain in which strategic pluralism has been studied (see Buss, 2003). The most commonly studied strategic pluralisms concern male versus female strategies and short versus long-term strategies, which are often framed as sex-specific (Buss & Schmitt, 1993). For instance, Haselton and Miller (2006) found that women are more attracted to creative intelligence in potential short-term mates during fertility peaks in their ovulatory cycle. This may be conceptualized as a sex-specific, short-term mating strategy.

Many of the authors who have contributed to this volume have conceptualized mating intelligence (MI) as the capacity to employ different optimal mating strategies under different conditions. For instance, DeBacker et al. (this volume) address how personal advertisements reflect general sex differences in mating strategies, as well as a rich assortment of sex-specific strategies for advertising one's own fitness and for assessing the fitness of potential others. Similarly, Figueredo et al. (this volume) consider strategic pluralism in the form of different life-history strategies that shape proclivities toward long versus short-term mating patterns. Nettle and Clegg (this volume) consider strategic pluralism in the form of different personality traits, such that both extremes of basic personality traits (e.g., neuroticism vs. emotional stability) reflect alternative mating strategies with their own distinctive fitness costs and benefits. Li's chapter considers strategic pluralism as a function of one's 'mate value' or 'mating budget,' investigating how people modify their mate preferences depending on the amount of 'mating currency' they possess. Finally, Weekes-Shackelford et al. suggest that the presence of children from a prior mateship should have major implications for optimal mating decisions (e.g., a single mother may focus more on good parenting qualities in choosing future mates).

In short, these chapters underscore the notion that there are many paths to success in human mating. Accordingly, MI, focusing on cognitive abilities in the mating domain, may be conceptualized in strategic terms. At a species-typical level, the rich and varied nature of human mating behaviors reflects a highly tuned intelligence that takes a vast array of fitness-relevant contingencies into account. For instance, Schmitt's (2005) work on variability in mating patterns across cultures suggests that the proclivity toward short-term mating strategies is strongly influenced by relevant qualities of the local social environment, such as the prevailing sex ratio (with males, for instance, behaving more promiscuously in places that have more females than males).

In addition to strategic pluralism at the level of species-typical mating intelligence, strategic pluralism may unfold at the level of heritable traits, or individually learned mating tactics. Further, even at the species-typical level where reliable mating mechanisms should be sensitive to many contextual variables, some individuals may be better at modulating their mating preferences and behaviors in reaction to those variables. This facet of MI represents the cognitive skills for choosing the right mating strategies given the circumstances—what could be called *meta-strategic MI*. Some individuals may be good at particular mating strategies (e.g., acting provocative vs. coy, acting committed vs. nonchalant), but may be very poor at knowing which strategy to use in a particular circumstance (e.g., they may act coy with a nervous introvert, or act nonchalant when presenting an engagement ring).

Meta-strategic MI concerns the ability to employ the right mating strategies given the situation at hand. Suppose, for instance, that there are two heterosexual males (let's call them Andrew and Christopher) at a particular engineering college (with a 4:1 male-to-female ratio). As products of the organic evolutionary process, they are (unconsciously) designed to optimize their mating success. They are each in stable, happy, long-term relationships (Andrew is with Melissa and Christopher is with Lauren). At a campus party one night, Andrew and Christopher run into two sexually attractive, flirtatious, and extraverted female students (Kathy and Kelly). Suppose that Andrew decides to keep his sexual desires in check while Christopher "makes a move on" Kathy. Several features of this scenario make Christopher's behavior less mating-intelligent thanAndrew's. Kathy is a popular extravert at a college party, so it is likely that Christopher's short-term play for Kathy will become known across campus. This may provoke Lauren toward jealousy and anger leading to a possible break-up. Christopher has much to lose from such a break-up: He is in a happy long-term relationship, and eligible women are rare in this particular environment, so he might have trouble replacing Lauren if she leaves him.

In this case, Andrew's behavior is smarter than Christopher's. He may have had the same sexual desires, but he was better attuned to his position and prospects within the local mating market (good current relationship, unfavorable sex ratio for mate-switching, hot-bed of gossip). His choice to not pursue his short-term desires was adaptive both for his immediate future (his current relationship with Melissa) and his long-term future (his sexual reputation, his prospects for marrying Melissa, etc.). Ultimately, the kinds of relatively intelligent choices made by Andrew here may lead to more mating success.

This analysis does not imply that long-term mating strategies are always superior to short-term strategies. (If the college's sex ratio were reversed, Kathy might be more likely to respond positively to Christopher's advances, and Lauren might be more forgiving of his attempted infidelity). Rather, the point here is that the decisions to pursue long versus short-term mating strategies should vary as a function of many contextual factors. An individual who is high in MI may be more adept at using short versus long-term strategies in ways that would have promoted reproductive success under ancestral conditions (if not modern conditions).

This meta-strategic dimension of MI mating mechanisms could be studied by examining mating-relevant choices that people make in real-world or hypothetical scenarios. For instance, as with ability-based measures of emotional intelligence (e.g., Bracket & Salovey, 2004), people could read scenarios (such as the Andrew/Christopher scenario above), in which mating-relevant contextual variables are manipulated, and their strategic choices are recorded. These choices could then be examined in terms of agreement with choices of other subjects making such judgments or of the options deemed most adaptive by a panel of experts on mating research. Each individual's meta-strategic MI ability could then be estimated and studied in future research. Meta-Strategic MI may emerge as a particularly important kind of cognitive ability when it comes to increasing mating success.

ACCURACY VERSUS ERROR IN CROSS-SEX MIND-READING

Some core components of MI concern Theory of Mind abilities (Baron-Cohen, 1999) as applied in the mating domain. Cross-sex and same-sex mind reading are needed to understand the mating psychologies of potential mates, sexual rivals, and interested on-lookers (e.g., friends, parents, children, siblings). For instance, a high-MI individual should be able to discern if a potential mate is sexually interested, is an honest long-term strategist, is someone with high subjective mate value, etc. Such social attributions are crucial to mating success in our highly social, highly talkative species.

However, when it comes to domains of social intelligence, raw accuracy may often be less intelligent—or at least less adaptive—than a proclivity toward adaptive biases in judgment, which minimize the expected *costs* rather than the raw *likelihood* of errors (Haselton & Buss, 2000; Haselton & Nettle, 2006). In particular, Haselton and her colleagues argue that mating-relevant biases, such as the tendency for males to overestimate the sexual interest of females, may be adaptive and may ultimately have been selected for precisely that reason. Because a 'miss' (failing to detect a woman's sexual interest when it is there) would be very costly (perhaps reducing reproductive success by one entire child), whereas a 'false alarm' (attributing sexual interest when it is not there) would be fairly cheap (entailing some wasted courtship effort), men should, from this perspective, be adaptively biased to minimize misses. Given a particular level of detection accuracy, such a pattern necessarily increases false alarms. Higher discrimination accuracy is of course always better, but in the real world, the accuracy of social attribution is always limited. Where accuracy is limited, adaptive biases should evolve to minimize the costs of errors and these adaptive biases should correspondingly be related to MI.

As described in Chapter 1, this error management perspective has important implications for research on the cross-sex and same-sex mind-reading elements of MI. In the initial research on MI conducted at SUNY New Paltz (Geher, DeWispelaere, Lavallee, & Musicaro, 2006), we created sex-specific indices of long-term MI and short-term MI modified from ability-based research on emotional intelligence (Mayer & Geher, 1996). We briefly describe this research here to provide an example of MI research dealing with cross-sex mind-reading.

A total of 481 (329 females; 152 males) young adults judged which personal ads (written by opposite-sex individuals) represented the most desirable short and long-term mates. All participants then engaged in a cross-sex mind-reading task by guessing which ads were rated most desirable by opposite-sex individuals. Overall, males were more accurate than females across both short and long-term judgments. (That is, men better understood what women wanted from male personal ads than women understood what men wanted from female personal ads.) A content analysis showed that males mildly overestimated the degree to which females focused on sexual qualities in short-term mates, whereas females more strongly over-estimated the degree to which males focused on sexual qualities in both short-term and long-term mates.

These errors are consistent with Haselton and Buss' (2000) Error Management Theory which suggests that *biased* (as opposed to *accurate*) social judgments should be typical when biases would have been evolutionarily adaptive. Recall that we propose mating mechanisms (such as the abilities to make adaptive mating-relevant judgments) to likely be somewhat g-loaded (while being *less* g-loaded than courtship display mechanisms). In support of this theory, we found a positive correlation between this male bias to 'overestimate sexual interest' and males' scores on an index of general intelligence (Yerkes, 1921), supporting a model of MI which includes adaptively biased cross-sex mind-reading.

In an interesting post-hoc analysis, we delved into the relationship between g and short-term mating judgments by males to address a question raised by Geoffrey Miller (2006; personal communication). Specifically, we investigated whether males were accurately matching the stated short-term preferences of females who were high in sociosexuality (Simpson & Gangestad, 1991), a construct roughly synonymous with promiscuity. Miller's rationale for this question was that high-sociosexuality women are most likely to acquiesce to advances for short-term encounters, whereas low-sociosexuality women are not. Although sociosexuality is hard to discern, men might benefit (i.e., minimize the fitness costs of sexual-interest attribution errors) by treating most women as high on sociosexuality until proven otherwise. This may be especially useful for males seeking casual sex.

We looked at the personal-ad preferences of high-sociosexuality women choosing short-term mating partners, with high sociosexuality defined as scoring more than one SD above the mean. There were only two items where high-sociosexuality women preferred a more sexually overt personal ad as desirable for a short-term partner compared with other women. Consistent with Miller's hunch, men who chose both of these sexually overt options as reflecting the short-term desires of women scored higher on our index of general intelligence than men who did not choose both of these options as reflecting the short-term desires of women.

These preliminary findings suggest that more intelligent males may overestimate women's sexual interest more often. Additionally, these results indicate that accuracy in knowing the short-term judgments of relatively promiscuous women and making the error of overgeneralizing those judgments to other women may be positively related to g for males. These findings suggest that certain kinds of accuracy and adaptive biases in cross-sex mind-reading—an important form of MI—may be associated with general intelligence.

The summary of this research here is intentionally brief, and is included mainly to provide a snapshot of research driven by the notion of MI. A key point is that raw accuracy in mating-relevant judgments may not necessarily be most closely associated with intelligence. Future empirical work on MI as a form of judgment and decision-making needs to carefully consider the success criterion being optimized by such decisions—expected net fitness payoffs may often be more important than some narrowly defined notion of 'accuracy.' When total accuracy is not likely or even plausible, *erroneous but adaptive* may be a good definition of intelligent.

This summary of our initial MI research suggests that future research on cross-sex mind-reading should not assume (as some marital therapists might) that 100 percent accurate telepathy and empathy is the gold standard of adaptive functioning. Systematic biases, omissions, blind spots, wishful thinking, and self-deceptions may often pay. The most biologically successful courtships and relationships may be characterized by a patchwork quilt of mutual insight and mutual ignorance. Further research should address the ways in which MI predicts accuracy in some domains, adaptive bias in others, and adaptive ignorance in still others. It should also explore the *g*-loadings and personality correlates of MI, and how MI predicts different forms of mating success (see later section dealing with issues tied to operationalizing this important outcome variable).

RESEARCH ON THE COURTSHIP-DISPLAY COMPONENT OF MATING INTELLIGENCE

Several of the chapters in this volume focus on the courtship-display component of MI (e.g., Kaufman et al.; Keller; Shaner et al.). Generally, the ideas included in these chapters are steeped in Miller's (2000a) theory of higher-order mental qualities as serving a courtship-display function and as having evolved via sexual selection through mutual mate choice.

Since the publication of *The Mating Mind* (Miller, 2000a), several studies have tested varied aspects of Miller's thesis (e.g., Haselton & Miller, 2006; Prokosch et al., 2005). With regard to the nature of MI, several hypotheses regarding the interface of human intelligence and courtship-displays used in human mating can be tested by future researchers. The variety of hypotheses that follow from extant research and theory on this topic is impressive in scope.

For instance, Shaner et al. (this volume) suggest several hypotheses regarding abnormal behavior and mating intelligence. These authors argue that several mental disorders, such as schizophrenia, have their etiologies rooted in high mutation loads, and that, across evolutionary time, people evolved to pay close attention to symptoms of such disorders, as cues of relatively low fitness (high mutation load) in potential mates. This theory, which conceives of mental disorders such as schizophrenia as the low-fitness extremes of fitness-indicator dimensions, leads to several novel hypotheses. For instance, it suggests that biases against individuals with mental disorders which act as (low) fitness indicators should be stronger in females (who are typically choosier than males), particularly during the relatively fertile parts of their ovulatory cycles.

Two important general issues that should be addressed by future research on the courtship-display components of MI—the structure of fitness-indicator dimensions, and the apparent positive manifold among fitness indicators—are discussed next.

The Structure of Fitness Indicator Dimensions. The fitness-indicator model suggests that we are particularly attuned to behavioral qualities of potential mates that reveal 'good' versus 'not so good' genes. In particular, Keller (this volume), Miller (this volume), and Shaner et al. (this volume) suggest that many attractive traits (e.g., facial symmetry, voice timbre, happy mood) evolved to be attractive because they signal that a potential mate has a low mutation load. Because any particular harmful mutation is likely to go extinct sooner or later, it is usually better to avoid having offspring who carry such mutations, by avoiding mates who display their manifestations. Thus, much of mate choice can be explained as an adaptive fear of heritable mutations—as *mutation-phobia.*

Researchers in this mutation-phobia camp suggest that overall genetic quality (the inverse of mutation load) exists on a continuum, roughly approximating a normal distribution. However, sometimes this continuous dimension may show up in a more categorical way, as the presence or absence of a particular behavioral trait or syndrome. Often, our mate preferences may have been shaped more to avoid mating with high-mutation-load individuals who have obvious physical or psychological problems, than to make very fine discriminations among individuals who seem more or less normal. Zebrowitz and Rhodes (2004) provide some evidence for this idea. They found that people could accurately predict overall health and intelligence for targets with relatively unattractive faces, but not for targets with relatively attractive faces. Facial attractiveness was predictive of health and intelligence only at the low-fitness extreme. These findings suggest an asymmetry between attraction toward high-fitness individuals and repulsion toward low-fitness individuals. Such an asymmetry suggests that for some fitness-indicator dimensions, there may be a curvilinear relationship between indicator quality and sexual attractiveness (concave-downwards, with rapidly diminishing returns above the mean of indicator quality). For example, someone with an IQ of 90 may be much more attractive than someone with an IQ of 70, but a potential mate with an IQ of 150 may be only a little more attractive than one whose IQ is 130.

As a thought experiment, consider college professors. Generally, professors are quite intelligent and creative. However, as one of our spouses pointed out in conversations during the writing of this book, not all professors would look great strutting on a Paris catwalk in this season's trendiest designer clothes. Intelligence may not be highly correlated with physical attractiveness at the upper end of the distribution. On the other hand, most average people would not look great in haute couture fashions either. The notion of an overall fitness factor suggests, rather, that professors, given their relatively high g (on average!), compared with the non-professorial counterparts, are relatively good looking (Miller, 2000b), free of psychological abnormality (Shaner et al., this volume), pleasant to listen to (Hughes, Dispenza, & Gallup, 2004) and pleasant-smelling (Thornhill & Gangestad, 1999). That is, the mutation-phobia camp suggests that there should be a 'positive manifold' (all-positive correlations) among fitness indicators—an idea addressed in detail in the next section.

Our alternative conception of fitness-indicator theory suggests that we are repulsed by high mutation loads (and low-quality fitness indicators) more than we are attracted to low mutation loads (and high-quality indicators). In this view of the world, some people are "messed up" in almost every way, but almost nobody is perfect in every way. If so, we can better understand how bright professors can so often be rather asymmetrical in body and abnormal in mind. Much more research needs to be done on the (probably nonlinear) functions that relate mutation load to mental fitness indicators, and that relate indicator quality to attractiveness in mating. A methodological issue arises here: If fitness indicators correlate differently at low-quality and high-quality extremes, then bright, healthy, college sophomores may not be the best and/or only population we should be studying for MI research on the display and judgment of fitness indicators! We will need to sample populations from all strata of society to have an honest chance of answering the MI questions we seek to ask.

The Positive-Manifold Principle. The courtship-display domain of MI, including costly, conspicuous displays of cognitive prowess in language, music, art, and humor (Miller, 2000a), may be thought of as reflecting a person's overall genetic quality (see Keller & Miller, 2006; Keller, this volume, & Shaner et al., this volume). An important characteristic of this fitness-indicator view concerns the positive-manifold principle, initially delineated by Spearman (1904) in describing the nature of general intelligence. In terms of g, Spearman's insights regarding the positive manifold speak to the consistently positive nature found among correlations between different intelligence indices.

In conceiving of g-loaded mental traits as having arisen from sexual selection processes, Miller (2000b) posits that g is basically an index of neurodevelopmental stability and brain efficiency that taps into an overall fitness factor (roughly, the first principal component of genetic quality across all fitness-related traits). Further, he proposes that the existence of this superordinate fitness factor should be manifest as a positive manifold (all-positive correlations) among fitness indicators in general, both physical and mental. As evidence of this notion, Miller cites research demonstrating positive correlations among disparate traits that are reasonably considered good fitness indices, including multiple aspects of intelligence, body symmetry, longevity, mental health, and physical health (see, e.g., Furlow, Armijo-Prewitt, Gangestad, & Thornhill, 1997).

This fitness-indicator conceptualization of MI is truly provocative (if unsettling!). It also has many important implications for future empirical work in the behavioral sciences. In his prior paper on this topic, Miller (2000b) delineates nine specific predictions, mostly concerning the positive-manifold among fitness indicators. An initial prediction is that factor analysis of fitness-indicator traits should demonstrate a super-ordinate, unifying factor with positive loadings across fitness indicators. Further, he proposes that the g factor should prove subordinate to the fitness factor in such an analysis, a finding that would be consistent with this notion of g as having a courtship-display function. See Miller (2000b) for a detailed rationale underlying this positive-manifold notion in addition to clearly articulated predictions. Future research on the positive-manifold model of fitness indicators should shed a great deal of light on the nature of the courtship-display components of MI.

OPERATIONALIZING MATING SUCCESS

Because of the nature of the MI construct, many research ideas that address MI share a common dependent variable: mating success. In light of the evolutionary reasoning that underlies MI, mating success is, in fact, a conceptual proxy for the more accurate index of the Darwinian success of a trait: reproductive success. In research on non-humans, reproductive success is often measured in terms of number of offspring produced—a straightforward and construct-valid index of success from an evolutionary perspective. However, for reasons described in this section, this index of evolutionary success is simply not appropriate when studying modern humans.

When considering Darwinian success in the animal world, reproductive success becomes a bit more complex than simply considering total number of offspring produced. Fisher (1915) suggested that the struggle to replicate should not only be measured by the number of offspring produced, but also by the success of these offspring in producing and rearing *offspring of their own*, who in return would also be able to produce offspring. Thus, *reproductive success* might best be thought of as the total number of descendants that an individual has (Hamilton, 1964).

Variation in reproductive success is the driving force behind evolution. "All selection is sexual selection in the sense that sex is the only means by which genes find their way from one generation to the next" (Ash & Gallup, this volume). In sexually reproducing species, there are often major sex differences in the nature of the elements underlying reproductive success. In humans, male reproductive success is generally limited by access to fertile females, while female reproductive success is limited by the resources she can acquire for herself and her offspring (Buss, 1989).

Pérusse (1993) investigated the relationship between education, occupation, and income (what he termed "cultural success") and reproductive success among men from Quebec. He hypothesized that males with higher cultural success would have more reproductive success (operationalized as number of offspring) than males with lower cultural success. However, the opposite was found: males with *less* cultural success actually left *more offspring* than males with more cultural success. Pérusse reasoned that the use of contraceptives and institutionalized monogamy underlied this discrepancy. He attempted to resolve this problem by using a contemporary proxy for reproductive success: mating success.

In Pérusse's subsequent research, mating success was operationalized as the number of consensual sexual partners, which should reflect attractiveness to the opposite sex. Pérusse (1993) reasoned that before contraception, a male's mating success would strongly predict his reproductive success (for arguments against this thesis, see Alcock, 1993). Pérusse proposed the following formula to estimate the number of potential conceptions (NPC) for a male in the absence of contraceptives (adopted from Kanazawa, 2003):

$$NPC = \sum_{i=1}^{n} [(1 - (1 - p)]^{P_i}$$

where n is the total number of female sex partners, p is the probability of conception per coital act, and P_i is the number of coital acts with partner i.

However, there are potential problems with this formula. First, the reproductive success of monogamous males is limited by one's partner's ability to produce offspring, no matter how many times they copulate (Bookstein, 1993). Second, the formula does not take into account the survivability of the offspring produced. These criticisms raise doubts as to whether Pérusse's (1993) formula is an accurate index of male reproductive success.

In an attempt to replicate Pérusse's (1993) findings with a larger, more representative sample, Kanazawa (2003) found that wealthy men, while not producing more offspring, did have sex more frequently with more partners than less financially secure males. Wealth had no such effect for females. These findings support for the theories of Trivers (1972) and Buss (1989) that females should value financial security in a potential mate.

Research suggests that in industrialized societies, there is a rift between MI and actual reproductive success (see Kanazawa, this volume). However, the problems created by this rift may be reduced, at least in studying males, by remembering that evolution has equipped males with psychological mechanisms leading them to act as if copulation, not reproduction, is their ultimate goal (Kanazawa, 2003). Before contraceptives, there was probably a near-linear relationship between copulation and reproductive success for males. Now that the use of contraceptives is widespread in contemporary industrial societies, the relationship between number of copulations and reproductive success has been virtually severed (Kanazawa, 2003). The problem is how to study traits (such as MI components) that evolved to promote reproductive success in the ancestral past. Pérusse's (1993) number of potential conceptions index seems to be a good first step to resolve this dilemma, but it has the problems mentioned earlier. Like many first steps, it travels in the right direction but doesn't arrive at the final desired destination.

Landolt, Lalumière, and Quinsey (1995) developed a self-perceived mating success scale, to measure individual differences in the ability to attract mates through a series of self-report items. The scale showed good internal reliability (Cronbach's alpha 0.83), and showed some convergent validity, correlating positively with self-reported "approximate number of sexual invitations received over the past year" and "over the past three years" (Landolt et al., 1995, p. 13). One obvious drawback is that this scale relies on self-report data, which may produce inaccurate results through memory biases and social desirability effects (Nisbett & Wilson, 1977).

Another self-report method to measure mating success is simply to ask how many sexual partners an individual has had in a given time period, or during his or her lifetime so far (e.g., Gangestad & Simpson, 1990; Rhodes, Simmons, & Peters, 2005). This method seems viable since an increase in the number of sex partners should be associated with traits that are seen as attractive by the opposite sex, but, as pointed out by Linton and Wiener (2001), "These kinds of data [number of partners, frequency of coitus and self-perceived mating success], however (unlike the potential conceptions index), fail to take into account the low probability of conception per copulation in humans" (p. 685). These authors suggest that it is important not only to take into account the low probability of conception per coitus, but also the possibility that the female will mate with competing males, further reducing the first male's chances of conception.

Linton and Wiener (2001) propose a slightly altered form of Pérusse's (1993) equation that takes into account the number of coital acts a female has with competing males:

$$NPC = \sum_{i=1}^{n} [(1-(1-p)]^{Pi} Pi/Ti$$

where n is the total number of female sex partners, p is the probability of conception per coital act, Pi is the number of coital acts with partner i and Ti is the number of coital acts with partner i plus the number of coital acts that partner n takes part in with competing males.

One severe limitation regarding the measurement of mating success is the lack of data on females. As suggested by Trivers (1972) and Buss (1989), female reproductive success is limited by the ability to secure resources for her and her offspring. A female's reproductive success is not measured in the number of fertile males available (Buss, 1989), but by the number of offspring who survive to produce offspring of their own (Trivers, 1972). The most reproductively successful males have the potential to leave many times more children than any female could. However females are always certain about their maternity, while males can never be completely sure of their paternity (Trivers, 1972). Accordingly, measuring the reproductive success of any female should be relatively easy, while accurately measuring the reproductive success of males may be harder due to the risk of cuckoldry. These differences relate back to parental investment—to reproduce, males only need to fertilize the female's eggs, while females must carry the offspring to term, run the risk of injury or even death during pregnancy, and care for the child until it can care for itself. So, successful females can never have as many offspring as the most successful males (Trivers, 1972). This reasoning suggests that measures of human mating success must be sex-differentiated. If males' reproductive success is influenced by access to fertile women, then a male's mating success should reflect his ability to mate with fertile women. If a female's reproductive success is measured by access to resources, then a female's mating success should represent the ability to procure resources from males.

In a recent attempt to model female mating success, Putz et al. (2004) suggested the following formula:

$$NPC = 1 - (1-p)^k$$

where p is the probability of conceiving a child per copulation and k is the number of copulatory acts since the females' last conception. With the use of contraceptives, this equation has a lot of drawbacks because many females can go for years without ever having a conception, and it does not take into account the genetic quality of the male.

Mating success has been used as a proxy for reproductive success given our contemporary use of contraceptives and monogamy (Pérusse, 1993). Evolution depends not on the number of copulations, or sexual partners, but on the number of offspring who survive to produce offspring of their own. As suggested by Pérusse (1993) and Kanazawa (2003), contraception makes current reproductive success a misleading index of mating success. It is clear that much more work needs to be done before the field has a commonly accepted methodology for quantifying the mating success of males and females. Future research on MI will likely benefit from better ways to operationalize mating success in sex-differentiated ways, that take into account the quantity and the quality of copulations, mates, and relationships. However, the MI model outlined in this chapter offers an integrated, theoretically derived, and research supported set of predictor variables that will be useful in assessing the potential utility of future mating success measures. While the MI construct proposed in this volume can benefit from future improvements in measuring mating success, we propose that MI as outlined in this chapter can be useful in evaluating the validity of the mating success measures yet to come.

CONCLUSION

The MI construct can lead to important research that connects human sexuality to human intelligence. In light of recent contributions in evolutionary psychology (e.g., Buss, 2005), we know that human mating is central to any understanding of the human mind. Further, Miller's (2000a) insights regarding the evolutionary origins of mating psychology and human intelligence provides a major step toward understanding how these domains of human functioning have been integrally linked across the evolutionary history of our species.

The integrative model of MI presented in this chapter is designed as a roadmap for researchers in this area. The primary contribution that this model presents concerns the distinction between mating-relevant cognitive domains that may be thought to primarily serve courtship-display functions (e.g., creative intelligence) and those which act as mating mechanisms (mating-relevant areas of human cognition that are not fitness indicators, such as cross-sex mind-reading). We hope that this model provides a useful framework for future research.

The origins and nature of human intelligence are eternally mystifying. Approaches to understanding the evolution of intelligence have been multi-faceted and contentious ever since Darwin's *The Descent of Man*. There is still no consensus among the varied perspectives (see Sternberg & Kaufman, 2002; Geher, Murphy, & Miller, this volume). Given its focus on the domains of human behavior that are most clearly linked to our evolutionary origins, the MI construct advanced in this book may provide important insights on the origins and nature of intelligence. Further, we hope that the integrative framework provided here may foster the development of common ground in our search for the evolutionary origins of human intelligence. History, of course, will be the ultimate arbiter regarding the theoretical and empirical utility of the MI construct. But should it prove useful, it may serve as bridge allowing safe passage of ideas and fruitful commerce between neighboring yet disparate disciplines—human intelligence, evolutionary psychology, social psychology, cognitive neuroscience, biological sciences, sociology, anthropology, and more.

ACKNOWLEDGMENTS

We are extremely grateful to many individuals whose assistance, guidance, and support were integral to this work. Geoffrey Miller has been exemplary as a collaborator on this project in general—and his suggestions regarding the empirical work on the cross-sex mind-reading element of mating intelligence described in this chapter were huge—as was his editing on this chapter. We also thank Jack Mayer, whose suggestions regarding the interface of emotional intelligence and human mating played a major role in the ideas presented here. Additionally, I (GG) thank my wife, Kathy, whose unofficial editorial work on this chapter was extremely helpful. We also thank New Paltz psychology department faculty member, Alice Andrews, for her support of this book and of all the SUNY New Paltz Mating Intelligence work that's been conducted thus far. We also thank David Buss who provided very helpful editorial comments on this chapter. Finally, we thank the many star students of SUNY New Paltz who helped with different elements of this project as research assistants, including: Michelle Coombs, Elisabeth Dewispelaere, Jason Diffenderfer, Kelly Fairweather, Rachel Fetters, Kimona Hanson, Krystle Hearns, Jill Lavallee, Justin Lee, Heather Mangione, Nilerisha Mollette, Regina Musicaro, and Uzoma Ugonabo.

REFERENCES

Alcock, J. (1993). Exadaptations. *Behavioral and Brain Sciences, 16*, 283–284.
Baron-Cohen, S. (1999). The evolution of a theory of mind. In M. C. Corballis & S. E. G. Lea (Eds.), *The descent of mind: Psychological perspectives on hominid evolution*. New York: Oxford University Press.

Bookstein, F. L. (1993). Converting cultural success into mating failure by aging. *Behavioral and Brain Sciences, 16*, 285–286.

Brackett, M. A., & Salovey, P. (2004). Measuring emotional intelligence with the Mayer-Salovey-Caruso Emotional Intelligence Test (MSCEIT). In G. Geher (Ed.), *Measuring emotional intelligence: Common ground and controversy*. New York: Nova Science Publishers.

Brackett, M. A., & Mayer, J. D. (2003). Convergent, discriminant, and incremental validity of competing measures of emotional intelligence. *Personality and Social Psychology Bulletin, 29*, 1147–1158.

Buss, D. M. (Ed.). (2005). *The handbook of evolutionary psychology*. New York: Wiley.

Buss, D. M. (2003). *The evolution of desire: Strategies of human mating*. New York: Basic Books.

Buss, D. M. (1989). Sex differences in human mate preferences: Evolutionary hypotheses tested in 37 cultures. *Behavioral and Brain Sciences, 12*, 1–49.

Buss, D. M., & Schmitt, D. P. (1993). Sexual strategies theory: An evolutionary perspective on human mating. *Psychological Review, 100*, 204–232.

Costa, P. T., Jr., & McCrae, R. R. (1992). *The revised NEO personality inventory and NEO five-factor inventory manual*. Odessa, FL: Psychological Assessment Resources.

Darwin, C. (1871). *The descent of man and selection in relation to sex*. London: Murray.

Figueredo, A. J., Vasquez, G., & Brumbach, B. H. (2005) The K-factor: Individual differences in life-history strategy. *Personality and Individual Differences, 39*, 1349–1360.

Fisher, R. A. (1915). The evolution of sexual preference. *Eugenics Review, 7*, 184–192.

Furlow, F. B., Armijo-Prewitt, T., Gangestad, S. W., & Thornhill, R. (1997). Fluctuating asymmetry and psychometric intelligence. *Proceedings of the Royal Society of London B, 264*, 1–8.

Gangestad, S. W., & Simpson, J. A. (1990). Toward an evolutionary history of female sociosexual variation. *Journal of Personality, 58*, 69–96.

Geher, G., DeWispelaere, E., Lavallee, J., & Musicaro, R. (2006). *Mating intelligence conceptualized as adaptive cross-sex mind-reading errors*. Poster presented at the 18th annual meeting of the Human Behavior and Evolution Society, Philadelphia, PA.

Geher, G., Derieg, M., & Downey, H. J. (2004). Required parental investment and mating patterns: A quantitative analysis in the context of evolutionarily stable strategies. *Social Biology*.

Hamilton, W. D. (1964). The genetical evolution of social behavior. I and II. *Journal of Theoretical Biology, 7*, 1–52.

Haselton M. G., & Buss, D. M. (2000). Error management theory: A new perspective on biases in cross-sex mind reading. *Journal of Personality and Social Psychology, 78*, 81–91.

Haselton, M., & Miller, G. F. (2006). Women's fertility across the cycle increases the short-term attractiveness of creative intelligence compared to wealth. *Human Nature, 17*, 50–73.

Haselton, M. G., & Nettle, D. (in press). The paranoid optimist: An integrative evolutionary model of cognitive biases. *Personality and Social Psychology Review*.

Hughes, S. M., Dispenza, F., & Gallup, G. G., Jr. (2004). Ratings of voice attractiveness predict sexual behavior and body configuration. *Evolution and Human Behavior, 25*, 295–304.

Kanazawa, S. (2004). General intelligence as a domain-specific adaptation. *Psychological Review, 111*, 512–523.

Kanazawa, S. (2003). Can evolutionary psychology explain reproductive behavior in the contemporary United States? *Sociological Quarterly, 44*, 291–302.

Keller, M. C., & Miller, G. F. (in press). Resolving the paradox of common, harmful, heritable mental disorders: Which evolutionary genetic models work best? *Behavioral and Brain Sciences.*

Landolt, M. A., Lalumière, M. L., & Quinsey, V. L. (1995). Sex differences in intrasex variations in human mating tactics: An evolutionary approach. *Ethology and Sociobiology, 16*, 3–23.

Li, N. (this volume). Intelligent Priorities. In G. Geher & G. F. Miller (Eds.), *Mating intelligence: Sex, relationships, and the mind's reproductive system.* Mahwah, NJ: Lawrence Erlbaum Associates.

Linton, D. K., & Wiener, N. I. (2001). Personality and potential conceptions: Mating success in a modern western male sample. *Personality and Individual Differences, 31*, 675–688.

Matthews, G., Zeidner, M., & Roberts, R. D. (2004). *Emotional intelligence: Science and myth.* Cambridge, MA: MIT Press.

Mayer, J. D., Caruso, D., & Salovey, P. (1999). Emotional intelligence meets traditional standards for an intelligence. *Intelligence, 27*, 267–298.

Mayer, J. D., & Geher, G. (1996). Emotional intelligence and the identification of emotion. *Intelligence, 22*, 89–113.

Miller, G. F. (2000a). *The mating mind: How sexual choice shaped the evolution of human nature.* New York: Doubleday.

Miller, G. F. (2000b). Sexual selection for indicators of intelligence. In G. Bock, J. Goode, & K. Webb (Eds.), *The nature of intelligence* (pp. 260–275). Novartis Foundation Symposium 233. Novartis Foundation: John Wiley.

Miller, G. F. (2006). Personal communication, June 9.

Nettle, D. (2005). An evolutionary approach to the extraversion continuum. *Evolution and Human Behavior, 26*, 363–373.

Nisbett, R. E., & Wilson, T. D. (1977). Telling more than we can know: Verbal reports on mental processes. *Psychological Review, 84*, 231–259.

Pérusse, D. (1993). Cultural and reproductive success in industrial societies: Testing the relationship at the proximate and ultimate levels. *Behavioral and Brain Sciences, 16*, 267–322.

Prokosch, M. D., Yeo, R. A., & Miller, G. F. (2005). Intelligence tests with higher g-loadings show higher correlations with body symmetry: Evidence for a general fitness factor mediated by developmental stability. *Intelligence, 33*, 203–213.

Putz, D. A., Gaulin, S. J. C., Sporter, R. J., & McBurney, D. H. (2004). Sex hormones and finger length: What does 2D:4D indicate? *Evolution and Human Behavior, 25*, 182–199.

Rhodes, G., Simmons, L. W., & Peters, M. (2005). Attractiveness and sexual behavior: Does attractiveness enhance mating success? *Evolution and Human Behavior, 26*, 186–201.

Schmitt, D. P. (2005). Fundamentals of human mating strategies. In D. M. Buss (Ed.), *The Handbook of Evolutionary Psychology*. New York: Wiley.

Simpson, J. A., & Gangestad, S. W. (1991). Sociosexuality and romantic partner choice. *Journal of Personality, 60*, 31–51.

Simpson, J. A., & Gangstead, S. W. (2000). The evolution of human mating: Trade-offs and strategic pluralism. *The Behavioral and Brain Sciences, 23*, 573–644.

Spearman, C. (1904). "General intelligence," objectively determined and measured. *American Journal of Psychology, 15*, 201–293.

Sternberg, R. J., & Kaufman, J. C. (Eds.) (2002). *Evolution of intelligence*. Mahwah, NJ: Lawrence Erlbaum Associates.

Thornhill, R., & Gangestad, S. W. (1999). The scent of symmetry: A human sex pheromone that signals fitness? *Evolution and Human Behavior, 20*, 175–201.

Trivers, R. (1972). Parental investment and sexual selection. In B. Campbell (Ed.), *Sexual selection and the descent of man*. Chicago: Aldine-Atherton.

Yerkes, R. M. (1921). Psychological examining in the United States. Memoirs of the National Academy of Sciences (15:890 pp. entire).

Zebrowitz, L. A., & Rhodes, G. (2004). Sensitivity to "bad genes" and the anomalous face overgeneralization effect: Cue validity, cue utilization, and accuracy in judging intelligence and health. *Journal of Nonverbal Behavior, 28*, 167–185.

Author Index

Page numbers in *italics* refer to the reference lists at the end of each chapter.
Page numbers in roman refer to citations in text.

A

Aaronson, C. J., 384, *382*
Abbey, A., 144, *153*
Abbott, M., 42, *66*, 128, 129, *132, 219*
Abed, R. T., 383, *386, 388*
Abelson, R. P., 265, *278*
Abrams, M. T., 315, *334*
Ackerson, L. C., 208, *219*, 376
Adami, H., 127, 131, *132*
Adler, H. M., 136, *153*
Aeschylus, 264, *278*
Afshar, Y., 56, *68*
Ahern, F. M., *72*
Aiello, L. C., 324, *332*
Aiken, L. S., 324, *332*
Alcalay, L., 39, 40, *74, 222*
Alcock, J., 163, *168*, 415, *419*
Alkire, M. T., 376, *389*
Allan, S., 39, 49, *69*, 383, *388*
Allen, L. M., 61, 62, 136, *155*
Allensworth, M., 213, *222*
Alliger, R. J., 215, *218*, 314, 327, *332*
Allik, J., 39, 40, 42, 53, 61, *74, 79, 100, 156, 213, 222*
Alvarez, H., 351, *362*
Ambady, N., 58, *66*, 269, *278*
American Psychiatric Association, 194, 206, *218*
Amos, T., 371, *386*
Andersen, B. L., 153, *153*
Anderson, C., 275, *278*
Anderson, J. R., 329, *332*
Andersson, M., 178, 182, *190*
Andreasen, N. C., 214, 215, *218, 221*, 314, 327, *332*
Andrews, P. W., 229, *254*, 383, *393*

Angleitner, A., 42, 58, *66, 83, 99*, 128, 129, *132, 143, 155, 332*
Ankey, C. D., *334*
Anstey, K. J., 374, *386*
Anthony, J. C., 207, *219*
Apicella, C., 42, *72*
Archer, J., 140, *153*, 369, *386*
Argiolas, A., 208, *221*
Armijo-Prewitt, T., 6, *30*, 416, *422*
Arndt, S., 215, *218*
Arnett, J. J., 46, *66*
Arnquist, G., 38, 41, 60, *66*
Aron, A., 39, *68*, 80, 95, 138, *157*
Arriaga, X. B., 272, *281*
Arseneault, L., 368, *386*
Ash, J. A., 316, *332*, 396, 417, *421*
Asherian, A., 42, *66*, 128, 129, *132, 219*
Aspi, J., 201, *220*
Aston, M. C., 17, *28*
Ault, L., 39, 40, 42, 53, 61, *74, 79, 100, 156, 213, 222*
Austers, I., 39, 40, 42, 53, 61, *74, 100, 156, 213, 222*
Avila, M., 127, 131, *132*
Avis, W. E., 81, *99*

B

Baare, W. F. C., 315, 327, *334, 374, 375, 391*
Bachner-Melman, R., 368, *386*
Baertschi, J. C., 315, *334*
Bailey, J. M., 6, 7, *31*, 40, 42, 53, 54, 56, *66, 71*, 108, 109, 111, 113, *118*, 121, *132*, 174, *190*, 369, *386*
Bainton, R. J., 208, *219*, 374
Baird, A. A., 347, *361*

425

Subject Index